Women and Politics

Women and Politics
The Pursuit of Equality

FOURTH EDITION

Lynne E. Ford
College of Charleston

WESTVIEW
PRESS

Westview Press was founded in 1975 in Boulder, Colorado, by notable publisher and intellectual Fred Praeger. Westview Press continues to publish scholarly titles and high-quality undergraduate- and graduate-level textbooks in core social science disciplines. With books developed, written, and edited with the needs of serious nonfiction readers, professors, and students in mind, Westview Press honors its long history of publishing books that matter.

Published by Westview Press
An imprint of Perseus Books, LLC
A subsidiary of Hachette Book Group, Inc.
2465 Central Avenue
Boulder, CO 80301
www.westviewpress.com

Every effort has been made to secure required permissions for all text, images, maps, and other art reprinted in this volume.

Westview Press books are available at special discounts for bulk purchases in the United States by corporations, institutions, and other organizations. For more information, please contact the Special Markets Department at the Perseus Books Group, 2300 Chestnut Street, Suite 200, Philadelphia, PA 19103, or call (800) 810-4145, ext. 5000, or e-mail special .markets@perseusbooks.com.

Design and composition by Eclipse Publishing Services

A CIP catalog record for the print version of this book is available from the Library of Congress

PB ISBN: 978-0-8133-5081-3
EBOOK ISBN: 978-0-8133-5082-0
10 9 8 7 6 5 4 3 2 1

For Frank, Grace, and Samuel

Contents

Chapter 8 – The Politics of Family and Fertility: The Last Battleground in the Pursuit of Equality?   327

Chapter 9 – Setting the Agenda and Taking Action: New Challenges in the Pursuit of Equality   397

List of Illustrations

Preface

The fourth edition of *Women and Politics: The Pursuit of Equality* is intended to serve as a core text for undergraduate and graduate courses on women and politics. When I first developed the course in my own department more than twenty-five years ago, a male colleague joked, "What will you cover in the second week?" On the contrary, I have found that the biggest challenge in teaching a course on women and politics is to introduce students to the vast history of women's movements, acquaint them with the scholarship on women as candidates, political leaders, and political participants, and still leave time to address contemporary policy concerns. This is particularly true given the explosion of high-quality scholarship on gender and politics. Never satisfied with a single book, I usually ended up using parts of five or six books at a significant cost to my students. In *Women and Politics: The Pursuit of Equality*, I integrate the major topics related to women's political engagement into a single text. Although there are now several core texts for a course on women and politics, very few provide thorough coverage of women's political participation and public policy issues in a single volume, as this one does. The history of women's entrance into the public sphere builds a strong foundation upon which contemporary progress in politics and policy areas is considered.

To provide coherence, I have created a strong central organizing theme that links topics across chapters but remains flexible enough to permit individual instructors to structure their course in a variety of ways. The book is organized around what I've termed the *paradox of gender equality*: the need to reconcile demands for equality with biological differences between women and men. I argue that, in trying to resolve the paradox, women have primarily followed two paths. One path advocates a *legal equality doctrine*, based on the belief that women and men must be treated the same in order to achieve equality. Therefore, differences must be erased by laws and public policies before equality can be achieved. Just as viable, another path focuses on women's differences from men. Advocates of this approach believe that treating men and women the same when they are in fact different is unfair. The *fairness doctrine* requires that law and policy account for the consequences of biological difference by treating men and women differently but fairly.

Resolving the paradox is complicated by the persistent and pervasive influence of the *separate spheres ideology*. Although this ideology impacts all women, it has affected different groups of women in different ways. Separate spheres ideology specifically excluded upper-class white women from employment and limited the type of employment opportunities and pay for low-income women and women of color in the workforce. Defining a contemporary role for women in the public sphere has been difficult because women's biological role in bearing children makes their traditional assignment to the home still seem "natural" to many people. Just as women's opportunities were once limited by the sharp demarcation between the private and public spheres, women today face conflicts created by a blurred line. Men and women alike are trying to sort out new gender roles even as the social construct of gender becomes more fluid.

Presenting the paradox of gender equality within the context of separate spheres ideology enables students to examine their own preconceived notions of the "appropriate" roles for men and women and to connect events in their own lives with the theories and scholarship presented in the book. This approach also helps students understand why issues of gender equality seem to reappear for successive generations of political activists to tackle. In each chapter, a special effort is made to focus on the diversity of experiences among women of different races, economic classes, sexual orientations, and political persuasions. The most compelling controversies of gender equality are often played out exclusively among women. Understanding how women differ from each other is as important as understanding how women are different from men. I've attempted to include as much scholarship as possible on the experiences of women of color, poor women, and women in other traditionally marginalized groups, including women who are opposed to equality altogether. Where such information is not available, I've challenged students to think carefully about why the gap in the research literature exists.

REVISIONS IN THE FOURTH EDITION

There are several important changes to this edition, beginning with a new publisher. I am pleased to be working with Westview Press for the first time. The fourth edition of *Women and Politics* maintains its solid framework, but material within chapters has been reorganized and streamlined to better present the book's content and arguments, and to avoid repetition across chapters. I have also added boldface key terms and a corresponding glossary.

The fourth edition includes significant updates to the scholarship, figures and tables, feature boxes, and current issues throughout the text. The 2016 primary and general election campaigns are covered extensively throughout. Women's candidacies, including Hillary Clinton's historic presidential campaign, are explored in depth. In addition, progress toward gender equality under eight years of the Obama administration is assessed. As feminists raising daughters, Michelle and

Barack Obama brought new attention to gender equality from the White House. Upon taking office in 2009, Obama signed the Lilly Ledbetter Equal Pay Act, and he remained a strong advocate for wage equality. He acted by executive order to extend family leave and sick days for federal workers. The White House convened several summits on work and family, campus sexual assault, and the status of women's rights. Yet during the same period, many states acted to limit women's access to reproductive health care and shrink the social safety net that disproportionately supports women and their children. Federalism means that the pursuit of women's equality is multifaceted and takes place across the several levels of government. There is extensive coverage of state policies affecting gender equity in education, employment, health, marriage and families, and fertility in the fourth edition. In response to several reviewers, this edition also includes more extensive coverage of issues relevant to conservative women and scholarship on conservative women's political behavior through Tea Party organizations, as Republican Party activists, and through conservative campus organizations.

The fourth edition includes international comparative content in a number of ways. Scholarship drawing on international data, case studies, and comparative analysis has been integrated wherever possible throughout the book. Finally, the policy chapters have been substantially updated to reflect changes in the domains of education, work, and family and fertility politics.

TEXT ORGANIZATION
The two dominant paths women have taken in resolving the paradox—the pursuit of legal equality and the pursuit of fairness—offer a way to organize women's politics historically as well as to present students with the live controversies of gender equality.

- Chapter 1 lays out the origins of the separate spheres ideology, distinguishes between sex as a biological designation and gender as a social construction, and details the roots of the legal equality and fairness doctrines. Both paths are presented as reasonable ways to resolve the paradox of gender equality on many issues. This chapter also acknowledges that women disagree as to which approach is the better way to proceed, and presents an overview of the major strands of feminism and their critiques. This section has been updated to reflect the new platforms for feminist voices and opportunities for organizing provided by social media. In reviewing the major strands of feminism, new emphasis on intersectionality has been added.
- Chapter 2 evaluates two major women's movements in the United States: suffrage and the Equal Rights Amendment. In both cases, the mechanism for change was a constitutional amendment. The contrast between the success of the suffrage movement and the failure to ratify the ERA illuminates the

differences between a legal approach to equality and women's interest in fair accommodations for biological differences. The histories of both movements present students with examples of women's political activism and highlight the contributions of young women and women of color in both movements. In the fourth edition, efforts to resurrect the Equal Rights Amendment are evaluated in light of the Supreme Court's marriage equality decision, the end of women's combat exclusion and their full integration into the armed forces, and the prevalence of gender-neutral restrooms—each offered by anti-ERA forces as an example of the dire consequence of ratification during the decade it was under consideration by the states (1972–1982).

• Chapter 3 examines women as voters and political participants. Although initially slow to enter electoral politics, women are now registered to vote at higher rates than men and have the power to dramatically shape elections. Social media has provided women with new ways to access political information and find allies, and it has increased their likelihood of donating money to political candidates. Young activists with Black Lives Matter and campus activism are featured. Chapter 3 addresses a variety of questions: How do women evaluate candidates? Which issues mobilize women's participation? Can female candidates mobilize women voters? In particular, how did Hillary Clinton's historic candidacy for president impact women's engagement with politics? What role do millennial women play as candidates and activists? Under what circumstances will women vote for other women? The fourth edition includes a substantial update on the impact and sources of the gender gap in presidential elections historically, in the battleground contests during the 2016 Democratic primaries, and in the 2016 general election.

• Chapter 4 covers women as candidates for political office, evaluating the differences between male and female candidates as well as differences among women in their approaches to running for elective office. Research demonstrates that when women run for office they are as likely as men to win, but they are substantially less likely to run in the first place—why? The barriers women faced in the 1990s have given way to a new, more gender-neutral campaign environment, but does this benefit women candidates or make winning more difficult? This edition includes the latest statistics on women officeholders at the local, state, and national levels, as well as the latest research on candidate emergence. The ways in which popular culture and socialization inform gender stereotypes is explored and then applied to evaluate the candidacies of women running for Congress and Hillary Clinton's presidential bid. New research on the political geography of women's electability is included in this chapter, particularly the ways in which Republican women face unique challenges as candidates. Initiatives to recruit and train women candidates have been updated. The questions Chapter 4 explores include: Why so few women in political office in the United States? Why has it taken so long for women to reach such a modest level of representation? Why has progress plateaued? The prospects for speeding up women's election to office through electoral gender quotas and gender gerrymandering are examined in this chapter.

- Chapter 5 evaluates women in public office—their behavior, their priorities, their style of governing, and their many accomplishments and challenges. The fourth edition includes updates on women officeholders and appointments throughout the executive branch and the judiciary. A new section on women in local government has been added. Women in the military has been included in this chapter, and coverage has been considerably expanded. Gender parity in officeholding is explored as a motivator of vote choice. Trends in the election of young people, women of color, and LGBTQ candidates are featured. The efficacy of policy organizations and "watchdogs" for gender equality is assessed.

- Chapters 6 through 8 focus on women and public policy. Chapter 6 examines education. Although Title IX is best known for opening athletic opportunities for women, it also opened doors to professional programs and eliminated quotas for women in "nontraditional" subjects such as math, science, and engineering. This chapter examines the link between education and income for women and men and explores the changing demographics of college admissions. New to this edition is an assessment of Title IX and the change in focus from a tool for access/equity to a tool to combat campus sexual assault. Student activism around campus sexual assault is featured in a new "Encountering the Controversies of Equality."

- Chapter 7 is focused on work, wages, and women's broad participation in the economy. The efficacy of federal antidiscrimination policies in eliminating second-generation discrimination is extensively considered. The limits to the legal equality approach are assessed relative to the persistence of the pay gap and occupational segregation. New to this edition is a section on low-wage workers and the impact of antipoverty initiatives for women. While there is no question that women are paid less than men, there is no single explanation or easy fix.

- Chapter 8 is dedicated to family and fertility issues. The fourth edition includes new material on marriage equality following *Obergefell v. Hodges* (2015) and the families created through same-sex marriages. New to this chapter is a section on the federal safety net for families. This chapter examines the complex ways in which biology and gender intersect, shaping the roles men and women play in families. What sort of help can individuals expect from government in balancing the demands of work and family life? Why is the United States one of only four nations in the world not to provide government support for paid family leave? The fourth edition includes updated information on abortion

politics, including extensive coverage of the labyrinth of restrictions adopted
by state legislatures. Also comprehensively addressed is the "war on women"
executed by limiting information on and access to contraceptives and reproductive health care. Efforts to defund Planned Parenthood by Republicans in
Congress and in state legislatures are discussed. Under "Threats to Women's
Autonomy," coverage of domestic violence has been expanded and threats of
violence to women online has been added. Technology and gender ideologies,
plus the spread of conscience clauses, are covered here as well.

- In conclusion, Chapter 9 evaluates women's progress in achieving equality and
challenges students to think about issues relating to women and politics that
they will face in their own lives. Material from throughout the book is drawn
into the analysis of women's progress, and students are invited to develop
an equality agenda for the future. A "Taking Action" feature links specific
resources to the book's summative conclusions and points students to direct
action strategies to promote gender equality.

TEXT FEATURES

The fourth edition of *Women and Politics: The Pursuit of Equality* provides a number
of features designed to encourage critical thinking. In each chapter, "Encountering the Controversies of Equality" presents students with a controversy or conflict
generated by the paradox of gender equality and prompts them to consider how it
could be resolved. For example, Chapter 6 explores men's and women's competing
Title IX claims in cases of sexual assault by looking at Emma Sulkowicz's *Mattress
Performance*. These boxes are intended to clarify the concept of the paradox and to
encourage students to appreciate the complexity of women's demands for gender
equality. By having students grapple with contemporary issues related to the core
themes of the text, the parallels between central issues facing women centuries ago
and issues facing students today become quite clear. These are also intended to
provoke discussion in class, and each feature includes critical-thinking questions.

In Chapters 2 through 9, "Point of Comparison" features specifically draw
attention to the ways in which countries vary on political norms, processes, and/or
empirical outcomes in issue areas related to the chapter's content. For example, the
"Point of Comparison" in Chapter 4 focuses on a form of positive discrimination,
electoral gender quotas, as a way to rapidly increase the proportion of women in
elective office. When viewed alongside Table 4.1, listing the ten countries with the
highest proportion of women serving in the lower house of the national legislature,
students are able to think more critically about quotas and discrimination—which
in the context of American politics have negative connotations—as worthy of consideration in advancing women's political representation.

In Chapter 9, the "Taking Action: What Can You Do?" section points female
and male students to relevant resources that will enable them to get involved and

take action to promote gender equality. The benefit to including this material in the final chapter is that it is more immediately tied to the summative information drawn from the previous eight chapters. As students are encouraged to develop a future agenda for women's equality and to find their unique role within that agenda, "Taking Action" gives them concrete steps to take. Finally, a "Spotlight on the 2016 Election" feature has been added to Chapters 3, 4, and 5 to incorporate the latest information from the election.

Each chapter also relies on contemporary scholarship from a number of disciplines, including political science, history, sociology, psychology, anthropology, philosophy, and the natural sciences. The interdisciplinary approach enriches the analysis and makes the text appropriate for women's studies courses as well as courses in political science. Although politics changes daily, I have presented the most current data available, including preliminary figures for women's participation as candidates and voters in the 2016 national election.

ANCILLARIES AND COMPANION WEBSITE

The fourth edition of *Women and Politics* is accompanied by an instructor's manual, test bank, and PowerPoint lecture slides for instructors using the book. The test bank includes approximately thirty test questions for each chapter in a mix of formats (multiple choice, fill-in-the-blank, short answer, and essay). The instructor's manual contains sample syllabi, sample classroom activities and discussion questions, and additional resource suggestions (readings, online resources, and films). The PowerPoint slides include basic lecture outlines that can be expanded to fit individual courses and the tables, figures, and photos from the book. Access to these resources can be requested at https://westviewpress.com/books/women-and-politics.

In addition, there is an open and free companion site for students with study questions for each chapter and links to online resources at https://westviewpress.com/ford4e.

ACKNOWLEDGMENTS

I could not have completed this book without tremendous support from a variety of sources. Ada Fung at Westview Press has provided invaluable guidance throughout the revision process. The fourth edition was completed while working full-time as an academic administrator, and I thank my Academic Experience colleagues at the College of Charleston for their interest, support, and encouragement. Since my day job is now outside my discipline, I am even more grateful for my enduring friendship with Kathy Dolan—a source of political wisdom and an ear for political venting. I owe my family—my husband, Frank Dirks, and my two children, Grace and Samuel Ford-Dirks—an enormous debt of gratitude for their love, encouragement, and patience.

When I wrote the first edition of this book, my daughter, Grace, was a newborn. As I finish the fourth edition, she has just been accepted to college. Only seventeen years old in November 2016, Grace accompanied me to the polls and held my hand as we voted for Hillary Clinton. We believed that later that night we would celebrate the election of the first woman president. Our disappointment is profound. When Hillary Clinton ended her primary campaign in 2008, young Grace and Samuel were confident that a woman would surely win the presidency "next time." That time has come and gone, and I am left to wonder whether "next time" will be within my lifetime. I hope so—and perhaps a student using this book will break that barrier.

As this is now the fourth edition of the book, I have benefited greatly from the feedback generously offered by the students, faculty colleagues, and reviewers who have taken the time to carefully read and consider previous editions of the book. Many of the important new directions in this edition come directly from their input.

I would also like to extend special thanks to those scholars who provided their insights and useful suggestions for the development of this text, including Benjamin Arah (Bowie State University), Mary Layton Atkinson (University of North Carolina, Charlotte), Leslie Baker (Mississippi State University), Michelle Brophy-Baermann (Rhode Island College), Michele DeMary (Susquehanna University), Sarah Gershon (Georgia State University), Lori Johnson (Mercer University), Mary-Kate Lizotte (Augusta University), Jennifer Sacco (Quinnipiac University), Julie Webber (Illinois State University), and others who wish to remain anonymous.

L.E.F.

CHAPTER 1

Two Paths to Equality

This is a book about women's use of politics and the political system in pursuit of gender equality. At its core, this book explores the complexity, tension, and controversy created by an overarching paradox in the unique nature of women's claims to equality. A paradox occurs when two apparently contradictory positions coexist. In this case, the paradox is this: How can demands for gender equality be reconciled with sex differences? Because "equal" often means "the same," how can men and women be the same if they are different?

The story of women's relationship to politics is therefore complex because the most direct path to gender equality is not clearly marked. In fact, this book argues that there are two well-worn paths women have traveled in pursuit of equality. On one hand, women have argued that equality is possible only when the differences between men and women are erased by laws that require men and women to be treated equally. We will refer to this path as the **legal equality doctrine**. The other path, what we will call the **fairness doctrine**, consciously recognizes the differences between men and women and argues that women will always be disadvantaged if they are not somehow compensated for the social, economic, and political consequences of those differences. What matters most to advocates of this second approach is that women are treated fairly—and fairness may require laws, policies, and practices that treat women differently from men.

The tension is evident in the disagreement among women themselves over which is the right path to take to improve women's status. Just because women share sex-linked biological characteristics with one another does not mean that they embrace a single understanding of gender equality, nor does it mean that they possess a group identity or group consciousness as women in a way that easily translates into political action. In this regard, feminism only adds to the tension. As an ideology, feminism has been ineffective as an organizing philosophy for women's

1

Box 1.1: Encountering the Controversies of Equality

How Should Female Veterans Be Memorialized?

Visit any town in America and you are likely to find a war memorial honoring those who fought for our nation. While there are more than two million living female veterans in the United States, there are very few memorials honoring women's military service. As new memorials are built, how should female veterans be represented?

The West Virginia Division of Veterans Affairs commissioned a statue honoring female veterans in 1999. When sculptor P. Joseph Mullins unveiled the design three years later, critics complained that it was not "feminine enough." The statue depicts a muscular woman wearing a casual uniform of pants and a T-shirt. "It would have been nice if we could have had a statue that looked more like a woman," said State Senator Anita Caldwell, vice chairwoman of the Senate Military Committee. State Senator Jon Blair Hunter, the committee's chairman, said the statue should "depict a woman in a skirt." The sculptor, himself a Vietnam veteran, said that depicting a woman in a skirt would have been inappropriate. The statue is "not a runway model and not a Playboy bunny," but rather a "nice, big, strong girl who's been through military training." After more than a decade of debate, the statue was finally installed at the state capitol in 2011.[1]

Meanwhile in New York, a statue erected in honor of female veterans located next to the State Museum generated the opposite reaction. The statue, intended by its creator to invoke "Lady Liberty," appears in a clingy, flowing gown.[2] A sash is draped over her left arm and a crown lies at her sandaled feet. State Senator Nancy Larraine Hoffman asked the governor to move the statue to another location and to replace it with "something more representative of the sacrifices women veterans have made." Margaret Bandy, one of the first women from New York to enlist in the Marines, said, "I think the statue misrepresents women in the military, especially today. I think the veterans deserve something less ethereal." Bandy enlisted in 1942 and served for three years as a drill

movements because feminism itself incorporates the equality paradox. Feminism promotes unity among women while recognizing diversity, and it pursues equality even while recognizing differences.

Controversy is inevitable anytime one group makes demands that require another group to relinquish power, resources, control, or the privileges they currently enjoy. **Patriarchy** literally means "rule of" (*arch*) "fathers" (*patri*). More generally, patriarchy characterizes the pervasive control men exercise over social, economic, instructor and company commander. "When you go to look at statues honoring men, they look like warriors. That's what we were too. I was fully willing to give up my life to defend my country."[3]

In Del City, Oklahoma, city officials erected a monument that includes five women in dress uniform—one from each branch of the service—holding hands while surrounding the American flag.[4] Nearby, another statue depicts a female National Guard soldier talking to her daughter, who is wearing her mom's uniform cap.[5] The Women in Military Service for America Memorial in Arlington National Cemetery does not include a depiction of a soldier.[6]

Source: "West Virginia's Female Veteran Memorial Statue Unveiling" by Governor Earl Ray Tomblin, (flickr.com/governortomblin) is licensed copyright © 2011 under CC BY-ND 2.0.

What do you think?

How is this controversy related to women's pursuit of equality and the paradox of gender? In deciding how military women should be represented, communities encounter the collision of women's real roles with the idealized image of women grounded firmly in the private sphere. What is the appropriate visual representation of women in today's military? What does each memorial representation tell us about women and men and the paradox of gender equality? Should future memorials be built to honor women in particular, or should we assume that any military memorial built today honors women as well as men?

and political power and resources. Feminism and women's movements directly challenge the privileged position of men and demand that women be viewed as individuals rather than simply as derivatives of their relationships to men. The long-standing and persistent belief that men and women naturally occupy separate spheres strengthens the power of patriarchy. The **separate spheres ideology** promotes the belief that because of women's role in reproduction, they are best suited to occupy the **private sphere** of home and family, whereas men are designed to occupy the **public sphere** of work and politics. Throughout the book, controversies about gender equality are most evident when women demand autonomy and work toward acquiring the rights and privileges that flow from eliminating the distinction between the public and private spheres.

This text employs the equality-difference paradox to examine women's historic and contemporary participation in politics. In doing so, it is important to state two caveats. First, accepting the equality-difference paradox as a framework for examining women's political integration in the United States does not mean that the legal equality doctrine and the fairness doctrine are the only two positions one might adopt. Dichotomies can sometimes be limiting in that they accentuate, or exaggerate, the positions at either end of a spectrum, while giving little attention to the space in between. History suggests that neither polar position provides an entirely satisfactory approach to the pursuit of gender equality. Similarly, neither position will provide a full explanation of women's successes and failures in working toward gender equality. Rather, it is the tension produced by the coexistence of the legal equality doctrine and the fairness doctrine that provides the most fertile ground on which to examine gendered society, women and politics, and the continuing controversies of equality. Second, equality is not the only goal of women's movements, nor is the equality-difference framework the only way to understand women's pursuit of gender equality. This framework, however, does provide a very effective way to explore the multitude of controversies associated with the pursuit of gender equality and to examine the diverse perspectives among women, as well as differences between women and men. Many of the most interesting debates explored in this text find women working in opposition to other women in defining and pursuing social, economic, and political goals. Finally, this is a book about women's engagement with politics in the United States, although insights drawn from women's experience in other political systems around the world can be found throughout the chapters.

POLITICS AND WOMEN'S PURSUIT OF EQUALITY

Why has it taken women so long to be recognized as important political actors? Why, in 2016, do women earn, on average, seventy-nine cents to a man's dollar, despite passage of the Equal Pay Act in 1963 and the Lilly Ledbetter Fair Pay Act in 2009? Why do many women, young and old alike, shy away from identifying as feminists yet express support for feminist positions? Why was allowing women to vote seen as the most radical demand expressed in the Declaration of Sentiments and Resolutions, adopted in 1848 at the first organized women's rights convention, in Seneca Falls, New York? Is the gender gap in contemporary electoral politics real, and if so, what does it mean? Why are women still petitioning government to address issues such as child care, work, and family leave; pay equity; control over reproduction; funding for women's health concerns; and rape and domestic violence when these very same issues were on the agenda at the Seneca Falls Convention? Answers to these questions lie in the controversies of gender equality created by the equality-difference paradox. Although women have been citizens of the United States since its founding, they have never shared equally with men in the rights or obligations of democratic citizenship.[1] Instead, women have struggled for admission to full and equal citizenship even while many argued that their particular brand of citizenship would be distinctively different from that of men.

The paradox of women's equality suggests that two paths toward the same end can coexist. Advocates of both legal equality and fairness have seen politics and the political system as a means to their preferred ends. The result has been a long history of disagreement among women about the surest path to full integration into public life and even about whether full public participation itself is desirable. Because women themselves hold different attitudes and opinions about their appropriate roles, their ability to effectively practice interest-group politics has been greatly diminished. If women could present a united front, their numbers alone would demand considerable respect and attention within the economy and from politicians at all levels of government. Women make up more than 53 percent of eligible voters in the United States. Unable to agree on unique sex and gender interests as women, or to disentangle gender interests from the powerful cross-pressures of race, ethnicity, class, motherhood, and sexuality, women's interests are allied with multiple groups and a reliable voting bloc has not materialized. Women's ability to speak with a single voice or act as a unified force on a single agenda is severely limited as a result. Thus women's relationship to politics and, more broadly, the development of women's movements have largely proceeded down two paths toward equality: one group advocating the legal equality doctrine and the other the fairness doctrine.

Feminists and nonfeminists alike find this division frustrating when a unified women's bloc would suit their needs. In 1920, both political parties worked feverishly to attract the female vote, and activists in the suffrage and women's rights movements worked diligently to turn out the women's vote in an effort to place their issues on the national policy agenda. When a coherent women's voice and vote failed to materialize, the parties eventually turned elsewhere, and activists were forced once again into an "outsider" strategy. Contemporary journalists, trying to discover pivotal voting groups in the national electorate, have variously labeled female voters as "soccer moms," "waitress moms," and "security moms." Obviously, these characterizations do not describe even the barest majority of women in the electorate, but the desire to understand women's political behavior and contribution to the nation by reducing their entire identity to a variation on motherhood is nothing new. Motherhood and women's unique role in nurturing future generations of citizens have exercised a powerful defining (and limiting) influence on women's relationship to politics.[2] In 1914, Congress passed a unanimous resolution establishing Mother's Day. The resolution's language emphasized mothers' contribution to the nation:

> Whereas the service rendered the United States by the American mother is the greatest source of the country's strength and inspiration . . . Whereas the American mother is doing so much for the home, for moral spirits and religion, hence so much for good government and humanity . . . Therefore, be it resolved that the second Sunday in May will be celebrated as Mother's Day.[3]

Women's role in good government in 1914, expressed by Congress in this resolution, was not one of direct action or participation but rather was limited to their functions in the private sphere of the home and in their socially defined roles as mothers and nurturers. While the constitutional right to vote in 1920 gave women a powerful form of direct participation, they were not newcomers to politics even then.

DEFINING WOMEN'S POLITICS

Defining politics beyond the traditional scope of electoral, party, or institutional behavior allows a more complete examination of women's political behavior. Until at least 1920, women had been legally excluded from many conventional forms of participation. As a result, an insider's definition of politics, focusing exclusively on political party activity, voting, campaigning, seeking office, or making direct contact with public officials, does not prove very useful in examining women's activism prior to suffrage or in understanding the complexity of women's politics today. Defining "politics" is in itself a political exercise, since any definition necessarily expresses some judgment about which participants, actions, and issues are legitimate. The pervasiveness of the separate spheres ideology and the power of patriarchy limited women's opportunities to engage in politics as it has been traditionally defined. Even though women were seen as outsiders prior to suffrage, the range of activities they undertook, the tactics they employed, and the issues they cared about were indeed political.

In pre-Revolutionary America, women organized public demonstrations to protest the high cost of food and household goods, and boycotted English tea to protest high taxes. To promote these activities, they formed organizations such as the Daughters of Liberty and the Anti-Tea Leagues. During the Revolutionary and Civil Wars, women participated both on the battlefield and in more traditional tasks consistent with their gender role, such as nursing, cooking, and sewing clothes for soldiers. Although not yet seated in power, women nonetheless lobbied those closest to them for early political recognition. Abigail Adams issued the now famous plea to her husband, John Adams, to "remember the ladies and be more generous and favorable to them than your ancestors. . . . If particular care and attention is not paid to the ladies, we are determined to foment a rebellion, and will not hold ourselves bound by any laws in which we have no voice or representation."[4] Rejected (or at best ignored) in the constitutional framework, women organized through voluntary associations and social movements.

Progressive women's organizations founded in the early twentieth century provided a model for the development of the welfare state in the 1930s, and women were integral in the abolition, temperance, and Progressive movements. When modern political campaigns began, women participated by performing duties "consistent with their temperament" (gender roles), by providing food, acting as hostesses and social organizers, and cleaning up afterward. Observers commented that in performing these duties women exhibited a partisan fervor equal to that of men.[5] Alexis de Tocqueville, noting in his essays that Americans were particularly preoccupied with politics, wrote that "even the women often go to public meetings and forget household cares while they listen to political speeches."[6] Although women were often relegated to support roles, they nonetheless participated in politics and acted politically long before they were awarded the franchise.

DISTINGUISHING SEX FROM GENDER

It is important at this juncture to distinguish between sex and gender. Individuals are assigned a **sex** at birth—male or female—typically based on physical characteristics and genitalia, but further defined by biological function and chemical hormones. Males and females differ most obviously in their unique contribution to human reproduction. Females alone can give birth and breast-feed. However, assigning women the job of raising children after birth is a socially defined gender role. **Gender** incorporates society's interpretation of sex-based characteristics and attaches a culturally constructed value to the differences and unique contributions of each sex. In a patriarchal culture, male characteristics are valued more highly than female qualities, and femininity is marginalized. This has significant implications for the ordering of society, the distribution of rights and power, and the creation of public policy. Although most contemporary scholars, scientists, politicians, and jurists no longer view biology as the sole determinant of human potential, our culture is not entirely free of the view that sex carries an immutable quality linked to social, political, and economic competence.

We now prefer to think of human behavior as a combination of nature (biology) and nurture (environment). The relative weight of biology and environment in producing an outcome is complex and subject to robust debate and research in a variety of disciplines. For our purposes, however, it is sufficient to state that simple sex differences do not create the greatest barriers to women's equality. Rather, it is how society interprets differences and values one quality over another that has the greatest impact on women's lives. Gender roles rather than sex differences will therefore be the focus of our inquiry in this book.

Gender, too, is an important and evolving issue, and is understood beyond the male-female binary today. Some people do not identify as either male or female; others identify as a blend of both, while still others identify with a gender but express their gender in ways that differ from stereotypical presentations. Gender "is the complex interrelationship between an individual's sex (gender biology), one's internal sense of self as male, female, both or neither (gender identity) as well as one's outward presentations and behaviors (gender expression) related to that perception, including their gender role."[7] Most often, when the term *gender* is used in this book it will be in reference to gender roles—the set of roles, activities, expectations and behaviors assigned to females and males by society.

THE FIRST PATH: THE LEGAL EQUALITY DOCTRINE

For as long as women and men have inhabited organized society, three assumptions have governed their relations: men and women have fundamentally different psychological and sexual natures; men are inherently the dominant or superior sex; and male-female difference and male dominance are both natural.[8] Whether understood as a deity's grand plan or as biology's destiny, the presumption that men and women naturally occupy different spheres has dominated political, economic, and cultural thinking for centuries. Aristotle, writing in *The Politics*, ascribed society's rule and command function to men since "women are naturally subordinate to men" and "the male is naturally fitter to command than the female, except when there is some departure from nature."[9] In the late nineteenth and early twentieth centuries, psychiatrists and philosophers claimed that education might actually be dangerous to a woman's reproductive system. Social Darwinists argued against women's suffrage, warning that because women are by nature the "nurturant and protective class," female voters might interfere with nature's progression by aiding the state in giving help to those who might otherwise not survive on their own (e.g., the poor, the sick, and the disabled).[10] While these theories may sound ludicrous, at their core lies a belief in a natural inevitability of sex and gender differences that enjoys support even today. This belief in the essential differences between women and men, more than any other perspective, distinguishes between the two paths to equality. Gender equality accomplished through legal doctrine cannot coexist with gender differences if these differences are grounded in essential human nature. Yet equality of rights for women is exactly what many feminists argue is the most basic human right of all.

Although the concept of equality lies at the very heart of a liberal democracy, even politics and constitutions cannot make men and women equal when people believe they are essentially and immutably different. How else could the US founders so eloquently write, "We hold these truths to be self-evident: That all men are created equal; that they are endowed by their Creator with certain unalienable rights . . ." in the Declaration of Independence while they ignored the interests of women and slaves? The answer lies in the presumption that a patriarchal society is natural and therefore unalterable through social, economic, or political means. Thus a gendered system—one in which gender is inextricably linked to power, prestige, and fundamental rights—has been a force in American politics since the nation's founding. It is embedded in the very documents that define our institutions and governing practices, if not in the precise language then in the founders' assumptions about human nature. The path toward gender equality pursued by advocates of the legal equality doctrine proposes to alter the assumption of natural differences between men and women by changing the laws that govern human behavior. The presumption is that once behavior is altered, a change in attitude is sure to follow.

Roots of Women's Claims to Legal Equality

Those who argued for women's political equality in the late eighteenth century most often based their claims on the liberal challenge to aristocratic rule and the Enlightenment's legacy of reason and human improvement. Political liberalism, or individualism, stresses the importance of rational thought, autonomous action, and choice on the part of each individual. An individual's status is therefore determined by that person's actions rather than by his or her station at birth. Gradually individualism gained influence to the point that restrictions on the voting rights of free males imposed by property requirements fell by the wayside with the election of Andrew Jackson in 1828. As individuals, free from the barriers to political agency imposed by the requirements of inherited wealth or title, native-born, middle-class white men were able to exercise greater economic and political power.

With this emphasis on individualism, education gained a prominent focus. Human beings were not purely subject to the whims of nature, liberals presumed, but open to developing their character through education and training. Individuals on equal footing would enter a social contract with one another to form a society of citizens. Unfortunately for women, early liberal theorists such as Thomas Hobbes, John Locke, and Jean-Jacques Rousseau excluded women from full citizenship. Hobbes and Locke were willing to grant women a somewhat ambiguous state of equality in nature, but not in politics. Rousseau assumed from the start that women lacked the natural capacities for full citizenship. All three believed that natural and biological differences between men and women precluded women's full participation in a social contract.[11] In this sense, contemporary political theorist Carole Pateman argues that a **sexual contract** predated a social contract.[12] A sexual contract required women to transfer their natural rights to men in exchange for protection, thereby leaving women without any independent rights to exchange with others in forming a social contract. Within this patriarchal arrangement, women could never be men's political equals.

Mary Wollstonecraft, philosopher and author of *A Vindication of the Rights of Men and A Vindication of the Rights of Woman*, denied any fundamental difference in character or nature between men and women. She argued that any weaknesses exhibited by women resulted from their faulty education and isolated social position. Wollstonecraft asserted that women would gladly trade their lofty yet isolated social position in return for their rights. Decades later, another liberal theorist, John Stuart Mill, published *The Subjection of Women* (1869). He too argued that a woman's "disability" in public life stemmed not from her sex alone but rather from her subjugation in marriage:

> The principle which regulates the existing social relations between the two sexes—the legal subordination of one sex to the other—is wrong in itself, and now one of the chief hindrances to human improvement; and that it ought to be replaced by a principle of perfect equality, admitting no power or privilege on the one side, nor disability on the other.[13]

Mill unfavorably compared women's fate in marriage to the institution of slavery, universally discredited among liberals. While slaves were coerced into service, Mill wrote, every aspect of society leads women to willingly enter a state of subjugation, and men's dominion over all and the intimacy men and women share make it impossible for women to cast off their bonds. Suggesting that at one time both slavery and monarchy seemed natural in America, Mill wrote: "So true it is that unnatural generally means only uncustomary, and that everything which is usual appears natural. The subjection of women to men being a universal custom, any departure from it quite naturally appears unnatural."[14] Mill did not propose any solutions to the problem of women's subjection in marriage, but like Wollstonecraft, he believed that the vote could emancipate women's minds and admit them to the public dialogue. As a member of the British parliament, he introduced and supported women's suffrage.

Patriarchy and Limits to Legal Equality

Patriarchal systems are ancient in origin and ubiquitous. Mill captured the pervasiveness of patriarchy's reach in this passage from *The Subjection of Women*:

> Whatever gratification or pride there is in the possession of power, and whatever personal interest in its exercise, is in this case not confined to a limited class, but common to the whole male sex. Instead of being, to most of its supporters, a thing desirable chiefly in the abstract, or, like the political ends usually contended for by factions, of little private

importance to any but the leaders; it comes home to the person and hearth of every male head of a family, and everyone who looks forward to being so. The clodhopper exercises, or is to exercise, his share of the power equally with the highest nobleman.[15]

Mill rightly recognized that all men were empowered by patriarchy, regardless of their individual ability to exercise their power and privilege wisely. Likewise, all women were disempowered by patriarchy, regardless of their innate abilities for leadership and for the wise exercise of power. Patriarchy assumed that all women, by nature, were incapable of equality, and therefore it limited women's claims to the natural and political rights flowing from individualism as described by liberal theorists.

Contemporary feminist scholar Adrienne Rich describes the patriarchal tradition's limits on women's opportunities this way:

Patriarchy . . . does not necessarily imply that no woman has power, or that all women in a given culture may not have certain powers. . . . Under patriarchy, I may live in *purdah* or drive a truck; . . . I may become a hereditary or elected head of state or wash the underwear of a millionaire's wife; I may serve my husband his early morning coffee within the clay walls of a Berber village or march in an academic procession; whatever my status or situation, my derived economic class, or my sexual preference, I live under the power of the fathers, and I have access only to so much of privilege or influence as the patriarchy is willing to accede to me, and only for so long as I will pay the price for male approval.[16]

Patriarchy, as Rich describes it, leaves room for women to exercise considerable discretion and choice, but only within a framework in which men control power, resources, and access to both. In other words, even when women believe they are making independent choices and aspiring to and achieving great professional success, they do so within the realm of choices that males allow. So what sorts of choices really exist for women within a patriarchal world? Patriarchy in this context poses serious problems for those who believe gender equality can best be accomplished by the legal equality doctrine. Can truly gender-neutral laws and policies exist when patriarchy is so pervasive?

Posing a slightly different but equally serious challenge for advocates of the legal equality doctrine, sociologist Sandra Bem contrasts patriarchy with the concept of androcentrism. **Androcentrism** is the practice of overvaluing the male experience and undervaluing the female experience. In an androcentric world, "males and the male experience are treated as a neutral standard or norm for the culture or the species as a whole, and females and female experience are treated as a sex-specific deviation from that allegedly universal standard."[17] Thus, feminists who aspire to equality as defined by the legal equality doctrine are faced with a fundamental dilemma: equality measured by whose standard? Can a standard be established apart from the dominance of the male experience? In a patriarchal system, the standard would appear to be whatever constitutes the male norm. Is the male norm an appropriate aspiration for women? Is it the appropriate standard for equality? Do we recognize the gendered character of standards of equality? More specifically, can laws based on the male experience adequately cover circumstances in the female experience? For many, particularly those who advocate the fairness doctrine, the answer is a resounding no. The male standard can improve women's situation only when women and men are similarly situated. In cases where men and women are differently situated, either because of biology or because of social norms, the male standard could actually mean additional burdens for women.

So while the legal equality doctrine as a path to gender equality has a solid basis in liberal democratic theory, making it an appropriate solution to the problems women face in gaining access to the public sphere, it is not without its theoretical or practical problems. The fairness doctrine addresses some of the problems inherent in the legal equality path but presents a different set of challenges for men and women seeking gender equality.

THE SECOND PATH: THE FAIRNESS DOCTRINE

Life in pre-Revolutionary America was largely agrarian and home-based. Women worked alongside men, and gender distinctions did not limit women's contribution or workday. However, as the means of production moved from the land to the factory, and as society was reorganized accordingly, specialization divided human laborers. At the time of the American Revolution, very few women were educated, and literacy rates among women were half those of men.[18] As childbearers, women were assigned to the private sphere of home and hearth. Although women had been integral to the maintenance and survival of the agrarian economy, the duties of the home were now defined as distinct from those of the productive economy and paid labor force outside the home. Opportunities for women to earn money or to control property were severely limited by law and practice. Women constituted the reproductive, unpaid labor force and men the productive, paid labor force. In this sense, they complemented each other and were said to occupy separate spheres.[19]

Separate Spheres Ideology

Women's role in the private sphere was, by definition, incompatible with full participation in society. Separate spheres ideology, although not originally defined by law, clearly identified the activities available for women as consistent with their primary role as childbearers and nurturers. Women's role within the home was raised to new heights of glorification for middle- and upper-class white women. The home was a woman's exclusive domain, giving her a certain degree of autonomy. Unpaid charitable and welfare activities, particularly those directed at women and children, were encouraged for all white women as appropriate extensions of the private sphere. For working- and lower-class white women and for women of color, the separate sphere limited their access to the productive labor pool and depressed the wages paid for their work.

Opportunities for work outside the home closely paralleled women's duties within the home. Immigrant women in the 1840s and 1850s, for example, worked in sex-segregated industries such as textile, clothing, and shoe manufacturing. Teaching, sewing, and later nursing were also seen as consistent with women's domestic responsibilities, although the pay was almost negligible. Enslaved women in the South were at the bottom of the hierarchy in every respect. They were subject entirely to the white male patriarchal ruling class and did not enjoy any of the privileges of autonomy that accompanied the separate station enjoyed by white women in the middle and upper classes.

Although the separate spheres ideology was ultimately quite constraining for all women, it did provide limited opportunities for middle- and upper-class women to gain experience in forming welfare associations. It afforded them growing access to education and made it possible for women to interact with other women in quasi-public settings. These interactions enabled women to view their condition in a critical light and eventually to organize for a greater role as women and to advocate for more rights in the public sphere. In this sense, the separate sphere was empowering for white middle-class women. However, because power in a capitalist economy flows from those who control valued resources (namely, money or goods), men continued to exercise decision-making power both within and outside the home. As separate spheres ideology found its way into court decisions and into the public's understanding of normal daily life, men used the ideology to solidify their control over women's lives and livelihoods.

Separate and Unequal Becomes the Law

Separate spheres ideology was reinforced and given the weight of law through *Bradwell v. Illinois* (1873). Myra Bradwell, a feminist active in women's suffrage organizations, passed the Illinois bar exam in 1869, but under Illinois law, females were not permitted to practice law, and the state's supreme court refused to allow her a license. Bradwell appealed to the US Supreme Court, claiming that the state of Illinois had violated her rights under the Fourteenth Amendment in denying her one of the "privileges of citizenship" (the privilege of practicing law). The US Supreme Court denied her claims and reaffirmed Illinois's power to determine distinct privileges for men and women under state law. In a concurring opinion,

Justice Joseph P. Bradley specifically noted the separate spheres ideology as justification for limiting women's role in the public sphere:

> Civil law, as well as nature herself, has always recognized a wide difference in the respective spheres and destinies of man and woman. Man is, or should be, woman's protector and defender. The natural and proper timidity and delicacy which belongs to the female sex evidently unfits it for many of the occupations of civil life. The constitution of the family organization, which is founded in the Divine ordinance, as well as in the nature of things, indicates the domestic sphere as that which properly belongs to the domain and functions of womanhood. The harmony, not to say identity, of interests and views which belong, or should belong, to the family institution is repugnant to the idea of a woman adopting a distinct and independent career from that of her husband. So firmly fixed was this sentiment in the founders of common law that it became a maxim of that system of jurisprudence that a woman had no legal existence apart from her husband, who was regarded as her head and representative in the social state. (83 U.S. 130, 21 L.Ed. 442)

Note that Justice Bradley relied on a series of assumptions in denying Bradwell's Fourteenth Amendment claim. First, he clearly delineated separate spheres and destinies for men and women, grounded not only in civil and common law but also in nature. Second, Justice Bradley said that the patriarchal family was not only natural but founded in "the Divine ordinance." Finally, he stated that the "law of the Creator" relegated women to the "offices of wife and mother." In other words, what is natural, ordained by the Creator, and made real through civil practice, the US Supreme Court cannot change. Furthermore, all women were captives of nature, the Creator, and common law, since the Court refused to address the privileges and immunities of adult women apart from their marital status:

> It is true that many women are unmarried and not affected by any of the duties, complications, and incapacities arising out of the married state, but these are exceptions to the general rule. The paramount destiny and mission of woman are to fulfil the noble and benign offices of wife and mother. This is the law of the Creator. And the rules of civil society must be adapted to the general constitution of things, and cannot be based upon exceptional cases. (83 U.S. 130, 21 L.Ed. 442)

Like Aristotle in an earlier time, the US Supreme Court treated all women as a group and ruled that even though there may be women whose exceptional abilities fit them for public life, society must be governed by the assumption that a woman's proper role is that of wife and mother. As such, women are dependent on men and cannot be treated as individuals in their own right. Although some women may have abilities that (but for their sex) would entitle them to practice law, society cannot be governed by such exceptions.

Later Court rulings would use the separate spheres ideology as a justification to protect women in the labor force and to accommodate their "special burden" by limiting their civic obligations (e.g., the vote, jury duty, military service). The Court rejected separate spheres ideology only during the last two decades of the twentieth century and then only piecemeal, not entirely. Although most would argue that both sex and race are immutable characteristics not subject to an individual's control, the Supreme Court still assumes that sex bears some relation to one's abilities; it does not, however, make similar assumptions about race. These distinctions and assumptions, embedded in the philosophy of law in the United States, will arise again in later chapters examining education, work, and family issues.

The Basis of Restricted Citizenship for Married Women

Bradwell's status as a *feme covert* (a woman "covered" entirely by her husband's legal identity) also contributed to her being denied the ability to practice law. Until the mid-1800s, **coverture**, imported to the colonies from the English legal tradition, defined married couples as one entity represented in civil society by the husband, thus complicating women's claims to equality and their challenges to the constraints of separate spheres ideology. English jurist William Blackstone wrote:

> By marriage, the husband and wife are one person in law: that is, the very being or legal existence of the woman is suspended during the marriage, or at least is incorporated and consolidated into that of the husband; under whose wing, protection and cover, she performs every thing. . . . [She] is said to be covert-baron, or under the protection and influence of her husband, her baron, or lord; and her condition upon marriage is called her *coverture*.[20]

A married woman could not execute contracts independently of her husband, nor could she buy or sell property, dispose of personal assets such as jewelry and household items, control the destiny of her children, or serve as their guardian apart from her husband's consent. Marital rape was inconceivable because husband and wife were one person. It was not until 1978, when New York included a spouse along with a stranger and an acquaintance in the list of perpetrators of rape, that marital rape was outlawed anywhere in the United States.

In 1805, the US Supreme Court articulated the nation's implicit understanding of a married woman's obligations to the state and her status as a citizen apart from her husband in the case of *Martin v. Massachusetts*. Anna Gordon Martin received approximately 844 acres of land from her father upon his death. As was the custom, her husband, William Martin, controlled the land during his lifetime, but the "right of remainder" meant that the land would pass to Anna's son James following her husband's death. However, the Massachusetts Confiscation Act of 1779 allowed the state to confiscate properties of individuals who fled with the British during the war, and Anna had fled with her husband.[21] At the close of the war, Anna's son petitioned for the return of the property, arguing that his mother, as a married woman, had had no choice but to follow her husband, and so could not have exercised the choice to stay in Massachusetts and retain her property. For that reason, the seizure of the property was illegal.

As inhabitants of the state (citizens), all women were subject to its laws, and single women were subject to taxation. The question before the Supreme Court was whether a married woman could have a relationship with the state distinct from that of her husband. Attorneys for the Martins argued that Anna, as a *feme covert*, was incapable of defying her husband by remaining in Massachusetts while he fled. They further argued that the state did not expect married women to act independently and could expect no assistance from them in defending the country: "So far are women from being of service in the defence of a country against the attacks of an enemy that it is frequently thought expedient to send them out of the way, lest they impede the operations of their own party."[22] Attorneys for the state crafted their argument based on the principles of natural law, reasoning that a precondition of citizenship was autonomous competence, and because women were considered citizens, they should also be responsible for their own actions even when their actions defied the theory of coverture marriage. They argued that "if patriarchy in politics is rejected, so too must patriarchy in marriage."[23] The Court ruled unanimously in favor of the Martins and returned the land to Anna's son. Although women might be citizens in a conceptual sense, marriage took away the privileges of citizenship in a real sense.

This line of reasoning was not merely a post-Revolutionary mind-set clouded by a tradition of coverture. In 1907, Congress passed a law stating that women who married aliens lost their citizenship even if they remained in the United States. The Supreme Court upheld the law as late as 1915, ruling in *Mackenzie v. Hare* that if a woman voluntarily married an alien, she must give up her citizenship and adopt the nationality of her husband. This law remained in effect until passage of the Cable Act of 1922, which stated, "The right of a person to become a naturalized citizen shall not be denied to a person on account of sex or because she is a married woman." This meant that American-born women who married aliens were treated as naturalized citizens, who could lose their citizenship if they lived abroad for two or more years. Even then, however, the law covered only marriages to men who were eligible to become naturalized citizens (excluding men from China or Japan, among others).[24] Thus, well into the twentieth century, a woman's marital status governed her relationship to the state, in terms of both rights and obligations.

This gendered construction of citizenship for women differed from male citizenship in important ways. The same line of reasoning that denied married women property, guardianship of their children, and independent thought and action found its way into debates over suffrage and subsequent Supreme Court rulings that rendered married women both sentimental and legal dependents of their husbands. The American Revolution challenged and abolished political patriarchy, yet even at the height of revolutionary spirit, familial patriarchy was continually reinforced through law, custom, and economic realities. Women remained in the same class as slaves and children when it came to extending the political rights of citizenship. Any attempt to challenge the natural order that kept women entirely in the private sphere was quashed.

The separate spheres ideology presents the most serious challenge to those who advocate the fairness doctrine as the most appropriate path to gender equality. The logic that believes the essential differences between men and women suit them for different roles in society cannot be overcome by law alone. Advocates of the fairness doctrine argue that trying to make men and women alike when they are in fact different is an unproductive approach to improving women's lives. Instead, they urge that women be treated fairly. However, the pervasiveness of a separate spheres ideology makes it difficult to argue that women should participate fully in the public sphere, while believing that women need protection from and accommodation for the burdens of their sex, which they bring with them to the public sphere. Like the legal equality doctrine discussed earlier, the fairness doctrine of gender equality is not without its theoretical and practical problems.

FEMINISM'S DIRECT CHALLENGE TO GENDER RELATIONS

Challenging long-entrenched gender roles and relationships is difficult even for the most committed individuals or groups. Gender exerts a powerful grip on each individual and on our social, political, and economic systems. Without some sensitivity to the power of gendered life, it is easy to miss the workings of this organizing system, since gendered life seems so "normal." The result is a system in which economic, political, social, and cultural forces interact with and reinforce one another in ways that continue to benefit one group and disadvantage the others. As participants in these interlocking systems, humans constantly reproduce the world we know through socialization, education, and role modeling as if we have no other choice. The effect is that the system continues as normal, becoming increasingly difficult to challenge as we each take our place within it. Those who suggest the system is corrupt or wrong threaten to upset centuries of tradition and custom that make life predictable and comfortable for the majority.

Feminism provides the most direct challenge to the gendered world, as well as to patriarchy, capitalism, and the sexist assumptions that women's difference from men renders them inherently inferior. Feminism is a complex and somewhat paradoxical ideology that defies a single definition. In fact, feminists are rarely in agreement with one another over the ultimate aims of feminism or the means to achieve them. Although many feminists exhibit a commitment to absolute legal and practical equality, some feminists have argued for separate spheres of influence and an emphasis on difference and complementarity rather than equality.[25] In an oft-quoted passage, Rebecca West wrote in 1913, "I myself have never been able to find out precisely what feminism is. I only know that people call me a feminist whenever I express sentiments that differentiate me from a doormat or a prostitute."[26] The lack of a single, well-articulated definition can lead to confusion, but the rich variety of perspectives accurately reflects the paradox of gender. Feminists of all descriptions wrestle with the same question: How can demands for equality and fairness be reconciled with sex differences?

As a word and concept, *feminism* is a relatively recent addition to the lexicon, emerging only in the 1910s to express a set of goals broader than those the suffrage movement embraced.[27] According to historian Nancy Cott, people in the nineteenth century talked about the "advancement of woman," the "cause of woman," or "woman's rights" and "woman suffrage." To our modern ears, the use of the singular "woman" sounds awkward, but "nineteenth-century women's consistent usage of the singular *woman* symbolized, in a word, the unity of the female sex. It proposed that all women have one cause, one movement."[28] Now in the twenty-first century, individualism is valued so highly that it would be rare to encounter anyone who believed that all women share a single cause. Modern feminism reflects these sentiments and, in doing so, embraces the paradox of gender equality that provides the foundation for the two paths to equality:

> Feminism asks for sexual equality that includes sexual difference. It posits that women recognize their unity while it stands for diversity among women. It requires gender consciousness for its basis yet calls for the elimination of prescribed gender roles. These are paradoxes rooted in the actual situation of women, who are the same as men in a species sense, but different from men in reproductive biology and the construction of gender. Men and women are alike as human beings, and yet categorically different from each other; their sameness and differences derive from nature and culture, how inextricably entwined we can hardly know.[29]

So, given this set of paradoxes, how might feminism be defined? Nancy Cott offers a very good three-part working definition of feminism:

- A belief in equality, defined not as "sameness" but rather as opposition to ranking one sex superior or inferior to the other, or as opposition to one sex's categorical control of the rights and opportunities of the other

- A belief that women's condition is socially constructed and historically shaped, rather than preordained by God or nature
- A belief that women's socially constructed position situates them on shared ground enabling a group identity or gender consciousness sufficient to mobilize women for change[30]

APPROACHES TO FEMINISM

As an ideology, feminism has spawned a number of different "brands," among them liberal feminism, radical feminism, Marxist-socialist feminism, global feminism, black feminism, gender feminism, third wave feminism, and intersectional feminism. Scholars differ on how to label and divide the complex terrain of feminist theory, but the preceding list is fairly representative of the major strands of feminist thought today. Philosopher Rosemarie Tong distinguishes among these theories based on the locus of women's oppression in each. For example, liberal, radical, Marxist-socialist, and global feminists (as well as ecofeminists to some extent) attribute women's subordination to macrolevel institutions, such as patriarchy, capitalism, or colonialism. Gender feminists, sometimes also called cultural feminists or maternal feminists, focus on the microcosm of the individual, claiming that the roots of women's oppression are embedded deep within a woman's psyche.[31] Third wave feminism developed in the early 1990s among young feminists interested in reclaiming the power of feminism and extending its reach and deepening its impact for women described as the daughters and granddaughters of second wave feminists. **Intersectionality**, a term coined by law professor Kimberlé Williams Crenshaw, draws attention to multiple sources of discrimination and oppression.[32] Although first used to describe how race and gender interacted in ways that marginalized rather than empowered black women, intersectional feminism now includes social identities beyond race.

Distinguishing between the strands of feminism and understanding the variety of feminist perspectives can sometimes seem overwhelming, but to simplify our discussion by examining only one or two feminist perspectives would perilously ignore the diversity among women themselves. Part of understanding why women do not always agree on the best way to advance their individual and collective status in society is grounded in the differing perspectives on what feminism means and how it should operate as an organizing philosophy for the women's movement. This section begins with a brief critical review of each approach to feminism.[33] It concludes by exploring the claim that feminism is dead and has been replaced by a postfeminist reality in the twenty-first century.

Liberal Feminism

Liberal feminism is perhaps the oldest strand of feminism, rooted in the same ferment that promoted individual autonomy over aristocratic privilege in the French

Revolution and the American Revolution. Liberalism stresses the importance of rational thought, autonomous action, and choice on the part of each person. Reason is what most clearly distinguishes humans from other forms of animal life. Autonomy empowers an individual to make choices in her or his own best interests, thereby elevating individual rights above the common good. Liberal theorists believe that the political and legal systems can be used to promote a liberal agenda for all people.

Early liberal feminists such as Mary Wollstonecraft, John Stuart Mill, and Harriet Taylor Mill stressed the importance of educating women, enfranchising women, and providing women equal access to both opportunities and resources in society. Liberal feminists tend to work *within* the existing political system and structures to eradicate all forms of sexual discrimination. Contemporary liberal feminists believe that by reforming the legal and political system to allow women equal access to opportunities and resources, men and women can achieve a state of equality. Liberal feminists target laws that distinguish between men and women based on sex. The Declaration of Sentiments and Resolutions, issued by women at the Seneca Falls Convention in 1848, was a liberal feminist document. It called for the reform of laws restricting women's right to hold property, to control resources, and to vote. The US suffrage movement and suffrage organizations, such as the National American Woman Suffrage Association (NAWSA), extended across three generations women's liberal feminist claims that suffrage was an integral step in achieving political and social equality. The Equal Rights Amendment (ERA) in the United States and the United Nations Convention on the Elimination of All Forms of Discrimination Against Women (CEDAW) are examples of contemporary legal reforms in this tradition.

During the early 1960s, President John F. Kennedy responded to feminists' concerns about equality for women by forming the Commission on the Status of Women. The commission studied various forms of discrimination against women, collected and made public new data on the condition of women, and spawned a number of state-based commissions that had similar missions. As a result of the data presented, the Equal Pay Act, promising equal pay for equal work, regardless of sex, was passed in 1963. Political action groups—the National Organization for Women (NOW), the National Women's Political Caucus (NWPC), and the Women's Equity Action League (WEAL), for example—were formed in the late 1960s to pursue the liberal feminist agenda. This agenda was based largely on a plan to demand enforcement of civil rights laws protecting women from discrimination. NOW and NWPC are still active today.

A contemporary example of liberal feminism is found in Sheryl Sandberg's *Lean In: Women, Work, and the Will to Lead*.[34] Sandberg is the chief operating officer of Facebook and founder of the Lean In Foundation. In the book Sandberg combines personal anecdotes with social science to encourage women to "lean in" to their ambition—to stay in the workplace and to aim for the top positions. She argues that the presence of more women in top corporate positions will transform the workplace in ways that benefit all women. Sandberg explores several issues on the liberal feminist agenda: the ambition double standard, the importance of a supportive life partner, the inverse relationship between a woman's success and likability, and the challenge of "having it all." Sandberg's message has been well received by the public and the media, and her network of "lean in circles" is reminiscent of consciousness-raising groups from the women's liberation movement decades earlier. Critics, however, charge that Sandberg's focus on individual achievement ignores the systemic barriers faced by many women.[35] The editors of *The Feminist Wire* write that Sandberg's form of corporate feminism works to "recreate the same old white heteropatriarchy that defines the American Empire." Feminist bell hooks expresses the fundamental critique of liberal feminism in labeling Sandberg's work "faux feminism": "There was never and is no simple homogenous gendered identity that we could call 'women' struggling to be equal with men. In fact, the reality was and is that privileged white women often experience a greater sense of solidarity with men of their same class than with poor white women or women of color."[36]

A variety of criticisms have been leveled against liberal feminism. Early and contemporary liberal feminists alike concentrate almost exclusively on the public sphere. Women's unpaid labor in the home, domestic abuse, marital rape, and traditional practices that discriminate against women in many cultures are not addressed within the liberal approach because they occur in the private sphere. These issues are labeled "personal" and therefore are not subject to public scrutiny or redress in the public policy arena. Radical feminists charge that liberal feminism has been co-opted by the male establishment since its goals are to reform the existing system rather than to replace it. Global feminists equate liberal feminists' embrace of individualism with Western values that do not fit well in other cultures where community is favored over the individual. Additionally, individualism makes sex solidarity and the development of a movement difficult, as liberal feminists have discovered repeatedly throughout history.

Politically conservative critics charge that liberal feminists, with their concentration on ending legal sex discrimination in society, are out of touch with mainstream women who still value marriage, motherhood, and family—all traditionally private sphere concerns. Finally, liberal feminism has been labeled racist, classist, and heterosexist. This last charge suggests that liberal feminism speaks only to concerns of white, middle- and upper-class, heterosexual women and ignores the realities of intersectionality. The history of the women's movement to date has offered ample evidence that the concerns of women of color, the working poor, and lesbians have been on the periphery of the agenda.

Radical Feminism

Whether you describe yourself as a liberal feminist dedicated to legal reforms in pursuit of equality or as a radical feminist dedicated to revolutionary change most likely depends on whether you see sexism as a form of oppression or as discrimination. Viewing sexism as a form of oppression emphasizes change affecting women collectively—a level of change possible only through a radical reordering of patriarchal society. Women's **oppression** refers to patriarchy's grip on all women, regardless of class, race, or sexual orientation. Ending oppression requires ending patriarchy, capitalism, and Western dominance. Viewing sexism as a form of discrimination emphasizes the individual. **Discrimination** refers to "the act of singling out a person for special treatment, not on the basis of individual merit, but on the basis of prejudices about the group to which the person belongs."[37]

Unlike liberal feminists, who believe that it is possible to produce systemic reforms that would yield women more rights (ultimately leading to equality of rights and the end of discrimination), radical feminists believe it is the "sex-gender system" itself that is the source of women's oppression.[38] **Radical feminism** is interested in women's liberation from the bounds of this system and therefore advocates for a total revolution. For this reason, scholars often classify women's organizations as either "reform-minded" or "revolutionary" and link them to liberal or radical feminist theory accordingly.[39] Radical feminist theory spawned a variety of activist groups in the 1960s. Many, although not all, were associated with the political left. Such radical organizations as the Redstockings, Women's International Terrorist Conspiracy from Hell (WITCH), the Feminists, and the New York Radical Feminists were among some of the largest groups formed.

Sexism, as the first form of human oppression, must take precedence over other forms of oppression and must be eradicated first. Beyond agreement on this basic issue, radical feminists differ on the best way to eliminate sexism. Radical-libertarian feminists believe that femininity, women's sex, and reproductive roles limit women's development. They often promote androgyny (eliminating masculine-feminine distinctions) as a way to overcome the limits of femininity and to break the socially constructed link between sex and gender. Radical-cultural feminists, on the other hand, believe that female-feminine qualities are vastly superior to male-masculine characteristics. Women should not try to be like men; rather, they should try to embrace women's essential nature. Therefore, culturally associated feminine traits—interdependence, community, sharing, emotion, nature, peace, and life—should be celebrated over hierarchy, power, war, domination, and death. Androgyny simply clouds the female nature with undesirable male qualities. For these reasons, radical-cultural feminists are often associated with lesbian separatism, a school of thought that rejects participation in male- and heterosexual-dominated institutions.

Critics of radical feminism often target the stark choices this approach asks women to make. Issues of separatism, lesbianism, and the promotion of reproductive technology over traditional means of conception and biological motherhood draw fire from politically conservative critics who charge that radical feminists are out to eradicate the family. Others criticize radical-cultural feminists' belief in the essential nature of women, charging that it unnecessarily polarizes men and women.

Marxist-Socialist Feminism

In contrast to liberal theory's emphasis on the individual, Marxist-socialist theory stresses the collective aspect of human development. Men and women, through production and reproduction, have collectively created society, which in turn shapes them. Capitalism and patriarchy work hand in hand, although Marxist-socialists believe that capitalism, more than sexism, is at the root of women's oppression. Women's economic dependence on men gives them little leverage in other aspects of society. However, rather than singling out women as the oppressed class, Marxist-socialist theories focus on the worker. A woman's situation can only be understood in terms of her productive work and its relationship to her life. In a capitalist system, women are exploited both in the marketplace (lowest-paying and most menial jobs) and at home (no wages for her domestic labor).

Marxist-socialist feminism advocates public policy that aims to redistribute wealth and opportunity. For example, some have argued that women should be paid a wage for their housework; others have concentrated their actions on issues of the workplace outside the home and the disparities in pay and position between men and women. The concept of "equal pay for equal work" does not cover women working in traditional occupations that are undervalued. Advocates of equal pay for jobs of comparable worth argue that wage inequities will persist as long as jobs are segregated on the basis of gender.

Critics of Marxist-socialist feminism most often point to the sizable gap between the ideal and the reality in contemporary Marxist-socialist regimes (those remaining and those recently dissolved). Within those regimes, women have filled the majority of low-status and low-paying occupations and, contrary to theory, are still taking primary responsibility for home and child care.

Global Feminism

The forces of colonialism and nationalism have conspired to divide the world into the "haves," known as the First World, and the "have-nots," known as the Third World. **Global feminism** seeks to expand feminist thought to include issues vital to women in the Third World. They argue that economic and political forms of oppression are every bit as severe as sexual oppression: "For global feminists, the personal and political are one."[40] The ways in which various forms of oppression interconnect and affect women has been the focus of many global feminists. Some charge that First World women are blinded by sexual oppression. As a result, they overlook their own complicity in the oppression of women that multinational corporations and exploitative labor practices cause. Others suggest that color, class, and nationality cannot be separated from sex when addressing the forms of oppression people face. Western feminists, they argue, have been too narrow in their agendas, particularly liberal feminists, who were guided by legal reforms in the public sphere. Political participation is a hollow victory for those who cannot feed their families, earn a living wage, control their reproduction, and live free of violence.

Cultural practices that Western feminists and others deem exploitative or damaging to women have presented the most vexing problems for global feminists. Dowry, bride price, female circumcision, and many religious customs are examples of practices that when taken out of a cultural context are indefensible in any feminist theory. However, the importance and power of culture, tradition, and religion make passing judgment on these and other issues problematic. Differences among women of various cultures present many challenges to global feminists who attempt to create a feminist theory and set of practices that unite rather than divide women.

Black Feminism

Most feminist anthologies use the term *multicultural feminism* to encompass the diversity of feminist thought among diverse populations. African American feminists in the United States, however, have been among the most vocal critics of the mainstream liberal feminist tradition, and so **black feminism** is included here as a unique category of feminist thought.

One of the thorniest questions arising in black feminist thought, according to Patricia Hill Collins, is *who* can be a black feminist.[41] Does authentic voice flow from one's race, one's experiences with the dual oppressions of race and gender, or one's ideas and ideologies regardless of race and gender? The core of the black feminist tradition encompasses several themes: the legacy of struggle, the experience born of multiple oppressions, and the interdependence of thought and action. Black feminists often express frustration that white women seem incapable of understanding the "multiple jeopardy" that black women face on a daily basis. Sexism cannot be separated from racism, classism, or any of the other "isms" women must deal with. To pursue a single-minded gender equality strategy is to ignore profound forms of oppression and to exclude women of color from the women's movement. Black women have experienced discrimination in the women's movement (discussed in greater detail in Chapter 2) and continue to press feminists to expand the definition of feminism. Alice Walker has offered the term **womanist** as an alternative to *feminist*, saying "womanist is to feminist as purple is to lavender."[42] A womanist is at heart a humanist pursuing political action as a means to human empowerment—including both men and women of all races, ethnicities, and abilities.

Critics of black feminism are most often African American women themselves. Some critics argue that black feminists have failed to confront sexism strongly enough as it occurs within the black community. Some black women have been reticent to press for stronger laws protecting women's interests, believing that black males are under siege by the dominant white community and would be disproportionately harmed in the process. In 1991, when lawyer Anita Hill charged Clarence Thomas, her former boss at the Equal Employment Opportunity Commission (EEOC), with sexual harassment, the nation was introduced to the divisions within the African American community and among black feminists. Hill's charges became public during Thomas's Supreme Court confirmation hearings before the Senate Judiciary Committee. Criticism of Hill and her decision to make her charges public came from a variety of quarters, but it was especially strong among blacks. They considered her "disloyal" and criticized her for potentially derailing a black man's chances for a seat on the Supreme Court. Public opinion polls revealed support for Hill among feminists, although 49 percent of American women (including both blacks and whites) either sided with Thomas or declared the dispute a "draw."[43] Further probing by pollsters found that Hill's Yale law degree and successful law career made her identity as a "black woman" problematic because it did not fit the stereotype many held.

Gender Feminism

Gender feminism, unlike any of the theories previously described, argues that the root of women's oppression lies somewhere at the intersection of biology, psychology, and culture. Gender feminists believe that the traits culture associates with women and femininity are superior in many respects to masculine traits, and therefore both men and women should strive to develop relational webs. The issues most closely associated with gender feminism include the superiority of women's moral development, women's ways of knowing and thinking, and women's mothering abilities. Because gender feminists argue that men and women are developmentally different, they are sometimes also known as *difference feminists*. However, difference in this case works in favor of women. Among the best-known gender feminists is Carol Gilligan, who challenged psychologist Lawrence Kohlberg's theory of moral development in her book *In a Different Voice*.[44] She argued that Kohlberg's widely accepted model did not account for differences between male and female moral development. While males resolve moral dilemmas using an ethic of justice, females use an ethic of care. While Gilligan did not at first argue that one was superior to the other, her work has been widely used to promote gender feminism's claim to women's moral superiority.

Maternalism, a subset of gender feminism, celebrates the power of women's reproductive capacity. Mothers in many Latin American nations, for example, have politicized motherhood in opposing dictatorships, raising sensitive political questions, and serving as visible reminders of the repression of immoral regimes. In the United States, mothers' movements are enjoying a contemporary resurgence. On Mother's Day 2000, tens of thousands of mothers marched on Washington, D.C., in the Million Moms' March to protest gun violence against children and to petition the government to take action in the form of tougher gun control legislation. The Mothers of the Movement is a group of African American women, each the mother of a son or daughter who died due to gun violence, while in police custody, or as a result of police actions. Their deaths attracted national media attention and helped to inspire the Black Lives Matter movement. At the 2016 Democratic National Convention, the Mothers of the Movement endorsed Hillary Clinton for president, saying she was the best candidate to make progress on police reform and gun violence prevention. After the convention they traveled together across the country, campaigning for Clinton and encouraging people to vote and to speak out for racial justice in African American communities.

Critics of gender feminism argue that associating women with caring reinforces the traditional view of women as nurturers, rather than the view of women as autonomous and strong. Particularly in relation to electoral politics, a nurturant posture of care has proven to be a somewhat limited virtue, depending on the domestic political climate in any one election. Others charge that labeling women as the only sex responsible for caring releases men from important social and familial obligations and unnecessarily polarizes men's and women's gender roles. Some also object to the nomenclature of maternal feminism, arguing that not all women are or aspire to be mothers.

Third Wave Feminism

In 1992, in the wake of the William Kennedy Smith rape trial and Anita Hill's testimony in the Clarence Thomas confirmation hearings, more than a hundred young feminists gathered in New York City and organized a network they called the Third Wave. Rebecca Walker is credited with coining the term in "Becoming the Third Wave," an essay published in *Ms.* magazine in 1992. The vision articulated by organizers was "to become the national network for young feminists, to politicize and organize young women from diverse cultural and economic backgrounds, to strengthen the relationships between young women and older feminists, and to consolidate a strong base of membership that can mobilize for specific issues, political candidates, and events."[45] **Third wave feminism** has a broad focus and integrates women's concerns with larger issues related to justice, including racism, poverty, and environmental issues. Betty Friedan, a founder of the second wave of feminism, said of the third wavers, "Young women are the true daughters of feminism; they take nothing for granted and are advancing the cause with marvelous verve. If they keep doing what they are doing, thirty years from today we may not need a feminist movement. We may have achieved real equality."[46]

In addition to newly formed organizations for young feminists' interests, several second wave organizations (such as NOW, the Feminist Majority Foundation, and the National Council of Women's Organizations) started new campus programs and outreach initiatives targeted at female millennials, the generation born roughly between 1977 and 1996. Feminist blogs such as *Feministe* and *Feministing*, among others, reach out to women beyond campus and organizational limits. "You cannot overestimate the impact of the Internet on feminism's outreach potential. We reach women who never had a class in women's studies, women in towns with no NOW chapter or any other explicit feminist organization," said Jessica Valenti, founder of *Feministing*.[47] Blogging has been called the new vehicle for feminist consciousness raising.[48] E-zines have acted as another form of women-only cyberspace.

More recently, third wave feminists have been at the forefront in challenging binary understandings of "male" and "female." Influenced by queer theory, young feminists argue that gender and sexuality are fluid categories. Gender identity, far from established at birth, is evolving and subject to individual expression. Sometimes associated with grrrl-feminism, third wave feminism celebrates individualism over artificial categories of identity, gender, and sexuality. Scholar Martha Rampton wrote that "grrrls of the third wave stepped onto the stage as strong and empowered, eschewing victimization and defining feminine beauty for themselves as subjects, not as objects of sexist patriarchy . . . the very notion of gender has been unbalanced in a way that encourages experimentation and creative thought."[49] Rampton described third wave feminism as conceiving reality "not so much in terms of fixed structures and power relations, but in terms of performance within contingencies. Third wave feminism breaks boundaries."

Some veteran feminists of the second wave express concern that third wave feminists are oriented around individual or personal expression rather than sharing the collectivist orientation necessary to agitate for political change. Kalpana Krishnamurthy, codirector of the Third Wave Foundation, says of the conflict, "I think that the impact of the feminist movement was in helping women to achieve a voice. Now we are articulating that voice in a multiplicity of ways."[50] Jennifer Baumgardner and Amy Richards, authors of *Manifesta*, say that young women today do take second wave feminism's gains for granted, that the liberation gained by the second wave infuses their lives like fluoride in water, giving them a certain degree of confidence. They caution, however, that young women also need to develop a political consciousness sufficient to confront today's challenges to equality. This strain of third wave feminism is echoed in the book *Catching a Wave*.[51] With essays grouped in a way that is designed to mirror the consciousness-raising process developed by second wave feminists to highlight social inequities and then to politicize readers to take action, this book argues that only by continually confronting the persistent structural inequalities in society can feminism retain its transformational power.

Intersectional Feminism

Emerging out of the shared space between second and third wave feminists, intersectional feminism is a critique of both in some respects. Intersectionality, according to *Washington Post* writer Christine Emba, has become a way to pose the question "Is feminism for everyone, or just the middle class?"[52] In many ways the question harkens back to a common critique of liberal feminism—that it largely left out women of color, immigrant women, and the poor. As "intersectionality" has emerged in the dialogue of popular culture and academia, its use has broadened beyond race and gender to include other overlapping social identities—sexual orientation, nationality, class, and disability, for example.

Intersectionality, according to Kimberlé Williams Crenshaw, was intended to reflect the ways in which existing antidiscrimination laws did not capture the intersection of race and gender that rendered black women invisible. She describes a 1976 discrimination suit against General Motors to highlight the problem. The company segregated its workforce by race and gender—there were black jobs and white jobs, jobs for women and jobs for men. "Neither the black jobs nor the women's jobs were appropriate for black women, since they were neither male nor white. Wasn't this clearly discrimination, even if some blacks and some women were hired?"[53] Her point is that antidiscrimination laws, arguably the greatest success of the legal equality approach, did not cover situations where the source of discrimination fell in the "intersection" of recognized or protected categories and therefore became invisible. "Intersectional erasures are not exclusive to black women," writes Crenshaw. "People of color within LGBTQ movements; girls of color in the fight against the school-to-prison pipeline; women within immigration movements; trans women within feminist movements; and people with disabilities fighting police abuse—all face vulnerabilities that reflect the intersections of racism, sexism, class oppression, transphobia, able-ism and more."[54] In this sense, intersectionality becomes about inclusion.

Critics of intersectional feminism argue that a focus on intersectionality is a new form of "identity politics," wherein each group advocates for inclusion without recognizing the ways their source of oppression is shared. The fight for equality becomes one of "us against them," where the phrase "check your privilege"—an expression most often used by social justice advocates and bloggers to encourage self-reflection on the many forms of invisible privilege (advantages) afforded to whites, males, heterosexual, and the able-bodied, to name only a few—becomes a form of bullying. Finally, some posit that without the law as an effective tool, intersectionality is a purely academic exercise that will not result in meaningful change.

Postfeminism?

Rather than embrace a third or even fourth wave of feminism, some (largely in the popular media) have argued that feminism has outlived its usefulness—or, to put it more bluntly, that "feminism is dead." Professor Mary Hawkesworth addresses the contradiction between the unprecedented growth of feminist activism around the globe and the recurrent pronouncement of feminism's death: "These textual accounts of death serve as allegorical signs for something else, a means of identifying a perceived danger in need of elimination, a way for a community to define itself through those it symbolically chooses to kill."[55]

The pronouncement of feminism's demise or failure has been a persistent media theme since the early 1970s, but what would it mean to be in a postfeminist era? Janelle Reinelt describes **postfeminism** as "a time when the residue of feminism is still with us in terms of its history and some of its commitments, but without the overarching umbrella of an organized social or political movement at either grass roots or national levels."[56] As Deborah Siegel, author of *Sisterhood Interrupted*, puts it, "The dilemma of my generation and those behind me is that we're caught between the hope for a world that no longer degrades women and the reality of a culture that is degrading. We see a few women breaking into the upper echelons of power, and we think things are great. It's confusing to be a daughter of feminism in a culture only half transformed."[57] Those who claim a fourth wave of feminism is under way point to the ways that issues central to the women's movement for decades are currently receiving attention in the mainstream press and politicians, including rape, violence against women, unequal pay, underrepresentation in positions of political and economic power, and workplace benefits such as sick leave and child care. Social media allows sexism to be called out and challenged in real time.

For many women, the reawakening came when the 2008 presidential primaries and general election campaign opened a new examination of gender matters. Media coverage of the two prominent women candidates in the field, Democratic senator Hillary Rodham Clinton and Republican governor Sarah Palin, focused new light on sex stereotypes largely thought extinct. When two men at a Clinton rally in New Hampshire yelled out "Iron my shirts!" the media reacted with amusement, not outrage. Sexism and sexist remarks by journalists and on-air pundits were pervasive throughout the primaries. Mike Barnicle on MSNBC described Clinton as "looking like everyone's first wife standing outside a probate court"; Jack Cafferty on CNN described her as "a scolding mother, talking down to a child." Glenn Beck of CNN observed, "There's something about her vocal range. . . . She's the stereotypical bitch, you know what I mean?"[58] On the Republican side, journalists were obsessed with Sarah Palin's appearance, and in September 2008, a company called Hero Builders released a highly sexualized Sarah Palin action figure dressed in a red push-up bra and a short schoolgirl tartan plaid skirt. As Kate Zernike observed in the *New York Times*, "A year ago, it all seemed so different. If the nation wasn't quite gender-blind, still, a woman stood poised to become president, didn't she?"[59] *Nation* columnist Katha Pollitt wrote that the "'sulfurous emanations' about Mrs. Clinton made [her] want to write a check to her campaign, knock on doors, vote for her twice—even though [I'd] probably choose another candidate on policy grounds."[60]

By the 2016 presidential contest, the media was more self-censoring, but sexism persisted in both political parties. As a candidate for the Republican presidential nomination, Donald J. Trump mocked fellow candidate Carly Fiorina's appearance ("Look at that face, would anyone vote for that? Can you imagine that, the face of our next president?").[61] Democrat Bernie Sanders's campaign manager chided the Clinton campaign for criticizing Sanders's campaign too aggressively: "Don't destroy the Democratic Party to satisfy the Secretary's ambitions to become President of the United States."[62] Bernie Sanders himself later claimed that Clinton was not qualified to be president. Countless news stories explored Hillary Clinton's "likability problem." Columnist David Brooks wrote that Clinton was disliked because she is a "workaholic" who "presents herself as a resume and policy brief." In other words, she wasn't fun.[63] Once the general election got under way, Republican Donald Trump questioned Hillary Clinton's stamina and claimed that she didn't "look presidential." After the first presidential debate, in which a majority of Americans believed that Hillary Clinton won by demonstrating a command of the issues and a presidential temperament, Fox News correspondent Brit Hume described her appearance as "composed, smug sometimes, not necessarily attractive."[64] Each of these examples calls attention to the prominent role gender plays in American elections and serves as a cautionary tale for any woman who might be considering a run for public office.

Do we live in a postfeminist world? Can women advance toward equality without an organized political movement sustained and energized by a feminist ideology? As you will see in the chapters ahead, women's pursuit of equality has been slow and progress has come incrementally. The catalyst for major progress has always been the tension created by women's political organizing for and against change.

USING POLITICS TO BRING ABOUT CHANGE

How will we know if and when women realize equality? Most likely the answer to this question depends in part on which path to gender equality you favor. If you favor the legal equality doctrine, you most likely believe that women's equality will resemble a gender-neutral state in which men and women exist as equals. If you favor the fairness doctrine, you probably believe that women are different from men and should remain so, but should not be disadvantaged by those differences. The central question of gender equality is this: Do differences between men and women require a sensitivity to sexual difference resulting in special provisions that compensate women for their biological role in childbearing, or does gender neutrality require that no distinctions of any kind be made on the basis of sex? In effect, an affirmative answer to one question or the other delineates the two paths traveled by activists in women's movements—both of which have been traveled in the name of improving women's status. While the two approaches may not be entirely mutually exclusive, their dual existence and favor among women have confounded the ability of women to exhibit sex solidarity around the issues of discrimination and gender inequality. Those who believe men and women are the same except for their sex-linked contributions to human reproduction are confident that gender-neutral laws can remedy the discrimination women face by eliminating sex-based barriers to opportunities in the public sphere. However, those who believe that men and women are essentially different are convinced that special legislation is the remedy for the social, economic, and political disadvantages women endure as a result of motherhood and traditional gender roles. Thus women are often most at odds with other women over their common interests.

Where does this leave women and the women's movement? Is feminism still relevant to women today? If so, what kind of feminism should guide women's political and social actions? A national survey in 2015 found that six in ten women and one-third of men identify as a feminist or strong feminist. Nearly 70 percent of those surveyed defined the feminist movement as "empowering."[65] The issues that rank as top priorities for women today include equal pay; domestic violence, sexual assault, and sexual harassment; child care; women's health care; family leave; drug and alcohol addiction; electing more women to political office; women in other parts of the world; and encouraging more women to pursue careers in math, science, and technology. Younger, unmarried, and minority women continue to experience economic stress following the recession that began in 2008, from which recovery has been slow. A higher minimum wage, paid sick days, paid family and medical leave, affordable child care, and ways to alleviate student debt are top issues on their agenda.[66] These issues will be addressed in the chapters that follow. Taken together, these issues make up a robust agenda for the next generation of feminists, both men and women.

Regardless of their chosen path and strategy, women have worked for nearly two centuries to gain access to the public sphere and to improve the quality of their lives. To effect this change, women have used such conventional forms of political participation as lobbying for constitutional changes, fighting for the right to vote, and pursuing elective office, as well as less conventional methods, including working in organizations outside government and protesting public and private sector inequities. In addition, women have lobbied for policy changes before state legislatures and the US Congress. At various times, the courts have facilitated or hampered their efforts. To quote the National Women's Equality Act (1998), women have "lobbied, litigated, picketed, marched, petitioned, engaged in civil disobedience, and boycotted to win women's rights."[67] However, women have still not gained full political, legal, social, economic, and educational equality. This book examines and analyzes women's political experiences, attitudes, and behaviors, and evaluates their successes as well as their failures to understand more clearly where women stand today in their pursuit of gender equality.

NOTES

Boxed feature notes appear at the end of the Notes section.

1 Linda Kerber, "The Paradox of Women's Citizenship in the Early Republic: The Case of *Martin v. Massachusetts*, 1805," *American Historical Review*, April 1992.

2 Maxine Margolis, *Mothers and Such: Views of American Women and Why They Changed* (Berkeley: University of California Press, 1984).

3 Ibid., 47.

4 Abigail Adams to John Adams, March 31, 1776.

5 Virginia Sapiro, *The Political Integration of Women: Roles, Socialization, and Politics* (Chicago: University of Chicago Press, 1983), 19.

6 Alexis de Tocqueville, *Democracy in America* (1835; reprint, New York: Doubleday, 1969), 243.

7 "Understanding Gender," Gender Spectrum, www.genderspectrum.org/quick-links/understanding-gender, accessed July 4, 2016.

8 Sandra Lipsitz Bem, *The Lenses of Gender: Transforming the Debate on Sexual Inequality* (New Haven, CT: Yale University Press, 1993), 1.

9 Aristotle, *The Politics of Aristotle*, trans. Ernest Barker (London: Oxford University Press, 1947), 43–45.

10 Bem, *The Lenses of Gender*, 11.

11 Suzanne M. Marilley, *Woman Suffrage and the Origins of Liberal Feminism in the United States, 1820–1920* (Cambridge, MA: Harvard University Press, 1996).

12 Carole Pateman, *The Sexual Contract* (Stanford, CA: Stanford University Press, 1988).

13 J. S. Mill, "The Subjection of Women," in *The Feminist Papers*, ed. Alice S. Rossi (Boston: Northeastern University Press, 1972).

14 Ibid., 201.

15 Ibid., 199.

16 Adrienne Rich, *Of Woman Born: Motherhood as Experience and Institution* (New York: Norton, 1976), 40–41.

17 Bem, *The Lenses of Gender*, 41.

18 It has been estimated that 70 percent of men in northern cities could read, compared to only 35 percent of women. See Linda K. Kerber and Jane Sherron De Hart, *Women's America: Refocusing the Past*, 4th ed. (New York: Oxford University Press, 1995).

19 Nadine Taub and Elizabeth M. Schneider, "Perspectives on Women's Subordination and the Law," in *The Politics of Law*, ed. D. Kairys (New York: Pantheon, 1982), 125–126.

20 William Blackstone, Chapter 15, in *Commentaries on the Laws of England*, book 1, vol. 4 (1765–1769).

21 Massachusetts Confiscation Act of April 20, 1779.

22 Linda Kerber, "The Paradox of Women's Citizenship in the Early Republic: The Case of *Martin v. Massachusetts*, 1805," 370.

23 Ibid., 375.

24 Ibid.

25 Imelda Whelan, *Modern Feminist Thought: From the Second Wave to "Post Feminism"* (New York: New York University Press, 1995).

26 Nancy Gibbs, "The War Against Feminism," *Time*, March 9, 1992, 51.

27 Nancy F. Cott, *The Grounding of Modern Feminism* (New Haven, CT: Yale University Press, 1987).

28 Ibid., 3.

29 Ibid., 5.

30 Ibid., 4–5.

31 Rosemarie Putnam Tong, *Feminist Thought: A More Comprehensive Introduction* (Boulder, CO: Westview Press, 1998), 5.

32 Kimberlé Williams Crenshaw, "Demarginalizing the Intersection of Race and Sex: A Black Feminist Critique of Antidiscrimination Doctrine, Feminist Theory and Antiracist Politics," *University of Chicago Legal Forum*, vol. 1989, issue 1, article 8, 139–167.

33 For a more complete description and historical account of each approach to feminism, see Tong, *Feminist Thought*; Whelan, *Modern Feminist Thought*; Allison M. Jagger, *Feminist Politics and Human Nature* (Totowa, NJ: Rowman and Allanheld, 1983); Susan Moller Okin, *Women in Western Political Thought* (Princeton, NJ: Princeton University Press, 1979); Shulamith Firestone, *The Dialectic of Sex* (New York: Bantam Books, 1970); Mary Daly, *Gyn/Ecology: The Metaethics of Radical Feminism* (Boston: Beacon Press, 1978); Nancy Chodorow, *The Reproduction of Mothering:*

Psychoanalysis and the Sociology of Gender (Berkeley: University of California Press, 1978); Carol Gilligan, *In a Different Voice* (Cambridge, MA: Harvard University Press, 1982); Patricia Hill Collins, *Black Feminist Thought: Knowledge, Consciousness, and the Politics of Empowerment* (Boston: Unwin Hyman, 1990); Robin Morgan, *Sisterhood Is Global* (Garden City, NY: Anchor, 1984).

34 Sheryl Sandberg and Nell Scovell, *Lean In: Women, Work, and the Will to Lead* (New York: Knopf, 2013).

35 For example, see the critique by Susan Faludi, "Facebook Feminism, Like It or Not," *The Baffler* 23 (2013); bell hooks, "Dig Deep: Lean In," *Feminist Wire*, October 28, 2013.

36 hooks, "Dig Deep: Lean In."

37 Virginia Sapiro, *Women in American Society*, 4th ed. (Mountain View, CA: Mayfield Publishing, 1999), 109.

38 Tong, *Feminist Thought*, 46.

39 There are, however, notable exceptions. Jo Freeman, for example, believes that it was a mistake to label some women's organizations as merely reformist since all groups were breaking away from established gender norms, an act "revolutionary" in itself. She'd prefer to divide branches of the movement into a "younger branch" and an "older branch." Barbara Ryan groups organizations within the movement into "mass movement" and "small groups."

40 Tong, *Feminist Thought*, 227.

41 Collins, *Black Feminist Thought*, 19.

42 Ibid., 37.

43 Tong, *Feminist Thought*, 222.

44 Carol Gilligan, *In a Different Voice*.

45 Beth Dulin, "Founding Project Challenges Young Feminists," *New Directions for Women* 21, no. 1 (1993): 33.

46 Joannie M. Schrof, "Feminism's Daughters," *U.S. News and World Report*, September 27, 1993.

47 Linda Hirshman, "Looking to the Future, Feminism Has to Focus," *Washington Post*, June 8, 2008.

48 Courtney E. Martin, "Why Feminists Fight with Each Other," *Alternet*, June 12, 2007. http://www.alternet.org/story/53844.

49 Martha Rampton, "Four Waves of Feminism," *Pacific Magazine*, Fall 2008.

50 Jennifer Friedlin, "Second and Third Wave Feminists Clash over the Future," *Women's eNews*, May 26, 2002.

51 Rory Dicker and Alison Piepmeier, eds., *Catching a Wave: Reclaiming Feminism for the 21st Century* (Boston: Northeastern University Press, 2003).

52 Christine Emba, "Intersectionality," *In Theory* blog, *Washington Post*, September 21, 2015.

53 Kimberlé Williams Crenshaw, "Why Intersectionality Can't Wait," *In Theory* blog, *Washington Post*, September 24, 2015.

54 Ibid.

55 Mary Hawkesworth, "The Semiotics of Premature Burial: Feminism in a Postfeminist Age," *Signs: Journal of Women in Culture and Society* 29, no. 4 (2004): 961–985.

56 Janelle Reinelt, "States of Play: Feminism, Gender Studies, and Performance," *Scholar and Feminist Online*, Summer 2003, Barnard Center for Research on Women.

57 Martin, "Why Feminists Fight with Each Other."

58 Susan J. Carroll, "Reflections on Gender and Hillary Clinton's Presidential Campaign: The Good, the Bad, and the Misogynic," *Politics and Gender* 5 (2009): 1–20.

59 Kate Zernike, "Postfeminism and Other Fairy Tales," *New York Times*, March 16, 2008.

60 Ibid.

61 Bryce Logan, "Donald Trump Mocks Rival Carly Fiorina's Face: 'Look at That Face, Would Anyone Vote for That?'" *Business Insider*, September 9, 2015.

62 Margaret Talbot, "Hillary Clinton Should be Allowed to Boast," *New Yorker*, April 22, 2016.

63 David Brooks, "Why Is Clinton Disliked?" *New York Times*, May 24, 2016.

64 Callum Borchers, "Fox News's Brit Hume Says Hillary Clinton Was 'Not Necessarily Attractive' During the Debate," *Washington Post*, September 26, 2016.

65 Seiyi Cai and Scott Clement, "What Americans Think About Feminism Today," *Washington Post*, January 27, 2016.

66 Greenberg Quinlan Roster Research, "Winning Women in 2016: Findings from a Web Survey of American Adults," February 17, 2016, www.americanwomen.org/research/document/American-Women-Survey-Millennial-Memo-02.18.16.pdf.

67 National Council of Women's Organizations, "National Women's Equality Act for the 21st Century," Proclamation in Seneca Falls, New York on July 17, 1998.

Box 1.1: How Should Female Veterans Be Memorialized?

1 Ashley B. Craig, "State Set to Commemorate Women's Veteran Memorial," *Charleston Gazette Mail*, November 9, 2011.

2 New York statue: www.ogs.ny.gov/global/images/ESP/womenVet.jpg.

3 Associated Press, "Women Veterans Criticize Statue Honoring Them," June 8, 2004.

4 Monument in Del City, Oklahoma: http://cdn2.newsok.biz/cache/r960-47ff577619178201b37f785c5c8a9441.jpg.

5 Statue of National Guard soldier with daughter, Del City, Oklahoma: http://journalrecord.com/tinkertakeoff/files/2014/11/141111-F-RI777-001.jpg.

6 Arlington National Cemetery: http://womensmemorialstore.com/store/media/banner.jpg.

CHAPTER 2

All Rights Are Not Equal: Suffrage Versus the Equal Rights Amendment

There have been two major points in American history when women have under-taken concerted action in the form of a movement in an attempt to effect a significant change in their public status. The first was the campaign for suffrage, especially between 1910 and 1920, the final phase of women's efforts. The second was during the 1970s, when women mobilized around the Equal Rights Amendment (ERA). In both cases, women eventually organized to achieve a single goal and were willing to make compromises on other important issues to realize that goal. In both cases, women constituted the majority of the proponents for and opponents to the change in their status. In both cases, women's support for, and opposition to, the vote and the ERA was grounded in their understanding of equality, their perspective on women's roles in the private and public spheres, and their concept of fairness. Women are not a homogeneous political force, and there is no sex solidarity among women regarding gender equality.

In the case of suffrage, the campaign was successful, albeit after more than seventy-two years of advocacy. When the Nineteenth Amendment reached the states for ratification, public attitudes had already changed. By then, women were viewed as independent from their husbands and fathers when it came to owning property and earning wages. Additionally, women already had full voting rights in fifteen states and presidential suffrage in another twelve. In effect, the constitu-tional change that gave women the vote followed a change that had already taken place in social attitudes. This was not so with the Equal Rights Amendment. The Constitution still has no equal rights amendment, even after nearly eighty years of episodic campaigning and an unprecedented thirty-nine-month extension to the ratification deadline granted by Congress in 1978. Why? What can we learn about women's relationship to politics and the controversies of equality in the con-trast? This chapter sets out to answer these questions, first by briefly examining the history of both movements, and then by analyzing the arguments for and against each change in light of the paradox of gender equality.

FROM SENECA FALLS TO SUFFRAGE: THREE GENERATIONS OF WOMEN WORK FOR THE VOTE

Although the vote is now considered the most basic act of citizenship, it took women more than seventy-two years of political activism to win the elective franchise. Three generations of women joined the cause, each believing that theirs would be the final effort required to convince enough state and federal legislators that women deserved and required political representation. Suffragists initially argued that admitting women to the political system would result in positive change. But within a generation, they discovered that it was more effective to argue that **suffrage** would not result in any change—positive or negative—but rather was required out of a sense of basic fairness. By the third generation, women were again divided over how to approach the civic gatekeepers. A younger group, led by Alice Paul, who was trained in militant tactics of political resistance, argued that women should not be begging the establishment for the vote; they should be demanding the right to vote. The more established suffragists, led by longtime activist Carrie Chapman Catt, believed that women would win the vote in time and that threatening politicians would only delay their victory. In the end, winning the vote required both approaches and a fundamental shift in public attitudes of legislators and average citizens alike. Women were admitted to the political franchise only after public opinion supported the view that women were capable of rational thought and action independent of their husbands.

Female Social Activists Discover the Suffrage Cause: 1840–1869

Many early advocates of equality and rights for women came to the cause via their dedication to the abolition of slavery or their experiences with other charitable societies.[1] In their drive to help others, women were able to transcend the line between private and public life and to share informally the "problems of their sex" with one another. As they labored for racial equality and political rights for African Americans, they became conscious of their own inequality. Historian Carol Ellen Dubois argues that women working in the abolition movement gained something even more significant than a discovery of their own second-class status: "What American women learned from abolition was less that they were oppressed than what to do with that perception, how to turn it into a political movement."[2] The seed for that political movement germinated with a sex discrimination incident at the World Anti-Slavery Convention held in London in 1840. Although women were part of the official US delegation, they were not allowed to participate in the proceedings and were relegated to seats in the balcony. It was here that Elizabeth Cady Stanton and Lucretia Mott began to discuss holding a meeting for the express purpose of discussing women's rights.

In 1848, Stanton and Mott issued a call for participation in a meeting organized to talk about the "social, civil, and religious rights of women."[3] More than 300 people participated in the two-day Seneca Falls Convention and ratified the **Declaration of Sentiments and Resolutions**, as drafted by Stanton. The meeting was odd by contemporary standards. Called to consider the question of women's equality, none of the conveners felt qualified to chair the meeting, and so the task fell to Lucretia Mott's husband, James. The taboo against "public women" fell away slowly, and subsequent conventions often relied on noted male abolitionists as speakers. Education activist Emma Willard, for example, always asked a man to speak on her behalf, or if forced to speak for herself, she did so while seated. Others delivered their remarks from behind a curtain. Historian Glenna Matthews refers to this phenomenon as the social geography of gender.[4] Elizabeth Cady Stanton, after speaking in public for the first time at Seneca Falls, added "access to the public lectern" to the other demands in the Declaration of Sentiments. Not until 1850, at a meeting in Salem, Ohio, was the social geography of gender transformed entirely. At that meeting, only women were allowed to speak, whether from the platform or the audience.

The Declaration of Sentiments mirrored the Declaration of Independence in form, word, and tone. These similarities suggest that the early advocates for women's rights based their equality claims in the liberal tradition of individualism. The Declaration of Sentiments began, "We hold these truths to be self-evident: that all men and women are created equal," and then listed eighteen injuries "on the part of man toward woman," including exclusion from the franchise, coverture in marriage, denial of property rights, lack of access to higher education, and the undermining of "confidence in her own powers . . . and [making] her willing to lead a dependent and abject life." The list was a curious mix of political and personal grievances against men. All of the resolutions passed unanimously at the convention with the exception of suffrage, which passed by a narrow margin (see Chapter 9 for the resolutions adopted by the convention).

Of all of the demands, the franchise was the most radical and controversial among the conference participants, as well as among women throughout the country. Even Lucretia Mott counseled Stanton against including suffrage in the resolutions, saying, "Thou will make us ridiculous. We must go slowly."[5] Frederick Douglass, former slave and noted abolitionist leader, reassured Stanton and promised to speak in favor of the suffrage resolution. Paula Giddings notes that "although the Black woman's contribution to the women's suffrage movement is rarely written about, Blacks, including women, had a more consistent attitude toward the vote than Whites, as Blacks had fewer conflicts about women voting . . . one would be hard pressed to find any Black woman who did not advocate getting the vote."[6] The reticence among Seneca Falls conventioneers to immediately embrace women's suffrage was a bellwether of the long struggle ahead. Of all those in attendance at Seneca Falls, only nineteen-year-old Charlotte Woodward lived long enough to exercise her right to vote.[7]

Box 2.1

Declaration of Sentiments

When in the course of human events, it becomes necessary for one portion of the family of man to assume among the people of the earth a position different from that which they have hitherto occupied, but one to which the laws of nature and of nature's God entitle them, a decent respect to the opinions of mankind requires that they should declare the causes that impel them to such a course.

We hold these truths to be self-evident: that all men and women are created equal; that they are endowed by their Creator with certain inalienable rights; that among these are life, liberty, and the pursuit of happiness; that to secure these rights governments are instituted, deriving their just powers from the consent of the governed. Whenever any form of government becomes destructive of these ends, it is the right of those who suffer from it to refuse allegiance to it, and to insist upon the institution of a new government, laying its foundation on such principles, and organizing its powers in such form, as to them shall seem most likely to effect their safety and happiness. Prudence, indeed, will dictate that governments long established should not be changed for light and transient causes; and accordingly all experience hath shown that mankind are more disposed to suffer, while evils are sufferable, than to right themselves by abolishing the forms to which they were accustomed. But when a long train of abuses and usurpations, pursuing invariably the same object, evinces a design to reduce them under absolute despotism, it is their duty to throw off such government, and to provide new guards for their future security. Such has been the patient sufferance of the women under this government, and such is now the necessity which constrains them to demand the equal station to which they are entitled.

The history of mankind is a history of repeated injuries and usurpations on the part of man toward woman, having in direct object the establishment of an absolute tyranny over her. To prove this, let facts be submitted to a candid world.

He has never permitted her to exercise her inalienable right to the elective franchise.

He has compelled her to submit to laws, in the formation of which she had no voice.

He has withheld from her rights which are given to the most ignorant and degraded men—both natives and foreigners.

Having deprived her of this first right of a citizen, the elective franchise, thereby leaving her without representation in the halls of legislation, he has oppressed her on all sides.

He has made her, if married, in the eye of the law, civilly dead.

He has taken from her all right in property, even to the wages she earns.

He has made her, morally, an irresponsible being, as she can commit many crimes with impunity, provided they be done in the presence of her husband. In the covenant of marriage, she is compelled to promise obedience to her husband, he becoming, to all intents and purposes, her master—the law giving him power to deprive her of her liberty, and to administer chastisement.

He has so framed the laws of divorce, as to what shall be the proper causes, and in case of separation, to whom the guardianship of the children shall be given, as to be wholly regardless of the happiness of women—the law in all cases, going upon a false supposition of the supremacy of man, and giving all power into his hands.

After depriving her of all rights as a married woman, if single and the owner of property, he has taxed her to support a government which recognizes her only when her property can be made profitable to it.

He has monopolized nearly all of the profitable employments, and from those she is permitted to follow, she receives but a scanty remuneration. He closes against her all the avenues to wealth and distinction which he considers most honorable to himself. As a teacher of theology, medicine, or law, she is not known.

He has denied her the facilities for obtaining a thorough education, all colleges being closed against her.

He allows her in Church, as well as State, but a subordinate position, claiming Apostolic authority for her exclusion from the ministry, and, with some exceptions, from any public participation in the affairs of the Church.

He has created a false public sentiment by giving to the world a different code of morals for men and women, by which moral delinquencies which exclude women from society, are not only tolerated, but deemed of little account in man.

He has usurped the prerogative of Jehovah himself, claiming it as his right to assign for her a sphere of action, when that belongs to her conscience and to her God.

He has endeavored, in every way that he could, to destroy her confidence in her own powers, to lessen her self-respect, and to make her willing to lead a dependent and abject life.

Now, in view of this entire disfranchisement of one-half the people of this country, their social and religious degradation—in view of the unjust laws above mentioned, and because women do feel themselves aggrieved, oppressed, and fraudulently deprived of their most sacred rights, we insist that they have immediate admission to all the rights and privileges which belong to them as citizens of the United States.

In entering upon the great work before us, we anticipate no small amount of misconception, misrepresentation, and ridicule; but we shall use every instrumentality within our power to effect our object. We shall employ agents, circulate tracts, petition the State and National legislatures, and endeavor to enlist the pulpit and the press in our behalf. We hope this Convention will be followed by a series of Conventions embracing every part of the country.[1]

Within months of the Seneca Falls meeting, women's rights conventions were held in other cities, beginning in Rochester, New York. Susan B. Anthony, a tireless crusader for suffrage later in the movement, was slow to join. She heard about the Rochester meeting from her mother and sister, but she was already immersed in the abolition and temperance movements, and felt those causes were more consistent with her Quaker beliefs. In 1851, when men in Akron, Ohio, directly challenged women's ability even to hold such conventions, let alone demand civil and political rights, a former enslaved woman named Sojourner Truth responded forthrightly from the floor. Truth's indignant oratory reflects her dual oppression as a black former slave and as a woman:

> Well, children, where there is so much racket there must be something out of kilter. I think that 'twixt the Negroes of the South and the women at the North, all talking about rights, the white men will be in a fix pretty soon. But what's all this here talking about?

> That man over there says women need to be helped into carriages, and lifted over ditches, and to have the best place everywhere. Nobody ever helps me into carriages, or over mud-puddles, or gives me any best place! And ain't I a woman? Look at me! Look at my arm! I have ploughed, and planted, and gathered into barns, and no man could head me! And ain't I a woman? I could work as much and eat as much as a man—when I could get it—and bear the lash as well! And ain't I a woman? I have borne thirteen children, and seen them most all sold off to slavery, and when I cried out with my mother's grief, none but Jesus heard me! And ain't I a woman?

> Then they talk about this thing in the head; what's this they call it? ["Intellect," whispered someone near.] That's it, honey. What's that got to do with women's rights or Negroes' rights? If my cup won't hold but a pint, and yours holds a quart, wouldn't you be mean not to let me have my little half-measure full?

> Then that little man in black there, he says women can't have as much rights as men, because Christ wasn't a woman! Where did your Christ come from? Where did your Christ come from? From God and a woman! Man had nothing to do with Him. . . .

> If the first woman God ever made was strong enough to turn the world upside down all alone, these women together ought to be able to turn it back, and get it right side up again! And now they are asking to do it, the men better let them.[8]

IMAGE 2.1: *Sojourner Truth (1797–1883), abolitionist and women's rights activist.*
Source: Courtesy of the Library of Congress, Rare Book and Special Collections Division, rbcmil scrp1000203.

Women's rights and abolition shared a common philosophical claim to equal rights, and the movements were closely linked until divisions surfaced over the Civil War amendments. The start of the war all but suspended the campaign for women's rights. Women in the North and South dedicated themselves to their respective causes, but most suffragists at the time supported the Union effort. In 1863, Stanton and Anthony organized the Women's Loyal National League in the North to promote the emancipation of all slaves through constitutional amendment.[9] The amendment proposed universal suffrage and was intended to include freed slaves and women. Many abolitionists objected to women's inclusion in the suffrage clause, fearing that it would cause the amendment to fail. The Republican Party argued that an attempt to enfranchise women would jeopardize efforts to enfranchise black men in the South.[10] The Thirteenth Amendment (1865) was ratified without any mention of the franchise. Attention then turned to the Fourteenth Amendment, which granted citizenship rights to freed slaves.

The **American Equal Rights Association (AERA)** was formed in 1866 to advance the cause of universal suffrage, and many active in the organization believed that suffrage was already implied in the language of citizenship. Several prominent African American reformers held leadership positions in the AERA, including Harriet Purvis, Sarah Redmond, and Sojourner Truth.[11] Black men and women active in the movement clearly linked women's rights with the vote and focused their efforts on universal suffrage and universal reforms. However, the AERA was embroiled in a battle between those whose first priority was black male suffrage and those who were dedicated first to women's suffrage. The tension found a target in the Fourteenth Amendment. The proposed wording of the Fourteenth Amendment meant that the word *male* would appear in the Constitution for the first time, thereby establishing two categories of citizens: male and female. Suffragists disagreed among themselves as to how they ought to react to the language of the proposed amendment. Anthony and Stanton believed that the amendment should be defeated unless it included women, while others, including Lucy Stone, argued that it was "the Negroes' hour, and that the women must wait for their rights."[12]

Those who believed in the precedence of women's suffrage could not get past the willingness of others to accept the word "male" in the text of the Fourteenth Amendment and the exclusion of women from the Fifteenth Amendment, which removed race as a disqualifier for the franchise. Having been told to wait their turn during the ratification of the Thirteenth and Fourteenth Amendments, woman suffragists saw the Fifteenth Amendment as their last opportunity to be included in the postwar reconstruction of the nation via constitutional amendment. White female suffragists left the AERA, blaming male abolitionists for sacrificing women in the name of expediency. Black women "remained quiet or divided among the prevailing forces."[13] The disunity resulted in the dissolution of the AERA and the formation of two rival organizations for women's rights in 1869: first the **National Woman Suffrage Association (NWSA)**, led by Stanton and Anthony, and later the **American Woman Suffrage Association (AWSA)**, led by Lucy Stone and Henry Ward Beecher. The NWSA turned its immediate attention to the fight over women's inclusion in the Fifteenth Amendment and divorced itself entirely from the Republican Party and the "Negro suffrage" question, whereas the AWSA continued to support the Fifteenth Amendment as written and vowed to support a Sixteenth Amendment dedicated to women's suffrage.[14]

Historian Rosalyn Terborg-Penn, writing about African American women's participation in the early suffrage movement, argues that the schism within the movement and black women's reaction to the divide reveals how "they were often torn between identifying with racial priorities or gender priorities."[15] In the process, black women are frequently left out of accounts of the divisions, and black males are often blamed. The racist overtones of Stanton's and Anthony's woman-first claims have been ignored in many contemporary accounts, according to Terborg-Penn, and worse still, feminist historical accounts written in the 1970s and 1980s justify white suffragists' racism as expedient "but often [do] not justify the pro-'Negro suffrage' male behavior as expedient."[16]

The disagreement with abolitionists and the divide among suffragists is significant because it signaled an end to women's quest for universal suffrage and a start to the often ugly nativist and racist rhetoric and action that characterized some claims to the vote for women. Women dove into social activism, dedicated to the universality of natural rights and to full citizenship rights and privileges grounded in the liberal tradition for all adults. However, their negative experiences with allied groups in the formative years of the rights movement pushed women toward exclusivity and self-interest, transforming the women's rights movement into a women's suffrage movement. In a broader sense, it also forced them to give up the philosophical and moral high ground, and to sacrifice forever the most radical notion of all: transforming the social and political structure itself.

Suffragists Disagree over Amending the US Constitution: 1870–1910

Having been divided primarily over strategic disagreements rather than deeper ideological differences, the NWSA and AWSA advanced along similar paths, courted many of the same potential constituents, and advocated many of the same arguments in favor of women's suffrage. There were some differences, however. The NWSA worked for both a federal amendment and state referendums. Of the two organizations, the NWSA was more revolutionary because it at first refused to admit men, attacked the institution of marriage, and published essays on "free love" in its journal, *The Revolution*.[17] Elizabeth Cady Stanton, in particular, targeted the church as a primary source of sexism in society, which led her to reject the Bible.[18] In the 1870s, NWSA used such confrontational tactics as attempting to vote, sponsoring female candidates, and mounting protests at public events.[19] The AWSA maintained its working relationship with abolitionists of both sexes, and its membership reflected a more conservative, middle- and upper-class slice of society. AWSA's publication, the *Woman's Journal*, supported the institutions of family, church, and marriage. For the most part, women's efforts in both organizations to educate the public and legislators involved petitioning legislatures, testifying before legislative committees, giving public speeches, and conducting public referendum campaigns. African American women's voices became more evident in their own right during the period between 1870 and 1890.[20] Never abandoning the cause of universal suffrage, their calls for change incorporated demands for both suffrage and basic civil rights for all black people.

Divisions between the two organizations and the NWSA's embrace of "free love" tarnished the women's suffrage organizations' claims to moral superiority. In the void, the **Women's Christian Temperance Union (WCTU)** took up the cause of suffrage. Frances Willard, WCTU president from 1879 to 1897, linked suffrage to temperance by arguing that only women could be counted on to cast the votes necessary to prohibit the sale and consumption of alcohol. Alcohol abuse was a leading cause of domestic violence, abandonment, and poverty for women and children. The WCTU was larger than any women's suffrage organization and contributed vast resources to the cause during Willard's presidency.[21] The combination of efforts yielded success. Two western territories, Wyoming and Utah, granted women the vote, and state legislatures in other regions (except for the South) considered women's suffrage legislation. Political scientist Lee Ann Banaszak calculated that, on average, "in every year between 1870 and 1890, 4.4 states considered legislation giving women the vote."[22]

From 1869 to 1874, NWSA members urged female activists to adopt a more revolutionary strategy. Missouri suffragists Virginia Minor and her husband, Francis, took the lead in developing a reinterpretation of the Fourteenth Amendment and applying its definition of citizenship to enfranchise women.[23] Victoria Woodhull, calling this strategy the "new departure," urged delegates at the 1871 NWSA convention in the District of Columbia to adopt the tactic in their own communities.[24] African American suffragist Mary Ann Shad Cary, having studied law at Howard University, constructed a legal argument applying the Fourteenth and Fifteenth Amendments to black women as well as black men. In testimony before the House Judiciary Committee, Cary argued that if women were denied the vote, the emancipation amendments would leave women free in name only. She called for an amendment to strike the word "male" from the Constitution.[25] By other accounts, African American women reacted to their personal exclusion from suffrage by working to influence the political decisions of their male kin and friends. Jewel Prestage notes, "According to one [Louisiana] state politician and former state senator, they followed their men from morning to night telling them how to vote, formed a large segment of the audiences at political meetings, and evidenced a deep interest in all that pertained to politics."[26]

Several women attempted to vote in the November 1872 election. Sojourner Truth was turned away from the polls in Battle Creek, Michigan. Susan B. Anthony and a small group of women voted in Rochester, New York. Anthony was arrested several weeks later and charged with "illegal voting." Rather than pay her fine and win her release, Anthony instead applied for a writ of habeas corpus in an effort to get her case before the US Supreme Court. Anthony used her trial and conviction to plead the case of women's suffrage before the court of public opinion:

> Yes, your honor, I have many things to say; for in your ordered verdict of guilty, you have trampled underfoot every vital principle of our government. My natural rights, my civil rights, my political rights, are all alike ignored. Robbed of the fundamental privilege of citizenship, I am degraded from the status of citizen to that of a subject; and not only myself individually, but all of my sex, are, by your honor's verdict, doomed to political subjection under this so-called Republican government.[27]

Although the judge at Albany refused to issue the writ and raised her bail to $1,000, Anthony remained steadfast. Unfortunately, her attorney did not. Writing a personal check for her bail, attorney Henry Selden scuttled any chances for Anthony to present her case to the Supreme Court. When Anthony asked Selden if he realized what he had done by paying her bail, he replied, "Yes, but I could not see a lady I respected put in jail."[28] Misplaced chauvinism denied Anthony the opportunity to make her case to the Supreme Court.

In the same election, Virginia Minor in Missouri cast her vote illegally and was arrested. But unlike Anthony's, Minor's case was eventually heard before the Supreme Court. She argued that in denying her the vote, the state of Missouri had denied her rights under the Fourteenth Amendment guarantee to the privileges and immunities of citizenship. The right to vote, she claimed, is a privilege of citizenship. The Court rejected her claim in *Minor v. Happersett* (1875). While admitting that women may be citizens, the Court said that not all citizens are voters. The Court based its opinion on the fact that the federal Constitution does not explicitly grant women the right to vote ("if it had been intended to make all citizens of the United States voters, the framers of the Constitution would not have left it to implication") and the fact that no new state added to the Union after ratification had granted suffrage to women.[29] Without constitutional instruction, the states could decide for themselves who had the privilege of voting. In closing, the Court said: "If the law is wrong, it ought to be changed; but the power for that is not with us. . . . No argument as to woman's need of suffrage can be considered."[30] The *Minor* ruling led suffragists to conclude that a legal strategy would not advance their cause, and therefore they were left with only two choices: a federal amendment or constitutional amendments in each state. By 1877, the NWSA had rededicated itself to a federal constitutional amendment. This time, however, the goal was not universal suffrage, but rather women's suffrage.

By 1890, old animosities between the NWSA and AWSA had faded sufficiently for the two to merge. The new organization, the **National American Woman Suffrage Association (NAWSA)**, elected Elizabeth Cady Stanton president. Stanton served only two years before she was forced out after publishing the *Woman's Bible*, a feminist reinterpretation of the Bible. Anthony, Stanton's replacement, found herself at the helm of a younger, more moderate membership. The merger did not immediately inject new enthusiasm or success into the movement. In fact, suffrage leaders referred to this period as "the doldrums."[31] After Utah and Idaho enfranchised women in 1896, no other state gave women the vote until 1910, when Washington acted. NAWSA's membership had fallen to fewer than 100,000.[32] Women's rights organizations had been formed in most states by then although there were very few in the South. Southern white women were slow to form rights organizations and many insisted that their organizations be segregated by race. In an attempt to bring Southern women to the cause, NAWSA adopted a questionable policy allowing the states to determine for themselves the membership qualifications of their affiliated organizations. Thus segregated organizations flourished in the South. Once again, suffragist leaders sacrificed a basic organizing principle in favor of expediency. This time, women's suffrage gave way to "white women's suffrage" in an effort to bring in southern states. These efforts to exclude

African American women did not go unchallenged. The NAACP, formed in 1909, mobilized at the behest of African American suffragists to put pressure on Alice Paul and other white suffrage leaders.

During this time women established literary and social organizations as well, eventually leading to the women's club movement.[33] African American women also organized into clubs, initiating the **black women's club movement**. Most of the early black women's clubs (1880s–1895) were formed to deal with local issues facing women of color and not affiliated with national organizations. In 1896, the largest national black women's clubs merged to form the National Association of Colored Women (NACW), a federation of women's clubs with Mary Church Terrell at the helm as president. The rise of the NACW coincided with the disenfranchisement of black males in the South, and so issues on its agenda included Jim Crow laws and lynchings, as well as women's suffrage.[34]

Toward the end of the century, many of the founding leaders of the movement—Stanton, Stone, and Anthony—were aging or had died. Carrie Chapman Catt briefly replaced Anthony as president of the NAWSA in 1900, before Dr. Anna Howard Shaw assumed the role in 1904. Shaw represented the "intergenerational" leaders of the suffrage movement and provided a bridge between the pioneers and the new younger leadership, including Alice Paul and Lucy Burns. Shaw concentrated the NAWSA's efforts on state referendums and on lobbying state legislatures, forgoing a federal amendment for a time.

The Final Push: 1910–1920

With the new century came new challenges for women's rights organizations. A multitude of clubs and organizations were mobilizing in favor of and in opposition to women's suffrage. Hundreds of African American women's clubs mobilized for the vote during the years 1900 to 1920, both in states that had already granted women the vote and in states that still prohibited women from voting. It was nearly impossible to coordinate efforts and strategies, and in the end it was two openly divergent strategies that together delivered women's suffrage.

The NAWSA continued to organize, petition, and lobby in the states. Emmeline Pankhurst had been pioneering direct protest tactics in the English suffrage movement. Harriet Stanton Blatch (Elizabeth Cady Stanton's daughter), Alice Paul, and Lucy Burns traveled to England to participate in this new method of campaigning for women's suffrage. Upon their return, Paul and Burns lobbied the NAWSA to return to a federal amendment strategy. Although the NAWSA formed a Congressional Committee in 1912, support for a federal strategy was so meager that the committee was given an annual budget of ten dollars.[35]

Paul and her followers, referred to as the "new suffragists" by some scholars,[36] differed from the "old suffragists" in that they viewed the fight for suffrage as a means to "challenge a social system that attempted to refute their feminist

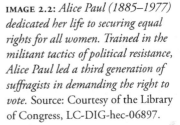

IMAGE 2.2: *Alice Paul (1885–1977) dedicated her life to securing equal rights for all women. Trained in the militant tactics of political resistance, Alice Paul led a third generation of suffragists in demanding the right to vote.* Source: Courtesy of the Library of Congress, LC-DIG-hec-06897.

ideology and deny them their identities."[37] Rather than begging for their rights, they intended to demand them. The NAWSA grudgingly agreed to support the Congressional Committee's proposal (in name only, since they refused to give Paul any funds) to hold a massive parade in Washington, D.C., designed to coincide with Woodrow Wilson's presidential inauguration. Paul was convinced, contrary to the NAWSA leadership, that if suffrage was to become a reality, the focus must be on a federal amendment. Congress must be convinced to pass legislation and send it on to the states. However, Congress was unlikely to act without some prodding, a task Paul assigned to the president of the United States. The March 3 parade was intended to put both Congress and President Wilson on notice that women would not wait any longer for action on the suffrage question.

Paul and the NAWSA's Congressional Committee devised a strategy by which local suffrage organizations would sponsor (and pay for) their own parade participants. When Howard University women volunteered to march in the college section of the parade, some white marchers threatened to pull out. To Paul's credit, she did not back down. Instead she found sympathetic white male marchers to provide a protective buffer for the Howard women. Some 8,000 marchers, including twenty-six floats, ten bands, and five squadrons of cavalry with six chariots, participated in the parade.[38] More than half a million people watched as the parade headed down Pennsylvania Avenue toward the White House. Although the NAWSA's Congressional Committee had sought additional police protection

Box 2.2 – Encountering the Controversies of Equality

Two Means to the Same End:
Alice Paul and Carrie Chapman Catt

The leaders of the women's suffrage movement are enjoying renewed public attention in the wake of women's recent electoral gains. The PBS documentary *Not for Ourselves Alone*, written and produced by Geoffrey Ward and Ken Burns, introduced thousands of viewers to Susan B. Anthony and Elizabeth Cady Stanton for the first time. Both of these pioneering women were dead long before the Nineteenth Amendment was ratified. The final battle for women's suffrage was led by Carrie Chapman Catt (1859–1947) and Alice Paul (1885–1977), but in dramatically different styles.

Catt worked her way through Iowa State University, serving as a school principal and later as one of the nation's first female school superintendents. She began her suffrage work with the Iowa Suffrage Association upon the death of her first husband. The prenuptial agreement signed before her second marriage, to George Catt in 1890, guaranteed her four months each year to work on suffrage activities. Known for her strong organizational skills, Catt took the helm of the National American Woman Suffrage Association (NAWSA) in 1917 and implemented the "Winning Plan," which combined a careful congressional lobbying strategy for a federal amendment with continued efforts to win suffrage in individual states. Catt believed that Congress would act only when women in enough states had the votes to make them listen. She further believed that rational appeals and careful persuasion would lead Congress and President Wilson to support suffrage in ways that punishing Democrats at the polls would not. She urged NAWSA members to remain nonpartisan in their calls on lawmakers. After the Nineteenth Amendment was ratified, Catt founded the League of Women Voters, a nonpartisan organization dedicated to educating women for full civic participation.

for the marchers, the superintendent of police refused, saying it was a job for the War Department, not the police department. Trouble started when spectators began insulting participants and pushing the crowd into the parade line. As police stood idle, the situation deteriorated into a near riot. In all, 175 calls for ambulances were sent out, and more than 200 people were treated at local hospitals.[39] A subsequent Senate investigation turned up numerous examples of police ineptitude and complicity with the rioters.

The publicity generated by the parade and Paul's claims that the police and top civilian officials had conspired to break up the parade brought unparalleled attention

Alice Paul, born to affluent Quaker parents, graduated from Swarthmore College in 1905 and earned a master's degree from the University of Pennsylvania in 1907 and a Ph.D. in 1912. Her studies combined her overlapping interests in economics, political science, social work, and women's equality. She would also go on to earn three law degrees. While pursuing a graduate fellowship in England, Paul met the Pankhurst sisters and was introduced to the militant tactics of the British suffrage movement. When she returned to the United States in 1910, she brought with her the direct and aggressive methods of the English suffragettes. Paul was convinced that suffrage rights needed to be taken and demanded, not begged for. Initially working within NAWSA as chair of the Congressional Committee, Paul organized a massive suffrage demonstration in Washington, D.C., held the day prior to Woodrow Wilson's inauguration. She believed that the party in power and incumbent politicians should be held accountable for their lack of support for suffrage. After being ousted from NAWSA, Paul organized the National Woman's Party to facilitate women's direct political action. She, too, had a gift for organizing. She coordinated the actions of hundreds of women who demonstrated in front of the White House and engaged in hunger strikes while imprisoned. Her friend Lucy Burns said of Paul, "Her great assets, I should say, are her power to make plans on a national scale; and a supplementary power to see that it is done down to the last postage stamp."[1] Paul's methods were viewed as controversial and radical.

What do you think?

Under what circumstances is direct action necessary in pursuit of women's equality? Evaluate Catt's and Paul's respective strategies in light of what you've learned about the history of the suffrage movement and the political climate between 1917 and 1920. Ultimately, which strategy was more effective in moving the Nineteenth Amendment toward ratification? Would one strategy have been as effective without the other? Why or why not?

to the suffrage cause. Not all of it was positive. Newspaper editorials chided the female participants for their unruly behavior, and such criticism made NAWSA's leadership nervous. In the leaders' minds, the Congressional Committee, and not the NAWSA, was pursuing a federal strategy. The NAWSA was still committed to a state-by-state campaign. Conflict between the Congressional Committee and the NAWSA leadership escalated. Allegations and conspiracy theories (none of which were ever proven) began surfacing that Paul and her supporters were working to undermine the state campaign by focusing exclusively on the federal amendment and on financial improprieties.

Frustrated, Paul broke with NAWSA and established the Congressional Union (CU) as an independent organization in 1914. The CU's first action was to hold Democratic Party elected officials responsible for the failure of federal suffrage legislation. The CU targeted Democratic congressmen in close races and actively campaigned against candidates who did not support enfranchising women. Following the same logic, Paul turned her attention to Woodrow Wilson. She organized pickets in front of the White House and called on Wilson to pressure Congress to consider and pass the federal amendment (known by then as the Susan B. Anthony Amendment). On January 10, 1917, the first "Silent Sentinels" appeared.[40] These were women who stood motionless holding banners that read "Mr. President, What Will You Do for Woman Suffrage?" and "How Long Must Women Wait for Liberty?" These suffragist picketers were the first picketers ever to appear before the White House.

The NAWSA did not specifically endorse the pickets and took a wait-and-see attitude under Carrie Chapman Catt's new leadership. Catt, who had replaced Shaw as president in 1915, made reforming the organization her first priority. Although Shaw led with great intelligence and moral authority, she did not have Catt's political savvy or her skills in managing the unwieldy NAWSA bureaucracy. Catt's first action was to obtain the allegiance of the national and state association leaders. Her goal was to "enable campaigners in the field and lobbyists in Washington to feel a united organization behind them."[41] Catt did not believe that the NAWSA or the suffrage question should be tied too closely to either of the two major political parties and instead pursued a nonpartisan strategy through ratification and beyond.

At first the pickets attracted public sympathy, and donations poured in from women nationwide. In 1917, Alice Paul transformed the Congressional Union into the **National Woman's Party (NWP)** and stepped up efforts to call attention to women's disenfranchisement. While other suffragists were concerned with the country's war on Germany, NWP picketers carried signs reading "Kaiser Wilson, have you forgotten your sympathy with the poor Germans because they were not self-governed? Twenty million American women are not self-governed. Take the beam out of your eye."[42] As the rhetoric heated up, police began arresting picketers, some of whom were physically attacked by daily crowds of onlookers. Each time police arrested a marcher or a woman was felled by attack, another woman was there to take her place. States sent delegations to the picket lines, and those who couldn't picket sent donations to support those marching in their place. When jailed, women refused to pay their fines and remained in jail. In an attempt to scare off new picketers, prison terms of up to sixty days were imposed. The women engaged in several hunger strikes to protest their unjust incarceration. Prison officials responded by force-feeding them through the nose, a dangerous and terribly painful practice. Public reaction was swift and overwhelmingly sympathetic to the

IMAGE 2.3: *March 3, 1913. Suffrage Parade down Pennsylvania Avenue, Washington, D.C. The procession included twenty-six floats, ten bands, five mounted brigades, three heralds, and more than 8,000 marchers. Women from countries that had enfranchised women marched first in the procession, followed by the pioneers in the US struggle. They were followed by sections celebrating working women by occupation, state delegations, and finally, a separate section for male supporters of women's suffrage.* Source: Wisconsin Historical Society, Photo ID WHi-3782.

suffragists, prompting early releases. Women released from prison capitalized on the public's sympathy by campaigning for suffrage in their prison garb.

The NWP's militant tactics offended many within and outside the movement, including many NAWSA members. Under Catt's leadership, the NAWSA was pursuing what it labeled the "Winning Plan": a state strategy for a federal amendment. Under Catt's plan, each state would be accorded resources and attention in proportion to its chances of passing a state constitutional amendment. Members also lobbied Congress to pass the Anthony Amendment. Catt believed that in time President Wilson could be persuaded to support the federal amendment, and she feared that the NWP's tactics would only antagonize him and drive him farther from the cause.[43] The "Winning Plan" was carefully orchestrated so that the NAWSA was perceived as "playing by the rules," contrary to the NWP. Catt and others in the NAWSA believed that Paul's tactics were hurting suffrage as a whole.

Most scholars attribute the amendment's final passage to a combination of efforts. "Between 1910 and 1920 an average of 15 states considered suffrage legislation each year, and there were more state referenda on women's voting rights than in the previous forty years combined," writes Banaszak.[44] As women won suffrage in an increasing number of states, pressure mounted on Congress to pass the Nineteenth

Amendment and to send it to the states for ratification. In 1918, the federal amendment failed in the Senate by two votes after passing the House of Representatives. Later that year, the NAWSA demonstrated the significance of the women's vote by targeting and defeating two antisuffrage incumbents in the Senate. As a result, the Nineteenth Amendment was sent to the states in 1919. The battle for ratification was waged in the states for fifteen months. The NAWSA state network, built as part of the "Winning Plan," proved invaluable in mobilizing men and women to pressure state legislatures for timely ratification. On August 26, 1920, by a one-vote margin in the legislature in Tennessee, the final state to ratify the amendment, the Anthony Amendment was added to the Constitution.

Tennessee tested women's ability to directly confront opponents and their tactics. It took pressure from President Wilson to convince Tennessee's governor to call the legislature into special session to consider the amendment. Court challenges to the amendment had been dismissed, clearing the way for the summer session called for August 9. Opponents poured into Nashville, and the state suffrage association issued a call for help to the national associations. The NAWSA and the NWP worked together to poll for support across the state. At first it looked promising, but support eroded in the face of well-funded and well-organized opposition. "Legislators who had expressed favorable sentiments toward woman suffrage were threatened with the ruin of their business and political careers, some were all but kidnapped, and they were all systematically plied with liquor."[45]

The Senate quickly passed the amendment and sent it to the House, where it stayed for ten days. During those ten days, members of the opposition were alleged to have bought votes, tried to break the quorum, appealed to "Negro phobia" and states' rights claims, and threatened legislators that a favorable vote would lead to their political death. Suffrage forces relentlessly counted votes in the House, and when the bill finally reached the floor on August 18, it was two votes short of passage. An attempt to table the bill resulted in a tie and then failed when an opponent, Representative Banks Turner, turned proponent. When the final vote was called, it was the youngest member of the chamber, twenty-four-year-old Harry Burns, who cast the surprise yea vote. In his pocket was a letter from his mother, an active suffragist:

> Hurrah! And vote for suffrage and don't keep them in doubt. I notice some of the speeches against. They were very bitter. I have been watching to see how you stood, but have noticed nothing yet. Don't forget to be a good boy and help Mrs. Catt put "Rat" in Ratification.[46]

The amendment passed, 49 to 47, just in time for twenty-six million women of voting age to participate in the 1920 elections. Writing in 1920, Mary Church Terrell observed: "By a miracle the 19th Amendment has been ratified. We women now have a weapon of defense which we have never possessed before. It will be a shame and reproach to us if we do not use it."[47]

OPPOSITION TO WOMEN'S SUFFRAGE

Traditional opponents to suffrage included the liquor industry, big business, and the church. The liquor industry held significant power in US politics, particularly in state legislatures. Its direct interest, however, was preventing Prohibition rather than preventing women's suffrage. Since many women suffragists were also temperance advocates, the liquor industry believed keeping women away from the voting booth would be in its best long-term economic interests. Businesses, primarily textiles and agriculture, which would be directly affected by women's voting on progressive reform agendas, were a welcome ally for antisuffragists. A relative latecomer to the antisuffrage coalition was the Catholic Church. Suffrage opponents initially shied away from the church because of fears of foreigners and papists. The Catholic Church opposed suffrage primarily on ideological grounds, arguing that the church desired "to prevent a moral deterioration which suffrage could bring and feared the development of a political structure and social climate deleterious to Catholicism."[48] Like other hierarchically organized religions opposed to women's suffrage, the Catholic Church believed that a traditionally constituted society was ordained by God, and any move by either sex on the terrain of the other was viewed as unnatural and a threat to the universal order. The association of the birth control movement with women's rights and suffrage after 1885 only solidified Catholics' official opposition to a more public role for women.

Beginning in about 1880, female suffragists encountered their most vexing opponents: other women. Suffragists initially dismissed the "remonstrants" (as they were called) as inconsequential and misguided. Later these opponents were attacked as fronts for male corporate interests, particularly those of their wealthy husbands. To suffragists Carrie Chapman Catt and Nettie Rogers Shuler, the "antis" served to "confuse public thinking by standing conspicuously in the limelight while the potent enemy worked in the darkness."[49] They further dismissed antisuffragists as throwbacks to outdated gender norms. Associating antis with traditional gender relations spawned a destructive and false dichotomy between "true women" and "new women"—one that would surface again in the 1970s in relation to the Equal Rights Amendment.

Historian Susan Marshall laments the simplicity with which antisuffragists have been treated, arguing instead that their very existence is an important element in understanding women as political actors.[50] To suggest that the antis were merely fronts for more powerful males is to rob them of their autonomy and political agency, as well as to undermine the suffragists' own arguments about women's equality. The dichotomy between "modernists" and "traditionalists" or "careerists" and "traditionalists/homemakers" ignores the complex, changing social

Box 2.3 – Point of Comparison

Women's Voting Rights Around the World

The United States was neither the first nor the last to give women suffrage. New Zealand, the first nation to do so, granted suffrage in 1893, during the "doldrums" of the US suffrage movement. Katherine Sheppard, a prominent leader in New Zealand's suffrage movement, was also a founding member of the Women's Christian Temperance Union (WCTU), an indication of the global character of women's organizations and resources.[1] Female suffragists across nations were similar in their social status—educated and middle- to upper-class. Their goals and organizing ideologies differed, however; arguments for universal suffrage were limited by legacies of colonialism, slavery, and political authoritarianism, and in many instances by Catholicism. The US suffrage movement was exceptional in its size—matched only by the mass movement in the United Kingdom.

No matter where women demanded voting rights, they faced opposition. Women in Kuwait gained suffrage only in 2005 after forty years, even though in Kuwait women's literacy rate is 77.5 percent, women constitute a majority of university graduates, and women's labor force participation is very high. In 2015, women were permitted for the first time (by order of the late King Abdullah) to vote and to stand as candidates in local council elections in Saudi Arabia. Saudi Arabia is the only country in which women cannot drive and a woman's male "guardian," usually a father, husband, brother, or son, can stop her from traveling overseas, marrying, working, studying, or having some forms of elective surgery.[2]

For Critical Analysis

Examine the table below. For each time period, the country that granted women suffrage most recently is listed last. Are there any surprises? Can you detect any patterns? What was happening around the world in the post–World War II era that resulted in so many nations adopting women's suffrage?

Pre-WWI (1900-1914)	Inter-War (1915-1939)	Post-WWII (1940-1989)		Post-Cold War (1990-2015)
Australia	Austria	Dominican	Ghana	South Africa
Finland	Canada	Republic	Cambodia	Qatar
Norway	Georgia	Yugoslavia	Ethiopia	Bahrain
Denmark	Poland	Bulgaria	Nicaragua	Oman
	Russia	France	Peru	Kuwait
	Belarus	Jamaica	Egypt	Saudi Arabia
	Germany	Croatia	Mali	
	Netherlands	Hungary	Somalia	
	Sweden	Indonesia	Tunisia	
	Ukraine	Italy	Columbia	
	Albania	Japan	Honduras	
	Czech Republic	Guatemala	Zimbabwe	
	Slovakia	North Korea	Chad	
	United States	Macedonia	Guinea	
	Armenia	Panama	Madagascar	
	Lithuania	Romania	Morocco	
	Kazakhstan	Taiwan	Zaire	
	Ecuador	Venezuela	Rwanda	
	Ireland	Vietnam	Sierra Leone	
	United Kingdom	Argentina	Paraguay	
	Turkey	Mexico	Uganda	
	Chile	Pakistan	Zambia	
	Spain	Singapore	Congo	
	Sri Lanka	Belgium	Iran	
	Brazil	Israel	Kenya	
	Thailand	South Korea	Afghanistan	
	Cuba	Niger	Libya	
	Puerto Rico	China	Sudan	
	Philippines	Costa Rica	Switzerland	
	El Salvador	Greece	Jordan	
		Haiti	Mozambique	
		India	Portugal	
		Nepal	Nigeria	
		Bolivia	Iraq	
		Syria		

conditions most women faced at the turn of the century. Opportunities for new roles as well as the increasing economic pressure on families created by periodic recessions meant that women of all classes bridged the divide between private and public life by combining work and family obligations. According to Marshall, antisuffragists had their own gendered class interests that motivated them to undertake political action to "protect their own positions of privilege as elite volunteers, political appointees, and custodians of prosperity." The ideology of separate spheres, so evident in antisuffrage rhetoric, "enhanced their social influence as cultural arbiters, maintaining the exclusivity of elite social networks while simultaneously promoting new standards of domesticity that enhanced class control. . . . From their perspective, the franchise was an inferior form of power to that which they already enjoyed."[51] Antisuffragists' access to money, leisure, and extensive social networks enabled their political action, while "the confines of class mandated a circumspect public image."[52]

Numerous organizations dedicated themselves to preventing women's suffrage. Many of these were state-level organizations created in response to statewide women's suffrage referendum campaigns, including the Maine Association Opposed to Suffrage for Women and the Massachusetts Association Opposed to Further Extension of Suffrage to Women. The southern states were the last to grant women the vote, and for most it came only with the federal amendment. Groups such as the Southern Woman's League for the Rejection of the Susan B. Anthony Amendment linked the preservation of the southern "way of life" to protecting women's honor from degradation at the polling place. There were also more nationally focused groups, such as the National Association Opposed to Woman Suffrage; its national publication, *The Woman Patriot*, extended the antis' fight beyond ratification in 1920. The Daughters of the American Revolution supported post-ratification agitation by linking supporters of women's rights with the abolition of family relations.

The majority of those in support of suffrage and those opposed shared important characteristics, first among them being their sex. Like most of the suffragists of this era, women opposed to women's equality tended to be wealthy, well educated, and well connected to the political power elite. Historian Susan Marshall argues that it was only after suffragists turned to direct electoral strategies aimed at defeating state legislators and members of Congress opposed to suffrage and stepped up the populist state referendum campaigns that the antis lost their edge. As long as the decision remained in the hands of a few insulated elite male politicians, the antisuffragists were well positioned to exercise their brand of influence through kinship and shared class interests, even while maintaining an image of self-sacrificing womanhood.[53] Suffragists, however, were forced to adopt an expedient political strategy that moved them closer to antisuffragists' conservatism. This conservatism is evident in posters proclaiming "Votes for Mothers" and in suffragists' claim that women's unique gender-linked perspective would "clean house" in the political system. Gone were the demands for women's natural rights, and the suffrage movement succumbed to the **cult of domesticity** in the final years before ratification in an effort to expand its base of support—a calculated reaction to the success of the antisuffrage movement.[54]

POSTSUFFRAGE DIVISIONS: THE EQUAL RIGHTS AMENDMENT OR SPECIAL PROTECTIONS FOR WOMEN?

In the aftermath of suffrage, the NAWSA and the NWP savored the victory and reevaluated their missions. Much of the scholarly literature chronicles the demise of the organized women's movement in the period immediately following suffrage. Although membership in these two major women's organizations did decline somewhat, that was to be expected, since their organizational focal point had been accomplished. Historian Nancy Cott writes that the 1920s, rather than marking the end of feminism, signaled the end of the suffrage movement and the emergence of the early struggle of modern feminism. "That struggle was, and is, to find language, organization, and goals adequate to the paradoxical situation of modern women, diverse individuals and subgroups who 'can't avoid being women whatever they do,' who inhabit the same world as men, not in the same way."[55] The two paths to gender equality clearly emerged during the period immediately following the ratification of the Anthony Amendment.

Women associated with the NAWSA under Catt's leadership had been persuaded to act as nonpartisans in the battle for suffrage, and many remained active in the organization in its new nonpartisan incarnation: the League of Women Voters. Rather than directly entering electoral politics, the League dedicated its efforts to educating newly enfranchised women, studying national legislation and social policy, and participating in local civic matters. Catt's earlier admonition against allegiance to any one party held, and the League separated itself from partisan politics entirely, even refusing to endorse specific candidates or to promote women from within its own ranks as candidates.

Ironically, the period immediately following ratification may have yielded the largest "eligibility pool" of potential female candidates with prior political experience, education, and political interest in history, and yet that pool went untapped. The transition from nonpartisan reformers to partisan "insider pols" never took place. Some suffrage activists were offered positions in the Wilson administration but turned them down, suspecting tokenism. Other strong leaders who might have been viable candidates for national office turned their attention to suffrage battles in Europe and divorced themselves from American politics almost entirely. Even Alice Paul, who pushed hardest for the introduction of an Equal Rights Amendment, spent the better part of the 1920s abroad. Like the NAWSA, the National Woman's Party underwent substantial reorganization between 1920 and 1923. It too eschewed a partisan electoral agenda and instead focused on achieving complete legal equality between men and women. For the remainder of the decade, members pursued three avenues toward that objective: the Equal Rights Amendment; its international equivalent, the Equal Rights Treaty; and the Equal Nationality Treaty, dealing in a more limited way with citizenship rights.[56]

The history of the **Equal Rights Amendment (ERA)** is similar to that of the battle for suffrage, with one major exception: the ERA was not ratified. Once women had the vote, disagreements surfaced over how the vote could best be translated into political power so that women could exert influence over issues and legislation. Initially political parties courted women voters by offering reform proposals and including progressive planks in their party platforms designed to appeal to female voters. In 1921, for example, Congress passed the Sheppard-Towner bill for maternity and infant care. However, the gender gap that many predicted in 1920 did not actually materialize for another six decades. It wasn't until the election of Ronald Reagan in 1980 that women were significantly more likely than men to support Democratic candidates. When a women's voting bloc failed to materialize after two election cycles, the parties left women to themselves to set a political action agenda for the future.

The Fight for an Equal Rights Amendment: The First Generation

Not all women believed that the vote alone would bring about significant change. After all, the Thirteenth Amendment, which abolished slavery, was not enough to guarantee full citizenship rights to former slaves, thereby requiring the ratification of the Fourteenth and Fifteenth Amendments. Thus some suffragists argued that another constitutional amendment was required to guarantee women equal rights under the law. At a 1923 National Woman's Party convention called to identify state laws that discriminated against women, Alice Paul proposed the Equal Rights Amendment. Daniel Anthony, a Kansas representative and nephew of Susan B. Anthony, introduced it into Congress that same year.[57] The language read:

> Men and women shall have equal rights throughout the United States and every place subject to its jurisdiction. Congress shall have the power to enforce this article by appropriate legislation.

The rift between liberal feminists (advocates of the legal equality doctrine) and social reform feminists (advocates of the fairness doctrine) was always present in the movement, but the single-minded pursuit of suffrage obscured its importance. Historian Nancy Cott argues that the unity attributed to the women's rights movement during the decades preceding ratification was overblown and quite unrealistic to expect.[58] Each generation of women's rights activists has had divisions over strategy as well as divisions born of race, class, ethnic, and religious differences among women. It is no more realistic to expect women to agree with one another than it would be to expect all men to agree with one another on every issue and political strategy. In fact, some scholars argue that the Nineteenth Amendment actually freed women to disagree among themselves and to pursue a wide range of political interests as full citizens and active political participants.[59]

Introduction of the ERA brought to the surface the deep divide within both the women's movement and society as a whole—between those who believed that equality meant special treatment and enactment of protective legislation that considered the burdens women bore (consistent with the fairness doctrine) and those who believed that only gender-neutral law and policies could achieve equality (consistent with the legal equality doctrine). Those favoring the legal equality path argued that protective legislation, although superficially designed to discriminate in favor of women, in reality kept women from the best-paying jobs and denied them the ability to competitively negotiate the terms of their labor as individuals. Women who had worked tirelessly to see fair protective legislation enacted now accused NWP members of elitism, charging that they had never worked a twelve-hour factory shift, so they did not, and could not, understand the issues of working-class women. Labor unions quickly mobilized their membership in opposition to the ERA and remained opposed to the amendment until 1973.

The rift over the ERA was exacerbated by the ambiguity of feminism as an organizing ideology. NWP members themselves, arguably the strongest proponents of a legalistic, rights-based form of equality for women, held mixed views about women's maternal function in society. The NWP focused primarily on the similarities between men and women, but it also believed that the biological fact of motherhood led men and women to possess different values. On the one hand, motherhood was a force for justice in the world and a check on social and sexual debasement. Yet it also believed "motherhood has been the rod held over the backs of women to drive them into submission; it has been the chain to hold them in dependence and to close-rivet them to a condition of slavery."[60]

Women's moral superiority, which flowed directly from maternalism (actual or anticipatory) in the eyes of some NWP members, required that women be admitted to all quarters of society on an equal basis. Protective legislation proponents also used this same maternal role to argue for special compensatory measures for women only—laws that the NWP found inherently discriminatory and economically restrictive. When the NWP approached Alfred E. Smith, governor of New York, to speak in opposition to protective legislation, he replied, "I believe in equality, but I cannot nurse a baby."[61] For many, this summed up the dilemma of equal rights. Women wanted equal opportunities, particularly in the economic marketplace, but also in education, access to health care, and marriage and family law. Yet the biological differences that left women with a unique role in perpetuating the species could not be denied.

The crux of the debate over equal rights, both then and now, lies in how best to render the two compatible. The NWP and other liberal feminists argued that a blanket constitutional amendment was the only way to guarantee women equal opportunities across the board. Social reform feminists maintained that the only way to "make women equal" was to recognize and compensate women for their burdens related to childbirth and family responsibilities. To them, gender-neutral laws were inherently unfair to women because such laws would always be blind to women's maternity issues. The ERA provided a foil for the competing visions of women's role in society. In the end, opposition to the ERA from progressive organizations, such as the National Consumers League, labor unions, and prominent female reformers such as Eleanor Roosevelt, scuttled any chance the legislation had of a formal hearing before Congress in the 1920s.

Over the next three decades support grew slowly but steadily for the amendment. During the 1930s, the National Association of Women Lawyers and the National Federation of Business and Professional Women's Clubs became sponsors of the ERA. In 1940, the Republican Party supported the ERA in its party platform, and the Democrats followed suit in 1944. In 1950 and 1953, the Senate passed the ERA but attached the Hayden rider, which provided that the amendment "shall not be construed to impair any rights, benefits or exemptions now or hereinafter conferred by law upon persons of the female sex."[62] Women's organizations immediately declared the Hayden rider an unacceptable attempt to have it both ways by allowing states to retain laws providing special benefits for women in employment.

The Second Generation

In the 1960s, with the rise of the civil rights movement, the context in which the ERA was debated changed dramatically. When Congress passed the 1964 Civil Rights Act, it effectively removed the controversy over protective legislation from the debate surrounding the ERA and paved the way for its eventual consideration. The 1964 act sought, among other things, to alleviate racial discrimination in employment, education, and public accommodations. Title VII of the act dealt with banning discrimination in employment. As the bill moved closer to passage, southern conservatives offered an amendment they thought would surely kill the entire bill. Judge Howard Smith, a Democratic congressman from Virginia, proposed to amend Title VII to include sex in the employment discrimination section. He offered his amendment, he said, "in a spirit of satire and cajolery," and the House promptly designated the day "Ladies Day." Supporters of the civil rights bill feared that adding women to the employment discrimination section would defeat the entire bill. However, a group of Republican and Democratic women, having planned to offer a similar amendment themselves, joined Smith's coalition of conservative southern Democrats. No committee hearings were ever held on the potential impact of the Smith amendment, nor did anyone pay much attention since it was offered "in jest." The amendment passed the House (and was not touched by the Senate). When the Civil Rights Act was finally passed and signed into law later that summer, liberal feminists gained their most powerful tool yet to combat sex discrimination in the workplace. Since protective employment law designed for women only is inherently discriminatory, such laws quickly fell by the wayside and with them organized labor's opposition to the ERA.

In 1970, two forces brought the ERA to the forefront of Congress's attention. First, the Pittsburgh chapter of the **National Organization for Women (NOW)** disrupted Senator Birch Bayh's hearings on giving eighteen-year-olds the vote (ultimately the Twenty-Sixth Amendment), prompting Bayh to promise to hold hearings on the ERA the following spring.[63] Second, Congresswomen Martha Griffiths and Edith Green freed the ERA from twenty-two years of captivity in committee without a hearing.[64] Green capitalized on a concurrent campaign to expand the scope of Title VII of the Civil Rights Act to include discrimination in education by holding hearings on that topic that eventually became hearings on discrimination against women in all facets of life. The official record from the Education Subcommittee's hearings created a compelling case for equal rights. Representative Griffiths mounted a discharge petition to free the ERA from the inaction of the House Judiciary Committee, chaired by the very powerful octogenarian Emanuel Celler. A discharge petition is a procedural mechanism for circumventing committee inaction and bringing a bill directly to the floor of the House of Representatives. Discharge petitions are a bold move and rarely successful—of the 829 petitions filed prior to Griffiths's, only twenty-four bills were ever successfully discharged. Of those twenty-four, only twenty passed the House, and only two were enacted into law.[65] Griffiths not only managed to convince 218 House members to sign the discharge petition but also got 332 of the 435 members to vote for the discharge resolution on the floor, effectively removing the ERA from the Judiciary Committee's grasp.

On the Senate side, however, the resolution was amended to exempt women from the draft, effectively killing the chances for congressional passage of the ERA in 1970. It was not until 1972, after more than a year of successive hearings, failed amendment attempts, and wording changes, that both houses of Congress successfully passed the bill with the constitutionally required two-thirds majority, enabling the ERA to be sent to the states.[66] Ironically, Emanuel Celler's congressional career, which had begun in 1923, the same year the ERA was introduced for the first time, ended in 1972, the year Congress finally passed the ERA. The opponent who defeated him in the Brooklyn district primary was herself an ardent supporter of the amendment.[67] Unlike suffrage, the ERA enjoyed overwhelming bipartisan congressional favor. Supporters predicted ratification by the states in record time, and the first few months seemed to confirm their optimism. State legislatures competed with one another for the honor of being the first to ratify the ERA. Hawaii ratified the amendment on March 22, 1972—the same day the resolution passed the US Senate. Five additional states ratified the amendment over the next two days, and by early 1973 twenty-four more states were added to the list. By 1977, however, only thirty-five states of the thirty-eight required to add the amendment to the Constitution had ratified it. A rare extension to the ratification deadline was granted in 1978, giving proponents until 1982 to gather the remaining three affirmative state votes. When the extended ratification deadline expired on June 30, 1982, not a single state had been added, and several states were actively working to rescind their prior ratification as the amendment died. The language of the defeated ERA read:

1. Equality of rights under the law shall not be denied or abridged by the United States or any State on account of sex.
2. The Congress shall have the power to enforce, by appropriate legislation, the provisions of this article.
3. This amendment shall take effect two years after the date of ratification.

Two weeks after the extended ratification deadline expired, the amendment was reintroduced in Congress, and it has been introduced in each Congress since that time.

Women Opposed to the Equal Rights Amendment

There is no question that forces opposed to the ERA were better organized and more effectively mobilized within individual states than pro-ERA organizations were immediately after congressional passage. Pro-ERA groups were located primarily in Washington, D.C., enabling them to lobby effectively for congressional passage. Once the resolution went to the states, however, these organizations lacked a network of state-based chapters that could work effectively for ratification. In contrast, opposition groups were founded primarily in the states and worked almost exclusively at the state level to oppose ratification.

Two national organizations were formed to oppose the ERA and remain active even today: the **Eagle Forum**, founded in 1972 by Phyllis Schlafly, and **Concerned Women for America (CWA)**, founded in 1979 by Beverly LaHaye. CWA developed a national network of anti-ERA prayer chains that weekly sought God's direct intervention. **Stop-ERA**, a Schlafly spinoff from the Eagle Forum, was dedicated specifically to the antiratification campaign in the states and has long been suspected of having direct ties to the John Birch Society. Other John Birch Society ad hoc groups, such as HOTDOG (Humanitarians Opposed to Degrading Our Girls) in Utah and POW (Protect Our Women) in Wisconsin, formed in the unratified states. Stop-ERA also spawned ad hoc groups, including AWARE (American Women Already Richly Endowed), Scratch Women's Lib, and the League for the Protection of Women and Children.[68] Most of these spinoff opposition groups were organized on the principle of protecting what were perceived as traditional family values. Operating from their self-appointed position as true defenders of women's interests, Eagle Forum and CWA leaders charged that the feminist agenda "deliberately degrades the homemaker."[69] They warned women that ratification of

IMAGE 2.4: *Phyllis Schlafly (1924–2016), founded STOP ERA in 1972, the year the Equal Rights Amendment was sent to the states for ratification. Schlafly, pictured in the foreground, is demonstrating against the ERA in front of the White House. White House pickets were pioneered by suffragists campaigning for women's equal rights.* Source: Courtesy of the Library of Congress, LC-DIG-ds-00757; Bettye Lane, photographer.

the ERA would radically alter the balance of power within families and would free men from their traditional economic obligations to their families.

Schlafly and LaHaye were both relatively privileged, well-educated women who headed organizations with multimillion-dollar budgets. Yet these women denounced careers for other married women. Both movements claimed the separate spheres ideology as the source of women's fulfillment as well as God's plan for human survival. Anti-ERA forces ignored the new economic realities that often drove women into the paid workforce, and charged that married women who worked outside the home did so for selfish, narcissistic reasons, threatening the health and safety of their children and family stability. Schlafly skillfully harkened back to the rhetoric of the antisuffrage campaign by labeling the ERA the "extra responsibilities amendment," a claim reminiscent of the charge that voting constituted an "unfair burden" on women already laden with home and child care responsibilities. Like the antisuffragist leaders of the 1910s, anti-ERA leaders, although elites themselves, successfully portrayed the ERA as harmful to nonprofessional women and the poor.

Both the CWA and the Eagle Forum attracted a base of members from the middle and lower middle classes and convinced them that ideal womanhood is characterized by the virtue of occupying a distinct and separate private sphere. Influence over men and the power to control men, they argued, flows from this privileged position, not government protection. "True women" are characterized by an attractive femininity that empowers them to speak for women, unlike the "Amazons," "feminoids," or feminist "freaks" of the "third sex." By legitimizing an expanded political role for women, historian Susan Marshall concludes, "the feminist movement has bequeathed a much larger legacy to contemporary political culture: the mobilization of conservative women. . . . They serve as ironic testimony to feminist assertions of female equality."[70]

The Failure of the ERA

The debate that prevented the ERA from receiving congressional attention in the 1920s largely centered on economic and workplace issues, particularly special protective legislation that compensated women in the workplace for the additional burdens of caring for children and a family. Equal pay, equal access to educational opportunities, and the right to advance in employment were all tied intimately to the economic debate. Proponents argued that freeing women to act as individuals in the marketplace would empower them to be more effective advocates of their self-interest at home and in politics. They also believed that the ERA would strike down oppressive marriage and divorce laws; provide access to birth control information; allow women the right to make contracts distinct from their husbands, to control their children, to maintain their names in marriage, and to exercise independent citizenship; equalize moral standards and treatment of sexually transmitted diseases; and even out penalties for sexual offenses.[71]

Opponents, however, successfully convinced a majority of men and women that the ERA would radically change the way society was organized along gender lines. Moreover, they asserted, this reorganization would not only have an impact on the workplace but, more importantly, would also affect the home and potentially the marital bed. This was more change than most citizens at the time were willing to accept. Opponents did not have to invest much in organized opposition because there was never a consensus in favor of the ERA in the 1920s, even among feminists active in major women's organizations. Most women favored fair treatment within the family and society at large. They did not view absolute legal equality as promised by the amendment as fair to women since the law might require that women be treated the same as men were. Any compensatory advantage women gained through progressive employment would be lost, and for many women, this was not the sort of equality they favored.

The climate in 1972 was quite different. Issues of women's vulnerability in the workplace had largely been settled in the courts. Additionally, protective legislation aimed solely at women had been struck down as incompatible with Title VII of the 1964 Civil Rights Act. The issue of equal pay was broached by the Equal Pay Act of 1963. The debate now centered on home protection and the preservation of traditional family values, including women's right to the role of primary caregiver and homemaker. By 1972, a considerable number of women had entered the paid workforce (43.9 percent of women, comprising 38.5 percent of the total paid workforce),[72] yet women opposed to the ERA voiced fears that full-time homemakers would be forced into the paid labor force. They argued that a change in the rules of gender relations would be inherently unfair to women and would lead to a rise in divorce rates, family and child abandonment, and poverty among women and children. They were, in effect, arguing that the separate spheres ideology protected women from the unfair burdens of the paid labor force.

In addition, the Supreme Court acted on the issue of abortion in 1973. Arguably, abortion was not directly related to the substantive content of the ERA, but opponents nonetheless used the *Roe v. Wade* decision to argue that ratification would inevitably lead to on-demand, government-funded abortions. Conservative groups effectively linked people's unease with the federal government's involvement in the abortion issue, cautioning that the ERA would give the federal government the power to enter private and family life. The conservative movement, organized largely by the fundamentalist Christian right, gained strength and new members by linking abortion and states' rights issues to the ERA. By 1982, the year the ERA officially died, more than 50 percent of married women were in the paid workforce. For African Americans, the figure topped 60 percent.[73] For these women, the glorification of the separate spheres ideology by ERA opponents was divorced from their reality, as they were not free to advocate for the right to be a full-time homemaker.

Surprisingly few scholarly studies have been published on the failure of the Equal Rights Amendment. Jane Mansbridge's *Why We Lost the ERA* (1986) is probably the best-known book on the subject. She argues that the ERA's failure can be attributed to a variety of causes, including a backlash against Supreme Court decisions in the 1960s and 1970s, particularly *Roe v. Wade*; the political mobilization of fundamentalist Christians; the gender imbalance in the state legislatures of nonratifying states; the emergence of new ultraconservative, anti-ERA leadership in the Republican Party (Ronald Reagan first among them); and a general deceleration in progressive reforms of all types during the 1970s.[74] Mary Frances Berry, in *Why ERA Failed* (1986), compares the ERA to other successful and unsuccessful campaigns to ratify amendments that attempted to make major changes in American life. Berry argues that in order for the ERA to have succeeded, a majority of voters would have had to recognize that a problem existed that had not been remedied by the courts, state legislatures, or Congress, and which could be solved only by changing the Constitution.[75] Despite the ERA's defeat, women who became politicized during the ratification fight, regardless of which side they were on, remained active in politics, ushering in the second wave of feminist (and antifeminist) political activity.

IMAGE 2.5: *Young women representing the Feminist Majority gather in front of the US Supreme Court to demonstrate their support for the re-introduction of the Equal Rights Amendment. One legislative proposal would remove the deadline for ratification while another would re-start the ratification process from the beginning.* Source: Courtesy of Feminist Majority; photo by Jessica Johnson.

The Equal Rights Amendment Reborn?

The Equal Rights Amendment would have become the Twenty-Seventh Amendment to the Constitution if three-fourths of the states had ratified it by June 30, 1982. Instead, the "Madison Amendment," governing congressional pay raises, which was sent to the states for ratification in 1789, became the Twenty-Seventh Amendment in 1992.[76] ERA supporters argue that acceptance of the Madison Amendment means that Congress has the power to maintain the legal viability of the ERA and the existing thirty-five state ratifications. If so, only three more states need to ratify the amendment to make the ERA a part of the US Constitution. The legal rationale for the "three-state strategy" was developed by three law students in an article titled "The Equal Rights Amendment: Why the ERA Remains Legally Viable and Properly Before the States," published in the *William & Mary Journal of Women and the Law* in 1997.[77] The Congressional Research Service analyzed this legal argument and concluded that the acceptance of the Madison Amendment does imply that ratification of the ERA by three more states could allow Congress to declare ratification accomplished.

Since 1995 ratification bills have been introduced in one or more legislative sessions in nine of the unratified states (Arizona, Arkansas, Florida, Illinois, Mississippi, Missouri, Nevada, Oklahoma, and Virginia), but none has achieved final passage. In 2016, for example, the Virginia state senate voted to ratify the

ERA, but a House committee failed to report the resolution for a full vote, killing the ERA's chances for another year. State affiliates of the national ERA Coalition have formed in unratified states, and young activists are using social media, such as Twitter, to generate renewed pressure on state and federal lawmakers. "Equal means equal" is the slogan of this new effort to see the ERA ratified.[78]

Representative Carol Maloney (D-N.Y.) has introduced the Equal Rights Amendment in the House of Representatives in every congressional session since 1997. Each time a companion bill has been introduced in the Senate. Both versions reproduce the language passed by Congress in 1972 but do not include ratification deadlines. If passed by a two-thirds vote in the House and Senate, the ERA would need to restart the ratification process in the states and win ratification in three-fourths of the state legislatures (for a total of thirty-eight). Proponents argue that this "start from scratch" strategy would avoid any protracted legal battles over whether a state's prior ratification still stands. Coincident to Maloney's bill, a second bill is regularly introduced in the House and Senate that would lift the 1982 deadline from the 1972 version of the Equal Rights Amendment, thus allowing unratified states the freedom to consider the amendment; this is consistent with the three-more-states strategy. In both cases, the legislative resolutions have been assigned to House and Senate committees but have never reached a full vote in either chamber.

Legislative proponents of the ERA are typically Democrats, but Representative Cynthia Lummis, a conservative Republican from Wyoming, has joined the fight. "My state currently has the largest gap in pay between men and women of any state in the nation," she says. "My state has fallen behind in understanding the importance of equal pay for the same job, for equal work. So it makes clear to me that these rights should not be taken for granted."[79] Lummis remains a steadfast opponent of abortion rights, believing the two issues to be separate. She further believes that the ERA would protect against sex-selective abortion, an issue important to fellow conservatives.

Is an Equal Rights Amendment Necessary Today?

Very few people argue against the Equal Rights Amendment as a matter of principle today. In polls, more than 90 percent of Americans agree that the Constitution should include equal rights for men and women.[80] Anti-ERA organizations from the previous ratification fight feared that the constitutional amendment would result in women in combat, unisex bathrooms, and same-sex marriages. In fact, each of these social changes has come to pass since then—propelled by changing public attitudes about sex, gender roles, and sexual orientation. Today's opponents worry that the ERA would eliminate a parent's option to enroll a child in a single-sex school, or lead to the demise of single-sex organizations for youth such as the Girl Scouts and Boy Scouts. Others object to being seen as a "victim" of discrimination and prefer to address instances of unequal treatment as individuals. As one woman wrote on the "Women Against Feminism" Facebook page, "If I experience sexism, I stand up for myself and move on. Bitching about it will get me nowhere."[81] Finally, a long-standing argument by opponents has been that federal law (e.g., the Equal Pay Act, Title IX, and the Violence Against Women Act) and antidiscrimination protection offered by the equal protection clause of the Fourteenth Amendment are sufficient tools to combat sex discrimination, leaving no reason to alter the Constitution.

Today's ERA supporters are quick to point to a January 2011 interview by the late Justice Antonin Scalia in *California Lawyer*.[82] Scalia argued that when debating the Fourteenth Amendment, Congress did not intend equal protection to apply to sex discrimination. He said, "Certainly the Constitution does not require discrimination on the basis of sex. The only issue is whether it prohibits it. It doesn't." The Fourteenth Amendment, adopted in 1868 as one of three post–Civil War amendments, was intended to prohibit the states from denying freed slaves (any person) "equal protection of the laws." It wasn't until 1971 that the Supreme Court applied the equal protection reasoning to a case involving sex discrimination.[83] Even today, the standard of review for sex discrimination cases, called "intermediate scrutiny," is lower than that used to evaluate claims of racial discrimination, which is "strict scrutiny." The equal protection clause has proven inadequate in addressing systematic bias and private forms of discrimination.

Federal legislation adopted specifically to prohibit discrimination on the basis of sex has also fallen short in eradicating the source of discrimination it was designed to address. Since the 1963 Equal Pay Act, for example, the wage gap has only narrowed from 59 cents to 79 cents to men's $1. It took the 2010 Affordable Care Act to end discriminatory practices in health insurance coverage for women. Prior to this law, women paid about $1 billion more than men a year for coverage in the individual health insurance market, and only 3 percent of those plans included maternity coverage. Without a clear constitutional basis for gender equality, the protection embodied in each federal law is subject to interpretation by the states and revision by the courts. ERA advocates point to state laws limiting reproductive rights and the Supreme Court's ruling in *Burwell v. Hobby Lobby* (2013) in which individual religious freedoms prevailed in allowing a business to refuse comprehensive birth control coverage in the company health plan.

For others the ERA remains an important statement of the nation's core values. When invited to name an amendment she would make to the Constitution if offered the chance, Justice Ruth Bader Ginsberg selected the Equal Rights Amendment: "It means that people are equal in stature before the law. We have achieved this through legislation, but legislation can be repealed. . . . That principle belongs in our Constitution."[84] Nearly all of the 100 constitutions around the world written since 1980 include either a reference to gender equality rights or a prohibition against discrimination on the grounds of gender.[85] Although the United States has yet to ratify the international Convention on the Elimination of All Forms of Discrimination Against Women (CEDAW), it did ratify the International Covenant on Civil and Political Rights (ICCPR) in 1992. The ICCPR commits the United States to "ensure the equal right of men and women to the enjoyment of all civil and political rights," including "equal protection" from sex discrimination.[86]

Support for constitutional equality remains high in the United States. Public opinion polls demonstrate historically high public support for the issue, but also suggest that mobilizing public support in favor of ratification will be difficult. While 96 percent of respondents support constitutional equality for women and men and 88 percent want the Constitution to explicitly guarantee equality, 72 percent of the public mistakenly believe that the Constitution already includes the Equal Rights Amendment.[87] Young women, in particular, are shocked to hear that a prohibition against sex discrimination is not included in the Constitution.

THREE POLITICAL LESSONS ABOUT GENDER EQUALITY

The battles waged to win suffrage (successful) and to pass and ratify the Equal Rights Amendment (not so successful) have taught us three valuable lessons about achieving gender equality.

1. A change in social norms and attitudes about women must precede a legal change, particularly in the case of a constitutional amendment.

The biggest obstacle to enfranchising women was the prevailing social attitude that women were not autonomous beings.[88] For women to be seen as competent in the public sphere, the power of the separate spheres ideology and coverture had to be overcome in the minds of those with the power to change existing law. It is no surprise, then, that it took so long for women to gain the vote. Centuries of socialization and custom and generations of attitudes had to be significantly altered so that adult women could be viewed as independent actors capable of making informed decisions apart from their fathers, brothers, and husbands. By the time the Nineteenth Amendment was ratified, women already had full voting rights in fifteen states, presidential voting rights in another twelve, and the right to participate in local and school elections in several others.[89] The full effect of the coverture doctrine was diminished when several states passed married women's property acts in the 1840s, giving free married women the right to control property for the first time. This single change—a woman's right to control her own property—was perhaps more democratizing than suffrage itself. Property gave women access to wealth, power, and additional rights that flowed from property ownership, such as the right to enter into and enforce contracts.

Coverture's grip on women's citizenship was, however, more difficult to sever and serves as an example of the principle that rights granted can be taken away. In the 1880s, Congress acted to link a woman's citizenship automatically to that of her husband. If a foreign-born woman married an American, she automatically gained US citizenship. But if an American-born woman married a foreign man, her US citizenship was stripped from her and she became an alien in her own country. Congress did not equalize citizenship rights until 1934.[90] So while the ratification of the Nineteenth Amendment was law following a change that had already taken place in attitude and practice, it also offered women constitutional protection for their voting rights and, by extension, the protection of other granted rights, since they now had a tool by which to hold legislators accountable.

By the time the Equal Rights Amendment passed both houses of Congress by the required two-thirds majorities in 1972, supporters believed that women's equality had achieved the same "bygone conclusion" status as suffrage had. They were wrong. Unlike the vote, which was a well-defined, single political act, equality was a much more ambiguous concept. While suffragists began their fight by arguing that admitting women to the voting population would radically change America for the better, they quickly learned to argue instead that votes for women would actually produce little noticeable change, and they could point to experience in suffrage states as evidence. Arguing that granting suffrage was really an issue of fairness was more palatable and successful than arguing that it would be an agent of change. Advocates of the ERA also tried to argue that fairness required an extension of equal rights to women. Because these rights did not take on a concrete form, it was difficult to persuade people that the radical changes to daily life predicted by Phyllis Schlafly and other ERA opponents would not come to pass. The ambiguity of equal rights allowed the opposition to suggest that ERA ratification would bring about unisex toilets, wives and daughters in military combat, and homosexual marriages. Despite the lack of evidence that any of their predictions would come true, proving otherwise was impossible.

In addition, people who supported women's equality but who were not ERA activists could point to more than a decade of change for the better through legislative action and favorable decisions by the courts. Why clutter the Constitution with rights already granted? Supporters were unable to convey the complexities and vagaries of relying on the courts and legislatures, which were historically unreliable. As long as other federal venues could be pursued, a constitutional change was unlikely.[91] In short, ERA supporters were unsuccessful in convincing the American public that the ERA would simply affirm the country's commitment to women's rights in ways that were consistent with current values. Furthermore, anti-ERA forces were very successful in raising fears about radical social change, the federal government's active intrusion into personal lives, and loss of the traditional family. The ERA was dead.

2. The role that states play in the pursuit of gender equality should not be underestimated.

Another lesson from the contrast between the fight for suffrage and that for the ERA has to do with the role that states play in determining women's rights. The United States is organized as a federal system with power shared between the national government and fifty state governments. As a result, each state plays a significant role in defining the rights and privileges of its citizens. Although the supremacy clause of the Constitution constrains states to act within the bounds set by the national government, in the absence of national action the states may act alone. Therefore, the laws regarding women's rights differ by state. Two states (Utah and Wyoming) not only gave women the right to vote but also extended equal legal rights when those states first joined the union. Nine other states adopted their own ERAs in the 1970s, while another eight have included language resembling the Fourteenth Amendment's equal protection clause in their state constitutions. This leaves a patchwork of rights for women wholly dependent on their residence. (In Chapters 6, 7, and 8, the policy implications of federalism are explored further.) Those working for suffrage were able to convince the public and three-fourths of the state legislatures that the right to vote was so fundamental to a functioning democracy that it could not be left to each state to decide. The wisdom of this strategy came only after decades of working in the states on suffrage referendums and state constitutional amendments.

Proponents of the ERA were not successful in making a similar case. They were also slow to realize the power each state held in determining the fate of the federal amendment, and so they delayed in organizing a state-based ratification strategy. Missing from the ERA ratification strategy was a 1970s version of Carrie Chapman Catt's "Winning Plan" that recognized the value of cultivating early allies in the states and state legislatures. Any subsequent fight for an ERA will enjoy the advantages (and disadvantages) of social media networks and the immediacy of electronic communication that may make embedded state activists less essential.

3. All women are not alike. There is no sex solidarity in pursuit of gender equality.

Women do not constitute a homogeneous population, and individual women may have multiple, intersecting identities that influence their political perspectives. Women proved to be some of the most vociferous opponents of both suffrage and the Equal Rights Amendment, much to the surprise of many female supporters. The same fault lines that divide the social, economic, and political interests of men divide women from one another. Empirical evidence from the 1970s and 1980s suggests that women do not act politically on the basis of shared interests with other women. "On most issues and candidacies that are seemingly relevant to gender, women do not differ materially from men, and both genders show considerable disunity," write social psychologist David Sears and political scientist Leonie Huddy.[92] In other words, gender does not bind women as a group any more than it binds men to one another in constructing and enacting a political agenda. While developing sex solidarity on a limited set of issues may be possible, the pursuit of gender equality is clearly not one of them. Women have developed alliances with African Americans and others similarly disadvantaged by the status quo only to break away when they felt their interests were being subsumed by those of other groups. Because women of different social, racial, or economic groups rarely interact as equals, they have difficulty making gender and common experiences as wives, mothers, and daughters a basis for political solidarity.[93]

The political equality promised women by the Nineteenth Amendment is only now slowly emerging as we move through the first part of the twenty-first century. Suffragists argued that the vote could also be used as a tool to extend women's rights and equality in the social and economic spheres; however, that has proven a slow, incremental process. The broad-brush equality in all spheres promised by the ERA threatened too much unpredictable change too quickly for many women. Equality and fairness are sometimes two different, albeit related, concepts. Suffragists started their campaign in 1848 by claiming in the Declaration of Sentiments that men and women are created equal and therefore eligible for the same rights and privileges of citizenship. This line of reasoning did not get very far since it said that men and women are the same and therefore should be accorded the same rights. ERA opponents convinced Americans that changing the "rules" (otherwise known as social norms) midway through the game was "unfair" to women who had remained at home to raise their children and support their husbands' careers; to suggest that men and women be treated equally (the same) meant that women would be responsible for earning a living, paying child support, planning for retirement, and maintaining a mortgage. To many, this was incomprehensible.

The relationship between political, social, and economic equality is complex and illuminates the fault lines in how women's equality is understood and accepted. In order for political equality to be extended to them, women had to make significant progress in crossing the divide between the public and private spheres and demonstrate their social and economic competence. However, once granted the vote, some women saw an opening to extend equality of rights even further, while others viewed the vote as an end in itself. With the death of the ERA in 1982, and little sign of it being resurrected soon, women in America are once again faced with the prospect of fighting over equality issue by issue. The paradox that characterizes women's equality—the desire to eliminate sex-specific laws and classifications, on the one hand, and the desire to recognize women's differences, on the other— ensures that the debate will continue for some time. Suffrage for women guarantees that women will be active on all sides of the debates, from inside the political system and as outside activists. Suffrage does not ensure that all women will act on a single agenda or set of interests.

CONCLUSION

It is with some sense of irony that scholars marked women's entrance into the electorate at precisely the moment the power of the vote declined.[94] Women's experience with politics prior to the Nineteenth Amendment (and even after they won the vote) was primarily a nonpartisan model based in voluntary associations. Whether political parties themselves declined in importance or whether women viewed partisan activity as a "male model" and therefore chose a different strategy, women and partisan politics have been slow to mix. After suffrage was ratified, activists pursued a divided agenda consistent with the two paths to equality: one branch proposed the ERA and pushed for gender-neutral legal reforms, while the other remained dedicated to nonpartisan civic participation in pursuit of fairness and inclusion in the existing social, political, and economic system. Although the language of equality remained important to both groups, there was little agreement on the meaning of full equality for women or on a strategy in pursuit of gender equality. Feminism as an ideology provided little guidance or cohesion in this regard.

Women and men were divided over the role women should play in politics and in society. In the fight for suffrage and legal equality, the National Woman's Party adopted the view that women would achieve equality only when they were so fully integrated into politics, society, and the economy that sex no longer served as a useful way to classify citizens. This is consistent with the legal equality doctrine. Other women, some active in the League of Women Voters, viewed eradicating sex classifications as dangerous for women. They viewed women's role in public life as every bit as important as men's but distinctively female in its character. This perspective (which is consistent with the fairness doctrine) sees women as society's caretakers, government's watchdog, and politics' conscience. Some women supported neither path because they viewed any move by women to participate in public affairs as a violation of God's plan and dangerous to the well-being of the traditional family. That these themes dominated the debates over the failed ERA some fifty years after the Nineteenth Amendment was ratified suggests that the controversies of equality have not yet been settled. Chapter 3 continues the examination of the two paths in pursuit of women's equality by looking at women as voters and participants in the political process.

NOTES

Boxed feature notes appear at the end of the Notes section.

1 Glenna Matthews, *The Rise of Public Woman* (New York: Oxford University Press, 1992).
2 Carol Ellen Dubois, *Feminism and Suffrage: The Emergence of an Independent Women's Movement in America 1848–1869* (Ithaca, NY: Cornell University Press, 1978), 32.
3 Jeffrey D. Schultz and Laura van Assendelft, eds., *Encyclopedia of Women in American Politics* (Phoenix, AZ: Oryx Press, 1999), 205.
4 Matthews, *Rise of Public Woman*, 117.
5 Eleanor Flexnor and Ellen Fitzpatrick, *Century of Struggle: The Woman's Rights Movement in the United States*, enlarged ed. (Cambridge, Mass.: Harvard University Press, 1996), 70.
6 Paula Giddings, *When and Where I Enter: The Impact of Black Women on Race and Sex in America* (New York: Bantam Books, 1984), 39.
7 Flexnor and Fitzpatrick, *Century of Struggle*, 70.

8 Elizabeth Cady Stanton, Susan B. Anthony, and Matilda Joslyn Gage, eds., *History of Woman Suffrage* (Rochester, NY: Charles Mann, 1881), 1:116. Sojourner Truth could neither read nor write, so Frances D. Gage wrote down part of the speech. Gage tried to capture Truth's unique dialect and speaking style in her record, but that has been dropped here. Some feminists today have accused white suffragists of recording Truth's words in ways that best served their cause and in the process robbing her of her "authentic voice." See Rosalyn Terborg-Penn, *African American Women in the Struggle for the Vote, 1850–1920* (Bloomington: Indiana University Press, 1998), for more on this debate. The most complete biography of Sojourner Truth is by Nell Irvin Painter, *Sojourner Truth: A Life, a Symbol* (New York: Norton, 1996). Painter has argued that Gage embellished Truth's oratory to create a feminist symbol. In fact, we will never know for sure what Sojourner Truth actually said at the Akron meeting (or at any other time in her life), since she could not write down her own thoughts and words.

9 Barbara Ryan, *Feminism and the Women's Movement: Dynamics of Change in Social Movement, Ideology, and Activism* (New York: Routledge, 1992).

10 Aileen S. Kraditor, *The Ideas of the Woman Suffrage Movement: 1890–1920* (New York: Norton, 1981).

11 Terborg-Penn, *African American Women in the Struggle for the Vote*, 24.

12 Kraditor, *Ideas of the Woman Suffrage Movement*, 3.

13 Terborg-Penn, *African American Women in the Struggle for the Vote*, 26.

14 Lee Ann Banaszak, *Why Movements Succeed or Fail: Opportunity, Culture, and the Struggle for Woman Suffrage* (Princeton, NJ: Princeton University Press, 1996). See also Ryan, *Feminism and the Women's Movement*, 20.

15 Terborg-Penn, *African American Women in the Struggle for the Vote*, 27.

16 Ibid.

17 Regarding the ban on men, Terborg-Penn wrote (in *African American Women in the Struggle for the Vote*, 34) that Stanton and Anthony eventually relented in the face of potential women members' strong opposition to the antimale stance. She reported that although males were grudgingly admitted, no male was permitted to hold office in the organization.

18 Banaszak, *Why Movements Succeed or Fail*, 7.

19 Ibid., 8.

20 Terborg-Penn, *African American Women in the Struggle for the Vote*, 36.

21 Barbara Sinclair Deckard, *The Women's Movement: Political, Socioeconomic, and Psychological Issues* (New York: Harper and Row, 1983).

22 Banaszak, *Why Movements Succeed or Fail*, 8.

23 Terborg-Penn, *African American Women in the Struggle for the Vote*, 37.

24 Ibid., 38.

25 Ibid., 39.

26 Jewel L. Prestage, "In Quest of African American Political Women," *Annals of the American Academy of Political and Social Science* 515 (May 1991): 92.

27 Stanton, Anthony, and Gage, eds., *History of Woman Suffrage*, vol. 2.

28 Geoffrey C. Ward and Ken Burns, *Not for Ourselves Alone: The Story of Elizabeth Cady Stanton and Susan B. Anthony* (New York: Knopf, 1999), 144.

29 *Minor v. Happersett*, 88 U.S. 162 (1875).

30 Ibid.

31 Flexnor and Fitzpatrick, *Century of Struggle*, 275.

32 Ryan, *Feminism and the Women's Movement*, 28.

33 Ibid., 26.

34 Terborg-Penn, *African American Women in the Struggle for the Vote*, 91.

35 Ryan, *Feminism and the Women's Movement*.

36 Christine A. Lunardini, *From Equal Suffrage to Equal Rights: Alice Paul and the National Woman's Party, 1910–1928* (New York: New York University Press, 1986).

37 Ibid., 17.

38 Ibid., 29.

39 Ibid., 31.

40 Flexnor and Fitzpatrick, *Century of Struggle*, 275.

41 Ibid., 273.

42 Ibid., 277.

43 Ibid., 271.

44 Banaszak, *Why Movements Succeed or Fail*, 11.

45 Flexnor and Fitzpatrick, *Century of Struggle*, 315.
46 Ibid., 316.
47 Terborg-Penn, *African American Women in the Struggle for the Vote*, 136.
48 Jane Jerome Camhi, *Women Against Women: American Anti-Suffragism, 1880–1920* (Brooklyn, NY: Carlson Publishing, 1994), 111.
49 Susan B. Anthony and Ida Husted Harper, eds., *The History of Woman Suffrage* (Rochester, NY: Charles Mann, 1902), 4:xxix.
50 Susan E. Marshall, *Splintered Sisterhood: Gender and Class in the Campaign Against Woman Suffrage* (Madison: University of Wisconsin Press, 1997), 529.
51 Ibid., 224.
52 Ibid., 12–13.
53 Ibid., 226–227.
54 Ibid., 229.
55 Nancy F. Cott, *The Grounding of Modern Feminism* (New Haven, Conn.: Yale University Press, 1987), 10.
56 Susan D. Becker, *The Origins of the Equal Rights Amendment: American Feminism Between the Wars* (Westport, CT: Greenwood Press, 1981).
57 Doris Stevens, *Jailed for Freedom: American Women Win the Vote*, ed. Carol O'Hare (1920; reprint, Troutdale, OR: New Sage Press, 1995).
58 Nancy Cott, "Across the Great Divide: Women in Politics Before and After 1920," in *Women, Politics, and Change*, ed. Louise A. Tilly and Patricia Gurin (New York: Russell Sage Foundation, 1990), 153–176.
59 Marjorie Spruill Wheeler, ed., *One Woman, One Vote: Rediscovering the Woman Suffrage Movement* (Troutdale, OR: New Sage Press, 1995), 355.
60 Becker, *Origins of the Equal Rights Amendment*, 51.
61 Ibid.
62 Jane J. Mansbridge, *Why We Lost the ERA* (Chicago: University of Chicago Press, 1986), 9.
63 Ibid., 10.
64 Gilbert Y. Steiner, *Constitutional Inequality: The Political Fortunes of the Equal Rights Amendment* (Washington, DC: Brookings Institution, 1985), 13.
65 Ibid., 15.
66 For a more detailed account of the congressional debates over the ERA, see Mansbridge, *Why We Lost the ERA*, 8–19; Steiner, *Constitutional Inequality*, 1–25.
67 Steiner, *Constitutional Inequality*, 22.
68 Janet K. Boles, *The Politics of the Equal Rights Amendment: Conflict and the Decision Process* (New York: Longman, 1979).
69 Marshall, *Splintered Sisterhood*, 232.
70 Ibid., 235.
71 Becker, *Origins of the Equal Rights Amendment*, 53.
72 Bureau of Labor Statistics, *Handbook of Labor Statistics*, Table 2, "Employment and Earnings," January 1997.
73 Cynthia B. Costello, Shari Miles, and Anne J. Stone, eds., *The American Woman: 1999–2000* (New York: Norton, 1998), 294.
74 Mansbridge, *Why We Lost the ERA*. See also Mansbridge, "Organizing for the ERA: Cracks in the Façade of Unity," in *Women, Politics, and Change*, ed. Tilly and Gurin, 323–338.
75 Mary Frances Berry, *Why ERA Failed: Politics, Women's Rights, and the Amending Process of the Constitution* (Bloomington: Indiana University Press, 1986), 2–3.
76 Amendment XXVII: "No law, varying the compensation for the services of the Senators and Representatives, shall take effect, until an election of Representatives shall have intervened."
77 Allison Held, Sheryl Herndon, and Danielle Stager, "The Equal Rights Amendment: Why the ERA Remains Legally Viable and Properly Before the States," *William and Mary Journal of Women and the Law*, Spring 1997, 113–136.
78 Jessica Neuwirth, *Equal Means Equal: Why the Time for an Equal Rights Amendment Is Now* (New York: New Press, 2015); *Equal Means Equal*, documentary film directed by Kamala Lopez, 2016, http://equalmeansequal.com.
79 Jessica Ravitz, "The Politics of Feminism: An Unlikely Partnership," CNN, April 16, 2015.
80 Neuwirth, *Equal Means Equal*, 8.
81 Quoted in Ravitz, "The Politics of Feminism."
82 "Legally Speaking: Antonin Scalia," *California Lawyer*, January 2011.

83 *Reed v. Reed*, 404 U.S. 71 (1971).

84 Jessica Ravitz, "The New Women Warriors: Reviving the Fight for Equal Rights," CNN, April 16, 2015.

85 Helen Irving, *Gender and the Constitution: Equity and Agency in Comparative Constitution Design* (New York: Cambridge University Press, 2008), 166.

86 Martha F. Davis, "The Equal Rights Amendment: Then and Now," *Columbia Journal of Gender and the Law* 17, no. 3 (2008): 439.

87 *The ERA Campaign*, no. 5 (July 2001).

88 Ryan, *Feminism and the Women's Movement*, 33.

89 Kristi Anderson, *After Suffrage: Women in Partisan and Electoral Politics Before the New Deal* (Chicago: University of Chicago Press, 1996), 50.

90 Virginia Sapiro, *Women in American Society*, 4th ed. (Mountain View, CA: Mayfield Publishing, 1999).

91 Mansbridge, *Why We Lost the ERA*, 35. See also Berry, *Why ERA Failed.*

92 David O. Sears and Leonie Huddy, "On the Origins of Political Disunity Among Women," in *Women, Politics, and Change*, ed. Tilly and Gurin, 252–253.

93 Louise A. Tilly and Patricia Gurin, "Women, Politics, and Change," in *Women, Politics, and Change*, ed. Tilly and Gurin, 24–26.

94 See Suzanne Lebsock, "Women and American Politics, 1880–1920," in *Women, Politics, and Change*, ed. Tilly and Gurin, 35–62.

Box 2.1: Declaration of Sentiments

1 Elizabeth Cady Stanton, Susan B. Anthony, and Matilda Joslyn Gage, eds., *History of Woman Suffrage* (Rochester, NY: Charles Mann, 1881), 1:67–74.

Box 2.2: Two Means to the Same End: Alice Paul and Carrie Chapman Catt

1 Christine Lunardini, *From Equal Suffrage to Equal Rights: Alice Paul and the National Woman's Party, 1910–1928* (New York: New York University Press, 1986), 10.

Box 2.3: Women's Voting Rights Around the World

1 Pamela Paxton and Melanie M. Hughes, *Women, Politics, and Power: A Global Perspective* (Thousand Oaks, CA: Pine Forge Press, 2007).

2 Angus McDowall, "Saudi Arabian Women Vote for the First Time in Local Elections," Reuters, December 12, 2015.

CHAPTER 3

Suffrage Accomplished: Women as Political Participants

O nce the legal barrier to the ballot was removed, women entered the electorate slowly, although African American women reportedly registered in large numbers in the South.[1] By and large, women voted similarly to men, but initially in smaller numbers. This slow start led one commentator to declare women's suffrage a colossal failure. Women's suffrage was not a failure but rather a casualty of unrealistic expectations—both positive and negative. "Men said that woman suffrage had promised almost everything and accomplished almost nothing when neither of these were true."[2] There are some remarkable historical examples of women forming voting coalitions in order to effect social change in their communities. In Nashville, Tennessee, African American and white women formed an alliance to demonstrate their power in expanding government's role and to promote a progressive political agenda.[3] The vote opened the door to the public sphere and a corresponding host of politically relevant activities.

Now, more than ninety-six years after gaining the vote, women are more likely than men to register to vote and to actually vote; they are as likely as men to engage in a whole range of extra-electoral activities. Women are, however, less likely than men to donate large sums of money to campaigns, to express interest in running for elective office, and to be recruited for office by political party elites. Also, the forces that attract women to politics are different from those that attract men. The vote did not make women think alike, act alike, or view issues of gender equality similarly. As we saw in Chapter 2, women differ from one another along roughly the same social, economic, and political lines that divide men. These differences influence women's levels and types of political engagement. This chapter examines women's political participation in the electorate as voters, partisans, and members of political organizations. In the process we will analyze how women's participation differs from men's and how women differ from one another as they pursue gender equality through political participation.

IMAGE 3.1: *The Sewall-Belmont House, in Washington, D.C., was headquarters for the National Woman's Party beginning in 1929 and functioned as an "embassy for women." Today the Belmont-Paul Women's Equality National Monument and Museum houses archives and artifacts documenting suffrage and women's rights campaigns.* Source: Courtesy of the Library of Congress, LC-DIG-highsm-09850; Carol M. Highsmith, photographer.

WOMEN ENTER THE ELECTORATE AS VOTERS

After ratification of the Nineteenth Amendment, procedures had to be clarified before women could actually cast their ballots. For instance, states had to change their laws and practices to allow women to register, and the pace of change varied by region. Women in Mississippi and Georgia, for example, did not vote in the November 1920 election because the state registrars upheld the existing four-month residency requirement.[4] Because counties and states did not always keep records of voting registration rates and hardly ever noted the sex of the voter in their records, little data are available to evaluate women's suffrage during the first decade following ratification.

As with other new groups of voters, it took time for women to develop voting habits, including accepting the idea that voting was appropriate behavior for women. Interviews with nonvoting women in Chicago conducted in 1923 found that more than 10 percent still believed it was wrong for a woman to vote.[5] In the years that followed ratification, African American women in the North continued to participate in politics but, feeling they had been abandoned by both white feminists in the final hours of the suffrage fight and by the Republican Party, they became disillusioned with national politics and concentrated on local politics.[6]

Although many attribute decreases in overall voter turnout during the 1920s to women entering the eligible electorate but not actually casting a ballot, some evidence contradicts that notion. It now seems just as likely that political parties experienced a dealigning period during which partisans of both genders moved away from the existing political parties and were therefore not attracted to vote for a party's candidate.[7] Sophinisba Breckinridge conducted the first empirical study of women's political participation in 1933.[8] In *Women in the Twentieth Century*, Breckinridge examined registration rates of men and women in Illinois, the only state to keep records separated by sex. Between 1914, when Illinois granted women presidential suffrage, and 1931, women's registration rates in Chicago increased by 10 percent, whereas men's decreased by the same percentage. The resulting "male advantage" in registration in 1931 was just 16 percent.[9]

A recent book, *Counting Women's Ballots: Female Voters from Suffrage Through the New Deal*, uses a methodology called ecological inference to overcome the lack of records and exit polls. Combining evidence from the US Census and voting records, authors J. Kevin Corder and Christina Wolbrecht estimated the percentage of women and men who voted in their sample of ten states.[10] In states with competitive elections, women voted at higher rates than in states where the outcome was more certain. When every vote counted, political parties and candidates worked to mobilize every voter, including women. Corder and Wolbrecht also found that in states with high barriers to voting—poll taxes, literacy tests, and long residency requirements—women, and particularly African American women, were affected to a greater degree than men. In short, the context of the election affected turnout as much or more than gender did. As we will see in this chapter, much the same is true today.

Women Voters Outnumber Men at the Polls

By 1980, the gap in registration rates had narrowed considerably, with 80 percent of men and 77 percent of women registered to vote. Women's registration rates surpassed those of men in the 1984 election and have remained higher in every subsequent national election. The 1965 Voting Rights Act was the catalyst for African American women's dramatic increase in voter registration, particularly in the South. Although registration figures by gender are not available for the period prior to 1975, later voter participation figures suggest that women were well represented among the newly registered southern voters.[11] Since 1980, the proportion of female voters has surpassed the proportion of male voters in every presidential election. In 2012, 63.7 percent of eligible female voters cast ballots compared to 59.8 percent of eligible male voters. Final turnout figures for 2016 were not available at the time of publication of this edition. The absolute number of women voting has also been higher than that of men in every presidential election since 1964. In real numbers, 9.8 million more women than men cast votes in the 2012 presidential contest.[12] In nonpresidential years, women have been outvoting men since 1986. In the midterm election of 2014, 43 percent of women eligible to vote turned out, compared to 40.8 percent of men.

TABLE 3.1: Young Women and Men Voting in Presidential Elections

Year	Ages 18–24		Ages 25–29		All Ages	
	% WOMEN	% MEN	% WOMEN	% MEN	% WOMEN	% MEN
2012	44.5	37.9	54.6	47.0	63.7	59.8
2008	52.0	45.1	59.0	50.2	65.6	61.5
2004	49.7	43.8	56.5	48.1	65.4	62.1
2000	38.2	34.0	49.9	43.7	60.7	58.0
1996	38.1	33.0	48.6	41.0	59.6	57.1
1992	49.0	44.8	57.7	52.2	66.3	64.6
1988	40.6	37.1	50.0	45.0	61.4	59.9
1984	44.9	40.7	56.3	51.7	63.5	61.7
1980	43.2	40.7	55.2	52.9	61.9	61.5

Source: "Young Women and Politics" Center for American Women and Politics (CAWP), Eagleton Institute of Politics, Rutgers University, 2016.

Estimates of men's and women's voting habits are generally based on post-election surveys. This methodology relies on individuals' correct recollection of whether they actually voted on Election Day. While remembering such information seems like a simple task, the considerable social pressure to fulfill one's civic duty to vote causes many people to misreport having voted, thereby slightly inflating the turnout statistics. Evidence from vote validation studies has shown that men are slightly more likely to misreport voting than are women, making the gap between male and female turnout rates potentially even larger.[13]

The Sociodemographics of Women Voters: Age, Race, and Education

The gap between men and women at the polls varies depending on a number of sociodemographic characteristics, such as age, race, and education. The level of women's participation in any given election is also influenced by the same sociodemographic factors. Take age, for example. Young people are often criticized for their lack of political engagement and their failure to vote once they turn eighteen. Among young men and women between the ages of eighteen and twenty-nine, the female advantage holds in voter turnout statistics (see Table 3.1). The 2016 Democratic primaries, and particularly Bernie Sanders's candidacy, captured the attention of young voters. Other mobilizing forces, such as Black Lives Matter activism in response to police-on-civilian violence, movements to pressure universities to remove legacies of the Confederacy, and protests against college rape culture may have led more college students to engage politically. Respondents to UCLA's annual CIRP freshman survey in 2015 demonstrated the highest levels of political engagement evident in fifty years (see Figure 3.1). Nearly one in ten students entering college in 2015 expected to

FIGURE 3.1: Percentages of First-Year College Students Who Intend to Influence the Political Structure (1974–2015)

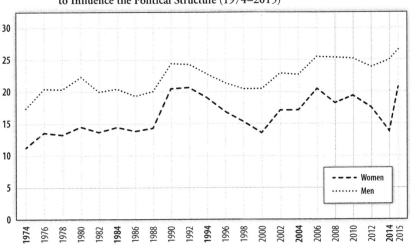

Source: *The American Freshman: National Norms*, Higher Education Research Institute, UCLA.

participate in student protests while in college. For students of color, the percentage was even higher (16 percent of black students and 10.2 percent of Latino students). Almost 40 percent of incoming freshmen said they want to become community leaders, and 22.3 percent of students hope to influence the political structure. A sizable majority (59.8 percent) said there was a very good chance that they would vote in a local, state, or national election while in college.[14]

The Center for American Women and Politics tracks gender differences on the question of influencing the political structure (see Figure 3.1). Males consistently attach more importance to influencing the political system than females (26.6 percent of men, 20.7 percent of women). Young men also express ambition for public office more often than women of the same age. Richard Fox and Jennifer Lawless surveyed 4,000 high school and college students and conducted more than 100 in-depth interviews to investigate young people's ambition.[15] Among high school students, the gap is relatively small, but it grows larger as students move from high school to college. Lawless and Fox find that in high school, males and females have similar socializing experiences—their parents encourage them to think about politics and public office in similar ways. By college, the percentage of women who say they received encouragement from a parent to run for office drops, falling below that for men, and women are more likely than men to evaluate themselves as "not qualified" to run. Although their research confirms the survey of entering freshman that found both men and women want basically the same things from their lives, including taking action to improve their community, men are significantly more likely to see that action in explicitly political terms than women as early as age eighteen. This is consistent with other research demonstrating that women tend to be less politically engaged overall than their male counterparts, although women are more likely to report plans to participate in a community action program than are men in college.

Why do young women outvote men but express less ambition toward other forms of political engagement? A study of young people between the ages of eighteen and twenty-five found that more women than men viewed voting as a responsibility (23 percent of women versus 20 percent of men), while more men saw voting as a choice (35 percent of men versus 31 percent of women).[16] In the 2012 election, an estimated 20.5 million people under thirty voted. Although people between eighteen and twenty-nine represented 21.2 percent of the population that was eligible to vote in 2012, the number of people in that age group who actually voted that year represented only 15.4 percent of all those who cast ballots—5.8 points below the group's eligibility rate. This figure is much lower than for any other age group, meaning that young people underperformed relative to their total proportion among eligible voters.[17] This has been consistently true since 1996 and was likely to remain the case in 2016, although individuals at the top edge of this age group are facing their third election as young adults and might be expected to become more consistent voters. Young voters are now the most racially and ethnically diverse segment of the electorate, and the most educated. According to a Harvard University Institute of Politics poll conducted in advance of the 2016 election, 61 percent of voters under thirty supported Hillary Clinton; 25 percent of young voters favored Donald Trump. Final figures for 2016 were not available at press time for this edition, but exit polls showed that Clinton won 55 percent of the youth vote to Trump's 37 percent. Young people mirror older generations in the issues they find more pressing: 64 percent identified the economy as the most important issue, and 39 percent indicated that combating the spread of terrorism was among the top three issues. Other key issues included reducing inequality (34 percent), uniting the country (31 percent), dealing with immigration (27 percent), and reducing the role of money in politics (23 percent).[18] However, even though the issues were the same, many young voters complained that the presidential campaigns did not frame the issues in a way that spoke directly to them. Voters under thirty were more likely than older voters to express concerns about lesbian and gay rights and about keeping abortion legal.

Organizations such as Rock the Vote have been working to register and mobilize young women and men since 1990. Rock the Vote's 2016 campaign, "Truth to Power," aimed to register an additional two million voters before November and increase turnout among voters under thirty in key battleground states. Rock the Vote typically uses a variety of celebrity ads and public service announcements. Independent Journal Review and Rock the Vote created a campaign video featuring twenty-year-old model Kendall Jenner changing in and out of popular fashion trends reflecting significant years in voting history as well as an ad in which Jenner

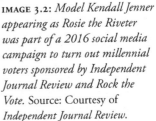

IMAGE 3.2: *Model Kendall Jenner appearing as Rosie the Riveter was part of a 2016 social media campaign to turn out millennial voters sponsored by Independent Journal Review and Rock the Vote.* Source: Courtesy of *Independent Journal Review.*

appears as Rosie the Riveter. "Kendall has a larger social media reach than each of the presidential candidates, and using her voice to encourage millennial voters is a great thing," said Alex Skatell, Founder and CEO of *Independent Journal Review.* In 2016 Rock the Vote also partnered with the dating app Tinder on "Swipe the Vote," which allows users to swipe left or right on issues to get "matched" with their ideal candidate. The top three matches were Bernie Sanders (37.8 percent), Hillary Clinton (37.6 percent), and Ted Cruz (14.3 percent). Donald Trump matched with only 8.1 percent of Tinder users.[19] Several women's organizations created summer initiatives designed to register and mobilize young women in November. The American Association of University Women (AAUW) launched "It's My Voice. I Will Be Heard" as a campaign to "harnesses the power of AAUW members to register and turn out millennial women voters nationwide at a time when, research shows, young women are less likely to vote."[20] A coalition of organizations banded together under the slogan "We Won't Wait 2016" to hold 500,000 "kitchen table conversations" intended to encourage women of color to be vocal about issues that are important to them. The National Federation of Republican Women organized a bus tour designed to register Republican women to vote and call attention to female candidates running in down-ballot races.

Anticipation of a high turnout for young women and men in November 2008 was based on their record-high participation during the primary season. Youth voter turnout in the 2008 primaries and caucuses was nearly double that in the

2000 primaries. In the 2008 general election, an estimated 22 million voters under thirty participated—an increase of 2 million over 2004. The gap between female and male young voters was nearly eight percentage points. Youth turnout was highest in Washington, D.C. (76 percent), Minnesota (68 percent), and Iowa (63 percent). In Washington, D.C., for the first time anywhere, young people voted at a higher rate (by three percentage points) than their adult counterparts. Researchers and political pundits alike attribute the record-high 2008 turnout among young people to the excitement generated by Barack Obama's historic candidacy. Turnout rates fell to more normal levels in 2012. In 2016, young voters in the primaries overwhelmingly preferred Bernie Sanders to either Hillary Clinton or Donald Trump. Based on primaries in the twenty-one states voting before June 1, 2016, the *Washington Post* reported that Democrat Bernie Sanders won 2 million more votes from those under thirty years of age than Clinton and Trump combined.[21]

In recent years, women under forty-five voted at significantly higher rates than did men in the same age group.[22] However, among those fifty-five and older, the percentage of women voting declined while the percentage of male voters held steady, thus reversing the gender advantage seen in younger age cohorts. Among citizens between sixty-five and seventy-four years of age, 74.4 percent of men reported voting in the 2012 election, compared to only 72.7 percent of women. Men seventy-five years or older outvoted women by a margin of six points in 2012.[23] Researchers are not sure why women's participation tends to decline after age fifty-five, when arguably they would have more, not less, resources and time to dedicate to politics.

Among African American voters, the gender gap in voter turnout has been consistently larger than in the population at large. Researchers attribute higher participation rates among African American women than men to a feminist identity developed through intersectional experiences with both race and sex discrimination, and to strong ties with their community and church.[24] In 2012, for example, 70 percent of black women voted, compared to 61 percent of black men. This gap is 6.5 points larger than that of the entire population.

Finally, education has long played a big role in predicting and explaining differential levels of civic engagement. For example, in the 2008 election, individuals with college experience voted at significantly higher rates than those without (62.1 percent compared with 35.9 percent). Table 3.2 displays the relationship between education level, sex, and voter registration and turnout for young voters ages eighteen to twenty-four. For both men and women, the higher the level of education, the more likely they are to be registered and to have voted in the 2012 presidential election. Only for those with no education beyond a high school diploma do men outpace women in registration (56.3 percent of men, 43.6 percent of women) and voting (52.3 percent of men, 47.6 percent of women). At all other levels of education, women significantly outperform men.

TABLE 3.2: Registration and Voting by Sex and Educational Attainment (Ages 18–24)

	Registered to Vote		Voted		All Eligible Citizens	
					REGIS-TERED	VOTED
	WOMEN	MEN	WOMEN	MEN		
HS diploma	43.6	56.3	47.6	52.3	34.8	12.0
Associate's degree (or some college)	52.7	47.3	52.8	47.0	49.1	20.5
Bachelor's degree	59.3	40.6	62.9	37.1	58.3	29.3
Advanced degree	54.4	45.5	55.5	44.4	48.5	21.6

Source: US Census Bureau, Current Population Survey, "Table 5. Reported Voting and Registration, by Age, Sex, and Educational Attainment: November 2014."

Why People Choose to Vote or to Abstain

Other factors beyond gender influence a person's decision to vote or to abstain. Since voter turnout in the United States is consistently lower than in most other developed nations, researchers have studied the motives and behaviors of voters for several decades to answer the question of why people *don't* vote. To cast a ballot, citizens must register to vote, which often means navigating a complex bureaucratic process. The 1993 National Voter Registration Act (NVRA), also known as "Motor Voter," made registering somewhat easier. The NVRA requires states to allow citizens to register to vote at the same time as they do other business with the state, such as register a car, renew a driver's license, or apply for some forms of government benefits. Although this program registered more people and created a slightly more diverse voter pool in terms of education, age, and race, the NVRA's effects on actual voter turnout were not as great as had once been predicted. In 2008, nearly 3 million registered voters could not vote because of problems related to their voter registration record. A study of in-person voters from the 2012 election similarly found that millions of voters experienced registration problems at the polls. In any given election year, roughly 30 percent of the eligible population is not registered to vote by the deadline. To ease the burden of registration, more than half of the states now allow online or electronic registration—saving money in the process as well.[25] Oregon and California have taken this a step further and adopted automatic voter registration in 2015. In those states, all people eligible to vote are automatically registered when they interact with a government agency (such as the Department of Motor Vehicles) unless they decline. Twenty-nine additional states are currently considering automatic registration.

Political scientists have also investigated why people *do* vote. After years of studies and countless theories, the answer remains a mystery. Some political scientists posit that citizens undertake a rational calculation of the costs and benefits of voting. If the benefits outweigh the costs, citizens appear at the polls. However, the benefits one person derives are difficult to determine since, according to some calculations, a voter is more likely to be struck by lightning on the way to the polls than to change an election's outcome.[26] So the benefits of voting are more often such intangibles as altruism or a sense of duty fulfilled. The costs vary depending on an individual's circumstances. For women, the costs may be higher than for men since women are still considered the primary caregivers for children and elderly parents, and they are more likely to have jobs with less flexible schedules or that pay on an hourly basis, all of which affect the time that women have to go to the polls. And yet women vote at higher rates than men, so other factors must be at work. Most likely, voting is a standing decision or a habit that individuals develop as they become integrated into the social and political life of their communities. Voting, in this context, is an act of social participation or civic involvement. In general, voters are connected to the larger society and to their communities in ways that nonvoters are not.[27] Women have a history of community-based involvement, and this tradition may help explain why women are more likely to vote than men.

In the 2008 and 2016 presidential elections, particularly during the Democratic primaries, there is some evidence that women were drawn to the polls by the prospect of voting for a woman with a strong chance to win the nomination. Likewise, in 2008 Republican voters had a historic opportunity to vote for a ticket that included a woman vice presidential candidate for the first time. Nearly a quarter century earlier, the last time a woman held a place on a national presidential ticket, Democratic vice presidential candidate Geraldine Ferraro reported that "women across the country have told me what a huge personal impact my nomination had on their lives." Exit poll data from the 1984 presidential race found that 23 percent of women agreed that Ferraro's candidacy had made them more interested in politics.[28] As a candidate, Hillary Clinton intentionally targeted women and called upon all voters to break the "highest and hardest glass ceiling in America." In 2008 Clinton said, "I am in this race for all the women in their nineties who've told me they were born before women could vote and they want to live to see a woman in the White House. For all the women who are energized for the first time, and voting for the first time."[29] In 2016, Clinton would often note that if she won the White House, "finally fathers will be able to say to their daughters, 'You, too, can grow up to be president.'"[30]

THE GENDER GAP

Pick up a daily newspaper during the months preceding an election and you'll find evidence that journalists and politicians alike perceive the gender gap to be a powerful political phenomenon.[31] The **gender gap** occurs when women as a group vote significantly different from men. The term originated during the 1980 presidential election, when the victor, Republican Ronald Reagan, ran a campaign dominated by his opposition to the Equal Rights Amendment and abortion and his support of "traditional family values," which many interpreted as a return to traditional roles for women. The Republican Party's continuing affinity for these themes is presumed to have alienated many women voters throughout the 1990s and well into the twenty-first century.[32]

The gender gap is calculated by subtracting the percentage of men who voted for a particular candidate from the percentage of women who voted for the same candidate (or vice versa), not by looking at how one candidate did among either women or men alone. Although after 1980 the gender gap referred to the greater likelihood of women voting for a Democratic Party candidate, a candidate cannot be said to have lost an election because she or he lost the "women's vote." Conceptually, when a single candidate fares well among female voters, for example, her opponent fares equally well among male voters. "By definition, the Republicans' 'problem with women' is exactly the same size as the Democrats' 'problem with men.'"[33] But since the size of the gender gap in recent presidential contests and in a number of high-profile congressional races was larger than the margin of victory, women have become the target of appeals by both parties. Add to that the fact that more women than men have actually cast votes in every election since 1964, and few politicians can afford to ignore the potential of women's electoral power.

The Gender Gap's Impact in Modern Elections

The Center for American Women and Politics (CAWP) at Rutgers University distinguishes between the women's vote and the gender gap. Although the terms are often used synonymously, the concepts are different. The women's vote refers to the division of support among women in a single contest, whereas the gender gap is the difference between men's and women's support for candidates in a race. "This distinction is important because even when women and men favor the same candidate, they usually do so by different margins, resulting in a gender gap."[34] Although women have tended to favor Democrats, the gender gap isn't a guarantee of victory for Democratic candidates. In the 2014 midterm elections, the Republican Party increased its share of seats in the House of Representatives and also took control of the US Senate, but a gender gap remained. Republicans attracted 52 percent of the national vote, while 47 percent of people voted for Democrats, but Republicans still suffered from a significant gender gap characterized by the Pew Research Center as wide as at any point over the last fifteen years. Women were 10 points less likely to support Republicans; the gap had been 8 points in 2012, 6 points in 2010, 5 points in 2008, and 4 points in 2006.[35]

Susan Hansen's analysis of the 2012 election found that voters regard the Democratic Party as more supportive of equality for women and reproductive rights. This proved to be "a highly effective wedge issue" that the Democrats were able to effectively exploit.[36] Perception of Democrats as "better for the interests of women" was strongly significant in explaining votes for Obama. Since the electorate is divided into roughly equal portions of Democrats, independents, and

Republicans, neither party can win an election without appealing to voters outside the party.[37] The Democrats' position on gay marriage also attracted Republican voters. Notes political scientist Susan B. Hansen, "The Republican Party thus faces a significant dilemma; the GOP is further away from voters' positions than the Democrats on both abortion and equality for women, and its opposition to gay marriage is increasingly out of step with Americans' liberalizing opinions. Demographic trends favor the Democrats, with growing numbers of seculars, younger voters, those with advanced degrees, divorced or unmarried individuals, and minorities."[38]

The contemporary gender gap generally ranges from 7 to 12 percentage points in congressional elections, and hovered at about 7.8 percentage points on average in presidential contests from 1980 to 2012 (see Table 3.3). President Bill Clinton enjoyed a significantly larger gender gap in 1996. The gap in 2000 was similarly large, but Democrat Al Gore lost the election to Republican George W. Bush. Men and women were clearly divided in their preferences for president, with a majority of women (54 percent versus 42 percent of men) voting for Al Gore and a majority of men (54 percent versus 43 percent of women) voting for George W. Bush. Despite the gender gap in favor of Democratic candidate John Kerry, President Bush increased his overall share of the women's vote in 2004. President Bush's ability to attract 48 percent of the women's vote (up from 43 percent in 2000) was a major factor contributing to his margin of victory in the popular vote.[39] Susan Carroll, senior scholar at the Center for American Women and Politics, says that Kerry was "so concerned with establishing his commander-in-chief credentials"; as a consequence, he did not address other issues important to women, including health care, job security, and retirement benefits. "He made many women wonder, 'Do you really understand the kind of difficulties I'm having?'"[40]

In 2008 women strongly preferred Barack Obama to John McCain (56 percent for Obama, 43 percent for McCain), while men split their votes about evenly between the two candidates (49 percent for Obama, 48 percent for McCain). Thus, the gender gap in 2008 was about 7 percentage points, identical to the gap in 2004. Senator Obama, however, drew more female voters in 2008 than Senator John Kerry did in 2004. Obama enjoyed support from a clear majority of female voters (56 percent), while Kerry attracted only a bare majority of women (51 percent) in 2004. By contrast, Senator John McCain did worse with women voters, attracting only 43 percent of their votes compared to George W. Bush's 48 percent in 2004. Obama pulled 46 percent of white women compared with 41 percent of white men, and 68 percent of Latino women versus 64 percent of Latino men. There was no gender gap for African American voters—both sexes overwhelmingly supported Barack Obama (96 percent of black women and 95 percent of black men). When Obama sought reelection in 2012, the gender gap contributed to his victory over Mitt Romney. Women constituted the majority of voters (53 percent), and 55 percent of women cast a vote for Obama. President Obama's share of African American

TABLE 3.3: Gender Gap in Presidential Elections, 1980–2016

Year	Presidential Candidate	Women	Men	Gender Gap
2016	Donald Trump (R)	42%	53%	11 pts.
	Hillary Clinton (D)	54%	41%	
2012	Barack Obama (D)	55%	45%	10 pts.
	Mitt Romney (R)	44%	52%	
2008	Barack Obama (D)	56%	49%	7 pts.
	John McCain (R)	43%	48%	
2004	George W. Bush (R)	48%	55%	7 pts.
	John Kerry (D)	51%	41%	
2000	George W. Bush (R)	43%	53%	10 pts.
	Al Gore (D)	54%	42%	
	Ralph Nader (Green)	2%	3%	
1996	Bill Clinton (D)	54%	43%	11 pts.
	Bob Dole (R)	38%	44%	
	Ross Perot (Reform)	7%	10%	
1992	Bill Clinton (D)	45%	41%	4 pts.
	George H. W. Bush (R)	37%	38%	
	Ross Perot (Reform)	17%	21%	
1988	George H. W. Bush (R)	50%	57%	7 pts.
	Michael Dukakis (D)	49%	41%	
1984	Ronald Reagan (R)	56%	62%	6 pts.
	Walter Mondale (D)	44%	37%	
1980	Ronald Reagan (R)	46%	54%	8 pts.
	Jimmy Carter (D)	45%	37%	
	John Anderson (I)	7%	7%	

Source: "Election 2016: Exit Polls." The *New York Times*, November 8, 2016; Kelly Dittmar, "The Gender Gap: Gender Differences in Vote Choice and Political Orientations," Center for American Women and Politics, Eagleton Institute of Politics, Rutgers University, July 17, 2014.

and Latina women increased, but his support among white women declined slightly (52 percent of white women supported Romney, while 42 percent voted for Obama). Women made the difference in several swing states. In Ohio, Obama lost to Romney by 10 points among independents (another prized group), but he won by 12 points among women. In Pennsylvania, there was a 16-point gender gap in Obama's favor.

The impact of the gender gap depends wholly on the proportion of men and women voting in any single election. Because women have been turning out in both higher proportions and larger numbers than men have in recent elections,

a gender gap favoring women is a determining force in the outcome of these elections. However, gender differences do not make up the largest gap within the
electorate. The gaps in voting behavior created by race (consistently 50 points
between whites and blacks; Obama attracted 95 percent of the African American
vote in 2012), ethnicity (71 percent of Hispanic and 73 percent of Asian voters
supported Obama in 2012), and economic differences (19 points between the rich
and poor in 2012) surpass gender in size, if not in significance.

Likewise, gender does not act in a vacuum, as we have noted repeatedly throughout this volume. In some cases, voters' intersectional identities may align to produce
a stronger attachment to one political party over another, but in other cases intersectionality may mean cross-cutting pressures that move voters into the independent
category. We do not yet fully understand the impact of intersectionality on voting
or the gender gap in American politics, but it is a robust new area of research.[41] The
gender gap attracts media attention because a political "war of the sexes" is more
socially acceptable than competition between the races or economic classes. In addition, women constitute a larger potential pool of voters with a proven track record
of turnout than voters in other categories, and so they are easier to profile and study.

Sources of the Gender Gap

A definitive source of the gender gap continues to elude scholars, but evidence supports a number of theories. Some attribute the gap to the changing employment
circumstances and attitudes of women,[42] while others attribute it to the changing
politics of men.[43] More broadly, scholars explain the different candidate preferences of men and women as differences in policy preferences, most especially those
regarding government social welfare spending and the importance of a government
"safety net." Additionally, "women's issues," such as abortion and women's rights,
along with "men's issues," such as the use of force and military expansion, have
been investigated as root causes of the gender gap. Perceptions of the economy,
either in general (most important to women) or in regard to an individual's personal finances (most salient to men), have been shown to differ by gender.[44]

By the time people went to the polls in November 2008, the economy and
energy were considered the top issue priorities by nearly all voters.[45] Women were
significantly more pessimistic than men in their outlook on their economic future.
Women were more likely to say they were falling behind economically, with a
majority (60 percent) reporting that their income was falling behind the cost of
living. Fifty-nine percent of women versus 46 percent of men were concerned
about "achieving their economic and financial goals over the next five years" as the
fall campaign got under way. When asked about equality of opportunity relative
to employment and the economy, an overwhelming majority of men believed
that they compete with women on a level playing field, with only about half
of women saying the same. Not surprisingly, then, women supported a larger

role for government in solving problems and meeting the needs of people—most especially in providing families with economic security, enforcing equal pay and equal opportunities, ensuring universal access to health care, expanding access to contraceptives and sex education to avoid unintended pregnancies, and ensuring that parents have access to affordable quality child care.[46] This gender difference over the size and scope of government continued through 2012 and into 2016.

Even when men and women hold the same policy positions, the levels of salience may differ to the extent that a single issue may determine the vote for one gender while being relatively unimportant to the other gender's final decision. This is most evident in the issue of abortion. While men and women do not differ significantly in their relative positions on abortion policy, the salience of the issue acts as a political mobilizing force for women but not for men.[47] During the 2012 election, the Republican Party was accused of waging a "war against women" over the issues of abortion, contraception, and rape—a "war" that manifested itself in a variety of ways. In 2011, state lawmakers had introduced more than 600 bills restricting abortion and passed a record ninety-one into law. Several states considered "personhood amendments" stating that life begins at conception and that the unborn are entitled to all of the protections guaranteed by the Fourteenth Amendment to persons "born in the United States." Republicans in Congress and in several states continued their efforts to defund Planned Parenthood because some affiliates perform abortions—and they have only intensified these efforts over time. Efforts to cover access to contraception, including Plan B, under the Affordable Care Act were met with objections from religious nonprofits and educational institutions (churches were already exempt). Attempts to find a compromise resulted in the Republicans holding hearings featuring an all-male panel of religious leaders and excluding Sandra Fluke, a Georgetown Law student whom the Democrats had put forth as a witness. Republicans on the campaign trail were forced to deal with controversial statements about rape made by Senate candidates. Missouri's Todd Akin said that abortion in the case of rape was unnecessary because in cases of "legitimate" rape, "a woman's body has ways of shutting the whole thing down" and preventing pregnancy. Richard Mourdock was in the lead in Indiana until he said, "Even when life begins in that horrible situation of rape, that is something God intended to happen," and ruled out exceptions for rape in restrictive abortion laws. Finally, the Republican Party Platform included a Human Life Amendment banning all abortions with no exceptions. In her analysis of the 2012 vote, Susan Hansen found that these issues as well as gay marriage cost Republicans votes and widened the gender gap in national elections for Congress and the presidency.[48]

In every post-9/11 election, the economy, security, and the "war on terror" have been among voters' top three issues. In 2004, George W. Bush relied on the threat of terror to increase his support among married women with children—dubbed "security moms" by the media. Although women's organizations moved quickly to debunk the myth of the "security mom," Republicans continued to appeal to this group of women.[49] A January 9, 2016, *Wall Street Journal* headline read: "A Revival of 'Security Moms' Would Stand to Benefit GOP."[50] Women tend to worry more than men about their personal and economic security largely because they are more likely to be victims of crime at home and are more likely to live on the economic margins. However, this concern about personal security does not necessarily translate into political preferences in the national security realm.[51] In fact, men were more likely than women to make terrorism and security a part of their voting calculus. In 2008, the economic downturn eclipsed the Iraq War and the "war on terror" for both men and women, but women consistently expressed a deeper sense of economic vulnerability that likely translated into greater issue saliency for the economy in their vote choice.

In the aftermath of the 2004 election, pundits attributed George W. Bush's reelection to his ability to attract "security moms" to the Republican ticket and the Democrats' failure to win back "NASCAR dads." Implicit in these labels is the assumption that parents have political interests that are distinct from those of voters without children—and that parenthood moved voters in a more conservative direction that benefited Republicans. However, researchers Laurel Elder and Steven Greene find little empirical support for the claims.[52] In fact, data from the 2004 election demonstrate that there was no "mother gap" on issues concerning security—in other words, women with children voted no differently than women without children. The only issue on which mothers were substantively distinctive from other women was on issues of social welfare; mothers favored greater access to health care and government support for jobs. Fathers did not differ on any issue from nonfathers, leading Elder and Greene to conclude that "it seems almost pointless to talk about 'dads' as a distinct political entity at all."[53]

In 2016, single women, Latinas, and millennial women were the voters most watched by pollsters and coveted by candidates. Unmarried women were most focused on economic issues, including equal pay, college affordability, and paid sick days. Single women also indicated a willingness to support candidates who pledged to protect a woman's access to reproductive health and birth control and less likely to support candidates who opposed a woman's right to abortion. And unmarried women "across the political spectrum outright reject[ed] a candidate who disparages women, even if they share[d] policy positions with that candidate."[54] In 2016, there were more than 58 million single women eligible to vote, and for the first time the number of single women exceeded married women among eligible voters. Latina women were driven by issues related to money and family. They expressed highly polarized feelings about the political parties and the presidential candidates. Latina voters overwhelmingly expressed support for Hillary Clinton, with 84 percent viewing Donald Trump negatively. Millennial women worried most about bills and expenses, followed by caring for a family and affordable health care.[55]

Box 3.1–Spotlight on the 2016 Election

The Glass Ceiling Remains: Are Women Voters Responsible?

If we learned anything from the 2016 presidential election, it is this: there is no group solidarity among women voters. Donald Kinder and Alison Dale-Riddle's analysis of the 2008 Democratic primaries should have served as a caution: they found that "group solidarity among women ha[d] little or nothing to do with support for Hillary Clinton."[1] Just a month prior to the 2016 election, favorability ratings for Obama were stronger than for Clinton among women professing a strong gender identity; women who did not perceive gender as an important part of their identity (40 percent in one pre-election survey) were especially anti-Clinton.

Kelly Dittmar, scholar at the Center for American Women and Politics, argues that the media narrative that women abandoned Clinton is incomplete at best, and at worst incorrect.[2] According to exit polls, the majority (53 percent) of white women voted for Donald Trump, a man comedian Samantha Bee referred to as a "vial of weaponized testosterone." However, a majority of white women have supported the Republican presidential candidate in every election since 2004. Hillary Clinton did win a majority (51 percent) of college-educated white women and, for the first time for a Democrat in twenty years, a majority of votes from married women. Clinton also won 94 percent of black women's votes and 86 percent of Latinas' votes.

Why wasn't this enough to secure the presidency? Hillary Clinton won 54 percent of women's votes, a performance Dittmar characterizes as "on par with Democratic presidential candidates in the past two decades." But Clinton isn't like any previous Democrat; she is a woman. Throughout the campaign Donald Trump demeaned women, bragged about assaulting women, questioned Clinton's stamina and qualification for the presidency, and called Clinton a "nasty woman" in the final presidential debate. None of that was enough to convince women to set aside party or their ambivalence about this particular female candidate and vote for Hillary Clinton to become the first woman US president.

The 2016 election was atypical in many ways, but female voters predictably cast their votes as partisans and not in solidarity as women.

Although men and women encounter the same set of issues in the same political context, they react differently to the political environment. Women and men experience changes in society, politics, and the economy differently and therefore exhibit different political responses to these changes. For example, as the percentage of women who head households increases, the gender gap increases, leading researchers to conclude that economic vulnerability as the result of social and economic changes increases women's Democratic partisanship.[56] Simultaneously, the partisan differences between men and women shape politics, as they "affect the kinds of issues on the political agenda, the nature of ensuing policy debates and the nomination process, as well as elections themselves."[57] While there is indeed evidence of a persistent gender gap, it is dynamic in nature. Its source is multifaceted and complex; its size is dependent on the behavior of strategic politicians, trends in the nature of families, and economic conditions; and its impact must be contextualized in the specific nature of each election cycle.

GENDER DIFFERENCES IN POLITICAL PARTICIPATION BEYOND THE BALLOT

One unique feature of the US political system is the sheer number of opportunities to engage in political activity apart from elections. For our purposes, we define political participation as "activity that has the intent or effect of influencing government action—either directly by affecting the making or implementation of public policy or indirectly by influencing the selection of people who make those policies."[58] For example, an individual might work on a campaign, donate to candidates or an important cause, serve on a local board or commission, contact public officials, join political or interest-based organizations, or volunteer for a community-based organization. Some forms of participation require resources, whereas others ask for nothing more than interest. Passionate interest sometimes results in protests or other unconventional forms of participation. Women who petitioned for suffrage rights engaged in protests to attract attention in the absence of power and access to other important political resources.

Political participation is not equally distributed throughout the population. Ironically, those who stand to benefit the most from working on a cause or for a candidate (e.g., the poor, minorities, women) often participate less frequently than others. Conventional wisdom holds that women participate beyond the ballot box at lower rates than men do. However, a closer examination reveals that if demographic characteristics are held constant, men and women participate at roughly equal levels across many, but not all, forms of political activity.

Do Men and Women Specialize in Forms of Political Participation?

In the largest study of its kind, political scientists Sidney Verba, Kay Schlozman, and Henry Brady surveyed more than 15,000 Americans by telephone and then interviewed more than 2,500 in person to understand voluntary civic participation.[59]

The researchers used the data to compare men's and women's behavior in traditional political activity and other forms of volunteerism to test the hypothesis that men and women specialize in different types of political engagement. In examining political participation,[60] they found that women engaged in an average of 2.0 political acts, while men undertook 2.3, a minor but statistically significant difference.[61] Generally speaking, men are slightly more actively involved than woman in traditional forms of political engagement—the largest differences appear in making a campaign contribution, contacting a government official, and affiliating with a political organization.[62]

The picture is slightly different for nonpolitical voluntary activities, but perhaps not as different as we might have expected. For nearly two centuries, women have participated at the periphery of politics through community and religious organizations. However, the data here show that men and women engage in about the same number of nonpolitical activities, with a few notable exceptions. Women are more likely than men to attend church and donate their time and money to the church. However, once men and women get involved, the amount of time and money they give is significantly different. Men give more hours to the church than women do, whereas women give more hours to politics than men do. When it comes to money, men contribute more frequently and are likely to contribute larger sums both to the church and to political causes and candidates.

A more recent examination of civic engagement among young people suggests that the picture may be changing with future generations. Girls and young women are ahead of their male counterparts in several forms of civic engagement, including volunteering, membership in community organizations, and voting. Post-college, women are overrepresented in programs such as AmeriCorps and Teach for America.[63] However, women are less likely to talk frequently about politics with family and friends. Young women assign less importance to the value of keeping up with political news and express less interest in holding elective office in the future. Most troubling are the findings that young women are less likely to believe they are above average in leadership skills and that the "confidence gap" widens between the first and last years of college. So, although we have seen elsewhere in this volume that Americans associate valuable leadership qualities with women—honesty, intelligence, and creativity—young women do not express such confidence in themselves.

Access to Monetary and Political Resources

Do men have access to more monetary resources and do they use those resources to greater political effect than women? Previous research has shown that the propensity to give and the amount contributed depend on both total family income and the portion of family income derived from the respondent's income. Women's mean family income is lower than men's, and women's personal share of family income is lower even in cases where both spouses work outside the home. Not only have women given in smaller amounts, but they have given less consistently. They also tend to give for ideological reasons (to support a cause) rather than for economic reasons.[64] However, early data on the 2016 elections suggest that women are playing a larger role as political donors. "Forty-three percent of all reported contributions to federal candidates for this election have come from women," according to an analysis of Federal Election Commission (FEC) data reported in May 2016.[65] Women also provided one-fifth of all individual contributions to super PACs up to that point in the election, compared to just 1 percent in 2010. The shift can be attributed to cultural and economic changes for women: "More women are founding their own companies or rising to lead family businesses, or have already sold or retired from them, a common springboard to the upper reaches of political fundraising."[66] Although most of the donor activity among women is directed toward Democratic candidates, women are playing a more significant role among Republican donors as well.

The emergence of women's political action committees (PACs) dedicated to soliciting funds from women in favor of electing women have provided a new and highly instrumental way to channel women's campaign contributions. For example, **EMILY's List** (Early Money Is Like Yeast—that is, "it makes the dough rise") was founded in 1985 to recruit, fund, and elect Democratic prochoice women to federal office. Ninety-four percent of EMILY's List contributors are women. In the 2014 cycle, the group reported more than $8 million in federal election spending to the FEC, and were anticipating raising and spending even more in 2016. "Our network of over 3 million members are fired up about 2016. We are ready to elect the first woman president—and more Democratic women up-and-down the ballot, from coast-to-coast," EMILY's List executive director Jessica O'Connell said in a May 2016 statement.[67] EMILY's List donors donated more than $200,000 to Clinton during the first month and a half of her campaign, according to FEC filings. That is nearly half of the $550,689 the group raised during the entirety of Clinton's first presidential bid in 2008, according to the Center for Responsive Politics. The Ready for Hillary super PAC formed and began raising money even before Secretary Clinton announced her candidacy. Once the campaign was under way, the PAC transferred its social media followers over to EMILY's List—including its 2.2 million Facebook and 145,000 Twitter followers.

Levels of Political Interest Among Men and Women

Researchers have long believed that interest motivates political activity.[68] Women in previous generations were conditioned to believe that politics was a "man's world" and therefore beyond the scope of their interest. Perhaps this legacy continues even today. Significant gaps in interest and attentiveness to politics remain between men and women. Sixty-one percent of college-educated women but only 36 percent of similarly educated men find politics too complicated to understand, according to a study conducted by the University of Pennsylvania's Annenberg Public Policy Center.[69] Nineteen percent of women between the ages of eighteen and twenty-nine talked about politics frequently with family and friends, whereas 22.8 percent of men in the same age group engaged in political discussion. Similarly, there is about a ten-point gap favoring men in those who believe keeping up to date with political affairs is important.[70] Women and men are equally likely to watch cable news and read a newspaper, but researchers Jennifer Lawless and Richard Fox found that men were two-thirds more likely than women to watch late-night shows such as *The Daily Show*, and that they were significantly more likely than women to access political news and political blogs on the Internet.[71]

At the root of this gender difference may be a political knowledge gap. Researchers remain puzzled as to why women answer fewer questions on political knowledge correctly than men. Using a national sample of adults, researchers at the Annenberg Center asked thirteen questions about the major presidential candidates' backgrounds and their positions on issues to test political knowledge during the 2000 primary campaign. In addition to analyzing the number of correct answers, researchers also paid attention to how often respondents answered incorrectly or stated that they did not know an answer. Men were more likely to answer correctly, whereas women were more likely both to answer incorrectly *and* to state that they did not know an answer. The knowledge deficit for women persisted even when several sociodemographic variables, such as level of education, age, race, income, marital status, party identification, and media exposure, were statistically controlled for. Simply being male added one correct answer out of the thirteen knowledge items in the scale.[72]

Rather than test actual knowledge, Mary Christine Banwart analyzed how informed young men and women *perceive* they are about politics.[73] Since previous studies have found that self-assessment of how much one has learned about a candidate predicts knowledge levels, and knowledge, in turn, predicts participatory behavior, this study hypothesized that a person's perceived level of information or knowledge will also influence his or her perspective on politicians and politics, as well as serve as a political motivator for action. Banwart conducted a national survey of college students one week prior to the November 2004 elections and found that males perceived themselves more informed about the election, but that interest levels between men and women did not differ significantly—both reported a high interest in the upcoming election. However, young women reported higher levels of political cynicism, defined as a "sense of powerlessness" and as the "feeling that government in general and political leaders in particular do not care about the public's opinions and are not acting in the best interest of the people."[74] Though this skepticism did not impact the vote in 2004 (more young women than men voted), Banwart notes that it still raises concerns regarding women's confidence in their role in other areas of politics, such as running for office and more actively seeking leadership roles. Interestingly, when the perceived level of knowledge is held constant between men and women, the difference in political cynicism disappears. Similarly, differences in political cynicism are erased when political interest is held constant between men and women. The study concludes, "Continuing to ask questions about why women and men differ in their perceptions of politics can lead us to a better understanding of the types of messages and information that work to generate an overall more informed, interested, confident, and engaged electorate."[75]

Kathleen Dolan challenged the definition of what constitutes knowledge and found that when the test questions related to gender-relevant domains of knowledge, the differences between men and women largely disappeared.[76] Political science scholarship has demonstrated that different domains of knowledge vary in relevancy for different groups. Canadian women, for example, know more than men about how to access various government benefits and services. Dolan employed a national sample of adults to test the hypothesis that women would be more likely to possess political knowledge relevant to issues of women's representation and would be more aware of women leaders than men. While men are more likely to know which party holds the majority in the House, women are more likely to know the percentage of women in Congress. Women are also less likely than men to underestimate women's representation. On other, more generic measures—identifying the Speaker of the House or naming a woman in Congress—there were no significant differences between men and women in the study. In part, therefore, the gap in political knowledge can be attributed to the ways knowledge is measured.

The consequences of the knowledge gap are varied. Differences in knowledge may result in different criteria for choosing candidates. Men may use pocketbook considerations, while women may rely on character or social policies as determinants.[77] Other studies find that women discuss politics less often with family and friends and are less likely to try to convince others how to vote. The ability to discuss politics and persuade others to act is based, to some degree, on political knowledge. If women do not take part in the flow of private and public political dialogue, their opportunity to exert influence over candidates, issues, and agendas will be reduced.[78]

EXPLAINING THE PATTERNS OF PARTICIPATION

The patterns of political participation present us with a puzzle: Women vote at higher rates than men do, but men exhibit more interest in, attentiveness to, and knowledge of politics than women. Among other forms of political participation, gender does not appear to exert a more significant influence than other factors related to a person's life circumstances. There are a variety of plausible explanations for the lingering gender differences in politics, including the power of socialization, real and perceived structural barriers to participation, and cultural counterpressures.

Socialization

The role of socialization is best characterized by Simone de Beauvoir's claim that "women are made and not born."[79] Socialization is the process by which we, first as children and later as adults, learn and internalize the values, norms, and expectations of the culture and society around us. **Gender socialization** is the process by which girls and boys learn to differentiate between the sexes and act according to the norms and expectations appropriate to their sex. As early as five years old, most children understand gender differentiation. Along with understanding that boys/men differ from girls/women biologically, children internalize the images of power and the sense of importance that separate the genders. Very quickly they describe the sexual hierarchy they see around them as "natural" or "normal."[80] Thus when boys show a stronger preference for "boys' toys" and same-sex playmates, researchers link their preference to the effects of this gender stratification.[81] Further, girls are more likely to wish that they were boys than the reverse. Researcher Ann Beuf asked sixty-three children, ages three to six, what they would do if they grew up as the opposite sex. More girls had thought about the possibility and had answers ready. The boys didn't even want to answer the question. When one boy was pressed, he said, "If I were a girl, I'd have to grow up to be nothing."[82] In similar research conducted by Myra Sadker and David Sadker, 42 percent of girls saw positive outcomes in becoming a boy, whereas 95 percent of the boys saw no advantage in becoming a girl. In fact, for 16 percent of the boys interviewed, becoming a girl was completely unacceptable. In the words of one boy, "I would stab myself in the heart fifty times with a dull butter knife."[83] At a very young age, children have already learned about the gendered world, including which gender is more valued by society. How do they learn the rules of gender hierarchy so quickly?

Gendered norms and expectations are communicated in a variety of ways. According to socialization research, agents of socialization, such as the family, school, peers, religion, and the media, play a role in shaping children's attitudes toward, knowledge of, and behavior in both gender and political roles. Early research on children and political learning found that the family transmitted the earliest messages about authority. In two-parent households, more prevalent in the 1950s and early 1960s, when this research was conducted, the father was labeled the authority figure and was assumed to transmit political information to his children. It was further assumed that if a father was absent, children's political sophistication would suffer. A more recent study, however, confirmed the role of the family in generating and passing on egalitarian political gender role attitudes.[84] Transmission of egalitarian attitudes was particularly strong between mothers and daughters, which the researchers credit, in part, for helping to create and sustain the gender gap in the younger generation.

Experiences in school reinforce the norms of democratic society. By high school, civics classes transmit specific political information to adolescents. Studies of textbooks have consistently found males depicted as the primary figures in political life, while females are rarely mentioned. When Ann Richards, governor of Texas from 1991 until 1995, was asked about the historical significance of her governorship, she replied that beyond any policy change she might facilitate, her picture would appear in textbooks and offer a role model for girls to emulate.[85] Gendered behavior is further encouraged through play with "appropriate" toys. Toy stores are shockingly clear in color-coding "boy" and "girl" aisles (in blue and pink, of course) and choosing displays ("hands-on" versus "look, don't touch"). Social psychologists confirm that children are equally serious about maintaining the separation: "One fourth-grade male reported that if he saw a boy playing with a doll, 'I'd yell at him first, but if he didn't stop, I'd punch him in the nose and call the police.'"[86]

Research done in the 1960s is now criticized for the way in which it interpreted differences between boys and girls on measures of political interest, knowledge, and awareness. Researchers, presumably viewing the data through their own gendered expectations, overestimated the size and significance of differences between primary-school boys and girls.[87] Additionally, the main body of political socialization research suggested that adult political behavior was a direct result of early childhood experiences, overlooking the possibility of change later in life. Only recently have researchers lengthened the time of observation to include adult experiences, such as those in the workplace, as well as the power of social, political, and economic events to reshape attitudes and behaviors.

Since politics in its traditional forms is limited to adults, how might gender socialization translate to political activity? Children learn through imitation, modeling, and apprenticeship opportunities. A White House Project Education Fund study found that the young men and women who are most engaged in politics are also involved and invested in their communities. They come from families in which their parents model civic behavior by voting. These young people are more likely to be registered to vote than those who are least involved in their communities. Those who indicated an interest in someday seeking political office themselves have gained leadership experience through school or other apprentice organizations, have been encouraged to run by adults or peers, are the most likely to believe that they can make a positive difference, and are the least likely to find politics too complicated.[88] The research suggests that providing girls with role models, mentors, and opportunities to practice politics before they reach adulthood makes a positive difference in women's interest and political ambition.

In anticipation of the 2008 election, the White House Project and the Take Our Daughters and Sons to Work Day Foundation launched a national campaign to encourage political participation among girls, entitled "Take Our Daughters to the Polls." The campaign encouraged parents, grandparents, and other adults to pledge to take a young girl to the polls on Election Day and released a viral video emphasizing the political power of girls across the country. "Children model their own dreams on what adults and society show them to be possible. By taking girls to the polls on Election Day, we teach them that they are a valuable part of the political process, and that their voice and their vote can make a difference," said Marie Wilson.[89]

Another initiative to encourage girls' political participation is the Barbie for President doll, first released in April 2000 and rereleased in 2004 and 2008 by Mattel in conjunction with the White House Project and Girls, Inc.[90] The doll was a part of the White House Project's "Go Vote. Go Run. Go Lead. Go Girl" initiative, which ended in 2013. In 2016 Mattel partnered with She Should Run to release an all-female ticket in a variety of skin tones, face shapes, and hair colors. "The President and Vice President dolls continue our efforts to expose girls to inspiring careers that are underrepresented by women," said Lisa McKnight, the general manager and senior vice president of Barbie for Mattel. "We see this doll set as a timely and topical platform to further the conversation around female leadership."[91] To that end, girls are directed to the Barbie website for an accompanying worksheet intended to inspire girls to consider politics and other leadership positions.[92]

Structural Barriers to Women's Participation

Political scientists have long confirmed that certain characteristics make some citizens more likely to participate in politics than others. For example, education, income, and certain occupations are good relative predictors of the frequency and types of citizen participation. Since women lag behind men on several economic indicators and have only recently matched men on years of formal education, lingering barriers to women's full participation remain, reinforcing the gaps found between male and female participation.

One additional factor distinguishes women from one another: gender consciousness, or a feminist identity. A group consciousness that ties an individual woman's interests to those of other women and provides an outlet for her discontent over gender inequities has been found to facilitate women's participation and to set those women apart from others.[93] Feminist consciousness may be shaped by generational forces. Those who come of age during eras of active public feminism—for example, those who turned eighteen during the early 1970s (the start of the second wave of feminism) or during the Clinton administration in the 1990s—are more likely not only to develop a feminist consciousness but also to act on it by supporting collective action advocating feminist policies. Those who come of age in more conservative periods (e.g., the Reagan or George W. Bush administrations) may also support feminist policies but are less likely to develop a feminist consciousness leading to support for and engagement in collective action.[94]

The years preceding the 2016 election, with a woman running for president, were especially ripe for developing a feminist consciousness. British actor Emma Watson, speaking as a UN Global Goodwill Ambassador, delivered a speech about feminism at the United Nations Headquarters in New York. Her remarks accompanied the launch of "HeForShe," a campaign for men and boys worldwide to advocate an end to gender inequality. She spoke about the role men have in helping women and girls achieve equal rights, and said that liberating men from stereotypes ultimately benefits women. Watson said, "I started questioning gender-based assumptions when at eight I was confused at being called 'bossy,' because I wanted to direct the plays we would put on for our parents—but the boys were not. When at 14 I started being sexualized by certain elements of the press. When at 15 my girlfriends started dropping out of their sports teams because they didn't want to appear 'muscly.' . . . I decided I was a feminist and this seemed uncomplicated to me."[95]

Cultural Messages: Counterpressures to Political Activity

Among the many potential barriers to women's participation are the daily messages present in popular culture and directed at shaping women's identity, expectations, ambitions, and habits. As we learned above, women remain less interested in politics and less knowledgeable about politics than men even today, nearly a hundred years since winning the vote. Powerful socialization forces in the nineteenth and early twentieth centuries led women to believe that politics was better left to men.[96]

However, contemporary media images of women in politics may be sending the message that women are "damned if they do and damned if they don't." In October 1992, Deborah Tannen, best known for her work on gender differences in communication styles, wrote an article for the op-ed page of the *New York Times* in which she addressed the "Hillary Factor." The term was originally coined to refer to the question of whether Hillary Rodham Clinton would help or hurt her husband Bill Clinton's chances to win the presidency. Tannen, however, took the term one step further, saying it represented the double bind that affects accomplished women who do not fit the stereotype of femininity and the expectations of motherhood. When, for example, the Clintons acted to protect their daughter's privacy by shielding her from the press, they were surprised to learn that a majority of Americans thought they were childless and held Hillary Clinton responsible for that misconception.

The "motherhood bind" has an impact on all women. As Tannen describes it, "If you're not a Mother, you're a Failed Woman. If you are a Mother, you can't have enough attention to pay to serious work. If you are paying attention to serious work, you must be a Bad Mother."[97] She goes on: "By what logic could it be scary rather than comforting for a president's wife, who everyone knows will have his ear, to be unusually intelligent, knowledgeable and accomplished? And to answer: by no logic at all. The hope was to incite emotions—fear and anger—that confront women who do not conform to the old molds." In the 2008 election, Alaska governor Sarah Palin faced many of the same questions about her suitability for the vice presidency based on her status as a mother of five relatively young children (see "Encountering the Controversies of Equality" on page 104).

Women face a variety of cultural expectations that may vary depending on their physical appearance, race, or ethnicity. In each case, men do not have the same expectations placed on them, and in each case there are significant political implications for women as a result. Ambrose Bierce once wrote, "To men a man is but a mind. Who cares what face he carries or what he wears? But woman's body is the woman."[98] Although Bierce was writing in 1911, consumer-spending statistics suggest his words still ring true. In 2014, Americans spent well over $12.9 billion on elective cosmetic surgery, and women accounted for 92 percent of all cosmetic procedures. The standards of beauty differ across cultures and vary over time, but women are universally expected to aspire to the current standards of beauty in ways that men are not. Men are referred to with the term *handsome*, connoting achievement and strength. Such terms do not accompany *beautiful*, which is applied only to females, scenes, or objects. This common terminology leads one set of researchers to conclude, "Men are instrumental; women are ornamental."[99]

These observations and statistics would be trivial if not for their consequences for how individuals are judged. In the classic "What Is Beautiful Is Good" study, psychologists asked college students to rate photographs of strangers on a variety of personal qualities. Those who were judged attractive were also more likely to be characterized as intelligent, flexible, interesting, confident, assertive, strong, outgoing, friendly, poised, and successful than those considered unattractive. Women were judged more harshly than men.[100] The same attributions are made when considering candidates seeking public office, with important implications for women candidates and voters.

Judging Competence by Appearance: Implications for Women

In a 2005 *Science* article, researchers noted that they were able to postdict the outcomes of more than 65 percent of the US Senate and House races in 2002 and 2004 by using inferences of competence based solely on candidate facial appearance.[101] Faces are a major source of information about other people. From a psychological perspective, researchers have found that rapid automatic inference from the facial appearance of political candidates can influence the way people process subsequent information about the candidates. When naive study participants were presented with pairs of black-and-white head-shot photographs of the winners and the runners-up from actual US Senate and House races, the candidate who was perceived as more competent won in 71.6 percent of the Senate races and 66.8 percent of the House races (if the subject recognized any of the faces, the pair was removed from analysis). To ensure that subjects were identifying competence rather than likability or some other trait, the researchers conducted a secondary analysis that asked subjects to evaluate candidates across seven traits. They found that the judgments rendered on the basis of a one-second exposure to the pairs of candidate photographs clustered into three distinct factors: competence (competence, intelligence, leadership), trust (honesty, trustworthiness), and likability (charisma, likability). Significantly, only the competence judgments predicted the outcomes of elections.

Box 3.2 – Encountering the Controversies of Equality

Female, Activist, Conservative, Republican . . . and Feminist?

When Phyllis Schlafly launched her campaign to stop ratification of the Equal Rights Amendment (ERA), she presented feminists with an enigma. Schlafly was a Phi Beta Kappa graduate of Washington University with a master's degree in government from Radcliffe College; she was married with six children; she was active in Republican Party politics and had been a candidate for Congress in 1952, when few women ran for office; and she was staunchly anti-feminist. Schlafly argued that ratification of the ERA would "threaten traditional gender roles in families and make women sexually and economically vulnerable,"[1] even though Schlafly herself seemed to be living life as a "liberated woman"— a goal of the women's movement for all women. Second wave feminists were convinced that women's equality would be achieved if government regulated discrimination in the workplace, provided funding for social welfare programs, and played a role in establishing universal child care. But this enlarged role for the government was anathema to the conservative ideology that promoted small government, a free market economy, and traditional family values.

Fast-forward to 2008, when Republican presidential nominee John McCain selected Alaska governor Sarah Palin to be his running mate. Palin introduced herself to Republican Party convention delegates as a "hockey mom" and appeared frequently on the national campaign trail with her husband and five children. Republican Michele Bachmann, a congresswoman from Minnesota and mother to five children, was the only woman candidate for president running in the 2012 primaries. Palin and Bachmann were at the leading edge of the Tea Party movement, a political resurgence of conservative activists expressing anger over the size and overreach of government (e.g., the Affordable Care Act), threats to national sovereignty (e.g., immigration), and a flailing economy (e.g., unemployment, national debt). Women are heavily represented at the national, state, and local grassroots levels as Tea Party leaders.

In *Tea Party Women*, Melissa Deckman argues that the Tea Party, like the anti-ERA movement decades before, provides conservative college-educated women who have workplace experience with the opportunity structure to become politically engaged. In this sense, conservative issues can become feminist issues using gendered motherhood and pro-family frames. As "kitchen table" conservatives, Tea Party women advocate for a balanced budget to protect their children's future. Gun rights become about protecting families. Government policies advancing equal pay and family leave and prohibiting discrimination on the basis of sex betray the idea that women are as capable as men. "It surprises some people to hear that I consider myself a feminist," says Sarah Palin. Palin traces her feminism to Enlightenment principles of individual justice and denounces "modern feminism" as antiwoman, portraying women as victims who need to rely on government to promote fairness in society.[2]

The Tea Party movement brings together elements of laissez-faire fiscal conservatism advocated by the Independent Women's Forum (IWF) and the social and religious conservatism advanced by Concerned Women for America (CWA) but remains noticeably distinct. Ronnie Schreiber has studied both long-standing organizations extensively and maintains that they represent distinct and rarely overlapping interests. Both groups, Schreiber argues, have extended the descriptive representation of women by providing "legitimacy to issue positions that would be dismissed if conservative men were the ones making the political claims."[3] Melissa Deckman summarizes the influence of Tea Party women: "By employing motherhood and other gendered rhetoric to pursue conservative economic policies and, to a certain extent, pro-gun legislation as well, Tea Party women put a conservative, gendered spin on a variety of public policies and challenge current public discourse about what constitutes women's interests, extending the concept of descriptive representation and perhaps even redefining elements of feminism in the process."[4]

The Tea Party movement, capitalizing and building upon the "Sarah Palin effect," has energized thousands of conservative female political activists, but do they have a mainstream political outlet in the Republican Party? The 2010 midterm election is sometimes referred to as the "Tea Party wave," since it swept control of the House from Democrats and ended Nancy Pelosi's run as the first female Speaker of the House. But, with a few notable exceptions, Republican women have not made substantial electoral gains in Congress or in state legislatures. Of the 104 women in the 115th Congress (2017–2019), only 26 are Republicans (21 in the House, 5 in the Senate).[5] Is the influence of the Tea Party here to stay? Donald Trump is not associated with the Tea Party movement, and yet he became the 2016 Republican Party standard-bearer. His candidacy presented Republicans with new challenges in attracting the support of women—both moderates and conservatives.

What do you think?

"The personal is political" was a rallying cry for second wave feminists who urged political action on previously private issues such as domestic violence, child care, and workplace equality. In what ways does this mantra also apply to today's conservative political activists' agenda, particularly the Tea Party movement? Can a conservative woman be a feminist? Why or why not? In what ways is gender equality enriched or threatened by conservative political activism?

Further exploring the gender implications arising from this study, researchers at Oklahoma State University reasoned that since candidate facial appearance affects voters' preferences and sex affects facial appearance, perhaps facial appearance and voter inferences have an impact on the electability of women.[102] Previous research has linked the "baby-face/maturity" facial dimension to perceptions of competence.[103] Researchers found that male faces are judged more mature, that candidates with "mature" faces are perceived as more competent, and that the perception of candidate competency affects vote choice. Additionally, sex conditions the perceptions—male subjects were more likely to rate mature-faced and male candidates as competent than were female subjects.

Overall, candidates perceived as competent had a higher probability of winning both simulated and real elections. However, even female candidates judged as mature-faced were not perceived as more competent than baby-faced men. Researchers attribute this finding to what we know about gender stereotypes—we prefer women, whether they are candidates or not, to appear feminine, but in the national electoral context, masculine traits are preferred. Therefore, a female candidate presenting a mature face may send voters conflicting cues that they cannot process—effectively creating yet another double bind for women candidates and officeholders.

Donald Trump, presumably unknowingly, called attention to this phenomenon during the Republican primary leading up to the 2016 presidential election. In a September 2015 interview with *Rolling Stone*, Donald Trump remarked on the appearance of Carly Fiorina, former CEO of Hewlett-Packard and the only woman among seventeen contestants for the Republican nomination. "Look at that face!" Trump said. "Would anyone *vote* for that? Can you imagine that, the face of our next *president*?" Trump later claimed that he was referring to Fiorina's persona rather than criticizing her appearance. Fiorina, responding to Trump's comments at a debate, noted coolly, "I think women all over this country heard very clearly what Mr. Trump said."[104]

The media facilitate the public's attention to appearance by focusing on female candidates' hairstyles and the color or design of their clothes, rather than on the content of their messages. George W. Bush campaign operative Mary Matalin described it this way: "Women in politics who look chic are perceived as frivolous. If you're pulled together that means you've been shopping . . . instead of laboring over papers. . . . Besides, every woman who looks good gets hit on, and after a while they just don't want to be hassled."[105] Josie Heath, a Democratic senatorial candidate in the 1990s from Colorado, claimed that she could describe her wardrobe during that period by reading her press clippings.[106] Following the 2000 presidential election, Katherine Harris, Florida's secretary of state, who was responsible for several significant decisions affecting the state's presidential ballot count, became the object of public ridicule based on her appearance. The *Washington Post* noted that Harris's lipstick was of "the creamy sort that smears all over a coffee cup and leaves smudges on shirt collars" and that she "applied her makeup with a trowel," and compared the texture of her skin to that of a plastered wall.[107]

As a candidate for the 2008 Democratic nomination for president, Hillary Clinton was ridiculed in the press for her "thick ankles" (noted by biographer Carl Bernstein), her laugh ("somewhere between a cackle and a screech," according to campaign consultant Dick Morris), her preference for suits with pants instead of a skirt, and her cleavage (the *Washington Post* noted an outfit in which the "neckline sat low on her chest").[108] This was not new to Clinton—in 1996 a website dedicated to her changing hairstyles received more than forty thousand hits a day. Clinton later turned criticism of her penchant for pantsuits into an advantage with a quip to David Letterman: "In my White House, we'll know who wears the pantsuits!" In 2013, a Reddit user posted an image of a "rainbow of pantsuited Hillary Clintons" that went viral.[109] And in 2016, a "Pantsuit Palette" T-shirt was available for sale on Clinton's campaign website.[110]

First Lady Michelle Obama presented the media and the American public with an interesting set of gender and cultural puzzles. Prior to Hillary Clinton, there had never been a First Lady with a postgraduate degree. Michelle Obama graduated from Princeton and earned her law degree at Harvard. She possesses a resume of professional accomplishments that include practicing law at the Chicago firm Sidley Austin (where she mentored a summer associate named Barack Obama), working with the city of Chicago to launch the youth mentorship program Public Allies, and a community relations position with the University of Chicago. Becoming First Lady effectively ended Michelle Obama's professional career, raising lots of questions among feminist columnists about what that meant for her personally and what it meant for women more generally. Katha Pollitt chronicled the media transformation of Michelle Obama from "fist-bumping radical to Mom-in-Chief," references to the two predominant frames used in coverage of her.[111] Michelle Obama's "bluntly spoken rejection of a simpleminded, Panglossian vision of America riled conservatives, from high-profile pundits to anonymous bloggers. *The National Review* featured a scowling picture of her on its April [2008] cover and characterized her as Mrs. Grievance and a 'peculiar mix of privilege and victimology.' A *Fox News* commentator famously characterized the Obamas' joyful fist tap the night Barack clinched the nomination as a 'terrorist fist jab,' while a satirical *New Yorker* cover depicted her with an Angela Davis 'fro and an AK-47," writes Geraldine Brooks.[112] Rebecca Traister decried the "momification" of Michelle Obama:

> This situation is not entirely unique. The battle to conform to wifely expectations was previously fought by Hillary Clinton, a woman who recently made a hell-bent run for exactly the same job her husband held in the years that she was forced to choke on her health plan and write books about the White House cat. . . . But Michelle [Obama] is in an

even tighter bind, in part because of the legacy left her by Hillary and her detractors. Powerful couples must now tread as far as possible from the 'two for one' talk, lest the female half get smacked with a nutcracker. But Michelle's power is potentially scarier than Hillary's could ever have been. She is not simply a smart and powerful woman, but a smart and powerful black woman.[113]

Yet nothing sparked more blogosphere commentary than David Samuels's March 15, 2009, essay in *New York Magazine*:

There are clear limits to Michelle's ambition. She went to excellent schools, got decent grades, and stayed away from too much intellectual heavy lifting, and held a series of practical, modestly salaried jobs while accommodating her husband's wilder dreams and raising two lovely daughters. In this she is a more practical role model for young women than Hillary Clinton, blending her calculations about family and career with an expectation of normal personal happiness.

"That Samuels, like a 1950s home ec teacher, advises 'young women' to keep their ambitions 'practical' if they want to be happy shows just how disturbing Hillary Clinton—or rather the nightmare fantasy of Hillary Clinton—has been to certain male psyches," writes Katha Pollitt.[114]

In much the same way as attractiveness, race and ethnicity modify expectations as well. Scholar Patricia Hill Collins writes that "portraying African American women as stereotypical mammies, matriarchs, welfare recipients, and hot mommas has been essential to the political economy of domination fostering Black women's oppression. Challenging these controlling images has long been a core theme in Black feminist thought."[115] Leaders in the women's movement were relatively silent during the congressional debate over welfare reform even when the tone and content became a thinly veiled racist attack on poor single mothers. African American women lag behind white women in winning legislative seats at both the state and federal levels.[116] Part of the reason is the lingering belief that black women are not serious and credible candidates.[117] To overcome this hurdle, more women of color need to seek and hold public office, but the obstacles are substantial. In political scientist Nadia Brown's research on the politics of appearance for black women state legislators, she collected feminist life histories from black women in the Maryland state legislature.[118] They told Brown that "their skin tone and decisions about how to wear their hair influenced how their colleagues and/or constituents viewed them." Most important, Brown's research explores the differences in appearances among black legislators in recognition of important intragroup differences. Since physical attractiveness of candidates is a heuristic cue for voters, this is important work in understanding how African American female candidates are perceived by others. Brown concluded that black women's legislative experiences are connected to what they look like. These experiences are linked to self-confidence, internal fortitude, and character building, which the women surveyed connected to their ability to overcome adversity.

Asian American women, Latina women, and Native American women have also been slow to ascend to public life. Besides having to overcome the previously described barriers, women in these groups (especially Asian and Latina women) face cultural expectations that limit their role to the home and family. Native American women, although historically active in tribal politics and fully integrated in many tribal systems of governance, have only recently explored public life beyond their communities of origin. Without role models to give voice to their concerns, women of color are also less likely to be involved in electoral politics as voters.

MOBILIZING WOMEN'S POLITICAL PARTICIPATION

Men and women approach politics similarly and from different perspectives depending on the activity and on life circumstances. While women vote at higher rates than men do, women remain less likely to donate money to a candidate, participate in political organizations, or seek elective office themselves. This chapter concludes by examining four factors that may increase women's political participation: events and issues, high-profile female candidates, organizations that target women, and the role of political parties.

Political Events, Issues, and Groups
That Stimulate Interest and Raise Gender Consciousness

Although many factors combined to make 1992 an especially good year for women in politics, one distinctly mobilizing event stood out: the Clarence Thomas Supreme Court confirmation hearings and Anita Hill's allegations of sexual harassment. Although this event is now a quarter century behind us, it remains a political and cultural touchstone. Sexual assault on college campuses and in the military along with the "war on women" are current examples of issues that stimulate women's engagement with politics, but no single event has galvanized women in the way that the Hill-Thomas hearings did in 1991.

On July 1, 1991, President Bush nominated Clarence Thomas to fill a vacancy on the US Supreme Court. On October 6, 1991, the Senate Judiciary Committee forwarded Thomas's nomination to the full Senate for a vote. That same day, however, Nina Totenberg of National Public Radio alleged that the committee had suppressed allegations of sexual harassment against Thomas brought by a University of Oklahoma law professor, Anita Hill. Hill had worked for Thomas at the Equal Employment Opportunity Commission (EEOC), the federal agency that enforces antidiscrimination policy. On October 8, Democratic congresswomen marched from the House to the Senate to demand an investigation. The Senate relented, and new hearings were called with Anita Hill as the primary witness. Her testimony before the Senate Judiciary Committee was televised, giving many voters, particularly female voters, a glimpse at the all-male, all-white committee. Interest in the hearings was intense: Senator Paul Simon reported receiving nearly 20,000 letters on the subject, compared to the fewer than 16,000 on the Gulf War. Millions watched the televised hearings; they had a larger audience than NFL games that were on at the same time.[119] Women were outraged at what many perceived as the unfair and condescending treatment of Hill. T-shirts proclaiming "I Believe Anita Hill," "He Did It," and "She Lied" sprang up across the country. An episode of the prime-time sitcom *Designing Women* was dedicated to the controversy. After the show's airing, CBS received more than 1,500 phone calls, mostly positive—the largest number in the network's history in response to a single show.[120]

The issue of sexual harassment separated men from women. Women, regardless of race or class, shared experiences similar in nature, if not in severity, to those described by Anita Hill. It appeared clear to even those most uneducated in fair-trial norms that the deck was stacked against Hill. Senator Arlen Specter stated that Hill's testimony "was flat-out perjury."[121] Male senators speculated openly on national television about various psychological disorders Hill might be suffering. The phrase "Men just don't get it" was born.

One of the first political victims of the Hill-Thomas hearings was Senator Alan Dixon, who lost his seat in the Illinois primary to political newcomer Carol Mosely Braun. Braun, one of several women moved by the Hill-Thomas debacle to seek public office, ultimately went on to win a seat on the Judiciary Committee. An unusually large number of seats opened up in Congress as a result of retirements and reapportionment, which further encouraged women to announce their candidacies. In all, twenty-two women sought Senate seats in 1992, compared to just eight in the previous election. A record four new women entered the Senate, raising the total to six in 1992, including Braun, who was the first African American woman to be elected to the Senate.[122] In the House of Representatives, forty-eight women were elected, nearly doubling the number of female members.

Facilitating this increase were a number of grassroots women's organizations whose membership also rose after the Hill-Thomas event. Membership in EMILY's List, an organization supporting pro-choice, Democratic female candidates, went from 3,000 to 23,000 in just one year. EMILY's List contributed more than $6 million to candidates in the 1992 elections, a fourfold increase over the elections of 1990.[123] The National Organization for Women (NOW) reported that anger over the Senate's handling of Hill's charges "has translated into 13,000 new members in the final months of 1991," and Feminist Majority reported receiving an unsolicited contribution of $10,000 after the hearings and a 30 percent rise in contributions overall.[124]

Recent films have reintroduced the public to Anita Hill and the Senate hearings, including the 2014 documentary *Anita*, directed by Oscar-winning Freida Mock, and the 2016 HBO TV movie *Confirmation*, starring Kerry Washington as Anita Hill and Wendell Pierce as Clarence Thomas. "Producers of the show felt the themes of gender and race would attract HBO viewers at a time when those themes continue to resonate nationally," observed the *New York Times* television critic. It is easy to think that the Anita Hill hearings and subsequent legislation and political action to regulate sexual harassment in the workplace would make other high-profile allegations unlikely, but in July 2016, Roger Ailes was forced to resign as chairman and chief executive of Fox News following allegations of sexual harassment spanning five decades. A former on-air host at Fox News, Gretchen Carlson, filed the first lawsuit, but she was quickly joined by more than twenty-five other women raising similar concerns.[125] The roles of Ailes and Fox News in the rise of the conservative wing of the Republican Party made sexual harassment a topic of conversation in the 2016 elections, but not to the same extent that it defined the elections in 1992.

In addition to issues in the news and events that take on political significance, groups play a role in amplifying women's political voices. New technologies enable groups to mine data to improve their effectiveness. All In Together (AIT) created the All In Together Action Center to enable individuals to quickly take action on political issues of interest by writing, calling, or tweeting their state and federal legislators, or signing petitions—all from a single website.[126] Platforms such as Change.org allow individuals to find and activate allies using social media. Change.org was started in 2007 by Ben Rattray to build social networking and fund-raising for nonprofits, and in 2010 the site added a petition tool. One of the first petitions was created by a woman from a township in South Africa. As a victim of "corrective rape" (intended to "cure" lesbians of their sexual orientation), she wanted the South African government to acknowledge "corrective rape" as a crime and take action to stop the abuses. Her petition attracted 170,000 signatures, and the South African parliament formed a national task force. For Rattray, this victory demonstrated the power of social media and social networks to connect like-minded citizens across geographic and cultural boundaries and direct their energy toward a specific, achievable demand for change.

Do Female Candidates Bring Women to the Voting Booth?

Can elections that feature women candidates be a mobilizing force for women in politics? As more female candidates appear on ballots for local, state, and national elections, will it stimulate higher rates of participation from women across the multiple dimensions of political engagement? The presence of women candidates can signal a greater openness in the system and more political opportunities for all. Women on the ballot send the message that politics is no longer an exclusively

Box 3.3 – Point of Comparison

"'Hey Baby!' Is Not My Name": Global Activism Against Street Harassment

A 2014 national survey found that 65 percent of women in the United States had experienced some form of street harassment, including verbal harassment or "catcalling" (57 percent), touching (23 percent), following (20 percent), or flashing (14 percent). Street harassment is defined as unwanted comments, gestures, and actions forced on a stranger in a public place without consent, and which are directed at a person because of their actual or perceived sex, gender, gender expression, or sexual orientation. Historians have found evidence of unwanted public attention in women's journals dating back to the 1800s. Men experience street harassment too—25 percent reported having this experience. In particular, LGBT men are more likely to be the subject of street harassment.

The Cornell International Survey on Street Harassment surveyed people from forty-two cities around the world and found that on average, 81.5 percent of women have been harassed before the age of seventeen. Ninety percent of British respondents said they were victims of street harassment between the ages of eleven and seventeen. Forty-seven percent of Indian women report that someone has exposed themselves to them. Researchers working within objectification theory, the idea that the way women are looked at and dehumanized affects their mental health and sense of self, have found that women often constrain or change their behavior because of past experiences with sexism.[1] In Germany, 80 percent of women reported having taken a different route to their destination at least once because of harassment.

Women around the world are harnessing the organizing power of social media and new technologies to stop street harassment and empower bystanders as allies. HarassMap.org in Egypt utilizes cell phone reporting and a mapping tool so that individuals can submit anonymous reports of harassment experienced or witnessed. Anyone who submits a report receives a reply providing information on how to access free legal services and psychological counseling. The organization uses the data to identify trends and to develop communication and intervention campaigns. Volunteers receive training through HarassMap Academy and then go into their own neighborhoods to convince people to stand up to sexual harassment. HarassMap is "working to encourage the entire community to stop allowing sexual harassment to happen with impunity and to change the atmosphere in their own neighborhoods to a safe and positive environment."[2]

Stop Street Harassment is an international organization with global affiliates.[3] Its Paris affiliate, Stop Harcèlement de Rue, recently teamed up with the rapid transit authority for a campaign to end harassment on public transportation in

Source: Courtesy of HarassMap; photo by Mostafa Abdel Aty.

Paris. The French government's High Council for Equality Between Men and Women released a report revealing that a staggering 100 percent of women surveyed in the Paris region said they had experienced harassment on public transit. A similar organization, Hollaback!, has affiliates in thirty-one countries and hundreds of cities and equips women to fight back against harassment in public space by documenting, mapping, and sharing information.[4]

Street protests like those sponsored during Meet Us on the Street's International Anti-Harassment Week offer an opportunity to raise collective awareness of the problem. Yet, in some areas of the world, activism can be as dangerous as the streets for women. An Afghan woman was almost lynched when she took to the streets of Kabul in metal armor covering her breasts and buttocks to protest against the sexual harassment faced by females. The eight-minute-long protest was poorly received by onlookers, who threw rocks and jeered.[5] Safe Cities global initiative and the UN Committee on the Status of Women have incorporated street harassment and sexual violence into their work and their public statements. NGOs, governments, and now global activists powered by technology are taking on street harassment in powerful new ways.

For Critical Analysis

In what ways have you and your friends experience street harassment? How do you react? In your judgment, how effective will the new reporting, mapping, and intervention technologies be to empowering women to combat street harassment? How else might women participate to open public spaces and ensure all women's safety?

male domain and that female participation is important and valued. In addition, women candidates are more likely to include issues of interest to women in their campaigns, thereby attracting their attention.[127] A study of gender and political participation in the United Kingdom found that women are significantly more likely to turn out and vote if they are represented by a woman, and are more likely to become involved in an electoral campaign on behalf of a female candidate. The study also found that women are more likely to agree with the statement that "government benefits me" if they are represented by a woman (49 percent, compared to 8 percent in constituencies with a male representative).[128]

Finding that much of the previous research investigated the impact of women on the ballot in 1992 (which came to be known in the media as the "Year of the Woman"), Kathleen Dolan examined national election data from 1990 to 2004 to examine whether the attitudes and behaviors of people living in states and districts with a woman candidate for the US Senate or House differ from those voting in elections where there are no women candidates. Her analysis covered different levels of office, differing conditions of competitiveness, different political party conditions, and a longer time frame of elections than previous research, and yet "the results show, overall, that there is little empirical analysis to support the assumption that symbolic representation is provided by women candidates or at least there is little support for the idea that their symbolic presence translates into any widespread increase in political attitudes and behaviors. . . . [W]e are left to conclude that the influence of women candidates is, at some level, a function of idiosyncratic circumstances of particular elections—such things as the mix of candidates, their positions, the issues of the day, media coverage, and public awareness."[129]

A study by Jennifer Wolak tried to control for all of the contextual and idiosyncratic aspects of individual races by conducting an experiment to investigate whether there is a direct psychological effect of candidate gender on voters' interest in political engagement.[130] Contrary to what we might have expected, Wolak found that "women's interest and engagement with the campaign is insensitive to the gender of the candidates, while men are less interested in participating in the election when the congressional candidate is female." This experimental finding confirms the findings in observational and survey methodologies of Dolan and others in suggesting that the mere presence of women in a campaign is not sufficiently powerful to attract women voters' interest or increase their sense of efficacy or psychological engagement. Wolak concludes, "If candidate gender energizes female voters, it likely is connected to the choices women candidates make in waging campaigns, any distinctive media coverage women receive because of their gender, variations in how parties and groups choose to mobilize voters when a woman candidate is on the ballot, any differences in the issue agendas of men and women candidates, or other campaign factors that are correlated with the gender of the candidate."

It may be the case that the power of female candidates is much like the power of more women in public office: the symbolic benefits are derived not from the one-on-one relationship of constituent to officeholder or voter to candidate, but from something more generalized.[131] In 2008, having Clinton as a viable candidate for the Democratic nomination for president and Palin's spot on the Republican ticket in the general election increased the media's focus on the lack of women in politics, shedding light on the fact that the United States lags behind other nations in electing a woman as head of state and in the representation of women at the legislative level. The gap between representative ideals and the gendered reality may have drawn women's attention to politics in a new way in that race.

Do women have an obligation to support women candidates? In her 2008 bid for the Democratic nomination for president, Clinton focused very little on her gender, believing instead that, as the potential first woman commander in chief, she had to run a strategic campaign fully cognizant of the double bind all female candidates face. She needed to appear agentic, competent, and capable of decision-making to be seen as viable for the highest office, but at the same time conform to gender expectations enough to be viewed as warm and likable.[132] (Barack Obama characterized Clinton as "likable enough" in a primary debate just prior to the New Hampshire contest.) The dominant theme of Clinton's 2008 campaign was "Tested and ready to lead in a dangerous world."

By contrast, in 2016 Clinton's message was that she was prepared to serve as a champion for all Americans and particularly for women. "Everyday Americans need a champion. And I want to be that champion," Clinton said in a video announcing her candidacy. "So I'm hitting the road to earn your vote—because it's your time. And I hope you'll join me on this journey." Throughout the primaries and in the general election campaign, Clinton emphasized pay equity, paid family and medical leave, a higher minimum wage, and access to affordable child care. It seemed that voters in 2016 were ready, if not eager, to hear about these issues from a woman candidate. "As far as the political culture and culture in general, this is as good a time as any for a woman to run for the highest office. There is a willingness now to promote pro-woman messages," said Jennifer Lawless, of the Women & Politics Institute at American University, in April 2015. "People are ready for a woman president. The question is this: Are they ready for Hillary as that woman?"[133]

In the 2016 presidential primaries, Hillary Clinton began the race with an air of inevitability surrounding her campaign, only to be challenged for the nomination by Vermont senator Bernie Sanders, a seventy-four-year-old white man. Leading up to the New Hampshire primary, Madeleine Albright, the first female secretary of state, generated controversy when she appeared to scold young women for not supporting Clinton. "We can all tell our story of how we climbed the ladder, and a lot of you younger women think it's all done. It's not done. There's a special place in hell for women who don't help each other!" Albright said. Feminist Gloria Steinem piled

IMAGE 3.3: *Political cartoonist Nick Anderson captures the hypocrisy of the Steinem and Albright comments.* Source: Nick Anderson Editorial Cartoon used with the permission of Nick Anderson, the Washington Post Writers Group and the Cartoonist Group. All rights reserved.

on in an interview later in the same week with talk show host Bill Maher, suggesting that young women were supporting Bernie Sanders because boys were: "When you're young, you're thinking: 'Where are the boys?' The boys are with Bernie." Both women attracted scorn for their comments: "Shame on Gloria Steinem and Madeleine Albright for implying that we as women should be voting for a candidate based solely on her gender," wrote one twenty-three-year-old woman.[134]

Sanders won the New Hampshire primary with 54 percent of the women's vote, compared with 46 percent for Clinton, and he went on to win the votes of 82 percent of women under thirty years of age. This surprising outcome sparked a series of press articles about the "generational divide" and the election's newest gender voter controversy—the battle between mothers and daughters.[135] According to data collected by CIRCLE, female voters ages seventeen to twenty-nine favored Bernie Sanders by a fairly large margin, with only 41 percent expressing support for Hillary Clinton. Support for Clinton increased with age: 68 percent of women ages thirty to fifty supported Secretary Clinton, as did 75 percent of women over the age of sixty.[136] Nineteen-year-old first-time voter Bridget Silha of Students for Sanders noted:

> A gap exists between women voters simply because of the times that we grew up in. Talking with older women, it is more common to notice their unequal status when they're talking with a man. With younger

women, you just walk into a room and speak your mind no matter who is a man or who is a woman. So, I believe that older women revere Clinton primarily because they see a woman in power and believe that they can combat this unequal status. Whereas younger women don't see the gender war as clearly.[137]

Molly Roberts, a senior at Harvard and a columnist for the *Harvard Crimson*, says that among certain segments of the liberal millennial population, Clinton's gender is not enough to make her a groundbreaker. "She might be a woman, but she is also white, and well-off, and straight. If she were black, or gay, or poor—as well as female, some young liberals might be more inclined to vote for her," she wrote.[138] In other words, Clinton doesn't fit into enough categories to be "exciting." Of course, the dynamics of the general election presented a much different point of contrast between Hillary Clinton and Donald Trump. Women overwhelmingly supported Clinton in pre-election polls (by a gap of 24 points in June 2016), but it would be hard to argue that Clinton's gender was the attraction. Trump's misogynistic comments and behavior led everyone to believe that the 2016 gender gap would be a chasm; it was not. Clinton attracted votes from constituencies traditionally aligned with the Democratic Party, but the promise of electing the first woman president was not enough motivation for Republican women to join them in voting for Clinton.

As evident from a variety of studies discussed in this book, voters clearly feel that female officeholders can offer something different from males. But they are hesitant to act on that belief at the polls, and women candidates are caught within the paradox. Voters say that they believe women in office might result in substantively different policies, which suggests that candidates might effectively appeal to this belief during the campaign. However, women voters also say that gender does not make any difference in their decision at the polls, so female candidates might be encouraged to campaign on the basis of no difference from male candidates. In focus groups for Sherrye Henry's *The Deep Divide*, about seven out of ten women (69 percent) said that the country would be different if more women held powerful positions. Forty-four percent believed this because they thought women in power would improve the quality of life, 14 percent believed women would formulate better economic policy, and 31 percent thought women would do a better job with social policy. Seventy-four percent of the women, including 67 percent of those who did not identify themselves as feminists, said that they thought having more women in powerful positions would lead to greater equality. However, when asked if they planned to vote for a woman "because another woman understands the problems women face, or does sex not make a difference," 74 percent said that sex did not make any difference. While the majority of these women believed that women in power would make some positive difference, they were unwilling to give women the advantage at the polls.[139] These findings reflect the power of the paradox of gender equality.

Women's Organizations

Groups such as the National Organization for Women (NOW) and the **National Women's Political Caucus (NWPC)**, as well as conservative organizations such as the Independent Women's Forum and Second Amendment Sisters, enjoy membership surges when highly publicized events remind women that the controversies of equality are not yet settled. "Women's organization" should not be construed to mean "feminist organization," although many explicitly political organizations dedicated to women share some feminist aims. NOW, for example, is an organization in the liberal feminist tradition. It was founded in 1966 in response to concern that the discrimination provisions of the 1964 Civil Rights Act and Title VII were not being properly enforced. NOW focuses on eliminating sexism in American society through legislation and court action. The NWPC, founded in 1971, is a bipartisan organization with the explicit goal of bringing more women, Republicans and Democrats alike, into office. Both organizations' activities are most consistent with the goals of the legal equality doctrine. NOW turned fifty in 2016 and has undertaken a number of initiatives to reflect on the past and adopt strategies for intersectional organizing at the national and local levels.

There is tremendous variety in organizations for women, and groups have been organized around every point along the ideological spectrum. Organizational involvement is intimately tied to participation in larger political arenas.[140] A member's contact with the organization extends her social network to include political activists and introduces political newcomers to the efficacy of political action in solving public problems. Further, in local chapters, members gain valuable political and leadership skills that allow them to access politics at all levels. In this way, associations may act as a feeder network to political party activity. Organizations may also facilitate citizen contact with public officials by encouraging letter-writing campaigns, visits to elected officials, or participation in organized demonstrations.[141] Women's organizations can mobilize women to vote and to participate in politics by drawing attention to important issues at stake in an election or to a contest between two evenly matched candidates.

Apart from mobilizing participation, women's organizations provide a wide range of services to members and nonmembers alike. The Internet provides women's groups even greater visibility and allows women around the world to access political information and resources twenty-four hours a day. Candidates and women who are thinking of seeking office can go online to access training seminars, consultants, and networks of volunteers. A majority of women serving in state legislatures today list a women's organization as an important source of support. Women's organizations have at times joined forces to propose policy agendas and to lobby for congressional action on women's issues. The National Council of Women's Organizations (NCWO) is a bipartisan network of leaders from more than 200 organizations representing more than 11 million women in the United States. Member organizations collaborate through substantive policy work and grassroots activism to address issues of concern to women across all age groups, including family and work, economic equity, education, affirmative action, corporate accountability, women and technology, reproductive freedom, women's health, and global progress for women's equality. The council proposes a National Women's Agenda every two years, corresponding to a new session of Congress.

Some active feminist organizations, such as MomsRising.org, operate largely online through a social media network, to advocate for progressive policies that benefit families. Paid sick leave, flexible work schedules, universal preschool, and enhanced maternity leave are at the top of their agenda. Other organizations, such as the **American Association of University Women (AAUW)**, provide research, data, and information to members. AAUW's reports on the wage gap and discrimination in the workplace have been key to advancing gender equity in education and the workplace. AAUW also runs campus-based leadership programs (such as "Elect Her") to encourage women to run for student government positions, particularly as president. Their "$tart$mart" workshops are designed to help women ready to graduate from college negotiate an appropriate starting salary, explicitly acknowledging that the wage gap starts with the first paycheck. The Feminist Majority Foundation, Planned Parenthood, the National Abortion Rights Action League, the National Coalition Against Violence, and CODEPINK are all examples of organizations that welcome members of both genders in their efforts to educate and mobilize for gender equality.

The Role of Political Parties

Although political parties made early overtures to female voters in anticipation of the immediate postsuffrage elections, they largely abandoned the "women's vote" when no such voting bloc materialized. Many women continued their activities with political parties, but, as political scientist Jo Freeman said, they entered mainstream parties "one room at a time":

> Party women had their own style of action. Whereas feminists had assaulted the citadel, and reformers had banged on the door, party women had infiltrated the basement of politics. But while their actions were incremental and only occasionally attracted notice, their numbers expanded and they helped bring about significant changes to the parties. They also built a base of well-informed women with years of party service who were quick to take advantage of the opportunities created by the new feminist movement that arose in the late 1960s.[142]

Both national political parties, as well as many state party organizations, created special women's auxiliaries designed to educate and mobilize female voters. Women's divisions proved both a facilitator and a ghetto for women interested in ascending to political power. At the same time that parties recruited women to organize other women, they denounced "sex solidarity" and encouraged their female organizers to do the same. Party loyalty was the first priority for parties. For party women, inclusion was the first priority. Party women, according to Freeman, were interested not in promoting a "women first" agenda but rather in receiving "equal rewards for equal service."[143] The odd waltz between parties and feminists continued with women and parties alike trying to argue both sides: parties tried to appeal to women by identifying women's issues in their platforms but appealing to their partisan loyalty first, while women worked tirelessly for the party but always held out the possibility of a women's bloc vote to motivate the party to listen to women. Attachment to political parties in general is on the decline, making it essential that new groups of voters be recruited into the ranks of the faithful. Women are certainly not a unified voting bloc, but statistics on the gender gap and women's voting history over the last several decades are evidence that the Democratic Party is perceived as the organization most closely aligned with women's interests. The Women's Leadership Forum (WLF) operates as the women's outreach arm of the Democratic Party.[144] Women played prominent roles at the Democratic National Convention in July 2016. Donna Brazile stepped forward as interim chair of the Democratic National Committee after Debbie Wasserman Shultz (D-Fla.) resigned from her position as chair before the convention started. Representative Marcia Fudge (D-Ohio) served as convention chairman. Women represented 2,887 of the 4,766 (61 percent) delegates to the Democratic National Convention.[145]

The National Federation of Republican Women (NFRW) provides a forum for women in the Republican Party. The 2016 presidential contest was challenging for many Republican women who were disappointed by the nomination of Donald J. Trump. Just prior to Labor Day, the traditional start to the presidential campaign, Donald Trump trailed Hillary Clinton by six points overall nationally but lagged among women by a margin of 58 percent to 35 percent. Among college-educated white women who identify as Republicans, Clinton led Trump by 30 points (57 to 27). Only 72 percent of Republican women supported Trump. But as the scholarship reviewed in this chapter confirms, party identification is the strongest indicator of vote choice. In the general election, Donald Trump won the votes of 91 percent of white Republican women.[146]

CONCLUSION

Women constitute a substantial political force in the abstract. However, a variety of historical and contemporary forces work to minimize the chances that women will act together as a unified group in politics. Despite the contemporary gender gap, a "women's bloc" did not materialize immediately following ratification of the Nineteenth Amendment, nor has it materialized in American politics since. Most likely, even the possibility of a women's voting bloc was the stuff of political myth-making or propaganda, depending on one's perspective. Women are divided by race, class, family status, and education in the same ways that men are politically stratified. Where men and women differ in their rates or modes of participation, resources are most likely at issue rather than gender. Women still lag behind men in their wages and have chosen not to allocate their monetary resources to electoral politics at the same levels as male donors. However, as some women have become more economically powerful they are increasing their role as political donors. It may be that 2016 is an aberration, driven by Hillary Clinton's historic position at the top of the Democratic ticket, but across both political parties women have exercised greater power as contributors.

Organizations, networks, and high-quality candidates addressing issues women believe are important may empower women as political participants in the future. Achieving gender equality, even if merely political equality, depends not only on women's ability to vote but also on their ability to express their collective will and interests effectively through other forms of political participation. The Internet has made access to political information on issues and candidates more available, and evidence suggests that women are heavy consumers of political websites and social networking tools. Access to the Internet may also increase the likelihood that women donate money to political candidates, parties, and PACs, thereby raising the volume of their collective political voice. Although women do not all vote for the same candidates or even in completely predictable patterns, the interest shown in attracting women voters is an important indication that women matter in politics. That so many of the registration and mobilization efforts in recent elections were undertaken by women's advocacy organizations suggests that the women's movement is enjoying a resurgence as well. However, gender equality does not easily translate into policy platforms or campaign promises, particularly considering the complexities introduced by the paradox and the two different paths to the realization of gender equality.

The 2008 presidential election was unique due to the historic presence of Hillary Clinton's candidacy for the Democratic nomination for president and Sarah Palin's nomination as vice president on the Republican presidential ticket. As a candidate, Hillary Clinton attracted more than 18 million votes in the primaries from both men and women. The 2012 presidential election was unique because of the unprecedented effort to mobilize women voters, largely in reaction to increasingly polarized positions on abortion and access to contraception and reproductive health care. Advocacy groups of all political and ideological persuasions worked to get women registered and to the polls. As a result, 62 million women voted, a marked increase over the 59 million who voted in 2000.

As the first woman to win a major party's nomination for president, Hillary Clinton frequently called attention to her gender during the 2016 campaign. Although pre-election polls had her leading Donald Trump among women by wide margins, on Election Day support from women was not enough to win her the presidency. Clinton won 54 percent of women's votes, a performance similar to Democratic presidential candidates in the past two decades. Pundits and pollsters contributed to a media frame that predicted that Republican women, turned off by Trump's misogynistic behavior, would cross party lines and vote for Clinton. However appealing the narrative was, it ignored decades of political science research that shows party tops gender in voter decision-making. Clinton won by overwhelming margins with women from groups traditionally associated with the Democratic Party: African American, Latina, and single women. She attracted more votes than expected from college-educated white women and from married women—groups who typically affiliate as Republicans. If there ever was an election where women had a reason to place gender before party, 2016 would certainly have been in contention, but it didn't happen. Do high-profile national female candidates mobilize women's political engagement in new ways? We don't know yet—we have only three election cycles to compare against more than two centuries of exclusion.

The fact remains that women make up 53 percent of the US population, constitute the majority of registered voters, and consistently vote at higher rates than men. In this sense, women's votes are key to winning elections for both male and female candidates. Empirical studies caution that female candidates and Democratic candidates should not take women's votes for granted, any more than male candidates or Republican candidates should write them off. Chapter 4 examines another form of political participation that could translate into the power to more directly set the political agenda: women as candidates for public office.

NOTES

Boxed feature notes appear at the end of the Notes section.

1 Jewel L. Prestage, "In Quest of African American Political Women," *Annals of the American Academy of Political and Social Science* 515 (May 1991): 95.

2 Jo Freeman, *A Room at a Time: How Women Entered Party Politics* (Lanham, MD: Rowman and Littlefield, 2000), 3.

3 Anita Shafer Goodstein, "A Rare Alliance: African American and White Women in the Tennessee Elections of 1919 and 1920," *Journal of Southern History* 64, no. 2 (May 1998): 219–246.

4 Kristi Anderson, *After Suffrage: Women in Partisan and Electoral Politics Before the New Deal* (Chicago: University of Chicago Press, 1996), 50.

5 Charles Merriam and Harold Gosnell, *Non-Voting: Causes and Methods of Control* (Chicago: University of Chicago Press, 1924), 36–37.

6 Rosalyn Terborg-Penn, *African American Women in the Struggle for the Vote, 1850–1920* (Bloomington: Indiana University Press, 1998), 137.

7 Anderson, *After Suffrage*.

8 Sophinisba Breckinridge, *Women in the Twentieth Century: A Study of Their Political, Social, and Economic Activities* (New York: McGraw-Hill, 1933).

9 Virginia Sapiro, *The Political Integration of Women* (Urbana: University of Illinois Press, 1983), 22.

10 J. Kevin Corder and Christine Wolbrecht, *Counting Women's Ballots: Female Voters from Suffrage Through the New Deal*. (New York: Cambridge University Press, 2016).

11 Prestage, "In Quest of African American Political Women," 97.

12 Turnout and registration statistics from "Gender Differences in Voter Turnout," fact sheet compiled by the Center for American Women and Politics, Eagleton Institute of Politics, Rutgers University, 2015.

13 Sidney Verba, Kay Lehman Schlozman, and Henry E. Brady, *Voice and Equality: Civic Voluntarism in American Politics* (Cambridge, MA: Harvard University Press, 1995), 254n.

14 Kevin Eagan et al., *The American Freshman: National Norms Fall 2015* (Los Angeles: UCLA Higher Education Research Institute, 2016).

15 Jennifer L. Lawless and Richard L. Fox, *Running from Office: Why Young Americans Are Turned Off to Politics* (New York: Oxford University Press, 2015).

16 Center for Information and Research on Civic Learning and Engagement, *Voter Turnout Among Young Men and Women* (Baltimore: School of Public Affairs, University of Maryland, May 2003).

17 Thom File, "Young-Adult Voting: An Analysis of Presidential Elections, 1964–2012," US Census Bureau, document P20-573, April 2014.

18 Harvard University Institute of Politics Summer 2016 Poll, http://iop.harvard.edu/survey/details /harvard-iop-summer-2016-poll.

19 Christine Birkner, "After 26 Years, Rock the Vote Is Still Driving Young People to the Polls," *AdWeek*, July 31, 2016.

20 AAUW Action Fund, "It's My Vote: I Will Be Heard," https://www.aauwaction.org/my-vote. Accessed August 2016.

21 Aaron Blake, "More Young People Voted for Bernie Sanders than Trump and Clinton Combined—by a Lot," *Washington Post*, June 20, 2016.

22 Richard A. Seltzer, Jody Newman, and Melissa Vorhees Leighton, *Sex as a Political Variable: Women as Candidates and Voters in U.S. Elections* (Boulder, CO: Lynne Rienner Publishers, 1997), 68.

23 Center for American Women and Politics, "Gender Differences in Voter Turnout."

24 Sandra Baxter and Marjorie Lansing, *Women and Politics: The Invisible Majority* (Ann Arbor: University of Michigan Press, 1980), 107–110.

25 Holly Maluk, Myrna Pérez, and Lucy Zhou, "Voter Registration in a Digital Age: 2015 Update," Brennan Center for Justice, New York University, 2015.

26 Nelson W. Polsby and Aaron Wildavsky, *Presidential Elections: Strategies and Structures of American Politics* (New York: Chatham House, 2000), 8.

27 Ibid., 9.

28 Lonna Rae Atkeson, "Not All Cutes Are Created Equal: The Conditional Impact of Female Candidates on Political Engagement," *Journal of Politics* 65, no. 4 (November 2004): 1040–1061.

29 Michael Nelson, "The Setting: Diversifying the Presidential Talent Pool," in Michael Nelson, ed., *The Elections of 2008* (Washington, DC: CQ Press, 2009).

30 Laura Barron-Lopez, "Hillary Clinton Leans In, Embraces Role of First Female President," *Huffington Post*, October 13, 2015.

31 Kathleen A. Frankovic, "Why the Gender Gap Became News in 1996," *PS: Political Science and Politics* 32, no. 1 (March 1999): 20–23.

32 Jeff Manza and Clem Brooks, "The Gender Gap in U.S. Presidential Elections: When? Why? Implications?" *American Journal of Sociology* 103, no. 5 (March 1998): 1235–1266.

33 Seltzer, Newman, and Leighton, *Sex as a Political Variable*, 4.

34 *Footnotes: A Blog of the Center for American Women and Politics*, http://www.cawp.rutgers.edu /footnotes/womenvote2014-tracking-gender-gap-and-women%E2%80%99s-vote-2014. Accessed August 2016.

35 Jocelyn Kelly, "As GOP Celebrates Win, No Sign of Narrowing Gender, Age Gaps," Pew Research Center, November 5, 2014.

36 Susan B. Hansen, "Sex, Race, Gender and the Presidential Vote," *Cogent Social Sciences* 2, no. 1 (2016), 1172936, doi:10.1080/23311886.2016.1172936.

37 Jeffrey M. Jones, "Democrat, Republican Identification Near Historic Lows," Gallup Politics, January 11, 2016.

38 Hansen, 13.

39 Votes for Women 2004, "Gender Gap Persists in the 2004 Election," www.votesforwomen2004. org. Accessed November 2004 (no longer available).

40 Robin Hindery, "Kerry and Women: Too Little, Too Late," *Women's eNews*, November 7, 2004.

41 Lisa Garcia Bedolla, Jessica L. Lavariega Monforti, and Adrian D. Pantoja, "A Second Look: Is There a Latina/o Gender Gap?" *Journal of Women, Politics and Policy* 28, nos. 3–4 (2006): 147–171.

42 Manza and Brooks, "The Gender Gap in U.S. Presidential Elections."

43 Karen M. Kaufmann and John R. Petrocik, "The Changing Politics of American Men: Understanding the Sources of the Gender Gap," *American Journal of Political Science* 43, no. 3 (July 1999): 864–887.

44 Susan Welch and John Hibbing, "Financial Conditions, Gender and Voting in American National Elections," *Journal of Politics* 54 (1992): 343–359.

45 "Issues and the 2008 Election," Pew Forum, August 1, 2008, www.pewforum.org/2008/08/21/publicationpage-aspxid1078/

46 "Poll Findings: Understanding What Women Want in 2008," National Women's Law Center and Peter D. Hart Research Associates, August 5, 2008.

47 Kay Lehman Schlozman, Nancy Burns, Sidney Verba, and Jesse Donahue, "Gender and Citizen Participation: Is There a Different Voice?" *American Journal of Political Science* 39 (1995): 267–293.

48 Susan B. Hansen, *The Politics of Sex: Public Opinion, Parties, and Presidential Elections* (New York: Routledge, 2014).

49 Greenberg Quinlan Rosner Research, "Re: The Security Mom Myth," accessed October 2004 at www.GreenbergResearch.com (no longer available); Dan DeLuce, "Pollsters Call 'Security Moms' a Myth," *Women's eNews*, October 12, 2004; Kim Gandy, "The Perils of Polling," National Organization for Women, www.now.org/news/note/100104.html, accessed October 2004 (no longer available).

50 Aaron Zitner, "A Revival of 'Security Moms' Would Stand to Benefit GOP," *Wall Street Journal*, January 9, 2016.

51 Greenberg Quinlan Rosner Research, "Re: The Security Mom Myth," 8.

52 Laurel Elder and Steven Green, "The Myth of 'Security Moms' and 'NASCAR Dads': Parenthood, Political Stereotypes, and the 2004 Election," *Social Science Quarterly* 88, no. 1 (March 2007): 1–19.

53 Ibid., 16.

54 "Unmarried Women in the 2016 Elections," American Women, January 28, 2016, www.americanwomen.org/research/unmarried-women-and-the-2016-elections.

55 Greenberg Quinlan Rosner Research, "A Struggling Electorate: Findings from a National Survey of Voters," June 9, 2016, www.gqrr.com/articles/2016/6/21/a-struggling-electorate-findings-from-a-national-survey-of-voters.

56 Janet M. Box Steffensmeier, Suzanna DeBoef, and Tse-Min Lin, "The Dynamics of the Partisan Gender Gap," *American Political Science Review* 98, no. 3 (August 2004): 515–528.

57 Ibid., 527.

58 Verba, Schlozman, and Brady, *Voice and Equality*, 38.

59 For information on the sample and methodology, see Verba, Schlozman, and Brady, *Voice and Equality*, Appendix A.

60 Defined in this study as whether the respondent voted, worked on a campaign, made a campaign contribution, worked informally or in the community, served on a local governing board, contacted a government official, attended a protest, or was affiliated with a political organization.

61 Kay Schlozman, Nancy Burns, and Sidney Verba, "Gender and the Pathways to Participation: The Role of Resources," *Journal of Politics* 56, no. 4 (November 1994): 969.

62 Ibid., 968–969. In each case, the gender differences were statistically significant.

63 Kei Kawashima-Ginsberg and Nancy Thomas, "Civic Engagement and Political Leadership Among Women—a Call for Solutions," CIRCLE Fact Sheet, May 2013, www.civicyouth.org/wp-content/uploads/2013/05/Gender-and-Political-Leadership-Fact-Sheet-3.pdf.

64 Wendy Kaminer, "Crashing the Locker Room," *Atlantic*, July 1992, 58–70.

65 Nicholas Confessore, "Women Build Political Clout as Big Donors: A Potential Boon for the Clinton Campaign," *New York Times*, May 8, 2016.

66 Ibid.

67 Nicholas Confessore, "Women's Rising Influence in Politics, Tinted Green," *New York Times*, May 7, 2016.

68 Sidney Verba and Norman Nie, *Participation in America: Political Democracy and Social Equality* (New York: Harper and Row, 1972).

69 Kathleen Hall Jamieson, Richard Johnston, and Michael Hagen, "The Primary Campaign: What Did the Candidates Say, What Did the Public Learn, and What Did It Matter" Philadelphia: Annenberg Public Policy Center, University of Pennsylvania, March 27, 2000.

70 Kawashima-Ginsberg and Nancy Thomas, "Civic Engagement and Political Leadership Among Women—a Call for Solutions," 2.

71 Jennifer L. Lawless and Richard L. Fox, "Girls Just Wanna Not Run: The Gender Gap in Young Americans' Political Ambition," Women and Politics Institute, American University, March 2013.

72 Ibid.

73 Mary Christine Banwart, "Gender and Young Voters in 2004," *American Behavioral Scientist* 50, no. 9 (May 2007): 1152–1168.

74 Ibid., 1155.

75 Ibid., 1166.

76 Kathleen Dolan, "Do Men and Women Know Different Things? Measuring Gender Differences in Political Knowledge," *Journal of Politics* 73, no. 1 (January 2011): 97–107.

77 Michael R. Alvarez and Edward J. McCaffery, "Is There a Gender Gap in Fiscal Political Preferences?," paper presented at the American Political Science Association meeting, September 2000.

78 Susan B. Hansen, "Talking About Politics: Gender and Contextual Effects in Political Proselytizing," *Journal of Politics* 59, no. 1 (February 1997): 73–103.

79 Simone de Beauvoir, *The Second Sex* (New York: Knopf, 1952).

80 Sapiro, *The Political Integration of Women*, 40.

81 Paul H. Mussen, "Early Sex Role Development," in *Handbook of Socialization Theory and Research*, ed. David Goslin (New York: Rand McNally, 1969).

82 Katherine Blick Hoyenga and Kermit T. Hoyenga, *Gender-Related Differences: Origins and Outcomes* (Boston: Allyn and Bacon, 1993), 265.

83 David Sadker and Myra Sadker, *Failing at Fairness: How America's Schools Cheat Girls* (New York: Scribner, 1994), 84–85.

84 Nicole Filler and M. Kent Jennings, "Familial Origins of Gender Role Attitudes," *Politics and Gender* 11 (2015): 27–54.

85 Sue Thomas, *How Women Legislate* (New York: Oxford University Press, 1994), 56.

86 Hoyenga and Hoyenga, *Gender-Related Differences*, 266.

87 See Roberta S. Sigel, *Ambition and Accommodation: How Women View Gender Relations* (Chicago: University of Chicago Press, 1996), 9–17; Sue Tolleson Rinehart, *Gender Consciousness and Politics* (New York: Routledge, 1992), 21–27.

88 "Pipeline to the Future: Young Women and Political Leadership," findings on mobilizing young women, from a survey and focus groups conducted by Lake Snell Perry and Associates for the White House Project Education Fund, April 12, 2000, 22.

89 "National Take Our Daughters to the Polls Campaign Launched in Historic Year for Women's Political Leadership," press release, White House Project, October 16, 2008.

90 "Barbie Is Running for President!" press release, White House Project Education Fund, April 19, 2000.

91 Mike Snider, "New Presidential Barbie Has a Running Mate Too," *USAToday*, July 13, 2016.

92 Barbie and She Should Run, worksheet, 2016, http://assets.barbie.com/games-bin/Downloadables/others/you-can-be-a-leader-worksheet.pdf. Accessed August 2016.

93 M. Margaret Conway, Gertrude A. Steuernagel, and David Ahern, *Women and Political Participation: Cultural Change in the Political Arena* (Washington, DC: Congressional Quarterly Press, 1997).

94 Elizabeth Adell Cook, "The Generations of Feminism," in *Women in Politics: Insiders or Outsiders*, ed. Lois Duke Whitaker, 3rd ed. (Upper Saddle River, NJ: Prentice Hall, 1999), 45–55.

95 Rossalyn Warren, "Emma Watson Says That the View Feminism Is 'Man Hating' Has to Stop," *Buzzfeed*, September 21, 2014.

96 Gerhard Falk, *Sex, Gender and Social Change: The Great Revolution* (Lanham, MD: University Press of America, 1998), 175.

97 Deborah Tannen, "The Real Hillary Factor," *New York Times*, October 12, 1992.

98 Estelle Disch, *Reconstructing Gender: A Multicultural Anthology*, 2nd ed. (Mountain View, CA: Mayfield Publishing, 2000), 308.

99 Ibid., 306.

100 Kenneth Dion, Ellen Berscheid, and Elain Walster, "What Is Beautiful Is Good," *Journal of Personality and Social Psychology* 24 (1972): 285–290.

101 Alexander Todorov, Anesu N. Mandisodza, Amir Goren, and Crystal C. Hall, "Inferences of Competence from Faces Predict Election Outcomes," *Science* 308 (June 10, 2005): 1623–1626.

102 Rebekah Herrick, Jeanette Mendez, Sue Thomas, and Amanda Wilkerson, "Gender Effects on Competence Inferences Based on Facial Appearances," paper presented at the annual meeting of the American Political Science Association, Boston, August 2008.

103 Leslie A. Zebrowitz and Joann M. Montpare, "Appearance Does Matter," *Science* 308 (June 10, 2005): 1565–1566.

104 Stephanie Condon, "Republican Debate: Carly Fiorina Responds to Donald Trump's Comments About Her Face," CBS News, September 16, 2015.

105 Linda Witt, Karen M. Paget, and Glenna Mathews, *Running as a Woman: Gender and Power in American Politics* (New York: Free Press, 1993), 59–60.

106 Kaminer, "Crashing the Locker Room," 58–70.

107 For more on this story, see Caryl Rivers, "Commentary: Mockery of Katherine Harris Shows Double Standard," *Women's eNews*, November 29, 2000.

108 For an interactive review of attention paid to Hillary Clinton's appearance, see "A Brief History of Hillary Clinton's Body Politic," *New York Magazine*, October 3, 2007, http://nymag.com/daily /intel/2007/10/a_brief_history_of_hillary_cli.html.

109 Margaret Wheeler Johnson, "Hillary Clinton Pantsuit Rainbow: Reddit User Celebrates Hillz' Trademark Outfit," *Huffington Post*, May 23, 2013.

110 Brian Flood, "Hillary Clinton Voters Can Now Wear All of Her Pantsuits on 1 Shirt," The Wrap, June 21, 2016. http://www.thewrap.com/hillary-clinton-pantsuit-merchandise-tshirt-donald-trump -2016-presidential-election/

111 Katha Pollitt, "Media's Whiplash on Michelle Obama: From Fist-Bumping Radical to Mom-in-Chief," *Nation*, April 3, 2009.

112 Geraldine Brooks, "Michelle Obama and the Roots of Reinvention," *More Magazine*, October 2008.

113 Rebecca Traister, "The Momification of Michelle Obama," *Salon*, November 12, 2008.

114 Pollitt, "Media's Whiplash on Michelle Obama."

115 Patricia Hill Collins, *Black Feminist Thought* (London: Routledge, 1991), 67.

116 R. Darcy, Charles D. Hadley, and Jason F. Kirksey, "Electoral Systems and the Representation of Black Women in American State Legislatures," *Women and Politics* 13 (1993): 73–76.

117 Irene Natividad, "Women of Color on the Campaign Trail," in *The American Woman: 1992–1993*, eds. Paula Ries and Anne J. Stone (New York: Norton, 1992).

118 Nadia Brown, "'It's More than Hair . . . That's Why You Should Care': The Politics of Appearance for Black Women State Legislators," *Politics, Groups, and Identities* 2, no. 3 (2014): 295–312.

119 Charles J. Olgetree Jr., "The People vs. Anita Hill: A Case for Client Centered Advocacy," in *Race, Gender, and Power in America*, eds. Anita Faye Hill and Emma Coleman Jordan (New York: Oxford University Press, 1995), 142–176.

120 Anna Deavere Smith, "Anita Hill and the Year of the Woman," in *Race, Gender, and Power in America*, eds. Hill and Jordan, 248–270.

121 Ibid., 250.

122 A seventh female senator, Kay Bailey Hutchison, Republican from Texas, was seated after winning a special election to replace Senator Lloyd Bentsen after he was appointed secretary of the treasury.

123 Cynthia B. Costello, Shari Miles, and Anne J. Stone, eds., *The American Woman: 1999–2000* (New York: Norton, 1998), 97.

124 Toni Cabrillo et al., *The Feminist Chronicles* (Los Angeles: Women's Graphics, 1994), 143.

125 Manuel Roig-Franzia, Scott Higham, and Krissah Thompson, "The Fall of Roger Ailes: He Made Fox News His 'Locker Room' and Now Women Are Telling Their Stories," *Washington Post*, July 22, 2016.

126 All In Together, http://aitogether.org/the-opportunity.

127 Kathleen Dolan, "Symbolic Mobilization? The Impact of Candidate Sex in American Elections," *American Politics Research* 34, no. 6 (November 2006): 687–704.

128 Electoral Commission, *Gender and Political Participation*, research report, April 2004, referenced in Sarah Hall, "Political Gender Gap Deters Women Voters," *Guardian*, April 28, 2004.

129 Dolan, "Symbolic Mobilization," 699.

130 Jennifer Wolak, "Candidate Gender and the Political Engagement of Women and Men," *American Politics Research* 43, no. 5 (2015): 872–896.

131 Jennifer L. Lawless, "Politics of Presence? Congresswomen and Symbolic Representation," *Political Research Quarterly* 57, no. 1 (2004): 81–99.

132 Susan J. Carroll, "Reflections on Gender and Hillary Clinton's Presidential Campaign: The Good, the Bad, and the Misogynistic," *Politics and Gender* 5, no. 1 (March 2009): 1–20.

133 Nia-Malika Henderson, "Hillary Clinton's Gender Tightrope," CNN Politics, April 15, 2016.

134 Alan Rappeport, "Gloria Steinem and Madeleine Albright Rebuke Young Women Backing Bernie Sanders," *New York Times*, February 7, 2016.

135 See, for example, Amy Chozick and Yamiche Alcindor, "Moms and Daughters Debate Gender Factor in Hillary Clinton's Bid," *New York Times*, December 12, 2015.

136 Taylor Reid, "Hillary Clinton: Exploring the Generation Gap Among Women Voters," Michigan State University School of Journalism, May 16, 2016.

137 Ibid.

138 "Hillary's Woman Problem," *Politico*, February 12, 2016.

139 Sherrye Henry, *The Deep Divide: Why American Women Resist Equality* (New York: Macmillan, 1994), 320–322.

140 David Knoke, "The Mobilization of Members of Women's Associations," in *Women, Politics, and Change*, eds. Louise A. Tilly and Patricia Gurin (New York: Russell Sage Foundation, 1990), 383–409.

141 Ibid.

142 Freeman, *A Room at a Time*, 6.

143 Ibid.

144 "Women's Leadership Forum," Official Website of the Democratic Party, www.democrats.org//page/womens-leadership-forum.

145 Collier Meyerson, "So We Counted All the Woman and People of Color at the DNC and the RNC . . . ," *Fusion*, July 27, 2016.

146 Clare Malone, "Can Kellyanne Conway Get Donald Trump to Stop Alienating Women?" *FiveThirtyEight*, August 25, 2016.

Box 3.1: The Glass Ceiling Remains: Are Women Voters Responsible?

1 Michael Tesler, "Why the Gender Gap Doomed Hillary Clinton," *Washington Post*, November 9, 2016.

2 Kelly Dittmar, "No, Women Didn't Abandon Clinton, Nor Did She Fail to Win Their Support," Presidential Gender Watch 2016, Center for American Women and Politics, November 11, 2016.

Box 3.2: Female, Activist, Conservative, Republican . . . and Feminist?

1 Melissa Deckman, *Tea Party Women: Mama Grizzlies, Grassroots Leaders, and the Changing Face of the American Right* (New York: New York University Press, 2016), 12.

2 Ibid., 20.

3 Ronnie Schreiber, *Righting Feminism: Conservative Women and American Politics* (New York: Oxford University Press, 2008), 12. See also Schreiber, "Gender Roles, Motherhood, and Politics: Conservative Women's Organizations Frame Sarah Palin and Michele Bachmann," *Journal of Women, Politics and Policy* 37, no. 1 (2016): 1–23.

4 Deckman, *Tea Party Women*, 27.

5 Center for American Women and Politics, Fact Sheets, 2016.

Box 3.3: "'Hey Baby!' Is Not My Name": Global Activism Against Street Harrassment

1 See Jessica Valenti, "What Does a Lifetime of Leers Do to Us?" *New York Times*, June 5, 2016.

2 HarassMap, "What We Do," http://harassmap.org/en/what-we-do.

3 Stop Street Harassment, www.stopstreetharassment.org.

4 Hollaback!, www.ihollaback.org/about.

5 Ben Tufft, "Woman in Armour Protesting Against Sexual Harassment in Kabul Pelted with Rocks," *Independent*, March 8, 2015.

CHAPTER 4

Women Seeking Office: The Next Phase of Political Integration

As of 2016, a total of 313 women have served in the U.S. Congress since Jeanette Rankin was first elected in 1916; 278 of those in the U.S. House of Representatives. If all 278 women served together, they would make up just over half (63 percent) of the total 435 seats in the House.[1]

Nearly a hundred years after suffrage, what is the status of women in office? In 2016, women occupy 104 (19.4 percent) of the 535 seats available in the US Congress. A record eighty-four women serve in the House of Representatives in the 114th Congress (2015–2017) representing thirty-one states, with an additional four women serving as nonvoting delegates. Thirty-three representatives are women of color (eighteen African Americans, nine Latinas, and six Asian Americans or Pacific Islanders). In 2012, Tammy Baldwin was elected to the US Senate from Wisconsin as the first open lesbian. Congresswoman Nancy Pelosi, a Democrat from California, is minority leader in the House and served as the first woman Speaker of the House from 2007 to 2011, when Democrats held the majority. In the Senate, women hold 20 of the 100 available seats. Three states (California, New Hampshire, and Washington) are represented by two female senators each. Another two states (Mississippi and Vermont) have never sent a woman to either the House of Representatives or the Senate.[2] Although the number of congresswomen has nearly doubled in the last twenty years (from 57 in 1995 to 104 in 2015), at the current rate of progress the Institute for Women's Policy Research predicts that it will be 2121 before women achieve political parity.[3]

Women filled 24.6 percent of the available seats in state legislatures in 2016, and 75 (24 percent) of the 312 statewide elective offices available. Six women served as governor, 12 women served as lieutenant governor, 8 women served as attorney general, 13 as secretary of state, and 8 as state treasurer.[4] The 2016 general election did result in significant change at the state level. Women in 2017 hold roughly the

TABLE 4.1: Ten Highest-Ranking Countries for Women's Representation in National Legislature, Lower House (2016)

Ranking	Country	Proportion of Women Members, Lower House
1	Rwanda*	63.8%
2	Bolivia*	53.1%
3	Cuba	48.9%
4	Seychelles	43.8%
5	Sweden**	43.6%
6	Senegal*	42.7%
7	Mexico*	42.4%
8	South Africa**	41.8%
9	Ecuador*	41.6%
10	Finland	41.5%
. . .		
96	Kenya*	19.7%
97	**United States**	19.4%
98	Kyrgyzstan*	19.2%

Source: Inter-Parliamentary Union, "Women in Parliaments: World Classification," as of August 1, 2016, www.ipu.org /wmn-e/world.htm; Global Database of Quotas for Women, www.quotaproject.org/country.cfm.

* Legislated gender quotas in place.
** Voluntary gender quotas, adopted by the party.

same percentage of seats in the state legislatures and statewide offices.[5] In 2008, the New Hampshire state senate became the country's first legislative body with more women than men (women held thirteen of the twenty-four seats). In 2017, New Hampshire became the first state with an all-woman, all-Democrat congressional delegation (Senator Jeanne Shaheen, Senator Maggie Hassan, Representative Carol Shea-Porter, and Representative Annie Kuster). Local offices are much harder to track due to the sheer number of elected positions across the country. However, in cities with populations of 30,000 or more, 18 percent of mayors were women in 2016. Women mayors led 17 percent of medium-sized cities (population of 100,000–500,000), and 15 percent of big-city mayors were female (cities with populations over 500,000). Two of the nation's largest cities have been led by young African American women (Stephanie Rawlings-Blake in Baltimore and Muriel Bowser in the District of Columbia). In 2017, Stephanie Rawlings-Blake was succeeded by Catherine E. Pugh, an African American woman.

IMAGE 4.1: *Hillary Clinton arrives on stage in Philadelphia on July 28, 2016, the final night of the Democratic National Convention, to accept the nomination for president. She became the first woman nominated for president by a major party.* Source: SAUL LOEB/AFP/Getty Images.

At the highest levels of government, 2016 was a good year for women. Hillary Clinton became the first woman to win a major party's nomination for president. Prior to Hillary Clinton's campaign for the Democratic nomination in 2008, only three women had sought the presidential nomination of a major party, while a fourth got as far as an exploratory committee before bowing out. In 2016, Hillary Clinton again sought the Democratic nomination, while Carly Fiorina was the only woman in a crowded field of seventeen candidates for the Republican nomination. But compared to other developed nations in terms of the number of women in political office, the United States clearly lags behind (see Table 4.1 and Chapter 5 "Point of Comparison," page 204). Of 193 countries, the United States places ninety-seventh based on the percentage of women serving in the lower (or single) house of the national legislature.[6] A UN Development Report stated, "While it is true that no definite relationship has been established between the extent of women's participation in political institutions and their contribution to the advancement of women, a 30 percent membership in political institutions is considered the critical mass that enables women to exert meaningful influence on politics."[7]

By the end of 2016, forty-six countries had achieved a critical mass of 30 percent women in the lower house of their national parliaments. The international average stands at 22.8 percent for both houses combined, but this hides considerable variation.[8] Notably, among the democracies ranking highest for women's representation, nearly all employ proportionally based electoral systems. In countries with the greatest success in promoting women's representation, there is generally some form of quota system for candidacy by which women are guaranteed a minimum number of winnable positions available on candidate lists (see the "Point of Comparison" box on page 148). Countries with a substantially lower proportion of women have, almost exclusively, plurality or majoritarian systems, and none has any formal system to encourage or require women's candidacies.

In the United States, explanations for women's underrepresentation have included the following: the country was not ready for women in high office; voters, particularly women voters, would not support a woman candidate; women could not raise funds to mount successful campaigns; or party elites conspired to keep women from being nominated to winnable seats.[9] Today the reality is that women are as likely, or more likely, than men to win elections.[10] However, political geography, increasing party polarization, and voter attitudes continue to shape the conditions in which women are recruited as candidates and run a campaign. The slogan "When women run, women win" says it all—to move the needle on women's representation, more women must stand as candidates, and it has proven difficult to convince women to run.

Answering the question of why women lag behind as candidates constitutes a major portion of this chapter. We will also explore women's experience as they campaign for office and assess how women's campaigns are similar to and different from men's. This chapter concludes with a look at current initiatives designed to increase the number of women running for public office.

WOMEN CANDIDATES ARE AS LIKELY TO WIN ELECTIONS AS MEN . . . BUT CONTEXT MATTERS

The long-held belief that a woman has a poor chance of electoral victory is empirically unsubstantiated. That does not mean, however, that the myth does not continue to scare women away from running for office. "If women think the system is biased against them, then the empirical reality of a playing field on which women can succeed is almost meaningless," write Jennifer L. Lawless and Richard L. Fox.[11] Women and men with equivalent professional and political credentials perceive the electoral system quite differently. Women, for example, view local and congressional elections in their area as more competitive than men do; anticipate that they will have a harder time raising money; and perceive that it is more difficult for a woman to be elected than for a man. Likewise, more women than men (29 percent to 17) rate the odds of winning their first race as "very unlikely."[12]

The public shares the view that politics is uniquely inhospitable to women.[13] A 2014 Cooperative Congressional Election Study survey found that 60 percent of the public believe the media focus too much on a woman's appearance and 58 percent said that women candidates are subjected to sexist media coverage during the campaign. In the same study, 48 percent said that women must be more qualified than men to win and 31 percent expressed the belief that women don't win as often as men. A Pew Research Center study, "Women and Leadership," confirms the public's view that although women and men share key leadership traits that make them equally suitable for high political office, women are held to higher standards (38 percent agree), face an electorate not ready to vote for a woman (37 percent), and lack sufficient party support for a successful campaign (27 percent).[14] And yet multiple studies have found equivalent success rates for male and female candidates, leading to the conclusion that "a candidate's sex does not affect his or her chances of winning an election."[15] Where is the source of this disconnect and what consequences might it have for women considering a candidacy?

In *Women on the Run*, Danny Hayes and Jennifer Lawless explore what they call the paradox of women's representation.[16] Women are underrepresented at all levels of elective office, and with each subsequent election the number of women increases only incrementally. However, empirical evidence shows that when women run, they do just as well as men. Hayes and Lawless conclude that "the best evidence to resolve this seeming contradiction suggests that women are under-represented in the United States primarily because they are less likely than men to run for political office in the first place, not that they don't win when they do."[17] Acknowledging that perceptions of media bias, voter attitudes, and the expectation of a difficult campaign environment still dissuade women from seeking office, their research claims that two features of contemporary American politics have significantly leveled the electoral playing field: the declining "novelty" of female politicians and the polarization of the parties. "Today, male and female candidates have few reasons to campaign differently, the media have little incentive to cover them differently, and voters have no reason to evaluate them differently. As a result candidate sex plays a minimal role in the vast majority of US elections."[18] Hayes and Lawless test their claim with in-depth analysis of hundreds of US House races, including campaign advertisements, media coverage, and candidate messaging, and conclude that men and women run virtually identical campaigns governed substantially more by partisanship than by the candidate's sex. This is not to say that the US electoral system is gender-neutral or that there are not examples of sexist behavior; rather, Hayes and Lawless find no evidence of systemic gender bias in campaigns that would lead women to be disadvantaged in electoral outcomes.

In this section we will look at some of the structural factors that impact, and in some ways impede, women's candidacies for office, including political geography and district-level characteristics, increasing party polarization, incumbency and term limits, and single-member versus multimember districts.

The Political Geography of Women's Races

Even a cursory examination of the map in Figure 4.1 will demonstrate that female members of Congress are not evenly distributed across the United States. While in the 114th Congress there were twenty women serving in the US Senate,

FIGURE 4.1: **Percentage of Women in State Congressional Delegations, 2015**

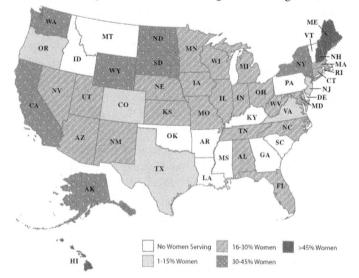

Source: Adapted from InsideGov, "One Interactive Map Shows the Best (and Worst) States for Gender Equality in Congress" February 20, 2015. http://members-of -congress.insidegov.com/stories/3554/female-representation-national-politics.

one-third came from three states where both senators were female (California, New Hampshire, and Washington). Likewise, the eighty-four women serving in the US House in the 114th Congress came from a handful of states.[19] Three states had never sent a woman to Congress (Delaware, Mississippi, Vermont), and thirteen states had no women among their congressional delegation in the 114th Congress. Of the 104 women in that Congress, 72 were Democrats and 28 were Republicans. The 115th Congress (2017–2019) includes 104 women; 21 women in the Senate and 83 women in the House of Representatives. In addition, the delegates from American Samoa, the District of Columbia, Guam, Puerto Rico and the US Virgin Islands are women. Lisa Blunt Rochester, a Democrat, was elected to the House from Delaware. These demographics suggest that district characteristics play an important role in electing women to office in addition to political party and gender.

Variation in the proportion of women serving in state legislatures as well as the apparent plateau in the growth of women serving has been attributed to a number of state-level characteristics. States with the lowest proportion of women serving tend to be clustered in the South or border southern states, where women were slower to exercise the franchise and where political parties are less open to recruiting women candidates.[20] By contrast, states in the top third for women state legislators tend to be in the West, where women gained political rights and the vote early and where open party structures encourage the recruitment of women.

An analysis by Political Parity of 23,709 candidates in congressional primaries and general elections found that women made up only 13 percent of the candidates between 1980 and 2012 and were more likely to be Democrats than Republicans (61 percent Democratic, 39 percent Republican). Female candidates were more likely to come from racially diverse, smaller districts that included a large urban area. Women of color were more likely to run in majority-minority districts: 61.5 percent of African American female candidates, 29 percent of Latina candidates, and 86 percent of Asian American female candidates have done so. Once through the primary, women of color (especially African American women) win general elections at a very high rate. This study also found that states with more women in their legislatures seem far more likely to encourage women to run in congressional primaries. Although having a woman in a top statewide office is not positively related to women's candidacy in congressional primaries, it is correlated with the percentage of women in the state legislature. Finally, this study found evidence of a "burst" effect for women in congressional elections, where "multiple women run for and are elected to office only after the first woman breaks through certain barriers."[21] Other scholars have labeled these breakthrough successes as political innovation districts. "Districts that have innovated by electing women are more likely later to have women candidates and representatives. In these districts, women are encouraged to run, and voters, witnessing the past success of women candidates, appear more ready to vote for them again."[22]

Political scientists Barbara Palmer and Dennis Simon defined "women-friendly" congressional districts and created an index of "women-friendliness" that takes into account partisanship and ideology, geographic factors, race and ethnicity, and socioeconomic factors to explain and predict where women are most likely to seek and win congressional office. Women have an easier time winning in open-seat contests (races without an incumbent), and Palmer and Simon discovered that some open-seat races are even more women-friendly than others.[23] "Female Democratic House members tend to win election in districts that are more liberal, more urban, more diverse, more educated, and much wealthier than those won by male Democratic members of the House; they come from much more compact, 'tonier,' upscale districts than their male counterparts," they write. Palmer and Simon also noted that female Republican House members tend to win election in districts that are, in essence, "less Republican"—less conservative, more urban, and more diverse.[24] These results are true for white women only; the African American women in Congress (all of whom were Democrats until Republican Mia Love was elected from Utah in 2014) come from districts that are similar to those electing African American men. This analysis is particularly useful in explaining the small number of Republican women elected to Congress and the increasing partisan gap among women: "The districts where Republican women are most likely to win the primary because they are female are the districts where they will have a hard time winning the general election because they are Republican." In other words, districts that have elected Republican women are very similar to districts that elect Democratic men. Prior to the 2010 census and reapportionment, the number of women-friendly districts had increased over time, largely as a result of the changing demography of the electorate. As constituencies have grown more racially and ethnically diverse and the proportion of voters with college degrees rises, political opportunities for women have increased.

Every ten years, following the census, congressional districts are redrawn and seats in the House of Representatives are reapportioned to reflect shifts in population. Redistricting following the 2010 census was heavily influenced by the REDMAP project, the Republican State Leadership Committee's strategy to invest in state legislative races to give Republicans the majority and then redraw state and congressional districts to lock in their partisan advantage. This practice of drawing districts to favor one political party, typically the majority party, is known as gerrymandering. It is typically accompanied by two other techniques: "packing," or loading partisans of the opposing party into a few districts, thereby producing a smaller number of seats delivered by more votes than necessary, and "cracking," or breaking up opposing partisan votes across many districts so that it is unlikely that they will have the numbers to win many electoral contests. Analysis of the 2012 elections demonstrates that these practices were highly effective—Democrats received 1.4 million more votes in contests for the House of Representatives, but Republicans won control of the House by a 234 to 201 margin.[25] The same is true for congressional elections in 2014. In Pennsylvania, for example, Democratic candidates attracted 44 percent of the vote, yet Democratic candidates won only five House seats out of eighteen. In other words, Democrats secured only 27 percent of Pennsylvania's congressional seats despite winning nearly half of the votes.[26] The consequence for women's representation is clear. Republican women are less successful at the primary stage in strongly conservative Republican districts, and REDMAP successfully created more Republican districts and concentrated Republican votes in ways that made Republican and Republican-leaning districts more conservative.

Partisan Polarization and the Lack of Republican Women Candidates

There was a time when women in Congress were roughly divided by party, but not anymore. In the 114th Congress, seventy-six women were Democrats and only twenty-eight were Republicans. The gap appears to have its origin in the primaries— Democratic women are more likely to run and far more likely to win their primaries than Republican women.[27] As parties have grown farther apart in ideology and on issue positions, they have become more internally cohesive: Republicans are more conservative and Democrats are more liberal, with little allowance for variation within the party. This puts Republican women considering a run for office in a difficult spot. As political scientist Ronnee Schreiber notes, "Republican women candidates must grapple with how well they 'fit' their party's image and how this affects their party leadership's willingness to support their candidacies."[28] This gap exists at the state level as well—states with more Republican voters have fewer women legislators.[29]

Research by Political Parity found a number of differences between women running in primaries as Democrats and those running as Republicans. First, Republican women lag behind their Democratic counterparts in raising money. Since parties tend not to pick a favorite or provide support during the primary phase of elections, candidates are on their own to tap into networks of donors or political action committees (PACs). Data from 2014 show that Democratic candidates were significantly more likely to raise at least $80,000 during the primary campaign and enter the general election with more cash on hand. Democratic women enjoy more infrastructure in the form of organizations such as EMILY's List. Women's PACs have helped recruit, train, and fund congressional candidates since the early 1970s, and the majority are dedicated to supporting Democratic candidates. There are a few PACs supporting Republican women, including VIEW PAC for congressional elections and Right NOW PAC for state legislative races. Smart Girl Politics and Voices of Conservative women emerged following the 2008 election to give more voice to the concerns of conservative women. Potential donors of both parties are more familiar with EMILY's List than with PACs promoting conservative women. Without broad familiarity and name recognition, an endorsement by a conservative women's PAC does not elicit the same funding signals to donor networks as the more familiar EMILY's List endorsements do for Democrats. Incumbents of both parties attract more donor funding in primaries and general elections, but Democratic women are more likely than Republican women to be incumbents.

There is also evidence that the Republican Party has dedicated less time than Democrats to developing and recruiting women candidates. In 2014, Democrats nominated twice as many women as Republicans did for House, Senate, and governor's races. Despite several high-profile victories, Republican men still account for 90 percent of Republicans in Congress. Joni Ernst, voted into the Senate as a Republican from Iowa, become the first women elected to federal office from that state. Martha McSally became the first Republican woman elected to the House from Arizona, and Utah's Mia Love is the first female African American Republican congresswoman. The challenge is increasing the number of Republican women willing to run in primaries. Although Political Parity's research showed that female Republican candidates were just as ideologically conservative as their male counterparts in 2014, women are often perceived as more moderate than men. As such, Republican Party leaders could have overlooked highly qualified female candidates as the party became more conservative. Additionally, among older men and voters in the South there is still a preference for men as candidates.[30] Increasing ideological coherence may have also driven Maine's Olympia Snowe from the Senate. In an essay published in the *Washington Post*, Snowe wrote that "while our constitutional democracy is premised on majority rule, it is also grounded in a commitment to minority rights," and the modern Senate has become a body where "everyone simply votes with their party and those in charge employ every possible tactic to block the other side."[31] Recruiting and running more women candidates with varied ideological perspectives is essential to engaging centrists.[32]

Incumbency and the Potential of Term Limits

Incumbency poses a serious problem to women challengers—one that could be remedied by term limits. Term limits enforced at the state level (term limits enacted by states for congressional seats were ruled unconstitutional) would require an officeholder to give up his or her seat after having served a preset number of terms in office. While term limits are a relatively recent reform, the effects are already being felt in some state legislatures as longtime incumbents are forced to leave office. Fifteen states have term limits in place for state legislatures; six others either repealed the measure or were forced by the courts to rescind term limits. Initially reformers argued that term-limit-induced retirements would increase the number of open-seat contests, thereby potentially improving the climate for female candidates.[33] This theory was supported by speculative research and research based on simulations and forecasting that suggested that term limits would benefit groups that serve for a limited time anyway (male incumbents serve for an average of 13.8 years, compared to 11.9 years for female incumbents) and that term limits would have the greatest impact in opening leadership positions to women. As Assemblywoman Carol Migden of California, chair of the Appropriations Committee, noted: "Most people don't get [appointed to] Appropriations in six years . . . but I got it in six months. Who says term limits aren't working?"[34] Similar successes in Maine have been reported by the *Wall Street Journal*: "As part of the increased turnover—40 percent of the legislators are freshmen—Maine has its first female House speaker and half of the legislature's leaders are women, the most ever."[35]

Research beyond speculation and modeling became available as the first states (California, Colorado, and Oklahoma) implemented term limits. California became the first state to "retire" an entire assembly of incumbent members in 1996. In evaluating the impact of term limits on women's progress in the California assembly, Stanley Caress cautioned, "term limits do not provide women candidates with an advantage if they already are well represented in a legislature's membership."[36] This turned out to be the case in 2016 in Oklahoma, a state with very few women in the legislature, where half of the women serving were not running again because of term limits. "Term limits have not proven to open up the system," said Cindy Simon Rosenthal, professor at Oklahoma University.[37]

Term limits have also had limited impact in terms of consistently moving women into leadership positions within the chamber. A case study comparing six pairs of term-limited and non-term-limited states concluded: "While it appears that in some states and political climates, such as California, term limits may prove to be very beneficial to women's success and help them capture these positions, in the overall analysis of these states, women seemed to be as successful gaining legislative leadership positions in non-term-limited states as those with limits."[38] Earlier research by the Center for American Women and Politics found that women gained seats through term limits only when there were organized efforts to recruit, support, and fund women candidates for state legislative seats.[39] Since that is the principal challenge of increasing the number of women in office, term limits alone are not likely to yield large increases in women or minority legislators. Gary Moncrief, a political scientist studying legislators, commented, "The logic [of term limits] was impeccable, the empirical evidence not at all. The problem is there aren't as many women running as we expected."[40] Term limits are in effect in fifteen states, while in six other states term limits have been repealed. Overall, the increase in female representation has been smaller in states with term limits than in those without, making term limits an inadequate remedy to the incumbency advantage held by men.

Single-Member Versus Multimember Districts

The electoral system itself is another source of potential bias or discouragement for women candidates. Most people take it for granted that elections are neutral contests, at least as far as the formal rules are concerned. However, political arrangements are not neutral.[41] African Americans and other minority groups have challenged electoral systems, though women have not. Research comparing electoral contests in which representation was chosen through single-member districts versus multimember districts has found that more women ran and more women were elected through multimember systems. Researchers have identified four main reasons women have done better in multimember districts. First, party and community leaders who are under some pressure to respond to interests in a district are more sensitive to including and supporting women candidates. Second, voters may be more comfortable voting for a woman if she is among a slate of candidates than if she is their only representative. Third, running as a woman among a group of candidates may produce some novelty value and attract more publicity and ultimately more votes. Finally, women are more willing to run for office in multimember districts since there is no specific opponent and women would therefore be running on their own qualifications and program ideas.[42]

Political scientists R. Darcy, Susan Welch, and Janet Clark examined state legislatures in the United States in an effort to empirically test the theory that women fare better under some electoral systems than others. Since states are constitutionally free to adopt any election method, there are a variety of experiences to examine. They found that in states that use both single-member and multimember district systems, women ran in greater proportions in multimember districts, and in seventeen out of twenty-one cases the proportion of women running and winning in multimember districts was about double the proportion of those running and winning in single-member districts. Further, in states with all single-member districts, the proportion of women elected was less than in states with multi-member or mixed systems.[43]

THE KEY TO MORE WOMEN IN OFFICE: MORE WOMEN CANDIDATES

The decision to seek political office is not one that can be empirically tested or objectively quantified. It is an intensely personal decision, and studies show that family, friends, and confidants have usually had more of an impact on potential candidates than national parties or other organizational appeals.[44] There are, however, some factors that all candidates take into consideration when deciding whether to seek public office. Many of these factors play differently for men and women. The first and foremost calculation has to be the chance of winning the election.

Perception of Electability

As noted earlier in this chapter, the public believes that women have a tougher time winning elections than men do. This belief is based in part on assumptions that women face discrimination from the election gatekeepers—the party elites responsible for recruitment of new candidates—and that they will experience bias in media coverage and on the campaign trail. Although these perceptions may or may not be true in any single contest or even overall, their power lies in the fact that women may not see themselves as viable candidates and party leaders may not see women as viable candidates. Gender bias in favor of men percolates throughout society. A 2013 Gallup poll found that 35 percent of those surveyed would prefer a male boss, while only 23 percent would prefer a female boss. The preference for a male boss was strongest among females.[45] As early as middle and high school, girls and boys express a preference for male political leadership and are more trusting of peer leadership exercised by males on the student council than they are of females' leadership.[46]

Women in politics have had to walk a tricky line. Urged to smile more and shout less, they have to find a balance between demonstrating a passionate commitment to the issues and being labeled as shrill and emotional. We saw this play out in the 2016 presidential election: Donald Trump said that Hillary Clinton, a former senator and former secretary of state, did "not look presidential," and her personal ambition for the presidency was characterized by Bernie Sanders's campaign manager as threatening to the Democratic Party. Conservative women interested in a candidacy run up against traditional gender role expectations and a masculinized Republican Party.[47] Black women are less likely to be encouraged to run and more likely to be discouraged from running. Once a candidate, they are more likely to face primary competition and encounter challenges raising money relative to black men candidates.[48] For African American women considering a candidacy, it may seem like a high-risk, low-reward proposition.[49] It is against this backdrop of gender bias in society that women assess the likelihood of their electoral success, even as we recognize that stereotypes are easing and the evidence in support of women's full integration into public life is stronger than ever before.

Studies find that women are more likely than men to carefully consider their qualifications for office. Women also often undervalue their credentials, while similarly situated men tend to overestimate their qualifications. These factors contribute to the power of the pipeline thesis, which argues that there are fewer women candidates and office holders because there are not enough women in the pipeline, that is, the group of vetted potential candidates that meet the formal and informal requirements to hold elective office. Although age, citizenship, and residence are the only formal qualifications for most offices, informal requirements might include name recognition, level of education, experience in political office, occupational prestige, and even marital status. They are all taken into consideration in creating the eligibility pool from which viable candidates are drawn, but these informal requirements can be more difficult for women to meet.

The characteristics of electable candidates depend in part on the level of the office in question (national, state, or local). The higher the office, the more experience, education, and professional prestige are expected. Candidates for the US Senate are drawn from a select pool of individuals, many of whom come from corporate boardrooms, the ranks of senior management, prestigious law firms, institutions of higher education, and the US House. Women have only recently broken into this select group, and their numbers remain small: twenty-one women act as CEOs of Fortune 500 companies, women constitute roughly 19.9 percent of board members of Fortune 500 companies and only 18 percent of the partners of large law firms, women make up only 19 percent of full professors at doctorate-granting institutions, and women are only 19.3 percent of the House of Representatives. For some, this suggests that the reason for women's lack of representation in politics rests with their small numbers in the pipeline to office. As more women enter the public sphere overall, so the theory goes, there will be more female candidates and therefore more women elected to office. The pipeline thesis is problematic, most notably because the number of candidates for office has not kept pace with women's advances in the fields most likely to produce political candidates—education, law, business, and community activism.

Political Ambition and Candidate Emergence

> Women, even in the highest tiers of professional accomplishment, are substantially less likely than men to demonstrate ambition to seek office. These results hold regardless of age, partisan affiliation, income and profession.[50]

In addition to being qualified, a potential candidate has to express a desire to run for office. Political ambition has been the subject of considerable scholarship on women candidates, and some of the most significant new research challenges both the eligibility pool and pipeline theses in explaining why so few women seek office in each election cycle. Research by Richard Fox and Jennifer Lawless suggests that the theories may rest on a fundamentally flawed assumption: that women respond to political opportunities in the same ways men traditionally have.[51]

Little attention had been paid to the process by which gender affects men's and women's emergence as candidates for public office until Lawless and Fox published *It Takes a Candidate* in 2005. Lawless and Fox conducted a national survey of 3,700 potential candidates in the eligibility pool (men and women with the same personal characteristics and professional credentials in business, law, education, and political activism) for all levels of office. They found that women overall were less likely than their male colleagues to consider running for office, even though they shared eligibility pool credentials for success and surpassed men in their interest in politics.[52] Although statistically significant gender differences characterized the consideration of running for office, the major differences appeared at the next stage of the process. Men were 50 percent more likely to have actually undertaken any one of a number of steps necessary to mount a campaign (e.g., investigated how to place their name on the ballot, or discussed running with potential donors, party or community leaders, or family and friends). As a result, 7 percent of the men and less than 4 percent of the women from the eligibility pool won an elected position.[53] Lawless and Fox resurveyed more than 2,000 of the original respondents in 2008 and found that "despite the historic events of the last seven years—such as the war in Iraq, frustration with the political process, and the emergence of a more diverse group of political candidates and leaders—overall levels of political ambition for women and men have remained fairly constant."[54]

So what explains women's lack of political ambition? Lawless and Fox investigated a number of factors related to traditional gender socialization, political culture, family responsibilities, and self-perceived qualifications, based on the original survey and interviews. They did not find any empirical support for the traditional barriers to women's entry into politics: women's ambition is not depressed by political culture, family structure, primary caretaking responsibilities, or ideological motivations. Rather, women's self-perceptions of their qualifications for office and the degree to which they receive encouragement to run are central to predicting whether women will seek political office. When women perceive themselves as "very qualified" to hold an elected position, they are significantly more likely to consider running. The impact of self-perceived qualifications on the decision to seek office for women is nearly double that for men. As Senator Susan Collins (R-Me.) said, "Far too often, smart, capable women simply talk themselves out of running for office. . . . [A] woman will think that in order to discuss trade policy, she needs a PhD in economics; a man who sells Hondas considers himself an expert."[55]

Both men's and women's ambition for office increases when they receive encouragement, particularly when it comes from both political *and* nonpolitical sources.

In some cases, simply being asked to run may be an important contributor even to the first thoughts of seeking office. Gary Moncrief and Peverill Squire found that 37 percent of women, compared to 18 percent of men, had never thought of running for office before someone asked them.[56] Despite the impact encouragement has on the decision to run, 43 percent of men, compared to 32 percent of women, had been encouraged to run by a party leader, an elected official, or a political activist. In this respect, "vestiges of patterns of traditional gender socialization in candidate recruitment hinder the selection of women candidates."[57] Laurel Elder also found evidence that role models play an important role in moving women from being potential candidates to actually running.[58] Women were far more conscious than men were of women politicians, and there is evidence that female role models have a unique and positive impact on women's political interest, knowledge, and engagement.

Although women who run for office are just as likely as men to emerge as winners, the winnowing process in candidate emergence described by Lawless and Fox yields a smaller number of female candidates. The pool of candidates who actually run, therefore, looks very different from the eligibility pool of potential candidates. There are a number of interesting implications for these findings. First, looking only at the end of the electoral process is not a very good gauge of the ways in which gender operates in candidate recruitment and elections. The women who ultimately decide to run have already overcome a number of barriers and may, as a result, actually be *more* qualified than the men they compete against. In this respect, the electoral contest may be less gender-neutral than first imagined. Second, relying on the inevitable advance of women in the professions will not be sufficient by itself to produce more women candidates or elected officials. Both the eligibility pool and pipeline theses must be reexamined relative to advancing women from being qualified candidates to actually running for office.

Political Ambition in Young Women

In a study conducted for the White House Project Education Fund, researchers interviewed young women and men to learn more about the pipeline of the future. The study found that young people, particularly women, are extraordinarily dedicated to their communities and to solving problems within them. Although they hold negative attitudes about politics and politicians in general, more than four in ten young adults would consider running for office themselves. Young women are more inclined to get involved in politics if they believe they will be able to accomplish their goals and address issues they care about through political involvement. Young women who have held leadership positions in their school or community and who have been encouraged to seek office are far more likely than other women to express a desire to seek political office. Encouragement has twice the power of any other factor in predicting whether a young woman will consider running for office. Therefore, young women are especially susceptible to being cultivated for elective office.[59]

For many women, an obvious place to gain leadership experience and experience with elections is in university student government. In terms of advantages and barriers to seeking leadership positions, men and women in college are as similarly situated to each other as they will ever be. However, while women are elected as representatives to student government and fill about half of these positions, they are underrepresented in presidential or vice presidential positions. Nearly three-quarters of student government presidents and vice presidents are male. A study found some evidence that having a female student government faculty advisor was positively correlated with females in leadership positions in student government. The ratio of female to male students enrolled on campus was not positively correlated with female student leadership. Because this was a largely descriptive study, the researchers were not able to explore the reasons behind women's under-representation in student government leadership.[60]

One such reason may be that the gender gap in political ambition begins well before a woman is old enough to seek state or national elective office. In 2013 Jennifer L. Lawless and Richard L. Fox surveyed 2,100 college students between the ages of eighteen and twenty-five. Not only did they find a gender gap in political ambition, but they discovered that the size of the gap is comparable to the one they found in the study of men and women already working in pipeline professions.[61] Nearly half (47 percent) of their sample of college students had at least considered the possibility of running for political office, but men were twice as likely as women to have thought about a candidacy "many times," while women were 20 percentage points more likely than men to never have thought about running for office. Twice as many men as women declared a "definite" plan to seek public office (14 percent compared to 7 percent). Compared to working professionals in the eligibility pool from Lawless' and Fox's previous research, the gender gap in political ambition between male and female college students is comparable if slightly larger. Among college students, 57 percent of men and 37 percent of women have at one time considered running for office—a 20-point ambition gap. For working professionals in both the 2001 and 2011 samples, the political ambition gap between men and women was 16 points.[62]

Lawless and Fox's research points to five factors that contribute to the gender gap in political ambition among college students. First, males are more likely than females to be socialized by their parents to think about politics as a career path, even though students of both sexes report growing up in households where politics was discussed and news about current events and politics was central. Still, 40 percent of male college students compared to 29 percent of female college students said they received encouragement from a parent to run for political office. Mothers and fathers were equally likely to encourage boys more than girls to consider running for office and to express a preference for their daughter to pursue a nonpolitical career. Second, while the family plays a critical role in the political socialization of children, the pronounced male advantage extends beyond the family to include teachers, coaches, friends, and extended family members. College men are markedly more likely to receive encouragement to pursue politics from multiple sources.

Third, college men and women appear to have different experiences at school, which shapes their political ambition. Young men are more likely to enroll in a political science class, participate in political activity while in college, and discuss politics with friends. For example, men are significantly more likely to be active in college Democratic or Republican organizations and to have run for a student government office. Women are less likely to surround themselves with politics in college. Fourth, men are more likely to have participated in competitive sports in college (varsity or intramural), to have played sports growing up, and to say that winning is very important. Playing organized sports "either provides an opportunity to develop, or reinforces the propensity toward, a competitive spirit," and these characteristics are related to running for office later in life.[63] Finally, Lawless and Fox found that young women are less likely to believe they are qualified to run for office. When encouraged to think about a time after graduation when they were established in their careers, men were more than twice as likely as women to believe they would be qualified to run for political office. This is quite similar to the results for working professionals. College women also suffered more doubts about whether they possessed the relevant skills for running for office—public speaking, for example. Thirty-five percent of men, compared to 29 percent of women, expressed confidence in their public speaking skills; 22 percent of men, compared to 14 percent of women, said they knew a lot about politics.[64]

A survey of 4,000 high school students found that 89 percent have no interest whatsoever in seeking political office.[65] This leaves 11 percent of the sample potentially interested in public office at some time in the future. These students shared a number of important characteristics—they came from households where politics was discussed and being informed about current events was important. They were also three times more likely to have been encouraged to consider running for office one day by friends or family, and they were more likely to be engaged in extracurricular activities associated with politics. Now consider this 11 percent in light of the findings on the size of the political ambition gap between men and women in college: the winnowing begins prior to college, making the pool of young women interested in political office even smaller. Convincing young men and women that public service is important, attractive, and right for them is a tall order. If women are less likely to be encouraged to consider a life in politics, the prospect of filling the 500,000-plus elected positions in the United States in a way that would approach gender parity is bleak. What might change the negative perception young people hold about politics? One avenue might be the effect of positive political role models.

The Power of Role Models

When women and minorities see people like themselves in office, they become more politically engaged and empowered. The presence of African American and Latino/a officeholders boosts voter turnout and, among Hispanic voters specifically, reduces feelings of political alienation.[66] Christina Wolbrecht and David Campbell examined the influence of women in elected office on adolescent girls' anticipated involvement—their intention to be politically active in adulthood.[67] They hypothesized that the presence of visible female role models makes young women more likely to express an intention to engage in political activity as adults. They found that the presence of more women in office positively corresponds to a smaller gap in anticipated involvement. In explaining the role model effect, they posit the following explanation:

> Specifically, our analysis leads us to suspect that the presence of female role models changes how adolescent girls perceive not gender roles in general or the system as a whole, but simply their own relationship to the political system. Having seen women successfully pursue elective office they are able to envision themselves as active participants in the political process. . . . [T]he presence of role models helps girls make the leap from psychological political engagement to an intention for actual political activity.[68]

In a subsequent study that included adults as well as adolescents, Wolbrecht and Campbell found that the presence of women as members of parliament (MPs) had an impact on the aspirations of women and girls, although the influence was strongest on adolescent girls. This study found that where there are more female MPs, adolescent girls are more likely to discuss politics with friends and to say that they will participate in politics as adults. Adult women are more likely to actually participate and to discuss politics.[69] Finally, they examined the role model effect in the United States, where the proportion of women in the national legislature is very small, by testing the hypothesis that girls are more likely to express an intention to be active in politics when they see women running for high-profile offices. Visibility is the critical component here, and it takes several forms in the analysis—visibility associated with a high-profile office (the presidency, for example), the viability of the candidate, and the extent to which gender is salient in the election. Similar to other research, they find that the more women politicians are made visible (usually by the national media), the more likely adolescent girls are to indicate an intention to be politically active. The role model effect here leads to greater likelihood for political discussion within girls' homes, enriching the overall political socialization environment.[70]

Capitalizing on Hillary Clinton's run for the Democratic nomination in 2007–2008, Nancy Pelosi's election as Speaker of the House in 2007, and Sarah Palin's vice presidential candidacy in 2008, researchers examined whether highly visible national female role models had any effect on anticipated political involvement of young women and men.[71] They also considered the role model effect at the state level to see if female candidates for governor and US Senate in 2006 increased the anticipatory political behavior of young people. In every case, the effect was conditioned by partisanship and ideology. Young women expressed higher levels of anticipated political involvement relative to men during the period corresponding to the election of Nancy Pelosi as Speaker and Hillary Clinton's candidacy for the 2008 Democratic nomination. However, the statistically significant role model effect associated with Pelosi and Clinton was limited to liberal women and Democratic women. There was also an increase in anticipated political involvement among conservative women associated with Palin's vice presidential candidacy, but there was no evidence of a Palin role model effect on other groups of young women (Republican, Democratic, or liberal). At the state level, there was evidence of a role model effect from women campaigning for governor and US Senate on both young women and young men. For young men, there was a positive effect if there was also congruence in ideology, but for young women, the positive effect did not require a shared ideology or party. In sum, high-profile women candidates have the potential to increase political participation among young women and to a lesser degree among young men. As we have observed repeatedly, context matters, and any effect is the product of the interactions between gender, partisanship, and ideology.

The results of these studies pose a kind of chicken-and-egg problem. The presence of more women officeholders and more visible and viable female candidates provides role models that in turn make it more likely that young women will discuss politics in the present and plan for a political life of engagement in the future. In 2016, for example, a national online poll conducted by the *New York Times* found that Hillary Clinton's candidacy prompted a quarter of young women ages fourteen to seventeen to say they were more likely to seek positions of political leadership.[72] The role model effect persists across nations, racial and ethnic groups, and age. Officeholders who are women of color have a distinctive effect on encouraging other minority females to engage with politics and run for office.[73] Therefore, we would expect that over time, the remaining gap in various forms of political engagement beyond voting that still persist between males and females would close. However, to get girls involved, there have to be more women political role models. As we have noted throughout this chapter and Chapter 3, increasing the number of women politicians in the United States has been a long, slow, incremental process. There exist institutional mechanisms such as electoral gender quotas that would more rapidly increase the number of visible female role models, but they have not

Box 4.1 – Point of Comparison

The Power of Positive Discrimination: Electoral Quotas to Advance Women in Office

Throughout the book, we have used the term discrimination in a negative context to refer to the ways in which women are treated unequally because of their sex or gender, usually resulting in some identifiable harm. But in some countries, positive discrimination in the form of electoral gender quotas has resulted in a greater share of political representation for women. Its use is widespread, with 110 countries employing gender quotas in some form, whether voluntary, legislative, or through reserved seats. Quotas work—Senegal doubled the number of women serving in parliament through the adoption of quotas in 2012.[1]

All electoral systems employ some kind of quotas. While we do not have gender quotas in the United States, we do have quotas intended to reflect population density and geographic diversity. Gender quotas are designed to enhance women's participation and representation. "Gender quotas ensure that women constitute a specific number or percentage of the members of a body, be it a candidate list, a parliamentary assembly, a committee or the government."[2] The quota system places the burden of recruitment not on the individual woman but on those who control the recruitment process. When quotas are effectively implemented, the proportion of women in politics increases rapidly. Even when quotas are temporary measures, women are elected at higher rates following their removal.[3]

There are different types of gender quotas. The primary distinction is between constitutional (e.g., Nepal, the Philippines, and Uganda) and legislative (e.g., Belgium, Bosnia-Herzegovina, Serbia, Sudan, and many parts of Latin America) quotas, which are officially mandated for all political parties participating in elections, versus voluntary political party quotas (e.g., Argentina, Bolivia, Ecuador,

been seriously considered in the United States. Thus, the factors that influence a woman's decision to stand for election, including recruitment strategies by political parties, become all the more crucial.

Political Parties: Allies in Recruiting Women?

Political parties serve a unique role in recruiting potential candidates to run in primary elections, where voters select one candidate to represent their party in the general election. Scholars have long suspected that party leaders are biased against women, but research to back up those suspicions has produced mixed results. Denise

Germany, Italy, Norway, and Sweden), which are designed to guarantee the nomination of a certain number or proportion of women. A "zipper"-style system alternates an equal number of women and men on a party list. "Double quotas" (used in Belgium and Argentina) ensure that women are not relegated to the bottom of party lists. Quotas can be introduced at any level of the political system—federal, national, regional, or local. Gender quotas may apply to the number of female candidates proposed by a party for election, or they may take the form of reserved seats in the legislature. Quotas can also be "gender-neutral" in the sense that they merely specify that neither gender should occupy more than 60 percent and no less than 40 percent of the seats, for example.

Although electoral gender quotas have been very effective in rapidly increasing the share of representative seats held by women in diverse settings, they are controversial for a variety of reasons. Quotas represent a shift from one kind of equality to another—from "equal opportunity" or "competitive equality" to "equality of result." Thus the idea of quotas can appear in conflict with other values such as fairness, competence, and individualism. Gender quotas are most easily introduced in proportional representation electoral systems, but they have been successfully introduced in some mixed systems or even majority systems.

For Critical Analysis

In the United States, the word *quota* carries a number of negative connotations because it is perceived to be in conflict with values associated with individualism, but is it? Consider that quotas require a political party to take seriously all likely candidates and not those they are most comfortable with or those who have stood for prior election. The United States has yet to elect more than 20 percent women to the Congress, yet the world average is 22.8 percent and the average for the Americas is 27.7 percent. The United States would have to elect another fifty women to achieve our region's average. Why not try quotas? What do you see as the advantages and disadvantages?

Baer calls political parties the missing variable in women and politics research.[74] Research using party financial contributions to candidates as a proxy measure of party support for women candidates has found no evidence of bias.[75] Bias, however, was detected in a study conducted by David Niven in which both county-level party chairs and potential women candidates were interviewed about their experiences and preferences.[76] Niven hypothesized that because in some states as many as 97 percent of county-level party chairs are male, male attitudes toward potential women candidates may take the form of assumptions about women as a group. This phenomenon is known as the outgroup effect. A prior study of male and female state legislators found some evidence of the outgroup effect. Younger, less experienced males were encouraged by the party to run for office, while only those women who had extensive party experience and a strong background were considered acceptable candidates. In other words, party elites judged males on their potential, but not females. In interviewing potential women candidates, Niven discovered that 64 percent of those who ran for state legislative or congressional seats had experienced some form of discrimination at the hands of party leaders. Niven found support for the claim that this perception of bias was real, and he attributed its cause to the outgroup effect. Party elites consistently recruited and preferred potential candidates they judged most similar to themselves. This is significant because 85 percent of the same women reported that they would not seek higher office if their party was unsupportive.

Other studies have found that in recruiting candidates for office, party elites tend to look for candidates similar to themselves in order to ensure shared values.[77] Since women are seen as part of the "other" group, they do not pass the similarity test during the initial screening. Another phenomenon explored by these studies is the distribution effect—that is, the way men and women are distributed across jobs and occupations results in abstractions about the sexes in general. As a result, men are judged more likely to succeed based on the prevalence of men in occupations viewed as feeders for political office. Women experience this bias in a number of different contexts, such as being chosen as candidates only for unwinnable contests while being overlooked for races in which the party has a good chance of winning the seat. In 1974, when Barbara Mikulski first ran, unsuccessfully, for the US Senate, she told a television audience that Maryland's Democratic Party appeared "very happy to support a woman against someone who they thought couldn't be beat . . . [It was] 'Okay, good old Barb. . . . Let her take the nosedive for the party.'" But when the seat seemed to be winnable, "like most women candidates, I was not considered a good investment."[78]

In a 2006 study of negative recruitment at the state legislative level, researchers found additional evidence that political elites continue to value men's political leadership more than women's. In this case, although both men and women received encouragement, women were significantly more likely than men to receive a negative response to their prospective candidacies. In particular, men receive encouragement from political elites to run in favorable districts (races their party is likely to win) and discouragement from political elites to run in unfavorable districts (races their party is unlikely to win), while women receive the opposite message. Unfortunately, women were more apt than men to value the input they received from party elites.[79]

Political scientist Kira Sanbonmatsu analyzed how party affiliation affects the recruitment of women to run for the lower houses of state legislatures.[80] She found that the incentive structure for women candidates differs for Democrats and Republicans. This suggests that there is not a single path to office, but rather paths that vary by party. The differential roles that political parties play in recruiting women to office are based on distinctly different eligibility pools and opportunity structures. Sanbonmatsu found that the traditional party organization serves as a barrier for both Republican and Democratic women; however, when there is a Democratic majority in the lower house, Democratic women candidates are negatively affected, while Republican women are not. Democratic women are less likely to enjoy party support during a primary, regardless of region, turnover, and legislative professionalism. This study suggests that in situations where it is difficult for the party to find candidates, they may actively seek women to run. When seats are competitive, on the other hand, "the party role may be to referee political ambition rather than cultivate it, and the party may be less likely to seek out women candidates."[81] Thus, not only do men and women approach the decision to run differently, as Fox and Lawless found, but women's experiences with party gatekeepers may differ depending on their party.

In US congressional primaries, candidates are required to act as entrepreneurs, building a following among likely voters, raising money, creating a campaign organization, and designing a winning strategy. Even though primaries are designed to winnow the field to one candidate in each party competing in the general election, political party organizations play a very small role in contemporary primary contests. Political parties tend not to provide resources in primary campaigns, creating a "candidate-centered" model that may pose additional challenges for women. A recent study of primaries for the US House of Representatives found no evidence of widespread, aggregate bias against women candidates.[82] However, that does not mean party primaries are gender neutral. Women constituted only 8 percent of the total House candidates during the period under study (2,648 women). Eighty-seven percent of all primary races were exclusively male, while 12 percent included one woman (1 percent included more than one woman). Women running in congressional primaries are disproportionately Democrat. The study's authors attribute this party imbalance to several factors, chief among them that voters perceive female candidates as more liberal than male candidates (regardless of party), giving Democratic primary contestants an edge with partisan Democrats but disadvantaging Republican women among primary partisans, who tend to come from the party's more conservative base. There is some evidence that Democratic Party activists are more active in identifying and recruiting women to run, in addition to the direct participation of Democratic national political action committees and political organizations (EMILY's List, for example) that are more active than their Republican counterparts.

Overall, women win primaries at rates comparable to men (57 percent of the time for women, 59 percent of the time for men). Republican men tend to win more often than Republican women (63 percent win rate for men, 60 percent for women). Women face more crowded primaries and draw more challengers when they compete for reelection as incumbents. In all Republican primaries with a woman, the mean number of candidates is 3.9, while in Republican contests with-out a woman candidate, the mean number of candidates is only 2.2. The same pattern holds for Democrats—the mean number of candidates in a primary contest in which a woman competes is 4.3, compared to a mean of 2.5 for con-tests without a woman candidate. Female incumbent House members draw more competition from within their own party and in the other party's primary, and a female incumbent is more likely to draw a female challenger into the other party's primary contest. This may have some negative consequences over time—there is no progress toward increasing women's overall representation if female candidates replace only female officeholders. Finally, the overall number of women enter-ing congressional primaries has decreased over time. "Taken together, our results suggest that primary elections are not gender neutral," researchers conclude. "And it is likely that these primary election dynamics affect the initial decision to run for office."[83]

GENDER AND THE CAMPAIGN EXPERIENCE

Women who decide to seek public office know that they will face tough opposition in a primary or a general election, or maybe both. And yet women candidates are still sometimes unprepared for the level of combat a campaign entails. Nancy Pelosi, representative from California, has warned women, "Don't think of this as some League of Women Voters type of thing to do. It's brutal. It's tough. You are going for power. It's never been just given away. It's highly competitive trying to take power, and as long as you understand that and are ready to take a punch square in the face, then you'll love it."[84] Having made the decision to run for office, a woman has to mount a campaign for a primary or general election. Women are strategic about where, when, and how they run for office.[85] We know that women who run win their elections at the same rate as their male counterparts in politics. This good news is tempered by the fact that women are less likely than men to be candidates—they are less often recruited by their party to run, less likely to have their political ambitions encouraged by family and friends, and less confident in their own skills, abilities, and qualifications. A woman who declares herself a candidate for political office has already overcome a significant number of obstacles before the campaign begins.

In this section we will examine women's campaign experience. Fortunately, the days of outright voter hostility to women candidates are largely over. Hayes and Lawless found in *Women on the Run* that, at least in US House races, "voters' views of candidates are shaped almost entirely by long-standing party attachments, leaving little room for sex to matter."[86] And yet when Hillary Clinton was asked to compare the sexism in the 2016 presidential campaign with that of the 2008 primaries, she described it as "less virulent" but said that she still encountered people on the rope lines who told her, "'I really admire you, I really like you, I just don't know if I can vote for a woman for president.' I mean, they come to my events and then they say that to me."[87] Campaigning while female is still an experience worth examining.

Media Attention and Campaign Advertising

Press coverage of candidates is a crucial component of elections. "Because a small proportion of the electorate has the opportunity to meet candidates in person, voters rely on news coverage—and other forms of mass media, such as paid advertising—in forming their opinions of those running for office."[88] What, if any, responsibility does the media bear for women's underrepresentation in politics? Studies conducted in the 1990s found that male candidates received more total coverage and that the coverage was more substantive; the higher the office, the greater the gender discrepancies in coverage.[89] One study employing an experimental design that manipulated media coverage patterns in hypothetical news articles found that candidates whose coverage followed "female candidate" patterns were judged by voters as less electable and found to have weaker leadership skills than candidates receiving "male candidate" press coverage.[90]

Studies in the last decade find little to no difference in the *amount* of coverage male and female candidates receive, particularly in gubernatorial or US Senate races. However, some research indicates that there is still a difference in the *type* of coverage. Employing the lens of intersectionality, Orlanda Ward treated women of color who were running for office, including blacks, Latinas, Middle Eastern Americans, and Asian Americans, as a "political category" to examine the frequency and tone of press coverage as well as the explicit foregrounding of female candidates' gender in the 2012 general elections.[91] Ward found that minority women candidates attract less coverage than their white counterparts, and the coverage they do receive is significantly more likely to focus on their gender. Similarly, Sarah Gershon looked at press coverage in congressional campaigns and found that being a woman or minority alone did not negatively impact coverage; "however, faced with the 'double barrier' of race and gender, minority congresswomen often receive more negative and less frequent media coverage than all other representatives."[92] Not only are minority women candidates disadvantaged, but voters in their districts are denied important information as a result of this media bias. All women running for office are still more likely than men to receive coverage of their appearance, personality, and marital status than men.[93]

The media's focus on women's appearance, clothing, and personality traits are closely connected with impressions of leadership ability. In 2016, Theresa May became prime minister of Great Britain as a result of Brexit, Britain's referendum on membership in the European Union, and David Cameron's resignation. An article in the *New York Times* describing May's working style as a "'safe pair of hands,' not flashy and even dull" also notes that May has "made a calculated effort to show some inner life and spark by her choice of clothes, especially her kitten-heeled animal-print shoes." In defense of her choice of clothing, May remarked, "You can be clever and like clothes."[94] In a satirical nod to the press's obsession with Hillary Clinton's pantsuits, the headline for an article by Jenni Avins in *Quartz* in 2016 declared, "Hillary Clinton's Husband Wore a Fetching Pantsuit to Honor Her Nomination for US President."[95] Avins wrote, "Bill's stately-but-approachable appearance and middle-of-the road fashion choices make him a terrific candidate for the supporting role of first spouse of the United States. He may lack current first lady Michelle Obama's upper arm strength, but he makes up for it with a nice head of hair." It is funny precisely because it hews so closely to the tone and tenor of fashion coverage of women in politics. When Sarah Palin endorsed Donald Trump's candidacy, the press reported that she did so wearing a "sparkly Milly beaded silk bolero jacket" that "sold out soon after, despite its $695 price tag."[96] Molly Ball, a writer for the *Atlantic*, argued that it is not sexist to describe women politicians' clothes: "We have gone from a world in which Hillary Rodham Clinton strove to conform to gender norms by wearing headbands and baking cookies to one where she proudly declares herself a 'pantsuit aficionado.' The evidence does not support declaring any descriptive writing about female candidates off-limits. . . . Sometimes, a skirt suit is just a skirt suit."[97]

Dealing with the press is one of several campaign activities that can depress women's political ambition for office. Several organizations are dedicated to identifying sexist coverage and advising women candidates on how to handle press attention. The "Name It, Change It" project monitors press coverage and documents sexist treatment.[98] The campaign encourages women to call out sexism when they experience it, and there is some evidence that acknowledging mistreatment leads to positive change. However, calling out sexism can lead some to charge that female candidates are just playing the "woman card."[99] In raising questions about Hillary Clinton's qualifications for the presidency, Donald Trump said, "Frankly, if Hillary Clinton were a man, I don't think she'd get 5 percent of the vote. The only thing she's got going for her is the woman's card, and the beautiful thing is women don't like her."[100] The Clinton campaign effectively turned the tables with her retort: "If fighting for women's health care and paid family leave and equal pay is playing the woman card, then deal me in." Clinton also raised $2.4 million for her campaign in the three days following Trump's remark.

Campaign advertising through paid television ads and social media such as Twitter and Facebook allows candidates more control over their message. It is one of the main ways candidates communicate their message to voters—by one estimate nearly $4.4 billion was spent on television ads in the 2016 presidential contest. Shauna Shames found that female candidates for US House, US Senate, and governorships used "femininity" strategically as a marker of "outsider" status.[101] Other research finds that candidates of either gender can appeal to women voters with identity-based ads. Female candidates are able to prime female voters' gender identity. Identity appeals by male candidates persuade female voters of their positive traits, though male voters are generally unaffected by these appeals.[102] Hillary Clinton used this type of advertisement to effectively portray herself as a fighter for working women in the primaries against Bernie Sanders. In a series of ads, a working woman from an early primary or caucus state was featured discussing an issue that Hillary Clinton promised to address if elected, including equal pay for women, college affordability, and stagnant middle-class incomes. "The top 25 hedge fund managers make more than all the kindergarten teachers in America combined," Clinton says in one of the ads, which featured a teacher named Cheryl. "Join the fight for higher incomes. Join the fight for Cheryl."[103]

In the general election against Donald Trump, Clinton's ads took a more negative approach but were still designed to prime female voters' gender identity. A thirty-second ad the campaign debuted at the end of September 2016 showed girls and young women looking in the mirror as they hear Donald Trump describe various women as "fat," a "slob," and one who "ate like a pig." It ends with a woman's voice asking: "Is this the president we want for our daughters?" In addition to strategizing on the message, candidates and campaigns also carefully consider the voice that delivers the message. A study of men and women as voiceover announcers in political advertising found that 62.7 percent of political ads featured a voiceover by a man, while only 27.7 percent featured a woman's voice in narration.[104] Women's voices have been found to be more effective when discussing women's issues such as child care, health care, and education, and candidates tend to use female voiceovers when targeting women voters.

Negative campaign ads are now an accepted strategy for many candidates, but they can still be treacherous territory for women. In some circumstances, however, women may stand to benefit with voters by using negative ads. When a female candidate uses a "male" issue as the basis of an attack on her male opponent, she is judged more competent on the issue.[105] This suggests that negative advertising could be an effective tool to neutralize the disadvantages caused by stereotypes. Research suggests that women are more constrained than men in deciding whether or not to use negative advertising: "Women may adjust their strategy in response to citizens' stereotypes about preferred feminine behavior."[106] There is also a gender gap in relation to a number of other campaign tactics. In a study of 4,000 candidates at the local, state, and federal levels, candidates were asked whether they believed it was acceptable, unethical, or questionable to engage in a range of campaign strategies, including making factually true statements out of context, attacking an opponent in an attempt to discourage that candidate's supporters from turning out to vote, and engaging in push polling (calling voters under the pretense of taking a survey, but attacking the opponent instead). The gender gap widens when the office is higher, but in all cases women candidates were significantly more likely to oppose each of the activities.

As the number of women in competitive races has increased, so has the likelihood that women are the target of negative campaigning. Using an experimental design, researchers explored whether negative commercials aimed at women candidates had the same effect as negative commercials attacking men candidates. Subjects were presented with a television commercial for a US Senate candidate, based on a real 2006 race in North Dakota but with the candidate names and state changed so that respondents could not hold any preexisting attitudes about the candidates. Then they were asked to assess the candidates' traits and competence and ultimately to make a vote choice. Overall, the researchers found that negative commercials are far less effective at depressing evaluations of female candidates compared to male candidates. "When exposed to identical attacks on a candidate, citizens are more receptive to critical comments made about a male candidate compared to the exact same criticisms leveled at a female candidate. In other words, the gender of the candidate conditions people's reactions to negative messages about political candidates. . . . [T]he presence of gender stereotypes appears to soften the blow of negative attacks, leading people to discount attacks on women candidates, compared to identical attacks on male candidates."[107]

The Pressure to Raise Money

When asked what would prevent them from seeking political office, young men and women listed raising large sums of money for the campaign as the number one barrier.[108] Likewise, in the Lawless and Fox study, "soliciting campaign contributions" ranked second only to "potentially having to engage in a negative campaign" as a campaign activity so unpleasant that it would deter the respondents from running for office (29 percent of women versus 21 percent of men, a statistically significant gender difference). Women are not equally represented in prestigious companies that lead to large single donations, nor have they traditionally attracted equal amounts of PAC money. Conventional wisdom suggests that women have had a harder time than men in raising and spending money to get themselves elected to public office. But, similar to the perceptions of other forms of bias in the electoral system, this conventional wisdom is no longer borne out by empirical fact.

The 1990s appear to mark the turning point in women's prowess as fund-raisers. Political scientist Barbara Burrell studied major-party nominees for the US House over a number of years and found that as early as 1972, female candidates for the House began raising and spending nearly as much money as male candidates. In House races between 1974 and 1980, a period that saw the number of women candidates increase dramatically, women raised and spent about 75 percent of what men raised and spent. In 1988, women raised 119 percent of what men raised, and in 1992, they raised 111 percent and spent 108 percent of what men raised and spent.[109] A study of the 1994 US House and Senate elections showed no disadvantage for women candidates.[110] Although there is less scholarship on women candidates as political fund-raisers than on many other aspects of campaigns, the most recent studies have tended to find that women in general elections raise as much as men in similar contexts (level of office, challenger versus incumbent, etc.). A candidate's ability to raise money is critical in attracting the support of national party leaders and interest from political action committees and other affinity organizations. Women's interest organizations have been quick to recognize the value of early money to the success of women's candidacies: a PAC called Ready for Hillary began fund-raising on Clinton's behalf before she announced her 2016 candidacy.

The Women's Campaign Fund, founded in 1974, and the PAC associated with the National Women's Political Caucus were among the first to dedicate money specifically to electing women. In 1978, the National Organization for Women formed NOW-PAC, a PAC that contributes to both men and women based on their "feminist credentials."[111] EMILY's List (Early Money Is Like Yeast—that is, "it makes the dough rise"), founded by Ellen Malcolm in 1985, was one of the first partisan PACs. It supports prochoice Democratic women who have been carefully screened and judged to be strong candidates. Women have traditionally had the hardest time raising early money that in turn allows them to purchase television airtime for advertisements and increase their name recognition as well as ultimately their donor base. EMILY's List pioneered the practice of bundling, an effective and creative way to circumvent the Federal Election Campaign Act's $5,000 limit on PAC contributions to a single candidate. Members of EMILY's List write three checks of at least $100 to three candidates that have been vetted and their contests thoroughly analyzed by EMILY's List staff. Through bundling, candidates receive an envelope full of checks written directly to them, rather than to the organization, that can total far more than the $5,000 limit.

The first high-profile test for a women's PAC came in 1986, when Congresswoman Barbara Mikulski of Maryland decided to seek a vacant Senate seat by challenging a popular congressman and an incumbent governor in the Democratic primary. Donations from EMILY's List have been credited with allowing her to pay for an early poll that provided solid evidence of her support throughout the state. This evidence made it possible for her to raise additional funds and eventually win the primary and the Senate seat. Since that race, EMILY's List has become one of the largest and most powerful PACs in the nation. EMILY's List has evolved from a primarily mail and paper check operation to an online and social-media-savvy operation. In 2010, the first election cycle in which super PACs were permitted, EMILY's List launched a super PAC called WomenVote!, which spent $3.6 million in 2010, nearly $8 million in 2012, and more than $23 million in 2016 in competitive races in which EMILY's List had endorsed a candidate. The organization has had an 84 percent success rate in races where it invested funds in the three cycles. Since its founding, EMILY's List has helped to elect more than 100 prochoice Democratic women to the House, 19 to the Senate, 11 to governors' seats, and hundreds of women to state and

IMAGE 4.2: *EMILY's List founder and past president Ellen Malcolm (second from left) appears with Democratic candidates (L-R) Elizabeth Warren, Debbie Stabenow, Deborah Roos, Tammy Duckworth, Katie McGinty, Jeanne Shaheen and Val Demmings at the 2016 Democratic National Convention.* Source: Paul Zimmerman/Getty Images For EMILY's List.

local office. EMILY's List is also one of the largest financial resources for minority women seeking federal office.[112] In the 2014 cycle, the group reported more than $8 million in federal election spending to the Federal Election Commission.

Republican women responded by forming Women in the Senate and House (WISH) to support prochoice Republican candidates. WISH was then countered by an establishment group (formed by wives whose husbands were serving in the Bush administration) called the Republican Women's Leadership Network (WLN). The WLN's philosophy is more in keeping with the Republican Party's stand on abortion.[113] Another recent prolife addition is the Susan B. Anthony List, which reportedly distributed $15.25 million to prolife female candidates in the 2014 cycle. In 2016, three women founded Women Vote Trump, a super PAC committed to raising $30 million in support of Donald Trump's election as president.

National PACs have now spawned local and statewide affiliates dedicated to raising money for women who seek all levels of office. For example, the Los Angeles African American Women PAC (LAAAWPAC) was organized in 1990 as the first African American women's PAC in California. The organization supports women running for office, sponsors community forums, provides information on complicated ballot propositions, and awards the Power PAC Pioneer Award to women who make a difference in their community.[114] In 2009, the Center for American Women and Politics identified forty-eight PACs and donor networks that either give money predominantly to women candidates or have a predominantly female donor base (not including issue PACs)—fifteen with a national focus and the remaining thirty-three with a state- or local-level focus.[115] The number is likely much larger now, but there is no single source that compiles information about women's donor networks and PACs.

Super PACs have attracted the largest donors among women. In 2012, thirty-one women made it onto the list of the top 150 donors and gave super PACs a combined $70 million. Hillary Clinton raised a higher percentage of her campaign funds from women than any major-party presidential candidate in history, while Donald Trump raised less from women than any other major party's nominee.[116] In addition to raising and contributing money, many of these groups also engage in recruiting, training, and providing other forms of aid to female candidates. Efforts of such magnitude, largely made by women on behalf of women, illustrate the importance of electoral politics to the larger movement for women's equality.[117]

Voter Gender Stereotypes and the Campaign Experience

We now return to look at the conventional wisdom that gender stereotypes affect campaigns and voters employ gender stereotypes in making judgments about candidates relative to the office they seek. Female candidates, so the story goes, face an impossible task in that they must convince voters that they possess stereotypical masculine traits (toughness, competence, confidence) while not straying too far from accepted stereotypes about female traits (empathy, compassion, modesty). The use of stereotyping by voters to render a decision increases within three contexts. First, stereotyping is more common when a voter must make a decision but lacks information and has neither the time nor the motivation to get that information. Because many women are newcomers to politics and more likely to be challengers, voters are more likely to have information about male candidates and to rely on gender as a relevant cue. Second, stereotyping is more likely to occur when individual characteristics, such as gender, are especially salient. If, for example, a pool of candidates includes only one woman, gender stereotypes will be more prevalent and will exert more influence on a voter's ultimate decision. Finally, when voters are exposed to stereotyping in media accounts of a campaign, they are more likely to pay attention to gender characteristics and to interpret new information about the candidate in ways that are consistent with their preexisting gender stereotypes.[118] Researchers have demonstrated how gender stereotypes lead voters and the media to view men differently from women and therefore to judge them differently within a political context. As women candidates have become less of a novelty over the past two decades and as their presence in politics has normalized (particularly now that a woman has been a major-party contender for the presidency), the role of stereotypes is getting a fresh look. Because scholars disagree on some important points, this section of the chapter will present conflicting evidence.

As women entered politics in the 1990s in large enough numbers to study, researchers found that voters' gender stereotypes had primarily negative implications for women candidates, particularly those running for higher national office. Voters preferred male characteristics in candidates seeking higher office. Policy areas in which males were typically judged more competent, including the military and economics, held greater importance in voters' calculations of competence the higher the level of office. Competence in female policy areas, such as alleviating poverty, education, issues affecting children, and health care, were correspondingly viewed less favorably the higher the level of office. These findings may explain, in part, why voters expressed the most support for women candidates at state and local levels but were slower to back a woman for president or vice president during this period.[119]

For candidates in the 1990s and 2000s, navigating the terrain of voter attitudes shaped by gender stereotypes was difficult. Women interested in the highest national offices had to convince voters of their atypicality by emphasizing their "male traits," particularly in the years immediately following the September 11, 2001, terrorist attacks. This was not easy to do, nor are candidates in total control of the images and message presented to voters. In many electoral contexts, women may have benefited from emphasizing stereotypically "feminine" traits to differentiate themselves from other candidates, especially when there is a benefit to being the "outsider."[120] These circumstances include an anti-incumbent mood among voters, an electoral context dominated by political scandal, and economic conditions favorable for government expansion in education and health care. Under these circumstances, women can turn gender and gender stereotypes to their electoral advantage by running "as women."[121]

The political climate leading up to the elections in November 2008—wars in Iraq and Afghanistan, a "war on terror," and a shaky economy—did not look promising for women. When the 2008 presidential nomination contest began in 2007, it looked as though war and national security concerns would dominate the debate and shape voter choice. Hillary Clinton, the only woman in the presidential race for either party, had to anticipate how gender and voter gender stereotypes might work relative to these issues. Since we know from social-psychological research that women are perceived as "communal" (warm and selfless) but not very "agentic" (assertive, instrumental, capable of decision-making) and men are assumed to possess the opposite set of qualities, any woman seeking the presidency had to convince voters of her competence and leadership abilities without appearing so agentic that she is labeled insufficiently feminine.

The **Goldberg paradigm** refers to bias in perceptions of men's and women's behavior relative to stereotypical expectations. When women occupy a male-dominated role (such as politics) and behave "like men" within that domain, they are rated lower than their male counterparts, particularly when males are doing the rating.[122] The presidency, as the highest national office, is presumed to require agentic leadership. Thus, a woman seeking that position must walk a very fine line lest voters punish her for appearing "too masculine" at the very same time she is auditioning for the most masculine job in politics. Political scientist Susan Carroll observed that while Hillary Clinton's 2008 campaign strategy emphasizing experience, strength, mastery of policy details, and a readiness to "lead on day one" was the only choice open to her, given what we know about voter gender stereotypes, it left her vulnerable to critics who labeled her cold and not sufficiently "human." In a further irony, although women's candidacies are usually associated with outsider status, and female candidates in general tend to do well in political environments ripe for change (e.g., conditions of corruption, voter mistrust or dissatisfaction), Hillary Clinton lost the nomination to another candidate who "embodied change in his physical appearance and also embraced the mantle of change"—Barack Obama, an African American candidate with the campaign slogan "Change we can believe in."[123] Marie Wilson put it this way: "He's the girl in the race. Clinton came out tough; she voted for the war. Obama came out as the person bringing people together and offering messages of hope and reconciliation."[124]

Gender stereotypes further constrained Clinton in her ability to directly address her 2002 vote to authorize the Iraq War. By the Iowa caucus in January 2008, voters' fears of another terrorist attack had transformed into anger over the mounting human and material costs of the Iraq War, and they were starting to feel the effects of the declining economy. "A number of feminists and progressives felt that they could not support Hillary Clinton in the 2008 election because of her vote to authorize the Iraq War; so long as gender stereotypes persist, those feminists and progressives are likely to find it very difficult to support not only Hillary Clinton but also any woman who has a serious chance of winning the presidency," observed Carroll.[125] Thus, while there are multiple reasons that Barack Obama clinched the Democratic nomination over Hillary Clinton, it would be hard to say, as commentator Al Hunt did in June 2008, that "gender no longer is a big deal in American elections."

Voters may approach an electoral contest with a distinct preference for male or female candidates.[126] This "baseline gender preference" is a standing predisposition built on gender stereotypes about candidate traits, beliefs, issue competencies, and voter gender. "Individuals who think men are more emotionally suited for politics, who think that men are more likely to take their position on government spending, and prefer men to handle stereotypically male issues are more likely to prefer male candidates," observes political scientist Kira Sanbonmatsu.[127] One of the strongest predictors of preference for a female candidate is voter gender—women prefer female candidates. In addition, individuals who think women are more likely to share their position on abortion are more likely to prefer the female candidate, as are those who think women are better able to handle the issue of Social Security. Sanbonmatsu investigated the link between a general preference for a male or female candidate and vote choice in male-female contests. Using an experimental condition in which

Box 4.2 – Encountering the Controversies of Equality

Impossible Expectations:
Hillary Clinton's Candidacy for the Presidency

When Hillary Clinton conceded the Democratic nomination for president to Barack Obama in 2008, she reassured her supporters that one day a woman would be president. "Although we weren't able to shatter that highest, hardest glass ceiling this time, thanks to you, it's got about 18 million cracks in it," she said. "And the light is shining through like never before, filling us all with the hope and the sure knowledge that the path will be a little easier next time." In 2016, when Hillary Clinton ran again for president, was it easier? Will it ever be easier for a woman running for president?

In one sense, the nation's ambivalence over Clinton's candidacy is about Hillary herself. But as countless essays have commented, she represents the broader disjuncture in our struggle with gender equality. Could there have been another first female major-party nominee? Attacked for her ambition and characterized as unqualified, had she been elected she would have been among the most qualified presidents in the nation's history: only six presidents have also served as secretary of state, and only three have served both as secretary of state and in Congress.[1] The *New York Times*, in endorsing her, said that "voters have the chance to choose one of the most broadly and deeply qualified presidential candidates in history." Even Marco Rubio acknowledged in a Republican debate, "If this is a resume contest, Hillary Clinton is going to be the new president of the United States." But when a woman runs for president, is it ever a resume contest?

Call it the double bind or the business end of an unrelenting double standard, but when women pursue power, they are punished for it. When men seek power, they're perceived as more competent, while women seeking power face "contempt, anger, and/or disgust."[2] Whether negotiating a salary or seeking a promotion, women "caught in the act of asking for power" are not likable. A Google search

respondents were presented with biographies of two candidates running in a hypothetical primary race for the US House of Representatives, Sanbonmatsu asked voters to indicate which candidate they would support. Sanbonmatsu varied the sex of the first candidate to analyze the use of gender stereotypes expressed through the voters' baseline gender preference. When given the chance, voters with a female baseline preference were much more likely to vote for the female candidate than the identical male candidate. When presented with a male-male race, voters with a female baseline preference opted for a "change-oriented" male candidate (arguably on "Hillary Clinton's likability problem" produces close to 35,000 hits. Clinton is most popular when she exercises power, not when she seeks it. And so "Clinton is somehow not allowed to get it quite right; she's either too hard or too soft, too much or too little of a feminist. There's always something wrong, even if the particular something is hard to identify and endlessly open to parsing: her laugh, her voice, her ankles, her hair, her pantsuits, her marriage."[3]

Journalist Rebecca Traister observed in May 2016 about the forthcoming election matchup, "There is an Indiana Jones–style, 'It had to be snakes' inevitability about the fact that Donald Trump is Clinton's Republican rival. *Of course* Hillary Clinton is going to have to run against a man who seems both to embody and have attracted the support of everything male, white, and angry about the ascension of women and black people in America. Trump is the antithesis of Clinton's pragmatism, her careful nature, her capacious understanding of American civic and government institutions and how to maneuver within them."[4] What do women owe Hillary Clinton for her candidacy? A lot, says Emily Bazelon: "Whether or not we vote for Clinton, we all owe her for the unending work and breathtaking determination and sheer stubbornness that got the country to this moment."[5] For author Sady Doyle, saying nice things about Hillary Clinton is a way to "shift the cultural dialogue, to allow for a world where women aren't suffocated or crushed by our expectations of them—a world where Hillary, and every future female President or Presidential candidate, can focus on the task at hand, and not have to climb over a barbed-wire fence of hatred in order to change the world."[6] The historic moment wasn't just about Hillary Clinton, but it would have been impossible without her.

What do you think?

In what ways did sexism shape the 2016 campaign? Will there ever be a time when women candidates are not subjected to misogynistic slogans on T-shirts ("Life's a bitch, don't vote for one" or "Trump that Bitch")? In what specific ways was Hillary Clinton's candidacy for president inevitable and in what ways might it have been an anomaly?

a female characteristic). However, when the change-oriented male candidate was running against a female candidate, these voters chose the woman. "When given a chance to vote for a woman," she concludes, "these voters responded."

Kathleen Dolan examined how voters evaluated women candidates for Congress between 1990 and 2000.[128] In contrast to most studies testing the relevance of candidate gender to vote choice, which generally employ hypotheticals under experimental conditions, Dolan used data from the American National Election Study (ANES) to examine voter candidate evaluations in real elections. She found that gender is less central to the evaluations of congressional candidates over time: "Candidate sex, by itself, is not necessarily the primary influence on evaluations but instead may be interacting with other influences in the electoral environment." Over the six election cycles in Dolan's study, the ways in which voters evaluated women candidates and the patterns of who voted for them and why were not consistent. In some elections, women voters were more likely to support women candidates, but not in others; in some years, issues such as abortion or defense were related to choosing women, but not in all. Dolan concludes that the impact of a candidate's gender is, in part, conditioned by external forces. Two of the most important forces in shaping evaluations of women candidates proved to be political party correspondence and incumbency status—the two main influences in any congressional election, regardless of the gender of one or both candidates. The effects of issues, voter demographics, and the amount of gender information are limited when compared to the more traditional political influences.[129]

Deborah Jordan Brooks, writing in *He Runs, She Runs: Why Gender Stereotypes Do Not Harm Women Candidates*, concludes on the basis of a series of Goldberg experiments pitting identical hypothetical male and female candidates against each other under varied conditions that voters are even-handed in their judgments. She attributes this to the "leaders-not-ladies" theory, which posits that "female candidates will be judged on the basis of good leadership rather than the basis of good femininity, and thus do not face higher standards."[130] This study was conducted after the 2008 election, arguably a turning point for women in politics. Like Hayes and Lawless in *Women on the Run*, Brooks argues that when the media's version of women's campaign experience as negative goes unchallenged, the greatest harm is in dampening political ambition in women considering a run for political office. She argues that when the political elites learn to judge women as leaders first, women will be more likely to be recruited contributing to greater parity in the candidate emergence process. In a similar vein, Kathleen Dolan's book *When Does Gender Matter?* links voters' use of stereotypes in candidate evaluations to actual vote choices. Using a national panel survey from 2010, she finds that women running for legislative office are rarely subject to stereotyping that leads to gender-based discrimination at the polls. Even if voters expressed stereotypes, there was little impact on their vote. Just like in Dolan's earlier study, what mattered most in shaping voter behavior was not gender or stereotypes about gender, but rather party and ideology.[131]

A study by Monica C. Schneider and Angela L. Bos changes the terms under which stereotypes are defined and measured. They argue that female politicians are a group distinct from and significantly different from other females, and thus constitute a subgroup with potentially unique stereotypes. Similarly, it could be that male politicians are distinct from the larger group of men. Their study confirms the existence of unique traits associated with a subgroup of female politicians that differ from traits associated with women generally. However, female politicians are defined more by their deficits than their strengths: "In addition to failing to possess the strengths associated with being women (e.g., sensitive or compassionate), female politicians lack leadership, competence, and masculine traits in comparison to male politicians. They are, however, associated with several negative traits (e.g., uptight, dictatorial, ambitious), although not as highly as anticipated."[132] In short, the authors conclude, female politicians seem to be losing on all counts. This dire finding is tempered somewhat by the discovery that "the stereotypes associated with female politicians are extremely nebulous and lack clarity."

Perhaps the ambiguity expressed in this research is a reflection of the electorate's attempt to come to terms with political gender equality in an electoral arena where women are regular and active participants. The public's reaction to Hillary Clinton's 2016 campaign mirrors that same process. A highly accomplished and experienced candidate, Clinton fought the perception that her success and indeed her candidacy for the highest office were derived from her relationship to two men, both presidents—Bill Clinton and Barack Obama. Although women are a long way from parity as candidates or officeholders, they are no longer a novelty and show no signs of retreating to the sidelines. For some voters, that fact is an uncomfortable truth, while for others it is a sign of tremendous progress. Future advances for women in politics will depend on increasing the number of candidates at all levels of political office and in all aspects of public service.

INITIATIVES DESIGNED TO INCREASE THE NUMBER OF WOMEN CANDIDATES

A number of organizations have undertaken special initiatives to identify, recruit, train, and support women candidates. Since women are less likely than men to self-recruit, these programs are critical to increasing the number of women candidates. Some of these examples are targeted at women still too young to qualify for political office (or even to vote in some cases), but the research reviewed in this chapter makes clear that the gender gap in ambition and confidence begins well before the age of majority. Similarly, minority women may be even more systematically disadvantaged in terms of recruitment, campaign resources, press coverage, and voter stereotyping in ways we are only now beginning to understand. Training expressly designed around issues of intersectionality and differences among minority women have been found to be effective.[133] All women benefit from being identified as qualified for office and mentored to a candidacy. Examples of these diverse initiatives include:

- *IGNITE* was founded in 2010 to build political ambition when girls and young women are forming their identities and aspirations. IGNITE trains young women from high schools, colleges, and universities across the United States under the premise that young women are passionate about improving their communities but may not always understand the role of political leadership in that process. Training teaches young women how to think critically about policy and understand how to make change. IGNITE's network of elected women exposes young women to role models in elected office and provides opportunities for internships and jobs.[134]

- *National Federation of Republican Women Campaign Management School* trains Republican women through a series of two-day courses held throughout the country. The training focuses on developing a strategy and message, raising money, targeting voters, managing volunteers and communications. Similar training for Republican women is offered through state-based *Excellence in Public Service* programs, typically sponsored by a prominent Republican in the state. For example, the program in New Jersey is sponsored and named for Christine Todd Whitman. A message from the former governor articulates the mission of the program: "I firmly believe that government can best serve the interests of its citizens when they are fully represented. The more diversity in the process, the more likely the process will work. Women bring a very different perspective to issues because our life experiences are different, along with our priorities. By expanding the pool of talent, we are able to draw upon more of those experiences to make good policy."[135]

- *Right Women, Right Now* is an initiative of the Republican State Leadership Committee (RSLC) to identify, recruit, and support women candidates nationwide in order to help elect more Republican leaders who better embody the electorate of our country, where women are 53 percent of the voters. Right Women, Right Now offers candidate trainings, mentorship matchings, and digital organizing tools for candidates' campaigns for state-level office. Since its founding in 2012, the organization has elected 229 new women to office and aims to grow the largest caucus of Republican elected women in the country.[136]

- *Higher Heights for America* is headquartered in New York and dedicated to creating a pipeline of black women's leadership. Higher Heights is building a national strategy to mobilize one million black women and $1 million by 2020 in order to harness black women's collective economic and voting power. The organization supports role models through a program called Sistas to Watch and encourages women's candidacies.[137]

- *EMILY's List Political Opportunity Program*, established in 2001, is the EMILY's List training program for female candidates. Reacting in part to the loss of women's representation in legislatures altered by term limits and redistricting, the Political Opportunity Program (POP) is a series of state and local candidate training seminars designed to help women develop a strong fundraising base, pursue critical issue priorities, develop strong communication strategies, form key alliances with local advocacy groups, and build a grassroots network of support that will help women win progressively higher offices. The rationale for POP is tied directly to the Fox and Lawless study's finding that women are less likely than men to view themselves as qualified to run for office and less likely than men to receive encouragement to run for office.[138]

- *The Women's Campaign School at Yale University* is cosponsored by Yale Law School and the Gender Studies Program. Each year the school offers a four-day training session designed to teach a wide range of campaign skills and introduce participants to professionals in the campaign and political arena. The school also offers a regular series of one-day workshops that cover such topics as "Secrets of Successful Fund-raising," "Campaign Message and Strategy," and "Politics: The Uncommon Career Choice," among others.[139]

- *LatinasRepresent*, established in 2014, is a joint initiative of Political Parity and the National Hispanic Leadership Agenda (NHLA). LatinasRepresent was formed to highlight Latina underrepresentation in elected office nation-wide and to increase the number of Latina candidates and public officials. The organization's strategy is based on research that underscores the importance of engaging mentors and role models, strategic targeting, and broader recruiting of Latinas by political parties.[140]

- *Women Under Forty PAC* is a multiparty PAC that supports women under the age of forty who run for state and federal office. Discouraged by the low number of young women in political office, a group of interested women gathered in Washington, D.C., in January 1999 and organized WUFPAC. During the 2000 election cycle, WUFPAC focused on raising money and making contributions to women under forty running for Congress. WUFPAC now supports women seeking seats in their state legislatures. "We're trying to do everything we can to encourage young women to become more interested in politics, take politics more seriously and understand the impact of politics in their lives," says Susannah Shakow, president of WUFPAC. "We need to have more women in the pipeline in order to end up with more women who want to run for Congress."[141]

- *Running Start* was created to empower young women to run for political office. In 2016, Running Start trained its 10,000th participant. A nonprofit, nonpartisan organization, Running Start educates young women about the importance of politics in their lives and provides leadership training: "Our goal is to give young women a running start in politics so that they will run for elected office earlier, climb higher on the leadership ladder, and share more in the decision-making power of this country." Running Start works with high school, college, and young professional women through four programs: the Young Women's Political Leadership Program, Campaign College, Running Start/Walmart Star Fellowship Program, and Path to Politics Seminars.[142]

Box 4.3–Spotlight on the 2016 Election

Future Women Candidates: Will 2016 Mobilize or Paralyze Women's Political Ambition?

Research highlighted in this chapter reinforces the adage "when women run, women win." The key to electing more women to political office lies in convincing more women to become candidates. However, in 2016, Hillary Clinton ran for president as the first woman nominated by a major political party, and she didn't win. Will Clinton's experience serve as a catalyst for women candidates or as more evidence that the political deck is stacked against them?

In 1991 the country watched as an all-male Senate Judiciary Committee grilled law professor Anita Hill over allegations that Supreme Court nominee Clarence Thomas sexually harassed her when they worked at the Equal Employment Opportunity Commission. It was clear that many on the panel did not believe Hill's account, but her story reminded many women of their own experiences in the workplace. "You had people who decided they didn't like what they saw," said Georgetown University professor of government Michelle Swers. "In general in politics, anger is a very motivating factor." The 2016 election, she suggested, "may be another pivotal consciousness-raising event for women, 'deciding the only way to change things is to get into the halls of power.'"[1]

Organizations that recruit, train, and fund women candidates, such as She Should Run and EMILY's List, reported a high volume of interest following the election. "We have heard from women across the country who are raising their hands to be part of the solution," noted Marcy Stech from EMILY's List. On November 29, 2016, She Should Run tweeted, "Since Election Day, @sheshouldrun has seen a 4000%+ increase in the rate of women joining our programs." Political scientist Farida Jalalzai summed up the cautious optimism well: "That does not mean that Trump's election did not deal a big blow, but that it might anger some of us enough that it actually ends up motivating us to heighten awareness of discrimination and take action."[2]

Yet the misogyny on display in the 2016 election and the bitter campaign could have the opposite effect and reduce the number of women willing to run for office in the future. Hillary Clinton was nearly unmatched in experience and qualifications for the presidency, and yet she lost to a man who had never held political office of any kind. Will that feed women's insecurities about their own qualifications? Will the sexism expressed openly throughout the presidential campaign reinforce potential women candidates' perception that the political system is biased against them?

In the weeks immediately after the election, it is likely too soon to know how Clinton's loss and Trump's victory will impact female candidates' emergence, but the midterm congressional elections and state races in 2018 may tell us more.

CONCLUSION

There is a wonderful story from the turn of the century about a Member of Parliament in Britain who welcomed Lady Astor as she took her seat there, the first woman ever to be elected to that body. "Welcome to the most exclusive men's club in Europe," he said with a grin. "It won't be exclusive for long," Lady Astor replied, with an even larger smile. "When I came in, I left the door wide open!"[143]

The assumption underlying this chapter has been, of course, that it is desirable to increase the number of women in office and that this goal can best be accomplished by increasing the number of women candidates who seek office. This assumption may be challenged by those who are happy with the status quo, and so it should be addressed. Women should participate fully as citizens and rulers within government for a variety of important reasons. The quality of representation suffers when women are excluded from elective office or the political opportunity structure is such that only a particular type of woman is elected. Men and women hold different views on issues and exhibit different policy preferences for dealing with public problems. When women are absent from legislative bodies or executive administrations, their perspective is also absent, robbing the country of valuable insight. As long as society is gendered, women will live a different life from men. Compared to men, women are more likely to earn less money, to work in hourly wage jobs and in part-time rather than full-time positions, and to rely on government assistance to feed, house, and educate their children. They are less likely than men to carry health insurance for themselves or their children. Priorities born of these experiences play an important part in establishing the priorities for a nation.

Women have been candidates for political office in numbers large enough to systematically study since the early 1990s, and a good deal of the conventional wisdom surrounding women candidates has been informed by research conducted in the 1990s and 2000s. Research on women candidates, their campaign experiences, and their odds of victory conducted in the last five years paints a slightly different picture and suggests that the political environment is changing. While gender continues to play a significant role in recruiting women for office, in women's self-assessment of their qualifications for office, and in the candidate emergence process, it may play less of a role in campaigns and in the minds of voters casting their ballot on Election Day. Thus the old adage "when women run, women win" continues to be true, and now it applies to an increasingly diverse group of women. However, it will be difficult to achieve gender parity in our elected officials as long as women lag considerably behind men in their willingness to become candidates. Research reviewed in this chapter suggests that the roots of women's lack of political ambition are nurtured during childhood in school settings and in families and therefore will be hard to disrupt. Adult women can be convinced to run if recruited by a political party, encouraged by colleagues and friends, and equipped with the information needed to mount a successful candidacy. Candidate training and organizational supports combined with role models and fund-raising assistance have proven effective at increasing the number of women candidates.

What sort of changes must we make as a society so that girls grow up believing that politics is open to them and that public service is a career as worthy of consideration and planning as any other? One possibility is that having more women in visible positions of leadership and political office will normalize women's participation such that women's candidacies are no longer remarkable. For now, women are a long way from parity at any level of office and in any branch of government. In Chapter 5, we will consider how women govern once elected or appointed to a political office.

NOTES

Boxed feature notes appear at the end of the Notes section.

1 United States House of Representatives, Women in Congress, http://history.house.gov/Exhibitions-and-Publications/WIC/Historical-Data/Historical-Data---Nav.

2 "Women in the U.S. Congress 2016," Center for American Women and Politics, Eagleton Institute of Politics, Rutgers University, www.cawp.rutgers.edu/women-us-congress-2016.

3 "IWPR Quick Figures," Institute for Women's Policy Research. www.iwpr.org/press-room/press-clips/congress-wont-be-50-percent-women-until-2121.-what-is-the-hold-up-june-19-2014 file:///U:/My%20Documents/Documents%202015-2016/Women%20and%20Politics%20files/Chapter%204%20revisions/Q014.pdf.

4 Center for American Women and Politics, "Women in State Legislatures 2016," and "Women in Statewide Executive Elected Office 2016." FACTS, Accessed September 2016.

5 Center for American Women and Politics, "For Women in State Legislatures and Statewide Offices, Not Much Change," November 21, 2016.

6 Inter-Parliamentary Union, "Women in Parliaments: World Classification," as of August 1, 2016, http://www.ipu.org/wmn-e/classif.htm.

7 International Foundation for Election Systems, "Representation of Women in National Elected Institutions: Differences in International Performance and Factors Affecting This," paper prepared for seminar on Women's Political Representation in the Coming 2004 Election, June 2001, 3.

8 Inter-Parliamentary Union, "Women in National Parliaments," As of August 1, 2016, www.ipu.org/wmn-e/world.htm.

9 Richard A. Seltzer, Jody Newman, and Melissa Vorhees Leighton, *Sex as a Political Variable: Women as Candidates and Voters in U.S. Elections* (Boulder, CO: Lynne Rienner Publishers, 1997), 76.

10 Jody Newman, *Perception and Reality: A Study Comparing the Success of Men and Women Candidates* (Washington, DC: National Women's Political Caucus, 1994).

11 Jennifer L. Lawless and Richard L. Fox, *Men Rule: The Continued Underrepresentation of Women in U.S. Politics* (Washington, DC: Women and Politics Institute, 2012).

12 Jennifer L. Lawless and Richard L. Fox, "Why Are Women Still Not Running for Office?" *Issues in Governance Studies* no. 14 (May 2008): 1–20.

13 Danny Hays and Jennifer L. Lawless, *Women on the Run: Gender, Media, and Political Campaigns in a Polarized Era* (New York: Cambridge University Press, 2016).

14 Kim Parker, Juliana Menasce Horowitz, and Molly Rohal, "Women and Leadership: Public Says Women Are Equally Qualified, but Barriers Persist," Pew Research Center, January 14, 2015.

15 Seltzer, Newman, and Leighton, *Sex as a Political Variable,* 79.

16 Hayes and Lawless, *Women on the Run,* 6–7.

17 Ibid., 6.

18 Ibid., 7.

19 "Fast Facts: Women Serving in the 114th Congress, 2015–2017," Center for American Women and Politics, www.cawp.rutgers.edu/fast_facts/levels_of_office/Congress-Current.php.

20 Barbara Norrander and Clyde Wilcox, "Trends in the Geography of Women in the U.S. State Legislatures," in *Women and Elective Office: Past, Present, and Future*, 3rd ed., eds. Sue Thomas and Clyde Wilcox (New York: Oxford University Press, 2014).

21 Shauna Shames, "Where Women Win: Closing the Gap in Congress," Political Parity, 2014, 11.

22 Heather Ondercin and Susan Welch, "Women Candidates for Congress," in *Women and Elective Office*, ed. Thomas and Wilcox.

23 Barbara Palmer and Dennis Simon, *Breaking the Glass Ceiling: Women and Congressional Elections*, 2nd ed. (New York: Routledge, 2008).

24 Ibid., 178.

25 Sam Wang, "The Great Gerrymander of 2012," *New York Times*, February 2, 2013.

26 Lee Fang, "Gerrymandering Rigged the 2014 Elections for GOP Advantage," *Bill Moyers and Company*, November 5, 2014.

27 Shauna Shames, "3:1 Right the Ratio," Political Parity, 2015.

28 Ronnee Schreiber, "Conservative Women Run for Office," in *Women and Elective Office*, ed. Thomas and Wilcox.

29 Ibid., 115.

30 Ibid., 31.

31 Olympia Snowe, "Why I'm Leaving the Senate," *Washington Post*, March 1, 2012.

32 Shames, "3:1 Right the Ratio," 34.

33 See Joel A. Thompson and Gary F. Moncrief, "The Implications of Term Limits for Women and Minorities: Some Evidence from the States," *Social Science Quarterly* 74, no. 2 (1993): 300–309.

34 Amy H. Handlin, *Whatever Happened to the Year of the Woman? Why Women Still Aren't Making It to the Top in Politics* (Denver, CO: Arden Press, 1998), 158.

35 Ibid.

36 Stanley M. Caress, "The Influence of Term Limits on the Electoral Success of Women," *Women and Politics* 20, no. 3 (1999): 45–63.

37 Liz Farmer, "Term Limits Don't Lead to More Women in Politics," *Governing*, April 22, 2016.

38 Viola Wild, "Term Limits and Their Effect on Women's Leadership Opportunities in State Legislatures: A Case Study," *Michigan Journal of Public Affairs* 1 (Summer 2004).

39 Susan J. Carroll and Krista Jenkins, "Term Limits and the Representation of Women, Minorities, and Minority Women: Evidence from the State Legislative Elections of 1998," Center for American Women and Politics, Rutgers University, 1999.

40 Peter Slevin, "After Adopting Term Limits, States Lose Female Legislators," *Washington Post*, April 22, 2007.

41 Darcy, Welch, and Clark, *Women, Elections and Representation,* 140.<<AU: Need full cite>>

42 Ibid., 158.

43 Ibid., 163.

44 Paul Herrnson, *Party Campaigning in the 1980s* (Cambridge, MA: Harvard University Press, 1988).

45 Frank Newport and Joy Wilke, "Americans Still Prefer a Male Boss," Gallup, November 11, 2013.

46 Richard Weissbourd, "Leaning Out: Teen Girls and Leadership Biases," Making Caring Common Project, Harvard Graduate School of Education, 2015.

47 Schreiber, "Conservative Women Run for Office."

48 Susan J. Carroll and Kira Sanbonmatsu, *More Women Can Run* (New York: Oxford University Press, 2014).

49 Kelly Dittmar, "The Status of Black Women in American Politics," Center for Women and Politics, for the Higher Heights Leadership Fund, 2015.

50 Lawless and Fox, "Why Are Women Still Not Running for Office?" 1.

51 Richard L. Fox and Jennifer L. Lawless, "Entering the Arena? Gender and the Decision to Run for Office," *American Journal of Political Science* 48, no. 2 (April 2004): 264–280.

52 Ibid., 268–269.

53 Ibid., 269.

54 Lawless and Fox, "Why Are Women Still Not Running for Office?" 1.

55 Laurel Elder, "Why Women Don't Run: Explaining Women's Underrepresentation in America's Political Institutions," *Women and Politics* 26, no. 2 (2004): 27–56; Susan Collins, "Through the Glass Ceiling," in *Skirting Tradition*, ed. Lia Larson (Hollis, NH: Hollis Publishing, 2004), 96.

56 Kathleen Murphy, "See Jane Stop Running," *Stateline: Politics and Policy News,* June 18, 2004.

57 Fox and Lawless, "Entering the Arena," 273.

58 Elder, "Why Women Don't Run," 43–44.

59 "Pipeline to the Future: Young Women and Political Leadership," findings on mobilizing young women from a survey and focus groups conducted by Lake Snell Perry and Associates for the White House Project Education Fund, April 12, 2000, www.womensleadershipfund.org/programs /research.html#content.

60 Carol D. Miller, "Participating but Not Leading: Women's Under-representation in Student Government Leadership Positions," *College Student Journal,* September 2004.

61 Jennifer L. Lawless and Richard L. Fox, "Girls Just Wanna Not Run: The Gender Gap in Young Americans' Political Ambition," Women and Politics Institute, Washington, DC, 2013.

62 Ibid., 3.

63 Ibid., 11.

64 Ibid., 13.

65 Jennifer L. Lawless and Richard L. Fox, *Running from Office: Why Young Americans Are Turned Off to Politics* (New York: Oxford University Press, 2015).

66 Beth Reingold, "The Uneven Presence of Women and Minorities in America's State Legislatures— And Why it Matters," Scholars Strategy Network Key Findings, October 2012.

67 Christina Wolbrecht and David E. Campbell, "Do Women Politicians Lead Adolescent Girls to be More Politically Engaged? A Cross-National Study of Political Role Models," paper presented at the annual meeting of the American Political Science Association, September 2005.

68 Ibid., 24.

69 Christina Wolbrecht and David E. Campbell, "Leading by Example: Female Members of Parliament as Political Role Models," *American Journal of Political Science* 51, no. 4 (2007): 921–939.

70 David E. Campbell and Christina Wolbrecht, "See Jane Run: Women Politicians as Role Models for Adolescents," *Journal of Politics* 68, no. 2 (2006): 233–245.

71 Mack Mariani, Bryan W. Marshall, and A. Lanethia Mathews-Schultz, "See Hillary Clinton, Nancy Pelosi, and Sarah Palin Run? Party, Ideology, and the Influence of Female Role Models on Young Women," *Political Research Quarterly* 68, no. 4 (2015): 716–731.

72 Jessica Bennett, "Girls Can Be Anything, Just Not President," *New York Times*, November 10, 2016.

73 Kira Sanbonmatsu, "Why Not a Woman of Color? The Candidacies of US Women of Color for Statewide Executive Office," Oxford Handbooks Online, September 2015.

74 Denise Baer, "Political Parties: The Missing Variable in Women and Politics Research," *Political Research Quarterly* 46 (1993): 547–576.

75 See, for example, Barbara Burrell, *A Woman's Place Is in the House: Campaigning for Congress in the Feminist Era* (Ann Arbor: University of Michigan Press, 1994).

76 David Niven, "Party Elites and Women Candidates: The Shape of Bias," *Women and Politics* 19, no. 2 (1998): 57–80.

77 Kenneth Prewitt, *The Recruitment of Political Leaders* (Indianapolis: Bobbs-Merrill, 1970).

78 Linda Witt, Karen M. Paget, and Glenna Mathews, *Running as a Woman: Gender and Power in American Politics* (New York: Free Press, 1993), 217.

79 David Niven, "Throwing Your Hat out of the Ring: Negative Recruitment and the Gender Imbalance in State Legislative Candidacy," *Politics and Gender* 2, no. 4 (December 2006): 473–489.

80 Kira Sanbonmatsu, "Political Parties and the Recruitment of Women to State Legislatures," *Journal of Politics* 64, no. 3 (August 2002): 791–809.

81 Ibid., 805.

82 Jennifer L. Lawless and Kathryn Pearson, "Competing in Congressional Primaries," in *Legislative Women: Getting Elected, Getting Ahead,* ed. Beth Reingold (Boulder, CO: Lynne Rienner, 2008).

83 Ibid., 32.

84 Witt, Paget, and Mathews, *Running as a Woman,* 214.

85 Kira Sanbonmatsu, "Women Candidates and their Campaigns," Political Parity, 2015.

86 Hayes and Lawless, *Women on the Run,* 7.

87 Rebecca Traister, "Hillary Clinton's Campaign Was Never Going to Be Easy. But Did It Have to Get This Hard?" *New York Magazine,* May 30, 2016

88 James Devitt, *Framing Gender on the Campaign Trail: Women's Executive Leadership and the Press* (Philadelphia: Annenberg Public Policy Center, University of Pennsylvania, 2000).

89 Kim Fridkin Kahn, "The Distorted Mirror: Press Coverage of Women Candidates for Statewide Office," *Journal of Politics* 56, no. 1 (1994): 154–173.

90 Kim Fridkin Kahn, "Does Gender Make a Difference? An Experimental Examination of Sex Stereotypes and Press Patterns in Statewide Campaigns," *American Journal of Political Science* 38 (1994): 162–195.

91 Orlanda Ward, "Seeing Double: Race, Gender, and Coverage of Minority Women's Campaigns for the U.S. House of Representatives," *Politics and Gender* 12, no. 2 (June 2016): 317–343.

92 Sarah Gershon, "Women Race, Gender, and the Media Intersect: Campaign News Coverage of Minority Congresswomen," *Journal of Women, Politics and Policy* 33 (2012): 105–125.

93 Dianne G. Bystrom, Mary Christine Banwart, Lynda Lee Kaid, and Terry A. Robertson, *Gender and Candidate Communication* (New York: Routledge, 2004).

94 Steven Erlanger, "Theresa May's Style: Put Your Head Down and Get to Work," *New York Times,* July 13, 2016.

95 Jenni Avins, "Hillary Clinton's Husband Wore a Fetching Pantsuit to Honor Her Nomination for US President," *Quartz,* July 27, 2016.

96 Julia Baird, "Sarah Palin's Mustache," *New York Times,* February 26, 2016.

97 Molly Ball, "No, It's Not Sexist to Describe Women Politicians' Clothes," *Atlantic,* July 2, 2013.

98 "Name It, Change It" campaign website: www.nameitchangeit.org.

99 Erika Falk, "Clinton and the Playing-the-Gender-Card-Metaphor in Campaign News," *Feminist Media Studies* 13, no. 2 (2013); see also Gail Collins, "Trump Deals the Woman Card," *New York Times,* April 28, 2016.

100 Anne Gearan and Katie Zezima, "Trump's 'Woman's Card' Comment Escalates the Campaign's Gender Wars," *Washington Post,* April 27, 2016.

101 Shauna Shames, "The 'Un-Candidates': Gender and Outsider Signals in Women's Political Advertisements," *Women and Politics* 25, nos. 1–2 (2003).

102 Mirya R. Holman, Monica C. Schneider, and Kristen Pondel, "Gender Targeting in Political Advertisements," *Political Research Quarterly* 68, no. 4 (December 2015): 816–829.

103 Sam Frizell, "Hillary Clinton Champions Working Women in New Ads," *Time,* October 27, 2015.

104 Patricia Strach et al., "In a Different Voice: Explaining the Use of Men and Women as Voice-Over Announcers in Political Advertising," *Political Communication,* February 2015, 183–205.

105 Ann Gordon, David M. Shafie, and Ann N. Crigler, "Is Negative Advertising Effective for Female Candidates? An Experiment in Voters' Uses of Gender Stereotypes," *Press/Politics* 8, no. 1 (2003): 35–53.

106 Paul S. Herrnson and Jennifer Lucas, "The Fairer Sex? Gender and Negative Campaigning in the U.S. Elections," unpublished manuscript; the quote cited is from Peter L. Francia, Paul S. Herrnson, and Jennifer Lucas, "Campaign Ethics and Reform: What Candidates Say," *Campaigns and Elections,* June 2002, 45–47.

107 Kim L. Fridkin, Patrick J. Kenney, and Gina Serignese Woodall, "Bad for Men, Better for Women: The Impact of Stereotypes During Negative Campaigns," *Political Behavior* 31, no. 1 (March 2009): 53–77.

108 "Pipeline to the Future," 16.

109 Barbara Burrell, "Campaign Finance: Women's Experience in the Modern Era," in *Women and Elective Office: Past, Present, and Future,* ed. Sue Thomas and Clyde Wilcox (New York: Oxford University Press, 1998), 26–37.

110 Barbara C. Burrell, "Money and Women's Candidacies for Public Office," in *Women and American Politics: New Questions, New Directions,* ed. Susan J. Carroll (Oxford: Oxford University Press, 2003), 79.

111 Burrell, "Campaign Finance," 128.

112 EMILY's List: www.emilyslist.org/pages/about-us.

113 Witt, Paget, and Mathews, *Running as a Woman,* 139.

114 Los Angeles African American Women Political Action Committee, www.laaawpac.org.

115 "Women's PACs and Donor Networks: A Contact List," Center for American Women and Politics, Eagleton Institute of Politics, Rutgers University, May 2009.

116 Will Tucker, "Clinton Raises Historic Share—and Amount—of Campaign Cash from Women," *Open Secrets,* June 9, 2016.

117 Christine L. Day and Charles D. Hadley, *Women's PACs: Abortion and Elections* (Upper Saddle River, NJ: Pearson Prentice Hall, 2005), 7.

118 Kim Fridkin Kahn, *The Political Consequences of Being a Woman* (New York: Columbia University Press, 1996).

119 Leonie Huddy and Nayda Terkildsen, "The Consequences of Gender Stereotypes for Women Candidates at Different Levels of Office," *Political Research Quarterly* 43, no. 3 (1993): 503–525.

120 Shames, "The 'Un-Candidates.'"

121 Paul S. Herrnson, J. Celeste Lay, and Atiya Kai Stokes, "Women Running 'as Women': Candidate Gender, Campaign Issues, and Voter-Targeting Strategies," *Journal of Politics* 65, no. 1 (February 2003): 244–255.

122 Susan J. Carroll, "Reflections on Gender and Hillary Clinton's Presidential Campaign: The Good, the Bad, and the Misogynic," *Politics and Gender* 5, no. 1 (March 2009): 1–20.
123 Ibid.
124 Amy Sullivan, "Why Didn't More Women Vote for Hillary?" *Time*, June 5, 2008.
125 Ibid., 11.
126 Kira Sanbonmatsu, "Gender Stereotypes and Vote Choice," *American Journal of Political Science* 46, no. 1 (January 2002): 20–34.
127 Ibid., 26.
128 Kathleen A. Dolan, "Gender Differences in Support for Women Candidates: Is There a Glass Ceiling in American Politics?" *Women and Politics* 17, no. 2 (1997): 27–41.
129 Ibid., 160.
130 Deborah Jordan Brooks, *He Runs, She Runs: Why Gender Stereotypes Do Not Harm Women Candidates* (Princeton, NJ: Princeton University Press, 2013).
131 Kathleen Dolan, *When Does Gender Matter: Women Candidates and Gender Stereotypes in American Elections* (New York: Oxford University Press, 2014).
132 Monica C. Schneider and Angela L. Bos, "Measuring Stereotypes of Female Politicians," *Political Psychology* 35, no. 2 (2014): 260.
133 Kira Sanbonmatsu, "Electing Women of Color: The Role of Campaign Trainings," *Journal of Women, Politics and Policy* 36, no. 2 (2015): 137–160.
134 IGNITE: www.ignitenational.org.
135 National Federation of Republican Women Campaign Management School: www.nfrw.org/cms. Excellence in Public Service, Whitman Series: www.whitmanseries.org.
136 Right Women, Right Now: http://rslc.gop/about_rslc/rwrn.
137 Higher Heights for America: www.higherheightsforamerica.org.
138 Political Opportunity Program (POP): www.emilyslist.org/ do/pop.
139 The Women's Campaign School: www.yale.edu/wcsyale.
140 LatinasRepresent: https://latinasrepresent.org.
141 Women Under Forty Political Action Committee: www.wufpac.org.
142 Running Start: www.runningstartonline.org/home.
143 Olympia Snowe, "Too Often Met with Silence," in *Skirting Tradition*, ed. Lia Larson (Hollis, NH: Hollis Publishing Company, 2004), 63.

Box 4.1: The Power of Positive Discrimination: Electoral Quotas to Advance Women in Office

1 Vidar Helgesen, "Women in the Driver's Seat of Democratic Politics," International IDEA, March 8, 2013.
2 Drude Dahlerup, "Comparative Studies of Gender Quotas," paper presented at International IDEA workshop, February 2003.
3 Rikhil R. Bhavnani, "Do Electoral Quotas Work After They Are Withdrawn? Evidence from a Natural Experiment in India," *American Political Science Review* 103, no. 1 (February 2009): 23–35.

Box 4.2: Impossible Expectations: Hillary Clinton's Candidacy for the Presidency

1 Michael Arnovitz, "Thinking About Hillary—A Plea for Reason," *The Policy*, June 18, 2016.
2 Emily Bazelon, "What Women Owe Hillary Clinton," *New York Times Magazine*, July 29, 2016.
3 Margaret Talbot, "Hillary Clinton Should Be Allowed to Boast," *New Yorker*, April 22, 2016.
4 Rebecca Traister, "Hillary Clinton's Campaign Was Never Going to Be Easy. But Did It Have to Get This Hard?" *New York*, May 30, 2016.
5 Bazelon, "What Women Owe Hillary Clinton."
6 Sady Doyle, "Likable," January 2016, Tumblr post, http://sadydoyle.tumblr.com/post/13566458 6198/likable.

Box 4.3: Future Women Candidates: Will 2016 Mobilize or Paralyze Women's Political Ambition?

1 Isaac Stanley-Becker, "Hopes for a Female President Dashed, Women Take Running for Office into Their Own Hands," *Washington Post*, November 26, 2016.
2 Clare Foran, "Will Hillary Clinton's Defeat Set Back Women in Politics?" *Atlantic*, November 27, 2016.

CHAPTER 5

Women as Political Actors: Representation and Advocacy

Despite steady progress over the last twenty-five years and even more rapid gains in recent elections, the number of women in political office in the United States is still significantly smaller than the number of men. Does it matter if more men than women are in politics? Are we concerned about this issue from a purely numerical standpoint, or is it that women in office govern differently than men and are therefore better able to represent women's interests? How do we define "women's interests"? The paradox of gender equality is again a useful way to evaluate our expectations about the number of women in office as well as how we think women will (or should) behave once in office.

Those who believe that equality stems from the similarities between men and women view parity (equal numbers of men and women) as the standard for equality of representation in political office. Women in this regard act as role models, and a diverse, descriptively representative government lends legitimacy to its decisions and actions. A political institution such as Congress or a presidential administration appears to better represent the people when its membership reflects the characteristics of the population it serves. Alternatively, for those who believe that equality requires recognition of the differences between men and women, having women in public office is important because their unique perspective affects what they bring to the job and the ways they substantively represent women and their interests. Of course, as we've seen repeatedly, these perspectives are not mutually exclusive and, in the case of political representation, are quite complementary. Both paths in pursuit of equality embrace the goal of bringing more women into politics.

This chapter examines women as political actors in a variety of political roles (legislative, executive, judicial, military) and at different levels of government (local, state, and federal), some elected and some appointed. Chapter 4 reviewed a number of initiatives designed to increase the number of women candidates and, by extension, the number of women elected officials. Here we examine women's experience and behavior as legislators, judges, executives, and appointed public officials working as political insiders. This chapter also looks at women in the military because it has historically served as a laboratory for social change by "ordering" equality consistent with the legal equality doctrine. Racial integration in the military was accomplished by Executive Order 9981, issued in 1948 by President Harry S. Truman. More recently, Secretary of Defense Leon Panetta announced the end of women's combat exclusion in January 2013 with full implementation by January 2016. We will look at the ways in which men and women are similar and different as political insiders in each context. We will also examine the ways women differ from one another as political actors.

POLITICAL REPRESENTATION: WHY NUMBERS MATTER

On October 25, 1991, the National Women's Political Caucus ran a full-page ad in the *New York Times*. Under a pen and ink drawing of a diverse hearing panel made up entirely of women, the heading read: "What If . . ." "What if fourteen women, instead of fourteen men had sat on the Senate Judiciary Committee during the confirmation hearings of Clarence Thomas? . . . Sound unfair? Just as unfair as fourteen men and no women."[1]

As this advertisement illustrates, feminists believe that more women in office will translate into a more woman-friendly political system, which in turn will generate government actions more responsive to women's unique concerns. The ad further implies that it is "unfair" when one group in society dominates political representation so completely, and that women, if elected, will act differently than men once in office. This is a complicated set of expectations born of our conceptual understanding of political representation.

Contemporary political theorist Hannah Fenichel Pitkin describes four types of political representation: formal, descriptive, symbolic, and substantive.[2] **Formal representation** refers to mechanisms in a political system that ensure representation and allow citizens to hold representatives accountable for their actions. In the US political system, elections are the mechanisms of formal representation. This explains why women were so anxious to participate in elections as voters and ultimately as elected representatives.

The next three types of representation refer to how a person is represented. When demands for more women in office stem from claims of justice and equity, descriptive and symbolic representation are in play. **Descriptive representation** is when women represent other women simply by their presence in government. We assume that if someone shares one or more of our descriptive characteristics, such as sex, race, sexual orientation, or other defining features, that person will also share

WHAT IF?

What if 14 women, instead of 14 men, had sat on the Senate Judiciary Committee during the confirmation hearings of Clarence Thomas?

Sound unfair? Just as unfair as fourteen men and no women.

What if even half the Senators had been women? Women are, after all, more than half the population. Maybe, just maybe, women's voices would have been heard. Maybe the experiences and concerns of women would not have been so quickly dismissed or ridiculed. And maybe all of America would have benefited.

The behavior and performance of the United States Senate during the Clarence Thomas confirmation hearings demonstrated a stark truth: women are tragically under-represented politically. As long as men make up 98% of the U.S. Senate and 93% of the U.S. House of Representatives, women's voices can be ignored, their experiences and concerns trivialized.

The need for women in public office has never been more obvious. Or essential.

Men control the White House, the Congress, the courthouse and the statehouse. Men have political power over women's lives. It's time that women help make the rules, create the policies, and pass the laws about sexual harassment, day care, affordable health care, and hundreds of decisions that affect American families every day.

The National Women's Political Caucus is determined to even the odds. To hear the voices of women echo in the halls of power.

If you're angry about what you've witnessed in the United States Senate, don't just raise your fist, raise your pen. Join us. The goal of the National Women's Political Caucus is to increase the number of women elected and appointed to public office. We're the only national bi-partisan grassroots organization working across this country to recruit, train and elect women into office at all levels of government.

Turn your anger into action. Join us.

Count me in. I want to help the National Women's Political Caucus increase the number of women elected and appointed to public office.
Enclosed is my check payable to NWPC Inc. for:
( )$250 ( )$100 ( )$50 ( )$35 OTHER $_____

Name _____
Address _____
City/State/Zip _____
Please bill my ( ) Mastercard ( ) Visa Account #_____
Account Number _____ Expiration Date _____
Signature _____ Date _____
Contributions to NWPC are not tax deductible.
National Women's Political Caucus
1211 A Street, N.W., Suite 950, Washington, D.C. 20002

Paid for by the National Women's Political Caucus

IMAGE 5.1

Source: Courtesy National Women's Political Caucus.

and protect our interests. Our image and interests are mirrored by the representative who is "like us." **Symbolic representation** adds an emotional or affective component to representation. When women looked at the all-male, all-white Senate Judiciary Committee during Clarence Thomas's confirmation hearings, what they saw neither mirrored their image nor made them feel as if their interests were being represented, and the palpable disconnect produced a strong negative reaction in many. This was the case again in 2012 when an all-male panel of religious leaders, assembled by Chairman Darrell Issa (R-Calif.), testified before the House Oversight and Government Reform Committee on religious liberty and contraceptive coverage under the Affordable Care Act. The one woman scheduled to testify, Georgetown law student Sandra Fluke, was barred from appearing before the panel. Women's numeric representation in Congress, state legislatures, or other halls of power is important for symbolic reasons in the sense that women *stand for* other women. Women standing for women challenges the mental image of political leadership as male in its embodiment: "When we don't see women as leaders, we continue to think of leaders as men. . . . In a circular fashion, the absence of women as political leaders contributes to the continued absence of women as political leaders."[3] Recall from Chapter 4 the important function female role models play for women, especially young women and

IMAGE 5.2: *An all-male panel of religious leaders testifies before House Oversight and Government Reform Committee on contraceptive coverage under the Affordable Care Act (February 2012).* Source: AP Photo/Carolyn Kaster.

women of color, in motivating them to think about running for office themselves.[4] Research also demonstrates that descriptive representation enhances accountability between constituents and elected officials. Women represented by a woman in the US Senate know more about their senators' voting records and weigh that information more heavily in evaluating the quality of representation.[5]

Substantive representation occurs when women *act for* other women by pursuing distinctive interests and policy preferences unique to women. This is perhaps the most important form of representation, although it is also the most problematic to implement and to study. As we have seen repeatedly throughout this volume, women do not constitute a homogeneous group, so defining "women's interests" along a single dimension is nearly impossible. Women acting for other women will reflect the diversity of ideological perspectives, lived experiences, and issue positions among the women elected representatives. Rarely will all women adopt the same substantive position simply because they are women. In fact, many women in public office do not view themselves as acting for other women and may not emphasize their role as "women" in office. Three female Republican House members in the 114th Congress, for example, referred to themselves as "congressmen" rather than use the term "congresswomen," as most female members do. Descriptive representation, therefore, may not have any predictable relation to support for women's substantive interests.

Another way of conceptualizing women's representation of other women is through **surrogate representation**.[6] Given the small number of women elected to Congress, most female citizens are not represented by a woman. However, surrogate representation suggests that a representational relationship can exist outside the boundaries of an electoral district. In this sense, the relationship between the citizen and representative is based on a shared political party, ideological perspective, issue affinity, or group identity. Notes Susan J. Carroll, "This concept of surrogate representation is potentially of great significance in considering how women representatives may be helping to transform the institution of Congress and its policy agenda. To the extent that women members of Congress see themselves and act as surrogate representatives for women outside the geographic boundaries of their districts, they bring something distinctive to their roles as representatives, something that most men do not bring."[7] For example, in January 2015 House Republican leaders scheduled a vote on the Pain Capable Unborn Child Protection Act to coincide with the annual March for Life marking the anniversary of the Supreme Court's 1973 *Roe v. Wade* decision. The bill would have banned all abortions after twenty weeks of pregnancy. Republican leaders canceled the vote after concerns were raised by Republican women that a vote on the bill would add fuel to the charges of a "war on women" and further alienate key constituencies.

How Important Is Parity in Representation?

Arguably, substantive representation could exist without descriptive or symbolic representation. In other words, men could act for women's interests in the absence of parity. But do they? Women are not confident that men will do a good job, an impression confirmed by the legislative track record on issues such as child care, family leave, and equal pay. A survey of legislators in 110 countries found that 49 percent of women and 36 percent of men disagreed with the statement "Men can sufficiently represent the interests of women in politics."[8] Most of the bills related to "women's issues" are indeed more often introduced by female legislators.[9] The desire to represent women characterizes the orientations of both Republican and Democratic women. As former representative Leslie Byrne observed: "Most of us didn't come in as women's issues people, but what we have found when we got there is that if we didn't step in, those issues weren't addressed. I have always said that all issues are women's issues. But there are particular issues that affect women in greater proportions than others that don't seem to get the attention, and those are the ones you find yourself looking at just out of an issue of fairness."[10]

In 2016, women held 19.6 percent of the seats in Congress and 24.4 percent of the seats in state legislatures, and that small percentage often makes it difficult to get particular issues on the official agenda. Elizabeth Holtzman, elected to the House in 1973 when there were just sixteen women there (3.6 percent) and no women in the US Senate, reflected: "Politics helps determine the kind of society we'd like to live in. And when women are not included in that conversation, or when they're marginalized or drastically underrepresented, it has real-world consequences for our society, for women and our families."[11] It is impossible to tell for certain whether gender parity in representation would alter the public agenda, but some evidence suggests that it would.

Does the public desire gender parity? Might their preference for or against it be a factor in explaining the relatively slow progress toward parity in descriptive political representation in the United States? Research by Kathleen Dolan and Kira Sanbonmatsu explores the public's view of the ideal gender composition of government.[12] When asked "In your opinion, in the best government the U.S. could have, what percentage of elected officials would be men?" the most common response was parity (50 percent men, 50 percent women). The mean response was 60 percent men, leaving 40 percent of the seats for women (even this imbalance is far from the reality of the 77–23 percent proportion in Congress and 76–24 percent imbalance in the state legislatures). Indeed, 45 percent of the respondents gave a figure for their ideal level of men's representation of 60 percent or higher (11 percent of those questioned wanted a government that was 75 percent male; 8 percent preferred it be 80 percent male).[13] Less than 10 percent of the sample preferred a government made up of a majority of women. More women (12 percent) than men (7 percent) desired a majority-female "ideal government," but both women (44 percent) and men (47 percent) prefer government that is majority male. Thus, while the public would like a government with more women than currently serve in office, there is no evidence of an overwhelming desire to work toward a majority-female government.

In exploring the reasons for the public's preferences, Dolan and Sanbonmatsu found that gender stereotypes about male and female suitability for politics and perception of issue competency shape the public's definition of ideal descriptive representation. "Respondents who believe that women are better suited emotionally for politics and who believe that women are better able to handle crime are more likely to believe that men should be half of elected officials." They found that the experience of being represented by a woman did not affect support for higher levels of representation among men or women, raising questions about whether the public is truly interested in advancing women's share of descriptive representation in legislatures.

In a 2014 Gallup poll, 63 percent of Americans said the country would be better governed with more female political leaders. Only 13 percent of the respondents believed the government would be worse run with more women in political office.[14] Support for more women was highest among those eighteen to twenty-nine years old (73 percent) and lowest among married men (45 percent). Not surprisingly, unmarried women, liberals, and Democrats felt best about more women governing. These are the voters whose support Hillary Clinton most needed in the 2016 presidential election. As it turns out, positive gender stereotypes and an abstract desire for a more gender-balanced ideal government have less effect on actual vote choice than do the traditional predictors of political party and incumbency.[15] When voters are faced with a single contest in which they have the opportunity to vote for a woman and thereby potentially add to the overall numbers of women in office, the traditional predictors of vote choice still prevail. It is clear that attitudes about women in politics have ideological and personal value to voters; if women appeared in more contests on more ballots, would gender-positive attitudes be more determinant? Part of the answer may lie in the extent to which people believe female representation is unique.

Are Women Unique as Representatives?

Descriptive, symbolic, and substantive representation, although conceptually distinct, are interwoven in complex ways that form the assumptions we make and the expectations we hold for women in political office. Because of the power of sex role socialization, we believe women are different from men and possess distinct traits and characteristics that are stereotypically feminine (e.g., compassionate, conciliatory, compromising). Some feminists see this difference as empowering and therefore expect women to behave differently than men within political institutions, to pursue different policy solutions, to hold different attitudes, and to make political processes and institutions more responsive to women's particular concerns.

In elections where women have made significant gains, female candidates have been able to capitalize on voters' desire for change by promising that if elected, women would be different—whatever that means. The meaning of "different" is left to the voters' (and the media's) imagination, but the invitation to rely on positive stereotypes in evaluating women candidates and their promises is clear. Implicit in the message is also the suggestion that women will be not only different but *better* than men. Some of these expectations have been confirmed by research studies, while others have not. Simply electing more women to office will not directly translate into the adoption of feminist policies. There is considerable diversity among women as a whole, as well as among women officeholders.[16] Assuming that all women share some essential quality that can be translated into a single political voice ignores that diversity and, in effect, silences the interests of some women in favor of more dominant women's interests.[17] The idea that women do not share one common political voice is evident in conservative women's claims to stand for and act for women's interests. Ronnee Schreiber chronicles the rise of two conservative women's organizations—Concerned Women for America (CWA) and Independent Women's Forum (IWF)—and notes that in many ways the groups' very existence is paradoxical. Both organizations criticize feminists for making identity-based claims and for seeking to represent women as a whole, "because women are not a homogeneous group." And yet, she argues, both organizations employ the tactic of "'strategic essentialism,' deploying their 'womanhood' selectively to contest feminist claims of representation and to give conservative interests more legitimacy. That is, they act as and for women, even while recognizing the trappings of this strategy."[18]

An alternative perspective among feminists considers women's claim of difference somewhat dangerous because it recalls the theory of separate spheres that relegated women to second-class status and confined them largely to the private sphere purely on the basis of their perceived difference from men. If women encourage voters to rely on stereotypes and place an emphasis on difference, it may backfire when the electoral context or public mood changes. Former Supreme Court justice Sandra Day O'Connor, for one, was skeptical of the wisdom of women's claims to virtue and difference:

> The gender differences cited currently are surprisingly similar to stereotypes from years past. They recall the old myths we have struggled to put behind us. For example, asking whether women attorneys speak in a "different voice" than men do is a question that is both dangerous and unanswerable. . . . It threatens, indeed, to establish new categories of "women's work" to which women are confined and from which men are excluded.[19]

Others worry that women will be held to a higher standard and be judged ineffective in short order if they cannot alter the political system after taking office. Madeleine Kunin, former governor of Vermont, said, "We cannot expect the few women in political life to change the values and the rules of the game alone, although that is sometimes precisely the expectation."[20] Key in her warning is "the few." Even today, women still constitute the minority in Congress, in all fifty state legislatures, and in parliaments around the world. Some research suggests that until women make up a critical mass (defined most often as 30 percent), they cannot be expected to exert much influence over the institution in which they serve, at least based on sheer numbers.[21] Whether women are in fact different from men may be unanswerable, as Justice O'Connor claimed. Nonetheless, the perception of difference is a powerful force in American politics.

QUALITIES OF POLITICAL LEADERSHIP: HOW DO MEN AND WOMEN DIFFER?

According to a Pew Research Center survey of Americans on gender and leadership, a majority of Americans believe that women and men are equally capable of being good political leaders and see little difference between the sexes on key leadership traits. Honesty, intelligence, and decisiveness were identified by more than 80 percent of those surveyed as "absolutely essential" leadership qualities, followed by organization, compassion, innovation, and ambition.[22] Men and women tend to agree on the top three characteristics, but women place a higher value on compassion and innovation than men do. Women, particularly young women, are also more likely than men to say that ambition is absolutely essential for a leader to be successful. Sixty-three percent of millennial women (ages eighteen to thirty-three) identified ambition as essential, compared to 53 percent of millennial men.

In evaluating men and women as political leaders, survey respondents perceived few differences on the traits of intelligence, innovation, ambition, honesty, and decisiveness. Among those giving the edge to either men or women, respondents said that women hold an advantage over men when it comes to compassion, organization, honesty, innovation, and intelligence. Men were judged as more ambitious and decisive than women. Solid majorities of Republicans (75 percent) and Democrats (74 percent) say men and women are equally qualified for political leadership. Among those who see a gender difference, Republicans give the edge in leadership qualification to men (22 percent), with only 3 percent reporting that women make better leaders. Among Democrats, 16 percent say that women make better leaders, while 9 percent say that men are better political leaders than women.

Most Americans believe that men and women are equally qualified to be political leaders. But are there differences in the ways that male and female officeholders lead and legislate? In this section, we will evaluate whether men and women differ in their ideological outlooks on politics and whether women pursue policies that are distinctly different from the policy priorities of men.[23] We will then examine the results of research on gender and policy making, and investigate whether women adopt a particular style as political actors different from that of their male colleagues.[24]

Ideology and Attitudes

Studies across several decades have found that women officeholders at both the state and federal levels are more liberal than their male counterparts, regardless of their political party. In one of the earliest studies of women in Congress, political scientist Freda Gehlen found that female representatives were more likely than males to support progressive initiatives such as the 1964 Civil Rights Act and the Equal Rights Amendment.[25] Longitudinal analysis of women in office from 1972 to 1980 found that the nature of the issue and the influence of a representative's constituency were as important or more important than gender in explaining male and female representatives' voting behavior. Although women voted more liberally than men in the early 1970s, the size of the difference in voting records decreased over time and did not exist in some regions of the country. Researchers thus concluded that legislative districts that supported liberal policies were more likely to elect women legislators during the 1970s and 1980s.[26] What initially appeared to be gender differences in voting behavior were actually a result of unique characteristics of the relatively few women elected to Congress at the time.

Political scientist Barbara Burrell replicated this early longitudinal analysis of House voting patterns in three sessions of Congress between 1987 and 1992 to see whether gender differences between male and female legislators' voting

Box 5.1 – Encountering the Controversies of Equality

Would More Women in Government Reduce Corruption? It Depends

What is the relationship between gender and corruption? Are women inherently less corrupt than men? Will more women in government reduce corruption? Corruption is defined as the misuse of public authority for private gain, including the solicitation of bribes, embezzling public money, "sextortion," and other forms of political graft. If women are perceived to be more honest and trustworthy, then one might naturally assume that having more women in government would reduce levels of corruption. This relationship is known as the "fairer sex hypothesis,"[1] and it has enjoyed enough support in the research that Peru replaced men with women in the transit police in an attempt to reduce corruption and revive confidence in law enforcement.[2] But while multiple studies demonstrate that the public perceives women as less corrupt and corruptible, establishing a causal relationship between more women in government and less corruption has proven complicated.

There is little doubt that women disproportionately suffer the effects of corruption. Women make up 70 percent of the world's poor and 65 percent of the world's illiterate. Poor women depend on public services such as education and health care. Bribery is sometimes a prerequisite for receiving public services, and corruption diverts resources earmarked for public services into private pockets. Women are less able to personally disrupt corruption when they experience it or to hold public officials accountable because they lack political agency and resources.[3] Do women, by their presence in government, reduce corruption? At first glance, the answer appears to be yes. Countries with larger numbers of women in politics and the workforce have lower levels of corruption.[4] Upon closer inspection, however, it appears that this relationship is not universal—it holds in some countries but not others. Some research attributes the relationship to indicators of a liberal democracy (i.e., rule of law, freedom of the press, frequent and free elections). Even

records remained even after accounting for the fact that women may disproportionately represent more liberal districts.[27] She found, similar to research from prior decades, that liberal ideology is strongest among Democratic women who represent northern urban districts. However, even when controlling for political party and constituent factors, gender remained a significant point of departure in predicting a legislator's voting record across social, economic, and foreign policy though both women in government and liberal democracy are negatively related to political corruption, when both are included in the same statistical model, the effects of women in government disappear, while liberal democratic institutions remain very powerful. Sifting through these various and conflicting studies, UNIFEM concluded that "more women in politics are not the cause of low corruption, but rather, democratic and transparent politics is correlated with low corruption, and the two create an enabling environment for more women to participate in politics."[5]

Researchers agree that women are more risk-averse than men. Women are also more vulnerable to punishment due to explicit or tacit gender discrimination. Therefore, in public settings women are less likely to engage in corruption for fear of being caught and losing their jobs.[6] A new study by Justin Esarey and Leslie Schwindt-Bayer found that "the women's representation-corruption link was strongest when the risk of corruption being detected and punished by voters is high—in other words, when officials can be held electorally accountable."[7]

Corruption in government deters women from entering politics. As a consequence, there are few women in highly corrupt systems, and women therefore are not in positions that would allow them to combat corruption by investing in human development policy. As former US ambassador for global issues Melanne Verveer said, "It's not about having more women in politics and saying, 'Ah, that will change everything. . . .' It's about changing the gender imbalance and then we could do a better job of tackling our problems."[8] But gender parity in the United States and around the world remains elusive—on average, women constitute just 19 percent of government.

What do you think?

This book is organized around the paradox of gender equality—the question of how men and women can be equal if they are different. How does this apply to the relationship between gender and corruption? Empirically, governments with more women have lower corruption. Does that mean adding women will reduce the negative effects of corruption? In what ways is this issue complicated by systemic factors, perceptions of gender differences between men and women, and the realities of persistent barriers to women's election?

issues. Political party is a slightly greater determinant than gender. Democratic women make the Democratic Party more liberal, whereas Republican women moderate the Republican Party.

By the early 2000s, however, the voting records of men and women had largely converged within each party, with the biggest differences now visible between parties rather than between genders within parties.[28] Brian Frederick attributes the change to the entrance of more conservative women into the US House, coinciding with increased ideological polarization between the parties. Women elected to Congress under these conditions reacted strategically to the growing polarization to gain institutional power and rewards—behavior that Kathryn Pearson calls gendered partisanship.[29] Republican women in the House responded by taking extra steps to prove their partisan credentials and counter the stereotype that they are more liberal than their male counterparts. By contrast, the behavior of women in the Senate is conditioned by institutional norms that promote centrist, cooperative behavior, positioning women to work across party lines to shape legislation, and women senators remain more liberal than their male counterparts.[30]

In state legislatures, the trend is similar. Studies conducted in the 1990s found a gender gap on a variety of issues, from the death penalty to construction of nuclear power plants; however, the gap was largest on issues of abortion policy.[31] A 1995 study, for example, found that women were more ideologically liberal than men on almost all issues, although somewhat less so on fiscal matters. Women were far more likely to oppose the death penalty, mandatory prayer in schools, and tax cuts that also require a cut in government spending, and to support abortion rights.[32] Relative to their constituents, women remained consistently more liberal than men in either party, but as the partisan landscape changed in the early 2000s, so did women in state legislatures. Robert Hogan examined this trend and found partisan differences similar to those in the US House described above. Among Democratic state legislators, women were less conservative than men, but among Republican state lawmakers, women were slightly more conservative than men. Although many factors that influence legislative voting affect women and men similarly, political party has a more prominent effect among women.[33] Differences between men and women previously attributed to gender differences in ideology and attitudes now look like strategic behavior driven largely by the deepening conservatism of the Republican Party. This is particularly intriguing given the partisan advantage maintained by Democrats in the number of women elected at all levels. Of the 1,814 women who held a state legislative seat in 2016, 60 percent were Democrats and 39 percent were Republicans. In the US Congress, 73 percent of women serving in 2016 were Democrats and only 27 percent were Republican.[34]

Since there are fewer women serving, gender may be more salient to how women legislators perceive their political roles and the impact their gender has on their career and their effectiveness in office.[35] Among respondents in the Pew survey who saw an advantage to political leaders of one gender over the other, the largest gender gap was on the ability to work out compromises—41 percent of women, compared with 27 percent of men, said women are better at compromising. More women than men said that female leaders surpass men in being honest and ethical, working to improve quality of life for Americans, standing up for their beliefs despite political pressure, and being persuasive.[36] "We need more consensus-builders, we need people who will listen more, who are less ego-driven and partisan. I really believe if you had 51 percent women in Congress, the whole dynamic would change," said Senator Kirsten Gillibrand (D-N.Y.).[37] Women state representatives view themselves differently as well. They see themselves as more hardworking, more patient, more attentive to detail, better prepared in their daily tasks, and better equipped to deal with female constituents' concerns than their male colleagues. As for their work, they think of themselves as more interested in long-term implications of policy than in short-term effects and as driven more by the common good than by personal gain.

Susan Carroll's study on women in Congress provides interesting insights into how congresswomen view their representational roles and work styles. Of particular note is how women bridge ideological or party differences in order to work together. Carroll says, "The obligation most congresswomen feel to act as surrogate representatives for women seems to be rooted in their beliefs that there are underlying commonalities. . . . Most women in Congress, regardless of party or ideology or race or ethnicity, believe that there are ties that bind women together across divisions."[38] Retired senator Barbara Mikulski (D-Md.) agreed: "I would say what's different is we're interested in governing, not in winning arguments."[39] Retired senator Olympia Snowe (R-Me.) said, "Women are focused on outcomes, results, and getting the job done. Basically women don't spend a lot of time on the periphery of a problem. They generally like to delve into it and achieve the results and figure out what's the best way to achieve that outcome."[40] Women in the Senate have built comity across the partisan divide by meeting monthly for dinner and getting to know one another as people who can work together. "I think it's really one of the best things about the Senate," said Gillibrand. "Women really do seek each other out to form friendships outside of our working lives. And we appreciate each other as women first, as mothers and daughters, as sisters, as wives, I think it makes a difference in how we react toward each other. We're always willing to listen, we're always willing to think through an issue for someone, we're also looking for things to work together on."[41]

"Styles" of Political Behavior

Several studies have found that in carrying out their role as legislators, women spend considerably more time keeping in touch with constituents and helping constituents solve problems than men do. Within the legislature itself, women tend to be team players more often than men, spending more time building coalitions within and across political parties.[42] Analysis of women in the Senate, for example, found that over a six-year period (2009–2015), the average female senator cosponsored 3.79 bills with female counterparts of the other party, while the average male senator cosponsored just 2.16 bills with male members of the other party. Although there are fewer women in the Senate than in the House, "female legislators in House still cosponsor legislation with each other—both within their party and with the opposite party—more often than their male counterparts."[43] Partisan conflict is a form of intergroup conflict, and researchers have found that "men are more sensitive than women to intergroup conflict and competition. Consequently, men are more likely to experience 'intergroup anxiety' at the prospect of interaction with partisan opponents" and "to avoid cross-party political discussion, not listen when they [do] engage in such conversations, and reject information from outparty leaders."[44]

Women's interest in building bridges extends to their leadership styles. Researchers developed a typology of leadership along two major dimensions: leadership styles (command, coordination, and consensus) and leadership goals (power, policy, and process). Along each dimension qualities range from a narrow focus on the self to a broader focus on others and the system as a whole. Previous evidence suggests that women would be more likely to be found among the consensus- and process-oriented leaders. Interviews with ninety legislative leaders in twenty-two states found that women more often considered their leadership styles to be based on cooperation and consensus-building qualities, while men usually described their styles as strong, directive, and oriented toward power and control.[45]

Significantly, the trend toward professionalized legislatures (higher salaries, more days in session, larger staffs) is also producing a trend toward the feminization of leadership. The number of women in leadership positions has increased almost in proportion to the number of women serving in state legislative institutions. And as legislatures have become more professional, their members have become more resistant to autocratic leadership styles. Both male and female leaders are more prone to adopt a "female" style of leadership that emphasizes consensus building and broader concerns about the political system as a whole in response to underlying changes in the institutions themselves.[46] By contrast, a study of female committee chairs found that legislative professionalization produced a negative effect on the collaborative style favored by women.[47]

The committee chair is one of the most important leadership positions within legislative institutions. Legislatures divide the work of detailed policy development and scrutiny among committees that are charged with drafting legislation, holding hearings, reaching compromises on competing interests, and ultimately presenting the draft legislation to the full body for consideration. This makes committees a central force of power and influence within the institution. Political scientist Lyn Kathlene examined the gendered dynamics of verbal exchanges within committee hearings.[48] Female chairs spoke less, took fewer turns at speaking, and interrupted less frequently than male chairs. Male chairs influenced committee hearings by engaging in substantive comments more than females did and, in the process, interjected their opinions more often. In one out of six turns, men "interjected personal opinions or guided the committee members and witnesses to a topic of their interest."[49]

Researchers have also found that in situations where women constitute the minority in a deliberative group, the rules regarding how decisions are made impact whether or not their voice is heard. Under experimental conditions, when women are the numerical minority in deliberating groups instructed to decide by majority rule (in contrast to a unanimous decision), they are significantly less likely to speak and to be considered influential than men in their groups.[50] Taking this one step further, the researchers asked, "Does low descriptive representation inhibit substantive representation for women in deliberating groups?" Again, this depends on the way decisions are made. When women are in the numeric majority and the decision is by majority rule, "they are more likely to voice women's distinctive concerns about children, family, the poor, and the needy, and less likely to voice men's distinctive concerns." However, when women are in the minority (as they are in nearly every governing body), they are better off with a unanimous decision-making rule so that their perspective must be included. "If one had to pick the setting that yields the most forms of substantive representation for women, one should pick majority rule with many women."[51]

Leadership Roles

If we are to conclude that women make a substantial difference in politics, we must move past style and even policy outcomes to examine their impact on the institution itself. Do women, by their very presence, change the way Congress works? It is a difficult question to answer. One way to go about it is to investigate whether women change their male colleagues' behavior or significantly impact the way male legislators see politics. Another way to leave a lasting impact is for women to be fully integrated into the leadership structure, from committee chair to formal power positions such as Speaker of the House. Representatives in these positions play a central role in defining the legislative agenda and may serve either as facilitators or as gatekeepers for other members with leadership ambitions.

"Simply put, men continue to represent the face of the United States' political institutions," write Jennifer Lawless and Sean Theriault.[52] Colorado representative Patricia Schroeder was the first woman ever appointed to the House Armed Services Committee (93rd Congress, 1973–1974), and she recalls that her appointment was not met with enthusiasm by the chair, Edward Hebert of Louisiana:

> He didn't appreciate the idea of a girl and a black [Ron Dellums] forced on him. He was outraged that for the first time a chairman's veto of potential members was ignored. He announced that while he might not be able to control the makeup of the committee, he could damn well control the number of chairs in his hearing room. . . . He said that women and blacks were worth only half of one "regular" member, so he added only one seat to the committee room and made Ron and me share it.[53]

In the 114th Congress, women occupied a more limited set of leadership positions than in the sessions immediately preceding. Representative Nancy Pelosi (D-Calif.) was elected Speaker of the House of Representatives in the 110th Congress (2007–2009). Her election to the Speaker's post represented a first for women and shattered "not a glass ceiling but a marble ceiling" in the halls of Congress, Pelosi said.[54] Pelosi relinquished the Speaker's role when the Republicans won a majority of the seats in 2012.[55]

Since that achievement, there have been few significant gains in women's representation among the highest echelons of committee power in either house. Women have never chaired more than three committees in a single Congress. More significant is that only one woman has ever chaired one of the "power/prestige committees," which include the Appropriations and the Ways and Means committees in the House, and the Appropriations, Armed Services, Finance, and Foreign Policy committees in the Senate. Maryland senator Barbara Mikulski chaired the Senate Appropriations Committee from 2012 to 2015. In the 114th Congress, Representative Candice Miller (R-Mich.) is the only female committee chair. She chairs the House Administration Committee, one of twenty standing committees. In the Senate, Lisa Murkowski (R-Alaska) chairs the Energy and Natural Resources Committee. In the first Congress to boast 100 women, the lack of women selected for leadership positions in the Republican-controlled Congress attracted notice. "House Republicans Just Picked 21 Committee Chairs. 20 Are Men," wrote the *Atlantic*. The Democratic Congressional Campaign Committee's Emily Bittner had this to say in a statement: "With a leadership team that looks like an episode of *Mad Men*, we can expect House Republicans will continue their assault on women's health and continue to block economic progress for women on issues like equal pay."[56] By contrast, in the Democratic-controlled Senate in 2013, women chaired six of twenty committees, including the Senate Budget Committee (Sen. Patty Murray) and the Senate Intelligence Committee (Sen. Dianne Feinstein).

Worth far more than symbolism, women's ascension to leadership positions, particularly policy committee chairs, positions them to shape the legislative agenda and exert substantive policy influence. It took twenty-four years in the House of Representatives before Representative Patricia Schroeder had risen sufficiently in seniority to chair a subcommittee of the House Armed Services Committee. Among the limited number of women who have chaired committees, many have now retired (including Schroeder). Lawless and Theriault conclude that women's early retirements may work against their accumulating sufficient seniority to achieve powerful committee positions. Members of the House who have served for a long time without attaining powerful positions were more likely to retire than both long-serving powerful members and newly elected members.[57] Furthermore, the more satisfied members are with their careers, the longer they are likely to stay. Positional considerations played a more central role in women's decision to leave than was true for men.

Whereas men seem more or less satisfied by service in the House, women appear to need policy influence to satisfy their career goals. When their initial goals have been met and no new challenges in the form of substantive leadership positions present themselves, women are likely to leave the House, thereby foreclosing the additional power and influence that accrue with seniority. Thus women's numeric under-representation is exacerbated by the fact that women are less likely to hold leadership positions in Congress. If men and women did not differ in their policy priorities, perhaps it wouldn't matter. However, there is clear evidence that women and men in public office pursue distinct agendas.

Policy Priorities

What is women's role in defining and promoting women's interests? To argue that women alone are responsible for protecting women, children, and the vulnerable in society suggests again that women have some quality in their nature that men lack. Does this line of reasoning promote women's equality or relegate women to the sidelines of institutional politics? On one hand, women representatives focusing on "women's issues" would shine a brighter light on those issues and, in theory, lead to more policies that would benefit women. On the other hand, if only women focus on "women's issues," that both ghettoizes those issues and creates a separation between female and male officeholders.

The contemporary focus on women as "different" is in part fueled by psycholo-gist Carol Gilligan's work on the moral reasoning of men and women. Her book, *In a Different Voice*, provides theoretical fuel for political scientists to empirically test whether men's and women's approaches to policy making differ in substan-tive ways. Men view individuals as situated within a hierarchical and competitive world, value the protection of individual rights, and are more likely to solve prob-lems using an "ethic of justice." Alternatively, women view the world as a series of interdependent, connected relationships. Because Gilligan believes that women are more likely to see individuals in terms of their "symbiotic relationships" to others, she argues that women will approach problem solving from an "ethic of care." Numerous studies find that women are more likely than men to sponsor or cosponsor legislation about women's rights and reproductive health choices as well as bills dealing with children, health care, and welfare. When combined with the "difference" argument, we are returned to the central question of how substantive and descriptive representation are linked.[58]

Sociologist Rosabeth Moss Kanter found that when members of a minor-ity group made up 15 percent or less of the total membership of a group, the larger group perceived them as tokens. This token status changed their behavior, and these minority-group members tended to respond in "unnatural" ways. As minorities in organizations reached "tilted" status (between 15 and 40 percent of the whole) or approached a "balanced" status (defined as a 40–60 split), they were able to respond in an unrestrained fashion. Building on this theoretical framework, known in the scholarship as **critical mass**,[59] political scientist Sue Thomas hypothesized that as the percentage of women in a legislative body increases, so too does the likelihood that women legislators will sponsor more bills relating to women, children, and families. Likewise, in states with more women legislators, the passage rates for bills on women, children, and families will be higher.[60] Thomas found that in states with more than 20 percent women legislators, women gave priority to bills related to women, children, and families more often than men did. In states that had the lowest percentages of women in their legislatures, no bills related to women, children, and families were introduced by either men or women.[61]

Kathleen Bratton examined legislative behavior (agenda setting, bill sponsorship, number of women's interest bills passed) in three states over thirty years (1969–1999) and found little support for the expectation that women serving in legislative bodies where they have "token" status differ from their male colleagues. Indeed, she noted, "gender differences in agenda-setting behavior in some states narrow as the percentage of women in the legislature increases."[62] One explanation Bratton gives for why her findings appear contrary to Kanter's theory is that women may respond to their token status with overachievement. More likely, the legislative and political contexts are substantively different from the corporate world Kanter used to develop her theory. Women elected officials are interested in "women's issues"—they may have campaigned based on a women's agenda, and they are less likely to object to being singled out as a woman than females in the corporate world, where identity has less relevance to the substantive work. Overall, the aggregate results indicate that as the number of women in a legislature grows, the potential for changes in the lived experiences of female citizens improves.[63] Amy Caiazza's study linking women's representation and women-friendly policy also demonstrates a strong positive relationship between the proportion of women in legislative seats and executive positions across the fifty states and the adoption of policies favorable to women.[64]

There is also some evidence that women officeholders provide an important form of symbolic representation in the form of political empowerment. Women represented by other women are more interested in politics, participate more, and have a greater sense of efficacy and political competence.[65] Similarly, a study of men and women living in congressional districts served by female legislators found that women exhibited a sense of political empowerment, a sort of psychic benefit derived from being represented by a woman in Congress. Men, however, did not derive the same benefit. The statistical differences noted between men's empowerment when represented by a woman and alternatively by a man suggest that the effect on women is derived from a type of symbolic representation and not district-specific characteristics that could also explain the election of a woman. Interestingly, women do not appear to expect more in the way of tangible benefits when they are represented by a woman.[66] However, it remains to be seen whether women's satisfaction with mere symbolic representation will decline over time as female officeholders become a more integral part of governing. Presumably, tangible benefits could combine with symbolic empowerment to produce an even stronger relationship between the gender of constituents and their representatives.

WOMEN IN POLITICAL ROLES

In this section, we consider the experiences and influence of women political insiders in the three branches of government—executive, legislative, and judicial—at the local, state, and federal levels of government.

Women in Local Government

In May 2016, the Seattle City Council voted 5 to 4 against a land use deal that supporters argued would have positioned the city to attract a professional basketball team by building a new sports arena. Normally, a vote like this wouldn't attract much attention beyond the city. However, Seattle's city council is majority female, and the vote broke along gender lines, with all five no votes cast by women. They explained that "giving over city resources for the project without any promise that a National Basketball Association team would come—and with recent comments by league officials that no new franchise was likely—made the arena terms questionable, and that another location already owned by the city, should be considered."[67] As a result of their votes, the councilwomen were attacked in hundreds of emails and social media posts—most of which are too profane to print here. One email from a local male attorney read in part: "As women, I understand that you spend a lot of your time trying to please others (mostly on your knees) but I can only hope that you each find ways to quickly and painfully end yourselves. Each of you should rot in hell for what you took from me yesterday."[68] In an op-ed published by the *Seattle Times*, the five councilwomen addressed the situation directly: "The misogynistic backlash to our vote is an attempt to communicate a dangerous message: Elected women in Seattle do not deserve the respect necessary to make tough decisions without the fear of violence and racially and sexually charged retaliation." They continued, "Make no mistake: We are not deterred. We will not be silenced with threats, not today, not tomorrow and not ever."[69]

Unlike federal and state governments, where executive or legislative positions are limited by the small number of offices available, local government offers women thousands of opportunities for public service. According to the US Census Bureau, there are 89,476 local governments in the country. These include counties, municipalities (mainly cities or towns), townships (less extensive powers), school districts, and special districts (water, sewer, fire protection, etc.).[70] The Center for American Women and Politics estimates that in 2016, 18 percent of mayors of US cities with populations over 30,000 were women.

IMAGE 5.3: *Stephanie Rawlings-Blake, mayor of Baltimore and DNC Secretary, announces the opening of the Democratic National Convention on July 25, 2016 in Philadelphia. Ms. Rawlings-Blake chose not to seek re-election as mayor in 2016.* Source: © Li Muzi/Xinhua/Alamy Live News.

As the city size increases, the likelihood of a woman mayor decreases. In medium-sized cities (population of 100,000–500,000), 17 percent of mayors are women, while just 15 percent of big-city mayors are female (cities with populations over 500,000).[71]

Two of the nation's largest cities are led by young African American women. Stephanie Rawlings-Blake became the mayor of Baltimore in 2010, when Sheila Dixon resigned from office following her conviction for embezzlement. Rawlings-Blake was president of the City Council at the time. She was elected to a full term the following year, winning 84 percent of the vote. Rawlings-Blake chose not to seek re-election in 2016; her successor, Catherine Pugh is also African American. Muriel Bowser is mayor of the District of Columbia, elected in 2014 with 54 percent of the vote. Both cities are challenged by poverty, crime, and the need to improve schools. Annise Parker served three terms (2010–2016) as mayor of Houston, Texas. Parker was the first openly LGBT person elected mayor of a major US city. In her final year, she introduced the Houston Equal Rights Ordinance (HERO), banning discrimination based on sexual orientation and gender identity (criteria not covered by federal antidiscrimination laws) in city employment, city services, city contracting practices, housing, public accommodations, and private employment. Although HERO was passed by the Houston City Council, it was defeated by a ballot referendum. Parker was term-limited and left office in January 2016 but has expressed interest in running for another position.

Mayor and city council positions are primary pipeline offices for state and national positions. A study of women's pathways to the state legislatures found that prior experience on a local or county board or commission (other than a school board) was most common (38 percent), followed by service on a school board (26 percent). Sixteen percent of women elected for the first time to the state legislature had prior elected or appointed experience on a local council (county or city).[72] Pragmatically speaking, women local leaders gain valuable connections and skills necessary to win higher levels of office.

Researchers at Emory University explored the question of why women's descriptive representation in policy-making positions is higher in some cities than in others.[73] What explains where women get elected? In their examination of 239 cities with populations of 100,000 or more, the authors found that the election of women as council members and the election of women as mayors are interdependent, meaning that women's presence in one institution affects their success in winning a seat in the other. Preliminary results suggest that women's presence on a council is more important to electing a female mayor than vice versa. The urban political context also influenced the ability of women to win elective office. While scholars in the 1970s predicted that women would be elected mayor in small communities where the position held less prestige, today studies find that larger municipalities are more conducive to women's representation. Women are more likely to be elected in communities with highly educated residents. The presence of women's political organizations in urban areas also contributes to women's election.

Women's interest in seeking political office at the local level has been documented by several scholars. Contrary to what is seen in state and federal offices, there is no ambition gap between men and women when it comes to local officeholding. Women express as much interest as men in council-level and mayoral positions, and there is more ambition among women than men for seats on the local school board.[74] Before running for office, most women elected as mayor have been active in the community with women's or civic organizations, have gained campaign experience by working to elect another candidate, and have held at least one prior elected or appointed position. Unlike at the state and federal levels, political considerations (e.g., public scrutiny, funding, party support, prior experience) played far less of a role than personal considerations (approval of a spouse and their children's ages). Friends and family exercised unique influence in either encouraging or discouraging a woman's candidacy for mayor. Finally, women more often than men were motivated to seek the mayor's job by their concern over a particular public policy issue—particularly in larger cities.

Once elected, do women at the local level make a difference? The evidence of women's substantive impact is mixed. A study of mayors in cities with populations over 30,000 found more similarities than differences among men and women on policy issues and the use of power. Men and women differed on the budget, however. Female mayors were more willing than male mayors to change the budget process and admit that fiscal problems existed in their cities. In describing how they would change the budgetary process, women were more inclusive and sought to broaden participation in the process, whereas men pursued changes that would allow them to exercise more control over the process.[75] Adrienne Smith argues that it is not just the presence of women that matters but also the power of the position they hold relative to others in the same municipality. Cities led by women will be more likely to produce policy outputs associated with women's needs and interests. She found that "empowered female executives in municipal governments influenced expenditure decisions made as part of the federal Community Development Block Grant program," dedicating a higher percentage of funds to programs and services for child care, youth, abused and battered spouses, and abused and neglected children.[76] Mirya Holman, in her book *Women in Politics in the American City*, also finds strong support indicating that electing women matters to policy and spending decisions and to the political culture of the city.[77] Another study, however, found no effect at all of the gender of the mayor on policy outcomes, hypothesizing that the types of policies relevant to local government mitigate the potential policy changes that might come from electing a woman as mayor.[78] The researchers note that "economic responsibilities such as local taxation and the provision of basic services are the province of city government, while social issues such as abortion and gun control are not. If the gender divide is not wide on the issues central to local government, catering to gender differences is less useful as an electoral strategy."[79]

Beyond substantive outcomes, there is also evidence that having women in office at the local level matters for symbolic reasons. Women in local office serve as role models for other women thinking about running for office. This has proven true beyond the United States as well. In India, increased presence and visibility of female local politicians raised the academic performance and career aspirations of young women. In villages that had never had female political leaders, researchers found that parents were 45 percent less likely to expect daughters to continue beyond secondary school, and girls were 32 percent less likely than boys to express those aspirations. In villages where a female political leader had served for at least two terms, girls' educational aspirations were equal to those of boys, and parents were much more likely to expect their daughters to achieve the same level of education as their sons. "We think this is due to a role model effect: Seeing women in charge persuaded parents and teens that women can run things, and increased their ambitions," said Esther Duflo, coauthor of the study.[80] In India, West Bengal is a particularly good place to test this relationship because gender quotas are in place for elected positions on village councils, and one-third of village councils are randomly selected to be reserved for a woman chief councilor in every election.

Women holding local office, whether elected or appointed, are well positioned to exert influence in a variety of ways both substantive and symbolic. Political context—partisanship, the means of selection, the power of the position relative to others, and whether or not women constitute a majority or minority—all matter in explaining the relative strength of women's influence in government. While there is proof that women leaders at the local level can be empowering to some, the Seattle example attests that they can be threatening to others.

Women Executives in the States

Perhaps it is the singular nature of executive roles that explains why no woman has yet been elected president and so very few have been elected as governor. In 2016, only six of fifty governors were women, and almost half of the states had never elected a woman state executive. Given that governors are heavily represented in the eligibility pool for presidential candidates, the lack of women in the states' top job is troubling. Women are underrepresented in statewide office in general. Beyond governor, statewide offices include lieutenant governor, attorney general, state comptroller, secretary of state, state superintendent of education, commissioner of labor, commissioner of insurance, state treasurer, state auditor, and railroad commissioner, among others. Titles and opportunities vary widely by state, but women held only 24 percent of these positions in 2016.[81]

In explaining why so few women are elected governor, researchers have concluded that "voters appear to be more comfortable with women in typically 'feminine' statewide elective executive offices, such as state education official, than in more 'masculine' offices like governor."[82] Democratic women were more likely to secure the nomination in states where women have a strong presence in the state legislature, consistent with the eligibility pool argument. Jason Windett examined a period of thirty years (1978–2008) and discovered that women were more likely to enter primaries in states with more women in the legislature and a culture favorable to women in elective office.[83] Windett also found that male governors were more likely than female governors to have been recruited by their political party and to receive the party's backing. For example, Republican women were not often selected as the party nominee when an open seat was available. Kelly Dittmar surveyed political consultants on their perceptions of voter support for women candidates. Forty-three percent of Democratic campaign consultants believe it is more likely that voters will support a woman for US senator than for governor; one-third believe that voters are equally likely to support a woman in either position; and only 14 percent believe voters will be more likely to elect a woman as governor than as a US senator. By way of explanation, one consultant remarked, "It's more difficult for voters to envision a female candidate in an executive role, than as 1 of 100 senators."[84] Republican consultants were much more likely to think that voters would be just as likely to support a woman as a man for these two offices (72 percent).

Since there have been so few women governors, there is very little research on how women act in the gubernatorial role and their effectiveness as state executives.

In 2010, voters in South Carolina elected Nikki Haley as the first woman governor of the state; she is also the first minority woman (Indian American) to lead the state. Voters in New Mexico elected Susana Martinez governor, making her the first Latina governor in the country. Both women have been identified as rising stars in the Republican Party; both were widely discussed as possible vice presidential running mates in 2016, but neither governor wished to be considered for the Trump presidential ticket. Haley has focused her attention on economic issues in South Carolina, attracting international manufacturing giants to the state with generous financial incentives. Martinez was selected chair of the Republican Governors Association in 2016.

Women Legislators in Congress and in the States

"What would change if Congress were as lopsidedly female as it is male? Not much."
—The Fix blog, *Washington Post*, March 6, 2015

"What would change if there were more women in Congress? More than you think."
—Monkey Cage blog, *Washington Post*, March 7, 2015

A majority of the research on women in public office has been conducted on legislators. We have already covered some of that research (e.g., on policy priorities) above. In this section, we will focus on the impact of gender on how legislative business is conducted, the influence of intersectionality on women's experience and effectiveness as legislators, and the efficacy of a women's caucus in advancing gender equality.

The competing headlines from two *Washington Post* political blogs frame our inquiry nicely. Journalist Philip Bump, a contributor to *The Fix* posed the first question because the 114th Congress (2015–2017) was the most diverse in our history—albeit still 80 percent male and 80 percent white. Bump examined roll call votes and simulated the impact of a Congress that was 80 percent female by flipping the genders within each political party. Because the party majority remained the same, and because, as we've seen above, men and women are more like one another within parties now than they are different across genders, he found that a supermajority-female Congress would make little difference. In the second question, political scientist and contributor to *Monkey Cage* John Sides went beyond roll call votes in his thought experiment. By defining "congressional action" to include agenda setting, bill sponsorship, and issue selection, he found that the research to date would predict a different set of outcomes. It will be a long time until we have a true empirical test, since we know from Chapter 4 that even if all of the women who ever served in Congress were serving at this moment, women's representation would only hit 63 percent, far short of the 80 percent imagined here.

FIGURE 5.1: Percentage of Women in Elective Office, 1971–2015

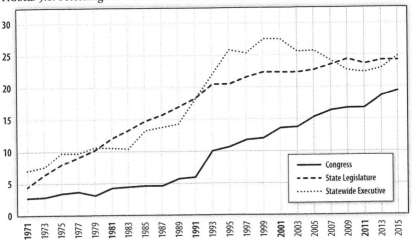

Source: Center for American Women and Politics, Eagleton Institute of Politics, Rutgers University.

The Impact of Gender on Legislative Business

Women's progress toward parity has been slow (see Figure 5.1) and at the state legislative level seems to have reached a plateau. Women continue to make gains in Congress, but the trend line here too is relatively flat. Whatever impact women have in legislative bodies, they act from a minority position. Widely cited research that coined the phrase "Jackie (and Jill) Robinson effect" suggest that women who overcome the odds and win a seat in Congress may be more ambitious or more qualified than their male peers, enabling them to outperform their male colleagues once elected.[85] Performance in this case was measured by the number of bills congressmen and congresswomen within a given district sponsored and the amount of federal dollars they were able to direct to their home districts over a twenty-year period (1984–2004). "On average, women sponsor about three more bills per Congress, which is a difference of roughly 17 percent relative to the member average of 18 bills and cosponsor about 26 more bills per congress than congressmen," the researchers noted. Women are also more successful in attracting federal dollars to their home district. Controlling for all sorts of factors that might account for increased funding, women bring home roughly 9 percent (approximately $49 million) more in federal spending. The "female effect" explains more of the variation in federal spending distribution than does membership in the majority party or seniority of the member.

For decades researchers have confirmed that women in Congress and in state legislatures are more likely than their male counterparts to sponsor legislation related to women's interests, particularly bills having to do with women's health, safety, and reproductive issues. In the 114th Congress, women were particularly active on the issue of sexual assault in the military. Democratic senators Kirsten Gillibrand (N.Y.) and Claire McCaskill (Mo.) each sponsored competing bills. Gillibrand's approach would have removed the decision to prosecute an alleged sexual assault from a commander in favor of an independent military prosecutor, arguing that keeping rape prosecution in the chain of command is part of the reason so few military sexual assaults are prosecuted (in 2014, there were 6,131 reports of sexual assault, but only 317 servicemembers were court-martialed and sentenced to confinement, for a 1-in-20 conviction and incarceration rate).[86] Gillibrand's bill was defeated in 2013, but she has indicated that she may reintroduce her bill. McCaskill's bill, which passed the Senate in March 2014 by a vote of 100–0, moved to eliminate the "good soldier" legal defense unless a defendant's character in the military is directly tied to the alleged crime. It would also allow sexual assault victims to weigh in on whether their cases should be prosecuted in a civilian court instead of in the military justice system. Finally, victims could use a confidential process to challenge any discharge or separation from the service that comes as a result of their cases. These differences in approach to the same problem came from within the same party and were hotly debated in the press. This example, and countless others, demonstrates the substantive value women bring to the legislature.

How women behave within the institution is also the subject of new research. Women of the Senate in particular have been characterized as collaborative problem solvers. Political scientists Jennifer Lawless and Sean Theriault found that women placed a higher value on civility than their male colleagues and were more likely to be proactive in finding ways to engage one another across the aisle and get to know each other as people. Studying two informal activities, the Secret Santa Gift Exchange and Seersucker Thursday, Lawless and Theriault found clear evidence that women differ from men when it comes to social engagement off the Senate floor. Women were "consistently more likely than men to participate in both activities designed to promote a sense of comity and collegiality" even though each activity was first introduced to the chamber by a male senator (Al Franken and Trent Lott, respectively).[87]

Having established that women appear to value collegiality more than men do, the researchers turned to the question of whether this impacted their legislative behavior. Media accounts of the female senators' role in finding a solution to the 2013 government shutdown aside, do women engage in the same type of legislative maneuvering that could effectively obstruct the legislative process and limit debate in favor of their bills? After examining procedural votes separately by party, Lawless and Theriault found little evidence that men and women differ in their procedural votes, concluding, "The data simply do not support the notion that women are more likely than men to be 'problem solvers' who vote with members of the other party when it comes to moving the legislative process forward."[88] Women, like men, are creatures of their district and, even more significant, of their political party.

Intersectionality and Minority Women Legislators

A growing body of research focuses on the intersection of gender, race, and ethnicity in shaping a legislator's behavior and effectiveness. Beth Reingold and Adrienne Smith investigate intersectionality's effect on welfare policy by comparing two approaches to understanding gender, race, and ethnicity. The additive approach assumes gender and race/ethnicity are distinct and independent. In this theoretical framework, female state legislators (regardless of race/ethnicity) would aim to mitigate the more restrictive and punitive aspects of welfare reform, similar to what African American and Latino legislators would do. The intersectional approach highlights the overlapping and interdependent nature of gender and race/ethnicity. Using this construction, Reingold and Smith hypothesize that legislative women of color would have the strongest countervailing effect on punitive aspects of state welfare reform, stronger than that of white women or of men of color. Their analysis reveals that "the impact of legislative women on welfare policy is highly contingent: depending on which women and which policies one examines, the presence and power of legislative women has a liberal effect, a conservative effect, or no effect. Across the policy dimensions, however, legislative women of color have a distinctive effect, one that is more consistent and consistently liberal than that of other legislative women or men of color."[89]

The research on intersectionality reminds us not to generalize too quickly about women's representation across race and ethnicity. Reingold and Haynie caution that to do so is to risk obscuring the representational advocacy provided by women of color, while privileging that provided by white women.[90] The researchers examined agenda-setting behavior of state legislators (male and female, African American, Latino/a, and white). No matter what definition of "women's interests" they employed, they found that "legislative women of color never appear disengaged from or significantly less committed to women's substantive representation than anyone else." Women in government articulate and act upon women's interests more so than men do, and that is true of all women.

African American women in Congress constitute a rather small but highly visible group. They face additional expectations about their behavior as legislators, and feel pressure to represent the interests of both women and African Americans. Their dilemma stems, again, from difficulty in defining a constituency based on some essential characteristic that may or may not unite them around a common agenda. "We're expected to be representatives on economic issues, health issues, housing issues, the issue of incarceration of black males and drugs," says Maxine Waters, a Democratic congresswoman from California. "But at the same time, because of the nature of this job and the nature of our work, it creates the need to be assertive. And sometimes [women lawmakers] are criticized for being too aggressive. Somehow, there is a desire for [women] to be tough, but not to show it, or to be aggressive, but to mask it in ways that men are not asked to do."[91] Eleanor

Holmes Norton, the nonvoting delegate from the District of Columbia, says that her preparation to represent dual interests stems from a lifetime's experience with both racism and sexism:

> Much of my view of women comes out of the life I've lived and the commitments I've made long before even thinking about running for Congress. Growing up in a segregated city and going to segregated schools raised my consciousness very early about [racial] discrimination. . . . The transfer of that from blacks to women was almost automatic. . . . By the time I got to Congress, my view on women and my feeling of responsibility for pressing forward their demands was very well formed. . . . This was just another place, another forum, to act on them.[92]

Fewer studies have been conducted on minority women's behavior as public officials, maybe because of the relatively small sample of minority officials to study. Of the 104 women serving in Congress in 2016, 33 were women of color: 18 African Americans, 9 Latinas, and 6 Asian Americans/Pacific Islanders. In addition, a black woman, an Asian American/Pacific Islander woman, and a Caribbean American woman served as delegates to the House from Washington, D.C., American Samoa, and the Virgin Islands, respectively. Women of color constituted 6.2 percent of the 535 members of the US Congress. In the state legislatures, women of color were 21.9 percent of the 1,815 total women who served nationwide.

The Role of a Women's Caucus in Facilitating Legislation for Women

Several studies note that an organized caucus for women's interests facilitates favorable legislation for women. Sue Thomas found that without gender balance or a critical mass of women in state legislatures, women's caucuses were instrumental in bringing attention to issues related to women, children, and families.[93] "When a caucus bands together, the result is political clout—a weapon with the potential to overcome skewed groups."[94]

In 1977, when only eighteen women (a little more than 3 percent) sat in Congress, fifteen women founded the Congresswomen's Caucus, later renamed the Congressional Caucus for Women's Issues (CCWI). Since its inception, the women's caucus has been a bipartisan organization cochaired by a Democrat and a Republican. To extend the caucus's influence, the Women's Research and Education Institute (WREI) was also founded in 1977 and remained organizationally linked to the caucus until 1985.[95] The CCWI provides two functions: to advocate for women and families, and to serve as an information clearinghouse on women's issues in Congress. The caucus has had several major legislative victories across nearly forty years of existence, including the Pregnancy Discrimination Act, the Family and Medical Leave Act, and the Violence Against Women Act, to name just three.[96]

In March 2016, three women representatives in the House announced the formation of a Congressional Caucus on Black Women and Girls, devoted to creating public policy that "eliminates significant barriers and disparities experienced by black women." The founders, US representatives Bonnie Watson Colman (D-N.J.), Robin Kelly (D-Ill.), and Yvette D. Clarke (D-N.Y.) noted in a press release that the CCBWG is the first of 430 registered congressional caucuses and member organizations that is specifically intended to make black women and girls a priority. Areas of action will include safety, economic opportunity, health concerns, justice, and participation in the electorate.[97]

Women in the Federal Executive Branch

Within the federal executive branch, there are permanent civil service jobs and political appointments. The Office of Personnel Management (OPM) is the human resources arm of the federal government. The Pendleton Civil Service Act of 1883 established a nonpartisan federal workforce, classifying certain jobs, removing them from the patronage ranks, and setting up the Civil Service Commission to administer a system based on merit rather than political connections. As the classified list was expanded over the years, it provided the American people with a competent and permanent government bureaucracy. By 1897, almost half of all federal employees were in classified positions. Today, with the exception of a few thousand policy-level appointments, nearly all federal jobs are handled within the civil service system. Although hiring is presumably based on merit, women still occupy a smaller percentage of the federal civil service workforce, have historically been overrepresented in the lower grades (meaning they are paid less), and are less likely than men to qualify for the preferences granted to veterans.

Women make up 43 percent of the federal workforce, slightly below the proportion of women in the workforce as a whole (47 percent). Fifty-eight percent of female federal workers are white, 24 percent are African American, 8 percent are Hispanic/Latina, and 6 percent are Asian American. Women make up 18.7 percent of all veterans working in the federal civil service. The Senior Executive Service (SES) was created to attract and retain talented senior management in government service. Women make up 34 percent of the SES—twice the share of women in private sector executive officer positions. The pay gap is smallest among this group; women in the SES earned 99.2 cents for every dollar their male counterparts made in 2014. Overall, female white-collar federal workers earn 87 cents for every dollar earned by a male white-collar federal worker.

There are more women among younger federal workers (ages twenty-five to forty-four), and women in this age group are more likely to be on a management track than women a decade ago. The federal government offers a number of flexible-workplace options, such as child care, working remotely, and alternative work schedules, that are attractive to both men and women. Women, however, express

Women World Leaders, 2016

Of 195 countries in the world today, seventeen nations are led by a woman president or prime minister. The table below lists the women who currently serve as president or prime minister of their country and the percentage of the lower legislative house held by women.

Country	Female Leader (Year Elected [E] or Appointed [A])	Percentage of Women in Lower House
Germany	Chancellor Angela Merkel (E, 2005)	36.5%
Liberia	President Ellen Johnson-Sirleaf (E, 2006)	11.0%
Chile	President Michelle Bachelet (E, 2006–2010; 2014)	15.8%
Bangladesh	Prime Minister Sheikh Hasina Wajed (E, 2009)	20.0%
Lithuania	President Dalia Grybauskaite (E, 2009)	21.3%
Trinidad and Tobago	Prime Minister Kamla Persad-Bissessar (E, 2010)	31.0%
Republic of Korea	President Park Geun-hye (E, 2013)	17.0%
Norway	Prime Minister Erna Solberg (E, 2013)	39.6%
Malta	President Marie-Louise Coleiro Preca (E, 2014)	12.9%
Croatia	President Kolinda Grabar-Kitarovic (E, 2015)	12.6%

Source: "Worldwide Guide to Women in Leadership," http://www.guide2womenleaders .com (data current as of October 24, 2016); Inter-Parliamentary Union, http://www.ipu .org/wmn-e/classif.htm (data current as of November 1, 2016).

slightly higher levels of satisfaction with each of these initiatives. "Our work-life policies are continually evolving to make the balance of caring for families and pursuing a career complementary rather than contradictory," said OPM director Katherine Archuleta in 2014.[98]

In addition to elective office, women also gain political power through appointments to governmental positions. Frances Perkins, appointed by President

Country	Female Leader (Year Elected [E] or Appointed [A])	Percentage of Women in Lower House
Namibia	Prime Minister Saara Kuugongelwa-Amadhila (A, 2015)	41.3%
Mauritius	President Ameenah Gurib-Fakim (E, 2015)	11.6%
Nepal	President Bidhya Devi Bhandari (E, 2015)	29.6%
Poland	Prime Minister Beata Szydlo (A, 2015)	27.4%
Marshall Islands	President Hilda Heine (E, 2016)	9.1%
Myanmar	State Councilor Aung San Suu Kyi (A, 2016)*	9.9%
Taiwan	President Tsai Ing-wen (E, 2016)	38.1%
Great Britain, UK	Theresa May (E, 2016)	29.6%
Austria	Doris Bures (E, 2016)	30.6%
Estonia	Kersti Kaljulai (E, 2016)	23.8%

* The country's constitution was written specifically to prevent Aung San Suu Kyi from becoming president, so the parliament created the post of state councilor, a role similar to prime minister.

For Critical Analysis

Look at the data in the table. What patterns do you notice? Are there any regional or geographic patterns? Is there a correlation between a female head of state and women in the legislature? The number of women world leaders has more than doubled since 2005, and many of these women are the first in their nation to hold the top political position. What do these data tell us about women and political representation? What other data might be useful to look at to analyze and understand women's rise to power around the world?

Franklin D. Roosevelt in 1933 as secretary of labor, was the first woman to serve in a presidential cabinet. Since the cabinet was established in 1789, there have been forty-eight female cabinet members (roughly 5 percent). When Bill Clinton was elected in 1992, he pledged to appoint a first-term cabinet that "looked like America." In keeping that promise, he named four women to cabinet positions, including Janet Reno, the first woman ever appointed attorney general. In

December 1996, Clinton named Madeleine K. Albright secretary of state, making her the highest-ranking woman to serve in the US government at the time. In 2001, George W. Bush appointed Condoleezza Rice national security advisor. Rice joined four other women in Bush's cabinet during the first administration and was appointed secretary of state in the administration's second term.

President Obama is credited with appointing the most demographically diverse administration in history. Women and minorities occupy 53.3 percent of the political appointments confirmed by the Senate in the Obama administration. President George W. Bush, by contrast, filled just 25.6 percent of positions with women and minorities, and Bill Clinton 37.5 percent.[99] The percentage of African Americans appointed to positions during two Obama terms is 14.4 percent, just one point higher than during Clinton's eight years. Notably, President Obama selected Loretta Lynch as US attorney general, making her the first African American woman to hold the position. The small increase in African Americans' share can be attributed to a combination of factors. President Clinton made it a high priority to recruit black appointees, and in the twenty years between Democratic administrations, African Americans have found attractive opportunities elsewhere, making government service less attractive. The largest diversity gains during the Obama administration have been made by members of the LGBT community. President Obama selected Eric Fanning as the first openly gay US secretary of the army; he was confirmed by the Senate in May 2016. In addition to Fanning, Obama has appointed six openly gay ambassadors and a number of transgender men and women to federal posts. President Clinton was forced to use a recess appointment to install James Hormel as ambassador to Luxembourg, making him the first openly gay US ambassador. Hormel's nomination faced strong opposition from Republicans in the US Senate.

In addition to diversifying appointments, the Obama administration used the power of the White House to call attention to women's issues in a number of other ways. In 2009, Obama established the White House Council on Women and Girls (CWG) to coordinate efforts across federal agencies and departments to ensure that the needs of women and girls are taken into account in all programs, policies, and legislation. In November 2014, the CWG released a report, "Women and Girls of Color: Addressing Challenges and Expanding Opportunity." A working group has been created to implement the report's recommendations in areas such as education, economic security, health, criminal and juvenile justice, and violence. The president created the position of White House advisor on violence against women, and established the post of director for human rights and gender in the National Security Council. In June 2016, President Obama convened the first United State of Women Summit to celebrate progress and to create an action plan to deal with issues such as violence, the wage gap, and the absence of educational opportunities for women around the world. At the summit, the White House announced $50 million worth of commitments to improve the lives of women and girls and to target key gender gaps in society. One of the announced initiatives is the White House Equal Pay Pledge, in which participating companies promise to conduct an annual gender pay analysis and to reassess their hiring and promotion processes to ensure equity. Well-known technology companies such as Airbnb, Amazon, Pinterest, Slack, and Spotify were among the first to sign the pledge.[100] "We have to remember that progress is not inevitable. It's the result of decades of slow, tireless, often frustrated, and unheralded work," Obama said.

Women, when they have held executive appointments, have traditionally served as secretary of labor, health and human services, housing and urban development, or education—offices consistent with women's traditional points of intersection between the private and public spheres. In order to expand women's sphere of influence by diversifying women's appointments, the National Women's Political Caucus established the Coalition for Women's Appointments, made up of about sixty women's professional and issue groups. The coalition identified qualified women candidates for appointed positions and provided the incoming Obama administration with "seven hundred resumes of highly qualified, individually vetted women, including many who filled break-through positions in the military, economic, and scientific areas, such as chief scientist at the National Aeronautics and Space Administration."[101] Similarly, the National Political Congress of Black Women (NPCBW), through its Commission for the Presidential Appointment of African American Women, created a talent bank of highly qualified African American women for top political appointments.[102] The Gay and Lesbian Victory Fund supplied the Obama administration with the names and resumes of qualified LGBT candidates during the 2008 transition. Today at the state level, there is a variety of coalitions and organizations identifying, preparing, and supporting women to serve in decision-making roles in executive cabinets and on boards and commissions. In California, for example, the Latina Appointments Collaborative works to get women appointed to city- and county-level boards and commissions. In the 2012 presidential election, Republican candidate Mitt Romney was ridiculed on social media for his reference to being given "whole binders full of women" by women's groups in an effort to diversify his administration as governor of Massachusetts. But in fact, advocacy groups have been very effective at helping diversify the pools of candidates considered for top political appointments at all levels of government.

In addition to providing role models for other women, there is evidence that women in appointed positions govern differently than men. President Jimmy Carter's female appointees were more feminist than his male appointees, while the women in the Clinton administration selected more women to serve under them than the men did.[103] On the other hand, analysis of women in the executive branch over several administrations since the 1960s suggests that women have had difficulty overcoming their "token" or "other" status to provide substantive governance on the basis of their gender.[104] Still, two female secretaries of state—Madeleine Albright

TABLE 5.1: Women Appointed to Presidential Cabinets

Appointee	Position	Appointed By	Dates
Frances Perkins	Secretary of Labor	F. D. Roosevelt	1933–1945
Oveta Culp Hobby	Secretary of Health, Education, and Welfare	Eisenhower	1953–1955
Carla Anderson Hills	Secretary of Housing and Urban Development	Ford	1975–1977
Juanita M. Kreps	Secretary of Commerce	Carter	1977–1979
Patricia R. Harris	Secretary of Housing and Urban Development	Carter	1977–1979
Patricia R. Harris	Secretary of Health and Human Services	Carter	1979–1981
Shirley M. Hufstedler	Secretary of Education	Reagan	1981–1985
Margaret M. Heckler	Secretary of Health and Human Services	Reagan	1983–1985
Elizabeth H. Dole	Secretary of Transportation	Reagan	1983–1987
Anne McLaughlin	Secretary of Labor	Reagan	1987–1989
Elizabeth H. Dole	Secretary of Labor	Bush	1989–1991
Lynn Morley Martin	Secretary of Labor	Bush	1991–1993
Barbara H. Franklin	Secretary of Commerce	Bush	1992–1993
Hazel R. O'Leary	Secretary of Energy	Clinton	1993–1997
Janet Reno	Attorney General	Clinton	1993–2001

Source: "Women Appointed to Presidential Cabinets," Center for American Women and Politics, Eagleton Institute of Politics, Rutgers University, 2015.

and Hillary Clinton—are strong examples of how women in the executive branch might prioritize women's issues. Albright was an active participant and leader in international conferences dedicated to improving women's rights, and she exhibited a sensitivity to women's concerns in shaping US policy toward refugees. And as secretary of state in the Obama administration, Hillary Clinton expanded upon that work. "I want to pledge to you that as secretary of state I view women's issues as central to our foreign policy," Clinton said at her confirmation hearing, "not as adjunct or auxiliary or in any way lesser than all of the other issues that we have to confront."

Clinton's feminist rallying cry as First Lady addressing the United Nations, "Women's rights are human rights," shaped her approach to foreign policy in several important ways. As secretary of state, Clinton introduced the International Council on Women's Business Leadership to help women launch businesses and find mentors in male-dominated fields and led the creation of the US National Action Plan on Women, Peace and Security, laying out strategies for partnering with women to prevent conflicts, for increasing and strengthening protections for women and girls

TABLE 5.1: Women Appointed to Presidential Cabinets *(continued)*

Appointee	Position	Appointed By	Dates
Donna E. Shalala	Secretary of Health and Human Services	Clinton	1993–2001
Madeleine K. Albright	Secretary of State	Clinton	1997–2001
Alexis Herman	Secretary of Labor	Clinton	1997–2001
Elaine Chao	Secretary of Labor	G. W. Bush	2001–2009
Gale Norton	Secretary of Interior	G. W. Bush	2001–2006
Condoleezza Rice	National Security Advisor	G. W. Bush	2001–2005
Ann Veneman	Secretary of Agriculture	G. W. Bush	2001–2005
Margaret Spellings	Secretary of Education	G. W. Bush	2005–2009
Condoleezza Rice	Secretary of State	G. W. Bush	2005–2009
Mary Peters	Secretary of Transportation	G. W. Bush	2006–2009
Hillary Rodham Clinton	Secretary of State	Obama	2009–2013
Janet A. Napolitano	Secretary of Homeland Security	Obama	2009–2013
Hilda Solis	Secretary of Labor	Obama	2009–2013
Kathleen Sebelius	Secretary of Health and Human Services	Obama	2009–2014
Sally Jewell	Secretary of the Interior	Obama	2013-2017
Penny Pritzker	Secretary of Commerce	Obama	2013-2017
Sylvia Mathews Burwell	Secretary of Health and Human Services	Obama	2014-2017
Loretta Lynch	Attorney General	Obama	2015-2017

during and after conflict, and for integrating the needs of women and girls into relief and recovery efforts. Under her leadership, the United Nations adopted a resolution mandating that peacekeeping missions protect women and girls from sexual violence in armed conflict. She also elevated the importance of maternal and reproductive health care around the world. Finally, she created the Office of Global Women's Issues within the Department of State and named the first US ambassador-at-large for global women's issues.[105] By nearly any measure, Hillary Clinton was effective as secretary of state in advancing a gender equality agenda and left the administration with a favorability rating of nearly 70 percent. Given the overt sexism evident in the 2008 campaign and her "likability problem," how did she garner so much support as secretary of state? Researchers Mary McThomas and Michael Tesler argue that Clinton successfully navigated the femininity/competence double bind as secretary of state by tapping into a wealth of support from "gender egalitarians." They note that future female candidates and cabinet officials could "garner support by embracing a feminist persona in order to capture the support of gender liberals."[106]

IMAGE 5.4: *Four women have served on the Supreme Court of the United States. Pictured (L-R) are Justice Sandra Day O'Connor (Ret.), Justice Sonia Sotomayor, Justice Ruth Bader Ginsburg, and Justice Elena Kagan.* Source: Steve Petteway, Collection of the Supreme Court of the United States.

Women in the Judiciary

To date, 112 justices have served on the US Supreme Court, and four have been women. President Ronald Reagan was responsible for breaking the gender barrier when he appointed Sandra Day O'Connor early in his first term. Her appointment was met with overwhelming enthusiasm and the Senate unanimously confirmed her appointment. President Clinton added the second woman, Ruth Bader Ginsburg, to the Court in 1993. O'Connor announced her retirement on July 1, 2005, leaving Ginsburg as the only woman on the Court until she was joined by Justices Sonia Sotomayor and Elena Kagan. Upon Justice David Souter's retirement in 2009, President Obama nominated federal appeals court judge Sonia Sotomayor, who, once confirmed, became the third woman and the first Latina to serve on the Supreme Court. Elena Kagan replaced retiring justice John Paul Stevens, resigning her appointment as solicitor general in the Obama administration upon confirmation by the Senate in May 2010.

Justice Ginsburg has openly advocated for more women to join her on the Court: "Women belong in all places where decisions are being made. I don't say [the split] should be 50–50. It could be 60 percent men, 40 percent women, or the other way around. It shouldn't be that women are the exception." Following O'Connor's retirement, Ginsburg was more vocal about her belief that her eight male colleagues might not understand the discrimination women face. For example, in a case involving a thirteen-year-old Arizona girl who was strip-searched by school officials looking for drugs, Ginsburg said, "They have never been a thirteen-year-old girl. It's a very sensitive age for a girl. I didn't think that my colleagues, some of them, quite understood." She was perturbed enough by her colleagues' lack of understanding in the Lilly Ledbetter pay discrimination case that she took the unusual step of reading her dissenting opinion from the bench and called upon Congress to reverse the Court (which they did at the start of the 111th Congress—see Chapter 7). The Court ruled in *Ledbetter* that women could not sue for pay inequities resulting from sex discrimination that had occurred years earlier. Ginsburg claimed that her male colleagues showed "a certain lack of understanding" of the bias women can face on the job. Similarly, in a case over awarding credit toward pension benefits during maternity leave, Ginsburg claimed, "Discrimination on the basis of pregnancy is surely discrimination on the basis of sex."[107]

Growth of Women in Law and the Judiciary

In 1970, women made up only 5.4 percent of law school students and only 4.7 percent of all attorneys. Because candidates for federal judgeships are generally twenty years out of law school, the pipeline for judicial appointments has only recently begun to fill with highly qualified women eligible for appointment to the federal bench. Title IX, discussed at length in Chapter 6, is largely responsible for eliminating quotas on the number of women admitted to law programs. In 2016, about half of all law degrees were awarded to women and about 35 percent of attorneys were women. Forty-five percent of associates in private law firms were women, and 21 percent of partners were women. In Fortune 500 companies, 24 percent of general counsel positions were held by women.[108] On average, a female lawyer earns 83 percent of a male lawyer's salary.

Only eight women had served as federal judges before 1977, when President Jimmy Carter unveiled his plan to diversify the federal courts. Carter added forty-one women to the judiciary, amounting to 16 percent of his judicial appointments. By comparison, the Kennedy and Johnson administrations were together responsible for appointing just four women to lifetime appointments; Nixon and Ford combined to add just two more women to the bench.[109] During President Bill Clinton's first term in office, 30 percent of his judicial nominees were women; in his second term, 28.7 percent of his nominees were women. President Obama has appointed 138 female judges—more than any other president to date. In 2016, 60 of the 170 active judges sitting on the federal courts of appeal were female (35 percent) and around 33 percent of US district court judges were women.[110] However, there are still six district courts around the country where there has never been a woman judge. Eighty-three women of color are currently serving as federal judges (10 percent), including forty-three African American women, twenty-six Hispanic women, eleven Asian American women, and one Native American woman. There are more than 18,000 seats on state courts in the United States; women hold 31 percent of the judgeships at the state level. In total, taking the entire judiciary at any level, women represent 27 percent of the bench.

Nicole Asmussen's research found that although recent presidents have actively sought women and minority nominees for the federal bench, their nomination process takes, on average, 27 percent longer and they are less likely to be confirmed than white male nominees (38.5 percent of female or minority nominations fail, compared to 29.3 percent for white males). This is not due to outright discrimination on the part of senators tasked with confirming judicial nominees. Rather, she finds that the pattern reflects a strategic cat-and-mouse game. She writes, "Senators are rather disinclined to oppose female and minority nominations because they face political costs for doing so. However, knowing this, the president exploits the situation by nominating women and minorities closer to his ideal judicial philosophy but more extreme than senators would normally be willing to accept if the nominee were a white male."[111] Her evidence suggests that Republican presidents in particular have pursued such a strategy, accounting for the delays and lack of success of female and minority nominations.

Does Gender Matter in the Judiciary?

Although there are more women attorneys and judges in the justice system today, research is somewhat mixed on whether gender matters in this context. While no one could disagree that the increased number of women in the judiciary is a significant form of descriptive representation, whether women jurists substantively represent women through their decisions is less clear. Some feminists argue that the presence of women in the legal system will have a profound impact because female lawyers and judges "bring a different perspective to the law, employ different methods, and reach different conclusions."[112] During his first opportunity to make a nomination to the US Supreme Court, President Obama acknowledged the importance of "life experience" in judicial decision-making:

> The process of selecting someone to replace Justice Souter is among my most serious responsibilities as President. So I will seek somebody with a sharp and independent mind and a record of excellence and integrity. I will seek someone who understands that justice isn't about some abstract legal theory or footnote in a casebook. It is also about how our laws affect the daily realities of people's lives—whether they can make a living and care for their families; whether they feel safe in their homes and welcome in their own nation.

I view that quality of empathy, of understanding and identifying with people's hopes and struggles, as an essential ingredient for arriving at just decisions and outcomes. I will seek somebody who is dedicated to the rule of law, who honors our constitutional traditions, who respects the integrity of the judicial process and the appropriate limits of the judicial role. I will seek somebody who shares my respect for constitutional values on which this nation was founded, and who brings a thoughtful understanding of how to apply them in our time.[113]

Judge Sonia Sotomayor, a daughter of Puerto Rican parents who was raised in a Bronx public housing project and later went on to graduate summa cum laude from Princeton University and earn her law degree from Yale Law School, was his choice. In announcing her nomination, he said, "When Sonia Sotomayor ascends those marble steps to assume her seat on the highest court in the land, America will have taken another important step towards realizing the ideal that is etched above its entrance: Equal justice under the law."[114] Instantly, not only did conservative opponents claim that she would be a "judicial activist" on the Court, but some latched onto a line from a 2001 lecture she delivered at the University of California, Berkeley, School of Law as evidence of Sotomayor's "racism." In that speech she noted, "I would hope that a wise Latina woman with the richness of her experiences would more often than not reach a better conclusion than a white male who hasn't lived that life." Within the full context of the speech, Judge Sotomayor was exploring the role that life experience plays in all judicial decisions, and she had been asked to speak directly to her life as a Latina jurist.[115]

Theories of feminist jurisprudence have been instrumental in reconceptualizing the way laws affecting employment, divorce, domestic violence, rape, reproductive rights, and sexual harassment are understood and interpreted. While researchers hypothesized that women judges would be more liberal than their male counterparts, studies comparing sentencing patterns of trial court judges, voting behavior on the US Courts of Appeals, and decisions in cases involving criminal procedure found no significant differences between men and women.[116] Arguably, difference is most important in areas directly affecting women's rights and claims to equality. Particularly because issues such as gender equality and reproductive rights involve judicially created rights, representation by women in all aspects of the legal system is important: "The constitutional and statutory bases of women's rights are limited, which leaves the protection of such rights to the federal courts."[117] Similar to the research on women in Congress, a study of appellate court judges found that the presence of one or more females on an appeals court panel tended to alter the behavior of their male colleagues, particularly on issues of most concern to women.[118]

Reviewing the existing scholarship on gender influence, Boyd, Epstein, and Martin found that in about one-third of approximately thirty previous studies, differences in the votes of male and female judges or differences in the votes of a panel of judges when one member is a woman could be identified. Their own study found that the probability of a judge ruling in favor of a plaintiff in a discrimination case decreases by 10 percent when the judge is a man. When a woman is on the panel, the likelihood that a male colleague will rule in favor of the plaintiff increases 12 to 16 percent. But law professor Deborah Rhode urges caution in drawing conclusions from such research: "Even if such research cumulatively suggests that the sex of a judge does influence the outcome of certain cases, sex is by no means a reliable predictor of the voting behavior of any particular nominee. Much depends on other aspects of a judge's background and how they influence his or her world view. . . . In short, the importance of diversity in judicial appointments should neither be overlooked nor overstated."[119] Sally Kenny, author of *Gender and Justice: Why Women in the Judiciary Really Matter*, writes that women judges simultaneously signify both business as usual and radical transformation. "I argue that, paradoxically, the more women judges look and behave like men, the more radical their presence on the bench can be because it normalizes women's authority and power. . . . [T]he more women are feminist, progressive, more likely to dissent and use outsider arguments, the more they bolster difference arguments that often lead to women's marginalization and exclusion."[120]

WOMEN IN THE MILITARY

In the last decade, more than 280,000 women have been deployed to Iraq and Afghanistan as the United States fought a global "war on terror" in three significant military engagements. As of April 2015, 161 women had lost their lives and 1,015 had been wounded in action as part of operations since the September 11, 2001, terror attacks. The Army alone reported eighty-nine women killed in the line of duty in Iraq and thirty-six in Afghanistan.[121] The military offers a unique setting in which to examine women's claims to equality and women's role in governing. Although the military is not a political office per se, security is an essential function of government. The military remains one of the most highly gendered environments even as it rapidly transitions to full gender integration using gender-neutral standards.

In 1994, Congress repealed the "risk rule," barring women from all combat situations and allowed each branch of the service to determine which positions would be open to women. Secretary of Defense Les Aspin advised, "Women should be excluded from assignment to units below brigade level whose primary mission is to engage in direct combat on the ground."[122] Combat was defined as "engaging an enemy on the ground with individual or crew-served weapons, while being exposed to hostile fire and to a high probability of direct physical contact with the hostile force's personnel."[123] As a result, thousands of previously restricted positions were opened to women, but many direct combat positions remained closed. Department of Defense and RAND Corporation studies demonstrated that women's integration was successful. Using interviews, surveys, and focus groups, the researchers probed issues of unit cohesiveness, readiness, and morale. While gender played some role in unit cohesiveness, this typically occurred only in units where conflict was already a problem. The presence of women was also cited as raising the level of professional standards. Morale was affected by gender in two areas: sexual harassment and a perception of a double standard related to physical standards.[124]

Deployment of women in Afghanistan and Iraq put the question of women in combat front and center. "Iraq has advanced the cause of full integration for women in the Army by leaps and bounds. They have earned the confidence and respect of male colleagues," said Peter R. Mansoor, a retired Army colonel.[125] These deployments stretched the limits of the law on women in combat roles. When commanders needed more soldiers for crucial jobs, such as bomb disposal and intelligence, they often resorted to bureaucratic trickery to attach women to a combat unit rather than assign them outright. According to retired Air Force Brigadier General Wilma L. Vaught, "You've got more women carrying weapons with the possibility that they'll use them to fight or defend themselves. That's one of the big differences between this war and others. Women haven't done this type of war before."[126] Another reason for the greater integration of women in the military is the culture of the countries where the most recent wars have taken place. In Afghanistan, for example, the cultural taboo against men looking at or speaking with Afghan women meant that the Army needed to create Female Engagement Teams (FETs). Women in the Army were recruited and trained to develop enduring, trust-based relationships with the Afghan women they encountered on patrols.

More than 9,000 female troops have earned Combat Action Badges during modern combat operations, including those in Iraq and Afghanistan, and hundreds more have earned valor awards, including the Silver Star, the Army's third-highest valor award. When Monica Brown, an eighteen-year-old Army medic from Lake Jackson, Texas, grabbed her kit and raced through enemy fire to save soldiers trapped in a burning Humvee in Afghanistan's Paktika province, she didn't worry about combat exclusions. "We weren't supposed to take her out on missions but we had to because there was no other medic," her platoon leader said. Brown received the Silver Star, the nation's third-highest award for valor, for her actions.[127] Senator Tammy Duckworth (D-Ill.) lost both legs in 2004 in Iraq when a rocket-propelled grenade struck the Black Hawk helicopter she was piloting. She dismisses concerns that women are not tough enough for combat: "When I'm asked if the country is ready for women in combat, I look down at where my legs used to be and think, 'Where do you think this happened, a bar fight?'"[128] According to a 2015 Rasmussen poll, a majority of American voters (52 percent) believe the growing role of women is good for the military, while only 12 percent believe that women's increased role will be bad for the military.[129]

Lawsuits are often the catalyst for change in the pursuit of gender equality. In 2012 the American Civil Liberties Union (ACLU) filed suit on behalf of four servicewomen against the Department of Defense for its **combat exclusion**— the blanket exclusion of women from combat jobs—which then limits women's opportunities for top leadership jobs and career advancement. However, it is more likely that the combat exclusion was rescinded by the Defense Department for more pragmatic reasons. In 2015, Defense Secretary Ashton Carter announced that all combat positions would be open equally to men and women. He noted, "To succeed in our mission of national defense, we cannot afford to cut ourselves off from half the country's talent and skills. We have to take full advantage of every individual who can meet our standards."[130] Female recruits tend to have more education and better test scores than men. As technology continues to advance, women have gained more opportunities. "U.S. military superiority is in our intelligence and technology. People who remain skeptical of having women fight for their country act like we're still attacking with fixed bayonets," says Linda DePaw of the Minerva Center, a military think tank.

Back in 2013, Defense Secretary Leon Panetta initiated the change by requiring each branch of the military to present a plan for the full integration of women, including combat positions. If military leaders believed that some jobs in their branch should remain closed to women, they bore the burden of justifying why an exception should be granted. Ultimately Secretary Carter's decision allowed for no exceptions, including the Marines and the Special Forces units within each branch of the service. The first two women graduated from the elite Army Ranger School in August 2015. Army Captain Kristen Griest, a military police platoon leader, and 1st Lieutenant Shaye Haver, an AH-64 Apache pilot, earned their Ranger tabs four months before Secretary Carter's decision made it possible for them to apply to join the 75th Ranger Regiment, an elite special operations force. Council on Foreign Relations senior fellow Gayle Tzemach Lemmon, who has reported on women in the military, said Griest's and Haver's achievement could increase women's interest in certain military positions and increase society's acceptance of women in military roles traditionally held by men. "The women who are out there performing the jobs, they are the people who are changing people's minds," said Lemmon.[131]

Martin Dempsey, chairman of the Joint Chiefs of Staff at the time the combat exclusion was dropped, shared an anecdote about his own encounter with change when he took over command of the 1st Armored Division in Iraq in 2003. On a trip outside of his headquarters, he introduced himself to his Humvee's crew. "I slapped the turret gunner on the leg and I said, 'Who are you?' And she leaned down and said, 'I'm Amanda.' And I said, 'Ah, OK,'" Dempsey recalled. "So, female turret gunner protecting division commander. It's from that point on that I realized something had changed, and it was time to do something about it."[132] Full implementation of the new directive will take time. Opponents worry that

IMAGE 5.5: *U.S. Army First Lt. Shaye Haver, left, and Capt. Kristen Griest, right, pose for photos with other female West Point alumni. Haver and Griest became the first female graduates of the Army's rigorous Ranger School.* Source: AP Photo/John Bazemore.

the military will weaken standards to make room for women, but Secretary Carter expressed confidence that "effective leadership and gender-neutral standards" can overcome any barriers to full gender integration. Because men and women will be held to the same gender-neutral standards, "equal opportunity may not always create equal participation."[133] Gender-neutral standards are important for making the political or legal case for women's full integration into the military, but moving forward may require more nuance consistent with the fairness doctrine.

Currently, 1.4 million Americans serve in the armed forces, and of those, about 15 percent are women. The Air Force and Navy have the highest proportion of women on active duty (19 and 18 percent, respectively) and the Marine Corps has the lowest (8 percent). The Army reports 13.6 percent women among enlisted personnel. Women today make up 6 percent of the military's top ranks. Sixty women were serving as generals and admirals in the active-duty military in 2015. Ann E. Dunwoody became the first four-star Army general in 2008, and in 2016, President Obama selected Air Force General Lori Robinson to be the head of US Northern Command. Robinson is the first woman to lead a unified combatant command, making her the highest-ranking woman in military history. The increase in the proportion of women in the military has resulted in changes in nearly all aspects of military life: training programs and physical fitness regimens, assignments, living arrangements, medical services, and veterans' benefits. New policies had to be created to address pregnancy, single parents in the military, child care during peacetime and deployment, dual-service marriages, sexual harassment, and sexual assault.

There are currently more than 1.8 million female veterans (roughly 8 percent of the veteran population) living in the United States. Female veterans suffer many of the same difficulties as male veterans upon returning from a war zone. In addition to combat-related injuries and mental trauma, women often report being victims of sexual assault while deployed or in training. And because women have long been officially barred from combat, those suffering from posttraumatic stress disorder (PTSD) faced a higher burden of proof. Swords to Plowshares, a veterans' service organization, say that female Iraq War veterans are among the fastest-growing population of homeless. Women returning from war face challenges in accessing appropriate medical care, since a majority of the veterans' hospitals and medical facilities are organized to care for male vets.

Women are also missing from the cultural portrayals of combat, making their isolation even more damaging. Gayle Tzemach Lemmon, writing in the *Atlantic*, says that "the victim narrative has overtaken all others in recent years when it comes to the story of women in uniform. There have been precious few depictions of women in uniform doing their actual jobs, most noticeably when it comes to the movies."[134] An exception is *Lioness*, a 2008 documentary directed by Meg McLagan and Daria Sommers that tells the gripping story of a group of female Army support soldiers who were among the first group of women to engage in direct ground combat with insurgents in Iraq.[135]

The issue of women in combat presents the paradox of gender equality in its starkest terms. Congress may well be forced to confront gender in future debates over military conscription. When President Jimmy Carter reactivated the draft registration process, Congress did not act on his recommendation to amend the act to include women. The Supreme Court ruled, in *Rostker v. Goldberg* (1981), that this decision to exempt women from registration "was not the 'accidental by-product' of a traditional way of thinking about females" and did not violate the due process clause. The Court reasoned that because of the combat restrictions on females at the time, men and women were not "similarly situated" for the purposes of draft registration. In an effort to force Congress to debate the issue of women in combat, US Representative Ryan Zinke (R-Mont. and a former Navy SEAL) introduced legislation in February 2016 requiring women to register for the draft. To his surprise, the bill moved forward quickly and without much objection, though it has not become law at this time. With combat restrictions now a thing of the past, should women be required to register with the Selective Service and be subject to conscription if a draft is ever reinstated? If Congress does not decide, the question will likely come before the Supreme Court for another hearing.

Box 5.3–Spotlight on the 2016 Election

A Change Election? No Increase for Women in Congress but Gains in Diversity

Although the 2016 election did not result in a woman president or change the proportion of women serving in Congress, the women who won will bring more diversity. "For all the talk of this being a change election, it was not a change election for women in politics," said Debbie Walsh, director of the Center for American Women and Politics.[1] Yet the 115th Congress includes thirty-eight women of color, an increase of five compared with the previous Congress. Thirty-four percent of the 104 women serving in Congress are women of color—thirty-five Democrats and three Republicans.

New women of color elected to the Senate include Catherine Cortez Masto from Nevada, Tammy Duckworth from Illinois, and Kamala Harris from California. Cortez Masto is the country's first Latina senator. Harris is the first Indian American to serve in the US Senate and the second African American woman elected to the Senate. Tammy Duckworth, an Iraq War veteran who lost both legs when the helicopter she was flying was hit by a rocket-propelled grenade, beat incumbent Republican Mark Kirk to become the first Asian American women to represent Illinois.

In the House of Representatives, Democrat Lisa Blunt Rochester is the first woman elected to Congress from Delaware and the first African American woman to represent Delaware. In Florida, Democrat Stephanie Murphy became the first Vietnamese American woman elected to Congress, beating twelve-term Republican incumbent John Mica. Orlando's police chief, Democrat Val Demmings, also won a seat in the House.

Although the 2016 election increased racial and ethnic diversity among women serving in the Senate and House, Republicans continued to lag behind Democrats in the number of women serving. Just five Republican women serve in the Senate, with twenty-three in the House. Representative Mia Love, who became the first black Republican woman in the House when elected in 2014, was reelected in 2016.

In the years leading up to the midterm elections in 2018, both political parties will likely work on strategies to recruit women candidates and to build on the successes of 2016 in bringing more women of color into politics.

CONCLUSION

Historically, women have been forced to act as outsiders in politics because of the legal and customary barriers to their direct participation as insiders. Contemporary female political actors, however, have a wide range of activities and strategies available in the pursuit of equality. Women elected to office who promise a different approach to governing do so in the hope of capitalizing on voters' positive gender stereotypes of women as moral, civic-minded, and dedicated to the interests of families, children, women, and those traditionally excluded from power. Outside the bounds of formal power, women continue to agitate for change here in the United States and globally. Women are more involved in politics, the political process, and governing than at any other time in our history. Still, there is work to be done in the pursuit of equality. The United States perceives itself as a global leader in securing women's rights, but the Senate refuses to ratify the Convention on the Elimination of All Forms of Discrimination Against Women (CEDAW) and has made only minimal progress in addressing other areas of critical concern.

As the number of women in local and state government, Congress, the executive branch, the judiciary, and the military grows, women will increasingly face the contradictions inherent in the pursuit of equality. Even while promising a "different voice," women have found themselves quickly confronted with the practicalities of functioning and governing within political institutions that may require behavior that is antithetical to their idea of "different." It will be important to watch this dynamic unfold as women's presence continues to grow in legislatures at the state and national levels. If women in government continue to be perceived as ineffective, or no more effective than men, in standing for the interests of women, then one of the primary arguments for women's election to positions of power will be undermined. The warnings of those wary of the "difference" argument's power to promote stereotypes and unreasonable expectations of women will resonate. Columnist Ellen Goodman, writing after the 1992 elections, asked: "How long before we read the first story asking why six women in the Senate haven't changed the institution?"[136] If anything, as the number of women in Congress has increased, the rich diversity among women has become more evident, which contributes to the mixed expectations for women's concerted behavior as a group. Working together across party and ideological lines, women have been able to add important issues to the public agenda. However, analysis presented in this chapter suggests that women's power beyond the agenda-setting stage of policy formation may still be limited by their lack of significant numbers and the influence that comes with leadership positions within institutions of government.

Up to this point, we have largely focused on how women have utilized politics to enter politics themselves, first as voters and later as public officials. The next three chapters of the book examine several broad policy areas to better understand how women shape and are shaped by public policies. The paradox of gender equality is integral to explaining both processes. Women shape public policy in a number of ways. In some cases, women's presence in legislative bodies makes it more likely that issues previously defined as private are transformed into public issues that can be addressed through the public policy process. Issues as diverse as domestic violence and quality child care have only recently been understood as problems that warrant attention in the public sphere. As activists and as officeholders, women can bring issues to the government's attention and influence the content of legislation. As administrators, they can influence how policy is implemented, enforced, and evaluated. The paradox of gender equality can be found squarely at the center of most debates over policy affecting women. Three broad policy areas at the heart of the paradox of gender equality are addressed in the following chapters: education, work, and family.

NOTES

Boxed feature notes appear at the end of the Notes section.

1 Harriet Woods, *Stepping Up to Power: The Political Journey of American Women* (Boulder, CO: Westview Press, 2000), 163.

2 Hannah Fenichel Pitkin, *The Concept of Representation* (Berkeley: University of California Press, 1967).

3 Georgia Deurst-Lahti and Dayna Verstegen, "Making Something of Absence: The 'Year of the Woman' and Women's Political Representation," in *Gender Power, Leadership, and Governance*, ed. Georgia Deurst-Lahti and Rita Mae Kelly (Ann Arbor: University of Michigan Press, 1998), 213–238.

4 Laurel Elder, "Why Women Don't Run: Explaining Women's Underrepresentation in America's Political Institutions," *Women and Politics* 26, no. 2 (2004): 27–56.

5 Philip Edward Jones, "Does the Descriptive Representation of Gender Influence Accountability for Substantive Representation," *Politics and Gender* 10, no. 2 (June 2014): 195.

6 Jane Mansbridge, "Should Blacks Represent Blacks, and Women Represent Women? A Contingent 'Yes,'" Politics Research Group, John F. Kennedy School of Government, Harvard University, 2000.

7 Susan J. Carroll, "Representing Women: Congresswomen's Perceptions of Their Representational Roles," paper presented at the conference "Women Transforming Congress: Gender Analyses of Institutional Life," Carl Albert Congressional Research and Studies Center, University of Oklahoma, April 13–15, 2000.

8 Inter-Parliamentary Union, "Equality in Politics: A Survey of Men and Women in Parliaments," Reports and Documents no. 54, 2008.

9 Craig Volden, Alan E. Wiseman, and Dana E. Wittmer, "Women's Issues and Their Fates in Congress," Working Paper 7-2013, Center for the Study of Democratic Institutions, Vanderbilt University, 2013.

10 Carroll, "Representing Women," 4.

11 Elizabeth Holtzman, "Not a Job for a Woman," *Politico*, June 29, 2016.

12 Kathleen Dolan and Kira Sanbonmatsu, "Gender Stereotypes and Attitudes Toward Gender Balance in Government," *American Politics Research* 37, no. 3 (May 2009): 409–428.

13 The data come from the 2006 American National Election Study (ANES) Pilot Study; see 414–415 for initial frequency results.

14 Justin McCarthy, "Americans Say Business Background Is Best for Governing," Gallup, July 21, 2014.

15 Kathleen Dolan, *When Does Gender Matter? Women Candidates and Gender Stereotypes in American Elections* (New York: Oxford University Press, 2014).

16 Jean Reith Schroedel and Nicola Nazumdar, "Into the Twenty-first Century: Will Women Break the Political Glass Ceiling?" in *Women and Elective Office: Past, Present, and Future*, ed. Sue Thomas and Clyde Wilcox (New York: Oxford University Press, 1998), 203–219.

17 Mansbridge, "Should Blacks Represent Blacks?"

18 Ronnee Schreiber, *Righting Feminism: Conservative Women and American Politics* (New York: Oxford University Press, 2008).

19 Linda Witt, Karen M. Paget, and Glenna Matthews, *Running as a Woman: Gender and Power in American Politics* (New York: Free Press, 1993), 268.

20 Ibid.

21 Sue Thomas, "The Impact of Women on State Legislative Policies," *Journal of Politics* 53, no. 4 (1991): 958–975.

22 Kim Parker, Juliana Menasce Horowitz, and Molly Rohal, "Women and Political Leadership: Public Says Women Are Equally Qualified, but Barriers Persist," Pew Research Center, January 14, 2015.

23 Barbara Burrell, "The Political Leadership of Women and Public Policymaking," *Policy Studies Journal* 25, no. 4 (1997): 565–568.

24 Debra Dodson, ed., *Gender and Policymaking: Studies of Women in Office*, Center for American Women and Politics, Eagleton Institute of Politics, Rutgers University, 1991.

25 Freda Gehlen, "Women Members of Congress: A Distinctive Role," in *A Portrait of Marginality*, ed. Marianne Githens and Jewel Prestage (New York: David McKay, 1977).

26 Susan Welch, "Are Women More Liberal than Men in the U.S. Congress?" *Legislative Studies Quarterly* 10 (February 1985): 125–134.

27 Barbara Burrell, *A Woman's Place Is in the House: Campaigning for Congress in a Feminist Era* (Ann Arbor: University of Michigan Press, 1997), in particular ch. 8.

28 Brian Frederick, "Are Female House Members Still More Liberal in a Polarized Era? The Conditional Nature of the Relationship Between Descriptive and Substantive Representation," *Congress and the Presidency* 36 (2009): 181–202.

29 Kathryn Pearson, "Gendered Partisanship in the U.S. House and Senate," paper presented at the conference "Legislative Elections, Process, and Policy: The Influence of Bicameralism," Vanderbilt University, October 22–24, 2009.

30 Brian Frederick, "Gender and Patterns of Roll Call Voting in the U.S. Senate," *Congress and the Presidency* 37(2010): 103–124.

31 Debra L. Dodson and Susan J. Carroll, "Reshaping the Agenda: Women in State Legislatures," Center for American Women and Politics, Eagleton Institute of Politics, Rutgers University, 1991.

32 John M. Carey, Richard G. Niemi, and Lynda W. Powell, "Are Women State Legislators Different?" in *Women and Elective Office*, ed. Thomas and Wilcox, 87–102.

33 Robert Hogan, "Sex and the Statehouse: The Effects of Gender on Legislative Roll-Call Voting," *Social Science Quarterly* 89, no. 4 (2008): 955–968.

34 Fact sheet compiled by the Center for American Women and Politics, Eagleton Institute of Politics, Rutgers University, 2016.

35 Sue Thomas, "Why Gender Matters: The Perceptions of Women Officeholders," *Women and Politics* 17, no. 1 (1997): 27–53.

36 D'Vera Cohn and Gretchen Livingston, "Americans' Views of Women as Political Leaders Differ by Gender," Pew Research Center, May 19, 2016.

37 Jaime Fuller, "A Conversation with Kirsten Gillibrand," *New York Magazine*, June 11, 2015.

38 Carroll, "Representing Women," 6–7.

39 Ailsa Chang, "Women on Capitol Hill Reach Across Party Lines to Get Things Done," NPR, May 8, 2014.

40 Susan J. Carroll, "Representing Women: Congresswomen's Perceptions of Their Representational Roles," in *Women Transforming Congress*, ed. Cindy Simon Rosenthal (Norman: University of Oklahoma Press, 2002), 61.

41 Fuller, "A Conversation with Kirsten Gillibrand."

42 Carey, Niemi, and Powell, "Are Women State Legislators Different?" 91.

43 Donte Stallworth, "Numbers Show Senate Women Get More Done than Men," *Huffington Post*, February 20, 2015.

44 Patrick R. Miller and Pamela Johnston Conover, "Why Partisan Warriors Don't Listen: The Gendered Dynamics of Intergroup Anxiety and Partisan Conflict," *Politics, Groups and Identities* 3, no. 1 (2015): 21–39.

45 Marcia Lynn Whicker and Malcom Jewell, "The Feminization of Leadership in State Legislatures," in *Women and Elective Office*, ed. Thomas and Wilcox, 163–174.

46 Ibid., 174.

47 Cindy Simon Rosenthal, "Determinants of Collaborative Leadership: Civic Engagement, Gender, or Organizational Norms?" *Political Research Quarterly* 51, no. 4 (1998): 847–868.

48 Lyn Kathlene, "Power and Influence in State Legislative Policy Making: The Interaction of Gender and Position in Committee Hearing Debates," *American Political Science Review* 88 (1994): 560–575.

49 Lyn Kathlene, "In a Different Voice: Women and the Public Policy Process," in *Women and Elective Office*, ed. Thomas and Wilcox, 198.

50 Christopher F. Karpowitz, Tali Mendelberg, and Lee Shaker, "Gender Inequality in Deliberative Participation," *American Political Science Review* 106, no. 3 (2012): 533–547.

51 Tali Mendelberg, Christopher F. Karpowitz, and Nicholas Goedert, "Does Descriptive Representation Facilitate Women's Distinctive Voice? How Gender Composition and Decision Rules Affect Deliberation," *American Journal of Political Science* 58, no. 2 (2014): 291–306.

52 Jennifer L. Lawless and Sean M. Theriault, "Women in the U.S. Congress: From Entry to Exit," in *Women in Politics: Outsiders or Insiders?* 4th ed., ed. Lois Duke Whitaker (Upper Saddle River, NJ: Prentice Hall, forthcoming).

53 Eleanor Clift and Tom Brazaitis, *Madam President: Shattering the Last Glass Ceiling* (New York: Scribner, 2000), 239.

54 Juliet Eilperin, "Nancy Pelosi Set to Be First Female Speaker," *Washington Post*, November 8, 2006.

55 "Women in Congress: Leadership Roles and Committee Chairs," Fact Sheet, Center for American Women and Politics, Eagleton Institute of Politics, Rutgers University, February 2015.

56 Daniel Newhauser, "House Republicans Just Picked 21 Committee Chairs. 20 Are Men," *Atlantic*, November 18, 2014; Nia-Malika Henderson, "In the 114th Congress, Men Will Chair 20 House Committees. A Woman Will Chair 1," *Washington Post*, November 19, 2014.

57 Lawless and Theriault, "Women in the U.S. Congress," 17.

58 Carol Gilligan, *In a Different Voice: Psychological Theory and Women's Development* (Cambridge, Mass: Harvard University Press, 1998).

59 Rosabeth Moss Kanter, *Men and Women of the Corporation*. (New York: Basic Books, 1977).

60 Sue Thomas, "The Impact of Women on State Legislative Policies," *Journal of Politics* 53, no. 4 (1991): 958–976.

61 Ibid., 967.

62 Kathleen A. Bratton, "Critical Mass Theory Revisited: The Behavior and Success of Token Women in State Legislatures," *Politics and Gender* 1, no. 1 (March 2005): 97–125.

63 Ibid., 122.

64 Amy Caiazza, "Does Women's Representation in Elected Office Lead to Women Friendly Policy? Analysis of State-Level Data," *Women and Politics* 26, no. 1 (2004): 35–70.

65 Angela High-Pippert and John Comer, "Female Empowerment: The Influence of Women Representing Women," *Women and Politics* 19, no. 4 (1998): 53–65.

66 Ibid., 62.

67 Kirk Johnson, "Majority-Female Council in Seattle Faces Backlash After Vote on Arena Deal," *New York Times*, May 8, 2016.

68 Erica C. Barnett, "What Happens When Female Politicians Try to Stand Up to Sports Fans," *Atlantic*, May 21, 2016.

69 Sally Bagshaw, M. Lorena Gonzalez, Lisa Herbold, Debora Juarez, and Kshama Sawant, "Seattle Women: Don't Let Hateful Voices Intimidate You into Silence or Inaction," *Seattle Times*, May 1, 2016.

70 US Census Bureau, 2012 Statistical Abstract, Table 428.

71 Mirya Holman, "Madame Mayor: Women's Representation in Local Politics," Political Parity, December 23, 2014.

72 Kira Sanbonmatsu, Susan J. Carroll, and Debbie Walsh, "Poised to Run: Women's Pathways to the State Legislatures," Center for American Women and Politics, Eagleton Institute of Politics, Rutgers University, 2009.

73 Adrienne R. Smith, Beth Reingold, and Michael Leo Owens, "The Political Determinants of Women's Descriptive Representation in Cities," *Political Research Quarterly* 65, no. 2 (2012): 315–329.

74 Susan J. Carroll and Kira Sanbonmatsu, "Entering the Mayor's Office: Women's Decisions to Run for Municipal Office," paper presented at the annual meeting of the Midwest Political Science Association, April 2010.

75 Lynne A. Weikart, Greg Chen, Daniel W. Williams, and Haris Hromic, "The Democratic Sex: Gender Differences and the Exercise of Power," *Journal of Women, Politics and Policy* 28, no.1 (2006): 119–140.

76 Adrienne Smith, "Cities Where Women Rule: Female Political Incorporation and the Allocation of Community Development Block Grant Funding," *Politics and Gender* 10 (2014): 313–340.

77 Mirya R. Holman, *Women in Politics in the American City* (Philadelphia: Temple University Press, 2014).

78 Fernando Ferreira and Joseph Gyourko, "Does Gender Matter for Political Leadership? The Case of U.S. Mayors," Working Paper 17671, National Bureau of Economic Research, December 2011.

79 Ibid., 21.

80 Lori Beaman, Esther Duflo, Rohini Pande, and Petia Topalova, "Female Leadership Raises Aspirations and Educational Attainment for Girls: A Policy Experiment in India," *Sciencexpress Report*, January 12, 2012.

81 "Women in Statewide Elective Office in 2016," Center for American Women and Politics, Eagleton Institute of Politics, Rutgers University.

82 Kira Sanbonmatsu, "Reaching Executive Office: The Presidency and the Office of the Governor," Political Parity, 2015.

83 Jason Harold Windett, "State Effects and the Emergence and Success of Female Gubernatorial Candidates," *Perspectives on Politics*, 2009, 519–536.

84 Kelly Dittmar, *Navigating Gendered Terrain: Stereotypes and Strategy in Political Campaigns* (Philadelphia: Temple University Press, 2015).

85 Sarah F. Anzia and Christopher Berry, "The Jackie (and Jill) Robinson Effect: Why Do Congresswomen Outperform Congressmen?" *American Journal of Political Science* 55, no. 3 (2011): 478–493.

86 Andrew Tilghman, "Military Sexual Assault Claims: 1 in 20 Lead to Jail Time," *Military Times*, May 13, 2015.

87 Jennifer L. Lawless and Sean M. Theriault, "Sex, Bipartisanship, and Collaboration in the U.S. Congress," Political Parity, 2016.

88 Ibid., 14.

89 Beth Reingold and Adrienne R. Smith, "Welfare Policy Making and Intersections of Race, Ethnicity, and Gender in the U.S. State Legislatures," *American Journal of Political Science* 56, no. 1 (2012): 131–147.

90 Beth Reingold and Kerry L. Haynie, "Representing Women's Interests and Intersections of Gender, Race, and Ethnicity in U.S. State Legislatures," in *Representation: The Case of Women*, ed. Maria C. Escobar-Lemmon and Michelle M. Taylor-Robinson (New York: Oxford University Press, 2014), 183–204.

91 Lisa Jones Townsel, "Sisters in Congress Prove They Have What It Takes to Bring About Change," *Ebony*, March 1997, 36–39.

92 Debra Dodson, "Representing Women's Interests in the U.S. House of Representatives," in *Women and Elective Office*, ed. Thomas and Wilcox, 130–149.

93 Sue Thomas, *How Women Legislate* (New York: Oxford University Press, 1994).

94 Thomas, "The Impact of Women on State Legislative Policies," 973.

95 Lesley Primmer, "The Congressional Caucus for Women's Issues: Twenty Years of Bipartisan Advocacy for Women," in *The American Woman, 1999–2000*, ed. Cynthia B. Costello, Sheri Miles, and Anne J. Stone (New York: Norton, 1998), 365–375.

96 "Caucus Accomplishments," Women's Policy, Inc., www.womenspolicy.org/our-work/the-womens-caucus/caucus-accomplishments.

97 Congressional Caucus on Black Women and Girls, https://watsoncoleman.house.gov/congressional-caucus-black-women-and-girls.

98 US Office of Personnel Management, "Women in Federal Service: A Seat at Every Table," 2014.

99 Juliet Eilperin, "Obama Has Vastly Changed the Face of the Federal Bureaucracy," *Washington Post*, September 20, 2015.

100 Issie Lapowsky, "At the White House's United State of Women Summit, a Call for More," *Wired Business*, June 14, 2016.

101 Woods, *Stepping Up to Power*, 2.

102 National Political Congress of Black Women, profile, www.npcbw.org.profile.html.

103 Susan J. Carroll and Barbara J. Geiger-Parker, "Women Appointed to the Carter Administration," Center for American Women and Politics, Eagleton Institute for Politics, Rutgers University, 1983.

104 MaryAnne Borrelli and Janet M. Martin, eds., *The Other Elites: Women, Politics, and Power in the Executive Branch* (Boulder, CO: Lynne Rienner, 1997).

105 Carmon Rios, "Five Times Hillary Clinton Put Women and Girls First as Secretary of State," Feminist Majority, April 20, 2016.

106 Mary McThomas and Michael Tesler, "The Growing Influence of Gender Attitudes on Public Support for Hillary Clinton, 2008–2012," *Politics and Gender* 12 (2016): 28–49.

107 Joan Biskupic, "Ginsburg: Court Needs Another Woman," *USAToday,* May 5, 2009.

108 American Bar Association, "A Current Glance at Women in the Law," May 2016.

109 Ruth Bader Ginsburg and Laura W. Brill, "Women in the Federal Judiciary: Three Way Pavers and the Exhilarating Change President Carter Wrought," *Fordham Law Review* 64, no. 2 (1995): 281–290.

110 National Women's Law Center, "Women in the Federal Judiciary: Still a Long Way to Go," 2009.

111 Nicole Asmussen, "Female and Minority Judicial Nominees: President's Delight and Senators' Dismay?" *Legislative Studies Quarterly* 36, no. 4 (November 2011): 592.

112 Richard L. Pacelle Jr., "A President's Legacy: Gender and Appointment to the Federal Courts," in *The Other Elites: Women, Politics, and Power in the Executive Branch,* ed. MaryAnne Borrelli and Janet M. Martin (Boulder, CO: Lynne Rienner, 1997).

113 "Obama's Remarks on the Resignation of Justice Souter," *New York Times,* May 1, 2009.

114 Peter Baker and Jeff Zeleny, "Obama Hails Judge as 'Inspiring,'" *New York Times,* May 27, 2009.

115 The full text of Sonia Sotomayor's lecture is at "Lecture: 'A Latina Judge's Voice,'" *New York Times,* May 14, 2009.

116 Sue Davis, Susan Haire, and Donald Songer, "Voting Behavior and Gender on the U.S. Courts of Appeals," *Judicature* 77 (1993): 129–133.

117 Pacelle, "A President's Legacy," 149.

118 Tajuana Massie, Susan W. Johnson, and Sara Margaret Gubala, "The Impact of Gender and Race in the Decisions of Judges on the United States Courts of Appeals," paper presented at the annual meeting of the Midwest Political Science Association meeting, April 2002.

119 Deborah Rhode, "In a 'Different' Voice: The Real Effect of Women on the Bench," *DoubleX,* June 10, 2009; Christine L. Boyd, Lee Epstein, and Andrew D. Martin, "Untangling the Causal Effects of Sex on Judging," paper presented at the annual meeting of the Midwest Political Science Association, April 2007.

120 Sally J. Kenney, *Gender and Justice: Why Women in the Judiciary Really Matter* (New York: Routledge, 2013).

121 Kristy N. Kamarck, "Women in Combat: Issues for Congress," Congressional Research Service, December 3, 2015.

122 "Military Service," in Lynne E. Ford, *Encyclopedia of Women and American Politics* (New York: Facts on File, 2008), 310.

123 Ibid.

124 "Military Readiness: Women Are Not a Problem," RAND Research Brief RB-7515, 1997.

125 Agnes Gereben Schaefer, Jennie W. Wenger, Jennifer Kavanagh, Gillian S. Oak, Jonathan P. Wong, Thomas E. Trail, and Todd Nichols, *Implications of Integrating Women into the Marine Corps Infantry* (Santa Monica, CA: RAND Corporation, 2015), 15.

126 Mona Iskander, "Female Troops in Iraq Redefine Combat Roles," *Women's eNews,* July 5, 2004; Lizette Alvarez, "G.I. Jane Breaks the Combat Barrier as War Evolves," *New York Times,* August 16, 2009.

127 Richard Sisk, "Women in Combat: Silver Stars, Combat Action Badges, and Casualties, Military.com, August 31, 2015.

128 Miranda S. Spivack, "Women in Combat: Will They Make for a Better Fighting Force?" *CQ Researcher* 25, no. 19 (May 13, 2016): 433–456.

129 "Support for Women in Combat Reaches New High," Rasmussen Poll, January 8, 2015.

130 Spivack, "Women in Combat," 440.

131 Gayle Tzemach Lemmon, "Missing in Action," *Atlantic,* August 4, 2015.

132 Sisk, "Women in Combat."

133 Spivack, "Women in Combat," 440.

134 Lemmon, "Missing in Action."

135 *Lioness,* www.lionessthefilm.com.

136 Witt, Paget, and Mathews, *Running as a Woman,* 269.

Box 5.1: Would More Women in Government Reduce Corruption? It Depends

1 Justin Esarey and Gina Chirillo, "'Fairer Sex' or Purity Myth? Corruption, Gender, and Institutional Context," *Politics and Gender* 9 (2013): 361–389.

2 Sabrina Karim, "Madame Officer," *Americas Quarterly,* Summer 2011.

3 Gwen Young and Kendra Heideman, "Women and Corruption: Perceptions Aside," Wilson Center, May 11, 2016.

4 Anne Marie Goetz, "Political Cleaners: Women as the New Anti-Corruption," *Development and Change* 38 (2007): 87–105; David Dollar, Raymond Fisman, and Roberta Gatti, "Are Women Really the 'Fairer' Sex? Corruption and Women in Government," *Journal of Economic Behavior and Organization* 46 (2001): 423–429.

5 Anne Marie Goetz, *Who Answers to Women? Gender and Accountability*, Progress of the World's Women 2008/2009 (New York: United Nations Development Fund for Women, 2008).

6 Janna Rheinbay and Marie Chene, "Gender and Corruption," Transparency International, March 2016.

7 Justin Esarey and Leslie Schwindt-Bayer, "Women's Representation, Accountability, and Corruption in Democracies," forthcoming in *British Journal of Political Science*, (November 21, 2016 version, http://jee3.web.rice.edu/gender-corruption-accountability.pdf).

8 Young and Heideman, "Women and Corruption."

Box 5.3:

1 Amber Phillips, "One Election Bright Spot for Democrats: Women of Color," *Washington Post*, November 10, 2016

▶ CHAPTER 6

Education and the Pursuit of Equality

Education is a critical resource for human advancement at the individual and societal levels. Education occupies a critical nexus for women between the private and public spheres. It isn't an accident that women won the right to be educated nearly a hundred years before they embarked on the campaign for suffrage. Education empowers individuals to act on the basis of their self-interest, which is why it has been treated as a restricted commodity. Early nineteenth-century Enlightenment theorists believed that education was crucial to developing the ability to reason and for attaining full citizenship. Therefore, only those who could become citizens needed to be educated, and that did not include women. Withholding education is a form of social control and a way of maintaining the status quo by ensuring that those at the bottom of the social hierarchy raise few objections.

Why educate women? Although this question may sound rhetorical today, in many countries and in some subcultures of the United States, education is still reserved almost exclusively for males, or after a certain level is limited to males. Girls in Afghanistan and Pakistan are the target of acid attacks and other forms of physical intimidation to dissuade them from going to school. Women's access to education in professional programs and in some institutions had been limited until Title IX, which was passed in 1972 as an amendment to the 1964 Civil Rights Act. Designed to address questions of gender equity in education by banning discrimination based on sex, Title IX receives the most public attention for what it has meant to girls' and women's athletics.

The American Association of University Women (AAUW) put the issue of gender equity in the classroom squarely before the public by issuing *How Schools Shortchange Girls*, a major research study that documented how girls were being unfairly disadvantaged by common classroom practices that gave preference to boys and valued boys over girls. Critics have charged that the situation is quite the

227

opposite: rather than schools cheating girls, as the AAUW report charged, boys are now at a disadvantage and are suffering from discrimination in education.[1] We will evaluate both arguments in this chapter. Finally, education is such a fundamental resource that its long-term influence is felt throughout a person's lifetime. We will examine the effect of education or the lack of it on women's status in the United States. The chapter concludes with an examination of issues in education facing future generations of citizens and policy makers.

A BRIEF HISTORY OF THE EDUCATION OF WOMEN

Education by its very nature empowers individuals, cultures, and nations to survive. From the beginning of human existence, informal education provided essential information about how to find and prepare food, build shelter, heal the sick, give birth to new life, and mourn the dead.[2] Access to formal education throughout time and regardless of place has been a restricted privilege. In ancient Greece, for example, athletics, music, and reading were the formal educational requirements for young males destined for full membership in the citizen class. By the Middle Ages, daughters of royalty were sometimes tutored, but it was not until the nineteenth century that even a few men beyond royalty received a formal education. "Formal education was considered irrelevant for most free citizens, dangerous for men of lower status and for women, and even illegal for enslaved black people."[3] With very few exceptions, education for elite women was restricted to music, foreign languages, and literature—all taught at home and for the express purpose of training women for their station in life.

The public debate over the character of women's education began in the seventeenth century in Europe and extended to the American colonies. The dominant philosophy regarding women's education sought not to enlighten and empower women, but rather to ensure they remained confined to their "fortune and condition." Women's training focused on building moral character and developing the necessary submissive nature and skills to maintain a marriage, run a household, and supervise children. Women in the colonies taught religion, but only to other women. Women were permitted to preach only to other women, and then only the words and thoughts derived from their husband's or minister's mind.[4] Women who demonstrated independence were often declared insane and a threat to social order. The most famous example is the prosecution of Anne Hutchinson by the conservative religious authorities of the Massachusetts Bay Colony. Her banishment was a direct result of Hutchinson's overstepping the bounds of women's proper role.

Although Enlightenment theorists were a powerful influence on the expansion of education as a social good, women's education was still relegated to "patient submissiveness to male authority." Jean-Jacques Rousseau, who argued for the importance of education, did not extend those same views to women's education. In *Émile* (1762), his treatise on the ideal education for a young man, Rousseau argued that the proper object of education for women was men. Anything beyond that was counterproductive since women's role and purpose was to marry and support their husbands, raise children, and manage the household. Educating women in reason and independence would not only be a waste but also would be a dangerous challenge to nature's designation of women as the object of men's pleasure.[5]

Catharine Macaulay and later Mary Wollstonecraft offered feminist critiques of Rousseau. In *Letters on Education*, published in 1790, Macaulay asserted that men and women needed to understand each other better. Through coeducation, both men and women would develop the physical and intellectual powers required to accept the political responsibilities of the liberal state. If educated similarly to men, women could shoulder their share of these responsibilities. Likewise, Wollstonecraft, in *Thoughts on the Education of Daughters* and later *A Vindication of the Rights of Woman*, advocated coeducation, insisting that women needed to develop independence, rationality, and competence. While she recognized that most women would become wives and mothers, she argued that women could best fulfill those roles if they first respected themselves as individuals.[6] While Wollstonecraft herself was labeled a radical, her ideas nonetheless suffused the philosophy of republican motherhood that emerged in post-Revolutionary America. Women should be good "republican mothers" able to educate the sons of liberty, argued leading educational theorists of the time. Judith Sargent Murray, writing as "Constantina," provided the first American feminist voice regarding the education of women, and was one of the first to challenge the prevailing notion that men and women were different by nature. Murray claimed that men and women were taught to be different:

> Will it be said that the judgment of a male of two years old is more sage than that of a female's of the same age? I believe the reverse is generally observed to be true. But from that period on what partiality! How is the one exalted and the other depressed, by the contrary modes of education which are adopted! The one is taught to aspire, the other is early confined and limited![7]

Access to education expanded in the United States throughout the 1800s. In the 1830s and 1840s, girls were admitted to free public elementary schools, particularly in the Northeast. Emma Willard opened the first college for women in 1821, the Troy Female Seminary. Prudence Crandall opened a similar academy for black women in 1833, only to be jailed and see her school burned to the ground.[8] Coeducational colleges developed in the 1830s, with Oberlin College in Ohio the first to admit both men and women, regardless of race. Women made up nearly one-third to one-half of the student body, and although allowed to mix freely with men in classrooms and during meals, they were primarily admitted to the "Ladies' Department." The women's course of study omitted Latin, Greek, and higher mathematics. Women students were expected to wash and repair the clothing of the male students, as well as take charge of the dining hall tasks. When Lucy Stone, a future leader in the suffrage movement, was admitted to Oberlin, she was permitted to take the regular four-year collegiate course only after first completing the program of equal length in the Ladies' Department.[9]

Wheaton College was founded as the first real women's college in 1834, followed by Mount Holyoke in 1837. Iowa was the first state university to admit women, beginning in 1855. In 1904, Mary McLeod Bethune opened a small school for black women in Daytona Beach, Florida, which later became Bethune-Cookman College. By 1873, 60 percent of all American secondary schools had mixed-sex classes, and by the late 1880s, the majority of teachers were women.[10] Women's progress in education provoked some to issue dire warnings about the consequences of "too much" education. In 1872, Dr. Edward Clarke of Harvard Medical School was invited to address the New England Women's Club in Boston. Several prominent women were in attendance, including Julia Ward Howe, Louisa May Alcott, and Lucy Stone. Dr. Clarke warned that education for women, and the mental exertion involved, could result in deadly physical consequences: "monstrous brains and puny bodies; abnormally active cerebration and abnormally weak digestion; flowing thought and constipated bowels."[11] The womb was especially at risk since it was already "housed in frail bodies 'diseased' by monthly bleeding." As historian Louise Bernikow notes, "Myths about the frailties of bodies that bled monthly assumed the form of restrictions on female athletics in our time, but they were rooted in 19th century desires to shut down that most dangerous organ, the female brain."[12]

As women joined the ranks of teachers in increasing numbers, the profession's prestige and salary began to fall. Kathryn Kish Sklar argues that the growth of mass education in the United States was accomplished cheaply as a result of low salaries for women. Low salaries were justified by three arguments: women did not have to support families, as men did; women deserved less pay since they would quit their jobs when they married; and women's salaries were determined by the market. But since women had few options beyond teaching, they accepted whatever salary was offered, no matter how low.[13] Most schools required that women leave the teaching profession once they married, but women's entrance into paid teaching positions opened avenues to other "suitable" occupations over time and accorded some women new public stature within their communities. As more women were educated, the number of women's clubs and organizations dedicated to improving and expanding education increased dramatically throughout the 1870s.

In the twentieth century, the science of homemaking was introduced to the curriculum through courses in home economics, nutrition, psychology, sociology, and even biology and chemistry. Educators reasoned that women needed mathematics in addition to courses in the natural sciences to help their children with their home-

IMAGE 6.1: *Mary McLeod Bethune with a line of girls from the school in Daytona Beach, Florida (1905).* Source: Black & white photonegative, 4 x 5 in. State Archives of Florida, Florida Memory.

work. The assumption that women's primary function was to marry and raise children remained dominant even as women entered higher education in greater numbers. Women's enrollment in college programs continued to ebb and flow throughout the century, dependent largely on the country's economic condition and men's needs. After World War II, for example, the percentage of women in higher education dropped substantially, reflecting the return of men to the classroom with federal assistance through the GI Bill. Women were encouraged to "return to normalcy," meaning that they were actively discouraged from seeking either education or employment beyond providing for the immediate needs of their family and home. By the early 1990s, women had surpassed men in enrollments in four-year colleges and universities in the United States, and the gap has continued to widen (Figure 6.1).

TITLE IX: LEGISLATING GENDER EQUITY IN EDUCATION

The first major piece of legislation to address gender equality in education was not passed until 1972, the same year that the Equal Rights Amendment was sent to the states for ratification. Although discriminatory educational practices based on race were addressed in Title VI of the 1964 Civil Rights Act, sex was not included anywhere in the Civil Rights Act except in Title VII, which dealt with employment. For many in the women's movement, issues of pay equity and employment discrimination were more overt and immediate barriers to women's equal status. While education plays an obvious and important role in preparing women for full employment, most schools were coeducational, thereby masking the many covert forms of educational discrimination against women. In 1970, President Nixon's

FIGURE 6.1: Earned Bachelor's Degrees by Sex, 1869–2019

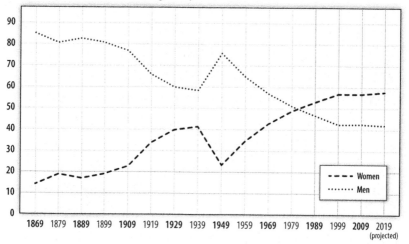

Source: US Department of Education, National Center for Education Statistics, "Degrees Conferred by Degree-Granting Institutions, by Level of Degree and Sex of Student: 1869–2022," Table 310, prepared 2012.

Task Force on Women's Rights and Responsibilities called discrimination in education "one of the most damaging injustices women suffer."[14]

Title IX, also known as the Educational Amendments of 1972, banned sex discrimination in education at all levels of formal education. The language of this legislation mirrored other equal protection legislation:

> No person in the United States shall, on the basis of sex, be excluded from participation in, be denied the benefits of, or be subjected to discrimination under any education program or activity receiving federal financial assistance.

Cosponsored by Congresswoman Edith Green and Senator Birch Bayh, the bill met little opposition from within Congress or from lobbyists when it was introduced. In fact, Green specifically asked women's organizations not to testify on behalf of the legislation, fearing the publicity would attract opponents and endanger the legislation's chances for passage.[15] While the legislation was designed to eliminate the crippling barriers in all sorts of educational programs, institutions, and curricula, the law is now almost exclusively described in relation to increasing women's access to sports programs—even in accounts of the women's movement or women's history.[16] The legislation specified that no federal funds could go to educational institutions that were already receiving federal dollars and practiced sex discrimination in any of their programs, including admissions, athletics, financial aid, counseling, facilities, and employment. Today, Title IX extends to issues of sexual harassment, sexual assault, pregnancy, and parenting.

Sexual and Gender Harassment

In 1992, the US Supreme Court ruled that a student could bring a Title IX claim for damages for a sexually hostile environment created by a teacher (*Franklin v. Gwinnett County Public Schools*). In *Davis v. Monroe County Board of Education* (1999), the Court ruled that schools may also be liable if one student harasses another student at school. Schools are obligated to take reasonable steps under Title IX to prevent and eliminate **sexual harassment**. A study by the AAUW found that 81 percent of students in public schools in grades eight through eleven had experienced some form of sexual harassment. Although girls were more likely to have experienced sexual harassment at some point in high school, boys reported experiencing sexual harassment "occasionally" or "often."[17] Unwelcome sexual comments, jokes, or gestures, whether in person or online, are the most common form of sexual harassment in middle and high school, experienced by 33 percent of all students in a single academic year.[18] Girls at all ages are more likely to be on the receiving end of sexual harassment, but the gender gap is greatest in the senior year of high school, with 69 percent of girls and only 39 percent of boys reporting that they had experienced sexual harassment during the school year.

Enforcing the prohibition against sexual harassment extends to **gender harassment**. The second most common form of in-person harassment experienced by middle and high school students is "being called gay or lesbian in a negative way."[19] Victims of gender harassment are targeted for failing to follow norms that are typical for their sex or gender or for openly expressing a non-heteronormative sexual orientation. Gender harassment is an attempt to enforce sex stereotypes. Students who do not conform to traditional gender norms are more likely than their peers to say they are called names, made fun of, or bullied at school (56 percent, compared to 33 percent).[20]

Sexual harassment, even noncontact encounters (verbal remarks or online messages), is different from bullying, and schools must deal with them as two separate problems. Susan Fineran, coauthor of a recent study on sexual harassment in grades five through twelve, says, "Title IX protects everybody in school against this kind of behavior, but as soon as you call something 'bullying,' then it's just viewed as ill behavior that one student does to another student. Sexual harassment is really an environmental problem for the school. The school needs to do something about stopping sexual harassment because they are legally bound to." Her study found that girls and sexual minorities were the groups most likely to be upset by sexual harassment and most likely to suffer low self-esteem, poorer mental and physical health, and experience trauma symptoms as a result.[21] Feeling unsafe at school has been correlated with declining academic performance, skipping school, and dropping out.

By one estimate, 67 percent of college students experience some form of sexual or gender harassment on campus, and nearly as many say they have witnessed another student being harassed on campus.[22] A majority of encounters are noncontact in nature (sexual remarks or electronic messages). Male and female students are almost equally likely to be the target of sexual jokes, comments, gestures, or looks. Male students are more likely to be called gay or a homophobic name. Both male and female students are more likely to be harassed by a man than a woman. More than one-third of college students do not tell anyone about their experiences; those who do confide in someone usually tell a friend. Less than 10 percent of all students report incidents of sexual harassment to a college or university employee. Sexual harassment on college campuses is serious and can lead to emotional damage and academic disruption for the victim, and contributes to a hostile learning environment for all students. For the university, sexual harassment and the failure to act when incidents of harassment are brought to their attention can be costly and harm their reputation.[23]

Campus Sexual Assault

Campus sexual assault is both a crime and a violation of the Title IX prohibition against sex discrimination. In the vast majority of cases, the perpetrator and the victim know each other and are enrolled at the same institution.[24] In 2011 and again in 2014, the US Department of Education (DOE) issued a letter to all institutions of higher education affirming that acts of sexual violence on campus are a form of sexual harassment prohibited under Title IX and providing guidance on compliance with the law's requirements. Title IX requires schools to address sexual violence promptly, thoroughly, and fairly, regardless of whether an incident is also reported to the police. All institutions must employ a **Title IX coordinator** whose responsibility it is to "help a school ensure that every person affected by its operations—including faculty, staff, and students—are aware of their legal rights under Title IX, and that the school and all of its employees, through its policies, procedures, and practices, complies with its legal obligations under Title IX."[25]

In addition, the **Clery Act** requires colleges and universities participating in federal student aid programs to report crimes that occur on campus (referred to as the Annual Security Report), provide "timely warning" of known risks to campus safety, and publicize campus safety policies. The Clery Act contains the Campus Sexual Assault Victim's Bill of Rights, which requires colleges to disclose educational programming, campus disciplinary process, and victim rights regarding sexual violence complaints. Parents and students can access campus crime statistics online through a portal maintained by the US Department of Education.

In 2013, the Campus Sexual Violation Elimination Act (**Campus SaVE Act**) broadened Clery Act requirements to cover all incidents of sexual violence on campus, specifically sexual assault, domestic violence, dating violence, and stalking.

SaVE also requires colleges to provide "primary prevention and awareness programs" for new students and employees in addition to ongoing violence prevention and awareness campaigns. SaVE includes minimum standards for institutional disciplinary procedures to ensure a prompt, fair, and impartial investigation and resolution and mandates that school officials receive annual training on domestic violence, sexual assault, and stalking. Under SaVE, both parties may have others present during an institutional disciplinary proceeding and any related meeting, including an advisor of their choice, and both parties must receive written notification of the outcome of all disciplinary proceedings at the same time.[26] Under the Clery Act, individuals are protected against retaliation by an institution or employee of an institution for exercising their rights under the act (Title IX also provides such protection).

Not everyone supports an activist role for the federal government in promoting campus sexual assault policies and procedures. Senator Lamar Alexander (R-Tenn.), chair of the Committee on Health, Education, Labor and Pensions, called the guidance by the Education Department "overreach." The Foundation for Individual Rights in Education (FIRE), an organization that promotes free speech and other liberties at universities, supports students who challenge their school's sexual assault disciplinary procedures. Critics allege that new campus procedures created in response to the Department of Education's guidance "lack the most basic elements of fairness and due process" and "are overwhelmingly stacked against the accused."[27]

Campus sexual assault remains an urgent problem for universities. However, estimates of the problem's magnitude are complicated by competing agendas and overlapping reporting requirements in the policies described above. The White House Task Force to Protect Students from Sexual Assault reports that one woman in five is sexually assaulted in college. Know Your IX, an antiviolence campus advocacy group, reports that 19 percent of women and 5–6 percent of men will experience sexual assault during college.[28] In June 2016, there were 246 ongoing investigations by the DOE Office of Civil Rights into how 195 colleges and universities handle sexual assault reports. The DOE regularly releases the list to reporters, and campus activists use the list to pressure schools to prioritize sexual violence. Several of these investigations have attracted significant national media attention.

An investigation found that Baylor University had ignored and mishandled several accusations of sexual assault on campus, many involving members of the football team, contributing to a cultural perception that football was "above the rules." ESPN's *Outside the Lines* broke the story of the university's failure to act on allegations of sexual assault, its failure to provide support for women who reported sexual assault, and a three-year delay in naming a Title IX coordinator, as required by law. Ultimately, Baylor's football coach was fired, five current or former Baylor University football players were accused of "acts of violence," and still others have been arrested, tried, and convicted of sexual assault. Kenneth Starr was demoted from the

IMAGE 6.2: *UC Berkeley junior Sofie Karasek, speaking, appears with other student survivors of sexual assault, Rep. Barbara Lee (far left) and Rep. Jackie Speier (far right) on campus in April 2014 to discuss sexual assault policies.* Source: Photograph of Sofie Karasek, taken by Nathaniel Solley, available at www.dailycal.org.

presidency by the Board of Regents, and subsequently resigned from the faculty of the Baylor School of Law as well.

Another reason for the difficulty in recording accurate data around campus sexual assault is the fact that a significant number of sexual assaults do not get reported. There are numerous reasons victims do not report their assaults, but some sexual assault survivors and advocacy groups point to low rates of arrest and conviction or leniency in punishing attackers as reasons. In March 2016, Brock Turner was convicted of raping an unconscious woman behind a dumpster. Two bystanders interrupted the assault and pinned Turner to the ground, holding him until the police arrived. Turner was a member of the Stanford University swimming program and had Olympic aspirations. Following the conviction, prosecutors in the case asked that Turner be sentenced to six years in prison (he could have received up to fourteen years), but Santa Clara County Superior Court judge Aaron Persky imposed a six-month jail sentence with probation, citing Turner's age and lack of a criminal history as the basis for his decision. "A prison sentence would have a severe impact on him," Persky said. "I think he will not be a danger to others."[29] Turner's light sentence and Persky's rationale for it sparked outrage. The victim, who has chosen to remain anonymous, wrote and then read aloud in court a twelve-page letter describing the impact Turner's attack had on her life; the letter was published by *BuzzFeed* and read by millions. Ashleigh Banfield, anchor of CNN's *Legal View*, read the letter live on the air. Vice President Joe Biden, who has been an outspoken advocate for preventing sexual assault, responded with an open letter also published by *BuzzFeed*: "It must have been wrenching to relive what he did to you all over again. But you did it anyway, in the hope that your strength might prevent this crime from happening to someone else. Your bravery is breathtaking."[30] Brock Turner was released in early September 2016 after serving half of his six-month sentence. In the same month, California governor Jerry Brown signed legislation that prevents courts from granting probation to people convicted in a rape or sexual assault involving a victim who was unconscious or too intoxicated to give his or her consent. "He got less than a semester in county jail," said Santa Clara County district attorney Jeff Rosen. "The next person that does something like this is going to be in prison for at least three years."[31]

A case at Brigham Young University illustrates the personal cost of reporting an assault for some victims. After reporting that she had been raped by a fellow student in his apartment, the female student received a letter from the associate dean of students: "You are being suspended from Brigham Young University because of your violation of the Honor Code including continued drug use and consensual sex, effective immediately." The honor code, signed by all BYU students, requires modest dress and prohibits drinking, drug use, same-sex intimacy, indecency, and sexual misconduct. Several women at Brigham Young have complained that before the university investigated their reports of sexual assault, they were investigated for violating the honor code by drinking alcohol or engaging in consensual sex. Although this clash of interests is largely limited to faith-based institutions, it points to the importance of amnesty clauses for all universities. Adele P. Kimmel, a lawyer at Public Justice, said, "All schools, including BYU, know that alcohol and drugs are often involved in sexual violence. If you're a school that wants to send a message to students that you're serious about preventing sexual violence, you should have an amnesty policy."[32]

The White House, politicians such as Senator Kirsten Gillibrand (D-N.Y.), and activists have taken steps to address the problem of campus sexual assault. The White House Task Force, cochaired by Vice President Joe Biden and presidential senior advisor Valerie Jarrett, was established in 2014 by President Obama in response to growing public concern over the pervasiveness of sexual violence on college campuses. The Obama administration has also launched a public-awareness campaign, "It's On Us," which encourages men and women to intervene before a sexual assault takes place. Schools in forty-eight states have active "It's On Us" chapters. Annie Clark and Andrea Pino, two University of North Carolina at Chapel Hill students, joined with other students to file a Title IX complaint with the Department of Education against the university alleging that the institution "routinely botched sexual assault and harassment complaints and mistreated victims."[33] Clark and Pino then founded End Rape on Campus (EROC), a nonprofit that they recently moved to Washington, D.C., where they are working with Senator Gillibrand to create educational initiatives and promote policy changes. EROC joins several other activist groups founded on campuses by survivors of sexual violence, including No Red Tape, Know Your IX, and Revoking Silence. (For more on campus sexual assault, see "Encountering the Controversies of Equality.")

Pregnant and Parenting Students

Prior to Title IX, pregnant students were almost always forced to leave school. Under Title IX, schools are prohibited from discriminating against pregnant and parenting students. Schools may not exclude a student from any educational program or activity, including extracurricular activity, on the basis of pregnancy. This also means that pregnant students may not be forced into separate schools. Schools must accommodate pregnant students to the same degree they would extend allowances for any other temporary disability, including granting a temporary leave from school. Pregnant student-athletes are permitted a one-year extension of the five-year period of eligibility.

While there have not been many court cases involving Title IX coverage of pregnant or parenting students, a number of pregnant students have brought suit after being denied admission to, or being dismissed from, the National Honor Society (NHS). The NHS invites students for membership based on a combination of academic achievement and moral character. In each of the NHS cases, the school claimed that the student's exclusion was based not on her pregnancy but rather on the fact that the student had engaged in premarital sex, a moral character issue. However, Title IX is a gender-neutral law. Thus it may permit discrimination on the basis of premarital sexual activity, but not against pregnant girls alone.[34] Male students would need to be similarly screened for sexual activity.

In 2003 Tara Brady became the first pregnant student-athlete to file suit under Title IX, alleging that her basketball scholarship was revoked after she became pregnant and decided to carry her pregnancy to term. A student-athlete and star basketball player at Sacred Heart University in Connecticut, she claimed that her coach told her that she would be a "distraction" and should leave the school, which she ultimately did.[35] A 2007 ESPN documentary described student-athlete pregnancy as an "underground topic" and featured stories of women forced to choose between their scholarship and their pregnancy. For example, one institution required female athletes to sign a document each year that included the statement "Pregnancy resulting in the inability to compete and positively contribute to the program's success will result in the modification of your grant-in-aid money."[36] Exposure of this discriminatory practice by ESPN led to its elimination.

Feminists for Life (FFL), an organization dedicated to systematically eliminating the root causes that lead to abortion, advocated for a "redshirting" policy for pregnant athletes. Redshirting is a form of medical leave for athletes that maintains both their scholarship and their eligibility. Pregnancy must be treated like any other temporary disability and students must be allowed to take a one-year leave without penalty and to have their prepregnancy status reinstated in full upon their return. In 2008 the National Collegiate Athletic Association (NCAA) responded to a growing number of issues related to pregnant and parenting collegiate athletes, and produced the NCAA Model Pregnancy and Parenting Policy tool kit to assist schools in complying with Title IX gender equity provisions. A survey found that 85 percent of Division I schools, 94 percent of Division II schools, and more than 98 percent of Division III schools lacked any written policy covering student-athlete pregnancy and parenting issues. The NCAA's policy is gender neutral; however, critics charge that the policy focuses primarily on the physical pregnancy and says very little about the needs of student-athletes who are new parents.

In many ways universities are behind in acknowledging that students may also be parents, even though one-fourth of all undergraduates (4.8 million in 2016) are raising children. Just half of four-year colleges and only 45 percent of community colleges provide access to on-campus child care. Students with children are especially at risk of failing to complete their degree—only 33 percent attain a degree or certificate within six years of enrolling.[37] A federally funded grant program administered through the US Department of Education was created to support low-income student-parents with campus-based child care services. In 2014, funding was provided to eighty-six colleges and universities to initiate campus-based child care options for parenting students. Data show that students enrolled at participating campuses have higher retention and graduation rates in addition to strong academic performance.

Title IX and Equity in Athletics

Title IX's impact on women's interest and participation in sports was immediate and has been overwhelmingly successful. In 1961, nine states actually prohibited interscholastic sports for females, presumably because of the stereotype that females were too delicate for physical activity and not suited for competitive sports. In 1971, only 7.5 percent of the nearly 4 million high school athletes were female. By 2011, the fortieth anniversary of Title IX, girls made up 41 percent of nearly 7.6 million high school athletes, representing a tenfold increase over participation levels in 1972.

The strongest opposition to Title IX came from college and high school athletic directors and coaches. The NCAA initially tried to lobby Congress to exclude athletics from Title IX coverage. When total exclusion failed, the NCAA argued, again unsuccessfully, that only the programs within an institution that actually received federal dollars should be subject to the equity provisions. Since few athletics programs at either the college or the high school level are direct recipients of federal dollars, this interpretation would mean a de facto Title IX exemption for athletics.

Box 6.1 – Encountering the Controversies of Equality

A Mattress as Alleged Crime Scene, Performance Art, Political Statement, and Maybe a Violation of Title IX

Not so long ago, campus sexual assault was not a topic of public discussion, nor was it the subject of much institutional attention. Although legal scholar Catherine Mackinnon first articulated the legal theory that sexual assault and harassment limit women's educational opportunities in 1977, it took a series of court cases in the 1990s to establish that Title IX applied in cases of sexual violence on campus. Still, universities were slow to establish procedures for adjudicating allegations of rape by one student against another. Enforcement by the US Department of Education (DOE) was ineffectual—not a single institution has ever lost federal funding as a result of a Title IX complaint and finding.[1]

Today's university campus is ground zero for the debate over Title IX's applicability to sexual assault. Columbia University student Emma Sulkowicz alleged that she was raped in her dorm room by another student during what she says began as a consensual sexual encounter in August 2012. Eight months after the incident, she filed a complaint with the university. The accused, Paul Nungesser, denied the allegations and was found "not responsible" by Columbia's internal disciplinary process using the "preponderance of evidence" standard of proof. Sulkowicz later filed a complaint with the local police, but the district attorney elected not to pursue the case. Although the disciplinary hearing process requires confidentiality, Nungesser's name was used in statements to the press by witnesses for Sulkowicz.

In April 2014, twenty-three students filed a federal complaint against Columbia and Barnard College, alleging violations of Title IX. They claimed that the institutions discourage students from reporting sexual assault, and complained that alleged perpetrators are not removed from campus and that sanctions, when imposed, are too lenient. Later that summer, Sulkowicz began *Mattress Performance (Carry That Weight)*, a senior thesis project supervised by a Columbia professor. She carried an extra-long twin mattress (similar to the one in her dorm room where she said the rape took place) whenever she was on campus; she could not ask for help in carrying it, but if help was offered, she could accept. Sulkowicz said the project would end when Nungesser was expelled from Columbia, even if that meant carrying the mattress until graduation. Although Columbia asked her not to do so, she carried the mattress onto the stage at commencement with the help of several other women. Throughout the project, several protests took place on campus featuring the mattress.

In April 2015, Paul Nungesser filed a Title IX lawsuit against Columbia University, its president, and the faculty member who supervised Sulkowicz's thesis, alleging that they exposed him to gender-based harassment and a hostile educational environment by allowing and condoning

Source: Andrew Burton/Getty Images.

the project. He argued that even though he had been cleared of any wrongdoing, the university enabled Sulkowicz to depict him as a rapist through her performance art. A US district court threw out Nungesser's case, but in August 2016 the 2nd US Circuit Court of Appeals reversed the lower court's ruling and allowed the case to move forward. The judge wrote, "A covered university that adopts, even temporarily, a policy of bias favoring one sex over the other in a disciplinary dispute, doing so in order to avoid liability or bad publicity, has practiced sex discrimination, notwithstanding that the motive for the discrimination did not come from ingrained or permanent bias against that particular sex."[2] If this ruling stands, it will undoubtedly open the door to more lawsuits by male students accused of sexual misconduct.

What do you think?

Title IX is a sex-neutral law. However, women are more likely to be victims of sexual assault and men are more likely to be perpetrators. Is it possible to design a sex-neutral adjudication process on campus? Have campus activists, who have pushed the issue of sexual assault to the forefront of the nation's attention, created a hostile environment that endangers due process protections for individuals accused of sexual misconduct? What protections are in place on your own campus for student survivors of sexual assault and students accused of sexual misconduct? Are they adequate to ensure that all individuals have free and unfettered access to full participation in the benefits of education?

The Office of Civil Rights, the primary enforcement agency, rejected the NCAA's efforts, maintaining that if any program took federal money, the entire institution was subject to Title IX compliance.

In 1974, the NCAA supported the Tower Amendment, which would have exempted men's intercollegiate football and basketball (the revenue-generating sports). A House-Senate conference committee rejected the amendment, leaving the NCAA to challenge the constitutionality of the gender-equity provision in the courts. Although that challenge was initially unsuccessful, a 1984 Supreme Court case, *Grove City College v. Bell*, temporarily gave Title IX opponents what they sought, ruling that only those programs receiving federal funds must comply with the statute. Congress acted (over President Ronald Reagan's veto) in 1988 to reinstate the original intent of Title IX by passing the Civil Rights Restoration Act. Four years later, in *Cohen v. Brown University*, a federal court ruled that Brown University had violated Title IX's provisions when it cut two women's teams and two men's teams. Although the university cut the same number of varsity teams for men and women, several women on the gymnastics team filed suit, claiming that the effect of Brown's action violated Title IX. Cutting the two women's programs had saved the university more than $62,000, while eliminating the two men's programs saved only $16,000. In other words, female athletes were disproportionately affected by the cuts.

Under Title IX, there are three ways an institution can show that it is providing equitable opportunities for women athletes. First, a school can show that the percentage of its female athletes is substantially proportionate to the percentage of women in its student body. Second, if there is not proportionality, schools are required to show that they are actively engaged in a meaningful process that will provide equity for women, typically by demonstrating a history of expanding opportunities for women to participate in athletics. The University of Maryland, for example, promoted its women's water polo team to varsity status in 2003 to create more scholarships and playing opportunities for female athletes on campus. By moving into compliance, the University of Maryland was able to return some scholarships to eight underfunded men's programs.[38] Finally, a school can demonstrate compliance by meeting the actual level of athletic interest among women.

This third provision has energized Title IX opponents, who claim that "studies consistently find higher rates of interest in athletic participation among males, be they eighth-graders or college students."[39] Brown University argued in its case that while 51 percent of its student body was female, only 38 percent of its intercollegiate athletes were women, suggesting that it was more than meeting the "interest test" required for compliance. It is difficult, however, to ignore the potential circuitousness of the interest argument. As law professor Robert C. Farrell counters, "It is hard to have a high level of interest in a sports program that doesn't exist." The US Court of Appeals agreed. In rejecting Brown University's "level of interest" argument, it stated, "To assert that Title IX permits institutions to provide fewer athletic participation opportunities for women than men, based upon the premise that women are less interested in sports than are men, is among other things to ignore the fact that Title IX was created to remedy discrimination that results from stereotyped notions of women's interests and abilities."[40]

Prior to Title IX, women made up 15 percent of college athletes but received just 2 percent of the total athletic budget. In 2011, more than 190,000 women participated in college athletics—about six times as many as in 1971. Today, women's participation rate in intercollegiate athletics is 43 percent of the 450,000 opportunities available.[41] But in what can only be seen as an unintended consequence of women's success in collegiate athletics, the number of female coaches has declined precipitously. Before Title IX, more than 90 percent of the coaches for women's teams were female. Universities often had a separate women's athletics program headed by a female athletics director. Post-1972, athletics departments merged, the number of female coaches began to fall, and the male coaches who followed were paid higher salaries. Today only 43 percent of NCAA women's sports teams have a female coach.[42]

In 2011 female student-athletes at Division I institutions received 48 percent of the athletic scholarships at those institutions. However, they received only 40 percent of total money spent on athletics despite making up 53 percent of the student body. Under Title IX, the total amount of scholarship aid made available to men and women must be substantially proportionate to their participation rate (although there is no requirement for equity in operating budget spending). The **Equity in Athletics Disclosure Act (EADA)**, passed in 2008, is one mechanism of enforcement. The EADA requires colleges and universities with intercollegiate athletics programs covered by Title IX to report data on athletic participation, staffing, and revenues and expenses, by men's and women's teams. According to EADA data, "46 percent of the Power Five conference schools have a proportional athletic aid gap of two percent or more—a gap considered non-compliant under Title IX without additional explanation or justification."[43] A media investigation into Title IX compliance by university athletic programs found a number of red flags and a general sense that "nobody is watching." According to Title IX attorney Kristen Galles, "the Department of Education has neither the resources nor the mandate to investigate or act upon the EADA data it collects, even when that data indicates that schools may be breaking the law."[44] Investigations begin only when someone files a complaint. After more than forty years of Title IX enforcement, the federal government has never taken funding away from an institution because of noncompliance with Title IX.

Title IX has long been labeled "unfair" to men because, in order to move toward compliance, some institutions have chosen to cut male sports programs. From the perspective of coaches and athletes whose budgets or prestige are likely to be reduced in the name of gender equity, Title IX promotes discrimination—a highly charged accusation. As John Weistart commented, "The particular rhetorical flourish that rallies these groups is the declaration that present policies under Title IX are 'affirmative action'—a not-so-subtle attempt to push the claims of women for recognition of their athletic aspirations into the swirl of anger that makes racial preferences such a political hot spot."[45] Although individual schools might have cut back on men's sports programs, nationwide very few schools reduced the number of male athletes by more than ten. Seventy-two percent of colleges and universities that have added women's teams have done so without cutting any teams for men.[46] In an ironic twist on the "fairness" claim, the US Olympic Committee was concerned enough about the decline in US medals in men's swimming and gymnastics to pledge $8 million leading up to the 2000 Olympic Games to help college conferences strengthen and restore their programs. Additionally, the Olympic Committee spent $4.4 million on men's gymnastics programs and built training centers in San Antonio, Minneapolis, and Salt Lake City for the men's sports that some colleges no longer offer.[47]

Unlike collegiate athletics, the laws in support of Title IX do not require high schools to publicly report gender breakdowns by sport, resources, and funding. "High school transparency" legislation has been introduced to require high schools to collect and report information on male and female sports, including participation opportunities, funding, and other resource allocation decisions.[48] This would be particularly helpful in identifying problems in urban schools. Research by the Women's Sports Foundation found that urban girls of color have some of the lowest rates of sports participation among all US adolescents. By the eleventh and twelfth grades, 84 percent of urban girls reported no physical education classes during the previous week. A Harris survey found that although 54 percent of boys and 50 percent of girls in the suburbs described themselves as "moderately involved" in athletics, only 36 percent of urban girls described themselves as "moderately involved" (compared to 56 percent of the urban boys).[49] To counter urban girls' lack of physical activity, the New York City public high schools established double-dutch jump rope as a competitive sport.[50] There are many benefits to competitive athletics for high school girls. Regular physical activity reduces the risk of obesity for adolescent girls. Women who played sports while young have a 7 percent lower risk of obesity twenty to twenty-five years later. In addition to combatting obesity, sports participation decreases the likelihood of a young women's chance of developing heart disease, osteoporosis, and breast cancer. All high school athletes are less likely to smoke cigarettes or use drugs, and female athletes have lower rates of sexual activity and pregnancy than their nonparticipating peers.

The impact of Title IX on women's participation beyond high school and collegiate athletics is also clear. On July 9, 1999, 90,185 people (including President Bill Clinton) crowded into the Rose Bowl in Pasadena, California, to see the US women's soccer team defeat China to win the World Cup. This was the largest crowd ever, across all sports, to watch a women's sporting event.[51] The 2011 Women's World Cup final broke the Twitter world record for number of tweets per second.[52] The 2015 Women's World Cup, with 26.7 million viewers tuning in across English- and Spanish-language broadcasts, was the most-watched soccer event in the United States.[53] A record 45 percent of athletes at the 2016 Rio Olympics were women, participating in 47.5 percent of the competitions. Twenty-eight women's sports were featured in Rio, including women's rugby for the first time and the reintroduction of women's golf. Fifty-three percent of the athletes on Team USA were women. American women won 27 gold medals and 61 of Team USA's 121 medals overall, a record of success attributed to Title IX. The International Olympic Committee (IOC) predicts gender parity in Olympic sports within a decade. However, only 24 of 106 IOC board members were women in 2016.[54]

Challenges Remain for Title IX

Over time, the most challenges to Title IX have arisen around its application to athletics and the fear that gains by women will result in losses by men. In February 2002, for example, the National Wrestling Coaches Association filed a lawsuit against the Department of Education alleging that the interpretation of Title IX embodied in the three-prong test for compliance is unlawful and authorizes intentional discrimination against male athletes amounting to "reverse discrimination" and "quotas."[55] On June 11, 2003, US District Court judge Emmet Sullivan dismissed the lawsuit, ruling that Title IX cannot be blamed for cuts to men's teams because educational institutions make decisions based on multiple unrelated factors. The court took further pains to recognize the importance of Title IX as a "landmark civil rights statute" with significant flexibility built into its implementing policies, negating the allegation of "quotas."

In June 2002, President George W. Bush appointed a fifteen-person Commission on Opportunity in Athletics to examine Title IX on eight specific questions. The first question asked if Title IX standards for assessing equal opportunity in athletics are working to promote opportunities for men and women, suggesting that the impetus for forming the commission in the first place was to determine whether implementation of Title IX is "unfair" to men. The commission held town meetings throughout the country to gather information before submitting a report to Secretary of Education Rod Paige. Several of the report's proposals threatened to dismantle Title IX protections and current interpretations of compliance requirements, including replacing the proportionality standard with a 50-50 standard (disregarding the actual proportion of male and female undergraduates); developing an interest survey and tying the percentage of opportunities for women to its results (in lieu of proportionality as the basic standard); eliminating nontraditional students (students older than twenty-four and any student with children) from the equation when calculating proportionality; and repealing the Equity in Disclosure Act, which requires public disclosure of financial and participation information by colleges and universities.[56]

Two female commission members, Donna de Varona (a two-time Olympic gold medal swimmer and chairperson of the US Olympic Committee's government relations committee) and Julie Foudy (former member of the US women's soccer team and president of the Women's Sports Foundation), issued a minority report:

> Our decision is based on (1) our fundamental disagreement with the tenor, structure and significant portions of the content of the Commission's report, which fails to present a full and fair consideration of the issues or a clear statement of the discrimination women and girls still face in obtaining equal opportunity in athletics; (2) our belief that many of the recommendations made by the majority would seriously weaken Title IX's protections and substantially reduce the opportunities to which women and girls are entitled under current law; and (3) our belief that only one of the proposals would address the budgetary causes underlying the discontinuation of some men's teams, and that others would not restore opportunities that have been lost.[57]

The three-part minority report presented the findings and recommendations that de Varona and Foudy believed the commission should have included, evaluated the commission's recommendations and gave an explanation for why they could not support them, and addressed the commission's process, which they believed was flawed. The minority report is quite detailed in estimating the potential impact the commission's recommendations would have on women's participation in athletics. In every instance, women would be substantially disadvantaged and would lose ground relative to the status quo.

On July 11, 2003, the Bush administration announced that there would be no changes to the way compliance is judged, and in fact, none of the recommendations from the Commission on Opportunity in Athletics were adopted. Largely due to the orchestrated efforts on the part of women's organizations to block any changes to Title IX, the Bush administration was forced to back down. "One year, one stacked commission, and the outrage of women's groups all over the country, and finally the Bush administration realizes the vast support for Title IX," said Eleanor Smeal, president of Feminist Majority. "Too bad it made us lose vital time and money that could be better spent enforcing Title IX."[58] Gerald Reynolds, assistant secretary for civil rights for the Department of Education, sent a letter to the country's educational institutions announcing the decision and detailing the commitment of resources to an educational campaign on Title IX compliance and aggressive enforcement of Title IX standards. Women's organizations interpreted the Bush administration's actions as recognition of the power of women's votes.

Title IX will mark fifty years in 2022. Its positive impact on opening access to women and promoting equity in all areas of education including athletics is indisputable. The next challenge will be to extend the principles of Title IX equity more broadly. The NCAA, the organization most closely associated with collegiate athletics, is a nonprofit organization that falls outside Title IX coverage. Thus when the University of Connecticut women's basketball team won its eleventh NCAA Division I national championship in 2016, the win earned zero dollars for its athletic conference or university. Meanwhile, for each game a team won in the NCAA men's tournament, the team's conference earned roughly $260,000 for the current year and for each of the next five years, making the total value of a win approximately $1.56 million. According to Smith College economist Andrew Zimbalist, "That sends a strong signal that the women's tournament is less significant and less worthy than the men's, and it's a policy that perpetuates a historical pattern of discrimination against women in institutions of higher education."[59]

Similarly, the US Soccer Federation, the governing body for soccer in the United States, pays the players on the men's and women's national teams differently. The women's national team won a third World Cup in 2015, yet according to a federal complaint filed with the Equal Employment Opportunity Commission by five members of the women's team, they earn 40 percent of what players on the men's national team earn. "The numbers speak for themselves," said Hope Solo, goalkeeper and one of the women filing the complaint. "We are the best in the world, have three World Cup championships, four Olympic championships."[60] The typical justification for the salary gap between male and female professional athletes is that the men draw bigger crowds and generate more money from ticket sales, corporate sponsorships, and television viewership. As women gained ground in professional sports they were told to be grateful for the opportunity to play and to get paid for doing it. "In this day and age, it's about equality. It's about equal rights. We believe now the time is right because we believe it's our responsibility for women's sports and specifically for women's soccer to do whatever it takes to push for equal pay and equal rights. And to be treated with respect," Solo said in an interview on NBC's *Today*.[61] The US Soccer Federation asked the government to dismiss the suit, saying there was no evidence the organization acted with a "discriminatory motive." Both the NCAA and the US Soccer Federation operate outside the bounds of Title IX's coverage, yet the equity imperative at stake in each challenge is consistent with the goals and intention of the federal law.

Title IX's Broad Impact on Access to Education

More women than ever before are enrolled in colleges and universities. In 1979, the number of women surpassed the number of men enrolled in college for the first time, and the upward trend has continued ever since. Most demographers expect that increase to continue, even as the proportion of male enrollees continues to decline.[62] Fifty-seven percent of the 20.2 million students enrolled at American colleges and universities in fall 2015 were female. For the first time since the US Census Bureau began collecting data on degree attainment, more women than men have a bachelor's degree. In 2014, 29.9 percent of men and 30.2 percent of women in the population have a bachelor's degree. Among African Americans the gap in educational attainment between men and women is even more substantial (see Table 6.1). African American women earned 67 percent of all bachelor's degrees, 70 percent of all master's degrees, and more than 64 percent of all doctorates awarded to African Americans. Black women account for 64 percent of all African American college enrollments in 2015.[63]

This trend is also not limited to the United States. Over the last decade, more than 70 percent of the increase in full-time undergraduates in the United Kingdom has been female. In Australia, women earn 52 percent of degrees compared with 48 percent for men, and 60 percent of University of Ottawa students are women. The roughly 60:40 ratio of women to men is close to the norm at most institutions of higher education. In the 1990s, women accounted for 100 percent of the enrollment growth at German universities and more than 60 percent in France and Australia.[64]

The Gender Gap in College Enrollment

Although the trend is clear, the reason for the decline in male enrollments is not. Part of the change can be attributed to an increase in academic and professional opportunities for women that require a bachelor's degree. Some ascribe the decline in male enrollments to a transitional economy and more non-college-related options for men. "Men have more options than women when they graduate from high school. There's the military, trade unions, and jobs that require physical strength," said one director of admissions. "A young woman who wants to have a career may think she has to go to college, whereas men see other alternatives."[65]

Another reason for the gender gap could be the significant differences in the expectations of young men and women regarding college graduation, a trend that has solidified over the past two decades. As the 1970s came to a close, the National Longitudinal Survey of Youth showed that fifteen- and sixteen-year-old males and females had statistically identical expectations of completing a four-year degree. In 1997, however, female respondents between the ages of twelve and seventeen were significantly more likely than males (ten points higher) to report that they expected to complete four years of college.[66] Given that educational expectations are highly correlated with ultimate educational attainment, we should expect the gender gap in enrollments to continue.

Colleges and universities must admit the best students in the applicant pool, and the majority of those are now female, as women tend to perform better than men in high school and in college. Higher education officials have expressed con-

TABLE 6.1: First Professional Degrees Awarded, by Sex and Race: 2012–2013

	Total*	Men	Women
DENTISTRY (DDS OR DMD)	5.1%		
White		34.0%	24.4%
African American		1.9%	2.5%
Hispanic		2.5%	3.5%
MEDICINE (MD)	17.2%		
White		34.8%	28.3%
African American		2.2%	4.1%
Hispanic		3.0%	3.2%
PHARMACY (PHARMD)	13.3%		
White		23.1%	36.1%
African American		2.8%	4.8%
Hispanic		1.7%	2.6%
VETERINARY MEDICINE (DVM)	2.6%		
White		18.6%	63.0%
African American		0.65%	1.9%
Hispanic		2.3%	8.2%
LAW (LLB OR JD)	46.6%		
White		40.9%	31.3%
African American		2.9%	4.4%
Hispanic		3.9%	4.2%

Source: National Center for Education Statistics, "Degrees Conferred by Postsecondary Institutions in Selected Professional Fields, by Race/Ethnicity and Field of Study: 2011–12 and 2012–13" (for males and females), Tables 324.60, 324.70 (Washington, D.C.: U.S. Department of Education, 2014).

* The "Total" column represents the number of degrees in that field as a percentage of all professional degrees awarded.

cern over the widening gender gap in college enrollments. Some institutions have started modifying their promotional material to appeal to male applicants, in an attempt to attract more men to campus. Other universities are using athletics, both varsity and intramural, to broaden the appeal of their campuses to male applicants. The University of Dallas brought back varsity baseball after a sixteen-year hiatus and added twenty-six men to the campus as a result. To attract more male applicants, Dickinson College in Pennsylvania included more pictures of male students and athletics in its admissions materials and highlighted its new physics, computer science, and math building. Dickinson also started a program in international business, in part to attract and retain more male students. Between 1999 and 2006, Dickinson went from 36 percent men in the incoming class to 44 percent men. The biggest factor in increasing the number of men on campus, according to Robert Massa, vice president for enrollment, was accepting a higher percentage of the males who applied. "The secret of getting some gender balance is that once men apply, you've got to admit them. So did we bend a little bit? Yeah, at the margin we did, but not to the point that we would admit guys who couldn't do the work," he said.[67]

At an annual meeting of the National Association for College Admissions Counselors, two panel discussions addressed the absence of men in the college applicant pool.[68] During these panels, titled "Where Have All the Men Gone?" and "Are Our Boys at Risk?," participants confirmed the trend in declining male enrollments but offered few solutions beyond giving preferential treatment to men in the admissions process. The idea of preferential treatment for male applicants was met with interest rather than scorn by other admissions counselors in the audience. The University of Pennsylvania has held a popular program, "Conference on College Men," for student affairs and admissions personnel. In the late 1990s, the University of Georgia began giving an edge in admissions to male applicants, but stopped in the face of a federal lawsuit.[69] In 2014, the College of William and Mary, a public institution in Virginia, admitted just 28 percent of female applicants compared to 42 percent of men who applied. The former dean of admissions acknowledged that admission decisions were influenced by gender: "We are, after all, the College of William and Mary, not the College of Mary and Mary."[70]

A report on the potential economic and social consequences of the gender gap in college enrollments warned that the "marginalization of men on the educational front will jeopardize the ability of men to perform vital economic and social functions that are key to strengthened family life and safe, stable and prosperous communities."

> Weaker educational attainment among men results in a reduction of the size of the skilled labor force—a resource that is vital to keep the nation's economic engine humming—and in labor productivity and economic growth. In the social arena, men play numerous roles: as husbands, fathers, breadwinners, and role models for young men.[71]

Educational choices have economic consequences for both men and women. On average, male college graduates earn at least $30,000 a year more than men with only a high school diploma (see Figure 6.2 on page 261), and the gap gets larger every year. And yet men account for 57 percent of the sixteen- to twenty-four-year-olds in the labor force who hold only a high school diploma. With an edge in education, women could presumably quickly close the salary gap and move into positions of power as heads of corporations and political leaders—that is, if and only if a college degree remains highly prized in the economic marketplace, and if and only if the economic disadvantage that comes purely from being female is somehow reduced. At a time when universities are competing with glitz and sports to attract male applicants and giving males a slight break on the admission standards, college-educated women in the full-time workforce still make only $10,000 more a year on average than high-school-educated men.[72]

Gender Gap in STEM

Why, despite the greater number of women than men enrolling in and graduating from college, does the gap between male and female earnings exist? One reason may be that men have a clear edge in their interest in advanced technology and computer skills. Career Training Foundation, a nonprofit organization that supports US trade and vocational schools, estimates that more than two-thirds of the people entering technology fields are male.[73] Girls still make up almost 90 percent of the students enrolled in classes leading to traditionally female occupations and only 15 percent of those in classes in traditionally male fields. Women make up a much smaller percentage of degrees awarded in the fields of computer and information sciences or engineering than in health or psychology (see Table 6.2). After Congress eliminated the funding for school guidance and equity counselors to eliminate sex bias and stereotyping in educational tracking, little has been done to assist individual boys and girls in choosing career paths. As the salaries for high-technology workers escalate and women lag behind men in choosing engineering, mathematics, and computer science as their major programs of study, the salary gap is, ironically, likely to increase even as women's edge in enrolling and earning bachelor's degrees continues to grow.

There is some evidence that women are making choices at the high school level that will give them a wider variety of choices in college. In content-specific courses at the high school level, girls continue to lag behind boys in entering science and higher mathematics courses in general. However, among the college-bound, girls caught up in the late 1990s and in some cases have exceeded boys in years of study in science and math. Among 2009 high school graduates, a higher percentage of females earned credits in algebra II, precalculus, advanced biology, chemistry, and health science. However, higher percentages of males earned credits in physics, engineering, and computer science. Although young women demonstrated skill and high achievement in these areas, they were still significantly less likely to list science or math among their favorite subjects and less likely than their male counterparts to say they liked math (53 percent of girls, 59 percent of boys) and science (59 percent of girls, 70 percent of boys).[74] Still, in the last ten years, the number of girls taking the AP Calculus AB exam has increased by nearly 60 percent, and the number of girls taking the AP Physics B exam has more than doubled. Girls now make up 48 percent of AP test takers in calculus, 47 percent

TABLE 6.2: Percentage of Bachelor's Degrees Conferred to Women by Field of Study

Field of Study	1969–70	1979–80	1989–90	1999–2000	2009–10	2013–14
Total*	43.1	49.0	53.2	57.2	57.3	57.1
Agriculture and Natural Resources	4.1	29.6	31.6	42.9	48.7	50.9
Accounting	8.7	36.1	53.3	60.4	N/A**	N/A**
Biological and Life Sciences	29.7	42.1	50.8	58.3	58.5	58.5
Business Management	9.0	33.1	46.5	49.5	N/A**	N/A**
Computer and Information Sciences	12.9	30.2	29.9	28.1	18.1	18.0
Education	75.3	73.8	78.1	75.8	79.5	79.4
Engineering	0.7	9.3	13.8	20.4	16.7	18.4
Health Professions	68.8	82.2	84.4	83.8	85.1	84.4
Mathematics	37.4	41.5	45.7	47.1	43.3	42.9
Physical Sciences and Science Technologies	13.6	23.7	31.3	40.3	41.0	39.3
Psychology	43.4	63.3	71.5	76.5	77.0	76.7
Social Sciences and History	35.9	43.6	44.2	51.2	49.4	49.0
Business	N/A	N/A	N/A	N/A	48.8	47.1

Source: US Department of Education, National Center for Education Statistics, Digest of Education Statistics, Table 290, "Bachelor's, Master's and Doctor's Degrees Conferred by Degree Granting Institutions, by Sex of Student and Discipline Division: 2009–2010," https://nces.ed.gov/programs/digest/d11/tables/dt11_290.asp. Updates for 2013–14 from Table 318.30, https://nces.ed.gov/programs/digest/d15/tables/dt15_318.30.asp.

* Total percentage of bachelor's degrees awarded to women regardless of field of study; includes fields not listed in the table.
** The categories for fields of study changed such that Accounting and Management were no longer recorded as separate fields. Business now takes their place.

in chemistry, and 58 percent in biology. In 2016, two of the three top award winners in the Intel Science Talent Search were girls.

The percentage of girls taking the AP computer science exam remains significantly lower than that of other fields (18 percent). In 2013, zero girls took the AP computer science exam in two states, Mississippi and Montana. In California, home of Silicon Valley, only 22 percent of AP computer science exams were completed by women. A recent study by Dr. Supna Cheryan, a psychology professor at the University of Washington, attributes young women's avoidance of computer science to their fears of not fitting in: "At a young age, girls already hold stereotypes of computer scientists as socially isolated young men whose genius is the result of genetics rather than hard work."[75] Cheryan also found that interest in enrolling in computer science classes increases if they are shown a neutral classroom rather than one decorated with *Star Wars* posters, science fiction books, and technology magazines. Harvey Mudd College adopted strategies consistent with this research—creating separate introductory courses for those without programming experience and renaming them to remove the word *programming* from the title—and saw the percentage of female computer science majors increase from 10 to 40 percent in just four years. In an effort to fill the pipeline of students interested in taking computer science classes, some states now allow a computer science class to fulfill state requirements for math or science education. Universities in many states have created tech summer camps for elementary, middle, and high school students to generate early interest in these courses.

Science, technology, engineering, and math are collectively known as the STEM disciplines. The prevalence of STEM degrees increased between 2004 and 2014 at the bachelor's, master's, and doctoral levels, according to the National Student Clearinghouse, with a corresponding decrease in the proportion of students majoring in social sciences and psychology. Overall, 40 percent of bachelor's degrees earned by men and 29 percent earned by women are now in STEM fields. At the doctoral level, more than half of the degrees earned by men (58 percent) and one-third earned by women (33 percent) are in STEM fields.

However, between 2004 and 2014, the share of STEM-related bachelor's degrees earned by women decreased in all seven discipline areas: engineering; computer science; earth, atmospheric, and ocean sciences; physical sciences; mathematics; biological and agricultural sciences; and social sciences and psychology. The biggest decrease was in computer science: women now earn 18 percent of computer science bachelor's degrees, while in 2004, women earned 23 percent of computer science bachelor's degrees. A report sponsored by the L'Oreal Foundation analyzed data from fourteen countries and found that women are three times less likely than men to become scientists. Furthermore, just one in ten women holds the highest academic position in science disciplines, and just 3 percent of Nobel Prizes in science-related fields have been awarded to women.[76] Men still earn most of the degrees in computer sciences; earth, atmospheric, and ocean sciences; mathematics and statistics; physical sciences; and engineering. "In engineering and computer sciences—the fastest-growing STEM fields with the greatest workforce demand—the percentages of women have reached a plateau or dropped over the last decade," noted a 2009 article.[77] Attrition of female faculty in STEM fields is also higher than in other disciplines, leaving very few female professors to take on leadership roles or serve as mentors to undergraduates in the STEM pipeline.

Why are women leaving STEM? Researcher Sue Rosser found, contrary to conventional wisdom, that it is not because women lack interest or mental aptitude.

If that were the case, women in STEM disciplines would consistently underperform relative to male students in college and graduate school. In fact, "the data show the contrary: women outperform men academically; receive more awards; have higher graduation rates and better attitudes toward education." According to Rosser, two factors stand out in explaining why women exit from STEM careers: the need to balance career and family, and a lack of professional networks.[78] Other researchers found that single men and single women participate about equally in the STEM workforce. By contrast, a married female PhD is thirteen times less likely to be employed than a married male PhD. If a married female PhD has young children, she is 30 percent less likely than a single male PhD to be employed.[79] The lack of federal or institutional supports for childbearing and family care in the United States disadvantage women here relative to female research scientists in other countries who enjoy more generous supports, such as paid family leave and on-site day care. "Male faculty members who start families within five years of receiving their PhDs are 38 percent more likely to earn tenure than women who do the same," the researchers discovered. Put somewhat differently, "for every three women who take a fast-track (elite or research university) job before having a child, only one ever becomes a mother."[80]

The other reason women leave STEM fields comes from the lack of career networks and mentors. As we have noted in previous chapters, mentors play a unique role in encouraging young women to pursue nontraditional paths in politics and employment; STEM careers are no different. Women scientists have fewer graduate and postdoctoral students to support their work than men and less diverse networks. Women faculty report fewer referrals from collegial networks to work as paid consultants, serve on science advisory boards, and interact with industry. There have been some novel approaches to solving these problems. For example, Clare Booth Luce Professorships, funded by the Henry Luce Foundation and designed to advance the careers of women in science, engineering, and mathematics, provide funding to cover professional expenses—defined to include child care as well as conference travel and publishing expenses.

A 2012 study involving science faculty from research-intensive universities demonstrates that gender bias in favor of male students is pervasive among both male and female faculty.[81] The study prepared identical resumes for "John" and "Jennifer," with a cover page stating that the applicant had just received a bachelor's degree and was seeking a position as lab manager. Half of the faculty participants received John's resume and the other half received Jennifer's resume. Each faculty member was asked to rate the applicant on a scale of 1 to 7 in terms of competence, hireability, likability, and the extent to which the professor would be willing to mentor the student. Each was also asked to indicate a salary they would be willing to pay. Regardless of the faculty participant's age, sex, area of specialization, or level of seniority, the applicant named John was rated an average of a half point higher than Jennifer in all areas except one and was offered a starting salary of $30,328 compared to Jennifer's starting salary of $26,508. The only area where Jennifer scored higher than John was likability. "That faculty members reported liking Jennifer more than John makes the covert bias all the more insidious," writes Professor Eileen Pollack.[82]

These results mesh with the findings of similar studies indicating that people's biases stem from "repeated exposure to pervasive cultural stereotypes that portray women as less competent by simultaneously emphasizing their warmth and likability compared to men."[83] Title IX is a gender-neutral law written to guarantee that sex is not used as the basis for discrimination in access to education, participation in programs, and full enjoyment of the unique benefits of education. However, when the barriers to full participation are ingrained in pervasive cultural stereotypes, the effectiveness of the legal equality doctrine is significantly undermined.

WOMEN'S EDUCATIONAL EQUITY ACT

Title IX requires gender-neutral treatment of men and women in education. The results have been more opportunities for women and fewer overt barriers to college admission and career choices. However, without proactive counseling and intervention strategies designed to increase the numbers of girls in nontraditional courses of study, the opportunities created by Title IX are likely to go unrealized. In 1974, Congress passed the Women's Educational Equity Act (WEEA), authorizing funds to promote bias-free textbooks and curriculum, support research on gender equity, and revamp teacher training programs. In other words, WEEA was the legislative acknowledgment that a legal mandate for equality in education would not produce gender equity in education. The definition of gender equity in education addresses the chances for both females and males to learn in an environment free of limits:

> Gender equity is a set of actions, attitudes and assumptions that provide opportunities and create expectations about individuals, regardless of gender. Gender equity is a chance for females and males at learning regardless of the subject; preparing for future education, jobs, and careers; high expectations; developing, achieving and learning; equitable treatment and outcomes in school and beyond. Gender equity is linked to and supports race, ethnic, economic, disability, and other equity concerns.[84]

From the start, the effort was underfunded and largely ignored. It was not until the AAUW published its 1992 report, *How Schools Shortchange Girls*, that a credible effort to support WEEA materialized. Funding of $3 million a year was appropriated in most years through the 1990s. As part of the original legislation, a national Equity Resource Center was established as a clearinghouse for teacher training, developing equity curriculum materials, and conducting research related to gender equity in education. Conservative organizations lobbied against annual appropriations for WEEA. The Heritage Foundation, a conservative Washington think tank, issued a report in 2001 in which it argued that "focusing on non-existent problems like gender inequity diverts funds and attention from the real—and critical—problems in America's educational system."[85] Federal funding for WEEA was ended in 2004 by the George W. Bush administration.

EQUITY IN ACTION: HOW GIRLS AND BOYS EXPERIENCE SCHOOL

The AAUW's 1992 report called immediate attention to a long-standing gender equity problem. Although girls and boys attended the same classes within the same schools, their experiences differed dramatically. *How Schools Shortchange Girls* became a rallying cry for feminists to reexamine sexist attitudes in the classroom. As a result of the report, parents started paying more attention to their children's experiences in school.[86]

How Girls Are Shortchanged in School

In 1982, the Project on the Status of Education of Women, a research effort commissioned by the Association of American Colleges (AAC), reported on the **chilly climate** for women in college classrooms. The research detailed the often subtle ways faculty treated male and female students differently. It found that both female and male faculty were more likely to ask questions of male students, to focus more intently on the answers of male students, and to ask "higher-order" critical questions of men but not of women. In examples offered in class, males occupied the role of "professional," while women were more often the "client" or "patient," thereby making it difficult for women to view themselves in professional roles. Project researchers found more blatant examples of male faculty sexualizing female students and denigrating their future aspirations by treating them as less serious than those of male students. Similarly, they found that a male student's success was more often attributed to skill or ability, while a female student's success was attributed to luck or a less difficult task.

This chilly climate has harmed both men and women. Women, over time, may grow to view their presence in a class or program of study as peripheral, have little expectation of participating in class discussions, and learn that their capacity for full intellectual development or career aspirations is limited. Male students are disadvantaged by not being challenged by all of their peers. Also, reinforcing any negative views of women may make men's transition to the workplace more difficult and limit their ability to work with and view women as equals.[87]

In 1984, the same project released a study of the chilly climate facing women outside the classroom on college campuses. The study concluded that "even though men and women are presumably exposed to a common liberal arts curriculum and other educational programs during the undergraduate years, it would seem that

IMAGE 6.3
Source: Doonesbury © 1992 G. B. Trudeau. Reprinted with permission of UNIVERSAL UCLICK. All Rights Reserved.

these programs serve more to preserve, rather than to reduce, stereotypic differences between men and women in behavior, personality, aspirations and achievement."[88] The report went on to document experiences in support services, campus employment, admissions and financial aid counseling, campus health care, campus safety, and a lax attitude about harassment or degradation of women on campus that disadvantaged female students.

Both the AAC and AAUW reports peg the roots of the chilly climate to early educational disparities in elementary school classrooms. In 1973, Myra Sadker published *Sexism in School and Society*. In many respects it was the first such book, written for teachers but released to a wider audience that documented sex-segregated classes, gender bias in required textbooks, and sexist teaching and counseling practices. Myra Sadker, with her husband and intellectual partner, David Sadker, continued to research bias in the classroom and, in particular, teachers' treatment of students. They published their results in *Failing at Fairness: How Our Schools Cheat Girls*, which was released in 1994. Coupled with the AAUW report, educators and parents could not ignore the findings on the treatment of girls in the primary school classroom. Primary school teachers tended to talk more to boys than to girls, asked boys a greater number of "higher-order" questions, and worked with them to derive the answers rather than dismissing the first answer as wrong and moving on, as they did with the girls. Teachers were also more likely to give boys specific instructions on how to complete an assignment but showed girls how to do it or did it for them. Additionally, teachers were more likely to praise boys for the content of their thinking as it was reflected in their work, whereas they praised girls for their neatness. The Sadkers' work was based on thousands of hours of classroom observations, many of which were videotaped. In the tapes, viewers could see teachers encouraging boys to work harder to answer a question while silencing girls by quickly moving on after their answer was offered. The teachers were not acting maliciously; they were simply not aware of their actions or of the detrimental consequences of their actions for girls.

The Backlash: How Schools Cheat Boys

Concurrent with the release of the previously mentioned studies on girls' educational experiences were several popular books on the psychological and intellectual development of girls in adolescence. Mary Pipher's *Reviving Ophelia* and Peggy Orenstein's *Schoolgirls: Young Women, Self-Esteem, and the Confidence Gap*, which appeared in bookstores in 1994, detailed the precipitous decline in intellectual confidence, voice, self-worth, and ambition in girls after about eleven years of age. Wildly popular with parents, educators, and women's groups, the books served to intensify the focus on girls. Congress responded by passing the Gender Equity in Education Act in 1994, which authorized additional research on girls' development, gender equity issues in education, and strategies to counter bias where it exists.

Quietly at first, and then more stridently, advocates for boys began to object to all the attention showered on girls, presumably at the expense of boys. They cited US Department of Education statistics showing that girls get better grades than boys, have higher educational aspirations, participate in advanced placement classes at higher rates, and surpass boys in reading and writing skills. Studies of fourth, eighth, and twelfth graders show that girls are more "engaged" in school in almost all aspects. They are more likely to come to school prepared (with paper, pencils, books, and the like), and they are more likely to do assigned homework. By the time boys are seniors in high school, they are four times as likely as girls not to do their homework. Boys are more likely than girls to be suspended from school, to be held back a grade, and to ultimately drop out of school altogether. Boys are three times as likely as girls to be diagnosed with some form of learning disorder and more likely to be involved with crime, alcohol, and drugs. Although girls attempt suicide more often than boys, boys are more often successful.[89]

In 1997, the Public Education Network (PEN) released a new teacher-student survey administered in grades seven through twelve that seemed to directly contradict the findings of the AAUW-sponsored research: contrary to the premise that girls were suffering neglect in the nation's classrooms, the PEN study found that boys consistently underperformed on a number of indicators. "Contrary to the commonly held view that boys are at an advantage over girls in school, girls appear to have an advantage over boys in terms of their future plans, teachers' expectations, everyday experiences at school and interactions in the classroom."[90] Most striking is the boys' perception, expressed by more than 31 percent of the boys in the study, that teachers do not listen to what they have to say. In contrast, only 19 percent of the girls shared this perception. Other studies released in the late 1990s offered similar findings relative to boys' current state of affairs. In almost all cases, girls outperformed boys, particularly on indicators related to school and aspirations for a college education.

The cover story of the May 2000 issue of the *Atlantic Monthly* was an article by Christina Hoff Sommers titled "The War Against Boys." The article charged that the "crisis" in girls' education of the early 1990s was generated on false assumptions, based on "bad science," and concocted by "girls' partisans" for political purposes. The article prompted an outcry from many feminist quarters, including Carol Gilligan and David Sadker, who were the objects of Sommers's critique. The response from readers was "swift and substantial."[91] Both the article and the exchange of letters offer an extraordinary glimpse of the power of gender and the intensity with which gender operates in shaping our perceptions of important social questions, the facts gathered in order to answer those questions, and how those facts are interpreted in order to make public policy.

In May 2008, AAUW released a report reviewing forty years of data on achievement from the fourth grade through college. For the first time, the report analyzed gender differences within economic and ethnic categories. The headline-grabbing aspect of the report was that "there is no crisis for boys" in schools. Rather, "if there is a crisis, it is with African American and Hispanic students and low-income students, girls and boys," said coauthor Christianne Corbett. The report found a literacy gap in favor of girls, but that had not changed substantially in nearly thirty years. Similarly, the math gap favoring boys had persisted but not increased. Students, boys and girls, from families with a combined income of $37,000 or less were less likely to be proficient in math and reading. Gender differences varied significantly by race and ethnicity. Catherine Hill, director of research at the AAUW Educational Foundation, said that the study was undertaken to dispel myths about a "boy crisis" and so that educational policy can be guided by fact.[92] The report states:

> Girls' educational successes have not—and should not—come at the expense of boys. If girls' achievements come at the expense of boys, one would expect to see boys' scores decline as girls' scores rise, but boys' average test scores have improved alongside girls' scores in recent decades. For example, girls' average scores on the NAEP mathematics test have risen during the past three decades—as have boys' scores (indeed, older boys retain a small lead in math). Girls tend to earn higher average scores on the NAEP reading assessments, but this lead has narrowed or remained the same during the past three decades.[93]

There may well be another explanation for the mixed evidence on girls' and women's school experiences. Title IX became law in 1972, the AAUW report was based on schools in the mid- to late 1980s, and the statistics offered to counter its findings are from the late 1990s. Rather than "bad science," perhaps the new statistics on women's performance in education reflect an outcome of gender-equity policy.

Reports continue to confirm that although girls and women have made substantial gains since Title IX was passed in 1972, they are still underrepresented in mathematics, science, computer, and technology fields; men still earn the majority of advanced degrees in STEM fields; and men still occupy the majority of decision-making positions within universities and continue to earn higher salaries. Most scholars agree that gender equity in education is a pressing problem for both boys and girls. The odd mix of gender-neutral and gender-specific education policy currently on the books ensures that this debate will continue, with each side armed with gendered facts to support its pursuit of equality in education.

EDUCATION'S LONG-TERM IMPACT ON WOMEN'S PURSUIT OF EQUALITY

In previous chapters we've addressed the question of women's agency— their ability to act by themselves and for themselves. Education serves as a vital resource in enabling women to exercise their agency as it relates to participation in politics, fertility issues, health decisions for themselves and their children, and the assurance of economic stability within their families. A tremendous body of research literature links women's education, employment, and empowerment.[94] In the United States, women's median income has increased both in real terms and relative to men's income, largely as a function of the increase in women's level of education (see Figure 6.2).[95] In 2016, based on median annual earnings, women with a college degree earned 75 percent of what similarly educated men earned, while women with a high school diploma or the equivalent earned 77 percent of what similarly situated men earned. Better-educated workers, both male and female, tend to raise the productivity levels of firms in most industries, and are more likely than their less educated peers to be employed and to work more weeks and hours during the year.[96] In 2015, 69 percent of women with a bachelor's degree or higher but only 32 percent of those with less than a high school degree and 47 percent of those with a high school diploma or GED were employed full-time.[97]

Where once there was a "success gap," referring to the trade-off many women made between advanced education and marriage, these days the gap has narrowed considerably. In 1980, a woman with three years of graduate school education was 13 percent less likely to be married than a woman with only a high school education.[98] By 2014, rates of marriage among women with advanced degrees were higher than for women with a bachelor's degree.[99] The media continue to perpetuate the stereotype that advanced education somehow disadvantages women in their ability to marry if they choose to (e.g., *Newsweek*'s erroneous statistic that "a 40-year-old woman had a statistically higher chance of being killed by a terrorist than getting married"[100] or *New York Times* columnist Maureen Dowd's assertion that "men don't like to date successful women"[101]). However, empirical research demonstrates that while marriage rates for all groups fell to record

FIGURE 6.2: Median Annual Earnings and the Gender Earnings Ratio for Women and Men at Different Educational Levels, 2013

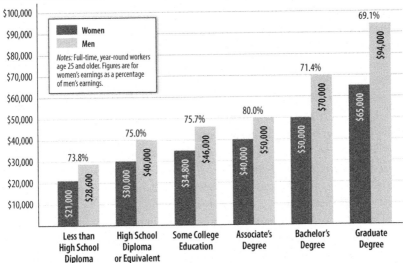

Source: Adapted from Institute for Women's Policy Studies, Status of Women in the States (Washington, D.C.: IWPR, 2015), http://statusofwomendata.org/explore-the-data/employment-and-earnings/employment-and-earnings.

lows in 2011, nearly two-thirds of adults with college degrees are married, while less than half those with some college education or a high school diploma are married.[102] Furthermore, only about half of first marriages are likely to survive at least twenty years, but college-educated women have an eight-in-ten chance of still being married after two decades.[103] Roughly two-thirds (65 percent) of men with a bachelor's degree could expect that, if they marry, their first marriage will last twenty years or longer, compared with 50 percent of men with a high school diploma or less. In addition, men with a higher level of education are more likely to get married in the first place when compared with less-educated men.

Comparative research documents that improvements in nutritional intake in households are a result of women's independent income. Research in India and elsewhere has shown a correlation between women's education, economic independence, and child survival rates.[104] Analysis by the UN Family Planning Agency has illustrated over the years that increases in educational attainment by women directly correlate with lower fertility rates, thereby easing the negative impact of population growth. Education also empowers women to use new communication technology to access information and to make their specific needs known to policy makers. As more women become policy makers themselves, there is evidence of a reciprocal impact on education for girls and women. In Bhopal, India, for example, the last four women leaders introduced compulsory education for girls that creates a standard for universal education for girls.

There remain challenges. Illiteracy among women persists as an international problem, although in the last decade the gap between men and women has closed somewhat. UNESCO estimates that globally 89 percent of men and 80 percent of women were able to read and write in 2011. But of the 17 percent of the world that remains illiterate, two-thirds of them are women. Throughout the world, girls are more likely to leave school early because of family obligations. Boys too leave school early but more often because of economic reasons, rather than to care for siblings or to perform unpaid household duties. Illiteracy rates among the young (ages fifteen to twenty-four) remain very high in countries where children are involved in economic activity. An estimated 122 million youth globally are illiterate, and 60 percent of these are female. When poor families have to choose which children will be educated, it is often girls who lose out.

Girls denied an education are more vulnerable to poverty, hunger, violence, abuse, exploitation, and trafficking. The positive impact of education, in the United States and around the world, is evident in women's health, earning potential and long-term economic stability, family stability, and an increase in the likelihood that women will ensure that their own children are educated. Finally, a better-educated and more literate female population should also increase civic engagement and voting rates and strengthen democracy.[105] "There is no better investment for a society than education, in particular girls' education," said the director-general of UNESCO, Koïchiro Matsuura. "Educating girls today has a lifelong impact on health, nutrition, employment and growth. Most fundamentally, education is a basic human right."[106] (For more on global education, see "Point of Comparison: Global Gender Gap Ranking and Educational Attainment.")

THE UNIQUE NATURE OF EDUCATION AS A PUBLIC GOOD

Although women today enjoy unprecedented access to education and high achievement within educational programs, their success has not gone unnoticed and is not universally celebrated. When education is viewed as a zero-sum game, improvements in educational opportunities and performance for women are interpreted by some as discrimination against men. Title IX's requirement that institutions receiving federal dollars treat men and women equally in all aspects of educational programming, including athletics, does not specify *how* to accomplish said gender equity. When universities choose to cut men's nonrevenue sports such as wrestling, swimming, or gymnastics in order to add women's programs in a move toward equity, it is an institutional decision, not one required by the policy. The perception is, however, that women's progress comes at men's expense. The controversy over how girls and boys are treated in the classroom has at its core the belief that when one sex is advantaged, the other must be disadvantaged.

Education is unique in the sense that it is a commodity with direct benefits for both society and the individual.[107] It is also a divisible or competitive good, meaning that it can be given to some and withheld from others. As we discussed earlier in this chapter, at one time women and African Americans were barred from schools and even from privately acquiring the knowledge and skills an education provides. Laws now guarantee access to education for all. However, education is also a good that can be consumed differently by individuals even when everyone has access to it in the same form. Sometimes this is an individual's choice, but in other cases, either through the socialization process or through subtle or not-so-subtle messages, individuals are directed to consume the good differently. Patterns of course enrollment suggest that men and women have consumed and may still consume education differently. The consequences of policy and individual choices around education are exhibited in the demographic characteristics of our population. Education plays a direct role in health, life expectancy, occupation and income, family size, and the quality of life citizens enjoy. Because of its importance, education remains a top policy priority in presidential campaigns and in successive sessions of Congress.

In the coming years, policy makers will be faced with making decisions about education policy that will have direct gender implications. For example, school vouchers offer one way to give parents more say in their children's education. Vouchers would allow parents to enroll their children in the school of their choice, and the federal dollars dedicated to education would follow that child. In practice, this would mean that parents could choose to enroll their children in parochial schools with assistance from the government. It remains unclear how this might impact existing policy that requires gender equity in all aspects of an institution that receives federal funds. How might gender issues be treated in a Catholic school's curriculum or in a school that adheres to fundamentalist Christian tenets? Where school vouchers are adopted, will there be Title IX issues? How strictly will the provisions of Title IX be enforced when they conflict with other educational goals? As we have seen in the discussion above, Title IX has come under heightened scrutiny because it is perceived as aiding women and girls at the expense of men and boys, even though the legislation itself is gender neutral.

CONCLUSION

Women were granted access to formal education nearly a century before they were granted access to the vote. Both of these rights have become powerful tools in the pursuit of equality. Because of the unique character of education as a public good that benefits society and the individual, and because education is such a fundamental resource and linked to myriad quality-of-life indicators, education policy is contested ground. This chapter looked at the way public policy can lead society

Box 6.2: Point of Comparison

Global Gender Gap Ranking and Educational Attainment

The most fundamental prerequisite for empowering women in all spheres of society is educational attainment. Without education of comparable quality and content to that given to boys and men, and education "relevant to existing knowledge and real needs, women are unable to access well-paid, formal sector jobs, advance within them, participate in, and be represented in government and gain political influence."[1] In some industrialized countries ranked near the top, women now represent a supermajority of all university students. "Ironically, as this trend has been identified it has immediately been labeled as worrisome: social analysts are starting to warn against the 'feminization of education' and the apparent alienation of men from schooling."[2]

The World Economic Forum produces the Global Gender Gap Index, which ranks 145 economies based on how well they are leveraging their female talent pool, according to economic, educational, health-based, and political indicators. A score of 1 on the Gender Equity Index indicates equality.

For Critical Analysis

This chapter makes the claim that education is positively related to gender equality. In what ways do the data here confirm this relationship around the world? When women are prevented from attending school, what are the potential consequences for society? How might education rates for women be raised around the world?

toward a more equitable distribution of educational access and content. Title IX has proven to be a powerful tool for changing the nature of education in the United States. Its detractors charge that gender equity laws are unfair to males because they require that limited resources be redistributed among both males and females. This does, in many cases, require that exclusive privileges once granted to males alone be shared. Gender equity in education, at its most basic level, requires that boys and girls share equally in consuming the resources required to develop skills and

Country	World Economic Forum Global Gender Gap Ranking	Gender Equity Score (1= Equality)	Adult Literacy		Girls' Share, Primary Enrollment	Women's Share, Tertiary Enrollment
			Women	Men		
TOP FIVE						
Iceland	1	.881	99%	99%	98%	103%
Norway	2	.850	98%	98%	100%	94%
Finland	3	.850	98%	98%	99%	101%
Sweden	4	.823	99%	99%	99%	79%
Ireland	5	.807	99%	99%	95%	72%
. . .						
United States	28	.740	99%	99%	91%	103%
. . .						
BOTTOM FIVE						
Iran	141	.580	83%	91%	96%	65%
Chad	142	.580	32%	48%	75%	1%
Syria	143	.568	81%	92%	61%	31%
Pakistan	144	.559	46%	70%	67%	10%
Yemen	145	.484	55%	85%	81%	6%

Source: World Economic Forum, "Global Gender Gap Report 2015," accessed at http://reports.weforum.org/global-gender-gap-report-2015/rankings; Augusto Lopez-Claros and Saadia Zahidi, *Women's Empowerment: Measuring the Global Gender Gap* (Geneva: World Economic Forum, 2005).

acquire knowledge. It also requires careful attention to the process of education to ensure that boys and girls are learning in a bias-free atmosphere. Finally, gender equity in education requires that society present both boys and girls with the full complement of life's opportunities beyond formal education. The next chapter examines how education is linked to work and wages. Education has permitted women to move from the private sphere to the public sphere, although as Chapter 7 shows, the move is far from complete.

NOTES

Boxed feature notes appear at the end of the Notes section.

1 See, for example, Christina Hoff Sommers, "The War Against Boys," *Atlantic*, May 2000); "Why Girls Do Better at School than Boys," *The Economist*, March 5, 2015.

2 Hunter College Women's Studies Collective, *Women's Realities, Women's Choices*, 2nd ed. (New York: Oxford University Press, 1995).

3 Virginia Sapiro, *Women in American Society: An Introduction to Women's Studies*, 4th ed. (Mountain View, CA: Mayfield Press, 1999), 146.

4 Ibid.

5 Nannerl O. Keohane, "'But for Her Sex . . .': The Domestication of Sophie," *University of Ottawa Quarterly* 49 (1980): 390–400.

6 Hunter College Women's Studies Collective, *Women's Realities*, 374.

7 Judith Sargent Murray, "On the Equality of the Sexes," in *The Feminist Papers*, ed. Alice S. Rossi (Boston: Northeastern University Press, 1988), 18.

8 Sapiro, *Women in American Society*, 148.

9 Hunter College Women's Studies Collective, *Women's Realities*, 382.

10 Kathryn Kish Sklar, "Catherine Beecher: Transforming the Teaching Profession," in *Women's America*, eds. Linda K. Kerber and Jane de Hart Mathews (New York: Oxford University Press, 1982), 140–148.

11 Louise Bernikow, "December 16, 1872: Dr. Edward Clarke Tells Women to Take It Easy," *Women's eNews*, November 30, 2004.

12 Ibid.

13 Sklar, "Catherine Beecher."

14 President's Task Force on Women's Rights and Responsibilities, *Task Force Report: A Matter of Simple Justice* (Washington, DC: GPO, April 1970), 7.

15 Joyce Gelb and Marian Lief Palley, *Women and Public Policies: Reassessing Gender Politics* (Charlottesville: University of Virginia Press, 1996), 99.

16 See Ruth Rosen, *The World Split Open: How the Modern Women's Movement Changed America* (New York: Viking Press, 2000).

17 National Coalition for Women and Girls in Education (NCWGE), "Title IX at 30: Report Card on Gender Equity," June 2002, 41, www.ncwge. org/title9at30-6-11.pdf.

18 Catherine Hill and Holly Kearl, "Crossing the Line: Sexual Harassment at School," (Washington, DC: AAUW, 2011).

19 Ibid., 12.

20 "The Next Generation of Title IX: Harassment and Bullying Based on Sex," National Women's Law Center Fact Sheet, June 2012), www.nwlc.org/sites/default/files/pdfs/nwlcathletics _titleixfactsheet.pdf.

21 Tara Parker-Pope, "Sexual Harassment at School," *New York Times*, May 1, 2008.

22 Hollaback!, www.ihollaback.org/resources/harassment-on-college-campuses.

23 Catherine Hill and Elena Silva, *Drawing the Line: Sexual Harassment on Campus* (Washington, DC: AAUW Educational Foundation, 2006).

24 "Statistics on Gender-Based Violence," Know Your IX, http://knowyourix.org/statistics. Accessed June 2016.

25 "Not Alone: The First Report of the White House Task Force to Protect Students from Sexual Assault," April 2014, www.notalone.gov/assets/report.pdf.

26 "The Campus Sexual Violence Elimination (SaVE) Act," Clery Center for Security on Campus, http://clerycenter.org/campus-sexual-violence-elimination-save-act. Accessed June 2016.

27 Samuel R. Bagenstos, "What Went Wrong with Title IX?" *Washington Monthly*, September-October 2015).

28 "Statistics on Gender-Based Violence."

29 Liam Stack, "Judge Aaron Persky Under Fire for Sentencing in Stanford Rape Case," *New York Times*, June 7, 2016.

30 Tom Namako, "Joe Biden Writes an Open Letter to Stanford Survivor," *BuzzFeed*, June 9, 2016.

31 Sarah Larimer, "In Aftermath of Brock Turner Case, California's Governor Signs Sex Crime Bill," *Washington Post*, September 30, 2016.

32 Jack Healy, "At Brigham Young, a Cost in Reporting a Rape," *New York Times*, April 26, 2016.

33 Richard Perez-Pena, "Students Initiate Inquiry into Harassment Reports," *New York Times*, March 7, 2013.

34 NCAA Model Pregnancy and Parenting Policy, www.ncaa.org/wps/ncaa?ContentID=39941.

35 Joanna Grossman, "A New Lawsuit by a Female Athlete Tests Title IX's Protection Against Pregnancy Discrimination," *FindLaw Commentary*, May 6, 2003; "Pregnant Student Athlete Files Title IX Suit Claiming Discrimination," *Ms. Magazine Online*, May 27, 2003; NCWGE, "Title IX at 30," 55–58.

36 Lindsay Rovegno, "Athletes Often Forced into Heartbreaking Decisions," ESPN, May 12, 2007.

37 "The Role of the Federal Child Care Access Means Parents in School (CCAMPIS) Program in Supporting Student Parent Success," Institute for Women's Policy Research Fact Sheet, February 2016.

38 Emily Badger, "In the Spirit of Title IX: U-Md. Makes Cheerleading a Sport," *Washington Post*, September 27, 2003.

39 George J. Bryjak, "The Ongoing Controversy over Title IX," *USA Today Magazine*, July 1, 2000, 62.

40 *Cohen v. Brown University*, 991 F. 2d. 888. 1993; F. Supp. 185 (D.R.I. 1995).

41 NCWGE, *Title IX at 40: Working to Ensure Gender Equity in Education* (Washington, DC: NCWGE, 2012).

42 "Report: Number of Female Coaches in Women's Sports Plummeted After Title IX," ESPNW, May 6, 2016.

43 Kevin Trahan, "'Nobody's Watching': Are Major College Sports Programs Treating Title IX like a Suggestion?" *Vice*, June 15, 2016.

44 Ibid.

45 John Weistart, "Equal Opportunity? Title IX and Intercollegiate Sports," *Brookings Review* 16, no. 4 (1998): 39–43.

46 Donna de Varona and Julie Foudy, "Minority Views on the Report of the Commission on Opportunity in Athletics," submitted to Secretary Rod Paige, February 2003, 8.

47 Karen Goldberg Goff, "Does Athletic Equity Give Men a Sporting Chance?" *Insight on the News* 15, no. 2 (January 11, 1999): 38.

48 Alicia Wong, "Where Girls Are Missing Out on High School Sports," *Atlantic*, June 20, 2015.

49 Katie Thomas, "A Team's Struggle Shows Disparity in Girls' Sports," *New York Times*, June 14, 2009.

50 Carla Murphy, "Girls' Sports Opportunities MIA in City Schools," *Women's eNews*, March 18, 2009.

51 "Attendance Numbers for USA 1999 Set New Marks," July 11, 1999, *Soccer Times*, www.soccertimes.net/worldcup/1999/jul11.htm.

52 NCWGE, *Title IX at 40*.

53 Chris Isidore and Brian Stelter, "Women's World Cup Victory Nabs Record Ratings," CNNMoney, July 6, 2015.

54 Zachary Crockett, "More Women Will Compete in Rio 2016 than in Any Other Olympics," *Vox*, August 5, 2016.

55 Joanna Grossman, "On the Thirtieth Anniversary of Title IX, We Need to Preserve, Not Reverse, Its Guarantee of Equity for Women in College Athletics," *FindLaw Commentary*, June 18, 2002.

56 Christine Grant, "Briefing Paper No. 3," NCWGE, accessed at http://www.ncwge.org/archive/statements/TitleIXbriefing/pressbriefing3.pdf.

57 de Varona and Foudy, "Minority Views."

58 "Women's Rights Groups Win Title IX Victory," *Ms. Magazine Online*, July 14, 2003.

59 Andrew Zimbalist, "The NCAA's Women Problem," *New York Times*, March 25, 2016.

60 Andrew Das, "Top Female Players Accuse U.S. Soccer of Wage Discrimination," *New York Times*, March 31, 2016.

61 "U.S. Women's Team Files Wage-Discrimination Action vs. U.S. Soccer," ESPN, April 1, 2016.

62 Shannon Dortch, "Hey Guys: Hit the Books," *American Demographics* 19, no. 9 (September 1997): 4–10.

63 "Black Women Students Far Outnumber Black Men at the Nation's Highest-Ranked Universities," *Journal of Blacks in Higher Education*, 2016, www.jbhe.com/news_views/51_gendergap_universities.html.

64 Wendy Berliner, "Where Have All the Young Men Gone?" *Guardian*, May 18, 2004.

65 Ibid., 6.

66 John R. Reynolds and Jennifer Pemberton, "Rising College Expectations Among Youth in the United States: A Comparison of the 1979 and 1997 NLSY," *Journal of Human Resources* 36, no. 4 (Fall 2001): 703–726.

67 Tamar Lewin, "At Colleges, Women Are Leaving Men in the Dust," *New York Times*, July 9, 2006.

68 "Notebook," *Chronicle of Higher Education* (October 20, 2000): A29.

69 Michael Fletcher, "Degrees of Separation: Gender Gap Among College Graduates Has Educators Wondering Where the Men Are," *Washington Post*, June 25, 2002, A01.

70 John Birger, "Why Getting into Elite Colleges Is Harder for Women," *Washington Post*, July 30, 2015.

71 Andrew Sum, Neeta Fogg, Paul Harrington, et al., "The Growing Gender Gaps in College Enrollment and Degree Attainment in the U.S. and Their Potential Economic and Social Consequences," paper prepared for the Business Roundtable, Center for Labor Market Studies, Northeastern University, 2003, 5–6.

72 Institute for Women's Policy Studies, *Status of Women in the States*, 2015, "Employment and Earnings," http://statusofwomendata.org/explore-the-data/employment-and-earnings/employment -and-earnings.

73 Ibid.

74 Brittany C. Cunningham, Kathleen Mulvaney Hoyer, and Dinah Sparks, "Gender Differences in Science, Technology, Engineering, and Math (STEM) Interest, Credits Earned, and NAEP Performance in the 12th Grade," National Center for Education Statistics, NCES 2015-075, February 2015.

75 Eileen Pollack, "What Really Keeps Women out of Tech," *New York Times*, October 10, 2015.

76 Allie Bidwell, "More Students Earning STEM Degrees, Report Shows," *US News and World Report*, January 27, 2015.

77 Sue V. Rosser and Mark Zachary Taylor, "Why Are We Still Worried About Women in Science?" *Academe*, May-June 2009.

78 Ibid.

79 J. Scott Long, *From Scarcity to Visibility: Gender Differences in the Careers of Doctoral Scientists and Engineers* (Washington, DC: National Academies Press, 2001).

80 Yu Xe and Kimberlee Shauman, *Women in Science: Career Processes and Outcomes* (Cambridge, MA: Harvard University Press, 2005).

81 Corinne A. Moss-Racusin et al., "Science Faculty's Subtle Gender Biases Favor Male Students," *Proceedings of the National Academy of Sciences* 109, no. 41 (2012).

82 Eileen Pollack, "Why Are There Still So Few Women in Science?" *New York Times Magazine*, October 3, 2013.

83 Eileen Pollack, *The Only Woman in the Room: Why Science Is Still a Boys' Club* (Boston: Beacon Press, 2016).

84 Information referenced in Paula M. Fleming, "The Women's Educational Equity Act Resources for Ongoing Efforts," *Equity and Excellence in Education*, vol 33, 2000.

85 Krista Kafer, "Wasting Dollars: The Women's Educational Equity Act," Heritage Foundation Backgrounder Report #1490, October 11, 2001.

86 American Association of University Women, *How Schools Shortchange Girls: A Study of Major Findings on Girls and Education* (Wellesley, MA: Wellesley College Center for Research on Women, 1992).

87 Roberta M. Hall and Bernice R. Sandler, "The Classroom Climate: A Chilly One for Women," Project on the Status and Education of Women, Association of American Colleges, 1982.

88 Roberta M. Hall and Bernice R. Sandler, "Outside the Classroom: A Chilly Campus Climate for Women?" Project on the Status and Education of Women, Association of American Colleges, 1984.

89 Sommers, "The War Against Boys."

90 Public Education Network, *The Metropolitan Life Survey of the American Teacher, 1997: Examining Gender Issues in Public Schools* (Rochester, NY: Louis Harris and Associates, 1997).

91 See both the article and the reader letters at http://theatlantic.com/ issues/2000/05/sommers.htm.

92 Christine Corbett, Catherine Hill, and Andresse St. Rose, *Where the Girls Are: The Facts About Gender Equity in Education* (Washington, D.C.: American Association of University Women, 2008).

93 Ibid., 22.

94 United Nations Development Programme, *Women's Political Participation and Good Governance: 21st Century Challenges* (New York: United Nations Development Programme, 2000).

95 Cynthia Costello and Barbara Kivimae Krimgold, eds., *The American Woman 1996–1997: Women and Work* (New York: Norton, 1996), 23.

96 Sum, Fogg, Harrington, et al., "The Growing Gender Gaps."

97 U.S. Department of Labor, Women's Bureau. "Labor Force Participation Rate by Educational Attainment and Sex: 2015 Annual Averages," www.dol.gov/wb/stats/latest_annual_data.htm #labor.

98 Kelly DiNardo, "Marriage Rates Rise for Educated Women," *Women's eNews*, April 6, 2004.

99 Richard V. Reeves, Isabel V. Sawhill, and Eleanor Krause, "The Most Educated Women Are the Most Likely to Be Married," Brookings Institution, August 19, 2016.

100 Megan Garber, "When *Newsweek* 'Struck Terror in the Hearts of Single Women'" *The Atlantic*, June 2, 2016.

101 Maureen Dowd, "What's a Modern Girl to Do?" The *New York Times Magazine*, October 30, 2005.

102 D'Vera Cohn, Jeffrey S. Passel, Wendy Wang, and Gretchen Livingston, "Barely Half of U.S. Adults Are Married—A Record Low," Pew Social Trends, December 14, 2011.

103 Wendy Wang, "The Link Between a College Education and a Lasting Marriage," Pew Research Fact Tank, December 4, 2015.

104 Amartya Sen, *Development as Freedom* (New York: Knopf, 1999).

105 UNICEF, *The State of the World's Children 2004* (New York: UNICEF, 2003).

106 UNESCO, "Girls Are the Focus of World Day Against Child Labor," June 10, 2009, accessed at http://portal.unesco.org/geography/en/ev.php-URL_ID=11388&URL_DO=DO_TOPIC&URL _SECTION=201.html.

107 Margaret M. Conway, David W. Ahern, and Gertrude A. Steuernagel, *Women and Public Policy: A Revolution in Progress*, 2nd ed. (Washington, DC: Congressional Quarterly Press, 1999), 19.

Box 6.1: A Mattress as Alleged Crime Scene, Performance Art, Political Statement, and Maybe a Violation of Title IX

1 Nina Burleigh, "Confronting Campus Rape," *Rolling Stone*, June 4, 2014.

2 Christina Cauterucci, "Court Rules Former Columbia Student Suspended for Alleged Rape Can Sue for 'Anti-Male Bias,'" *Slate*, August 2, 2016.

Box 6.2: Global Gender Gap Ranking and Educational Attainment

1 Augusto Lopez-Claros and Saadia Zahidi, *Women's Empowerment: Measuring the Global Gender Gap* (Geneva: World Economic Forum, 2005), 5.

2 Joni Seager, *The Penguin Atlas of Women in the World*, 4th ed. (New York: Penguin Books, 2009), 30.

CHAPTER 7

Women and Work: In Pursuit of Economic Equality

Even more than education, work exemplifies the contradictions of the paradox of gender equality. Although separate spheres ideology may have faded over time as the primary organizing principle of gender relations, its legacy is very much alive today in how women and men experience work. Title VII of the Civil Rights Act of 1964 makes it illegal to restrict jobs to one sex or the other based purely on sex or stereotypical assumptions about gender-linked abilities, but gender segregation is pervasive throughout the labor force. The economy is organized into "men's jobs" and "women's jobs" that are eerily consistent with the division of labor between the public and private spheres. The four largest occupations for women—secretaries, teachers, nurses, and home health aides—are each at least 80 percent female. Carpentry, one of the largest occupations for men, is 97 percent male. In legislation having to do with technical and vocational training, the federal government defines nontraditional fields as "occupations or fields of work for which individuals of one gender comprise less than 25 percent of individuals employed."[1] In 2012, nontraditional occupations for women employed only 6 percent of all women but 44 percent of all men; nontraditional occupations for men employed 5 percent of men but 40 percent of women.[2] If all occupations enjoyed the same level of prestige and pay, the concentration of one gender in a few occupations would not disadvantage women, but that is not the case. There are consequences to maintaining a gendered economy.

The median annual income for all full-time male workers in 2015 was $50,383, compared with $39,621 for all full-time female workers. Women's income constituted 79 percent of men's, putting the annual earnings wage gap at roughly 21 percent.[3] For women of color, the wage gap is even larger. African American women's earnings are 64 percent of those of white men, and Latina women earn just 54 percent.[4] Moreover, even when men and women were similarly educated and working in the same profession, women were likely to be paid less than men. Women's 2015 median weekly earnings in the legal profession, for example, were estimated at $1,717, compared with an estimated $1,914 for men. Women constitute 36 percent of all lawyers in the United States, yet only 18 percent of the equity partners and 21 percent of all partners.[5] Women represent 25 percent of the senior-level executives in Fortune 500 companies (up from 15 percent in 2009) and earn roughly 85 percent of the salaries of their male counterparts. Women's overrepresentation in low-paying, service-sector jobs also contributes to their high poverty rates. Many who work full-time and are the sole breadwinners for their families bring in earnings of less than $15,000 a year.[6] Are the disparities between men and women in employment a result of socialization and education, employment discrimination, negative public attitudes about women's work, or women's choices?

This chapter examines women's entrance into the labor force and assesses the power of the paradox of gender equality in shaping their experiences over time. Employment policies consistent with the legal equality doctrine have been very effective in expanding occupational choices for women and in limiting forms of workplace discrimination including sexual harassment. Gender-neutral policies in employment are designed to guarantee women equal pay for substantially equal work, equal access to Social Security and other employment-related benefits, and equal access to opportunities for advancement within their careers. The Equal Pay Act of 1963 guarantees that men and women will be paid equally for doing the same job. Title VII prohibits discrimination on the basis of sex and gender identity in hiring and employment. Affirmative action policies are meant to ensure that women cannot be ignored in hiring and promotions.

The reality of women's experience, however, suggests that gender-neutral policies do not aid in balancing the responsibilities of work and family, nor do they credit women for the impact of their family responsibilities on their earnings throughout their lifetimes, particularly in determining retirement income. Some public policies were designed at a time when very few women were active in the paid labor force. Social Security, for example, was designed for a male breadwinner with a female dependent, but today the Social Security Administration is "neutral with respect to gender—individuals with identical earnings histories are treated the same in terms of benefits."[7] The research reviewed in this chapter will show that gender-neutral policies work best for women who most closely follow the traditional male model of employment—that is, women who are unmarried without children and therefore unencumbered by caregiving responsibilities. Gender-specific policies in employment that would account for ways in which women are more similar to one another than to men are nearly impossible to design without violating the prohibitions of sex discrimination so central to Title VII. As a result, women's experience with work remains highly gendered, regardless of their occupation, class, race or ethnicity, age, or level of education.

WOMEN ENTER THE WORKFORCE: A BRIEF HISTORY

Men and women have always worked. In preindustrial society, although men and women performed different tasks, both men's and women's work were necessary for survival.[8] There was little distinction between home and the workplace because they were often one and the same. In Colonial America, the home was the center of production, with men working in the fields and women tending to the home by cooking, cleaning, bearing and caring for the children, and manufacturing the goods the family needed to survive. What their families did not consume, women offered for sale, which brought in additional income for the family.[9] However, industrialization moved the means of production from the homestead to the factory, altering the division of labor between men and women and casting the value of labor in terms of money rather than the sustainability of the family. The value attached to gendered work became more starkly differentiated, so much so that participants in the Seneca Falls Convention in 1848 included among their demands issued in the *Declaration of Sentiments* women's ability to work and be fairly compensated.

Early in our nation's history, women entered the paid labor force in large numbers as teachers, seamstresses, domestics, or mill operators—occupations clearly consistent with their private-sphere roles. In 1860, women accounted for 10.2 percent of the free labor force. Almost one out of every ten free women over the age of ten was a wage earner. That women *could* work in less traditional venues was clearly demonstrated by female slaves. Not only did African female slaves work side by side with men in the fields, but they tended to domestic chores for their masters' families as well as for their own. Prior to the Civil War, the slave labor force included nearly 2 million women. Their entry into the paid labor force is reflected in the next census: in 1870, 13.7 percent of women worked for pay, making up 14.8 percent of the nation's total workforce. By 1910, one out of every five workers was a woman, representing three times the number of female wage earners in 1870.[10] Since 1870, the proportional increase in the number of employed women has exceeded the proportional increase of employed men in every decade.[11]

Domestic work dominated women's paid labor during the first phases of economic assimilation. In 1870, seven out of every ten women workers were servants. As new jobs opened in factories, retail stores, offices, and classrooms, the proportion of women working as domestic servants fell.[12] However, employment patterns were still segregated by sex. In industry, women were concentrated in the manufacture of cloth, clothing, food, and tobacco products. In the expanding white-collar sector, women were also relegated to a limited range of low-level jobs, such as teachers, nurses, office workers, salesclerks, and switchboard operators.[13] Women employed in these capacities were likely to be young, urban, unmarried, and the daughters of recent immigrants. The sole exception was the African

American woman worker, who might be of any age and was more likely to be married while employed.

White women's youth was evidence of work's temporary nature for women of this period. The average white woman worker assumed that she would stop working once she married. This attitude perpetuated the expectation that women worked to contribute to the family but not to independently provide for their own support. Women's short time in the labor force limited their earning potential since they were perpetual newcomers to the workforce, viewed as temporary and therefore not worth training for higher-paying skilled jobs. Thus women were relegated to the lowest-level jobs with little to no possibility of economic security or advancement.

Cultural pressure on women to adhere to the "domestic ideal" of hearth and home directly collided with increasing opportunities for women in the economy.[14] Even if employers were willing to accept women as full participants in the workforce, eligible for any job at any salary, the majority of the public was not. As Theodore Roosevelt wrote at the turn of the century, "If the women do not recognize that the greatest thing for any woman is to be a good wife and mother, why, that nation has cause to be alarmed about its future."[15] The history of women and work is characterized by the often conflicting forces of economy and culture. In times of crisis, the nation accepts and in fact relies on women's labor. But more often than not, once the crisis passes, women are expected to return to the domestic ideal. After recruiting women into the workforce in unprecedented numbers during World War II, the government implemented a "return to normalcy" campaign to convince women to leave the workforce and return to their responsibilities at home. By that time, however, most of the social prohibitions against married women working had fallen by the wayside, a direct result of women's wartime experiences. Women had learned to accommodate the dual burdens of work and family. Women's participation in the post–World War II labor force continued to increase, and by the late 1960s, nearly 40 percent of all women were employed outside the home.[16]

Women's labor history is also replete with contradictions about race and class. While middle- and upper-class white women aspired to and were in fact pressured to adhere to the domestic ideal, poor working-class women, along with women of color and recent immigrants, were not included in this ideal. Low salaries meant that most working-class men could not be their families' sole wage earner; this was particularly true for recently emancipated slaves. Survival often required women and children to enter the paid labor force and accept whatever low-paying, high-risk jobs were available. As white women moved from domestic labor to clerical and sales positions, African American women took their place. The proportion of African American women domestic workers increased from 38.5 percent in 1910 to 59.9 percent in 1940. Over the next two decades, African American women diversified their labor participation to include manufacturing and clerical work.

By the late 1960s, only 20 percent of working African American women were employed in private households.

Women's working conditions were also hampered by their exclusion from organized labor movements. During the first half of the nineteenth century, unions did not accept female members. By 1920, only 7 percent of women belonged to unions, compared with 25 percent of men.[17] Women in some industries attempted to form their own labor organizations (e.g., the Working Girls' Societies, the Women's Trade Union League). Women's unions tried unsuccessfully to alter the belief that women were temporary workers who were motivated only by the opportunity to earn "pocket money" to supplement their husband's income, or the notion that working women were selfishly pursuing a career at the expense of their family responsibilities at home. These attitudes about women's motivations for work persisted well into the twentieth century.[18]

By the mid-nineteenth century, approval of working women was conditional at best. Employment was acceptable only for women at opposite ends of the age spectrum, for those without children or whose children were grown, and for those who were willing to settle for part-time, low-wage positions. But by the 1960s, pressures of inflation collided with the rebirth of the feminist movement to produce an awakening among women as a group and within the larger public's consciousness. As a result, the proportion of all types of women in the workforce rose. The job prestige gap between white, African American, and Hispanic women continued to close. By 2012, two-thirds of African American women and three-fourths of white women held white-collar jobs. At present, a majority of all families across class and race (both with children and childless) are dual-earner families. Employed women in dual-earner couples contribute an average of 46 percent of annual family income, but the ambivalence over women's dual roles in the private and public spheres persists. The proportion of men and women in the paid workforce today is nearly even (53 percent male, 47 percent female), and yet two in five men still think women's place is in the home.[19]

GENDER SOCIALIZATION AND ATTITUDES ABOUT WORK

Gender specialization in work and the expectations for work relative to gender may develop in early childhood, built on a foundation of separate-spheres ideology. Studies show not only that girls over the age of five spend more time on household chores than boys do but also that girls begin doing chores at an earlier age.[20] Girls specialize in cooking and cleaning (jobs that are performed regularly), while boys are more likely to take out the garbage and help with yard work (jobs that are performed less frequently). Because parents view regularly performed chores, such as washing dishes, as contributing to the good of the family, they are usually done without pay (allowance), while such infrequent tasks as washing the car are likely to be compensated. Boys are more likely to find a neighborhood "market" for outdoor chores such as shoveling snow or raking leaves, but girls are less likely to earn money cleaning a neighbor's house (although girls may earn money by babysitting and are more likely to perform that task than their brothers). Children are likely to conclude that the tasks males occasionally perform have monetary value but the tasks females frequently perform do not. "Children have reason to think that boys labor for payment, while girls 'labor for love.' . . . The sexual division of children's play and labor induces both boys and girls to see housework and child care as women's responsibility, a responsibility that, ideally, is performed with love and pleasure. If housework, especially child care, is a woman's labor of love, equity does not come into the picture."[21]

In studies of the division of household labor between adults, women consistently perform more hours of labor in the home, regardless of race, class, education, and occupational status. In 2014, for example, women spent an average of 2 hours 9 minutes on household activities every day, while men spent an average of 1 hour 22 minutes on the same set of household tasks.[22] When women do not work in the labor force, they perform an average 38 hours of housework a week compared to men's 12 hours. The inequities are even greater among couples with children, although recent data suggest that millennials (individuals born roughly between 1980 and 2000) are more balanced in caring for their children. Fathers with children under thirteen spend an average of 3 hours per workday caring for their children (a figure that increased by a full hour between 1977 and 2008), while women spend slightly more, at 3.8 hours per workday (a figure that remained steady over the same period).[23] Somewhat surprisingly, men and women accept inequities at home as "fair." When married women who work outside the home are doing 66 percent of the housework, they judge the division fair. It is only when their portion of housework approaches 75 percent that they judge the distribution as unfair. Men, on the other hand, view it as unfair when they do roughly the same amount of housework (48 percent) and see the division as fair when they perform about 36 percent of the labor.[24]

Why have women willingly accepted this double burden of carrying the majority of the housework and child care on top of a full-time job outside the home? Again the answer can be found in the separate spheres ideology. Virginia Valian, author of Why So Slow? The Advancement of Women, suggests three reasons. First, both men and women see equity as a relevant concept in the workplace, but neither sees home as the workplace. Because taking care of the family is a labor of love for women, demanding equity makes a woman appear heartless. "Women have learned to help others directly, by caring for them, even if that help comes at their own expense. Men, on the other hand, have learned to help others indirectly, by earning money to provide material wellbeing and educational opportunities," Valian writes.[25] Second, because of years of socialization in non-overlapping roles, men and women define certain jobs as feminine and others as masculine, making it difficult for a man to retain his masculinity when performing "feminine" jobs in the home. Finally, men tend to compare themselves with other men, and women compare themselves with other women. And if men and women compare their own division of labor within their marriage with that of their parents, both husband and wife view themselves as better off than either of their parents. Both men and women believe (correctly in most cases) that contemporary men are doing substantially more than their fathers ever did, particularly in the area of child care. This relieves men of the responsibility for equal housework and denies women grounds (or so they perceive) for demanding a more equitable division of labor in the home.[26]

This leaves women to figure out ways to combine a professional career or full-time job with the demands of the home and children, and defines resolving work and family pressures as a female problem rather than a human one. Thus, the needs for higher-quality and more-affordable child care, family leave policies, and work hours that offer more flexibility are all defined as "women's issues" and are largely absent as considerations in the policies reviewed below. The burden of finding solutions in the absence of government action is squarely placed on women in most cases. If we are to make additional progress toward workplace equality, these issues must find a place on the public policy agenda as workplace issues and not women's or family issues.

LEGAL PATHS TO EQUALITY: FEDERAL ANTIDISCRIMINATION POLICIES

Women's work, as we saw earlier, is largely a function of the interplay of the economy and cultural sex role expectations. As the need for skilled workers surpassed the available male labor pool, more women entered the workforce and sought opportunities beyond those prescribed by traditional gender roles. They were aided in this by government—the National Manpower Council, the Department of Labor, and the Women's Bureau joined forces to explore ways to develop women's labor potential. In 1957, these organizations issued a report affirming that the principles of equality of opportunity and pay should apply to women as well as men.[27] The women's movement, largely dormant at this point anyway, did not immediately seize on this report as an opening because it was experiencing internal divisions over the pursuit of equal opportunities at the expense of protections for women workers. In this sense, the first equal employment laws were not a direct result of actions by the women's movement but, rather, happened despite inaction and division within the movement.

The two paths to equality stemming from the paradox of gender equality were both evident as the government struggled with how to extend equal employment rights to women. On one hand, a strictly gender-neutral approach guaranteed legal equality for men and women in the workplace, assuming that men and women experienced the workplace in similar ways. In passing the **Equal Pay Act** of 1963,

Congress guaranteed women equal pay for work equal to that of male employees. **Title VII of the 1964 Civil Rights Act** prohibits discrimination against both men and women in employment on the basis of sex (it says nothing about gender identity). Alternatively, gender-specific policies, such as protective legislation safeguarding women from long hours or dangerous working conditions and accommodating their "special burden" of bearing and raising children, recognize differences between men and women. Such protective legislation was popular with progressives and social-reform feminists in the early twentieth century, but liberal feminists argued that it would in fact disadvantage and stigmatize women.

The passage of Title VII ended for the moment the debate over which path the government would pursue, but it is not clear that the legal equality path has been most advantageous for women or that gender-neutral laws will eliminate the most intractable barriers to economic equality. An example of a policy consistent with the fairness doctrine is affirmative action. Women have directly benefited from affirmative-action policies that were set in motion by Executive Orders 11246 and 11375. With the exception of affirmative action, the history of gender antidiscrimination employment law in the United States is one that has been based on the legal equality doctrine. Legal equality is most effective in breaking through the initial barrier—ending sex-based job classifications and pay rates or extending women credit. But once the overt barriers have been removed, a web of cultural and social attitudes remain that have proven difficult to legislate away. In this section, we will review the major federal legislation designed to eliminate gender-based employment discrimination.

The Equal Pay Act of 1963

The Equal Pay Act of 1963 was not the government's first foray into regulating pay equity. Largely as a way to prevent employers from dampening wages by hiring women, at several points prior to 1963 the government required that women and men be paid equally. The Fair Labor Standards Act of 1938 prohibited classifying jobs and wages according to age or sex, provided a minimum wage for some job classifications, and required fair treatment for wage and hourly workers. Similarly, when women flooded the workforce during both world wars, government took action to alleviate the fear that women in men's jobs would depress wages. Policy dictated that women holding "men's jobs" be paid "men's wages." Hardly a statement on gender equality, the policy was designed to protect men's jobs and wage rates. Since attitudes about women working were still largely ambivalent, policy directed at equalizing wages based on a doctrine of equality did not surface until the Kennedy administration sent an equal pay bill to Congress. The Women's Bureau, led by Esther Peterson, argued that "fairness" dictated equal pay for men and women. Initially the Women's Bureau pursued "equal pay for comparable work," but it relented under pressure from employers who argued that defining

IMAGE 7.1: *President John F. Kennedy signs the Equal Pay Act into law on June 10, 1963.* Source: Abbie Rowe. White House Photographs. John F. Kennedy Presidential Library and Museum, Boston.

comparable work would invite excessive government intrusion. Given the persistence of the "dual labor force," both Congress and the law's detractors in industry were confident that an equal pay law within the context of a sex-segregated workplace would not jeopardize men's jobs or wages. By the time Congress took action, twenty-three states already had equal pay laws on the books.

The federal law requires that when men and women perform the same (or substantially the same) job in the same place and under the same conditions, they must receive equal pay.[28] However, seniority, merit, and measures related to the quantity and quality of the work provide a legal basis for pay differentials, as does "any other factor other than sex." Initially, the law, which was an amendment to the Fair Labor Standards Act, covered only wage and hourly employees and exempted employers with fewer than twenty-five employees. In 1972, the law's protections were extended to workers in small firms not covered by minimum-wage laws, professionals including teachers, and state and local government employees. Enforcement moved from the Department of Labor exclusively to the **Equal Employment Opportunity Commission (EEOC)** in 1978, but that move did not result in more stringent application of the law. Primarily, enforcement is the result of an individual or group of workers filing a claim with the EEOC.

The prevailing 19 percent wage gap in 2016, more than fifty years after the law was passed, suggests that both the law and its enforcement have not rectified the problem of wage discrimination. In 2010, President Obama established the National Equal Pay Task Force to ensure that the agencies responsible for equal pay enforcement are coordinating efforts and to improve the infrastructure for collecting data and reports on pay inequities. The administration also launched an "Equal Pay App Challenge" to encourage software developers to assist the National Equal Pay Task Force in developing new tools to educate users about the pay gap and new strategies to combat it. The winning application, Aequitas Mobile Application, empowers users with current wage data, interview, and resume and negotiation tools, and connects users to equal-pay-related social media discussions. OES Data Explorer provides easy access to US wage estimates by city, state, and job title from Bureau of Labor Statistics occupational databases. Both of these applications will promote discussion of the wage gap in addition to providing users with valuable data.

Title VII of the 1964 Civil Rights Act

Now singularly powerful in combating gender discrimination in employment, Title VII of the 1964 Civil Rights Act resulted from an amendment offered by Congressman Howard Smith, a conservative southern Democrat from Virginia. Smith was determined to undermine the prohibitions against race discrimination at the core of the act by suggesting that men and women should be treated equally in the workplace. He was sure that the inclusion of sex along with race, color, religion, or national origin would derail the bill in the Senate, if not in the House. Without the amendment, many argued, white women would have been the only workers unprotected from employment discrimination under federal law. While accounts of his precise motivations vary, the Smith amendment did, in fact, survive to become one of the most powerful federal antidiscrimination employment laws.

The inclusion of sex along with the other protected categories was opposed by several prominent women's organizations, including the President's Commission on the Status of Women, the Women's Bureau, and the American Association of University Women. Their opposition arose mainly in response to the issue of protective legislation for women and the recognition that special accommodations for women would no longer be permitted under Title VII.[29] The law has since been amended three times. The first change extended the authority of the EEOC and expanded coverage to include public employers and educational institutions. The second amendment, known as the Pregnancy Discrimination Act (1978), declared that classifications based on pregnancy and pregnancy-related disabilities fall within the meaning of "sex" under Title VII. Third, the Civil Rights Act (1991) amended Title VII to reverse the effects of several Supreme Court rulings in the late 1980s that made job discrimination suits harder to win.

The EEOC, now responsible for administering all of the nation's equal protection provisions, was created under the 1964 Civil Rights Act and charged with developing guidelines for Title VII's implementation. It was clear from the start that the EEOC was not going to be very ambitious in writing guidelines on sex discrimination. EEOC commissioners and staff expressed a general belief that the addition of sex to the law had been illegitimate. The commission's executive director, Herman Edelsberg, informed the press that "no man should be required to have a male secretary."[30] Women's organizations such as the newly formed National Organization for Women (NOW) rallied to pressure the agency to act more diligently. The specific provisions in Title VII most relevant to sex discrimination are found in section 703(a):

> It shall be an unlawful employment practice for an employer (1) to fail or refuse to hire or to discharge any individual, or otherwise to discriminate against any individual with respect to his compensation, terms, conditions, or privileges of employment, because of such individual's race, color, religion, sex, or national origin; or (2) to limit, segregate, or classify his employees or applicants for employment in any way which would deprive or tend to deprive any individual of employment opportunities or otherwise adversely affect his status as an employee, because of such individual's race, color, religion, sex, or national origin.[31]

An important exception to Title VII's coverage arises from what is called a **bona fide occupational qualification (BFOQ)**:

> Notwithstanding any other provision of this subchapter (1) it shall not be an unlawful employment practice for an employer to hire and employ employees . . . on the basis of his religion, sex, or national origin in those certain instances where religion, sex, or national origin is a bona fide occupational qualification reasonably necessary to the normal operation of that particular business enterprise.[32]

Like many policies passed by Congress, the basic provisions and language of Title VII have been subject to interpretation by the Supreme Court. Two of the statute's critical phrases have provided the basis for such cases. Title VII prohibits discrimination practices "because of sex." Congress did not specify exactly what it intended with this language, so the courts decided what it means through a succession of cases. In 1912, Justice Holmes best articulated for the Court the basic principle of the equal protection clause that allows some sex-based laws to stand, even today in the face of Title VII's prohibition of sex discrimination: "The Fourteenth Amendment does not interfere [with state legislation] by erecting fictitious equality where there is real difference."[33] Unlike race, which the Court views as an immutable characteristic that bears no relationship to job performance, sex is assumed to create real and meaningful differences in a man's or a woman's ability to get and hold some jobs. However, the determination of the relevance of sex differences to employment cannot, the Court ruled, be based on assumptions of women as a group or any stereotypical characteristics as a group and must be based in fact.

One of the first Title VII cases brought on the basis of sex was *Phillips v. Martin Marietta* (1971). Ida Phillips challenged the Martin Marietta Corporation's policy against hiring women with preschool-age children, although it had no such policy that affected the hiring of men. Two lower courts ruled that the employment policy did not violate Title VII since it did not rely solely on sex but also relied on a criterion "other than sex" (having preschool-age children). The Supreme Court rejected the "sex plus" criterion as a violation of Title VII's intent.

Several cases have been brought before the courts on the basis of the BFOQ exception to Title VII. One of the earliest, *Weeks v. Southern Bell Telephone and Telegraph* (1969), challenged a rule that prevented women, but not men, from holding positions that required lifting more than thirty pounds. Lower courts ruled that the company had based its decision to limit women's employment on stereotypes rather than on real abilities of its employees or applicants. Similarly, in *Rosenfeld v. Southern Pacific Company* (1971), the Ninth Circuit Court of Appeals ruled against Southern Pacific's policy of excluding women from certain "unsuitable" jobs because they involved irregular hours and lifting weights of up to twenty-five pounds, and because state laws limited working conditions for women under a variety of protective statutes. The court ruled that neither reason constituted a BFOQ because both relied on stereotypes of women's abilities rather than on a finding of fact.[34]

BFOQ defenses were invoked in a large number of early employment discrimination cases. Some of the most important rulings defining permissible BFOQ defenses have involved a male plaintiff bringing suit to open occupations previously limited to women. In *Diaz v. Pan American World Airways, Inc.* (1971), Celio Diaz applied for a job as a flight attendant, but was refused employment because of his sex. Pan Am's policy of hiring only women as cabin attendants raised the question of whether an employee's sex in situations where the public expected to find one sex or the other constituted a legitimate BFOQ. The Supreme Court reversed a lower court's support for the policy, ruling that Title VII permits sex to operate as a BFOQ only when it is reasonably necessary to the operation of a business. The Court left open the possibility that there might be some instances when "the essence of the business operation would be undermined by not hiring members of one sex exclusively," but ruled that Pan American had not argued that female flight attendants were essential to their business success.

Ten years after the Pan Am ruling, another case involving an airline's hiring policy refined the Court's test for business necessity. In *Wilson v. Southwest Airlines Company* (1981), Southwest Airlines argued that female flight attendants were necessary to the financial success of its business in the highly competitive aviation industry. Southwest Airlines had adopted a public relations campaign based on an image of female sexuality that catered to the almost exclusively male category of business travelers. Using the slogan "We're Spreading Love All over Texas," Southwest gained on its competitors throughout the 1970s. When sued for its refusal to hire male flight attendants, Southwest Airlines argued that in this case, sex operated as a BFOQ since their financial success depended on the appeal of their female flight attendants. In its decision, the Supreme Court created a two-pronged test based on two questions: (1) does the job require that the worker be of one sex only, and if so, (2) is that requirement reasonably necessary to the essence of the employer's business? In requiring affirmative answers to both questions, the Court sought to retain Title VII's intent. Since Southwest Airlines' primary business was providing safe air transportation, requiring flight attendants to be female was not reasonably necessary to the essence of safe travel. The Court concluded, "Sex does not become a BFOQ merely because an employer chooses to exploit female sexuality as a marketing tool or to better insure profitability."[35]

Under some conditions, sex does serve as a legitimate BFOQ, but they are few. For example, conditions of privacy may warrant one sex exclusively (a single-gender restroom attendant or undergarment fitter). Jobs that require "authenticity," such as an actor or actress playing a particular role in a movie or play, have been allowed under the BFOQ exception. The wildly popular Broadway musical *Hamilton* tried to claim race and ethnicity as a BFOQ in casting calls for productions in Chicago, Los Angeles, and San Francisco. However, the Actors' Equity Association objected, saying that a preference for "non-white actors and actresses" is inconsistent equal opportunity in theater. The show's creator, Lin-Manuel Miranda, has described *Hamilton* as "the story of America 'then' told by America 'now.'" Although the young, diverse cast and the hip-hop soundtrack are critical parts of *Hamilton*'s success, the producers revised their casting call to invite all races and ethnicities to apply.[36]

A 1977 Supreme Court ruling in *Dothard v. Rawlinson* disappointed most feminists. In rejecting a woman's bid to become a prison guard in an Alabama state penitentiary, the Court allowed Alabama to discriminate against qualified women applicants because of the dangerous conditions in Alabama's prison system. The Court stipulated that unconstitutional overcrowding created a danger to men as well as women, but it nonetheless held that "a woman's ability to maintain order . . . could be directly reduced by her womanhood. . . . There would also be a real risk that other inmates deprived of a normal heterosexual environment would assault women guards because they were women." This ruling was very narrowly written and did not even extend to most other state prisons that attempted to prohibit female guards. However, as Justice Thurgood Marshall pointed out in his dissenting opinion, the majority opinion "regrettably perpetuates one of the most insidious of the old myths about women—that women, wittingly or not, are seductive sexual objects."[37] Most jobs now have been ruled open to both sexes.

Six Chix

IMAGE 7.2

Source: *Six Chix* used with the permission of Ann Telnaes and the Cartoonist Group. All rights reserved.

The Supreme Court expanded "sex" to include "gender" over a series of cases that began with *Price Waterhouse v. Hopkins* (1989).[38] Ann Hopkins, a senior manager at the Price Waterhouse accounting firm, was denied partnership because she exhibited traditionally masculine traits. The firm went so far as to advise her to "take a course at charm school" and "walk more femininely, talk more femininely, wear makeup, have her hair styled and wear jewelry."[39] The Court found that Price Waterhouse had discriminated against Hopkins "because of sex" by insisting that she conform to sex stereotypes consistent with her gender. The Court wrote, "Congress intended to strike at the entire spectrum of disparate treatment of men and women resulting from sex stereotypes. . . . [A]n employer who acts on the basis of a belief that a woman cannot be aggressive, or that she must not be, has acted on the basis of gender." According to the Court's decision in *Price Waterhouse*, the term "sex" in Title VII encompassed both biological sex and gender: "If gender plays a role in an employer's decision to take an adverse employment action, they have committed sex discrimination."[40] Lower court decisions made clear that the prohibition against adverse employment actions based on gender stereotypes extended to men as well as women.

In 2004, the Sixth Circuit became the first federal court to extend the sex/gender stereotype theory to transgender plaintiffs. In *Smith v. City of Salem* (2004) and *Barnes v. City of Cincinnati* (2005), the court concluded: "Discrimination against a plaintiff who is transsexual—and therefore fails to act and/or identify with his or her gender—is no different from the discrimination directed against Ann Hopkins in *Price Waterhouse* who, in sex-stereotypical terms, did not act like a woman."[41] In 2012, the EEOC ruled that if an employer discriminates "based on gender identity, change of sex, and/or transgender status," the employer has engaged in disparate treatment "because of sex," thus violating Title VII. This ruling applied to all federal agencies.[42]

Less settled is whether discrimination on the basis of sexual orientation is covered by Title VII. The Employment Non-Discrimination Act (ENDA) was first introduced in Congress in 1994 and would prohibit discrimination on the basis of sexual orientation. Language was added in 2007 to include gender identity protections. Recognizing that ENDA was unlikely to pass in a Republican-controlled Congress, President Obama issued Executive Order 13672 in July 2014 to prevent discrimination in the civilian federal workforce on the basis of both sexual orientation and gender identity. The EEOC continues to accept claims of discrimination on the basis of sexual orientation.

In nearly every case, enforcement of Title VII occurs in reaction to a complaint filed by an individual or group with the EEOC. There are primarily three types of proof of discrimination. The first is proof of prior intent to discriminate, requiring written or sworn oral testimony that there was intent on the employer's part to discriminate against one sex in hiring, promoting, paying, or providing benefits. While there were blatant cases of intent throughout the 1970s, more recent cases have not presented such clear proof and have mostly fallen under either disparate treatment or disparate impact.

Disparate treatment refers to an employer deliberately favoring or disadvantaging one group protected under Title VII over another. In these cases, the burden of proof falls on the plaintiff, who must demonstrate with hard evidence that the disparate treatment is due to sex rather than some legitimate reason unrelated to sex. When a group files suit, evidence may take the form of statistics showing a pattern of discrimination in hiring over time or that women are underrepresented in the company's employee or applicant pool relative to those qualified to hold the position in the population at large. However, if an individual files suit, evidence can often be difficult to obtain.

Disparate impact cases arise where an employer's policies appear to be gender neutral but have the effect of treating men and women differently, such as minimum height requirements, the ability to lift a certain weight, or the need to travel for extended periods of time. A defense in this case requires the employer to prove that the requirements are related to the job and that they constitute a business necessity. In other words, if the qualifications for a position list the ability to lift more than seventy-five pounds, but in performing the job the employee is never asked to lift heavy loads, the business necessity defense is not legitimate and the qualifications constitute Title VII discrimination. As a result of the Civil Rights Act of 1991, the courts are now bound by legislation to hold employers responsible for demonstrating that their employment practices that may result in a disparate effect are related to a legitimate business necessity. The burden of proof lies with the defendant (the employer), and the plaintiff is not required to prove that the company intended to discriminate through its hiring practices.[43]

The most recent cases alleging sex discrimination under Title VII concern what legal experts refer to as **second-generation discrimination**—subtle, perhaps even unconscious bias against women. Stanford law professor Deborah Rhode said, "There are no smoking guns; much of it is what social scientists call micro-indignities—small incidents that viewed individually may seem trivial, but when viewed cumulatively point to a practice of insensitivity and devaluation that can get in the way of work performance."[44] This kind of discrimination can also discourage women from entering certain occupations historically dominated by men. "For women, a hostile environment, or one that demonstrates a lack of opportunity to grow or rise through the ranks, is undoubtedly a factor in career decision-making."[45]

Pregnancy Discrimination Act (1978)

An amendment to Title VII of the Civil Rights Act of 1964, the **Pregnancy Discrimination Act (PDA)** prohibits workplace discrimination on the basis of pregnancy. The impetus for the legislation was the 1976 US Supreme Court ruling in *General Electric v. Gilbert,* in which the Court ruled that a policy that distinguishes between pregnant and nonpregnant persons does not constitute sex discrimination against women.[46] The PDA effectively overturned the *Gilbert* decision. The first clause of the act clarifies that Title VII's prohibition against sex discrimination applies to discrimination "because of or on the basis or pregnancy, childbirth, or related medical conditions." The second clause says that employers must treat pregnant women the same as "other persons not so affected but similar in their ability or inability to work" in all areas of employment, including hiring, firing, seniority rights, job security, and fringe benefits. If the employer offers health insurance to employees, that must include coverage for pregnancy, childbirth, and related conditions. Employers who do not provide insurance for health or temporary disabilities are not required by the act to provide coverage for pregnant women.

The Pregnancy Discrimination Act is consistent with the legal equality approach, even though only women can get pregnant. The act specifically says that employers cannot treat pregnancy "more or less" favorably than other temporary disabilities. Therefore, pregnant women are not eligible for pregnancy-specific special accommodations. Prior to the Family and Medical Leave Act (1993), that meant that the PDA did not require an employer to provide paid or unpaid maternity leave or guarantee that a job would be protected following childbirth, even though the Supreme Court ruled that the PDA does not specifically prohibit employment practices that might favor pregnant women. California, New Jersey, Rhode Island, and New York (effective in 2018) are the only states that currently mandate paid family leave.[47]

In a setback to advances in antipregnancy discrimination, the US Supreme Court ruled 7–2 in *AT&T Corporation v. Noreen Hulteen et al.* that an employer does not violate the PDA by paying pension benefits calculated using prior standards that are no longer acceptable under current law. The plaintiffs in this case were four current or former female AT&T employees who took unpaid, uncredited maternity leave prior to the Pregnancy Discrimination Act's implementation in 1979. As a result, their pension benefits today are smaller than they would have been otherwise. Justice David Souter, for the majority, wrote, "Although adopting a service credit rule unfavorable to those out on pregnancy leave would violate Title VII today, a seniority system does not necessarily violate the statute when it gives current effect to such rules that operated before the PDA." Justice Ruth Bader Ginsburg said in dissent, "I would hold that AT&T committed a current violation of Title VII when, post-PDA, it did not totally discontinue reliance upon a pension calculation premised on the notion that pregnancy-based classifications display no gender bias." This case mirrors the 2007 *Lilly Ledbetter v. Goodyear Tire & Rubber Co.* case (discussed later in the chapter)—both deal with correcting employment discrimination retroactively to address current inequalities that arise from a past discriminatory act.[48]

In 2015 the US Supreme Court issued a 6-3 ruling in *Young v. United Parcel Service*,[49] the same year the EEOC issued its "Updated Pregnancy Discrimination Guidance."[50] Peggy Young was working as a UPS delivery driver when she became pregnant and was advised by her doctor against lifting objects weighing over twenty pounds. UPS requires that drivers be able to lift seventy pounds without assistance. She asked to be accommodated, but UPS did not reassign Young to another job, though it provided work reassignments when employees became injured on the job or lost their Department of Transportation driving certification, and for those with a disability covered under the Americans with Disabilities Act. Young alleged that UPS violated the PDA when it refused to accommodate her pregnancy-related condition. Lower courts ruled in favor of UPS, but the Supreme Court sent it back to the lower courts to reconsider under the guidance it offered in the decision. Justice Breyer's majority opinion essentially rejected the arguments of both Young and UPS, instead searching for a middle ground—pregnancy is not any more deserving of accommodation than other temporary disabilities, but if an employer accommodates workers who are similar to pregnant workers in their ability to work, it cannot refuse to accommodate pregnant workers simply because "it is more expensive or less convenient" to do so. Further, when an employer's accommodation policies impose a "significant burden" on pregnant workers that outweighs any justification for the policies, then a jury can conclude that the employer is intentionally discriminating against pregnant workers. The late Justice Antonin Scalia (joined by Justices Anthony Kennedy and Clarence Thomas) dissented, stating, "The right reading of the same-treatment clause prohibits practices that discriminate against pregnant women relative to workers of similar ability or inability. It does not prohibit denying pregnant women accommodations, or any other benefit for that matter, on the basis of an evenhanded policy."

The Pregnancy Discrimination Act has been in place for more than thirty years. Still, the EEOC received 3,543 complaints of pregnancy-related discrimination in 2015. Combined with more women working, the increase in pregnancy discrimination complaints can also be attributed to more pregnant women in the workplace. According to the US Census Bureau, women are working longer into their pregnancies and taking shorter maternity leaves. In 2008, 67 percent of women worked during a pregnancy and 73 percent of women returned to work within six months of a birth. A majority of women used paid or unpaid maternity leave rather than leaving the workplace entirely. The Supreme Court's logic in *Young v. United Parcel Service* demonstrates how difficult it is to treat pregnancy in the gender-neutral terms required by the legal equality doctrine. The Pregnant Workers Fairness Act, introduced to Congress in 2014, would require employers to provide pregnant workers with reasonable accommodations under a framework resembling the Americans with Disabilities Act.[51] The bill has not become law.

Affirmative Action Policies: Executive Orders 11246 and 11375

In 1965, President Lyndon Johnson signed Executive Order 11246, which required companies that do business with the federal government to take "affirmative action to ensure that applicants are employed, and that employees are treated during employment, without regard to their race, color, religion or national origin."[52] The Office of Federal Contract Compliance was established within the Department of Labor to enforce the order. Unlike Title VII, sex was not included in the original affirmative action order. However, pressure from women's organizations and others convinced President Johnson to sign Executive Order 11375 (1967), which included sex among the protected categories in affirmative action policies. Affirmation action policies have gone a step further than Title VII and the Equal Pay Act, both of which require employers to treat similarly situated men and women in a similar manner. Recognizing that today's inequalities are rooted in past discrimination, affirmative action policies require employers to consciously monitor their employment practices and take action if women are underrepresented or have been underrepresented in the past. Affirmative action is a proactive remedy to past discrimination. Critics of the policy have long referred to affirmative action as "reverse discrimination." The Supreme Court has made it very clear that a lawful affirmative action program "must apply only to qualified candidates, have a strong reason for being developed, and be narrowly crafted to minimize negative effects."[53] This means that an affirmative action program cannot legally promote unqualified candidates at the expense of qualified individuals, nor can it use quotas, contrary to popular anti-affirmative-action political rhetoric.

Despite affirmative action policies, studies consistently document the persistence of discriminatory treatment based on race and gender. Tests conducted by the Fair Employment Council of Greater Washington continue to find that

white applicants are favored over minority applicants who have identical credentials. Paired testers, one white and one black, are sent to apply for the same job.
Although the two people have identical work experiences, backgrounds, demeanor,
interviewing skills, and physical builds, the Fair Employment Council tests found
that almost half of the white testers received job offers, compared with only 11 percent of the African American applicants.[54]

Although many of the most vehement attacks on affirmative action policies
have come at the expense of racial minorities, women of all races stand to lose a
considerable tool in the pursuit of equality if the principles of affirmative action
are undermined or ruled unconstitutional. Studies show that African American
women, long relegated to the bottom of the ladder in hiring, salary, and promotion,
have gained in both employment opportunities and wages as a result of affirmative
action laws.[55] All women seem to have gained as a result of an increase in the public's
consciousness of equal opportunity and diversity in the workplace and in admissions to professional schools. The rise in the number of women entering law and
medical programs, while not directly due to affirmative action policies per se, can be
positively linked to greater awareness of gender balance in admissions.

During the 1980s, under President Reagan, a conservative Supreme Court did
significant damage in both practice and concept to affirmative action principles.
While the Civil Rights Restoration Act of 1988 and the Civil Rights Act of 1991
reversed many of the Court's more damaging rulings on federal equal employment opportunity law, it would nevertheless be fair to say that the climate in the
United States toward affirmative action remained hostile throughout the 1990s. In
November 1996, 54 percent of California's electorate voted for Proposition 209,
which prohibited the implementation of race- or gender-based affirmative action
programs and resulted in dramatic changes in admission practices in the state's
extensive college and university system.

On June 23, 2003, the US Supreme Court issued two decisions involving
class-action lawsuits filed on behalf of white students denied admission to the University of Michigan's undergraduate programs (*Gratz v. Bollinger*) and law school
(*Grutter v. Bollinger*). In *Gratz*, the Supreme Court ruled 6–3 that Michigan's
automatic award of 20 points toward admission to all minority applicants purely
because of race to be insufficiently "narrowly tailored to achieve the interest and
educational diversity that respondents claim justifies their program." Still, the majority opinion affirmed the concept of affirmative action and diversity as a compelling interest. In *Grutter*, a 5–4 decision upheld the law school admission program,
with the majority opinion noting: "Effective participation by members of all racial
and ethnic groups in the civic life of our Nation is essential if the dream of one
Nation, indivisible, is to be realized." The difference between the two cases is in the
role race played in the admissions decision relative to the consideration of other
individualized factors.

In *Gratz*, the automatic award of points toward a positive admission decision purely on the basis of race was ruled unconstitutional because it was not sufficiently individualized. The Court provided a clear statement about the appropriate use of race in admissions, holding that the individualized consideration of race must be the hallmark of a carefully designed admissions policy that promotes educational diversity. The ruling also effectively overruled major portions of the 1996 US Court of Appeals ruling in *Hopwood v. Texas*, and allowed institutions in Texas, Louisiana, and Missouri to use race-conscious admissions policies designed to advance educational diversity. State universities in Florida, Washington, and California are still prohibited by state law from considering race in the admissions process. However, many scholars cite the Court's rulings in *Gratz* and *Grutter* as evidence that assaults on the very concept of affirmative action to promote diversity will not get a friendly hearing.

The Supreme Court again narrowed the scope in which race can be used as one of a number of factors in college admissions in *Fisher v. University of Texas at Austin* (2013).[56] The Texas legislature passed a law requiring the University of Texas to admit all in-state high school seniors who ranked in the top 10 percent of their class. However, shortly after the 2003 *Grutter* ruling, the University of Texas identified racial and ethnic disparities between incoming classes and the state's population, and altered its race-neutral admissions policy. For Texas applicants not in the top 10 percent of their class, the university factored race into its admission decision. Abigail Noel Fisher, a white student who was not in the top 10 percent of her class and was not admitted to the University of Texas, argued that she was denied admission on account of her race while minority students with lower grade point averages than hers were admitted under the diversity plan. The district court and the Fifth Circuit Court of Appeals both sided with the University of Texas. But in a 7–1 decision, the US Supreme Court said that the lower courts erred in not applying the standard of "strict judicial scrutiny" to the university's admissions policy, noting that any policy that takes race into account must be "precisely tailored to serve a compelling governmental interest." University of Texas officials argued that their policy's use of race was narrowly tailored to pursue greater diversity.

The case returned before the Supreme Court in 2015 on another challenge following changes to the University of Texas program. With only seven justices voting (Antonin Scalia died in February 2016 and Elena Kagan recused herself because of her involvement in the case while working in the solicitor general's office), the Court rejected the new challenge. Justice Kennedy wrote: "Considerable deference is owed to a university in defining those intangible characteristics, like student body diversity, that are central to its identity and educational mission." But he went on, "It remains an enduring challenge to our nation's education system to reconcile the pursuit of diversity with the constitutional promise of equal treatment and dignity."[57] A majority of Americans continue to support gender and race affirmative action programs. However, a recent Gallup poll showed that there is more support for gender-based action (67 percent) than race-based action (58 percent).[58]

Affirmative action continues to be an important tool for women and minorities in pursuit of equality. A Department of Labor study estimated that 5 million minority workers and 6 million women are in higher occupational classifications today than they would have been without the affirmative action policies of the 1960s and 1970s.[59] The new frontiers of affirmative action policies for women and girls are closely related to expanding access to and interest in traditionally male-dominated fields, where salaries are often higher. Affirmative action policies also mitigate the impact of the "glass ceiling." Although women as a group have made significant gains over the last decade in combating sex discrimination in employment, the rates of progress differ considerably by age, race, ethnicity, and disability. Sex discrimination charges filed with the EEOC increased by 12 percent overall in a decade, yet claims filed by African American women increased by 20 percent and those filed by Hispanic women increased by 68 percent. The study found similar variations by group on sexual harassment claims, pregnancy discrimination suits, retaliation claims, and age discrimination charges.[60]

The Lilly Ledbetter Fair Pay Act of 2009

When Lilly Ledbetter retired from Goodyear in 1998, she received an anonymous note revealing the salaries of her fifteen colleagues (all male and some with less seniority). Only then did she realize that she was the victim of pay discrimination, and she attributed her pay inequity to her sex. At first her salary was similar to that of her male colleagues, but over time she received smaller raises even though her performance ratings were positive. Because subsequent raises are often a percentage of the last base rate of pay, the cumulative effect was substantial. "Ledbetter was paid $3,727 per month; the lowest paid male area manager received $4,286 per month, the highest paid $5,236."[61]

Ledbetter filed an equal pay complaint with the EEOC under Title VII. Goodyear argued that Ledbetter filed her complaint too late (the 180-day statute of limitation having passed long before), and when the case came before the US Supreme Court, the majority of the Court agreed. The majority opinion, written by Justice Samuel Alito, applied a very narrow interpretation of the 180-day statute of limitation requirement. The Court claimed that it was incumbent on Ledbetter to file charges year by year, each time Goodyear failed to increase her salary commensurate with the salaries of male peers. Justice Ginsburg, in her dissenting opinion, which she read aloud from the bench, took the majority to task for its failure to understand the nature of pay discrimination and women's experiences in the workplace:

> Pay disparities often occur, as they did in Ledbetter's case, in small increments; cause to suspect that discrimination is at work develops only over

time. Comparative pay information, moreover, is often hidden from the employees' view. Employers may keep under wraps the pay differentials maintained among supervisors, no less the reasons for those differentials. Small initial discrepancies may not be seen as meet for a federal case, particularly when the employee, trying to succeed in a non-traditional environment, is averse to making waves.[62]

Citing precedent she claimed the majority ignored, Ginsburg argued that the "unlawful practice" is the current payment of salaries "infected by gender-based (or race-based) discrimination," which occurs whenever a woman's paycheck is less than a similarly situated man's. In other words, gender-based wage disparities are most often the "cumulative effect of individual acts." The majority identified only the "pay-setting decision," discrete from prior and subsequent decisions, as the "unlawful practice." Lilly Ledbetter's salary fell 15 to 40 percent behind those of her male coworkers as a result of the repetition of pay decisions undervaluing her work. Under the Court's ruling, "each and every pay decision she did not immediately challenge wiped the slate clean. Consideration may not be given to the cumulative effect of a series of decisions that, together, set her pay well below that of every male area manager. Knowingly carrying past pay discrimination forward must be treated as lawful conduct."[63] Ginsburg argued that the majority issued a "cramped interpretation of Title VII" at odds with the statute's broad and robust protection against workplace discrimination, and she urged Congress to "correct this Court's parsimonious reading of Title VII."

The reaction to the *Ledbetter* decision was swift. Women's advocates decried the decision as a setback for women and a setback for civil rights. Business groups applauded what they called a "fair decision," one that the US Chamber of Commerce said "eliminates a potential wind-fall against employers by employees trying to dredge up stale pay claims."[64] Lilly Ledbetter was invited to speak to the delegates at the Democratic National Convention held in Denver, Colorado, on August 26, 2008 (Women's Equality Day). She said:

> I'm here to talk about America's commitment to fairness and equality, and how people like me—and like you—suffer when that commitment is betrayed. How fitting that I speak to you on Women's Equality Day, when we celebrate ratification of the amendment that gave women the right to vote. Even as we celebrate, let's also remind ourselves: the fight for equality is not over. I know that from personal experience. I was a trailblazer when I went to work as a female supervisor at a Goodyear tire plant in Gadsden, Alabama. . . . Despite praising me for my work, Goodyear gave me smaller raises than my male co-managers, over and over. . . . Those differences affected my family's quality of life then,

IMAGE 7.3: *President Barack Obama signs the Lilly Ledbetter Bill as Vice President Joe Biden, Secretary of State Hillary Clinton, a bipartisan group of Congress persons, and Lilly Ledbetter stand behind, in the East Room of the White House in Washington, D.C., on January 29, 2009.* Source: Official White House Photo by Joyce Boghosian.

and they affect my retirement now. When I discovered the injustice, I thought about moving on. But in the end, I couldn't ignore the discrimination. So I went to court.[65]

Democrats in the House of Representatives filed the first version of the Lilly Ledbetter Fair Pay Act immediately after the Supreme Court's ruling and subsequently passed the bill, but it was defeated in the Senate by Republicans who claimed it would lead to frivolous lawsuits. The House and Senate versions were reintroduced at the start of the 111th Congress in January 2009, and with expanded Democratic majorities in both houses, the bill passed before the month was over. President Barack Obama signed the bill into law, the first of his presidency, on January 29, 2009, effectively nullifying the Supreme Court's decision.

The law amends the Civil Rights Act of 1964 by stating that the 180-day statute of limitation for filing an equal pay lawsuit regarding pay discrimination resets with each new discriminatory paycheck. In signing the bill into law, President Obama said, "I sign this bill for my daughters, and all those who will come after us, because I want them to grow up in a nation that values their contributions, where there are no limits to their dreams and they have opportunities their mothers and grandmothers never could have imagined." While certainly an important tool for pursuing wage discrimination litigation in the courts, the new law does little to enhance the effectiveness of the Equal Pay Act or to redress any of the issues Justice

Ginsburg raised in her dissent. The Paycheck Fairness Act (discussed in the section on the wage gap), if passed by Congress, would offer much more powerful protection against wage discrimination.

THE IMPACT OF FEDERAL POLICIES ON WOMEN'S WORK EXPERIENCES

There is ample evidence that the major federal policies previously described have not entirely eliminated discrimination in employment for women, nor have they fundamentally altered the ways in which men and women experience the workplace. The "dual labor force" is still intact even in the face of advances that women have made in the professions. Women are still more heavily concentrated in "women's jobs" at the low end of the pay and prestige scales, which are less likely to carry the benefits that provide health care for women and their families. The wage gap remains real, even accounting for occupational differences and education. The WAGE (Women Are Getting Even) Project estimates that over a lifetime (roughly forty-seven years of full-time work), the wage gap amounts to a $700,000 loss for a high-school-educated woman, a $1.2 million loss for a college-educated woman, and a financial penalty of more than $2 million for women with graduate or professional degrees.[66] Workplace climate issues were raised in a very public way in both Clarence Thomas's Senate confirmation hearings and in President Clinton's impeachment hearings in the House of Representatives and trial in the Senate. More recently, sexual harassment allegations led to the resignation of Roger Ailes, chairman and CEO of Fox News, in 2016. Sexual harassment remains a very real threat to many women's security and advancement, even though stricter laws have been established to punish offenders. In this section, we will examine how contemporary women enter and experience the workplace three decades after the major federal equal employment laws were passed.

Advances in Professions but Occupational Segregation Still Rules

The combination of Title IX (see Chapter 6) and federal affirmative action goals has motivated professional programs to examine their admissions policies and the gender balance in their classrooms. Title IX eliminated quotas for women in specific programs, allowing women to compete for admission on their merits. The result was a steady increase in the number of women enrolled in law, medicine, engineering, science, and dentistry postgraduate programs. Between 1974 and 1994, overall job growth was fastest for managers and other professionals; in 1994, 7 million women held managerial and professional positions, almost double the number in 1974.[67] In 1990, the typical employed woman was more likely to be in an administrative support job than in a managerial or professional job. In 2000, just a decade later, the reverse was true.[68] Today, 41 percent of employed women are classified as management or professionals, with another 30 percent working in sales and office positions.[69]

Virginia Valian examined men's and women's advancement in the professions using both aggregate data (all men and women) to examine trends and cohort data (men and women born in the same year) to compare men and women with identical education and backgrounds. She made sure to note similarities in human capital, a variable that represents education, experience, and other qualifications, and which is often used to dismiss the size of the wage gap. Valian found that men in business, medicine, government, and the law advanced more easily than women in the same professions.[70] In 1978, two women were heads of Fortune 1000 companies in the United States—a number that remained unchanged in 1994. In 1996, four women headed up Fortune 1000 companies. Ten years later, in 2016, women held twenty of the CEO positions at Fortune 500 companies (4 percent).

Why so few? When Valian examined the relative progress made by men and women in the same cohort who had college degrees and MBAs, she found that men were promoted more quickly and advanced to higher salary grades more quickly than women were. She noted a similar situation for engineers, concluding: "In engineering, as elsewhere, men accumulate advantage more easily than women do."[71] Women were overrepresented in lower-prestige ranks, and men were overrepresented in higher-prestige ranks, even though both the men and the women had identical training, education, and experience. Alice H. Eagly and Linda L. Carlie employ a labyrinth metaphor to explain why a few women reach the highest leadership positions, but the majority do not: "For women who aspire to top leadership, routes exist but are full of twists and turns, both unexpected and expected."[72] Among the barriers creating walls in the labyrinth, Eagly and Carli include vestiges of sex discrimination, particularly related to marriage and parenthood, which promote men's careers and stymie women's. There remains a resistance to women's leadership born of the clash between communal and agentic qualities that put women in a bind (see Chapter 4 for an application of this theory to female political candidates). Personal qualities and dominant behavior that are attributed to effective leadership or leadership potential in men often lead to women being vilified or labeled negatively. If women are too communal, they don't "have what it takes"; if they are too agentic, they aren't likable and warm. Self-promotion is not rewarded in women; since being modest and considerate is socially expected of women, they do not receive any additional points in leadership potential if they display this behavior, while in men it is viewed as "impressive." Women in leadership are acutely aware of these contradictions. A Catalyst study of Fortune 1000 female executives found that 96 percent of them said that developing "a style with which male managers are comfortable" was either critical or fairly important.[73]

Another explanation for the barrier that prevents otherwise qualified women from attaining the highest positions has been labeled the **glass ceiling**.[74] When Carly Fiorina was appointed president and CEO of Hewlett-Packard, she proclaimed that there was no glass ceiling for women, only to later characterize it as a "dumb thing to say." After her firing in 2005, she published a memoir, *Tough Choices*, in which she detailed the ways in which the corporate world is still a difficult place to be a woman. In an interview with *Salon*, she noted, "I thought when I went to HP that we had come further than we had. I hoped I was advancing women in business by putting women in positions of responsibility. But it's clear that we don't yet play by the same rules and it's clear that there aren't enough women in business, and the stereotypes will exist as long as there aren't enough of us."[75] Women of color have characterized the glass ceiling as more of a **concrete ceiling**. The metaphor is intended to convey how difficult it is for women of color to penetrate their advancement ceiling; unlike white women, women of color cannot even see through the concrete to "catch a glimpse of the corner office."[76] Surveys of women of color in management reveal that a lack of networking opportunities is perceived as the number one barrier to advancement. A vast amount of research literature documents the power of the old-boy network in excluding women's participation in the types of informal informational exchanges that result in client referrals and overall advancement in an organization.[77]

The glass ceiling has barely been cracked in boardrooms. In 2014, women occupied 19.2 percent of the seats in US boardrooms—80 percent were white, 12 percent African American, 4.4 percent Latina, and 3.7 percent Asian. Women hold a larger share of seats at European stock index companies. In Norway, for example, women hold 35.5 percent of board seats.[78] A study by Catalyst found men and women equally ambitious for top corporate leadership positions. Fifty-five percent of female respondents and 57 percent of male respondents aspired to their organization's top position. Similarly, roughly equal numbers of men and women reported that they did not want the top job (26 percent of female executives, 29 percent of the males). Having children made no difference to the level of ambition expressed by women or men. Ambition was particularly strong among individuals in line positions (82 percent of women and 77 percent of men). The survey also found that men and women shared similar advancement strategies (consistently exceeding performance expectations, successfully managing others, seeking high-visibility assignments, and demonstrating expertise) and have experienced similar barriers to advancement (displaying a behavioral style that is different from an organization's norm, lacking general management or line experience, and lacking awareness of organizational politics).[79] The differences uncovered were between men's and women's experiences. Women reported encountering gender-based stereotypes, exclusion from informal networks, lack of role models, and an inhospitable corporate culture.

A related phenomenon is the **glass cliff**. A study cited by BBC News found that women are often promoted to leadership positions once a company is doing badly. Given a choice between a male candidate and a female candidate at such times, companies were much more likely to choose the female candidate. The author of the study labels the trend a "new form of subtle discrimination."[80] Still, a recent report by Catalyst suggests that women at the top benefit the company financially: "On average, companies with the highest percentage of women in top management outperform companies with the lowest percentage."[81]

Women currently earn 47.3 percent of all the law degrees in the United States and make up 36 percent of American attorneys. Women account for 35.5 percent of federal circuit court of appeals judges and 33 percent of federal district court judges, and three women serve as justices on the US Supreme Court. Women hold 27 percent of all federal and state judgeships. Minority women are further underrepresented, making up less than 3 percent of the profession and less than 1 percent of law firm partners. The American Bar Association's Commission on Women in the Profession concluded that "in both law firms and corporate legal departments, women of color receive less compensation than men and white women; are denied equal access to significant assignments, mentoring and sponsorship opportunities; receive fewer promotions; and have the highest rate of attrition."[82] Women attorneys in 2016 earned a median income of $82,680, compared to men's median earnings of $99,580 (calculated as salary without bonus or other incentive pay).[83]

Exacerbating the slow progress for women in the legal field is the perception, particularly among men, that "full equality is upon us or just around the corner. Only 3 percent of male lawyers think that prospects for advancement in the legal profession are greater for men than for women."[84] A study by the American Bar Association (ABA) suggests that most attorneys equate gender bias with intentional discrimination. However, the major barriers to women's advancement uncovered by the study include unconscious stereotypes, inadequate access to support networks, inflexible workplace structures, sexual harassment, and bias in the justice system.[85] The problem is as much a sticky floor as it is a glass ceiling—the income gap between male and female lawyers begins during the first year of practice and widens from there.[86] According to the National Association for Law Placement, in 2016 only about 18 percent of the partners at major law firms nationwide were women, a figure that has risen only slightly since 1995, when about 13 percent of partners were women.[87]

The attrition rate for women attorneys is more than double that of men within the first two years and thereafter, and it is even higher for women of color. Eighty-five percent of minority female attorneys in the United States will quit large firms within seven years of starting their practice. Deborah Rhode, author of the ABA's report "The Unfinished Agenda" and a professor at Stanford Law School, argues that women who aspire to leadership roles in firms face "double standards and double binds." Women are rated lower, particularly by male evaluators, when they adopt a typically "masculine" style of authority. Women attorneys suffer from a presumption of incompetence and are therefore held to higher standards than their male counterparts, especially if they are mothers: "Those who want extended leaves or reduced schedules appear to be lacking as professionals. Those who seem willing to sacrifice family needs to workplace schedules appear to be lacking as mothers." Workplace structures fail to accommodate family commitments. Even though more than 90 percent of firms report allowing associates part-time schedules, only 3 to 4 percent of lawyers actually use them. Finally, women in law (as in business and electoral politics) lack access to mentors and supportive networks.[88]

Today, more women are choosing careers in medicine. Nearly a third of all practicing physicians are women, and they account for more than 60 percent of pediatricians and more than 51 percent of obstetricians/gynecologists. Forty-six percent of all physicians in training and almost half of all medical students are women, according to the Association of American Medical Colleges (AAMC). More than 60 percent of trainees in dermatology are women, and the number of female general surgery trainees is now 38 percent. Two-thirds of black applicants to medical school are women. But while the number of women physicians is rising, women make up a little more than a third of full-time academic medicine faculty, and women remain less likely than men to be full professors in medical schools.[89]

In terms of salary, women fare better when pay is based on hourly wages, with female doctors earning nearly 87 percent of male doctors' earnings. However, 55 percent of women, compared with 42 percent of men, practice in the three lowest-paying specialties—pediatrics, general practice, and general internal medicine. Conversely, only 14 percent of women work in the four highest-paying fields (radiology, general surgery, anesthesiology, and subspecialty surgery), compared with 27 percent of men.[90] Valian found that men and women choose specialties that are congruent with gender expectations and that senior medical staff encouraged young medical students to choose specialties that conformed to gender roles. Like their counterparts in law, women in medical school find a predominantly male faculty, even though in 2015 women made up more than 48 percent of the applicants. As the Association of American Medical Colleges notes, "The number of women entering medical school has led to the premature conclusion that gender equality has been achieved."[91]

In computer science and technology, gains made by women in the 1980s and early 1990s have actually eroded. Even with projected growth of 15–20 percent between 2012 and 2022, the vast majority of computer science jobs will be pursued and filled by men. As STEM-related industries as a whole add more than 1.7 million jobs in the coming years, there continues to be a notable absence of women in the field. As noted in the previous chapter, this trend begins well before entering the job market: girls account for more than half of all advanced placement (AP) test takers, yet boys outnumber girls four to one in taking computer science exams.[92] Although women constitute nearly half of the workforce, they hold just 13 percent of the science and engineering jobs.[93] Women at the top of the educational attainment ladder have made significant inroads into previously male-dominated professions and nontraditional occupations; women and men with at least a four-year degree are considerably more likely to work in occupations that are better integrated in terms of gender than are men and women with lower levels of education. However, the movement toward even greater occupational integration stalled in the 1990s; a phenomenon scholars correlate with a "complete stop" in 1990 to the twenty-year trend in gender integration of college majors.[94] This slowdown or near-stop in gender integration of occupations is true across race and ethnicities as well: "Hispanic men and women are the least likely to work in the same occupations, Asian American men and women, the most likely."[95] Overall, occupational segregation by gender is much stronger than occupational segregation by race. However, gendered occupational segregation is even more pronounced for women of color. For example, 62 percent of Latina women were clustered into just two job categories—service occupations and sales and office occupations (compared to 57 percent of African Americans, 51 percent of whites, and 44 percent of Asian women clustered in the same categories).[96] Only 35 percent of African American women and 26 percent of Latinas were employed in higher-paying management, professional, or related jobs, compared with 48 percent of Asian women and 43 percent of white women. As we will see later in the chapter, occupational gender segregation plays a significant part in the wage gap.

Improvements to the Quality of the Workplace: Ending Sexual Harassment

Sexual harassment is a form of gender discrimination in employment and educational institutions that is covered under Title VII and Title IX, respectively. The EEOC defines **sexual harassment** as

> unwelcome sexual advances, requests for sexual favors, and other verbal or physical conduct of a sexual nature constitute sexual harassment when (1) submission to such conduct is made either explicitly or implicitly a term or condition of an individual's employment; (2) submission to or rejection of such conduct by an individual is used as a basis for employment decisions affecting such individual; or (3) such conduct has the purpose or effect of unreasonably interfering with an individual's work performance or creating an intimidating, hostile, or offensive working environment.[97]

The EEOC's regulation encompasses the two most common types of harassment: quid pro quo (an exchange of favors) and creating a hostile environment. The standards for applying Title VII to allegations of sexual harassment in the workplace were developed by a series of federal circuit court decisions and the EEOC before a case ever reached the Supreme Court.

In 1986, ruling in *Meritor Savings Bank v. Vinson*, the Court outlined a pattern of proof of hostile environment cases, in which the plaintiff must show that (1) she was subjected to unwelcome sexual conduct, (2) it was based on her sex, (3) it was sufficiently pervasive or severe to create an abusive or hostile work environment, and (4) the employer knew or should have known of the harassment and failed to take prompt and appropriate remedial action.[98] The Court specifically took note of the EEOC guidelines in deciding the *Meritor* case, which prompted the lower courts to do the same.

In determining the character of "unwelcome" sexual advances and the severity of an abusive or hostile work environment, the courts have tended to use a "reasonableness standard." This means that, under similar circumstances, would a "reasonable person" in the harasser's position have known the behavior was unwelcome? Feminists objected to this standard, arguing that harassers are usually men and that men do not have a good track record when it comes to understanding the seriousness of sexual harassment or the difference between "teasing" and "harassment." The courts later adopted a standard of reasonableness from the victim's perspective, noting that the previous standard ran the risk of reinforcing the prevailing level of discrimination. In *Ellison v. Brady*, the Ninth Circuit Court of Appeals adopted the perspective of a "reasonable woman." In its ruling, the court was careful not to establish a higher level of protection for women (a fear expressed by some liberal feminists), noting: "A gender-conscious examination of sexual harassment enables women to participate in the workplace on an equal footing with men. By acknowledging and not trivializing the effects of sexual harassment on reasonable women, courts can work toward ensuring that neither men nor women will have to 'run a gauntlet of sexual abuse in return for the privilege of being allowed to work and make a living.'" Thus, when a male plaintiff alleges a hostile environment, the standard would be that of a "reasonable man."

The courts' willingness to hold an employer accountable for the behavior of its managerial and supervisory employees has prompted most businesses and schools to develop policies on sexual harassment. These policies include guidelines on how to report incidents of harassment and procedures for an internal resolution of the complaint. A victim of sexual harassment may file a sex discrimination claim with the EEOC. In the nine months following the televised Anita Hill–Clarence Thomas hearings in 1991, the EEOC reported a 60 percent increase in the number of complaints. Included in the Civil Rights Act of 1991 are provisions allowing victims of sexual harassment to sue for monetary damages (up to $300,000). In the 1993 case *Harris v. Forklift Systems*, the Supreme Court ruled that a victim of sexual harassment need only demonstrate impairment of work or education to prove that an environment is hostile, even though lower courts had been heading toward requiring evidence of severe psychological harm.

In 1998, the Court heard *Oncale v. Sundowner Offshore Services*, the first case to consider whether Title VII applies to sexual harassment between persons of the same sex. Joseph Oncale worked for a Louisiana offshore oil company. Oncale claimed that other male employees, including two with supervisory authority over him, had psychologically and physically abused him. All of the men involved were heterosexual. The company defended the behavior of its employees and characterized the content and intensity of the behavior as "simply hazing" and the product of an all-male environment. Ultimately, Oncale quit and filed suit. The lower federal courts dismissed the case, saying that Title VII does not apply to claims of same-sex harassment. In a unanimous ruling for the Supreme Court, Justice Antonin Scalia wrote that Title VII protected men from discrimination and that its protection against sexual harassment extended to same-sex conduct. The Court applied the "reasonable person" standard in determining that the behavior was so severe that it could be classified as sex discrimination.[99] Thus sexual harassment results from gender-based hostility manifested as sexualized conduct, normally between a woman and a male employer or authority figure, but not exclusively so. *Oncale* suggests that it is the hostility and the severity of the behavior, even if directed at a member of one's own sex, that makes sexual harassment illegal under Title VII. Two cases decided after *Oncale* indicate that the courts will continue to apply the protections of Title VII to cases in which individuals are harassed for not exemplifying the gender norms expected of their sex. In other words, illegal sexual harassment can also include victimization of males for not being "manly" enough.[100]

One might think that twenty-five years after sexual harassment was brought to the public's attention by the Clarence Thomas Senate confirmation hearings and subsequent policy actions, high-profile cases of sexual harassment would be a thing of the past. Not so. In July 2016, allegations that Roger Ailes, chairman and CEO of Fox News, had sexually harassed women for decades thrust the issue back into the news. Former Fox anchor Gretchen Carlson filed the first lawsuit against Ailes on July 6, 2016. Due to the widespread media attention and an internal investigation by the network, more than twenty-five women came forward with similar stories, including popular on-air personality Megyn Kelly. Ailes was said to have frequently made inappropriate comments to women in private meetings and asked them to twirl around so he could examine their figures; and there were persistent rumors that Ailes propositioned female employees and Fox interns for sexual favors. "The fact that these incidents of harassment were so common may have contributed to why no one at Fox came forward or filed a lawsuit until now. Ailes's attitudes about women permeated the very air of the network, from the exclusive hiring of attractive women to the strictly enforced skirts-and-heels dress code to the 'leg cam' that lingers on female panelists' crossed legs on air. It was hard to complain about something that was so normalized," noted an article in

New York Magazine.[101] Ailes was fired by the network's owner, Rupert Murdoch, and left Fox News on July 21, 2016. That sexual harassment had become so much a part of a major network's culture that it went unreported is evidence of the limits of law and policy to intervene.

A new area of harassment takes place outside the office setting—harassment of women online. An Australian study conducted in 2016 confirmed that harassment of women online is at risk of becoming "an established norm in our digital society."[102] The Australian researchers found that among women under thirty, 76 percent had experienced some form of abuse or harassment online, ranging from unwanted contact, **trolling**, and cyberbullying to threats of rape and death. One in four women had received general threats of physical violence, and one in four lesbian, bisexual, and transgender women had experienced online harassment. While men also experience online threats, women received twice as many threats involving sexual violence or death. Although most of the women surveyed believed the problem was getting worse, they also felt helpless to stop it, and only 10 percent ever reported the threats to police.

A Pew Research Center report found that in the United States, the incidence of online harassment and abuse is similar to that documented by Australian researchers, but that only 5 percent ever reported the problem to police. In part the lack of reporting stems from a perceived disconnect between the online world many young professionals now occupy full-time and the face-to-face world of law enforcement and the judicial system. Journalist Amanda Hess writes about feminism and Internet culture, earning her a fair share of online harassment and physical threats. When she reported a particularly scary set of threats in 2014, the officer taking the report asked, "What is Twitter?"[103] Video game designer Brianna Wu attracted a firestorm of abuse when she talked about online harassment in an interview. Law enforcement told her to "turn off her computer and walk away."

Congresswoman Katherine Clark (D-Mass.) has introduced a number of bills designed to elevate the problem of online harassment and abuse among the priorities of the FBI and other law enforcement agencies. She sponsored the Interstate Swatting Hoax Act of 2015, a bill designed to punish "swatting," when someone deceives law enforcement into responding to a made-up emergency in order to harass the target of the swat. In March 2016, she introduced the Cybercrime Enforcement Training Assistance Act, a proposal that would provide federal grant money to local law enforcement for the prevention, enforcement, and prosecution of online crimes against individuals.[104] Women have reacted by creating women-only spaces on the Internet. The past two years have seen a proliferation of invitation-only listservs, private Slack channels, and closed Facebook groups with names like "Girls Night Out," "Female Founders," and "No Boys Allowed."[105]

THE WAGE GAP: THE LEGAL EQUALITY DOCTRINE'S ULTIMATE TEST

While Title IX and Title VII opened doors to education and employment in well-paying professions previously limited to men by custom or quota, the Equal Pay Act, the first among the major federal equality initiatives, has not effectively guaranteed women equal pay. Regardless of occupation, experience, skills, age, or education, a pay gap remains, although it varies in size. Race and ethnicity increase the wage gap relative to white men, regardless of women's experience or education. There is no question that progress has been made in closing the gap, but as you can see in Figure 7.1, the slope of each line is relatively flat, meaning that progress has been incremental and the gap remains.

The wage gap is a complicated social and economic phenomenon with multiple sources and no easy solutions. In this section we will review several of the leading causes of the wage gap, including occupational segregation, time spent on work, education and experience, and discrimination. (We will cover the presence of children as a major contributor to the wage gap—a penalty for mothers, but an enhancement for fathers—in Chapter 8.) Next, we will assess ways to close the remaining wage gap, including legislation on comparable worth and wage transparency, encouraging careers beyond traditionally gendered occupations to alleviate occupational segregation, and workplace practices that reduce discrimination. Adjusting the minimum wage is also a way to address the gender gap, and that is discussed in greater detail later in this chapter. Policies that hold employees harmless for taking time off to care for themselves (paid sick leave, annual leave) or for a family member (family and medical leave) and flexible work arrangements will be discussed in Chapter 8.

There are a variety of ways to display the size of the gender wage gap. The oft-reported wage ratio of 79 percent (often expressed as a wage gap of 21 percent) is based on men's and women's annual median earnings for people who work a minimum of thirty-five hours a week (full-time) and all year. In 2014, men's median earnings were $50,383 compared to women's median earnings of $39,621.[106] However, this calculation does not account for differences in occupations, and it is less sensitive to how much individuals work than an hourly wage calculation. Based on hourly median earnings, men's median hourly earnings were $14.39 per hour compared with women's median hourly earnings of $12.18 in 2014.[107] This works out to a wage ratio of 85 percent, or a wage gap of 15 percent. Sixty percent of workers are paid hourly; the benefit of using median hourly earnings is that it captures both full-time and part-time work. Expressing the wage differential in hourly earnings rather than annual earnings does not include jobs that pay a salary, primarily management or professional occupations. There are a variety of other ways to calculate the differences between men's and women's pay, but together they demonstrate that while the wage gap has narrowed over time, it has not been eliminated. There are several potential sources of the remaining pay differential.

FIGURE 7.1: Wage Gap by Gender, Race, and Ethnicity, 1975–2014

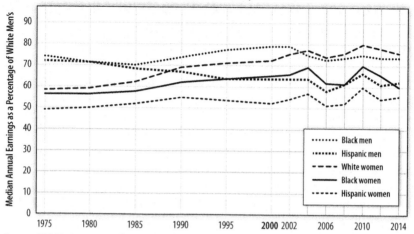

Source: US Department of Labor, Bureau of Labor Statistics, Women's Bureau, "Highlights of Women's Earnings," Statistics and Data, 1975–2015; Institute for Women's Policy Research, "The Gender Wage Gap," by year 2008–2014.

Sources of the Wage Gap

Earlier, we discussed occupational segregation (which economists also call occupational crowding) as a central feature of women's experience in the gendered economy and a major contributor to the wage gap. Occupations dominated by men pay more than occupations where the vast majority of employees are women. Twenty-six of the thirty occupations with the highest earnings are male dominated, while twenty-three of the thirty occupations at the bottom of the earnings scale are female dominated. Even though women have made progress in entering nontraditional careers, most of that change happened prior to the 2000s, and in some of the most common occupations for women there has been little change at all: "Women were more than nine in ten pre-school and kindergarten teachers, hair dressers and cosmetologists, and dental hygienists in 1972, and they are more than nine in ten now."[108] Economists have developed an index to measure the change in occupational segregation over time—it compares the share of women in each individual occupation to the share of women in the labor force overall and then calculates how many women (or men) would have to change occupations to get to a state where each individual occupation mirrors the distribution of men and women in the economy as a whole. Using this methodology, researchers calculated that half of women or half of men would have to change occupations for there to be gender parity across occupations.[109] One study by economists Francine Blau and Lawrence Kahn attributes 51 percent of the wage gap today to sex-segregated jobs.[110]

If men and women redistributed themselves to achieve a state of parity, would the wage gap disappear? Probably not; as women enter a previously male-dominated field, the pay declines. In a large study based on US Census data from 1950 to 2000, researchers found that when "women moved into occupations in large numbers, those jobs began paying less even after controlling for education, work experience, skills, race and geography."[111] This study examined two possible hypotheses drawn from sociology and economics: queuing and devaluation. Queuing characterizes a situation in which both men and women might like to work in highly compensated occupations, but employers prefer men and discriminatory hiring practices result in women clustering in low-wage occupations. Devaluation posits that it doesn't really matter whether men and women are attracted to or assigned to specific occupations because the discriminatory effect happens after the hire, when assigning pay: "Employers ascribe a lower value for the work done in occupations with a high share of females and consequently set lower wage levels."[112] During the period of study, as more women became recreation workers, median hour wages declined 57 percent. Wages declined as women became designers (34 percent drop) or biologists (18 percent drop). But wages rose as more men entered a field previously dominated by women. In short, women are clustered in the lowest-paying occupations, whether they gravitate there to find more flexibility or because they are driven there by employers' preference in hiring males for higher-paying jobs. And a shift by women from traditional to nontraditional occupations would not erase the pay gap because it is women who are devalued and not the work itself.

A long-standing explanation for the pay gap has to do with human capital—the skills, education, and experience a worker brings to the job. Prior to the 1970s, there was a sizable gap between men and women in human capital. Today, however, women earn more than half of all bachelor's, master's, and doctoral degrees awarded by US colleges and universities. As we noted in Chapter 6, educational attainment is positively correlated with earnings. For all workers, the educational wage gap is quite clear—college graduates earn more than twice what high school graduates earn. Economists predict that within just a few years, a majority of all jobs in the United States will require vocational training or education beyond a high school diploma. Experience in the labor pool is another form of human capital, and the market rewards continuous years of uninterrupted work. Although women are more likely than men to take a short leave for the birth of a child, both men and women now expect to work throughout their lifetimes. A majority of women are in the paid labor force, and a majority of women with children are working. Indeed, much of the decline in the wage gap has been associated with women's increased education and experience. However, as women surpass men in education and experience, the impact on the wage gap runs in the other direction. "Once we hold differences in men's and women's experience constant, the pay gap

Box 7.1 – Point of Comparison

The Global Gender Wage Gap

Accrding to the World Economic Forum's (WEF) 2015 Global Gender Gap Report, it will take approximately 118 years until the global pay gap between men and women is closed. According to the latest figures, the average full-time salary for a working woman is $11,102 a year—little more than half the male average of $20,554. Women's average salary today almost matches men's average salary in 2006 ($11,351; women's pay then was $6,117).[1] These figures are part of the WEF's annual report on all aspects of the gender gap, which also covers education, health, and political empowerment. The WEF Global Gender Index ranks 145 countries on economic participation, educational attainment, health, and political engagement. Global averages inevitably mask huge differences between countries and even regions.

In the table below, you will find data from two sources—the WEF Global Gender Index and the Organization for Economic Cooperation and Development (OECD). The OECD includes thirty-five developed nations. The OECD Gender Wage Gap for full-time employment is calculated as the difference between male and female median wages divided by male median wages.

For Critical Analysis

There is no country with a zero wage gap. There is no country in the world in which women's median wages exceed men's median wages. This chapter has explored a number of explanations for the wage gap. Given the figures before you, will we reach a point where women and men earn equal wages? Why or why not?

actually widens; 20 years ago taking account of differences in education narrowed our estimates of the pay gap," notes a report produced by the National Equal Pay Task Force.[113] In research on the role of employment experience in explaining the gender wage gap, Michal Myck and Gillian Paull found an inverse relationship between experience and compensation for women. In other words, as women gained more experience, the relative value of experience to setting wages diminished.[114]

At no time are men and women more like one another in education and experience than at college graduation. A study by the American Association of University Women (AAUW) examined the gender pay gap for college graduates. One year out of college, women working full-time earn only 80 percent as much as their male colleagues. To be sure, the choice of major in college and occupational field

Country	Gender Wage Gap (OECD) %	Full-Time Equivalent Employment Rates W% / M% (OECD)	WEF 2015 Economic Participation and Opportunity	WEF 2015 Gender Equality Ranking
New Zealand	5.6	57 / 83	30	10
Belgium	5.9	48 / 67	34	19
Denmark	6.8	54 / 67	20	14
Norway	7.0	58 / 71	1	2
Hungary	8.7	54 / 69	62	99
Greece	11.3	40 / 64	87	87
Ireland	12.8	70 / 93	26	5
Germany	13.4	53 / 80	38	11
Slovak Rep	14.8	57 / 68	93	97
Iceland	14.5	70 / 93	5	1
OECD Avg.	15.5	57 / 88	—	—
United States	17.9	57 / 77	6	28

Sources: World Economic Forum (WEF), *Global Gender Gap Report 2015*, www3.weforum.org/docs/GGGR2015/cover.pdf; Organization for Economic Cooperation and Development (OECD), Gender Equality Data Portal, www.oecd.org/gender/data.

plays a role in the size of the gap; however, even between men and women with the same major and in the same occupation, a pay gap remains. In education, a female-dominated major, women earn 95 percent as much as their male colleagues just one year after graduation. In biological sciences, a mixed-gender major, women earn only 75 percent as much as men. In mathematics, still largely a male-dominated field, women earn 76 percent as much as their male colleagues.[115] The gender gap widens significantly as men and women approach midcareer (ages thirty-five to forty-four). The pay ratio for early-career women (ages twenty-five to thirty-four) went from 68 cents in 1979 to 92 cents in 2011 before falling back to 90 cents in 2016. A midcareer woman would have experienced a 58 cent pay ratio in 1979 and now earns just 81 cents to a midcareer man's dollar. In 2014, the pay ratio for the two oldest groups of working women was estimated at 77 cents for those forty-five to fifty-four and 76 cents for those fifty-five to sixty-four.

Time spent on work is often cited as the principal difference between men and women working full-time and year round. Men work more hours and are more likely than women to work overtime. Economists call this overwork, defined as consistently working at least fifty hours per week. A 2014 study based on Bureau of Labor Statistics between 1979 and 2009 examines the role of overwork in explaining the plateau in closing the wage gap. As men increased their overwork and earned overtime compensation for the extra hours, their income relative to women's increased. Although, theoretically, egalitarian attitudes today mean that both men and women can extend their work hours, the researchers argue that women face "essentialist" expectations for intensive mothering that limit their ability to increase their wage with overwork: "In the context of rising relative wages for overwork, gender essentialism about caregiving may exacerbate the motherhood penalty in wages and stagnate the gender wage gap trend by limiting mothers' ability to benefit from these rising prices."[116] The Pew Research Foundation confirms that mothers more than fathers reduce work hours to care for a child or other family member (42 percent of mothers, 28 percent of fathers).[117] In recognition of this reality, economist Claudia Golden argues that increasing workplace flexibility is one of the last remaining hurdles for women to achieve parity in the workplace.[118]

What about the effect of discrimination and bias in hiring, work assignment, and promotion? Just as forms of sexual harassment have become more subtle, so too has bias in employment decisions. Removing gender information reduces the bias. Claudia Goldin and Cecelia Rouse found that if women auditioned for symphony orchestras from behind a screen so that their sex was not evident, they were more likely to be hired.[119] In a variety of studies, researchers have demonstrated that among identical resumes where only the name is changed, gender impacts whether the applicant is hired, the starting salary offer, and the interview panel's overall assessment of the candidate on qualities such as competence and likability. Recall the bias exhibited by STEM faculty in hiring students for a laboratory manager's position in a study included in Chapter 6.[120] Similar findings are reported across occupations and across disciplines in academia.

Even if a woman successfully navigates bias in the hiring process, once employed she may find herself judged as less competent and less "likable" than her male colleagues. This bias is exhibited by both male and female employers. Examining the workplace experiences of transgender people offers another field experiment in which to measure gender bias. Researchers have documented that while transgender people have the same human capital after their transition, their workplace outcome often changes radically. Average earnings for female-to-male transgender workers increase slightly following their gender transitions, while average earnings for male-to-female transgender workers fall by one-third. A loss of earnings is often accompanied by a loss of authority and rise in harassment. Alternatively, becoming a man often brings an increase in respect and authority.[121]

Another set of explanations for the wage gap has to do with women's behavior in applying for competitive jobs and bargaining for salary once an offer has been extended. Economists have found that women are less likely to apply for jobs described as competitive or for jobs where the compensation is based on individual performance in a competitive atmosphere. Women tend to be attracted to positions that promise certainty in compensation and the opportunity for team-based work.[122] Another intriguing explanation for the residual wage gap comes from research on women's willingness to negotiate salary. Linda Babcock and Sara Laschever used experimental conditions to test whether an individual's sex was correlated with his or her willingness to bargain. For example, volunteers in a laboratory setting were asked to play the word game Boggle and were told that they would be paid anywhere from $3 to $10 for their time. After playing the game, each subject was given $3 and asked if the sum was acceptable. Male subjects were eight times more likely than female subjects to ask for more money. When the conditions of the experiment were changed slightly so that all of the subjects were explicitly told that their payment was negotiable (thus giving them tacit permission to bargain), the gender gap remained. Only 58 percent of the women, compared to 83 percent of the men, asked for more money. Finally, in a survey of master's degree graduates about their actual first job offers, the researchers found that four times as many men as women had negotiated for a higher salary rather than simply accepting the first offer (51 percent of the men, compared to 12.5 percent of the women). Those who negotiated were rewarded with an average salary 7.4 percent higher than those who had not bargained.[123]

However, this finding is tempered somewhat by research that identified perceptual bias against women who tried to negotiate.[124] Both men and women in this study were likely to subtly penalize women who asked for a higher salary. Volunteer subjects were asked to decide whether they would hire each of the candidates. Although both men and women were negatively affected by bargaining, the size of the negative impact for women was twice that for men. Likewise, when asked to rate whether they would be willing to work with each of the candidates, male volunteers tended to rate negatively women who had negotiated, but they were less likely to similarly penalize men; female volunteers rated negatively both men and women who bargained and preferred those who accepted the offered salary. Overall, women who negotiated were perceived as "less nice." Similar studies found that male and female job applicant behavior was modified by the sex of the employer making the job offer—women were more likely to negotiate if the offer came from another woman. Thus, "there is an economic rationale to negotiate, but you have to weigh that against the social risks of negotiating. Those risks are higher for women than for men."[125] Given this research, advocates for pay equality have recommended training and coaching women to be more effective at negotiation or banning bargaining altogether. As interim CEO of Reddit, Ellen Pao banned the practice of salary negotiation. As an article in the *Atlantic* pointed out, "Pao argued that negotiation was always going to be a man's game, and that instead of asking women to behave like men, just ban the practice."[126]

There are those who believe the wage gap is attributable to women's choices, presumably independent of or in full knowledge of the variables we have just reviewed. Conservative economist Diana Furchtgott-Roth testified before the EEOC that "the average wage gap is not proof of widespread discrimination, but of women making choices about their educational and professional careers in a society where the law has granted them equality of opportunity to do so." Labeling the wage gap a product of the popular media culture's "women as victims" theory, Furchtgott-Roth and Christine Solba of the ideologically conservative American Enterprise Institute and the Independent Women's Forum argue that self-selected statistics and anecdotal evidence have led women and policy makers to believe a myth that stems from faulty methodology and an unwillingness to admit that women have made progress in the last three decades.[127] But as we have seen, for women and men with the same education, continuous years in the workforce, age, and occupation, the adjusted wage gap still exists, although it is much smaller.

In Search of a Resolution to the Wage Gap Problem

For each likely cause of the wage gap, we have briefly mentioned a potential remedy. In this section, we will review more formal ways to address the persistence of gender-based pay differentials, including legislation and executive orders on comparable worth and salary transparency, actions by states, and changes to the structure of paid employment. **Equal Pay Day**, celebrated in April, marks the day each year on which women as a group "catch up"—in other words, how far into a second year women must work to earn what men earned in one year. It is an occasion to call attention to the wage gap and to examine progress toward closing the wage gap between women and men. African American women are paid, on average, just 64 percent of what white men are paid each year. Black women's Equal Pay Day is celebrated as a day of action in August as a result.

One way to close the gap would be to focus on **comparable worth** and **pay equity** rather than equal pay for equal work. The Equal Pay Act of 1963 has done little to address the effects of employment patterns contributing to the wage gap (occupational segregation, differential pay within occupations due to gender bias, etc.) that lead so many women to do women's work for women's wages. Advocates of the original Equal Pay Act gave up the words "equal pay for comparable work" in order to get the bill passed. In recent years the concept of comparable worth has returned as a public policy issue. Comparable-worth legislation would ensure that women who work as prison matrons, for example, would be paid the same as men who work as prison guards. Similarly, 911 dispatchers would receive the same pay as emergency operators at the fire department, a social worker's wages would equal those of a probation officer, and a nursery worker who tends children would not be paid less than a nursery worker who tends plants.[128] In an attempt to garner public support, advocates of comparable worth have adopted the rhetoric of "paycheck fairness." As we have seen repeatedly, a change in the status or conditions women face is much more likely to be accomplished in the name of "fairness" than in the pursuit of "sameness." Some opponents of comparable worth still worry that men's wages will be depressed under such an arrangement, while others recognize the large redistribution of income that would be required to eliminate the dual labor market.

The **Paycheck Fairness Act**, a bill that was first presented in Congress in 1997 and has been introduced in ten successive sessions of Congress without becoming law, would strengthen the penalties that courts may impose for equal pay violations and provide compensatory as well as punitive damages, in addition to back pay, to individuals denied equal pay for equal work. In addition, this bill would authorize class action lawsuits and would direct the Department of Labor to provide public information about strategies for eliminating wage discrimination and to issue guidelines for evaluating comparable jobs. Employees would be able to share pay information, something that is still grounds for dismissal in many workplaces, without employer retaliation. The bill also establishes a competitive grant program to develop salary negotiation training for women and girls. Lisa Maatz of AAUW distinguishes between the Ledbetter Equal Pay Act and the Paycheck Fairness Act this way: "Ledbetter provides the legal basis for the ability to seek redress for discriminatory pay practices; the Paycheck Fairness Act gives individuals the tools to find out that they're being discriminated against in the first place." Opponents to the Paycheck Fairness Act claim that revealing salary information violates privacy; that the wage gap may not exist, and if it does, it is a product of women's choices; and that the legislation would encourage employers to hire only men in order to avoid lawsuits.

President Obama used executive orders in several cases where Congress has failed to act. In 2014 Obama took action to prevent federal contractors from retaliating against employees who choose to discuss their compensation. He also signed a presidential memorandum requiring federal contractors to submit summary data on their employees' compensation, broken down by sex and race, to the Department of Labor. The data are meant to encourage compliance with equal pay laws and to target enforcement. Salary transparency increases wages and shrinks the pay gap. Britain in 2015 introduced a plan requiring companies with 250 employees or more to publicly report their own gender pay gap; Prime Minister David Cameron said that the disclosures "will cast sunlight on the discrepancies and create the pressure we need for change, driving women's wages up."[129] Austria and Belgium have similar requirements. There is good reason to believe this approach will work. In 2014, five companies voluntarily released pay gap data. One of those companies, PricewaterhouseCoopers, did an analysis and found that most of its pay disparity was due to a lack of women in senior positions, so the firm undertook a study of whether it was promoting employees fairly. The company found, "the grade just below partner was 30 percent female, yet only 16 percent of those promoted to partner were women. A year later, the percentage of women promoted to partner had more than doubled."[130] The analysis also found that men passed over for a partnership were routinely offered a retention bonus to encourage them to stay with the company, but women were not. Joanne Lipman observed that there are potential cost savings to be realized in publishing salary data. Companies routinely spend billions of dollars to train employees to recognize unconscious bias, while addressing salary inequities is likely to cost only a fraction as much.[131] American company Salesforce conducted an internal audit and found that female employees were paid less, so the company spent $3 million on adjustments to ensure pay equity. There is every reason to believe that salary transparency would benefit racial and ethnic minorities as well as women.

The wage gap varies by state—it ranges from 35 percent in Louisiana to 10 percent in Washington, D.C. Several states, most notably California, New York, and Massachusetts, have recently passed laws designed to close the wage gap. The California Fair Pay Act of 2015 requires employers to pay equally for "substantially similar work," even if the titles are different or even if men and women work at different job sites. The law also prohibits retaliation against employees who ask about or discuss wages with coworkers. Employees can challenge pay differentials and employers will have to demonstrate that wage differences are due to factors other than sex (e.g., merit or seniority) and that the differences are directly and reasonably related to the job.[132] Massachusetts is the most recent state to adopt a pay equity law. Under the statute, employers may not ask applicants about their salary histories until after they make a job offer that includes compensation, unless the applicants voluntarily disclose the information. It is a common practice for employers to use previous salary information to establish the current offer; since women are often paid less than men, this practice exacerbates women's pay differentials. The Massachusetts law requires equal pay for comparable work and defines comparable as "substantially similar" in skill, effort, responsibility, and working conditions regardless of title. The law also bans salary secrecy and retaliation in ways similar to the California law.[133] The Massachusetts law goes further than any federal action or any other state law to advancing women's pay equity and closing the gender wage gap. Examining the effectiveness of the new law may provide the evidence that Congress needs to take similar action on behalf of the entire workforce.

THE CONSEQUENCES OF A GENDERED ECONOMY

Throughout this chapter, we have examined the ways in which women and men experience work and the economy. In lots of ways, these experiences have converged, but in some important ways the gendered economy produces winners and losers.

Women in the Low-Wage Economy and Poverty Rates

Two-thirds of low-wage workers, who work in jobs that typically pay $10.50 per hour or less, are women.[134] Eighty percent of women working in the low-wage workforce have at least a high school diploma, but only 10 percent have earned a bachelor's degree. The majority are twenty-five to forty-nine years old and single; 47 percent are women of color. Half the women in the low-wage economy work full-time, and a majority work all year.[135] Women in the United States are 35 percent more likely than men to be poor, with single mothers at highest risk.

Washington, D.C., and twenty-nine states had minimum wage rates higher than the federal minimum of $7.25 in 2016, according to the National Conference of State Legislatures. For the six states with no legislation on minimum wage rates (New Hampshire, Alabama, Louisiana, Mississippi, South Carolina, and Tennessee), the national rate applies.[136] New York and California each raised the minimum wage to $15 per hour in 2016. In Oregon, the state legislature passed a series of increases to the state minimum wage scheduled to take effect between 2016 and 2022. Starting with 2023, the state minimum wage rate will be indexed to inflation based on the Consumer Price Index. In addition to the new standard minimum wage, the Oregon law differentiates between urban Portland and non-urban counties.[137] Fifteen dollars per hour is widely viewed as a living wage, high enough for workers to afford a basic standard of living (food, shelter, transportation, insurance, etc.). Of course, whether $15 per hour will really cover living expenses depends on where you live. The living wage for one adult in New York City is calculated at $14.52, but for one adult with one child it rises to $28.24. Municipalities have sometimes worked independently from a state to determine a wage that is generous enough to attract and support a skilled workforce and simultaneously low enough to appeal to employers. Several state legislatures have recently tried to preempt local ordinances to raise the minimum wage, citing the need for consistency.

Occupational segregation contributes to women's poverty—6.5 million women work in occupations that have median earnings for full-time work that are lower than the federal poverty threshold for a family of four, which was $462 per week in 2015.[138] These occupations are also characterized by fluctuations in demand for labor, meaning that women may not always be able to get fifty-two weeks of work. Five of the most common occupations for women (employing 8.3 percent of all women working full-time)—home health aides, cashiers, maids and household cleaners, waitresses, and personal care aides—have median earnings

Box 7.2 – Encountering the Controversies of Equality

The Underside of Globalization: Are Immigrant Women Becoming the New "Wife" at Home?

According to the United Nations Population Fund, the number of people living outside their country of birth has almost doubled during the last fifty years. Of the more than 125 million people in need of humanitarian assistance worldwide, 75 percent are women and children.[1] Millions of women from poor countries in the global south migrate north to do "women's work." Barbara Ehrenreich and Arlie Hochschild label this pattern a worldwide gender revolution. As male wages and overall earning power have fallen, women have increased their share of market participation to "make up the gap" in both rich and poor countries. "The lifestyles of the First World are made possible by a global transfer of the services associated with a wife's traditional role—child care, homemaking, and sex," they write.[2] As women in the United States and other developed nations have increased their roles in the public sphere by increasing their hours and commitment to paid labor, there is a gap in caregiving in the private sphere created by their absence. "The 'care deficit' that has emerged in the wealthier countries as women enter the workforce *pulls* migrants from the Third World and postcommunist nations; poverty *pushes* them."[3]

Only nineteen of sixty-five countries surveyed by the International Labour Organization (ILO) have specific laws or regulations governing domestic work, leaving migrant women vulnerable to a wide range of abuses. Women who are desperate to find work are easy prey for traffickers. Trafficked women are forced into sex work, domestic roles, or sweatshop labor. Human trafficking is the third-most-profitable criminal enterprise in the world (after arms and drugs). An estimated 800,000 humans are trafficked across international borders each year—up to 80 percent are women, half are children.

below the federal poverty line. Only one of the most common occupations for men (cooks, employing 1.3 percent of all men working full-time) has median earnings below poverty level. Another group of workers labor in occupations with median earnings at around 150 percent of the poverty level, placing them squarely within the working poor but earning too much to qualify for public support. For women, these occupations include retail sales, receptionist, and teacher's assistant, and for men these occupations include grounds maintenance workers, stock clerks, and janitors. In July 2016, Jamie Dimon, CEO of JPMorgan Chase, announced a raise from $10.15 per hour to a range of $12 to $16.50 (depending on region) for the

Lest one believe that the global transfer of female labor is exclusively pulled by women, Ehrenreich and Hochschild note that although American women took on more hours of paid work outside the home, they maintained (and slightly increased) the hours dedicated to child care and household chores, while men only slightly increased their share of the domestic burden. "So, strictly speaking, the presence of immigrant nannies does not enable affluent women to enter the workforce; it enables affluent *men* to continue avoiding the second shift."[4]

Low wages paid to workers in the private sector increase pressure on the public sector to provide increased public assistance to fill the gap. The lack of paid family leave, publicly funded child care, and universal access to health care in the United States shifts the communal responsibility for caregiving to the private sector. With nobody home and no public support, caregiving in the United States has increasingly been outsourced to female migrant laborers—women who have left their own children and families. "A lot of these immigrant women are fleeing economic situations in their home country that have created an impossible set of choices. The women who care for our loved ones simply can't take care of their own," says Ai-jen Poo, the director of the National Domestic Workers Alliance, a support and advocacy network.[5] "This trend toward re-division of women's traditional work throws new light on the entire process of globalization."[6]

What do you think?

In what ways is the global transfer of female labor an issue of gender equality? When women migrate, their children rarely accompany them, making it highly likely that a poor woman will raise the children of an affluent woman even as her own children are raised by relatives or in orphanages in her home country. In what ways does this disjuncture demonstrate the impossibility of entirely reconciling the separate spheres for women? In some ways, the reality of women's labor migration is decidedly antifeminist in its character—what supports one woman's social advancement involves the sacrifice of another woman's labor—or is it?

bank's lowest-wage workers—bank tellers (87 percent women) and customer service representatives (65 percent women). Critics calculated the cost of this gesture at $150 million a year, or less than 1 percent of JPMorgan's $24 billion profit. Dimon himself earns $27 million per year.[139] Although not a grand solution, it is a public recognition of the wage penalty associated with occupational segregation.

Women and children account for 70 percent of the nation's poor. Federal and state antipoverty programs have suffered as a result of the sustained economic downturn and public attitudes that favored reducing government-provided support and shrinking the safety net. Temporary Assistance for Needy Families (TANF), the primary policy for addressing families in poverty, includes a requirement that recipients work, although the high cost and limited availability of high-quality child care limits many women's opportunities for work that might lead to independence and freedom from poverty (see Chapter 8 for more on TANF).

Pursuing Equality in a Recession and Afterward

Can women make progress toward gender equality in recessionary times? It depends. A recession is not gender neutral. Old challenges such as occupational segregation in part-time and low-wage jobs that typically do not provide health care benefits means that although women have been more likely than men to keep their jobs, they are not getting ahead financially.

Prior to the onset of the Great Recession (December 2007–June 2009), women were steadily increasing their share of labor force participation, while men's economic activity declined overall but still remained higher than for women. In 2007 men's and women's economic lives were more similar than at any previous time in history, but the impact of the Great Recession was gender-specific in many ways. Men and women entered the recession with similar levels of unemployment, 5.1 and 4.9 percent respectively, but as of December 2009, the unemployment rate for women had climbed to 8.8 percent, while the rate for men was 11 percent.[140] Women are less likely than men to be covered by unemployment insurance and receive benefits. This is because women tend to work more intermittently, because family responsibilities can force women to leave employment for reasons that disqualify them from receiving unemployment benefits, and because in many states workers who seek part-time work are not eligible for unemployment insurance. The economic stimulus package passed by Congress in 2009, known as the American Recovery and Reinvestment Act (ARRA), specifically encouraged states to change unemployment insurance requirements to reduce sources of gender disparity. As a result, sixteen states reformed benefit structures to be more accessible to women and to part-time, low-wage workers of both genders.[141]

During the Great Recession, significant layoffs and rising unemployment in manufacturing and construction—sectors heavily dominated by men—increased women's share of the overall workforce (49.1 percent) and the likelihood that a woman was the breadwinner in her family. However, the persistence of the wage gap and sluggish job growth in the sectors most likely to be occupied by women (education, health care, and the service sector) meant that women's earnings did not increase to match their new role as their family's sole wage earner. In the typical dual-earner family, a woman contributed roughly 35.6 percent of the total family income in 2008. Therefore, in recessionary times, women may be safer in their jobs but find it nearly impossible to support their family on their wages alone.

Beyond employment, women were one-third more likely than men to have subprime mortgages, nearly 60 percent of impoverished children were living in female-headed households, and the poverty rate was higher among women than it was among men of any race. In nearly 44 percent of African American families with children, a woman was the primary breadwinner (including families headed by working single mothers and married-couple families in which the husband is unemployed).[142] Forty percent of married Latinas bring in more than half of their families' income, and 23 percent of Latinas are the family's primary breadwinner. Women workers still bore the burdens of the **double shift** even though they were more likely to have an unemployed male partner at home. According to economists Alan B. Krueger and Andreas Mueller, "unemployed men's child care duties are virtually identical to those of their working counterparts, and they instead spend more time sleeping, watching TV and looking for a job, along with other domestic duties."[143] Historically, the gendered division of labor in households has been resistant to change. While men have increased their share of domestic labor and child care over the last twenty years, they have not done so in direct proportion to a decrease in employed women's time on household tasks. To cover the gap, families outsource—they dine out, hire cleaning services, and pay for child care. "As declining incomes force families to cut back on these outlays," says Heidi Hartmann, chief economist at the Institute for Women's Policy Research, "women will most likely pick up the slack."

As the economy recovered in 2009, the ARRA focused on job creation related to "shovel-ready" infrastructure projects and secondarily in support for state and local governments, education, and health. Critics charged that women were largely excluded from the jobs creation aspect of the president's stimulus proposal. Linda Hirshman, for example, asked in a December 2008 *New York Times* op-ed, "Where are the new jobs for women?"[144] The White House estimated that 42 percent of the jobs created by the stimulus package would go to women, especially those in fields such as education and health care, where federal spending would bridge state and local budget gaps. Yet, this particular approach would have no impact on low-wage occupational segregation and the lifetime effects of the wage gap. Instead advocates urged Congress and the White House to use the recession as an opportunity to invest in training women for high-paid nontraditional employment and to provide incentives for government contractors to fill a portion of newly created jobs with women and minorities, noting, "The economic crisis has the potential to radically change how certain employers conceive of women workers, but government must provide the leadership and incentives."[145]

As the country climbed out of the recession, economists assessed the changes to the labor force. Initially, it appeared that men gained and women lost. Between June 2009 and May 2011, men had gained 786,000 jobs and lowered their unemployment rate to 9.5 percent. Women, by contrast, continued to lose jobs, and their unemployment rate increased slightly to 8.5 percent.[146] It was not initially clear why women fared worse in this recovery. One explanation is that women were more heavily concentrated than men in government jobs (federal, state, and local), an employment sector negatively impacted by the recession. Another possible explanation is that men were more willing to seek employment in occupations where women had been heavily concentrated—professional and business services and education and health services—and employers gave the edge to men in hiring. By 2013, women were enjoying a larger share of the recovery. The national unemployment rate for women was 6.8 percent, compared with 7.7 percent for men, and women had regained all of the jobs lost during the recession.[147]

One trend to watch in the coming years is the continuing decline in prime-age (twenty-five to fifty-four years old) men's labor force participation. Today, one in six prime-age men are either unemployed or out of the workforce altogether. "According to a report from White House economists, non-working prime-age men skew young, are less likely to be parents, are disproportionately black and less educated, and are concentrated in the South."[148] Although there are many possible explanations (e.g., they are enrolled in school, on disability, parenting, or in prison), the most likely is that job sectors historically dominated by men, such as manufacturing, mining, and construction, have experienced a long decline, and these sectors are not likely to return to previous levels. Meanwhile, the private sector has shifted to jobs more likely to be done by women—personal care aides, home health aides, medical secretaries, and marketing specialists. Harvard economist Lawrence Katz says, "Some of the decline in work among young men is a mismatch between aspirations and identity. Taking a job as a health technician has the connotation as a feminized job."[149] A post-recessionary economy may offer both men and women the opportunity to reexamine their skills, plans for the future, and pursue nontraditional occupations thereby reducing occupational segregation and improving wages for all.

Women in Retirement: Social Security and Private Pensions

The current Social Security system was established under the Social Security Act in 1935. Numerous changes have been made since its inception, but the basic philosophy has remained intact. The Social Security system is an example of a gender-neutral law because it does not treat men and women differently in the law itself, though men and women experience the system quite differently as a result of differences in employment and wage patterns. Social Security is particularly important for women because women are 60 percent less likely than men to have a private pension, and when they do, the average size is about half that of men's.[150] They also live longer than men, and because of pay inequities and time spent away from work to raise children, women have lower lifetime earnings than men. Women reaching the age of sixty-five in 2015 are expected to live, on average, an additional 21.6 years compared with 19.3 for men.[151] Women make up 56 percent of Social Security beneficiaries age sixty-two and older and approximately 66 percent of beneficiaries age eighty-five and older.[152]

Without Social Security, the poverty rate for women over sixty-five would be nearly double its current rate.[153] As it is, nearly 70 percent of all poor old people are female. However, there is tremendous variation by race and ethnicity. In 2003, the poverty rate for white women was 10 percent (nearly double that for white men). Among elderly African American women, the poverty rate was 27.4 percent (compared with 17.7 percent for African American men), and it was 21.7 percent for Hispanic women age sixty-five and above (compared with 16.6 percent for Hispanic men).[154] Social Security contributes 60 percent of retirement income for the average woman and 100 percent for one in five women. Despite this greater reliance, older women's benefits are lower than older men's benefits. The average annual Social Security benefit for older women in 2015 was $13,500, while for men it was $17,600.[155]

Although some adjustments to the laws have been made to recognize women's increased participation in the labor force, the Social Security system is premised on the 1930s traditional gender roles in families, which characterizes a tiny fraction of today's families. Social Security was intended to be a supplement to private pension plans and savings accumulated over the course of a lifetime, but only about half of men and a quarter of retired women earn additional income from private pensions. Social Security is a pay-as-you-go system, meaning that current payroll taxes are used to pay benefits to current retirees. Social Security benefits are based on the thirty-five years of highest taxable earnings of at least $520 each quarter of the year. The benefit formula is a progressive calculation, and the five lowest-earning years (including those with zero earnings) in an individual's working life are dropped. A married person is eligible for the larger of either 100 percent of his or her own benefit or 50 percent of his or her spouse's benefit. A woman whose benefit, based on her own work record, is less than or equal to the spousal benefit she could claim is said to be "dually entitled" and does not gain additional benefit from having worked. A man is similarly entitled to benefits from his wife's accounts, but in reality nearly all who use the spouse's benefit are women. This may change if more men opt to help raise children by either reducing the number of hours they work or by leaving the paid labor force entirely for a period of time.

For women currently working, this provision raises some interesting equity questions. Leanne Abdnor, author of the Cato Institute's report "Social Security Choices for the 21st Century Woman," argues that Social Security has an outdated benefit structure that has failed to keep pace with the changing nature of US families.[156] Abdnor contends that single women and women in dual-earner couples are unfairly being asked to subsidize the benefits of stay-at-home married women who do not pay Social Security taxes. Abdnor advocates giving women, particularly young women in the workforce, more control over their retirement savings through personal retirement accounts. By doing so, some portion of a working woman's retirement income would be hers alone and would not go toward subsidizing women who do not work outside the home. Other women's organizations oppose privatizing Social Security, even though they admit that the system is perhaps unfair to working women and should be updated to account for changes in work patterns and family structure. The Institute for Women's Policy Research report on women and Social Security recommends adopting minimum benefits and child-care credits as a way of treating all women more equitably. Minimum benefits would give credit for time spent in the labor force rather than the amount contributed through Social Security taxes, thereby benefiting low-wage workers, many of whom are women. Child care credits would give women who stay home to raise their children credit within the retirement system for the unpaid work of caregiving.[157] Because Social Security provides women with far more than simple retirement benefits (disability benefits are especially important for women of color) and because Social Security benefits are progressive (benefiting most those who earned least), most women's organizations argue against anything that will siphon money out of the current system, although most also advocate some type of reform to maintain solvency.

Advocates of the equality doctrine favor redefining women's roles so that they claim benefits equivalent to men's. They worry that policies that acknowledge and accommodate women's persistent and disproportionate share of unpaid care work (e.g., the family service credit noted above) or time outside of the paid labor force will simply perpetuate traditional gender roles by linking new benefits to old duties. Advocates of the fairness doctrine argue that any social retirement system must take into account the unequal amounts of unpaid work that women perform outside the formal economy and claim that the basis for retirement rewards needs to be reexamined. Both groups agree that the current Social Security system, although somewhat antiquated in its assumptions about gender and work, continues to be an effective antipoverty program for women in their twilight years. Social Security consumes 24 percent of the annual federal budget. Social Security provided benefits to 2.3 million spouses and children of retired workers, 6.1 million surviving children and spouses of deceased workers, and 10.8 million disabled workers and their eligible dependents in December 2015.[158] The program remains an essential resource for Americans and a critical antipoverty program for women and their families.

CONCLUSION

In this chapter we have covered a lot of topics related to work, the economy, wages, retirement, and the different ways men and women experience the labor market over the course of their lifetimes. It is clear that society has not resolved its ambivalence over women in the full-time workforce, even though the majority of women overall and the majority of women with small children are full-time year-round participants in the economy. Antiquated notions of why women work reinforce

pink ghettos of low-wage occupations primarily held by women and also depress women's wages overall. The wage gap not only deprives women and their families of income now and cumulatively over a forty-seven-year work life, but also reduces retirement benefits.

While Title VII and Title IX have opened doors to women's employment and educational opportunities, the Equal Pay Act has been largely ineffective in equalizing wage rates for men and women. The Lilly Ledbetter Fair Pay Act (2009) does not guarantee equal pay; it merely provides women a longer time period in which to seek a legal remedy once pay discrimination is discovered. The Paycheck Fairness Act would provide more transparency in pay scales and more powerful legal remedies, but it does not fully adopt a theory of comparable worth. States such as California and Massachusetts are the first to embrace a comparable-worth framework for the pursuit of wage equality, and they have adopted laws that require salary transparency and protect employees from retaliation if they discuss their pay or ask questions about differences in pay between employees.

Is a gender-neutral approach to employment policy effective for women, or does gender neutrality merely increase the burden on women who work full-time in both the paid and unpaid labor sectors? Our analysis in this chapter suggests that the policies adopted in the 1960s and still subject to interpretation by the courts today have not been sufficient to change the character and existence of the dual labor market, the wage gap, or the "glass ceiling" and "sticky floor" problems. A majority of women entering the workforce today will hold a wage-earning job until retirement. Women work out of economic necessity and because they find it fulfilling. As we have noted in previous chapters, until public attitudes catch up with the realities of women in the workforce, public policy is unlikely to address the most pervasive problems women face in achieving real economic equality. Law has been ineffective at combating second-generation discrimination. In the next chapter, we will examine the formation of families, fertility policies, and the ways in which women's participation in the labor force has demanded changes from men, children, and society at large.

NOTES

Boxed feature notes appear at the end of the Notes section.

1 Defined in the Carl D. Perkins Vocational and Technical Education Act of 2006 and the Workforce Investment Act of 1998.
2 Ariane Hedgewisch and Heidi Hartmann, "Occupational Segregation and the Gender Wage Gap: A Job Half Done," Institute for Women's Policy Research, January 2014.
3 "Women's Earnings and Income," Catalyst, April 8, 2016.
4 Milia Fisher, "Women of Color and the Gender Wage Gap," Center for American Progress, April 14, 2015.
5 American Bar Association, Commission on Women in the Profession, "A Current Glance at Women in the Law," May 2016.
6 "Facts About Women and the Minimum Wage," US Department of Labor, March 19, 2015.

7 Social Security Administration Fact Sheet, 2012, www.ssa.gov/news/press/factsheets/ss-customer/women-ret.pdf.

8 Eleanor Flexnor and Ellen Fitzpatrick, *Century of Struggle: The Women's Rights Movement in the United States* (Cambridge, MA: Harvard University Press, 1996).

9 Sharlene Hesse-Biber and Gregg Lee Carter, *Working Women in America: Split Dreams* (New York: Oxford University Press, 2000), 18.

10 Nancy Woloch, *Women and the American Experience* (New York: Alfred A. Knopf, 1984), 220.

11 Julie A. Matthaei, *An Economic History of Women in America: Women's Work, the Sexual Division of Labor, and the Development of Capitalism* (New York: Schocken Books, 1982).

12 Woloch, *Women and the American Experience*, 221.

13 Ibid., 220.

14 Ibid., 221.

15 Maxine L. Margolis, *Mothers and Such: Views of American Women and Why They Changed* (Berkeley: University of California Press, 1984), 195.

16 Hesse-Biber and Carter, *Working Women in America*, 37.

17 Rosalyn Baxandall, Linda Gordon, and Susan Reverby, *America's Working Women: A Documentary History—1600 to the Present* (New York: Vintage Books, 1976), 255–256.

18 Ann Gordon, Mari-Jo Buhle, and Nancy Schrom, "Women in American Society: An Historical Contribution," *Radical America* 5, no. 4 (1971): 3–66.

19 Kristin Smith, "Women as Economic Providers: Dual Earner Families Thrive as Women's Earnings Rise," University of New Hampshire, Carsey School of Public Policy, National Issue Brief #84, Summer 2015.

20 J. J. Goodnow, "Children's Household Work: Its Nature and Functions," *Psychological Bulletin* 103 (1988): 5–26.

21 Virginia Valian, *Why So Slow? The Advancement of Women* (Cambridge, MA: MIT Press, 1998), 33.

22 American Time Use Study, Bureau of Labor Statistics, "Household Activities," 2014, www.bls.gov/TUS/CHARTS/HOUSEHOLD.HTM.

23 Ellen Galinsky, Kerstin Aumann, and James T. Bond, "Times are Changing: Gender and Generation at Work and Home," Families and Work Institute: 2008 National Study of the Changing Workforce (revised August, 2011), 14.

24 Ibid., 40.

25 Ibid., 44.

26 Ibid.

27 National Manpower Council, *Womanpower* (New York: Columbia University Press, 1957).

28 Equal Pay Act of 1963, 77 Stat. 56 (1963).

29 J. Ralph Lindgren and Nadine Taub, *The Law of Sex Discrimination*, 2nd ed. (Minneapolis, MN: West Publishing, 1993), 145–146.

30 Cynthia Harrison, *On Account of Sex: The Politics of Women's Issues, 1945–1968* (Berkeley: University of California Press, 1988).

31 Ibid., 146–147.

32 Ibid., 174.

33 *Quong Wing v. Kirkendall*, 233 U.S. 59, 63 (1912).

34 Lindgren and Taub, *Law of Sex Discrimination*, 177.

35 *Wilson v. Southwest Airlines Company*, 517 F. Supp. 292, 301, 302 (N.D. Tex. 1981).

36 David Ng, "'Hamilton' Musical Runs into Trouble over 'Non-White' Casting Notice," *Los Angeles Times*, March 20, 2016.

37 *Dothard v. Rawlinson*, 433 U.S. 321 (1977).

38 *Price Waterhouse v. Hopkins*, 490 U.S. 228 (1989).

39 Ibid.

40 Eric S. Dreiband and Brett Swearingen, "The Evolution of Title VII—Sexual Orientation, Gender Identity, and the Civil Rights Act of 1964," Jones Day, Cleveland, OH, April 2015.

41 *Smith v. City of Salem*, 378 F.3d 566 (6th Cir. 2004); *Barnes v. City of Cincinnati* 401 F.3d. 729, 733 (6th Cir. 2005).

42 Dreiband and Swearingen, "The Evolution of Title VII," 10.

43 *Griggs v. Duke Power Company*, 401 U.S. 424 (1971).

44 Vauhini Vara, "The Ellen Pao Trial: What Do We Mean by 'Discrimination'?" *New Yorker*, March 14, 2015.

45 Bourree Lam, "Debating the Gender Pay Gap," *Atlantic Monthly*, August 10, 2016.

46 *General Electric v. Gilbert*, 429 U.S. 125 (1976).

47 "State Family and Medical Leave Laws," National Conference of State Legislators, July 19, 2016.

48 Joanna Grossman, "*AT&T v. Hulteen*: The Supreme Court Deals a Blow to Once-Pregnant Retirees," *FindLaw Commentary*, May 26, 2009; *United Auto Workers v. Johnson Controls, Inc.*, 499 U.S. 187 (1991).

49 *Young v. United Parcel Service*, 575 U.S. ___ (2015)

50 EEOC, "Updated Pregnancy Discrimination Guidance," June 25, 2015.

51 National Partnership for Women and Families, "Fact Sheet: The Pregnant Workers Fairness Act," June 2015.

52 Executive Order 11246, 30 F.R. 12319, 1965.

53 Jocelyn C. Frye, "Affirmative Action: Understanding the Past and Present," in *The American Woman 1996–1997: Women and Work*, ed. Cynthia Costello and Barbara Kivimae Krimgold (New York: Norton, 1996), 35.

54 Ibid., 37–38.

55 Roberta Ann Johnson, "Affirmative Action and Women," in *Women in Politics: Outsiders or Insiders?* ed. Lois Duke Whitaker, 3rd ed. (Upper Saddle River, NJ: Prentice Hall, 1999), 334–352.

56 *Fisher v. University of Texas at Austin*, 570 U.S. ___ (2013).

57 Adam Liptak, "Supreme Court Upholds Affirmative Action Program at University of Texas," *New York Times*, June 23, 2016.

58 Rebecca Riffkin, "Higher Support for Gender Affirmative Action than Race," Gallup Politics, August 26, 2015.

59 National Partnership for Women and Families, "Affirmative Action Helps Boost Women's Pay and Promotes Economic Security for Women and Their Families," accessed at www.civilrights.org/equal-opportunity/fact-sheets/women.html.

60 National Partnership for Women and Families, *Women at Work: Looking Behind the Numbers Forty Years After the Civil Rights Act of 1964* (Washington, DC: National Partnership for Women and Families, 2004).

61 *Lilly M. Ledbetter v. The Goodyear Tire & Rubber Company, Inc.*, 550 U.S. 618 (2007), Justice Ruth Bader Ginsberg, dissenting.

62 *Lilly M. Ledbetter v. The Goodyear Tire & Rubber Company, Inc.*, 550 U.S. 618 (2007), Justice Ruth Bader Ginsberg, dissenting, 2–3.

63 Ibid., 19.

64 Robert Barnes, "Over Ginsburg's Dissent, Court Limits Bias Suits," *Washington Post*, May 31, 2007.

65 "Pay Equity Pioneer Lilly Ledbetter Addresses the DNC," *PBS NewsHour*, August 26, 2008.

66 National Committee on Pay Equity, www.pay-equity.org/info-time.html; WAGE (Women Are Getting Even), www. wageproject.org. Accessed July 2016.

67 Cynthia B. Costello, Shari Miles, and Anne J. Stone, eds., *The American Woman 1999–2000: A Century of Change—What's Next?* (New York: Norton, 1998).

68 Cynthia B. Costello, Vanessa R. Wight, and Anne J. Stone, eds., *The American Woman: 2003–2004: Daughters of a Revolution—Young Women Today* (New York: Palgrave Macmillan, 2003), 253.

69 Department of Labor Statistics, "Occupations," www.dol.gov/wb/stats/leadoccupations.htm. Accessed July 2016.

70 Valian, *Why So Slow?*, 190–191.

71 Ibid., 198.

72 Alice H. Eagly and Linda L. Carli, "Women and the Labyrinth of Leadership,"*Harvard Business Review*, September 2007, 63–71.

73 Ibid., 67.

74 Federal Glass Ceiling Commission, *Good for Business: Making Full Use of the Nation's Human Capital* (Washington, DC: Government Printing Office, 1995).

75 Rebecca Traister, "The Truth About Carly," *Salon*, October 19, 2006.

76 Sheila Wellington, quoted in "Women of Color Report a 'Concrete Ceiling' Barring Their Advancement in Corporate America," Catalyst Accessed July 2016. .

77 See Hesse-Biber and Carter, *Working Women in America*, 163–173.

78 "S&P 500 Board Seats Held by Women by Race/Ethnicity," Catalyst, 2016.

79 Catalyst, "Women and Men in U.S. Corporate Leadership: Same Workplace, Different Realities?," 2004.

80 Paul Rincon, "Women Looking over Glass Cliffs," BBC News, September 6, 2004.

81 Quoted in "More Women Join World's Workforce, Obstacles Persist," *Breaking Through the Glass Ceiling: Women in Management*, International Labor Office, updated 2004.

82 Liane Jackson, "Minority Women Are Disappearing from BigLaw—and Here's Why," *ABA Journal*, May 1, 2016.

83 American Bar Association, "A Current Glance at Women in the Law," May 2016.

84 Ibid., quoting Deborah Rhode, chair of the ABA Commission on Women in the Profession.

85 Deborah L. Rhode, "The Unfinished Agenda: Women and the Legal Profession," ABA Commission on Women in the Profession, 2001, 5.

86 ABA Commission on Women in the Profession, "A Current Glance of Women in the Law 2003," accessed July 2016.

87 National Association for Law Placement, www.nalp.org. Accessed July 2016.

88 Rhode, "The Unfinished Agenda," 14.

89 "The Good and Bad Statistics on Women in Medicine," *Wall Street Journal*, October 29, 2015; see also Association of American Medical Schools, "The State of Women in Academic Medicine," 2014. www.aamc.org/members/gwims/statistics.

90 Valian, *Why So Slow?*, 208.

91 Ibid.

92 Danielle Kurtzleben, "AP Test Shows Wide Gender Gap in Computer Science, Physics," *U.S. News & World Report*, January 14, 2014.

93 Karen West, "Breaking the Code: Women Add New Perspective to Software Engineering," *Seattle Business Magazine,* June 2015.

94 Hedgewisch and Hartmann, "Occupational Segregation and the Gender Wage Gap," 7.

95 Ibid.

96 Milia Fisher, "Women of Color and the Gender Wage Gap," Center for American Progress, April 14, 2015.

97 Dorothy McBride Stetson, *Women's Rights in the USA: Policy Debates and Gender Roles*, 2nd ed. (New York: Garland Publishing, 1997), 317.

98 Lindgren and Taub, *Law of Sex Discrimination*, 217.

99 Susan Gluck Mezey, *Elusive Equality: Women's Rights, Public Policy, and the Law* (Boulder, CO: Lynne Rienner, 2003), 148.

100 *Doe v. City of Belleville*, 119 F.3d563; *Rene v. MGM Grand Hotel*, 305 F.3d1061.

101 Gabriel Sherman, "The Revenge of Roger's Angels," *New York Magazine*, September 2, 2016.

102 Elle Hunt, "Online Harassment of Women at Risk of Becoming 'Established Norm,' Study Finds," *Guardian*, March 7, 2016. See also Adrienne Lafrance, "When Will the Internet Be Safe for Women?" *Atlantic Monthly*, May 20, 2016; Maeve Duggan, "Online Harassment: Summary of Findings," Pew Research Center, October 22, 2014.

103 Lafrance, "When Will the Internet Be Safe for Women?"

104 Ibid.

105 Caitlin Dewey, "How Do You Stop Online Harassment? Try Banning the Men," *Washington Post*, April 14, 2016.

106 Carmen DeNavas-Walt and Bernadette D. Proctor, "Income and Poverty in the United States: 2014," US Census Bureau, September 2015, 41, Table A-4.

107 Ibid.; US Bureau of Labor Statistics, Highlights of Women's Earnings, 2014, Table 15.

108 Hegewisch and Hartman, "Occupational Segregation and the Gender Wage Gap: A Job Half Done," 1.

109 Ibid., 5.

110 Francine D. Blau and Lawrence M. Kahn, "The Gender Wage Gap: Extent, Trends, and Explanations," NBER Working Paper 21913, January 2016.

111 Claire Cain Miller, "As Women Take Over a Male-Dominated Field, the Pay Drops," *New York Times*, March 18, 2016.

112 Asaf Levanon, Paula England, and Paul Allison, "Occupational Feminization and Pay: Assessing Causal Dynamics Using 1950–2000 U.S. Census Data," *Social Forces* 88, no. 2 (2009): 865–892.

113 Council of Economic Advisors, "Fifty Years After the Equal Pay Act," Report of the National Equal Pay Task Force, April 2015.

114 Michal Myck and Gillian Paull, "The Role of Employment Experience in Explaining the Gender Wage Gap," Institute for Fiscal Studies, July 2004.

115 Judy Goldberg Dey and Catherine Hill, "Behind the Pay Gap," AAUW Educational Foundation, April 2007.

116 Youngjoo Cha and Kim A. Weeden, "Overwork and the Slow Convergence in the Gender Gap in Wages," *American Sociological Review* 79, no. 3 (2014): 1–28.

117 Pew Research Center, "Mothers, More than Fathers, Experience Career Interruptions," September 30, 2015.

118 Claudia Golden, "A Grand Gender Convergence: Its Last Chapter," *American Economic Review* 104, no. 4 (2016): 1091–1119.
119 Claudia Goldin and Cecelia Rouse, "Orchestrating Impartiality: The Impact of 'Blind' Auditions on Female Musicians," *American Economic Review* 90, no. 4 (September 2000): 715–741.
120 Corrine A. Moss-Racusin et al., "Science Faculty's Subtle Gender Biases Favor Male Students," *Science*, vol. 109 no. 41, August 2012.
121 Kristen Schilt and Matthew Wiswall, "Before and After: Gender Transitions, Human Capital, and Workplace Experiences," *Berkeley Electronic Journal of Economic Analysis and Policy* 8, no. 1 (September 2008): Article 39.
122 Jeffrey A. Flory, Andreas Leibbrandt, and John A. List, "Do Competitive Workplaces Deter Female Workers? A Large-Scale Natural Field Experiment on Job-Entry Decisions," *Review of Economic Studies*, October 2014.
123 Linda Babcock and Sara Laschever, *Women Don't Ask: Negotiation and the Gender Divide* (Princeton, NJ: Princeton University Press, 2003).
124 Hannah Riley Bowles, Linda Babcock, and Lei Lai, "Social Incentives for Gender Differences in the Propensity to Initiate Negotiations: Sometimes It Does Hurt to Ask," *Organizational Behavior and Human Decision Processes* 103, no. 1 (2007): 84–103.
125 Hannah Bowles, quoted in Shankar Vedantam, "Salary, Gender and the Social Cost of Haggling," *Washington Post*, July 30, 2007.
126 Bouree Lam, "How Do We Close the Wage Gap in the US?" *Atlantic*, March 9, 2016.
127 Diana Furchtgott-Roth and Christine Solba, *Women's Figures: An Illustrated Guide to the Economic Progress of Women in America* (Washington, DC: AEI Press and the Independent Women's Forum, 1999).
128 Ellen Goodman, "Equal Pay Struggle Continues," *Times-Picayune*, March 16, 1999.
129 Joanne Lipman, "Let's Expose the Gender Pay Gap," *New York Times*, August 13, 2015.
130 Ibid.
131 Ibid.
132 Patrick McGreevy and Chris Megerian, "California Now Has One of the Toughest Equal Pay Laws in the Country," *Los Angeles Times*, October 6, 2015.
133 Bryce Covert, "Massachusetts Becomes First State Ever to Ban Employers from Asking for Salary Histories," *Think Progress*, August 1, 2016.
134 Anne Morrison and Katherine Gallagher Robbins, "The women in the Low Wage Workforce May Not Be Who You Think," National Women's Law Center, September 2015.
135 Ibid.
136 National Council of State Legislatures, Minimum Wage Chart, www.ncsl.org/research /labor-and-employment/state-minimum-wage-chart.aspx. Accessed July 2016.
137 Oregon Minimum Wage Rate Summary, www.oregon.gov/boli/WHD/OMW/Pages /Minimum-Wage-Rate-Summary.aspx. Accessed July 2016.
138 Institute for Women's Policy Research, "The Gender Wage Gap by Occupation 2015," Publication C440, August 2016, 5.
139 Mark Gimein, "Jamie Dimon's Self-Congratulatory Pay-Raise Announcement Is Good for Working Women," *New Yorker*, July 14, 2016.
140 Heidi Hartmann, Ashely English, and Jeffrey Hayes, "Women and Men's Employment and Unemployment in the Great Recession," Institute for Women's Policy Research, Publication C373, February 2009.
141 Ibid.
142 Dana Goldstein, "Pink Collar Blues," *American Prospect*, June 8, 2009.
143 Catherine Rampell, "As Layoffs Surge, Women May Pass Men in Job Force," *New York Times*, February 6, 2009.
144 Linda Hirshman, "Where Are the New Jobs for Women?" *New York Times*, December 9, 2008.
145 Goldstein, "Pink Collar Blues."
146 Rakesh Kochar, "Two Years of Economic Recovery: Women Lose Jobs, Men Find Them," Pew Research Center, July 6, 2011.
147 Abha Bhattaral and Sarah Halzack, "Women Are Faring Better than Men in Wake of the Recession," *Washington Post*, September 22, 2013.
148 Derek Thompson, "The Missing Men," *Atlantic*, June 27, 2016. See also "The Long-Term Decline in Prime-Age Male Labor Force Participation" Executive Office of the President of the United States, June 2016.
149 Thompson, "The Missing Men."

150 Madonna Harrington Meyer and Pamela Herd, *Market Friendly or Family Friendly: The State and Gender Inequalities in Old Age* (New York: Russell Sage Foundation, 2007).

151 Social Security Administration, "Fact Sheet: Social Security Is Important to Women," 2015.

152 Ibid.

153 Women 4 Social Security, www.women4socialsecurity.org.

154 Meyer and Herd, *Market Friendly or Family Friendly*, 2.

155 Joan Entmacher and Katherine Gallagher Robbins, "Women and Social Security," National Women's Law Center, February 2015.

156 Leanne Abdnor, "Social Security Choices for the Twenty-First-Century Woman," *CATO Project on Social Security*, February 24, 2004.

157 Marianne Sullivan, "Women Sharpen Views on Social Security," *Women's eNews*, March 9, 2004; National Women's Law Center, "Women and Social Security Reform: What's at Stake," May 10, 2002.

158 "Policy Basics: Where Do Our Federal Tax Dollars Go?" Center on Budget and Policy Priorities, March 4, 2016.

Box 7.1: The Global Gender Wage Gap

1 Juliette Jowit, "Women Will Get Equal Pay . . . in 118 Years," *Guardian*, November 18, 2015.

Box 7.2: The Underside of Globalization: Are Immigrant Women Becoming the New "Wife" at Home?

1 United Nations Population Fund, "Ten Things You Should Know About Women and the World's Humanitarian Crises," 2016, http://www.unfpa.org/news/10-things-you-should-know-about-women-world%E2%80%99s-humanitarian-crises.

2 Barbara Ehrenreich and Arlie Russell Hochschild, *Global Woman: Nannies, Maids, and Sex Workers in the New Economy* (New York: Henry Holt, 2002).

3 Ibid., 8.

4 Ibid., 9.

5 Rachel Aviv, "The Cost of Caring," *New Yorker*, April 11, 2016, www.newyorker.com/magazine/2016/04/11/the-sacrifices-of-an-immigrant-caregiver.

6 Ehrenreich and Hochschild, *Global Women,* 11.

CHAPTER 8

The Politics of Family and Fertility: The Last Battleground in the Pursuit of Equality?

F amily policy and issues of reproduction and fertility pose the greatest challenges to feminists when choosing a path toward equality. Gender neutrality in family law or in policies related to pregnancy often obscures the ways in which women are disadvantaged. For example, a law that prevents firefighters from breast-feeding their babies between calls affects only women, although it presumably applies to all firefighters. In *General Electric v. Gilbert* (1976), the Supreme Court ruled that a policy that distinguishes between pregnant and nonpregnant persons does not constitute sex discrimination against women, though this was later overturned by the Pregnancy Discrimination Act of 1978.[1] A legal equality doctrine is difficult to adopt in family and fertility policies because in many cases women's biological differences are paramount and are magnified by socially constructed gender roles. Yet laws that apply only to women and are based on their reproductive functions are often discriminatory in their application and can disadvantage women.

This chapter begins by surveying the laws that apply to the formation, maintenance, and dissolution of families constructed through marriage. Although nearly half of all marriages end in divorce, marriage remains the primary mechanism by which families are defined and recognized under federal and state law. These laws are expanding to incorporate same-sex marriages following the Supreme Court's ruling in the 2015 case *Obergefell v. Hodges* affirming marriage equality. An increase in single-parent households, the majority of which are headed by women, may require more of the social safety net, but single-female households are no longer limited to the poor. More women choose to remain single today; the proportion of women who were married dropped below 50 percent for the first time in 2009.

We then turn to an examination of reproductive policy. The presence of children in a woman's life directly challenges her autonomy. By regulating access to contraception, abortion, and reproductive health services, a state can regulate

327

women's sexuality, reproductive, and life choices. States have added a complex web of restrictions on legal abortion, and as a consequence, 87 percent of counties in America lack an abortion provider. We will evaluate under what circumstances the state has a legitimate interest in regulating reproduction and how such regulations affect women's claims to autonomy.

Surrogacy, contract pregnancy, and in vitro fertilization present society with a new set of issues and raise new questions. Sex is conceptually different from gender, but emerging fertility technology could further blur or entirely erase the lines between sex and gender. Will fertility technologies liberate women from their biological role in reproduction in ways that promote equality, or will the science of fertility and reproduction serve as another form of patriarchal control? Should women be able to contract freely for their reproductive labor, just as men are constitutionally free to contract for their productive labor? What impact will changes in reproductive technology have on defining and forming families in the United States? This chapter considers women's attempts to reconcile their role within families with their expanding role in the public sphere. As we'll see, public policy in this area both assists and hinders women's pursuit of equality.

DEMOGRAPHICS OF MODERN AMERICAN FAMILIES

American families today are quite diverse, leading the Pew Research Center to proclaim that "there is no longer one dominant family form in the US."[2] The traditional patriarchal family model of two parents—a male breadwinner and a stay-at-home mother—with two or more children characterizes less than a quarter (about 22 percent) of all US households today. "There hasn't been the collapse of one dominant family structure and the rise of another. It's really a fanning out in all kinds of family structures—different is the new normal," says Philip Cohen, a sociologist at the University of Maryland.[3]

The 2015 census counted 124 million households in the United States. The most common type of household is the two-wage-earning married couple with or without dependents. In 1960, 90 percent of children lived in a two-parent family, while 8 percent lived in a mother-headed household and 1 percent lived only with a father. By 2014, nearly one-quarter of children lived in a single-parent, mother-headed household, with 4 percent living in a father-headed single-parent household. In 2015, 66.9 million opposite-sex couples lived together—60.1 million (90 percent) were married and 6.8 million were not. Eighty-five percent of Asian American children lived with two parents, as did 78 percent of white non-Hispanic children, 70 percent of Hispanic children, and 38 percent of African American children. About 9 percent of all children lived in a household that included a grandparent, and 23 percent of those had no parent present. In 2015, a majority of women reported living in a household without a spouse (51 percent). According to the US Census Bureau's 2014 population statistics, gay and lesbian couples accounted for

FIGURE 8.1: Households by Race and Type in 2015

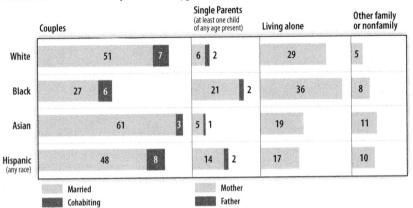

Source: US Census Bureau, Current Population Survey, Annual Social and Economic Supplement, 2015.

just over 783,000 households—48 percent were male-male households and 52 percent were female-female households.[4] Since 2010, the Census Bureau has been working to improve its measure for same-sex married and unmarried but coupled households.[5]

American men and women are marrying later in life. In 2016, the median age at first marriage was around twenty-seven for women and twenty-eight for men. In 2012, the Pew Research Center reported that about one in five adults twenty-five and older had never been married—about 42 million people. According to Current Population Survey data, about a quarter (24 percent) of never-married young adults ages twenty-five to thirty-four are living with a partner. In a national survey, Pew researchers asked people to choose which of the following statements best reflects their opinion: "Society is better off if people make marriage and having children a priority, or society is just as well off if people have priorities other than marriage and children." Just 46 percent of respondents indicated that society is better off when people prioritize marriage and children.[6]

The divorce rate in 2015 for first-time marriages was 42 percent, but almost 80 percent of divorced people remarry, creating blended families. "Although at any point in time a majority of children may be living with two biological parents, the prevalence of divorce and remarriage, along with non-marital fertility, ensures that more than half of all children will spend some time before they graduate from high school living outside the 'traditional' nuclear family," reports the Council on the Contemporary Family.[7] The divorce rate slowed considerably in the early part of the 1990s, perhaps because men and women were marrying later.[8]

The share of never-married adults (twenty-five and older) has gone up for all major racial and ethnic groups in the United States, but the rate of increase has been most dramatic among African Americans. Among African Americans, the share of adults who have never been married rose from 9 percent in 1960 to 36 percent in 2012. Since 1980, the share of Hispanic adults who have never married has doubled (from 12 percent to 26 percent). For Asian Americans, the share of never-married adults has gone up from 13 percent in 1980 to 19 percent in 2012.[9]

FORMING FAMILIES THROUGH MARRIAGE

Marriage is both an individual choice and a social expectation. For women, the institution of marriage has historically been the most oppressive force in denying them the rights, privileges, and obligations of full citizenship. As discussed in Chapter 1, a husband's identity entirely subsumed his wife's under coverture marriage—John Stuart Mill characterized it as a form of slavery. Upon entering coverture marriage, a woman became wholly subject to her husband's will and dependent on his willingness to provide support for her and their children. She relinquished control of all property and assets that she might have inherited from her family, and any assets that the couple might have accumulated during their marriage were considered the husband's property exclusively. Throughout most of the nineteenth century, women's invisibility under coverture denied them political, social, and economic rights in the public realm. Although coverture has largely disappeared as the standard for modern marriage, its vestiges remain in the patriarchal traditions and laws associated with forming a family through marriage.

Family policy is not covered under the Constitution and has largely been left to the states. Laws regarding marriage usually have to do with establishing a minimum age for males and females to marry, specifying property rights, providing for custody and care of children produced within a marriage, and setting the conditions under which a couple may divorce. Until *Obergefell v. Hodges* determined that the right to marry extended to same-sex couples, the decision to allow or forbid same-sex marriage was also left up to the individual states. Marriage laws are intended to promote social order and protect property interests, but for the most part the character of family life once the family unit is formed is considered a private matter and not subject to the intrusions of public policy in the same ways that education and employment are. However, for women, the private nature of the family has often left them largely unprotected from the power of patriarchy.

Individuals who come together in marriage, or even those who choose to live together without being married, can more or less negotiate their own gender roles with minimal state interference for as long as the union holds. However, they cannot escape the gender roles built into the US tax code; the consequences of a largely absent family support system even in the face of women's increased participation in the labor force; insurance regulations; or laws regulating divorce, child custody, and support. Partners in same-sex marriages face additional ambiguity, as a multitude of laws must be changed to reflect marriage equality. Legal marriage carries with it access to a variety of benefits: the right to share medical benefits, inherit a pension, or access spousal Social Security benefits. Legal marriage also carries a variety of social and cultural benefits as well as the privileges extended to individuals related by kinship. For example, if a friend invites you to a dinner party, you would not assume that the invitation includes your housemate, but you probably would assume that it includes your spouse. Legal marriage bonds two previously unrelated people in powerful ways. Privileges extended to "next of kin" go to a spouse before any blood relative. Other family constellations, while increasingly prevalent in the United States, have not been as widely recognized by law or supported by public policy.

A Brief History of Marriage and Marriage Traditions

Political scientist Dorothy McBride Stetson characterizes the development of modern marriage as the result of three theories: unity, separate but equal, and shared partnership.[10] Unity, which rendered husband and wife one legal entity, characterized marriage through the early 1900s. It was slowly replaced by the "separate but equal" theory, where each individual made a different but equally important contribution to the union. This period, which lasted throughout the 1960s, was defined by traditional sex roles in which the male was the family breadwinner and the female was in charge of the home and children. Women in this capacity were glorified by the **cult of domesticity** and were urged to invest themselves in homemaking with the same fervor that a male invested in his paid employment. An explosion of consumer goods and new household appliances relieved women of much of the drudgery of housework and reinforced the primacy of the woman's role as household manager.

While the "separate but equal" theory meant that a woman was not considered a legal dependent of her husband within a marriage, she was severely disadvantaged should her marriage dissolve. Women who stayed at home found themselves without the education or training, employment history, or job skills necessary to support themselves and their children, and without the credit history necessary to qualify for a mortgage or even to rent housing should their marriage end in divorce. The courts most often required a husband to support his ex-wife with alimony and child support payments, but her standard of living declined substantially, even with such court-ordered monetary support. Furthermore, most states granted a divorce only if one party was determined to have been at fault as a result of serious abuse, neglect, abandonment, or adultery. No-fault divorce, permitting a couple to part without publicly establishing blame, was first established in California in 1969. As more women entered the labor force and increased their overall participation in the public sphere, the theory of marriage characterized as an equal partnership became the norm.

The equal partnership theory was defined in 1970 by a National Organization for Women task force as "an equal partnership with shared economic and household responsibility and shared care of the children." The transition from "separate but equal roles" to "shared but equal roles" is hardly complete, as Chapter 7 revealed, and most marital relationships remain asymmetrical. While the majority of state laws now recognize men and women as equal partners in a marriage, reality has not yet caught up with the law. Both men and women struggle to balance the need for two incomes with the problems created by the absence of a full-time family caretaker and household manager. Public policy has not kept pace by providing family support structures, even though the laws regarding marriage, divorce, child custody, and support have become, for the most part, gender neutral. In this case, gender-neutral policy does not disadvantage women's rights specifically but rather disadvantages women and men within the family unit in daily life.

Although the notion of a marriage contract is largely outdated, the concept of rights and obligations in a legal marriage retains some viability in the law. Originally, marriage contracts detailed the duties and obligations of both parties in a marriage. The husband was responsible for support, and in return the wife owed her husband household, domestic, and companionship services.[11] As you might recall from Chapter 2, anti-ERA forces objected to a blanket legal equality for women under the Equal Rights Amendment, fearing that husbands would no longer be obligated to provide financial support for their wives and families. Today most courts obligate spouses to support one another according to circumstances rather than generalized gender roles. Although most marital obligations were unenforceable in court, there were and still are consequences for women stemming from this contractual conception of marriage and the theory of unity.

Until the **Equal Credit Opportunity Act** was passed in 1974 (and since amended in 1977 and 1988), women were routinely denied credit because lenders assumed that, married or unmarried, women were not economically responsible individuals. When a woman married, many credit card lenders automatically canceled cards that were in her birth name and reissued joint accounts in her husband's surname. If the marriage dissolved, through divorce or death, women did not qualify for credit since their credit history was based on their husband's. Women were often required to have a man (husband, father, brother) cosign loan agreements. When applying for a mortgage or joint credit with her husband, a wife was required to provide information about her birth control practices and her intentions to bear children. Only half the wife's salary was included in calculating assets to determine a couple's mortgage, based on the assumption by lenders that women were not autonomous economic entities. The Equal Credit Opportunity Act, as amended, requires lenders to base their credit decisions solely on an individual's ability to repay the debt, rather than on sex, race, national origin, or age. Further amendments in 1988 opened the door to commercial lines of credit for women entrepreneurs.

Coverture and the theory of unity rendered the husband and wife one person in the eyes of the law. As such, husbands and wives could not sue each other in civil court nor be compelled to testify against each other in criminal court. Courts did not want to settle disagreements between a husband and wife. Over time, the private nature of family and marriage reinforced this **interspousal immunity**, even though other legal changes granted women independent public standing, including the ability to make contracts. Interspousal immunity has complicated a battered woman's ability to bring civil suits against her husband, and because of the private nature of marriage, domestic violence has been ignored until recently. Due to the conjugal rights inherent in the marriage contract, a wife could not charge her husband with rape. Today marital rape is illegal in all fifty states..

Violence within a marriage raises questions of justice. Philosopher Susan Moller Okin argues that marriage and the family as currently practiced in the United States are unjust institutions.[12] While she acknowledges that talking about justice is difficult in such an intimate and private setting, it should nonetheless govern marital unions and the families that result. Okin believes that the roots of injustice can be found in the vulnerabilities created by traditional expectations of women, both in paid labor and in the family. She argues that the "division of labor within marriage (except in rare cases) makes wives far more likely than husbands to be exploited both with the marital relationship and in the world of work outside the home." Traditional gender role expectations developed in childhood have led both men and women to anticipate a certain division of labor within a family, based on the "husband as provider, wife as full-time caregiver" model, which in most cases does not mirror reality. Since the majority of women (including mothers of small children) are in the paid workforce, they end up doing a disproportionate share of the labor at home and outside the home (since they work longer hours for less pay).

Women are disadvantaged in the workplace because the professions or occupations that provide the flexibility needed to raise children are often in traditionally female occupations, which pay less. Even if that isn't the case, women find themselves in professional settings that assume a full-time "wife" at home and that do not support combining work and family in any sort of equitable manner. At home, they must deal with the unequal distribution of labor within the family. Even as wage earners, women assume the majority of child care and household chores—the unpaid work of a family. In most cases, Okin argues, this imbalance of power is a nondecision—assumed rather than determined.[13] Reality no longer reflects the expectations born of traditional gender roles. Since what a family should be differs from what many families experience, we should strive to create diverse expectations that allow all types of families to flourish and do not make one sex vulnerable to power differentials that result from an asymmetrical division of labor.

Legacies of Patriarchy in Contemporary Marriage

American culture is devoid of public rites that symbolize the passage from child-hood to adulthood, except for marriage. It is no surprise, then, that a lot is invested in the marriage ritual and ceremony. It might come as a surprise, though, how many of the traditions and customs are a legacy of unity marriage theory or coverture.

Young girls are socialized early to anticipate and plan for their "dream" wed-ding, with the cost traditionally borne by the bride's father. The ceremony itself is a mix of civil and religious symbolism. White, the traditional color of a woman's gown, symbolizes purity, and the veil worn by many brides is a holdover from the days when the wedding was the first time a bride and groom met. The ring exchange originally symbolized the exchange of property that was negotiated in a marriage contract. Weddings are usually public celebrations where friends and relatives join in recognizing the new union by contributing money and gifts for the couple's joint household. Although weddings now come in all varieties—from very traditional to religious to purely civil ceremonies—the symbolism remains an im-portant aspect of joining two individuals in legal marriage. However, these symbols also reproduce the patriarchal culture that has oppressed women within marriage for centuries, although most would not recognize them as such today.

Some people incorrectly assume that women are legally required to take their husband's surname, but this custom is actually a result of common law or tradition. A holdover from the days of unity in marriage, a woman's adoption of her husband's name signals a new identity in marriage for women, but not for men. Women are known as Miss, Ms., or Mrs., a "social marker" for women's identities. Each carries information about marital status or, with "Ms.," a refusal to be traditionally labeled. Men, regardless of age or marital status, are simply addressed as "Mr." Customarily (and in a few states, legally), children produced in a marriage are registered with the state under the husband's last name. The use of **patronymics** (father's names) was important in establishing the continuity of lineage and property rights. This sex-based requirement, which is for women only, was upheld by the US Supreme Court as recently as 1971.[14]

Today women are more likely to keep their birth name than they have been in any of the last four decades. According to a *New York Times* survey, 22 percent of all women marrying in the 2010s elected to retain their birth name. An additional 10 percent or so chose a third option, such as hyphenating their name or legally changing it while continuing to use their birth name professionally.[15] By compar-ison, the percentage of women who married and kept their names in the 1970s until the beginning of this decade varied between 13 and 18 percent. Women are marrying later in life, are more likely to have cohabited before marriage, and are more educated than in any previous decade. Sociologists also point to women's presence on social media as a factor against a name change. In reviewing Harvard alumni surveys, economists found that each year that women delayed marrying or having children was associated with a 1 percentage point decline in the probability that they would change their names.[16] Among racial and ethnic groups, white native-born women are the most likely to adopt their husband's name. Asian and Hispanic women were among the least likely to change their name at marriage.[17]

Domicile laws establish an individual's rights within a defined territory (most often a state) for the purposes of benefits and obligations. Since most laws regarding the family are state based, establishing permanent residency is significant—income taxes, college tuition, and marital property laws depend on domicile. Many states follow the common law, which assumes that a husband's residence constitutes the primary residence of a family—a relic of unity theory of marriage. In the days when men provided sole financial support for the family, giving them precedence in the choice of domicile may have made sense. But as women enter the workforce on a more equal basis, where a family sets up residence is now subject to negotiation. The rise of commuter marriages, defined as couples who spend at least three nights apart each week for a minimum of three months, has caused domicile laws to change. The number of commuter marriages, initially necessitated by two professional careers, has increased in recent years as a result of the declining economy and rising unemployment. According to the US Census Bureau, the number of couples who live apart has more than doubled since 1990, increasing to an estimated 3.5 million married couples (including military families).

Although property rights were invested entirely in the husband during coverture, married women's property acts enacted in the 1800s permitted women to acquire and control property. In reality, however, because women were still relegated to the home and unpaid labor in the home by the separate spheres ideology and tradition, laws that allowed them to acquire property, enter into contracts, or engage in business were initially limited. In common-law property states, husbands and wives are entitled individually to control property—that is, whoever holds the title owns the property. In many cases, however, because full-time homemakers had no visible source of income, the courts ruled that jointly acquired property or assets (including a joint bank account) were the husband's property. The courts also paid close attention to who paid the bills in two-income families. Women sometimes found themselves without assets if they assumed responsibility for such consumables as food and the husband paid the mortgage and purchased durable goods, such as the family automobile. In community property states, both the husband and wife equally control assets acquired in marriage. Nine states—Arizona, California, Idaho, Louisiana, Nevada, New Mexico, Texas, Washington, and Wisconsin—have some form of community property laws. Although exceptions have been made for individual inheritance or assets accumulated prior to the marriage, the courts in community property states view a couple as one economic unit.

In many cases, courts used to give husbands control over the ongoing management of community property, but this has since been changed to reflect the idea of marriage as an equal partnership.[18]

Divorce

Divorce contributes significantly to poverty rates among women; this stems from the interplay of private and public patriarchy. Within a marriage, women contribute their unpaid labor, and if they work outside the home, their earnings provide less than one-third of the family income in most households. When a marriage ends in divorce, a woman's standard of living falls because her single wage must provide for herself and her children. A ten-year study in California estimated that after divorce women's standard of living declined by 73 percent, while men's rose on average by 42 percent.[19] Men are also more likely to remarry and to do so more quickly than women. One study estimated that the total family income of a divorced woman and her children was less than 50 percent of the family income prior to divorce, but as the custodial parent, she needed approximately 80 percent of the total family income before the divorce to maintain the family's standard of living.[20]

Since marriage is a state-sanctioned legal union, only the state can legally dissolve a marriage. Eighteenth-century feminists sought reforms to divorce law to escape abusive and dangerous marriages at a time when civil law did not recognize divorce. The state exercised its prerogative to encourage marriage even at the expense of women's physical safety and happiness. Prior to California's adoption of no-fault divorce laws in 1969, most states required the party seeking a divorce to prove legitimate grounds for a separation—most often battering, abuse, abandonment, and adultery. Evidence of fault was required even when both parties agreed to divorce. Reforms to state divorce laws began in the late 1960s and generally followed California's lead in adopting no-fault divorce laws. No-fault divorce is now available in all fifty states, although its application and disposition are very different. Irreconcilable differences or separation are most often the grounds for contemporary divorce. States that recognize separation as grounds may require a couple to live in separate residences for a time (usually six months to two years) before granting a divorce.

In recent years, states have become alarmed at the rising divorce rates (just under 50 percent of first marriages now end in divorce), and in response they have renewed efforts to legislate marriage and divorce policy. For the most part, states have not returned to fault-based divorce, although some states have extended the waiting period for divorce or have required couples to get counseling when children are involved. Most states, however, have concentrated on encouraging couples to be more careful before entering into marriage in the first place. Some states now require couples counseling before issuing a marriage license. Louisiana went a step further and created voluntary "covenant marriages." Couples who choose a "covenant marriage" agree to seek counseling if problems develop in their marriage and will be allowed to seek a divorce only under certain severe circumstances (sexual abuse, adultery, abandonment) or after a two-year separation, very similar to the grounds of fault-based divorce. Arizona and Arkansas have since adopted similar legislation, and several other state legislatures have policies under consideration. Couples with a "regular marriage" may retroactively petition the state for a covenant marriage by declaring in a written affidavit that "marriage is for life" and by agreeing to abide by the guidelines of a covenant marriage.

While real property assets are fairly easy to divide and most states require an equitable division of real property, benefits awarded by a third party (health insurance, pension rights, stock options) or an increase in earning capacity derived from a professional degree are more difficult to divide. Since most states have community property laws, any assets or property acquired during marriage are subject to equitable division by the court. More than half of the states consider pensions marital property and subject to division. Federal law covers access to Social Security or military pension benefits after divorce as long as the couple has been married for ten years or more. An employer is required to continue health insurance coverage for one year. The most difficult concept for the states to grasp, however, involves human capital. In the 1970s and 1980s, the popular press was full of stories about professionally successful husbands who were divorcing their wives after several decades of marriage, even though the wife had supported the family financially during her husband's years in law school or medical school. In almost all cases, the courts determined that earning capacity and educational degrees cannot be divided. However, several courts have used a man's earning capacity and a woman's contribution to developing his earning capacity to determine the amount of alimony payments. Others have required a husband to reimburse his wife for the cost of his education.

Alimony is yet another holdover from the theory of unity. A husband's obligation for financial support extended past the marriage if the husband sought the divorce or was determined to be at fault. During the 1970s, alimony laws were rendered gender neutral, allowing the courts to require support payments to either husband or wife. In *Orr v. Orr* (1979), the US Supreme Court ruled that sex-based alimony laws violated the equal protection clause of the Fourteenth Amendment. The end to fault-based divorce also diminished the presumption that alimony is compensation for harm. It is now rare that either spouse is ordered to make support payments indefinitely. Short-term payments may be ordered to ease the transition from marriage to a single-wage status. Alimony may also be awarded to allow a spouse to receive job training or earn a college degree, or as a one-time financial award. In many cases, gender-neutral, no-fault divorce laws have not benefited women, particularly those who pursued a traditional gender role within marriage. These women suffer a dramatic loss of income and social status when their marriage ends.

Child support is different from alimony. Both parents may be ordered to provide support for their children, regardless of the custody arrangements. Noncustodial parents are much less likely to actually pay court-ordered support (and are more likely to be fathers). Congress has reacted by strengthening enforcement of child-support provisions. In 1975, Congress created the Child Support Enforcement program to collect unpaid child support from noncustodial parents. While billions of dollars have been collected and redistributed, that amount represents a very small proportion of what is actually owed. In 1996, as a part of the welfare reform bill known as the Personal Responsibility and Work Opportunity Reconciliation Act, Congress created state and federal databases to help locate noncustodial parents. Motor vehicle, tax, and public utilities records have allowed authorities to track noncustodial parents across state lines. New penalty provisions revoke motor vehicle licenses, as well as professional and recreational licenses issued by the government, for nonpayment.

Marriage Equality

With a 5–4 decision in the 2015 case *Obergefell v. Hodges*, the US Supreme Court affirmed the right of same-sex couples to marry. The majority opinion, authored by Justice Anthony Kennedy, situated the right to marry in the due process and equal protection clauses of the Fourteenth Amendment, declaring that "the right to personal choice regarding marriage is inherent in the concept of individual autonomy."[21] By the time the *Obergefell* ruling was issued, thirty-six states, the District of Columbia, and Guam were issuing marriage licenses to same-sex couples, though thirteen states had banned gay marriage by constitutional amendment or state law and many of these states refused to recognize same-sex marriages performed in other states. Marriage equality was achieved through federal and state actions, but there are several issues left to resolve before same-sex couples enjoy all of the privileges marriage bestows on opposite-sex unions.

In 1993, the Hawaii Supreme Court ruled that denying marriage licenses to same-sex couples might violate the equal protection clause of the Hawaii Constitution.[22] Legislators in other states began to worry that if Hawaii allowed gay people to legally marry, their own state might be forced to recognize the union. Opponents of gay marriage pushed for constitutional bans on same-sex marriage, and several were quickly adopted. At the federal level, Congress passed and President Bill Clinton signed into law the Defense of Marriage Act (DOMA) in 1996. DOMA denied federal recognition to same-sex marriages and allowed states to ignore gay marriages performed in other states. Prior to DOMA, four states already had laws banning gay marriage (Maryland, New Hampshire, Wisconsin, and Wyoming). Vermont was the first state to pass a law that allowed full and equal civil legal status to gay and lesbian couples, although not the right to legally marry. Courts in Hawaii and Alaska attempted to recognize same-sex civil unions and give them the same legal privileges as heterosexual marriages; however, state constitutional amendments banning gay marriage overturned such rulings. In Massachusetts, seven gay couples filed suit, arguing that the Massachusetts constitution guaranteed them the right to marry. The state supreme court agreed and ordered the legislature to allow same-sex couples to marry by May 17, 2004.

Eleven states had constitutional amendments banning same-sex marriage on the November 2004 ballot, and they all passed. President George W. Bush pushed for an amendment to the federal constitution defining marriage as the legal union of one man and one woman, and although it was introduced in 2006, it never received a hearing in Congress. There was a good deal of confusion in California in 2008. The state Supreme Court ruled in June that restricting marriage to heterosexual couples violated the constitutional rights of homosexual couples, and thousands of same-sex couples were married. However, California voters approved Proposition 8 in November, banning gay marriage in the state. Proposition 8 was upheld by the California Supreme Court, but the court stipulated that the 18,000 marriages that had taken place between June and November remained legal. By 2010 gay couples could be legally married in just five states: Massachusetts, Connecticut, Iowa, Vermont, and New Hampshire.

In 2013, in *United States v. Windsor,* the US Supreme Court declared a portion of DOMA unconstitutional. Section 3 of the law prevented the federal government from recognizing gay marriages for the purposes of federal laws, benefits, or programs even when those couples were legally married in their home state. Justice Anthony Kennedy, writing for a 5–4 majority, noted that the act wrote inequality into federal law and violated the Fifth Amendment's protection of equal liberty. "DOMA's principal effect is to identify a subset of state-sanctioned marriages and make them unequal," he wrote.[23] This decision prompted the federal government to immediately extend federal benefits to married same-sex couples regardless of whether they had been married in a state where gay marriage was legal or were currently living in one. More than 1,100 federal regulations, rights, and laws are impacted by marital status. Interspousal immunity, visitation rights in federal prisons, military benefits and access to on-base housing, health and survivor benefits, and military family separation allowances were changed to include same-sex couples. Although *Windsor* did not erase the differences in marriage law between states, it provided federal judges with the reasoning to expand equal treatment in the many challenges issued to state laws. For example, in January 2014, the US Court of Appeals for the Ninth Circuit held that gays and lesbians cannot be excluded from juries, affirming that equal dignity extended to responsibilities as well as rights.

Obergefell provided the constitutional basis for marriage equality and thus made gay marriage legal everywhere in the United States. Even so, resistance remained strong in certain regions of the country. In Rowan County, Kentucky, for example, county clerk Kim Davis refused to issue marriage licenses to same-sex

IMAGE 8.1: *Demonstrators in support of same-sex marriage spell out 'LOVE' with balloons outside the US Supreme Court in Washington, D.C., before the Obergefell v. Hodges ruling. The court's decision, announced on June 26, 2015, recognizes a constitutional right for same-sex couples to marry.* Source: Andrew Harrer/Bloomberg via Getty Images.

couples under her signature, citing personal moral and religious objections to gay marriage. A US district court judge found Davis in contempt of court and jailed her for five days. Davis was released under the condition that she not interfere with the efforts of her deputy clerks, who had started issuing marriage licenses to all couples. Ultimately Kentucky passed a law removing clerks' names from marriage licenses, settling the question for Kim Davis personally. Davis viewed this as a victory: "I am pleased that I can continue to serve my community as the Rowan County Clerk without having to sacrifice my religious convictions and conscience."[24] But the larger question of whether an individual's religious convictions can deny others equal rights remains unresolved. The rise of conscience clause laws is discussed in the last section of this chapter.

The shift in public opinion favoring gay marriage has been rapid and broad. President Obama announced his support of gay marriage in 2012, following a period of public opposition and a preference for states to decide the question. After a decade of opposition, Hillary Rodham Clinton announced her support in 2013 in a video with the Human Rights Campaign. As a candidate for president, she made her "H" logo rainbow-colored, and the day the US Supreme Court heard oral arguments in *Obergefell*, she tweeted, "Every loving couple & family deserves to be recognized & treated equally under the law across our nation.

#LoveMustWin #LoveCantWait." According to Pew Research Center polling done in 2001, 57 percent of Americans opposed gay marriage while 35 percent favored it. Support for marriage equality has grown steadily every year, and in 2016, the proportions of those who favor versus those who oppose gay marriage have flipped. Today 55 percent of Americans support same-sex marriage, while 37 percent oppose it.[25]

Family policy, largely related to marriage and divorce laws, is administered almost exclusively by the states. This has resulted in an uncoordinated patchwork of laws and policies targeted at specific issues or populations. When federal legislation is layered on top of state statutes, the result is often more confusion than support for families. Determining what families need from government is all the more difficult because the idea of what a "family" is has changed faster than the laws that define and support families. Public and private employer policies aimed at parents and children necessarily exclude couples who choose not to have children. Does this unlawfully deny child-free couples a social or employment benefit? The political debate over "family values" is laden with values regarding which type of family constellation(s) should be rewarded or discouraged. Conservative Christians have entered politics in large numbers during the last decade to influence policy in favor of the "traditional family"—though even this group acknowledges that traditional families now include two wage earners.

SUPPORTING FAMILIES WITH WORKING PARENTS

Families of all types have long put pressure on those in office for more help in accommodating the stresses associated with juggling work and family. Family policy can come in several forms, including cash benefits or social insurance to boost the family's standard of living (health insurance, education, Social Security, or employment); indirect cash transfers such as tax credits or deductions for dependent children, family allowances, and means-tested family benefits; employment benefits for workers with families (maternity and parental leave); direct services to families (on-site child care, after-school programs); housing subsidies for families with children; or legislation that is consistent with the state's population policies (access to contraception, abortion services, infertility treatments, or adoption). The United States has a large number of policies at the state and federal levels that affect families, including the Family and Medical Leave Act (1993), the first parental leave policy enacted in the United States. However, dominant attitudes that support family autonomy and limited government involvement as well as the reinforcement of traditional gender ideologies have limited the coherence and reach of family policy.

The issues associated with balancing work and caring for families loom large for individual families, particularly for women within families, but receive very little positive public attention. Mona Harrington, author of *Care and Equality:*

TABLE 8.1: International Maternity Leave Benefits, Selected Countries by Region

Country	Length of Leave	Percent of Wages Paid	Provider of Coverage
Congo	15 weeks	100	50% employer, 50% social security
Kenya	2 months	100	employer
Morocco	14 weeks	100	social security
Nigeria	12 weeks	50	employer
Somalia	14 weeks	50	employer
South Africa	4 months	45–60	unemployment insurance
Argentina	90 days	100	social security
Bahamas	13 weeks	100	40% employer, 60% social security
Brazil	120 days	100	social security
Chile	18 weeks	100	social security
Cuba	18 weeks	100	social security
Haiti	12 weeks	100 for 6 weeks	employer
Honduras	10 weeks	100 for 84 days	33% employer, 67% social security
Mexico	12 weeks	100	social security
Venezuela	18 weeks	100	social security
Bangladesh	16 weeks	100	employer
Cambodia	90 days	50	employer
China	90 days	100	social security

Source: International Labour Organization, 2014, accessed at http://www.ilo.org.

Inventing a New Family Politics, argues that a serious politics of family care must "explicitly link economics and the function of caretaking. It must begin with a clear view of the unfair allocation to women of the major costs of caretaking and clear recognition of the critical deficits in the present care system. And then, with the whole picture of these systemic costs and deficits firmly in mind, the liberal community must work on the invention of a new care system."[26] Most important, Harrington says, care must be thought of as a public issue—one of our national social issues. The need for socially supported care in the United States runs across all income levels, not just those at the bottom. Because of the focus on poverty programs as the only means of public family support, the idea of family care as solely a private responsibility goes unchallenged. Implicit, then, is the assumption that all other families—middle- and upper-income—can provide or, more likely, purchase all of the care services they require. The problem is that we have not

TABLE 8.1: International Maternity Leave Benefits, Selected Countries by Region *(continued)*

Country	Length of Leave	Percent of Wages Paid	Provider of Coverage
India	12 weeks	100	employer, social security
Iran	90 days	66.7 for 16 weeks	social security
Iraq	62 days	100	social security
Israel	14 weeks	100	social security
Saudi Arabia	10 weeks	50 or 100	employer
Australia	18 weeks	fed. min. wage*	social security
Austria	16 weeks	100	social security
Canada	up to 50 weeks	55 for 50 weeks	unemployment insurance
Denmark	52 weeks	100 up to a ceiling	social security
France	16–26 weeks	100	social security
Germany	14 weeks	100	social security to a ceiling, employer
Italy	5 months	80	social security
Japan	14 weeks	60	social security, health insurance
Portugal	120/150 days	100/80	social security
Spain	16 weeks	100	social security
United Kingdom	39 weeks	90 for first 6 weeks; flat rate for 33 more weeks	social security
United States	12 weeks	0	

*Proposal pending approval

devised any "equality respecting system to replace the full-time caretaking labor force of women at home."[27]

Whether a country has adopted a policy relating to family support depends on a number of factors, including structural economic factors (capitalist versus socialist economy); need created by changing social and economic factors; and the activity of family advocacy groups, employers and business owners, women's organizations, and religious groups. These "policy inputs" influence the "policy output" in each country and help explain why there are differences across national boundaries.[28] In comparison to other nations, the United States fares poorly on the Work, Family and Equity Index developed by the Project on Global Working Families to measure governmental performance in meeting the needs of working families around the world.[29] The United States performs well in equitable right-to-work policies but falls short on supporting families. Of the 196 countries included in the International Labour Organization (ILO) "Maternity and Paternity at Work" study, only seven countries do not provide paid maternity leave: Surinam, Marshall Islands, Micronesia, Tonga, Palau, Papua New Guinea, and the United States (see Table 8.1).[30] The ILO recommends women be guaranteed fourteen weeks of paid maternal leave. At least 107 countries protect working women's right to breastfeed; in at least seventy-three countries, breastfeeding breaks are paid. There is no such right to breast-feed, paid or unpaid, in the United States. A Department of Labor study found that employed women who received twelve weeks or more of paid maternity leave were more likely to start breastfeeding their baby and continue to breastfeed for at least six months, as recommended by the American Academy of Pediatrics, than women who did not get any paid leave. Research confirms a positive relationship between paid maternity leave and economic growth. "European countries view paid leave for mothers as an investment in their economy. Countries can either work with half of their workforce or compete with their full workforce, which requires paid maternity leave," says Jody Heymann, a public health scholar.[31] The absence of paid maternity leave disproportionately affects women at the lower end of the economic spectrum and particularly those in the low-wage workforce. A 2012 Department of Labor study found that 23 percent of women who left work to care for an infant took less than two weeks off, substantially increasing health risks for both mother and child.

Without a federal policy, where you live in the United States and whom you work for determine the benefits you receive as a family. Only 12 percent of US workers in the private sector can get paid family leave through their employer, according to the Department of Labor. A number of those without access to paid leave have turned to crowdfunding websites to raise money for maternity leave.[32] In 2004, California became the first state to provide up to six weeks of paid family leave (up to 55 percent of a worker's wage) financed through the state's disability insurance fund. New Jersey and Rhode Island also provide paid family leave financed by a payroll deduction. San Francisco became the first US city to require employers of more than twenty people to cover the 45 percent of a worker's wage that the state of California does not. In April 2016, New York passed a paid family leave bill that when fully implemented will provide up to twelve weeks of paid leave. Beginning in 2018, the support will be 50 percent of an employee's average weekly wage, capped at 50 percent of the statewide average weekly wage; and when fully implemented in 2021, it will cover 67 percent of a worker's average weekly wage, capped at 67 percent of the statewide average weekly wage.[33]

In the private sector, tech companies have led the way—Twitter, Facebook, and Google provide paid family leave packages as an employee recruitment and retention incentive. However, a Harvard Business School survey in 2014 found that of nearly 4,000 corporate executives across a range of industries, 60 percent of male executives had a spouse who did not work outside the home, compared with 10 percent of the women.[34] With the majority of top executives able to focus exclusively on work, it is little wonder that paid family and medical leave, paid sick leave, and workplace flexibility issues have gained little traction in the United States. In a study of 1,000 male managers, men in traditional marriages were more likely to have negative attitudes toward women in the workplace than men in dual-income marriages.[35] Researchers also found that the managers tended to evaluate work-life policies on the basis of their own experiences. "It is not hard to see how senior men with wives at home end up perpetuating the ideal male work model," writes Anne Weisberg in the *New York Times*.[36]

Paid Family and Medical Leave

The **Family and Medical Leave Act (FMLA)** allows workers to take up to twelve weeks of unpaid leave to bond with a newborn, newly adopted, or newly placed child; to provide care for a seriously ill child, spouse, or parent; or care for their own serious health condition, without fear of losing their jobs. Most now believe it does not go far enough and needs to be strengthened, but when Representative Patricia Schroeder of Colorado first introduced the bill in 1985, no one would join her as a cosponsor. After eight years of legislative debate and two George H. W. Bush presidential vetoes, the FMLA was signed by President Clinton in 1993. Amendments to the act have extended the protections to allow workers with family in the military to take time away from work to attend to situations arising from a parent, spouse, son or daughter's foreign deployment and up to twenty-six weeks of leave to care for a servicemember with a serious injury or illness.

However, FMLA only applies to what the legislation refers to as "covered employers." These include private sector employers with fifty or more employees, all public agencies, and all public or private elementary and secondary schools. An employee is eligible for FMLA leave if he or she has worked for a covered employer for at least twelve months, has worked at least 1,250 hours during the twelve months immediately preceding the leave, and works at a location where the employer has at least fifty employees within seventy-five miles. These regulations mean that roughly 60 percent of the American workforce is actually covered by FMLA.[37] A majority of those who are eligible and use FMLA leave do so for personal health reasons—issues that would likely be covered by a paid sick leave policy. Less than 10 percent of FMLA is used for pregnancy-related issues and 6.8 percent for the care of a new child. At any given time, only 10 percent of covered employees nationwide are on unpaid FMLA leave. Policies such as FMLA that mandate job-guaranteed leave but do not require wage replacement are of limited value to most workers, particularly the working poor. The FMLA did, however, assert a public interest in family care and opened an important door.

The issue of paid family and medical leave has become a significant part of the current political dialogue and was a feature of the 2016 presidential campaign.

Box 8.1 – Encountering the Controversies of Equality

Need a Baby Boom? Come to Terms with Gender Equality

The Italian government designated September 22, 2016, as "Fertility Day," and Health Minister Beatrice Lorenzin launched a social media campaign designed to remind Italians of the "beauty" of parenthood, warn them of threats to fertility, and educate them on ways to increase fertility. One message contained an image of a woman holding an hourglass with the words "Beauty has no age. But fertility does." Another read "Fertility is a common good."[1] The campaign was immediately criticized as sexist and offensive to women, particularly since young women applying for jobs in Italy still encounter a practice called *dimissioni in bianco*, where they are asked to sign undated letters of resignation that allow employers to dismiss them if they become pregnant.

The total fertility rate for Italy in 2015 was 1.42 children per woman—not high enough to maintain its current population (the replacement rate is 2.1), let alone grow the population. Anything below replacement rate indicates a population decreasing in size and growing older. Global fertility rates are in general decline, and this trend is most pronounced in industrialized countries, especially Western Europe. Governments pay close attention to fertility rates and population trends. Economic growth is fueled, in part, by new workers with new ideas, and the social safety net is funded through taxes generated by a strong economy.

"The trouble with the Fertility Day campaign isn't that the low birthrate won't cause real problems, it's that those problems shouldn't be women's to solve," writes journalist Claire Zillman.[2] Consider the situation in France and in Scandinavian countries. The fertility rate in France is 2.01, and more than 1.8 children per

---

The Obama administration has been a strong advocate for paid leave. As part of his annual budget proposal for fiscal years 2016 and 2017, the president urged Congress to provide six weeks of paid parental leave to federal employees. In January 2015, with an executive order, Obama directed federal agencies to advance up to six weeks of paid sick leave to federal employees for the care of a new child or ill family member. Funding for his proposal to provide up to twelve weeks total of paid leave would come from employees' accumulated sick and administrative leave.[38] A previous executive order required federal contractors to provide up to seven days of sick leave for employees to use for themselves or to care for an ill family member. Defense Secretary Ash Carter announced in 2016 female

woman are born in Sweden, Norway, and Finland, compared to a European Union average of 1.58. Social demographers attribute the differences to changing attitudes about gender equality and women at work. "The fertility rate is high in European countries where family norms are flexible, women feel free to work, pro-child policies are generous and childcare is well organized—in short, in countries that have come to terms with gender equality," reported an article in the *Guardian*.[3] The employment rate for women ages twenty-four to fifty-four is 83.4 percent in France, 84.4 percent in Finland, 85.6 percent in Denmark, and 87.5 percent in Sweden. In 2002, the European Union set a target for member states to provide formal care facilities for a third of all preschool children. In France, well over half of all children under three are in some form of collective care; the figure is over 65 percent in Denmark. The map of the fertility rate in European countries overlaps with the map of women who work outside the home and the map of child care facilities. By contrast, direct financial support or incentives to boost fertility rates have shown limited effects.[4]

Italian prime minister Matteo Renzi seemed to acknowledge this reality. "If you want to create a society that invests in its future and has children, you have to make sure the underlying conditions are there," he said, citing the need for good jobs and child care services.

What do you think?

Are you surprised that the modern recipe for high fertility rates is relaxed attitudes toward nontraditional families, a large proportion of women in the workforce, and state-provided child care? Up until the 1980s, it was the opposite—high fertility correlated with low employment for women. What has changed? How might these changes impact your personal decisions? What role should governments play in encouraging fertility? If the US government undertook a campaign similar to Italy's Fertility Day, what do you imagine the reaction would be?

members of the military can take twelve weeks of paid maternity leave—an increase of four weeks.

Voters are paying attention. According to surveys conducted for the National Partnership for Women and Families in 2016, 76 percent of voters support establishing a national paid family and medical leave policy. Women (85 percent), voters under thirty (68 percent), unmarried women (76 percent), African Americans (85 percent), Latinos (67 percent), and voters making under $30,000 a year (71 percent) are strongly supportive of this initiative. Although Democratic and independent voters express the highest level of support, a strong majority of Republicans (57 percent) are also in favor of paid family and medical leave. After learning about the current FMLA, nearly eight in ten voters say it is important for elected officials to update the law to guarantee access to paid family and medical leave.[39]

Paid family leave was the subject of speeches at both national party conventions in 2016. Ivanka Trump, daughter of Republican nominee Donald Trump, addressed the convention delegates, saying, "At my father's company, there are more female than male executives, women are paid equally for the work that we do, and when a woman becomes a mother she is supported, not shut out." She went on to advocate for equal pay and child care. Although these positions resonated well with those in attendance, they were not as clearly articulated in the 2016 Republican Party platform.[40] Hillary Clinton, by contrast, offered a number of proposals on affordable child care and paid family leave, and proposed tax credits for unpaid caregivers. Work-family balance issues were prominently featured in the Democratic Party platform.[41]

The status quo isn't working for women or men in dual-career households. *Daily Beast* columnist Connor P. Williams recently wrote, "Want to open the boardroom doors for women? Encourage—heck, praise—dads who stay home with their children."[42] According to Pew, only 4 percent of households in 2015 could be characterized as "mother-only employed," compared with 28 percent "father-only employed," with the balance, 66 percent, dual income households. Four in ten Americans still believe it is "extremely important" for a father to provide income for his children, while just 25 percent say the same about mothers. Fathers and mothers were equally likely to report that parenting is extremely important to their identity and a rewarding experience. Although much of the work-family balance research and discussion focuses on women, 52 percent of dads in the Pew survey said that it is difficult to balance the responsibilities of work and family.[43] Relative to their own parents, both mothers and fathers today spend more time with their kids. Forty-six percent of fathers say they spend more time with their children than their own parents spent with them, but 48 percent say that it is still not enough time.

Paid (and unpaid) paternity leave is less available than paid maternity leave in the United States. And although several large companies currently offer fathers paid leave, very few take it. Fifteen percent of US companies provide some paid time to new fathers, but many are reluctant to use it for reasons ranging from a fear of losing status at work to stereotypes of a father's role in the family. Approximately 85 percent of men take some time off from work following the birth of a child, but most take at most a week or two.[44] Paternity leave is beneficial to all involved. A Columbia University study found that fathers who take longer leaves are more involved with child care months after returning to work. Mothers also benefit—more generous and equitable parental leave polices mean that mothers are more likely to return to their jobs once their maternity leave is over. Some countries, such as Sweden and Portugal, have mandatory leave for fathers.

At the very least, new fathers do not have to worry about an earnings penalty associated with parenthood. Married mothers of minor children experience the largest wage gaps. Whereas marriage and children are associated with higher earnings among men, women suffer a **motherhood penalty** that results in a loss in wages and benefits at the rate of about 4 percent per child. This gap cannot be explained by human capital, family structure, family-friendly job characteristics, or differences among women that are stable over time.[45]

In addition to depressed wages, mothers suffer from inherent bias at other stages of the employment process. Cornell University's Cognitive Bias Working Group published a study in 2007 that confirmed this bias against mothers.[46] Volunteer subjects and a sample of real employers were asked to evaluate a group of equally qualified male and female job applicants on the basis of their resumes, some of which had a cue about parenthood. The bias against mothers but not fathers was striking among both the volunteer subjects and the actual employers. Mothers were consistently rated as less competent and less committed, and they were held to higher performance and punctuality standards. Mothers were 79 percent less likely to be hired, and if hired, they received a starting salary offer $11,000 lower than nonmothers. Women without children were more than twice as likely as equally qualified mothers to be called for interviews. Fathers fared the best and were offered the highest starting salaries of any group (including men who were not fathers).

Child Care

Child care became a politicized issue when two women were forced to withdraw their nominations for attorney general of the United States under the newly elected Clinton administration in 1993. Zoe Baird, the first female nominee for attorney general, withdrew her nomination because of allegations related to her nanny's employment and payroll taxes. Kimba Wood, President Clinton's second choice for the post, was also forced to step down over similar issues related to her child care arrangements. Clinton's third choice, Janet Reno, was not subject to this line of inquiry since she was unmarried and without children. No previous nominee had ever been questioned about his child care arrangements during Senate confirmation hearings.

Twenty years later, President Barack Obama identified affordable, high-quality child care as a "must-have" in his 2015 State of the Union address: "It's time we stop treating child care as a side issue, or as a women's issue, and treat it like the national economic priority that it is for all of us."[47] Research demonstrates the positive impact high-quality early childhood education can have for all children: improved cognitive skills, school readiness, and positive social outcomes. For at-risk children, participation in early care programs leads to higher IQs at age five, increased high school graduation rates, higher incomes, and lower rates of crime and use of social services in adulthood.[48] The demographics of the full-time workforce have changed dramatically over the last forty years, but the social support structures to help families care for children, the elderly, or the ill have not changed substantially. As with paid leave, the United States has no universal child care policy. For families with children between the ages of three and five, child care is the third-greatest expense after housing and food. In most states, the cost of center-based care exceeds the cost of a year of college. Finding adequate child care and paying for it is a widespread problem for all Americans, so why hasn't it become a political imperative?

The reasons are many. Elizabeth Palley and Corey S. Shdaimah, authors of *In Our Hands: The Struggle for U.S. Child Care Policy*, point to the lack of a good way to frame the case for child care as anything other than an individual parent or family responsibility.[49] Ambivalent public attitudes about mothers in the workplace robbed the issue of political immediacy—women (and men) were afraid to demand government support for the care they needed because it made obvious the reality that most mothers in all socioeconomic classes were working. Adopting a comparative perspective, Kimberly Morgan argues that differences in child care policies among Western industrialized nations are more likely explained by the role of organized religion in politics than by women's employment rates or the influence of left-wing political parties.[50] In countries such as France and Sweden, where "religious authorities have been subordinated to secular ones," the state has played a more active role in family policy. France and Sweden enacted public policy solutions to provide full-day care for infants and children. In countries where religion has more influence over politics (e.g., the Netherlands and the United States), "religious forces have succeeded in generating more opposition to shifting gender roles and the creation of government family policy." The United States has left the solution for this problem up to individual families and the private sector, with the minimal public subsidies that do exist being limited to the poorest families. Middle- and upper-class families are able to access care in the private sector precisely because the government has not intervened in the market to insist that day care centers be regulated more heavily or to set expectations for education, training, and wages for day care workers. As we discussed in Chapter 7, child care is an overwhelmingly female occupation and among the poorest-paid of all occupations. For these reasons and countless others, even though political candidates and elected officials talk about the need for accessible, high-quality child care, the United States still lags behind the rest of the industrial world in making it happen.

In times of national crisis (an economic depression or a war), when women were needed to work, the government has taken an active role in providing assistance with child care, only for that support to vanish once the crisis passed. During World War II, the government needed women in heavy industry and in white-collar jobs to replace the men sent off to war. It actively recruited women into wage work and facilitated women's entrance into the labor force by providing comprehensive child care centers. Not only did these nurseries tend children, but women were also able to drop off mending and the week's shopping list, and collect a ready-made dinner. Infirmaries cared for sick children, and a medical staff tended to immunizations and regular checkups. Facilities created under the Lanham Act of 1941 were in a sense accidental. The act allocated funds for the exigencies of wartime production, and the mobilization of the female labor force created a dire need for child care facilities. When the war ended, so did the national commitment to women's role in the paid labor force and to the support structures that made it possible.

Not only did the financial support disappear, the national rhetoric about the positive benefits of nursery education for children took a dark cold war turn. In the postwar "return to normalcy," individualized care at home was celebrated over state-run day care centers, which were characterized as providing "highly regimented, one-size-fits-all care that stifled the individuality of the child."[51] State-sponsored day care, successfully co-opted by the ideological right, became "sovietized" in the national mind-set. Publicly subsidized child care became more available in the 1960s but was tied to the growth in public housing and other programs designed to combat poverty.[52] Upper- and middle-class women were pressured to stay home with their children, as no child care was good enough to justify leaving their children to go off to work. But poor women were being told to join the workforce, as no child care was bad enough to justify providing public support for them to stay home with their children.[53]

Congress attempted to address the need for universal child care in 1971 in the Child Development Act, which would have created a network of child care facilities with fees based on a family's income. But the public's negative reaction prompted a presidential veto and shelved the discussion for nearly twenty years. In the 1990s, when it became evident that the majority of women and women with small children would participate in the full-time workforce and that women would work throughout the course of their lifetime, the government began to reexamine the issue. In 1990, Congress passed the Child Care and Development Act, which authorized funding in the form of block grants to states, allowing each state to decide how the money would best serve its needs. On one hand, this allowed states to experiment with child care strategies that were tailored to their unique constituencies and needs. Alternatively, by not providing uniform standards for quality, training, and services, the Child Care and Development Act did nothing to improve the accessibility or quality of child care nationally. Further, 75 percent of the block-grant funding was targeted for low-income families, which perpetuated the myth that child care was a class issue. In 2012, $11.4 billion in federal and state spending (less than in 2002) went toward improving child care quality and access, with 1.5 million children receiving assistance each month (the lowest number since 1998).

Over the last two decades there has been no significant progress in expanding care for all children. For two-paycheck families, reliable, high-quality child care remains scarce and exorbitantly expensive. The annual cost of center-based care for an infant ranges from $5,496 to $16,549, a cost that exceeds the average tuition of a four-year public university in thirty-one states and the District of Columbia.[54] The cost drops as the child ages, but not by much. Care for a four-year-old in a center can range from $4,515 to $12,320, and even home-based care is out of reach for many, with costs ranging from $4,039 to $10,727 depending on geographic location in the country. Because federal support for child care comes in the form of grants to states, there is great variation across states. In thirty-eight states, families with income above 200 percent of the federal poverty level ($39,580 a year for a family of three in 2014) cannot qualify for assistance. For those who do qualify, the waiting lists for spots can be quite long. As of 2014, eighteen states had established waiting lists or had frozen intake for families applying for child care assistance.[55] There is also great variation across states in access to four-year-old kindergarten, ranging in enrollment from 100 percent in the District of Columbia to just 12 percent of children in New Hampshire.

Paid Sick Leave and Flex Time

Approximately 160 countries provide mandatory paid sick days, with 127 nations providing a week or more each year. In the United States there is no such policy, effectively leaving 60 million workers, or 43 percent of the private industry labor force, without any paid sick leave. Thirty-eight percent of women workers in the private-sector do not have access to a single paid sick day. Business owners have been among the staunchest opponents of paid sick leave, arguing that it would amount to a costly government mandate, particularly during an economic recession. However, one of the consequences of not having paid sick leave is that employees feel compelled to go to work even when contagious or risk losing their job. A survey by the Center for WorkLife Law found that one in six workers said that they or a family member had been fired, suspended, punished, or threatened by an employer for taking time off to care for themselves or a family member. The National Partnership for Women and Families (NPWF) found that paid sick days actually reduce the business costs of employee turnover, absenteeism, and lack of productivity when an employee is sick on the job. The NPWF estimates that seven days of annual paid sick leave would yield a net savings of more than $8 billion to the national economy.

Five states plus an additional twenty-eight cities, one county (Montgomery County, MD), and Washington, D.C., have paid sick time laws on the books. Dr. Jody Heymann, founder of the Project on Global Working Families, argues that the United States is harming its economy by not adopting worker protections. A variety of advocates have urged the adoption of paid sick leave as an employment standard just like the federal minimum wage. The Healthy Families Act, sponsored in the House by Rosa DeLauro (D-Conn.) and in the Senate by Patty Murray

(D-Wash.), would mandate that employers with fifteen or more workers guarantee employees one paid hour off for every 30 hours worked, up to seven days each year. Paid sick days could be used to care for a child, parent, spouse or one's self. The bill was last introduced in February 2015 but Congress has not acted. President Obama twice campaigned for president on the issue of paid sick leave, and on Labor Day in 2015 he signed an executive order requiring federal contractors to give employees up to seven days of paid sick leave a year. Secretary of Labor Thomas Perez said, "While we have a ways to go to ensure every worker in America has paid sick leave, the executive order will provide additional paid sick leave to an estimated 828,000 workers. Nearly 437,000 of those currently receive no paid sick leave."[56] The executive order goes into effect January 1, 2017.

Workplace flexibility and scheduling policies are another way to support dual-earner families. The most common work arrangements include flextime, compressed workweeks, home-based work, and job sharing. Flextime allows the worker to vary the start and end times to a workday or to accumulate compensatory time to be used when needed. Scheduling predictability is particularly important to low-wage workers in fields such as hospitality, retail, and food and beverage, where a mix of daytime, nighttime, and weekend schedules is the norm. Seventy-four percent of hourly workers reported experiencing significant schedule fluctuations on a weekly or monthly basis. Students enrolled full- or part-time in college may experience similar pressures due to unpredictable schedules in combining education and work.

SAFETY NET FOR POOR FAMILIES

The single best predictor of poverty in America is gender. There are a variety of contradictory trends that contribute to the disproportionate number of women who live below the poverty line. Fewer women are married, although nearly half of all women have children. A single head of household with minor children, regardless of sex, is at a severe disadvantage since he or she will be required to do the unpaid labor of the household as well as work for a living outside the home. The problem is worse with a single female head of household because women's wages are lower than men's. Heads of households with children must either pay for child care, work part-time and provide some of the care themselves, or stay home to care for the children. With any of these options, a household's income is diminished. Although we are conditioned to believe that having a job is crucial to supporting one's family and contributing to the community, there is a shortage of jobs, particularly jobs that provide a living wage.

Welfare Policy: Temporary Assistance to Needy Families

Welfare policy in the United States began more than ninety years ago with state-level mothers' pension policies, which were designed to reduce the poverty of mothers without husbands. The New Deal then nationalized mothers' pensions with the Aid to Dependent Children (ADC) program, which was based on a number of assumptions about gender, poverty, and the need to lift single women "toward the norms of Anglo-American, middle-class culture."[57] ADC was modified to include a grant to mothers as well as children in 1950, and then it became **Aid to Families with Dependent Children (AFDC)** in 1962. Over time, the program's goals and focus shifted from ensuring that children did not grow up in poverty for lack of a male breadwinner to enforcing gender ideology and racial and cultural control.[58] As barriers to eligibility and moral supervision were lowered, more women of color joined the program, and the public's perception that women on welfare "don't deserve it" increased.

Pressure throughout the 1980s and 1990s to "end welfare as we know it" was rooted in a variety of myths about welfare recipients and cultural stereotypes about women in general—specifically African American women. Prior to national work requirements and time limits imposed by legislation in 1996, 43 percent of AFDC recipients either combined work with welfare or cycled between the two, and 56 percent of AFDC recipients were enrolled on welfare continuously for fewer than two years.[59] Furthermore, welfare payments alone never enabled a woman and her children to escape poverty. In 1996, the maximum AFDC benefit for a family of three in New York, the most generous state, was $703 a month, while the maximum payment in Mississippi, the least generous state, was $120 a month. In 1996, a family of three with an annual income of $12,980 ($1,082 a month) or less was considered below the poverty line. Even with food stamps, the combined benefit in the most generous state was only $935 a month—well below the poverty standard. The median combined payment per month was only 65 percent of the poverty line.[60] Welfare, although designated as an antipoverty program, did not "pay" women enough to escape poverty, did not provide incentives to get the education and training that would allow women to seek jobs above poverty-level wages, and did not address the fact that a single woman did not have a "wife" at home to care for her children while she was at work.

The reform package passed by Congress and signed by President Clinton in 1996, called the Personal Responsibility and Work Opportunity Reconciliation Act, had as its centerpiece an AFDC replacement known as **Temporary Assistance to Needy Families (TANF)**. The basic goal of the new program was to replace government assistance with earnings, ending the entitlement to public assistance. Funding would be distributed as block grants to the individual states for the design and administration of welfare programs. States were encouraged to design programs around work requirements, allowing recipients to keep a larger percentage of their wages and still be eligible for assistance, education, and training programs to develop job skills. States have imposed time limits on benefits ranging from two to five years (over a person's lifetime in most cases), increased efforts to collect child support from biological fathers, and given more attention to child care demands.

Since TANF was passed, the number of families receiving public assistance in most states has decreased, but likely not for the reasons the policy's authors intended. Nationwide, welfare goes to just 23 out of every 100 families who live below the poverty line, according to the latest data from 2014. That's compared to 68 out of every 100 poor families in 1996, the year welfare reform was passed. Although the number of people on welfare has declined, the poverty rate has not. Peter Edelman, a staunch critic of the 1996 reforms, characterized the policy's impact this way: "Welfare is no longer an entitlement. That means that it is basically a matter of local discretion. It is now very difficult to get on welfare."[61] Johns Hopkins University economist Robert Moffitt notes that although reforms probably dropped the welfare caseload by 20 percent by 2001, employment among single mothers only increased by about 4 percent.[62]

There have been a number of challenges associated with TANF. When welfare reform was first passed, work mandates for women focused on promoting self-sufficiency among single mothers. Congress also increased work support programs such as the Earned Income Tax Credit (EITC), raised the minimum wage, extended Medicaid for all children, and increased child care subsidies.[63] A robust and expanding economy in the late 1990s increased the availability of low-wage jobs, which led to growth in employment rates among poor women and a decrease in welfare rolls. However, two recessions later, the results are less promising. Poverty rates remain high among welfare leavers, in part because wages are so low and because the gender-based employment barriers that plague all women are especially salient for poor women. These include occupational segregation (38 percent of welfare recipients are employed in the service sector), longer hours for lower wages than similarly situated male beneficiaries, limited access to health care and other forms of employment-based benefits, and scarce and inadequate child care. Education is a strong predictor of wages and job type, but the number of high-school-educated unmarried mothers enrolled in college fell by 25 percent as a result of welfare reform. "The more heavily the women are working, and the more women are living in states that require a lot of work and don't count education as work, the less likely they are to be in school. They can't seem to do both, so 'work first' comes at the expense of education," notes an article in *Inside Higher Education*.[64]

TANF's broad goals—providing cash aid to the poor; promoting work, job training, and marriage; reducing out-of-wedlock pregnancies; and increasing two-parent families—left the states plenty of room for interpretation. Every federal TANF block grant dollar that a state doesn't spend on basic cash assistance can be used for other programs such as foster care, pre-K, and college scholarships—programs that are connected to reducing poverty but would otherwise have to be funded out of the state's own budgets. This makes it enticing for states to keep people off TANF caseloads. As sociologist Kathryn Edin notes, "States have used their flexibility in many cases to purge the rolls of people who would have been eligible for the program, and instead use the money to plug state budget holes or for other things that governors want to do that are politically popular." In Oklahoma, where the number of families in poverty who receive TANF has dropped by more than 80 percent since the 1996 reforms, the state currently spends just 9 percent of its TANF block grant on cash assistance for families. It spends nearly as much (5 percent) on programs to promote two-parent families and prevent out-of-wedlock pregnancy.[65] As such, women and children are living in dire circumstances. In their book *$2.00 a Day*, Kathryn Edin and Luke Shaefer describe women and children relying on homeless shelters and selling their own plasma just to get by and ending up in very frightening conditions that don't even look like America.[66]

As welfare has withered, food stamps have become far more important. In 2012, a three-person family in the median state could get more in benefits under the Supplemental Nutrition Assistance Program (SNAP) than it could under TANF.[67]

Food Security and Food Stamps

More than 29.7 million people in the United States live in a food desert, a low-income area without access to a supermarket that sells fruits, vegetables, and other whole foods. Public health researchers have linked food deserts to obesity since residents are often forced to buy high-calorie, high-sugar consumables from a more-accessible convenience store. In 2014, one in seven households were food insecure, meaning that at some point during the year the family had difficulty providing enough food for all family members due to a lack of resources.[68] The federal nutrition assistance program, the Supplemental Nutrition Assistance Program (food stamps), is particularly critical for children. In 2014, more than 15.3 million children (one in five) lived in a food-insecure household. The vast majority of these households are headed by adults who work: 34 percent by a single female earner and 25 percent by married dual earners. One-third of food-insecure households have annual incomes of at least two times the federal poverty level. These facts likely run contrary to your perception of who goes hungry in America.

Food stamps have been one of the most effective antipoverty programs, even though the benefit is solely for the acquisition of nutritious food. Women with access to SNAP have much higher economic self-sufficiency—a measure that includes completed education, employment status, earnings, and financial success—than those who did not.[69]

Social Insurance Programs

Social insurance includes a number of programs, including Social Security, unemployment insurance, and Medicare, that are designed to help workers and their families replace lost income due to unemployment, disability, retirement, or death. In 2015, the United States spent $900.5 billion on Social Security and $38.8 billion on unemployment insurance.[70] Access to health care through coverage under the Affordable Care Act is also considered a form of social insurance. Notice that these social insurance programs, while essential to providing a safety net for Americans, are benefits available only to people active in the workforce. A slightly different way to strengthen the safety net for poor families would be through universal basic income (UBI), a policy that would give every adult citizen an annual stipend ($10,000 is the figure commonly used in examples).

A feminist argument for UBI is that it is a way to provide income to caregivers for work done gratis now; this unpaid workforce is overwhelmingly female. The idea of a "stake in society" goes back to 1797, when Thomas Paine proposed giving every twenty-one-year-old a lump sum to neutralize the advantage of land inheritance.[71] Cost estimates make UBI an unlikely solution in the United States, to say nothing of the ideological objections to such a massive redistribution of wealth. But the implications for gender equality and for reducing poverty make it a good intellectual exercise nevertheless.

FERTILITY AND REPRODUCTION

This section explores the link between population and family policy: the issue of fertility. Fertility, reproduction, and issues of population growth or limits even more directly target women and are rarely gender neutral. When policy is crafted to be gender neutral, it rarely benefits women in their pursuit of equality. Unlike education, employment, or family support, where socially constructed gender ideologies are most profoundly related to women's disadvantages, fertility issues focus first on sex and secondarily on gender.

A woman's individual interest in regulating fertility and reproduction is directly connected to issues of private and public subordination. Yet since human reproduction is also social and cultural reproduction, controlling the quality and quantity of reproduction has long interested the state. It is the social aspect of reproduction that gives women socially constructed gender expectations that are related not only to childbearing but also to child rearing and motherhood. A state's survival depends on successive generations of children who have been properly guided to mature citizenship. A state's interest in regulating fertility and reproduction, therefore, is also directly related to women's subordination. In the United States, reproductive policy is not as explicitly stated as it is in other nations, yet it is present nonetheless. Such policies are complicated by the dominance of individualism and a liberal approach to policy creation. In most areas of US constitutional law, the interests of the individual outweigh the interests of the state, unless the state can prove a "compelling state interest" that would warrant intruding on individual rights. In the area of reproduction, however, it is less clear whether individual rights, and particularly women's individual rights, reign supreme.

The US Supreme Court has extended the individual's right to privacy to some reproductive decisions (birth control, access to abortion in the first trimester) but has not required the states to support these rights if an individual cannot afford to purchase them on the private market. Some areas of reproductive policy and decision-making do not conform well to a rights-based interpretation. Some argue that the right *not* to reproduce is every bit as fundamental as the right to reproduce. Christine Overall contends that a woman has no moral obligation to have a child against her will: "Women who do not have access to contraceptive devices and abortion services are, as a result of 'biological destiny,' victims 'of a sort of reproductive slavery.'"[72] But others, such as Sara Ann Ketcham, argue that there is an inherent asymmetry between the right not to reproduce and the right to reproduce that stems from reproduction's inclusion of other people. Therefore, the rights and interests of others (father, child, society) must also be taken into account in protecting an individual's right to reproduce.[73] The former perspective is most directly relevant to contraception and abortion rights, while the latter directly concerns the movement to endow the fetus with rights that are equal to those of the woman.

Individual Access to Contraception

The history of reliable contraception in the United States is a relatively short one. Only within the last forty years have women had access to methods of contraception that are safe, reliable, and entirely within their control. The Food and Drug Administration (FDA) approved an oral contraceptive for women (the pill) in 1960, the first new technology in contraception since condoms and diaphragms in the nineteenth century. The pill was followed by FDA approval of the sponge in 1983, the cervical cap in 1988, and, in 1990, a long-acting, reversible contraceptive implant known popularly as Norplant and effective for up to five years (no longer available in the United States). Depo-Provera, an injectable contraceptive that is effective for up to three months, had been widely used in other countries prior to its approval for use in the United States. Additionally, the FDA approved the sale of female condoms in the 1990s.

More recent forms of contraceptives include the vaginal ring (sold as Nuva-Ring), the patch, and a safer version of the intrauterine device (IUD). New oral contraceptives include extended-cycle birth control pills, such as Seasonale and Lybrel, which reduce the number of menstrual cycles per year. These methods are not without critics, and the most vocal are not from within the medical community. Some feminists argue that this method "medicalizes" normal body functions and that denying women regular menstrual cycles "infantilizes" them and robs young women of "that next stage of maturation."[74] Essure, a nonsurgical form of sterilization in which a microdevice is implanted in the fallopian tubes to block fertilization, was approved by the FDA in 2002.

Emergency contraception such as Plan B, when used within seventy-two hours of unprotected sex or contraceptive failure, can reduce the risk of pregnancy by as much as 89 percent. Making emergency contraception readily available would reduce the need for medical or surgical abortions, but gaining access in the United States has been a long and difficult process. The FDA approved Plan B for general use in the United States in 1999, but it was available by prescription only. Women's organizations pushed for an over-the-counter solution. Although an FDA advisory committee voted 23–4 to recommend approval of over-the-counter sale of emergency contraceptives, the FDA denied an application to switch Plan B to over-the-counter status in May 2004, citing concerns about its use by women under the age of sixteen. In 2006 the FDA approved Plan B as an over-the-counter medication for those age eighteen and older, and sales to seventeen-year-olds were approved on April 22, 2009. Several forms of emergency contraceptives are now available in drugstores without age restriction, although manufacturers are required to include on the label that "the use of these emergency contraceptives is intended for women ages 17 and older."[75]

The Guttmacher Institute estimates that the average American woman who wants two children spends about three decades of her life trying to avoid pregnancy and only a few years either trying to conceive or pregnant. There are 61 million women of childbearing age in the United States; about 43 million (70 percent) are sexually active but do not want to become pregnant. However, approximately 3 million women at risk for unintended pregnancy are not using any form of contraception. By age forty-five, more than half of US women have had one or more unintended pregnancies.[76] Availability and cost, along with side effects and safety concerns, are the most common reasons women offer for not using contraception or using it infrequently. Couples who do not use any method of contraception have an 85 percent chance of experiencing a pregnancy over the course of one year.[77] The proportion of sexually active women not using a method of contraception is highest among fifteen-to-nineteen-year-olds and lowest among women ages forty to forty-four.

Contraceptive use is high across racial and ethnic groups. Eighty-three percent of African American women use a contraceptive method, compared with 91 percent of Hispanics and whites and 90 percent of Asian women. There are few differences in contraceptive use among religious groups. Eighty-nine percent of at-risk Catholics and 90 percent of at-risk Protestants regularly use contraceptives; 99 percent of both groups have in their lifetime used contraceptives. The more a woman knows about contraception and her options, the more likely she is to choose a hormonal or long-acting reversible method. The pill and female sterilization are the two methods most commonly in use since 1982.

Development and dissemination of contraceptives depend in large part on the public's attitude toward sexuality, current birthrates, and the positive or negative consequences of population growth. Prior to the Civil War, many states permitted abortion until "quickening," but soon after the war's conclusion most states banned abortions. Succumbing to the pressure to reproduce and new restrictive attitudes toward sexuality promoted by organized religion, Congress passed the **Comstock laws** in 1873. These laws were ostensibly designed to control pornography but defined it as any information or product distributed for preventing conception or causing unlawful abortion—in effect likening contraception to obscenity and making it illegal to distribute information on contraception or contraceptive devices. Various social sectors supported restricting contraceptives, including doctors. In their eyes, contraception violated nature, bred immorality, damaged health, and violated the sanctity of motherhood.[78] Many women, particularly those in the middle and upper classes, viewed contraception as a direct challenge to marital fidelity and their corresponding sphere of authority. Poor and uneducated women were most disadvantaged by unintended pregnancies and thus were especially vulnerable to public campaigns devoted to suppressing information or medical services. Middle- and upper-class women had access to an informal but extensive network of information, to birth control devices illegally imported from Europe, and to relatively safe, but still illegal, abortions.

Birth control advocates such as Margaret Sanger and Emma Goldman worked directly with poor and working-class women, many of whom were recent immigrants. In addition to stressing that giving birth to too many children or not adequately spacing pregnancies was harmful to women's health, Goldman, a socialist active in the labor movement, was also interested in limiting child labor, which drove down wages for everyone.[79] Immigrants were the targets of a robust eugenics (selective breeding) movement that thrived by promoting fears of "race suicide" if the birthrate among the white middle class declined and poor immigrant populations increased unchecked. These seemingly contradictory interests forged a nascent birth control movement that directly violated the Comstock laws.

By 1914, Margaret Sanger, who had been radicalized by her experiences with the left and a year in France, began to publish a monthly newsletter called *Woman Rebel*, in which she eventually promoted contraception as a woman's right:

> A woman's body belongs to herself alone. It does not belong to the United States of America or any other government on the face of the earth. Enforced motherhood is the most complete denial of a woman's right to life and liberty. Women cannot be on an equal footing with men until they have full and complete control over their reproductive function.[80]

Many issues were confiscated by the post office under the Comstock laws. While the newsletter did not include information on contraceptive techniques, it did publish letters from desperate readers begging for information. In response, Sanger published a brochure entitled *Family Limitation: A Nurse's Advice to Women*.

Between 1914 and 1917, more than 160,000 copies were distributed, although Sanger fled to England during some of that time to avoid further prosecution under the obscenity laws. In 1916, Sanger opened the United States' first birth control clinic in Brooklyn, New York.

A court decision in 1918 allowed physicians to disseminate "advice to a married person to cure or prevent disease"—a clear reference to venereal disease and a cover for distributing contraception to married women. Medicalizing the birth control issue allowed Sanger to solicit support and cooperation from physicians, and in 1921 she formed the American Birth Control League (ABCL). By the 1940s, the ABCL gave way to the Planned Parenthood Federation of America in recognition of contraception's transformation into a "family planning" tool. In the 1960s, Planned Parenthood challenged a Connecticut law that banned the sale, advertisement, or manufacture of birth control devices and prohibited married couples from using contraception. In 1965, in *Griswold v. Connecticut,* the US Supreme Court declared that Connecticut's law was an unconstitutional violation of the right to privacy of married persons. In 1972, the Court extended the fundamental right of procreative choice and privacy to unmarried persons with its ruling in *Eisenstadt v. Baird.* The fundamental right to privacy established in the *Griswold* and *Eisenstadt* rulings was extended to cover a woman's right to abortion services in 1973 (*Roe v. Wade*).

The Politics of Insurance Coverage for Contraception

The Patient Protection and Affordable Care Act of 2010 (ACA) required new private health plans written on or after August 1, 2012, to cover contraceptive counseling and services for all FDA-approved methods without any out-of-pocket costs to patients.[81] The Department of Health and Human Services (HHS) regulations exempted some religious employers (e.g., churches)—an exemption also provided in many state laws. An "accommodation" was proposed for employers with religious affiliations (e.g., nonprofits and schools) but not eligible for the religious exemption. These employers could notify their health insurance company or the federal government of their objection and not be obligated to provide contraceptive coverage. Instead, a third-party provides the coverage so that the employee is not adversely impacted by the employer's religious affiliation.

As Elizabeth Deutsch wrote in the *New York Times,* "Access to reproductive care is central to equality between the sexes. By requiring employers' health plans to provide contraceptive coverage, the Affordable Care Act represents an important legislative link between sex equality and reproductive rights."[82] Of particular importance is the ACA's elimination of patient cost-sharing, which allows a woman to choose one method over another without regard to cost; this enables low-income women to select high-cost long-acting reversible methods. A 2015 study found that use of the pill, injectable contraception, and the vaginal ring all increased substantially between fall 2012 and spring 2014, as did the proportion of women paying zero out-of-pocket costs for care.[83]

In 2014, the US Supreme Court ruled in *Burwell v. Hobby Lobby, Inc.* that certain "closely held for-profit corporations" were to be exempt from the ACA's requirement that employers provide contraceptive coverage without cost to the employee.[84] Hobby Lobby, a business with more than 15,000 employees and 600 stores in 41 states, is owned by the Green family, evangelical Christians who believe that life begins at conception and that any birth control method that may result in the destruction of a fertilized egg is a form of abortion. Furthermore, they believe that paying for contraceptive choices that might destroy a fertilized egg through the company health plan makes them complicit in an immoral act. The majority opinion affirmed the basic principle that Americans have the right to hold religious beliefs and to not be forced by the government to act in ways that violate those beliefs. However, in this case an individual's religious beliefs would, in effect, deny female employees the benefits mandated by the Affordable Care Act. The 1993 Religious Freedom Restoration Act (RFRA), requiring strict scrutiny when a neutral law "substantially burdens a person's exercise of religion," provided the basis of this 5-4 decision. The Court said that the ACA's contraceptive mandate was not the least restrictive means to accomplish the administration's goal.

In 2016 several cases related to the ACA's contraceptive coverage mandate reached the court. The Court consolidated these cases into one, *Zubik v. Burwell,* which argues that the religious exemption in the ACA is itself an infringement on religious freedom. The religious nonprofits bringing the suit argue that applying for the religious exemption amounts to "facilitation of sin" because it initiates a process that allows employees to be covered (and therefore obtain the contraceptive method of their choice) through a third party. With only eight members and thus fearing a 4–4 deadlock, the Court ultimately remanded these cases back to the lower courts, asking that they seek a compromise acceptable to all parties.[85] This means (at least for the moment) that under some circumstances, an employer's religious beliefs can impact the contraceptive services available to its female employees.

Individual Access to Abortion Services

Today and in earlier eras, whether legal or illegal, abortion in practice is not limited to a particular type of woman. Nearly half of all pregnancies in the United States are unintended, and about 40 percent of these end in abortion. Based on current abortion rates, slightly more than one in three American women will have had an abortion before age forty-five. Overall, the abortion rate in the United States is falling; in 2011 the abortion rate reached its lowest point since 1973 with 16.94 abortions per 1,000 women ages fifteen to forty-four, down from a peak of 29.3 in 1981.[86]

Ninety percent of all abortions performed in the United States occur in the first trimester of pregnancy; 60 percent occur within the first eight weeks and 30 percent within the first six weeks. Each year, 2 out of every 100 women between the ages of fifteen and forty-four have an abortion—58 percent of them are in their twenties, 61 percent have one or more children, and 57 percent are economically disadvantaged. Fifty-four percent of women who had abortions were using contraception during the month they got pregnant. White patients accounted for 39 percent of the procedures, African Americans for 28 percent, and Hispanic women for 25 percent. Catholic women are 29 percent more likely than Protestant women to seek an abortion, although their overall rates of abortion are comparable to the national abortion rate. Fifty-nine percent of abortions in 2014 were performed for women who had previously given birth.

Of the 42 million abortions performed each year worldwide, more than 40 percent are obtained illegally.[87] An estimated 5 million women around the world are hospitalized each year for abortion-related complications, such as hemorrhage and sepsis. Complications due to unsafe abortion procedures account for an estimated 13 percent of maternal deaths each year (about 67,000). In areas of the world where abortion is illegal or inaccessible, women resort to a variety of unsafe abortion methods in attempts to terminate an unintended pregnancy (e.g., drinking turpentine or bleach; placing a foreign object, such as a stick, coat hanger, or chicken bone, into the uterus; jumping from the top of stairs or a roof).[88]

In the United States, abortion, much more so than contraception, has divided families, political parties, and the nation. Abortion rights were most clearly established in *Roe v. Wade* (1973), although by the time *Roe* was decided, more than thirteen states had reformed and liberalized their abortion laws. More than likely, state-level reforms would have continued had the Court not acted, but slowly and in a patchwork fashion. Almost everyone agreed that abortion reforms were necessary to protect women from physical injury and death at the hands of illegal abortionists. Just because abortion was illegal did not prevent it from occurring, and the dire consequences of botched abortions cut across all races and socio-economic groups.

Justice Harry Blackmun, writing for the seven-vote majority in *Roe v. Wade*, used the trimesters of pregnancy as benchmarks to balance a woman's privacy interests with the state's increasingly legitimate interests in protecting a fetus as it approached viability outside the womb. In the first trimester, a woman's right to make private choices is protected from state interference (although later decisions have allowed the state to regulate the conditions under which a woman exercises her right). During the second (fourth through sixth month) and third (seventh month through birth) trimesters, the state gains grounds to regulate abortions "in ways that are reasonably related to maternal health" or to restrict its use entirely by the third trimester, except when necessary to protect the life or health of the mother.

While the decision nationalized women's rights to a legal abortion within the first three months of a pregnancy, it also muddied other issues surrounding

Box 8.2 – Point of Comparison

Regulating Access to Legal Abortion

The Pew Research Center analyzed 196 countries and found that "nearly all nations (96 percent) allow women to terminate their pregnancies in order to save their lives."[1] The report goes on to note that "only six countries do not allow women to receive abortions under any circumstances." The circumstances under which abortions are regulated most often include saving a woman's life, preserving a woman's physical health and/or mental health, in case of rape or incest, because of fetal impairment, for economic or social reasons, and on request.[2]

- In six countries a woman is not permitted an abortion to save her own life: Chile, Dominican Republic, El Salvador, Holy See, Malta, and Nicaragua.
- Fifty countries (26 percent) allow abortions only to save the life of the mother.
- Eighty-two nations (42 percent) allow abortions when the mother's life is at risk as well as for at least one other specific reason, such as to preserve a woman's physical or mental health, in cases of rape or incest, because of fetal impairment, or for social or economic reasons.
- Three in ten countries, fifty-eight in total, allow abortions on request or for any reason, although many of these states do not allow women to terminate their pregnancies after a certain point (e.g., twenty weeks).

What are the implications for women in countries where abortion is so restricted as to make it nearly impossible to obtain? Consider the case of Ireland. A constitutional amendment adopted in 1983 permits abortion only to save the woman's life. A woman who obtains an abortion in Ireland outside the single permitted exception faces a decade in prison. As many as 150,000 women are believed to have traveled to England or other European countries where abortion is available since the Eighth Amendment was adopted. In August 2016, @TwoWomenTravel documented the experience of a woman seeking an abortion in England in twenty-eight live tweets,

reproductive rights by rooting the decision in privacy doctrine. In *Harris v. McRae* (1980), the Court held that the right to privacy does not compel states to pay for poor women's abortions. The separation of public and private, enunciated in *Roe* and *Harris*, was used in 1989 (*Webster v. Reproductive Health Services*) to allow states to prohibit abortions from being performed in public facilities or by public employees. The public-private distinction was used again in 1996 to uphold the thus reviving the debate about legal abortion in Ireland a month after a statement from the UN Human Rights Committee declared that Ireland's ban on abortion subjected a woman to cruel, inhuman, and degrading treatment.[3] The Coalition to Repeal Eight is an alliance of rights organizations working toward a referendum to repeal the Eighth Amendment.

In El Salvador, not only is abortion illegal without exception, but women who miscarry or experience complications during pregnancy can be jailed. Many of the women incarcerated in Ilopango Women's Prison, currently operating at 900 percent capacity, are there for that

Source: Courtesy of RepealEight

reason; the conditions there are described as a "living hell." Dennis Munoz serves as attorney for women imprisoned in Ilopango. "There is a war against women in this country," he explains, "and if you are poor and uneducated like a majority of women, you might be next."[4] Abortion became illegal in El Salvador in 1998 in all cases. Those who assist in an abortion face six to twelve years in prison, motivating those in medicine and law enforcement to aid in the criminalization of women whose pregnancies end in miscarriage or stillbirth.

For Critical Analysis

Under what circumstances do governments exercise a legitimate interest in restricting abortion? The two cases profiled here are countries heavily influenced by the Catholic Church. Should public policy reflect the belief systems of a country's dominant religion? Why or why not? El Salvador demonstrates the perils of imposing sanctions on those who provide for women's reproductive health. In what ways might you see similar trends in the United States? What are the consequences for women in these instances?

ban on the furnishing of abortion information and counseling to poor women by federally funded family-planning agencies (*Rust v. Sullivan*).

In other cases, the Court has allowed states greater leeway in establishing limits on a woman's right to abortion services as long as the regulations do not create an "undue burden" on the woman seeking an abortion. A state regulation is an undue burden "if its purpose or effect is to place a substantial obstacle in the path of a woman seeking an abortion before the fetus attains viability."[89] In 1992, *Planned Parenthood of Southeastern Pennsylvania v. Casey* upheld most of Pennsylvania's regulations, including an "informed consent" provision, a twenty-four-hour waiting period, and parental consent for women who were minors. The only provision the Court declared an "undue burden" was the requirement that women notify their husbands prior to having an abortion. Thirty-one states enforce parental consent or notification laws for minors seeking an abortion. Forty-five percent of minors who have had abortions told both of their parents, and 61 percent underwent the procedure with at least one parent's knowledge.[90]

Two decisions delivered at the conclusion of the Court's 1999–2000 term reversed its trend in recognizing more active regulatory action by the states. In *Hill v. Colorado* the Court considered the constitutionality of a statutory buffer zone (in this case eight feet) around abortion clinics and around individuals entering the clinics. Antiabortion protesters set up human barricades around abortion clinics and harassed women on their way in and out of the clinics, urging them not to "kill their baby." In this case, the free speech interests of the protesters were weighed against women's right to abortion services. The 6–3 majority in *Hill* upheld Colorado's "zone of separation" statute, arguing that the law was a reasonable restriction on the First Amendment right of so-called sidewalk counselors to protest, educate, or counsel outside a health care facility.[91] The second case, *Stenberg v. Carhart*, dealt with the issue of late-term abortions and a state's ability to prohibit all late-term abortions (called "partial birth" abortions by opponents). This case, decided by a 5–4 vote, turned on the question of a woman's health. Justice Stephen Breyer, writing for the majority, said, "A risk to a woman's health is the same whether it happens to arise from regulating a particular method of abortion, or from barring abortion entirely." This decision supported a doctor's determination of what is in the best interests of the woman's health over the state's outright ban on certain abortion procedures.

In 2000, the FDA approved the use of mifepristone, also known as RU-486, to terminate early pregnancies (forty-nine days or less). Since it first came on the market in 1988, RU-486 has been used in Europe and China by more than 620,000 women. Mifepristone blocks the effects of progesterone, a hormone essential for sustaining pregnancy, and prevents an embryo from attaching to the uterine wall during the earliest stages of gestation. With mifepristone, pregnancies can be terminated much earlier than with a surgical abortion and surgical complications are avoided. It is effective in about 95 percent of all cases. Under the terms of FDA approval, mifepristone should be distributed by physicians, who must also be able to provide surgical intervention in cases of incomplete abortion or severe bleeding (or they must have made plans in advance to have others provide such care). In March 2016, the FDA approved a lower dosage of mifepristone (fewer side effects) and allowed its use up to the tenth week of an unintended pregnancy—consistent with medical practice and the most recent scientific evidence.[92] In 2012, 21 percent of all terminations were accomplished by medical abortion.[93] Some states have adopted regulations to restrict the use of mifepristone since its initial FDA approval. Following the issuance of the 2016 guidelines, the Republican governor of Arizona, Doug Ducey, signed a bill that required doctors in his state to follow the old guidelines in an effort to restrict women's access to medical abortion.[94]

In 2016, the Supreme Court clarified what constitutes a "substantial obstacle" to obtaining an abortion in *Whole Women's Health v. Hellerstedt.*[95] In 2013, the Texas state legislature adopted HB 2, a law that introduced new restrictions on clinics providing abortion services. It mandated that physicians who perform abortions must have admitting privileges at a hospital no more than thirty miles away from the clinic. The law also required clinics to meet the same state requirements as ambulatory surgical centers (e.g., number of staff, size and layout of the clinic). The legislature claimed that the law's purpose was to protect women's health by ensuring that doctors and facilities providing abortions are qualified and safe. If HB 2 had been fully implemented, all but ten of Texas's abortion clinics would have been forced to close. When the first restriction took effect in November 2013, twenty-three of the forty-two abortion clinics in the state were forced to close.

A number of women's health clinics in Texas sued in federal court to stop the law, arguing that it imposed an "undue burden" on women seeking an abortion. At trial, the judge found no medical reason for the new requirements and observed that the effect of the law would make it extremely difficult for many women in Texas to obtain a legal abortion. The state appealed the ruling to the Fifth Circuit of Appeals, which concluded that it doesn't matter if the law actually makes women safer, only that the law intended to protect women's health. The case was then appealed to the US Supreme Court, where the Texas law was ruled unconstitutional. Writing for the majority in the 5–3 ruling, Justice Stephen Breyer found that both the admitting privileges and the surgical center requirements were substantial obstacles for women seeking an abortion. Texas failed to prove that these requirements advanced the state's interest in protecting women's health. In fact, the majority noted that abortions are safer than many other common medical procedures that are not subject to the surgical center requirements. The Supreme Court's ruling will impact similar restrictions imposed by other states but will likely not deter them from devising new regulations. Since 2011 almost three hundred abortion restrictions have been enacted, primarily by Republican-led state legislatures.[96]

Public Opinion on Abortion

Overall, US public opinion favors maintaining a woman's right to choose abortion. The Pew Research Center reports in 2016 that 56 percent of adults say abortion should be legal in all or most cases, compared with 41 percent who say it should be illegal all or most of the time.[97] These findings have been consistent for the past twenty years, with small fluctuations shaped by political or cultural events.

For example, antiabortion violence and state legislative restrictions tend to push opinion in favor of abortion rights. Among all US adults surveyed in Gallup's May 2015 Values and Beliefs poll, 29 percent favor legal abortion under "any circumstance," 13 percent favor legal abortion under "most circumstances," and another 36 percent say abortion should be legal in only a few circumstances. Nineteen percent of adults polled say that abortion should be illegal in all circumstances.[98] The Gallup poll also probed "prochoice" or "prolife" identification. Half of Americans identify as "prochoice," while 44 percent identify as "prolife." Favoring abortion rights does not necessarily mean a person chooses to adopt the politicized "prochoice" identity, since 77 percent of the public favors legal abortion, even if conditioned by circumstances. Slightly more women than men choose to identify as prochoice (54 percent women, 46 percent men; this represents a divergence along gender lines since 2011, when there were no differences found between men and women. More Democrats (68 percent) than independents (50 percent) and Republicans (31 percent) identify as prochoice.

Conditional support for abortion often depends on the circumstances presented by women seeking abortion. Support is highest for instances of rape or incest or when a woman's health is threatened by continuing the pregnancy. Support is lowest when the circumstances involve a woman's personal choice, such as the inconvenience of an unintended pregnancy to a career or education plans. Wendy Kaminer attributes these negative attitudes toward women who say they are not ready for the changes a child would require in their lives to an unwillingness to grant women autonomy: "The abortion debate is not simply about the nature of a human fetus; it is, in large part, about the nature of a woman. Is it natural for her to put motherhood second—or to choose not to become a mother at all? Is it natural for her to demand the same right to self-determination that fully democratic societies have always granted men?"[99]

Freelance journalist Amy Richards elicited a huge response to her 2004 *New York Times Magazine* story, "When One Is Enough." Thirty-four years old and unmarried, Ms. Richards discovered she was pregnant with triplets. "My immediate response was, I cannot have triplets. I was not married; I lived in a five-story walk-up in the East Village; I worked freelance; and I would have to go on bed rest in March. I lecture at colleges, and my biggest months are March and April. I would have to give up my main income for the rest of the year. There was a part of me that was sure I could work around that. But it was a matter of do I want to?" Ultimately, Ms. Richards decided to undergo selective reduction and aborted two of the three fetuses. She gave birth to a single healthy baby. The *New York Times* published an "Editor's Note" following the story, which read:

> Ms. Richards, who told her story to a freelance *Times Magazine* contributor, Amy Barrett, discussed her anxiety about having triplets, the

procedure to terminate two of the pregnancies and the healthy baby she eventually delivered; she expressed no regret about her decision. The column identified Ms. Richards as a freelancer at the time of her pregnancy but should have also disclosed that she is an abortion rights advocate who has worked with Planned Parenthood, as well as a co-founder of a feminist organization, the Third Wave Foundation, which has financed abortions. That background, which would have shed light on her mindset, was incorporated in an early draft, but it was omitted when an editor condensed the article.[100]

Why did the *New York Times* feel compelled to offer this editorial note? Is there a reason the story cannot stand on its own? Is part of the reason expressed in the observation "she expressed no regret about her decision"? The column generated several hundred letters to the editor. Of the ten the magazine published, only two, both written by men, could be characterized as supportive of Richards's decision. Most of the others commented on the seemingly detached or coldhearted manner in which she approached the decision to terminate two of the three fetuses.

The issue of abortion was introduced into the 2008 presidential campaign in a way that demonstrates its continuing complexity for the American public. Sarah Palin's addition to the Republican ticket created a decidedly prolife visual. Palin frequently campaigned with her then four-month-old infant, born with Down syndrome, and her pregnant, unmarried seventeen-year-old daughter. Palin's personal decisions on reproductive issues seemed to inject abortion into the campaign without the usual vitriol. In addition, her presence on the ticket placated conservative Republican voters who were worried about Senator John McCain's credentials on reproductive issues and embryonic stem cell research. While 13 percent of Americans in 2008 said they would vote only for a candidate who shared their position on abortion, 49 percent said it was "just one of many important factors" and 37 percent said it was not a major issue at all.[101] More than 65 percent of Americans continue to express support for maintaining the principal holding in *Roe v. Wade*, allowing women to choose abortion virtually free from state-imposed restrictions in the first trimester.

After the election, Sarah Palin spoke more openly about her decision to have a child at forty-four and to continue her pregnancy once she learned the baby would have Down's syndrome. Speaking at an Indiana right-to-life fund-raiser, she disclosed:

> I had found out that I was pregnant while out of state first, at an oil and gas conference. . . .

> Then when my amniocentesis results came back, showing what they called abnormalities. Oh, dear God, I knew, I had instantly an understanding

for that fleeting moment why someone would believe it could seem possible to change those circumstances. Just make it all go away and get some
normalcy back in life. Just take care of it. Because at the time only my doctor knew the results, Todd didn't even know. No one would know. But I
would know. First, I thought how in the world could we manage a change
of this magnitude. I was a very busy governor with four busy kids and a
husband with a job hundreds of miles away up on the North Slope oil
fields. And, oh, the criticism that I knew was coming. Plus, I was old . . .

So we went through some things a year ago that now lets me understand
a woman's, a girl's temptation to maybe try to make it all go away if she
has been influenced by society to believe that she's not strong enough
or smart enough or equipped enough or convenienced enough to make
the choice to let the child live. I do understand what these women, what
these girls go through in that thought process.[102]

Except, as Ruth Marcus of the *Washington Post*, concluded, "if it were up to Palin,
women would have no thought process to go through. The 'good decision to
choose life,' as she put it, would be no decision at all, because abortion would
not be an option." Like so much about Palin's candidacy, her decision about birth
versus abortion proved to be a political Rorschach test for the politicization of the
abortion issue. For Kim Lehman of Iowa Right to Life, Palin's remarks demonstrate the strength of her convictions: "She was tested, tried, and chose life. It goes
to show her character." For Elizabeth Shipp, political director at NARAL Pro-
Choice America, it demonstrates the importance of the right to choose for every
single woman: "If I didn't know better, I'd say Governor Palin sounds remarkably
pro-choice."[103]

In the 2016 presidential contest, abortion rights played a more muted role.
The Democratic Party platform supported abortion rights, and Hillary Clinton had
publicly championed Planned Parenthood and consistently advocated for women's
right to access abortion services: "I believe we need to protect access to safe and
legal abortion—not just in principle, but in practice. Any right that requires you
to take extraordinary measures to access it is no right at all."[104] The Republican
Party platform strongly denounced abortion, but Donald Trump's position was
less clear. A *Washington Post* headline in April 2016 read, "Donald Trump Took 5
Different Positions on Abortion in 3 Days." Early in his public life, Donald Trump
emphasized the importance of choice, even as he stated that he hated the concept
of abortion. But as a presidential candidate in 2016, he told MSNBC correspondent Chris Matthews that if abortion was ever made illegal, women receiving an
abortion should be punished. His campaign later walked back that statement, clar-
ifying that it would be the person performing the illegal abortion who would be

punished and not the woman. Trump also tweeted, "Like Ronald Reagan, I am pro-life with exceptions."

In the third presidential debate of the general election, the only debate in which a question on abortion rights was asked of the candidates, Donald Trump said he supported the federal ban on "partial-birth" abortion because, under the procedure, "in the ninth month you can take the baby and rip the baby out of the womb of the mother."[105] The Guttmacher Institute reports that only about 1.5 percent of all abortions take place later than 20 weeks following conception and that the vast majority occur prior to 24 weeks. Clinton, who voted against a federal ban on late-term abortion, defended the right to reproductive autonomy in this debate, saying:

> You should meet with the women I've met with; women I've *known* over the course of my life. . . . I've been to countries where governments either forced women to have abortions, like they used to do in China, or forced women to bear children, like they used to do in Romania. And I can tell you the government has no business in the decisions that women make with their families in accordance with their faith, with medical advice. And I will stand up for that right.[106]

What we know about the public's position on abortion is dependent on a pollster's ability to ask questions that elicit accurate responses. Tresa Undem's survey for the National Institute for Reproductive Health found that a majority of voters support a woman's access to abortion and want it to be easily accessible and affordable. More important, Undem found that voters were largely uninformed about state-imposed restrictions. Only 45 percent of adults polled were aware of the "recent trend of states passing laws making it harder for women to get abortion care." To try to understand what people know about restrictions on abortion, Undem conducted thirty-four focus groups in several states. The groups were made up only of people who had moderate views on abortion but favored restrictions under some circumstances. "We gave them a timeline of laws in their state from 1973 to now. No messaging, very neutral language," Undem says. "I've never in 15 years of doing focus groups seen a reaction like this. People were shocked and disgusted."[107] Sixty-three percent of people in the focus groups said that abortion laws are "going in the wrong direction," compared with only 20 percent who believed policy was going in the right direction.

Limiting Access to Abortion and Reproductive Health Care

While abortion services are legal within the first trimester, they are difficult to obtain for many women. The number of abortion providers declined another 4 percent between 2008 and 2011. In the United States today, 89 percent of all counties have no abortion services, and 38 percent of American women of reproductive age live in those counties. Mississippi, for example, is one of five states with a single abortion provider in the state (Missouri, North Dakota, South Dakota and Wyoming are the others). Nine out of every ten abortion providers are located in major metropolitan areas.

Joint federal-state Medicaid funding has restricted abortions for low-income women for nearly forty years. The 1977 Hyde Amendment forbids the use of federal funds for abortions except in cases of life endangerment, rape, or incest. Thirty-two states and the District of Columbia follow the Hyde guidelines; seventeen states have policies that direct Medicaid to pay for all or most medically necessary abortions (although thirteen have been directed to do so by court order).[108] Under the Affordable Care Act, states had the option to establish health care exchanges to make purchasing health insurance more affordable. Ten states restrict insurance coverage of abortion in all private insurance plans, including those that are offered through the ACA's health insurance exchanges. Twenty-five states restrict abortion coverage in plans offered through the exchange, and twenty-one states restrict abortion coverage in insurance plans for public employees.[109]

Federal and state Medicaid (health care funding for lower-income patients) is at the heart of the controversy over repeated efforts to "defund" Planned Parenthood, which today is the largest single provider of reproductive health services in the United States, seeing an average of 2.5 million patients a year. Services vary by clinic, but typically include birth control and long-acting reversible contraception; emergency contraception; breast and cervical cancer screening; pregnancy testing and pregnancy options counseling; testing and treatment for sexually transmitted infections; sex education; vasectomies; LGBT services; and abortion.[110] The overwhelming majority of Planned Parenthood's services involve screening for and treating sexually transmitted diseases and infections (42 percent), as well as providing contraception (34 percent). Abortion services account for roughly 3 percent of all services provided.[111] Title X (a federally funded family planning program) and Medicaid combine to provide $500 billion for women's health care at Planned Parenthood clinics. Title X does not permit money to be used to fund abortions; Medicaid may fund abortion services, but only in very limited circumstances, because of the Hyde Amendment. Three-fourths of Planned Parenthood patients are low-income and have no other primary health care provider.

In 2015, the antiabortion organization Center for Medical Progress covertly videotaped the conversations of Planned Parenthood employees who believed they were meeting with representatives of a biotechnology company. Planned Parenthood has made fetal tissue available to researchers. The Center for Medical Progress released the video and alleged that Planned Parenthood was selling aborted fetuses for profit. These allegations were dismissed as false in investigations by law enforcement and news organizations, but nevertheless fueled ongoing attempts to restrict government funding to Planned Parenthood in Congress and in several states. In 2015, Republicans in Congress voted to deny federal funding to Planned Parenthood eight times. Twelve states have passed laws to block state dollars from funding reproductive health services at Planned Parenthood clinics. Several state initiatives have been ruled unconstitutional in the courts because they target access to legal abortion specifically.

Beyond lack of funding for abortions and attempts to defund and discredit organizations such as Planned Parenthood, there are other ways in which women's access to abortion is limited, including through violence and intimidation. Although the first reported cases of violence at an abortion clinic occurred in 1977 (arson in St. Paul, Minnesota), clinics and providers have been regular targets of violence since the 1980s. More than 80 percent of all abortion providers have been picketed or seriously harassed. Doctors and other workers are subject to death threats, and clinics have experienced chemical attacks, arson, bomb threats, invasions, and blockades. In the late 1980s, Randall Terry founded Operation Rescue, an organization that blockaded clinic entrances, engaged in "sidewalk counseling" in an effort to dissuade women from seeking abortions, and publicized the faces of those entering clinics. Operation Rescue personnel displayed graphic photographs of aborted fetuses and chanted "stop the killing" as women tried to enter health clinics. Prochoice forces countered with clinic escorts and human shields to protect women from harassment. There were thousands of arrests as clinics increasingly became political battlefields.

In the 1990s, antiabortion activists turned to intimidation and harassment of individual doctors and their families by picketing their homes, following them, and circulating "wanted" posters. To date, more than 200 clinics have been bombed or experienced serious vandalism, and eleven abortion providers have been murdered. Dr. David Gunn was the first abortion provider to be killed, in 1993. Dr. George Tiller, described as the country's most prominent provider of late-term abortions, was killed inside his church in Wichita, Kansas, on Sunday, May 31, 2009. Although most antiabortion groups condemned the killing, Randall Terry called Tiller "a mass murderer who 'reaped what he sowed.'"[112] Tiller was also a frequent target of Fox News's Bill O'Reilly, who referred to him as "Tiller the Baby Killer" and alleged he was guilty of "Nazi stuff." Tiller had been shot once before in 1993 and suffered injuries to both arms. His clinic, Women's Healthcare Services, had been bombed, blockaded, fired on, and vandalized. In the summer of 1991, more than 2,000 arrests took place outside of the clinic. As one health care provider described, "The fear of violence has become part of the lives of every abortion provider in the country. As doctors, we are being warned not to open big envelopes with no return addresses in case a mail bomb is enclosed. I know colleagues who have had their homes picketed and their children threatened. Some wear bulletproof vests and have remote starters for their cars. Even going to work and facing

IMAGE 8.2: *Cecile Richards, President of Planned Parenthood Federation of America, testifies during a House Oversight and Government Reform Committee hearing on federal funding for Planned Parenthood (September 2015).* Source: Tom Williams/ CQ Roll Call.

the disapproving looks from co-workers—isolation and marginalization from colleagues is part of it."[113]

Overall there is a lack of doctors who can perform abortions. Although abortion is the most common ob-gyn surgical procedure, almost half of graduating ob-gyn residents have never performed a first-trimester abortion—in part because only 5 percent of US ob-gyn residency programs train future doctors to perform first-trimester abortions. A group of pro-choice medical students founded Medical Students for Choice in 1993 following the shooting death of Dr. David Gunn. The organization is a network of more than 10,000 medical students and abortion providers across the United States and Canada. Although the membership was "shocked" by Dr. Tiller's murder, the organization vowed that the killing has only strengthened its resolve to ensure that all women have a full spectrum of reproductive options. "Giving up would be a fate worse than death," said Miranda Balkin, a fourth-year medical student and board president of Medical Students for Choice. "My life is one life, but there are thousands of women who need reproductive choice."[114]

More states today recognize that although parent involvement is desirable when it comes to a minor child's health care, it is more important that children have access to critical medical services, including mental health care, drug and alcohol abuse treatment, and reproductive health care. The exception to this trend is abortion services. Thirty-seven states require some type of parental involvement in a minor's decision to terminate a pregnancy—a deterrent to abortion access. In most but not all instances, a judicial bypass option allows a minor to seek a court's permission rather than that of a parent.

Crisis Pregnancy Centers: No Health Care Available

Another tactic specifically intended to persuade women and prevent them from having an abortion are the so-called crisis pregnancy centers (CPCs) found in many communities large and small. According to the National Abortion Federation, there are as many as 4,000 CPCs nationwide, compared with an estimated 2,000 clinics that provide abortion services for women.[115] With names like Crisis Pregnancy Center, Pregnancy Aid, Birth Right, Open Door, or Pregnancy Counseling Center, these groups want to be the first contact a woman makes when she thinks she might be pregnant, so they can talk her out of considering abortion. CPCs often locate near high schools or near actual abortion clinics and advertise "free pregnancy testing" and "options counseling" to attract women who believe they might be pregnant.

The inside of CPCs look very much like a medical clinic, but they do not provide information about abortion services or contraceptives, nor do they refer women interested in obtaining an abortion to an appropriate facility. Instead, while women await the results of their pregnancy test, they are asked to watch antiabortion videos and provided with antichoice literature. Some women also report being harassed with phone calls or visits to their homes. State attorneys general in California, Maryland, Massachusetts, Minnesota, Missouri, New York, North Carolina, Texas, and Virginia have taken action against CPCs, documenting their intentionally misleading practices. Examples of misleading information provided by staff at crisis pregnancy centers include a claim that birth control and abortion increase the risk of infertility and breast cancer and that abortion causes mental illness. New York now requires that CPCs clearly disclose that they do not provide or make referrals for abortion or birth control and disclose in writing that the facility is not a licensed medical provider qualified to accurately diagnose or date a pregnancy.[116]

WOMEN'S RIGHTS VERSUS FETAL RIGHTS

Liberal theories grounded on individual rights provide one philosophical basis for feminists to make equality claims in a number of areas, as we've seen in previous chapters. Liberal feminists have been both lauded and derided for their emphasis on gaining equal status with men within the current political, social, and economic system. Critics of liberal feminism often point to the limits of using a male standard of equality to judge women's status. Successful claims advanced on the basis of the legal equality doctrine are most often made under the banner of fairness—that is, if men retain certain rights, privileges, or obligations that further their status purely on the basis of gender, fairness dictates that women be treated equally by erasing gender/sex from the statute or policy in question. Alternatively, the other approach in pursuit of equality argues that fairness requires the law to treat men and women differently. How do these two paths to gender equality apply to pregnancy, reproduction, and the regulation of emerging fertility technologies?

The rulings in *Griswold* and *Roe* ground women's reproductive liberty in the constitutional right to privacy. In this sense, privacy is understood as a limit on government's intervention in personal decisions or conduct. Individuals have a fundamental "right to be let alone," according to the decision in *Griswold*. However, the Court's ruling in *Harris*, that the government does not have to fund poor women's abortions through Medicaid, raises questions about whether a negative view of privacy is sufficient to guarantee women the fundamental right to personhood (autonomy) when it comes to making decisions about reproduction. A right to obtain an abortion that cannot be exercised solely because of one's inability to pay rings hollow for many feminists. Does government have an affirmative obligation related to the exercise of privacy rights?

Feminist legal scholar Catherine MacKinnon argued that locating women's reproductive rights in the privacy doctrine merely reinforces the subordination women experience as a result of the public-private dichotomy. The assumption that women can exercise autonomy within the private sphere is faulty, she argues, and she cites as evidence the lack of support for a woman's right to refuse sex. If unintended pregnancy is a result of unintended sex (she argues here that men control the sex act entirely), then privacy understood as a negative right rather than a positive duty for government to provide termination of the unintended pregnancy merely reinforces women's subordination as a group to men as a group.[117] In this sense, "*Roe v. Wade* presumes that government nonintervention into the private sphere promotes a woman's freedom of choice. . . . But the *Harris* result sustains the ultimate meaning of privacy in *Roe*: Women are guaranteed by the public no more than what we can get in private—that is, what we can extract through our intimate associations with men. Women with privileges get rights. . . . So women got abortion as a private privilege, not as a public right. . . . Abortion was not decriminalized, it was legalized."[118] MacKinnon charges that in the case of abortion specifically and reproductive rights more generally, the concept of "privacy" shields and protects the very source of women's subordination—the private sphere.

Within the private sphere, women are left to negotiate their rights as individuals who are segregated from the interests of women as a group. This, she argues, is why women cannot be effectively organized around the issue of abortion. "This is an instance of liberalism called feminism, liberalism applied to women as if we *are* persons, gender neutral. It reinforces the division between public and private that is *not* gender neutral. It is at once an ideological division that lies about women's shared experience and that mystifies the unity among the spheres of women's violation."[119]

Whether or not one accepts MacKinnon's line of reasoning, *Harris* poses an interesting dilemma. Privacy guarantees only the right to decide whether or not to terminate the pregnancy, not the ability to carry out the decision. The government in this case supports only one decision—the decision to continue the pregnancy. But how does this square with welfare reform provisions for a "family cap"—that is, a limit to public assistance when an additional child is born? It would seem that government now supports neither decision—or rather the law may support both decisions, but for poor women, reality permits neither.

When Rights Are in Conflict: State Intervention

There has been a growing trend toward greater state intervention in the lives of pregnant women in the name of fetal protection. This intervention includes state-compelled medical treatment, arrest, and incarceration of drug-addicted pregnant women under child endangerment laws or drug distribution penalties; workplace restrictions that apply to both pregnant and potentially pregnant women; and numerous conditions placed by states on the right to seek a legal first-trimester abortion. Central to each of these areas is the competition of rights between the woman and the fetus. Some scholars have argued that the extension of "rights" to a fetus is possible due to advances in technology that have allowed the public to see the fetus as it develops recognizably human features long before viability.[120] *Roe* tips the balance from the interests of the individual (the woman) to the state at the point of fetal viability. As technology has gradually moved the point of viability earlier in the pregnancy, in both reality and public perception, the state has taken a more aggressive role on behalf of the fetus, often at the expense of a woman's autonomy. More often than not, the public has been supportive of increased state intervention, especially when it comes at the expense of personal autonomy for poor women and women of color. With each new form of state intervention, the autonomy of all women is placed at risk.

Compelling pregnant women to undergo medical treatment can be seen as enforcing the woman's duty to care for the fetus.[121] In the case of *In Re A.C.*, a court of appeals held that a trial judge's actions that compelled a woman who was twenty-six and a half weeks pregnant and dying of cancer to have a caesarean section violated a long tradition of an individual's right to accept or reject medical treatment and to maintain bodily integrity. At twenty-six weeks, the woman entered the hospital knowing that her illness was terminal, and she agreed to palliative care to extend her life until her pregnancy reached the twenty-eighth week (forty weeks is a normal full-term pregnancy). Within four days, her condition worsened and she was unable to communicate further. The hospital immediately sought a declaratory judgment from the court to intervene for the fetus as *parens patriae*. The hospital's doctors testified that a fetus delivered at twenty-six weeks was viable and stood about a 50 percent chance of survival. But there was no evidence that the woman had consented to a caesarean delivery at twenty-six weeks, and her mother opposed intervention since she believed her daughter wanted to live to see the baby if delivered and that she would not have chosen to deliver a child with a substantial degree of impairment (which was likely, given the premature birth and the mother's medical condition). A trial court ordered the caesarean section, arguing that "the state has an important and legitimate interest in protecting the potentiality of human life."[122] The child died within two and one-half hours of the surgery, and the woman died two days later.

The appeals court based its reversal of the lower court's decision on several legal precedents, including an individual's right to make informed choices about treatment that includes the right to forgo treatment altogether and the court's inability to compel a person to permit significant intrusion on his or her bodily integrity even if the life of another person is at stake (e.g., compulsory bone marrow transplants for relatives). The court wrote, "It has been suggested that fetal cases are different because a woman who 'has chosen to lend her body to bring a child into the world' has an enhanced duty to assure the welfare of the fetus, sufficient even to require her to undergo caesarean surgery. Surely, however, a fetus cannot have rights in this respect superior to those of a person who has already been born."[123]

Regardless of the appellate court's holding, forced caesarean surgeries continue. Utah prosecutors charged a woman with murder for failing to undergo a caesarean-section delivery, a decision that allegedly resulted in the death of one of her unborn twins. As attorney Sherry Colb notes, this prosecution raises a significant question: "Are we, as a society, prepared to demand more of pregnant women than of anyone else?"[124] Looking at trends in state and federal law, the answer appears to be yes. Parents are not required under penalty of prosecution to donate a kidney to save the life of their child who has already been born. Many do, of course, but they are not legally obligated to do so. Ultimately, Utah dropped the capital murder charge against this woman, but not before she pled guilty to two charges of child endangerment for using cocaine during her pregnancy, placing her at risk of five years in prison. She was sentenced to eighteen months' probation and ordered to seek drug treatment.

A second area of states' attempts to regulate pregnant women's conduct is in regard to drug and alcohol use. Most often, drug- or alcohol-addicted women are identified for state intervention and punitive action after they have given birth to a child who tests positive for drugs or exhibits symptoms of fetal alcohol syndrome. Some states have required public hospitals to report such findings to law enforcement officials. These laws disproportionately impact poor women and women of color because they are more likely to seek prenatal care and deliver infants at public hospitals. Dorothy Roberts argues that hospitals that serve poor minority communities are among the few that have implemented infant toxicology tests. One trigger for testing is the mother's failure to obtain prenatal care, a factor highly related to race and income. In many cases, hospitals do not have formal screening criteria, but rely on hospital staff to identify women likely to be substance abusers and test their infants. Racial stereotypes result in tests being performed almost exclusively on African American women and their babies.[125]

State legislatures have recently enacted a number of provisions specifically designed to criminalize behaviors by pregnant women. In Utah, Governor Gary Herbert signed into law the Criminal Homicide and Abortion Revisions Act, which punishes pregnant women who "knowingly" commit acts that might result in miscarriages. A similar law in Texas would seek to punish any pregnant woman who ingests a controlled substance. Wisconsin criminalized legal abortion if it is obtained without first undergoing a vaginal probe.[126]

Fetal Protection Policies

Increased regulation of pregnant or potentially pregnant women can also take the form of workplace exclusions in occupations deemed hazardous to fetal development. Under the guise of protecting women's health, fetal protection policies have proliferated within the past two decades. The underlying philosophy of fetal protection policies is similar to that expressed in *Muller v. Oregon* (1908), a case in which the US Supreme Court upheld a limited workday for women only. Limiting working conditions (hours, minimum wage, and the like) for men was considered an arbitrary infringement on the right and liberty of the individual to contract in relation to his labor. The Court reasoned that because "healthy mothers are essential to vigorous offspring, the physical well-being of women becomes an object of public interest and care in order to preserve the strength and vigor of the race."[127]

Justification for contemporary fetal protection policies is now grounded in the "rights" and interests of the fetus rather than in broad social reproductive-policy goals. Exclusionary workplace policies that bar women from certain positions designated (by employers) as "hazardous" view individual women only within the context of reproduction. As many as 20 million women may have already been excluded from certain jobs, usually the highest-paying jobs, as a result of these exclusionary policies. Ironically, fetal protection policies are most often found in industries where women make up a small proportion of the total workforce, while the risks are greatest in industries where women constitute 75 to 80 percent of the workforce (e.g., semiconductors, textiles, and hospitals). The scientific evidence on which exclusionary policies are based is subject to debate and rarely considers paternal risk factors, either genetically at the point of conception or the risk of a man exposing a pregnant woman to toxins that are on his skin or clothing. Critics of exclusionary policies directed solely at women charge that such blanket policies fail to recognize women as individuals capable of making autonomous decisions and evaluating risks in employment. This "romantic paternalism" is strikingly similar to protectionist policies of the Progressive Era that were declared unconstitutional under Title VII.[128]

In *United Auto Workers v. Johnson Controls, Inc.* (1991), the US Supreme Court held that the fetal protection policies adopted by the company violated Title VII because they constituted disparate treatment on the basis of sex, since employees were classified by gender and reproductive capacity rather than by individual circumstances. In addition, Johnson Controls argued that it was permitted to bar fertile women to protect their potential offspring, justifying their policy with a bona fide occupational qualification (BFOQ) of "sterility." The company further claimed that the BFOQ was closely related to job skills and aptitudes because it was necessary to ensure the safe and efficient production of batteries.

The Court found that the policy was not justified under the BFOQ defense to sex discrimination, and said that an employer was not permitted to discriminate against women based on their *potential* for pregnancy unless that potential prevented them from doing their jobs. Treating all female employees as potentially pregnant constitutes discrimination on the basis of sex. The Court did not directly address questions of an employer's responsibility to provide a safe workplace for all employees regardless of sex, the argument about potential tort liability and business solvency, or the existence of fetal rights.

Fetal rights as applied to women's employment conditions pit the interests of an individual woman against societal interests. As Suzanne Uttaro Samuels, author of *Fetal Rights, Women's Rights: Gender Equality in the Workplace*, notes, "Like the dystopia in Atwood's *The Handmaid's Tale*, a society that allows employers to adopt fetal protection policies reifies women's procreative role while denigrating their other contributions. In such a society, women can never be the equals of men."[129]

Federally Imposed Restrictions on Abortion

During the first George W. Bush administration, Congress passed two laws intended to narrow the scope of women's exercise of abortion rights by elevating the status of the fetus. One was the 2004 Unborn Victims of Violence Act, also known as Laci and Conner's Law, after the Laci Peterson homicide. The legislation created a separate offense for killing or injuring an "unborn child" while committing a federal crime against a woman. Although the measure excludes voluntary abortion, it defines an unborn child as "a member of the species *Homo sapiens*, at any stage of development, who is carried in the womb." The specific language recognizes an embryo or a fetus as a person distinct from the pregnant woman, thereby creating separate legal rights for the fetus. Because of this provision, opponents charge that it is a back-door attack on reproductive rights and threatens to undermine the central holding in *Roe v. Wade*.[130]

The second was the Partial-Birth Abortion Ban Act of 2003, making it illegal for doctors to take overt action to abort a late-term fetus—a fetus in the second or third trimester. The bill makes no exemption for a woman whose health is put at risk by carrying the pregnancy to term, nor does it take into account ailments or deformities the child may suffer in life. Nebraska's similar late-term abortion law had already been declared unconstitutional by the US Supreme Court in *Stenberg v. Carhart* (2000). Three federal judges in three different locations have issued injunctions against the Partial-Birth Abortion Ban Act, citing the undue burden the law places on women's right to make their own medical decisions about abortion without interference from the government. US district court judge Robert Kopf noted, "While the procedure is infrequently used as a relative matter, when it is needed, the health of the woman frequently hangs in the balance." Neither the Nebraska statute struck down in *Carhart* nor the federal law contains a health exception. In addition, the judges cited the law's vagueness relative to the procedures being banned. US district court judge Phyllis Hamilton noted, "The term partial-birth abortion is neither recognized in the medical literature nor used by physicians who routinely perform second trimester abortions." She went on, "By referring to the procedure as 'infanticide,' Congress was being 'grossly misleading and inaccurate.' . . .Congress was aware that the abortion procedure banned by the bill applied to fetuses that were too young to live outside the womb."[131]

On April 18, 2007, in a 5–4 decision, the US Supreme Court upheld the federal Partial-Birth Abortion Ban Act of 2003 in *Gonzales v. Carhart*.[132] Justice Anthony Kennedy wrote the majority opinion and was joined by Chief Justice John Roberts and Justices Alito, Thomas, and Scalia. Justice Ruth Bader Ginsburg wrote a dissenting opinion that was joined by Justices Souter, Stevens, and Breyer. *Gonzales* marked the first time the Court had ever upheld a total ban on a specific abortion procedure; however, the central holding in *Roe v. Wade* was not overturned by this ruling. The ruling upholds the 2003 law as written, but left open the possibility that the law could be challenged again "as applied." In other words, if it could be demonstrated that the law in its application constituted a substantial obstacle to the abortion right, the Court might reexamine the holding.

Justice Ginsburg read her dissent from the bench, registering her extreme displeasure with the majority's holding and its basis. She called the ruling "an alarming decision" that refuses "to take seriously" prior rulings and precedent. She wrote, "The Court's opinion tolerates, indeed applauds federal intervention to ban nationwide a procedure found necessary and proper in certain cases by the American College of Obstetricians and Gynecologists. For the first time since *Roe*, the Court blesses a prohibition with no exception protecting a woman's health." Justice Ginsburg suggested that the majority's opinion was political rather than judicial in nature, noting that "the Court's hostility to the right *Roe* and *Casey* secured is not concealed. Though today's opinion does not go so far as to discard *Roe* or *Casey*, the Court, differently composed than it was when we last considered a restrictive

IMAGE 8.3: *Surrounded by lawmakers, US President George W. Bush signs legislation banning so-called partial birth abortions in Washington November 5, 2003. The law will prohibit doctors from committing an "overt act" designed to kill a partially delivered fetus and allows no exception if the woman's health is at risk, or if the child would be born with ailments.* Source: Reuters/Kevin Lamarque KL.

abortion regulation, is hardly faithful to our earlier invocations of 'the rule of law' and the 'principles of *stare decisis*.'" Ginsburg concluded her dissent:

> In sum, the notion that the Partial-Birth Abortion Ban Act furthers any legitimate governmental interest is, quite simply, irrational. The Court's defense of the statute provides no saving explanation. In candor, the Act, and the Court's defense of it, cannot be understood as anything other than an effort to chip away at a right declared again and again by this Court—with increasing comprehension of its centrality to women's lives.

Particularly troubling to Ginsburg and to feminist legal scholars is the language Kennedy employs in defense of the government's intervention in women's medical decision-making, even going to so far as to articulate a new government interest—protecting "the bond of love the mother has for her child."[133] The Court determined that abortion has serious harmful effects on women, including severe psychological consequences, even though this belief was based on "no reliable data," by the Court's own admission. Thus, the Court upheld the restriction as a way of protecting women from their own potentially harmful choices. Justice

Ginsburg charged that this reasoning "reflects ancient notions about women's place in the family and under the Constitution—ideas that have long been discredited." Further, the majority's opinion uses rhetoric that demonstrates hostility to a woman's right to choose and disdain for the medical profession. Justice Ginsburg wrote:

> Throughout, the opinion refers to obstetricians-gynecologists and surgeons who perform abortions not by the titles of their medical specialties, but by the pejorative label "abortion doctor." A fetus is described as an "unborn child," and as a "baby"; second trimester, pre-viability abortions are referred to as "late-term"; and the reasoned medical judgments of highly trained doctors are dismissed as "preferences" motivated by "mere convenience."

Legal scholars continue to warn, particularly after the Court's opinion in *Gonzales*, that we are perhaps one vote away from a majority decision overturning *Roe v. Wade.* Eight years of a prochoice president, Barack Obama, inoculated the Supreme Court against threats of an antiabortion appointment. As a candidate for president in 2016, Donald Trump promised that if elected he would appoint antiabortion justices. But as the history of judicial appointments demonstrates, no president can be entirely sure of an appointee's future opinions.

State-Imposed Restrictions on Legal Abortion

A woman's right to choose abortion and to legally access abortion services is already heavily conditional on the policies adopted and enforced in the state where she resides. Abortion is already largely inaccessible to the majority of women, and current state policies exacerbate these inequities in abortion access.[134] Eleven states still have pre-*Roe* abortion bans on the books—several of which could, in theory, be enforced if *Roe* is overturned. Louisiana, Mississippi, North Dakota, and South Dakota have laws that automatically ban abortion if Roe is overturned. Thirteen states retain, but do not enforce, abortion bans enacted prior to 1973 (Alabama, Arizona, Arkansas, Colorado, Delaware, Massachusetts, Michigan, Mississippi, New Mexico, Oklahoma, Vermont, West Virginia, and Wisconsin—although some of these provide exceptions for rape, incest, and/or to protect the life or health of the woman). In other states, policy makers are writing legislation that bans abortion under all or virtually all circumstances, in anticipation of a day when *Roe* no longer limits the restrictions states can impose on abortion. Still others have laws declaring their intent to ban abortion to the full extent allowed by the US Constitution.[135]

In the first half of 2016 alone, state legislators have introduced 1,256 bills relating to reproductive health and rights, 35 percent of which were to restrict access to abortion.[136] Between 2011 and August 2015, states enacted 287 new legal restrictions on access to abortion care. A review of existing abortion laws by the Guttmacher Institute identified nine broad categories of regulations and limitations on whether, when, and under what circumstances a woman may obtain a legal abortion.[137] Thirty-eight states require an abortion to be performed by a licensed physician, and nineteen states require an abortion to be performed in a hospital after a specified point in the pregnancy. Forty-six states allow individual health care providers to refuse to participate in an abortion, and forty-three states allow institutions to refuse to perform abortions. Thirty-four states require parental involvement in a minor's decision to have an abortion; twenty-two states require one or both parents to consent to the procedure, while ten states require that one or both parents be notified.

Among the newest trends is a "counseling" requirement, imposed by seventeen states, that may require information be given to a pregnant woman on at least one of the following: the purported link between abortion and breast cancer (six states), the ability of a fetus to feel pain (nine states), long-term mental health consequences for the woman (seven states), or information on the availability of ultrasound (six states). The veracity and accuracy of the information provided in these required counseling sessions are highly contested. For example, there is no medical science that supports a causal link between abortion and breast cancer, and experts disagree over whether a fetus has the ability to register pain. On June 27, 2008, the Eighth Circuit upheld a South Dakota law requiring doctors to inform patients seeking an abortion that the procedure will "terminate the life of a whole, separate, unique, living being." In a 7–4 decision, the court based its ruling in part on the majority opinion in *Gonzales v. Carhart* expressing concern that women be protected from a decision they might "regret." A dissenting opinion noted that the law was not about giving women information designed to assist their decision-making, but rather "expresses ideological beliefs aimed at making it more difficult for women to choose abortions."[138]

Twenty-four states now require a woman seeking an abortion to wait a specified period of time, usually twenty-four hours, between an exam or mandated counseling and the procedure. Both the counseling requirement and most especially the mandatory waiting period require a woman to make repeated trips to the facility in order to obtain a legal abortion. As Rachel Benson Gold notes, "Many of these policies, at their heart, are premised on the notion that women who intend to have an abortion (and, to some extent, the public at large) do not fully understand what an abortion really is—and that, if they did, they would behave differently." In fact, the majority in *Gonzales v. Carhart* (2007) all but invited states to reexamine the information provided to women prior to an abortion, specifically the information describing "the way in which the fetus will be killed," on the grounds that "a necessary effect of [such a requirement] and the knowledge it conveys will be to encourage some women to carry the infant to full term."[139] In the states that require women to receive specific information prior to an abortion, the Guttmacher Institute found only ten states in which the information generally conforms to the widely held principles of informed consent; information provided in the rest was "designed more to influence rather than inform the woman's decision." There is no evidence that state policies designed to persuade women to forgo a planned abortion are effective.[140] On the contrary, there is considerable proof that the content of pre-abortion information mandated in several states is misleading and misrepresents current medical knowledge.[141] The Guttmacher Institute now classifies twenty-seven states as "hostile" to abortion rights, with eighteen of those classified as "extremely hostile."[142]

One consequence of the rise in state restrictions on access to reproductive care and abortion has been the return of do-it-yourself (DIY) abortions. In a 2016 *New York Times* column, economist Seth Stephens-Davidowitz documented the positive correlation between clinic closures and Google searches for alternative methods of abortion. He writes that Google searches "show a hidden demand for self-induced abortion reminiscent of the era before *Roe v. Wade*. This demand is concentrated in areas where it is most difficult to get an abortion and it has closely tracked the recent state-level crackdowns on abortion."[143] In 2015, there were more than 700,000 Google searches looking into self-induced abortions, including about 160,000 searches for the abortion pill (many states require a physician to administer the first dose, making online pharmacy distribution illegal). The ten states with the highest rates of searches for self-induced abortions appear on the Guttmacher Institute's list of states that are "extremely hostile" to abortion rights, including Mississippi, which has one clinic and a population just under 3 million. Thirty-eight states now allow a person to be charged with homicide if she or he is believed to be responsible for the unlawful death of a fetus, and not all of these laws exempt the pregnant woman from being charged.[144]

Conscience Clause and the Right to Refuse

As we've discussed throughout this chapter, a woman's right to receive information and reproductive health services related to contraception and abortion has been restricted by others' claims to rights. In some cases, the "other" is another person (e.g., a spouse or partner, or a parent in the case of minors), an employer, a state official, or the federal government. Often these claims of competing rights involve deeply held personal beliefs about what is right and wrong. Although US political culture is characterized by the right of the individual, in the area of reproductive rights it is complicated as to *which* individual's rights prevail. Conscience exceptions or "right to refuse" policies are an example of this tension.

Conscience laws, adopted by federal and state governments following *Roe v. Wade* in 1973, allow health care professionals, clinics, and hospitals to refuse to provide services related to reproductive health without suffering legal consequences.

Forty-five states allow some health care providers to refuse to provide abortion services. In all cases, individual providers are covered under these provisions, and in thirteen states the law is limited to private hospitals, such as those affiliated with the Catholic Church. Twelve states allow health care providers to refuse to provide services related to contraception. In Arizona, Arkansas, Georgia, Idaho, Mississippi, and South Carolina, a pharmacist may refuse to dispense contraceptives. In eighteen states, doctors and health care providers can refuse to provide sterilization services.[145] Alternatively, some states have imposed an affirmative duty on pharmacists to dispense emergency contraception, but when challenged in court these laws have been found to violate the free exercise clause of the First Amendment and the equal protection clause of the Fourteenth Amendment.[146]

An individual denied access to legal contraception has been denied the constitutional right of privacy first recognized in *Griswold v. Connecticut* in 1965. Since pharmaceutical contraception is used almost exclusively by women, questions of unequal treatment arise. For low-income women or women in rural areas, a refusal to provide services or fill prescriptions may leave no other options.

THREATS TO WOMEN'S AUTONOMY

Throughout this book, women's claims to equality have been limited by the ways in which women as autonomous individuals are subsumed by the identity of another. In the early Republic, coverture marriage and separate spheres ideology conspired to render women nearly invisible in the public sphere. Civil, economic, and political rights were deemed unnecessary for women because they were "cared for" by men and male-dominated institutions. Obviously, women's rights have advanced considerably, and one might be tempted to declare victory. However, as you have seen in this chapter, the family and women's role in reproduction still impose limitations on women's autonomy. This section addresses still more threats to women's autonomy and thus her equality.

Domestic Violence

Domestic violence is an issue that sits at the intersection of the private and public spheres. The context in which domestic violence is defined affects the remedy available. Under coverture laws of marriage, men were allowed to administer "corrections" to their wives since they were legally responsible for their wives' debts and conduct.[147] Just as parents were entrusted with the discipline of their children, a husband as the patriarchal head of a family was entrusted with the discipline of his wife. The phrase "rule of thumb" is said to have arisen in this context—a husband's legitimate authority to use force against his wife or children was limited to the use of a stick no larger in diameter than his thumb. One of the temperance movement's causes was to stop women from being physically abused by their husbands. Drunken husbands not only spent the family's wages but also often returned from a night of drinking to physically assault their wives and children. Activists urged reform of divorce laws to permit women to escape domestic violence.

The 1970s battered-women's movement reflected the divide among feminists. Some argued that the best way to help women end the violence in their lives was to provide them with services (e.g., shelter, police protection, legal aid, and counseling) within the conventional social service sector. Other, more radical feminists believed that domestic violence stemmed from economic dependency and would not cease until the basic structural gender arrangements in society changed. They favored creating autonomous alternatives to the patriarchal family and economic structures.[148] Addressing domestic violence must begin by moving the definition of the problem from the private sphere to the public sphere. When women's battery is defined as a family problem, public institutions are unlikely to interfere. Thus, police departments have been slow to intervene in domestic disputes until recently. Today, one in three women and one in four men have been physically abused by an intimate partner. On a typical day, domestic violence hotlines nationwide receive approximately 20,800 calls. The impact on the individual and on the people around a victim of domestic violence includes higher rates of depression among victims, workplace absenteeism, and job loss, with an economic impact of $8.3 billion annually. [149]

A national coalition of feminist organizations successfully lobbied Congress to pass federal legislation on domestic abuse. The 1994 **Violence Against Women Act (VAWA)** charges the Justice Department with collecting data on domestic abuse, provides money to state and local governments to fund efforts to provide services to victims and abusers, and identifies domestic abuse as a gender-based crime; this has allowed victims to sue their batterers in federal court. VAWA has been reauthorized by Congress every five years since its passage. In 2013 reauthorization, more attention was paid to issues of dating violence and sexual assault on college campuses (see Chapter 6), Native American women's issues, and LGBT services for victims of domestic violence.

When NFL quarterback Michael Vick was indicted in 2007 and found guilty of animal abuse for his role in a dogfighting ring, he was suspended indefinitely without pay from the NFL. Feminists were astounded that the NFL has not acted with equivalent outrage when players are charged with domestic violence against women. Although some players have been arrested and convicted of spousal abuse (e.g., Ray Rice in 2014 and Johnny Manziel in 2016), not one has been permanently banned from the NFL. The NFL suspended Ray Rice for two games following his arrest after video surfaced of him dragging his unconscious fiancée from an elevator. But if the website TMZ had not released additional video showing him knocking her out with one punch, it's doubtful that NFL's weak punishment would have attracted as much outrage as it did. Domestic violence accounts for 48 percent of the arrests for violent crimes among football players, compared to

21 percent among American men ages twenty-five to twenty-nine.[150] The NFL has responded by producing a public service announcement, "No More," urging bystanders to intervene and by revising its personal conduct policy to immediately place players on paid leave pending the outcome of league investigations and criminal proceedings.

Of females killed with a firearm, almost two-thirds were killed by their intimate partners. The number of women shot and killed by their husband or intimate partner was more than three times higher than the total number murdered by male strangers using all weapons combined in single-victim/single-offender incidents.[151] Domestic violence compromises women's autonomy, and its prevalence worldwide is shocking—one-third of all women have experienced intimate partner violence. Education plays an important role in the prevention of domestic violence, and economically secure women are much more likely to leave unhealthy relationships. Ultimately, domestic violence is about the desire of one person to exert complete control over another.

Technology, Reproduction, and Gender Ideologies

Scientific advances in the technology of reproduction have increased the demand for applying such technology to infertility. Nearly 15 percent of all married couples have fertility problems.[152] Experts estimate that average male sperm count has fallen by more than 30 percent in the last half century, and nearly a quarter of men now have sperm counts that are low enough for them to be considered functionally sterile. Similarly, the number of women experiencing fertility problems has also grown. Of those who are currently sterile, 40 percent attribute sterility to fallopian tubes scarred by pelvic inflammatory disease and other low-level gynecological infections.

Changing social patterns have contributed to the growth of consumer demand for fertility technology as well. The wider acceptance of contraceptive use, abortion, and the growing trend among single women to bear and raise a child have all helped to dramatically decrease the number of infants available for adoption. The availability of fertility technology has increased the number of couples interested in producing a biological child rather than having to navigate the complicated procedures involved with domestic and foreign adoptions. In addition, more people have postponed marriage and parenting until after earning a degree and establishing their careers, and thus they have delayed childbearing until later in life, when infertility is more common for both men and women.[153]

Consumer-driven demand for fertility technology, while presumably grounded in the most intimate desire for a child, has been criticized for "commercializing reproduction" and creating a market in women's reproductive labor. Treating women's reproductive labor as a commodity similar to any other form of labor presents society with a wide array of conundrums that are only now beginning to surface in the form of public policy. One of the first public exposures to contract pregnancy was the "Baby M" case, in which Elizabeth and William Stern contracted with Mary Beth Whitehead to have her artificially inseminated with William Stern's sperm. Whitehead was promised $10,000 upon delivering the child. The specific terms of the contract were drawn up to avoid "baby selling" under New Jersey law. Although the baby was initially turned over to the Sterns and Elizabeth Stern was granted the right to immediately adopt William Stern and Mary Beth Whitehead's daughter, Whitehead subsequently changed her mind and sought custody of the child known in court documents as Baby M, arguing that the bond between mother and child was more powerful than any contract.

In 1988, the New Jersey Supreme Court sided with Whitehead and invalidated the surrogacy contract on the grounds that money exchanged for the purpose of adopting a child was illegal under New Jersey law and therefore the contract was unenforceable. The court invalidated Elizabeth Stern's adoption and restored Whitehead's parental rights, but awarded custody to William Stern. The outcome of this highly publicized case once again focused public attention on women's reproductive roles that conflict with social expectations. Those sympathetic to Whitehead's claims pointed to the Sterns' wealth, two-career status, and impatience with the adoption process as evidence that they were unfit as parents, compared with Whitehead, who already had children of her own and a stable marriage, and was motivated out of a desire to help infertile couples realize their dream. Elizabeth Stern, diagnosed with multiple sclerosis, was criticized for putting her own health interests ahead of having biological children.

Today the laws regarding surrogacy remain largely unsettled. Family law, including surrogacy, is primarily a state matter. Seventeen states have laws permitting surrogacy, but they vary tremendously. In twenty-one states there is neither a law nor a published case regarding surrogacy. In five states surrogacy arrangements are prohibited, meaning such contracts are unenforceable. California has the most permissive surrogacy law, allowing anyone to hire a woman to carry a baby; the birth certificate lists only the names of the intended parents and not the woman contracted for the pregnancy.[154] In states without specific legislation, judges are required to interpret family law as best they can. On average, about 2,000 babies are born in surrogate arrangements each year. One of the newest areas of surrogacy law involves embryo adoption. This situation arises when couples with viable embryos decide to allow them to be adopted by infertile couples rather than have them destroyed upon completion of their own assisted reproduction procedures. Unlike with surrogacy, genetic parents relinquish all rights to the embryo prior to implantation. The child born of the implantation is the child of the recipient couple and no further legal action is required to perfect the parent-child relationship.

Sometimes fertility technology makes headlines because of its unprecedented success. On January 26, 2009, Nadya Suleman gave birth to octuplets in California. Although the news was initially greeted with great curiosity and enthusiastic interest, the public's attitude changed when the mother's identity and broader circumstances became known. At the time of the birth, Suleman was single, unemployed, and living with her mother, and she was already the parent of six children, including twins, ranging in age from two to seven. Whereas other women who have given birth to multiples have been showered with gifts from large corporations, such as a lifetime supply of free diapers or baby food, or their own television show (e.g., *Jon and Kate Plus 8*), Suleman seemingly received only criticism that she was irresponsible and a "bad mother."

All fourteen of Suleman's children were born with the assistance of fertility technology, raising a number of ethical questions within the medical community. "It was a grave error, whatever happened," said Eleanor Nicoll, a spokeswoman for the American Society for Reproductive Medicine. "It should not have happened. Eight children should not have been conceived and born."[155] There are few regulations covering doctors and clinics that provide fertility assistance. Associations such as the American Society for Reproductive Medicine and the Society for Assisted Reproductive Technology have guidelines that call for no more than two embryos to be implanted in a woman in her early thirties; there is nothing in the guidelines about the number of previous children. The octuplets' birth led many in the medical profession to expect new legislation. The United States does not regulate family size, but if it were to do so, how many would it permit? Who would decide, and what would the implications be for women and gender equality? More important, what does this case and set of questions say about women's autonomy in the area of fertility?

The policy status of surrogacy, contract pregnancy, and in vitro fertilization techniques that result in embryos being created outside the womb is unclear. Sex and gender are interwoven, but rarely consciously disentangled, in the public dialogue on the social desirability of decoupling traditional heterosexual intercourse from reproduction. Regulations are substantially behind medical technology and are largely driven by a reaction to events already unfolding (e.g., cloning). The question of whether reproductive technologies liberate women or serve as yet another tool of patriarchal control dominates feminist literature on the subject. While technology seems to have helped infertile women, single women, and women without heterosexual partners bear children, it directly challenges our definition of family, our understanding of the link between sex and gender, and women's biological and sociological role in reproduction. Should society set a limit on the number of children in a "family"? Is surrogacy exploitation akin to prostitution? Should women be able to contract for their reproductive labor as freely as they do for other types of labor? Do reproductive technologies devalue women's reproductive role or liberate women from the subordination inherent in biological reproduction? These questions and more will face future generations of men and women, as well as policymakers and politicians.

CONCLUSION

A variety of issues related to the family will face future generations of citizens and policy makers. The very definition of what constitutes a family is being redefined today. Same-sex marriage has become legal since the *Obergefell v. Hodges* decision in 2015, but even before then, the country had been trending toward a more inclusive definition of family. New reproductive technologies have allowed same-sex couples, whether male or female, to genetically contribute to the conception of a "child of their own." Women's biological and sociological roles in relation to reproduction are less clear than they have ever been. How will these issues be resolved?

The policy process is not particularly well equipped to deal with such intimate and complex issues. The same claim to privacy that gives women choices in reproductive decisions also surrounds and isolates them as individuals subordinated within families in the private sphere. Domestic violence, marital rape, and poverty conditions have all been beyond the scope of politics and government action until relatively recently in our history. More so than in other issues we've discussed in this volume, family and fertility decisions present women with direct challenges to their autonomy. When women were defined solely within the private sphere, they were virtually invisible. As women have become more active in politics and the public sphere, they have transformed previously private issues significant to their lives and livelihoods into issues legitimate for public policy.

However, as government has become more involved in these issues, women's interests as autonomous individuals run the risk of being subsumed by larger social interests or by political ideologies that circumscribe their autonomy. Particularly in the area of reproduction and fertility concerns, women as individuals risk becoming an invisible interest in public policy debates. As we saw in Chapter 5, electing more women to public office does not in itself guarantee that women's interests will be promoted. As Laura Woliver states, "If we honestly discussed abortion within the territory of gender politics and women's rights and health instead of centering on fetal life, we would have to answer questions about how abortion is singled out for regulations that presume incompetent, selfish, misinformed female decision making instead of simply regulating abortion with the same health and safety provisions for other medical procedures."[156]

How will women and men resolve these tensions created by the paradox of equality? There is no clear path to women's equality in the family and in reproductive choices. The legal equality doctrine's gender-neutral approach does not seem appropriate when the issues are tied directly to women's biological sex as well as socially constructed gender roles. The persistence of patriarchal culture, however, makes it difficult to determine what fair treatment for women under the fairness doctrine is. Betty Friedan argued that the only way to resolve these seemingly intractable issues is to redefine the context of the problem from judging *equality* within a legal framework to judging it in the context of the substantive *quality* of men's and women's lives. This, she argues, calls for a reconceptualization of how to balance work (public sphere) and family (private sphere).[157] This new equality is not equality between men and women but equality in the substantive areas in which their lives converge. This is the challenge for the coming century as men and women continue their pursuit of equality.

NOTES

Boxed feature notes appear at the end of the Notes section.

1 *General Electric v. Gilbert*, 429 U.S. 125 (1976).
2 Kim Parker, Juliana Menasce Horowitz, and Molly Rohal, "Parenting in America," Pew Research Center, December 17, 2015.
3 Brigid Schulte, "Unlike the 1950s, There Is No 'Typical' U.S. Family Today," *Washington Post*, September 4, 2014.
4 US Census Bureau, 2014 American Community Survey, "Table 1. Household Characteristics of Opposite-Sex and Same-Sex Couple Households," www.census.gov/hhes/samesex/files/ssex-tables -2014.xlsx.
5 Rosemary Radford Ruether, "Diverse Forms of Family Life Merit Recognition," *National Catholic Reporter* 36, no. 32 (June 16, 2000): 19.
6 Wendy Wang and Kim Parker, "Record Share of Americans Have Never Married," Pew Research Center, September 24, 2016.
7 Shannon Cavanagh, "An Analysis of New Census Data on Family Structure, Education, and Income," Council on Contemporary Families, February 26, 2015.
8 Cynthia B. Costello, Shari Miles, and Anne J. Stone, eds., *The American Woman 1999–2000: A Century of Change—What's Next?* (New York: Norton, 1998), 190.
9 Wang and Parker, "Record Share of Americans Have Never Married."
10 Dorothy McBride Stetson, *Women's Rights in the USA: Policy Debates and Gender Roles* (New York: Garland Press, 1997), 178–183.
11 Virginia Sapiro, *Women in American Society: An Introduction to Women's Studies*, 4th ed. (Mountain View, Calif.: Mayfield, 1999), 392–393.
12 Susan Moller Okin, *Justice, Gender, and the Family* (New York: Basic Books, 1989).
13 Ibid.
14 *Forbush v. Wallace*, 341 F. Supp. 241 (1971).
15 Claire Cain Miller and Derek Willis, "Maiden Names, on the Rise Again," *New York Times*, June 27, 2015.
16 Alvin Powell, "A New Comfort Zone? Fewer Women Keeping Their Names on Marriage," *Harvard Gazette*, August 24, 2004.
17 Gretchen E. Gooding and Rose M. Kreider, "Women's Marital Naming Choices in a Nationally Representative Sample," *Journal of Family Issues* 31, no. 5 (2010): 681–701.
18 Stetson, *Women's Rights in the USA*, 192.
19 Lenore J. Weitzman, *The Divorce Revolution: The Unexpected Social and Economic Consequences for Women and Children in America* (New York: Free Press, 1985).
20 Hunter College Women's Studies Collective, *Women's Realities Women's Choices: An Introduction to Women's Studies* (New York: Oxford University Press, 1995), 249.
21 *Obergefell v. Hodges*, 576 U.S. ___ (2015).
22 *Baehr v. Lewin*, 852 P.2d. 44 (Hawaii 1993).
23 *United States v. Windsor*, 570 U.S. ___ (2013).
24 Corky Siemaszko, "Kentucky Clerk Kim Davis, Who Refused to Issue Marriage Licenses to Gays, Seeks to End Case," NBC News, June 21, 2016.
25 Pew Research Center, "Public Opinion on Same-Sex Marriage," May 12, 2016.
26 Mona Harrington, *Care and Equality: Inventing a New Family Politics* (New York: Oxford University Press, 1999), 48.
27 Ibid., 17.

28 Anne H. Gauthier, *The State and the Family: A Comparative Analysis of Family Policies in Industrialized Countries* (New York: Oxford University Press, 1996), 3–4.

29 Jody Heymann, Alison Earle, and Jeffrey Hayes, "The Work, Family and Equity Index: How Does the United States Measure Up?" Project on Global Working Families, Institute for Health and Social Policy, McGill University, 2008.

30 International Labour Organization, "Maternity and Paternity at Work," 2014.

31 Melissa Etehad, "The World Is Getting Better at Paid Maternity Leave. The U.S. Is Not," *Washington Post*, August 13, 2016.

32 Rita Rubin, "U.S. Dead Last Among Developed Countries When It Comes to Paid Maternity Leave," *Fortune*, April 6, 2016.

33 "Governor Cuomo Signs $15 Minimum Wage Plan and 12 Week Paid Family Leave Policy into Law," Office of the Governor, New York State, April 4, 2016.

34 Anne Weisberg, "The Workplace Culture That Flying Nannies Won't Fix," *New York Times*, August 24, 2015.

35 Ibid.

36 Ibid.

37 Council of Economic Advisors, "Nine Facts About American Families and Work," June 2014.

38 Kellie Lunney, "Obama Again Urges Paid Parental Leave for Federal Employees," *Government Executive*, February 9, 2016.

39 Lake Research Partners, "Findings from National Survey Shows Strong Support for Paid Family and Medical Leave," National Partnership for Women and Families, February 4, 2016.

40 Republican Party Platform, 2016, www.gop.com/the-2016-republican-party-platform.

41 Democratic Party Platform, 2016, www.demconvention.com/wp-content/uploads/2016/07/Democratic-Party-Platform-7.21.16-no-lines.pdf.

42 Conor P. Williams, "Fatherhood, Manhood, and Having It All," *Daily Beast*, June 28, 2014.

43 Kim Parker, "Six Facts About American Fathers," Pew Research Center, June 16, 2016.

44 Lauren Weber, "Why Dads Don't Take Paternity Leave," *Wall Street Journal*, June 12, 2013.

45 Michelle J. Budig, "The Fatherhood Bonus and the Motherhood Penalty," Third Way NEXT, n.d., http://content.thirdway.org/publications/853/NEXT_-_Fatherhood_Motherhood.pdf.

46 Shelley J. Correll, Stephen Benard, and In Paik, "Getting a Job: Is There a Motherhood Penalty?" *American Journal of Sociology* 112, no. 5 (March 2007): 1297–1338.

47 White House, "Remarks by the President in State of the Union Address," January 20, 2015.

48 Institute for Women's Policy Research, "The Need for Support for Working Families," Briefing Paper #B357, February 2016.

49 Elizabeth Palley and Corey S. Shdaimah, *In Our Hands: The Struggle for U.S. Child Care Policy* (New York: New York University Press, 2014).

50 Kimberly J. Morgan, *Working Mothers and the Welfare State: Religion and the Politics of Work-Family Policies in Western Europe and the United States* (Stanford, CA: Stanford University Press, 2006).

51 Susan J. Douglas and Meredith W. Michaels, *The Mommy Myth: The Idealization of Motherhood and How It Has Undermined Women* (New York: Free Press, 2004), 237.

52 See Janet C. Gornick, Marcia K. Myers, and Katerin E. Ross, "Supporting Employment of Mothers: Policy Variations Across Fourteen Welfare States," *Journal of European Social Policy* 7 (1997): 45–70.

53 Ellen Goodman, "Who Gets Blamed for Matthew's Death? The Working Mother, of Course," *Boston Globe*, October 26, 1997, E7.

54 "The Need for Support for Working Families," 5.

55 Ibid.

56 Jill Cueni-Cohen, "The Future of Paid Sick Leave," *Human Resource Executive Online*, April 19, 2016.

57 Gwendolyn Mink, "Welfare Reform in Historical Perspective," *Social Justice* 21, no. 1 (Spring 1994): 114–132.

58 Ibid., 117.

59 Heidi Hartmann and Roberta Spalter-Roth, "The Real Employment Opportunities of Women Participating in AFDC: What the Market Can Provide," *Social Justice* 21, no. 1 (1994).

60 Randy Albelda and Chris Tilly, *Glass Ceilings and Bottomless Pits: Women's Work, Women's Poverty* (Boston: South End Press, 1997), 13.

61 Peter Edelman, "A Call to Action: Taking a Stand Against Poverty and Inequality," keynote remarks delivered at the Equal Justice Conference, Minneapolis, MN, May 7, 2008, www.abanet.org/legalservices/dialogue/downloads/dialsu08.pdf.

62 Jordan Weissmann, "How Welfare Reform Failed," *Slate*, June 1, 2016.

63 Rebecca Blank, "Evaluating Welfare Reform in the United States," *Journal of Economic Literature* 40, no. 4 (2002): 1105–1166.

64 Doug Lederman, "Welfare Reform and Women's College Enrollment," *Inside Higher Education*, November 14, 2008.

65 Krissy Clark, "The Disconnected," *Slate*, June 3, 2015.

66 Kathryn Edin and Luke Shaefer, *$2.00 a Day: Living on Almost Nothing in America.* (New York: Mariner Books, 2016).

67 Weissmann, "How Welfare Reform Failed."

68 Diane Whitmore Schanzenbach, Lauren Bauer, and Greg Nanz, "Twelve Facts About Food Insecurity and SNAP," Hamilton Project, Brookings Institution, April 21, 2016.

69 Ibid., 9.

70 National Priorities Project, "Federal Budget Tipsheet: Social Insurance and Earned Benefits," June 5, 2015.

71 Judith Shulevitz, "It's Payback Time for Women," *New York Times*, January 8, 2016.

72 Robert Blank and Janna C. Merrick, *Human Reproduction, Emerging Technologies, and Conflicting Rights* (Washington, DC: Congressional Quarterly Press, 1995), 4.

73 Sara Ann Ketchum, "Selling of Babies, Selling of Bodies," in *Feminist Perspectives in Medical Ethics*, ed. Helen B. Holmes and Laura M. Purdy (Bloomington: Indiana University Press, 1992), 284–294.

74 Tracy Clark-Flory, "The End of Menstruation," *Salon*, February 4, 2008.

75 Dawn Stacey, "The History of Emergency Contraception," *VeryWell*, July 5, 2016.

76 Alan Guttmacher Institute, "Improving Contraceptive Use in the United States," 2008 Series, No. 1.

77 Guttmacher Institute, "Contraceptive Use in the United States," October 2015.

78 Nancy Woloch, *Women and the American Experience* (New York: Alfred A. Knopf, 1984), 365.

79 Ibid., 367.

80 Quoted in ibid., 369.

81 Guttmacher Institute, "Insurance Coverage of Contraceptives," June 2016.

82 Elizabeth Deutsch, "No Contraception, No Equality," *New York Times*, March 23, 2016.

83 Adam Sonfield, Athena Tapales, Rachel K. Jones, and Lawrence B. Finer, "Impact of Federal Contraceptive Coverage Guarantee on Out-of-Pocket Payments for Contraceptives: 2014 Update," *Contraception* 91 (2015): 44–48.

84 *Burwell v. Hobby Lobby*, 573 U.S. ___ (2014).

85 Dahlia Lithwick, "Supreme Court on Contentious Contraception Case: We're Not Gonna Decide," *Slate*, May 16, 2016.

86 Rebecca Wind, "U.S. Abortion Rate Continues Long-Term Decline," Alan Guttmacher Institute, January 17, 2008.

87 Alan Guttmacher Institute, "Facts on Induced Abortion Worldwide," October 2008.

88 Ibid.

89 *Planned Parenthood of Southeastern Pennsylvania v. Casey*, 112 S.Ct.2791 (1992).

90 Alan Guttmacher Institute, "Induced Abortion," Facts in Brief, 2000.

91 California Abortion and Reproductive Rights Action League, *"Hill v. Colorado*: Summary of the Court's June 28, 2000 Decision," www.choice.org/court2000/hillsummary.html.

92 Sabrina Tavernise, "New F.D.A. Guidelines Ease Access to Abortion Pill," *New York Times*, March 30, 2016.

93 Centers for Disease Control and Prevention, "Reproductive Health Data and Statistics," (2012) www.cdc.gov/reproductivehealth/data_stats.

94 Margaret Talbot, "The Pill That Still Hasn't Changed the Politics of Abortion," *New Yorker*, April 4, 2016.

95 *Whole Woman's Health v. Hellerstedt*, 579 U.S. ___ (2016).

96 Esme E. Deprez, "U.S. Abortion Rights Fight," *Bloomberg News*, July 7, 2016.

97 Michael Lipka, "Five Facts About Abortion," Pew Research Center Fact Tank, June 27, 2016.

98 Lydia Saad, "Americans Choose 'Pro-Choice' for First Time in Seven Years," Gallup, May 29, 2015.

99 Wendy Kaminer, "Abortion and Autonomy," *American Prospect* 11, no. 14 (June 5, 2000).

100 Amy Richards as told to Amy Barrett, "When One Is Enough," *New York Times Magazine*, July 18, 2004, 18.

101 Lydia Saad, "Abortion Issues Laying Low in 2008 Campaign," *Gallup*, May 22, 2008.

102 Ruth Marcus, "Palin's Personal Choice," *Washington Post*, April 20, 2009.

103 Ibid.

104 Emma Grey, "Hillary Clinton Has No Time for Bullsh*t About the 'Gender Card,'" *Huffington Post*, January 11, 2016.

105 Jennifer Ludden, "Fact Checking Trump's Statements on 'Partial-Birth' Abortion," National Public Radio, October 20, 2016.

106 Christina Cauterucci, "Hillary Clinton's Debate Answer on Abortion Is Why We Need More Women in Politics," *Slate*, October 19, 2016.

107 Irin Carmon, "Why It's So Hard to Measure Public Opinion on Abortion," MSNBC, January 22, 2016.

108 Guttmacher Institute, "State Funding of Abortion Under Medicaid," June 2016.

109 Guttmacher Institute, "Restricting Insurance Coverage of Abortion," June 2016.

110 Planned Parenthood Federation of America, www.plannedparenthood.org/learn.

111 Danielle Kurtzleben, "Fact Check: How Does Planned Parenthood Spend That Government Money?" National Public Radio, August 5, 2015.

112 Peter Slavin, "Slaying Raises Fears on Both Sides of Abortion Debate," *Washington Post*, June 2, 2009.

113 Marlene Gerber Fried, "Excerpts from Chapter 17," *Our Bodies, Ourselves*, 2005 edition.www .ourbodiesourselves.org/abortion.htm.

114 K. Aleisha Fetters, "Medical Students Fill Survivor Role for Dr. Tiller," *Women's eNews*, June 7, 2009.

115 National Abortion Federation, "Crisis Pregnancy Centers," 5aa1b2xfmfh2e2mk03kk8rsx-wpengine .netdna-ssl.com/wp-content/uploads/cpc.pdf.

116 Ibid.

117 Catherine A. MacKinnon, "Privacy v. Equality: Beyond *Roe v. Wade*," in *Mary Joe Frug's Women and the Law*, ed. Judith G. Greenberg, Martha L. Minow, and Dorothy E. Roberts, 2nd ed. (New York: Foundation Press, 1998), 737–742.

118 Ibid., 741.

119 Ibid., 742.

120 Robert H. Blank, "Reproductive Technology: Pregnant Women, the Fetus, and the Courts," in *The Politics of Pregnancy*, ed. Janna C. Merrick and Robert H. Blank (New York: Haworth Press, 1996), 1–18.

121 Dorothy E. Roberts, "Punishing Drug Addicts Who Have Babies: Women of Color, Equality, and the Right of Privacy," in *Mary Joe Frug's Women*, ed. Greenburg, Minow, and Roberts, 772.

122 *In Re A.C.*, Court of Appeals of the District of Columbia, *en banc*, 573 A.2d 1235 (1990).

123 Greenberg, Minow, and Roberts, *Mary Joe Frug's Women and the Law*, 754.

124 Sherry F. Colb, "Crying Murder When a Woman Refuses a C-Section: The Disturbing Implications of a Utah Prosecution," FindLaw, March 16, 2004.

125 Roberts, "Punishing Drug Addicts Who Have Babies," 772.

126 Michelle Goodwin, "The Pregnancy Penalty," *Health Matrix: The Journal of Law-Medicine* 26, no. 1 (2016).

127 J. Ralph Lindgren and Nadine Taub, *The Law of Sex Discrimination*, 2nd ed. (Minneapolis, MN: West Publishing Co., 1993), 39.

128 Robert Blank, *Fetal Protection in the Workplace* (New York: Columbia University Press, 1994), 99.

129 Suzanne Uttaro Samuels, *Fetal Rights, Women's Rights: Gender Equality in the Workplace* (Madison: University of Wisconsin, 1995), xi.

130 Keith Perine, "Fetal Protection Bill Cleared as Democrat's Substitute Fails," *CQ Weekly*, March 7, 2004, 744.

131 Sheila Gibbons, "Dim Coverage Given to Abortion-Ban Ruling," *Women's eNews*, June 23, 2004.

132 *Gonzales v. Carhart*, 550 U.S. 124 (2007).

133 Ibid.

134 Melody Rose, *Safe, Legal, and Unavailable? Abortion Politics in the United States* (Washington, DC: CQ Press, 2007).

135 Alan Guttmacher Institute, State Policies in Brief, "Abortion Policy in the Absence of *Roe*," June 1, 2009; Juliette Terzieff, "If *Roe* Falls, States Ready to Curb or Ban Abortion," *Women's eNews*, November 9, 2007.

136 Guttmacher Institute, "Laws Affecting Reproductive Health and Rights: State Trends at Midyear, 2016," July 21, 2016.

137 Alan Guttmacher Institute, "State Policies in Brief: An Overview of Abortion Laws," June 1, 2009.

138 Gretchen Borchelt, "Eighth Circuit Allows Politicians to Interfere in Doctor-Patient Relationship," June 27, 2008, blog, National Women's Law Center.

139 Rachel Benson Gold, "All That's Old Is New Again: The Long Campaign to Persuade Women to Forego Abortion," *Guttmacher Policy Review* 12, no. 2 (Spring 2009): 19.

140 Ibid., 22.

141 Harper Jean Tobin, "Confronting Misinformation on Abortion: Informed Consent, Deference, and Fetal Pain Laws," *Columbia Journal of Gender and the Law* 17, no.1 (2008): 111–153.

142 Guttmacher Institute, "The Number of States Considered Hostile to Abortion Skyrocketed Between 2000 and 2014," www.guttmacher.org/sites/default/files/images/2000-2014-maps-states .png. Accessed July 2016.

143 Seth Stephens-Davidowitz, "The Return of the D.I.Y. Abortion," *New York Times*, March 6, 2016.

144 Andrea Rowan, "Prosecuting Women for Self-Inducing Abortion: Counterproductive and Lacking Compassion," *Guttmacher Policy Review* 18, no. 3 (Summer 2015).

145 Guttmacher Institute, "Refusing to Provide Health Services," June 2016.

146 Claire Marshall, "The Spread of Conscience Clause Legislation," *Human Rights* 39, no. 2 (2013).

147 William Blackstone, *Commentaries on the Laws of England* (London: Strahan, 1803).

148 Gretchen Arnold, "Dilemmas of Feminist Coalitions: Collective Identity and Strategic Effectiveness in the Battered Women's Movement," in *Feminist Organizations: Harvest of the New Women's Movement*, ed. Myra Marx Feree and Patricia Yancey Martin (Philadelphia: Temple University Press, 1995), 276–290.

149 National Coalition Against Domestic Violence, "Domestic Violence Statistics," 2015.

150 Danielle Paquette, "Johnny Manziel Is the NFL's First Domestic Violence Case in 2016. He Won't Be the Last," *Washington Post*, February 9, 2016.

151 US Department of Justice, Bureau of Justice Statistics, "Homicide Trends in the U.S.: Intimate Homicide," January 25, 2010 www.ojp.usdoj.gov/bjs/homicide/intimates.htm.

152 Robert H. Blank, *Regulating Reproduction* (New York: Columbia University Press, 1990), 13.

153 Ibid., 15.

154 Tamar Lewin, "Surrogates and Couples Face a Maze of Laws, State by State." *New York Times*, September 17, 2014.

155 Ashley Surdin, "Octuplet Mother Also Gives Birth to Ethical Debate," *Washington Post*, February 4, 2009.

156 Laura R. Woliver, *The Political Geographies of Pregnancy* (Urbana: University of Illinois Press, 2002), 83.

157 Betty Friedan, *The Second Stage* (New York: Summit Press, 1986).

Box 8.1: Need a Baby Boom? Come to Terms with Gender Equality

1 Claire Landsbaum, "Italian Women Are Not Happy with Italy's Sexist 'Fertility Day' Campaign," *New York Magazine*, September 2, 2016.

2 Claire Zillman, "Why Italy's 'Fertility Day' Is a Sexist Mess," *Fortune*, September 2, 2016.

3 Anne Chemin, "France's Baby Boom Secret: Get Women into Work and Ditch Rigid Family Norms," *Guardian*, March 21, 2015.

4 Ibid.

Box 8.2: Regulating Access to Legal Abortion

1 Angelina Theodorou and Aleksandra Sandstrom, "How Abortion Is Regulated Around the World," Pew Research Center, October 6, 2015.

2 United Nations, "World Abortion Policies," 2011, www.un.org/esa/population/publications /2011abortion/2011wallchart.pdf.

3 Francis Mulraney, "Irish Women Live Tweet Abortion Journey, Get the World Talking About Ireland," *Irish Central*, August 23, 2016.

4 Lauren Bohn, "El Salvador's 'Abortion Lawyer,'" *New York Times*, September 12, 2016.

CHAPTER 9

Setting the Agenda and Taking Action: New Challenges in the Pursuit of Equality

Our examination of women's pursuit of equality has focused on the complexities, tensions, and controversies created by the paradox of gender equality—that is, how to reconcile demands for gender equality with sex differences between men and women. Two major paths have been forged in attempting to resolve the paradox and improve the status of women. The difference between the two approaches lies in how the implications of sex differences are understood. Legal equality doctrine advocates believe that women can never achieve equality as long as they are treated differently from men—that is, as inferior to men. By removing sex as a method of categorizing individuals, women will be free of the discriminatory institutional, legal, and political barriers erected purely on the basis of sex that have historically prevented them from full participation in society. Using the legal equality doctrine, women and men are made the same in the eyes of the law, and therefore cannot be treated differently (with a few remaining exceptions).

Critics of this approach argue that since men and women are in fact biologically different, erasing their legal differences but not their real differences will merely burden women further. Fairness doctrine proponents believe that sex differences have significant and persistent consequences for how men and women live in the world. Women are disadvantaged and equality is not meaningful when their unique biological role is ignored, as it would be under the legal equality doctrine. Using the fairness doctrine, laws that recognize and accommodate women's physical differences will thereby promote women's equality in reality. Gender, the evolving social construction of sex, complicates both approaches to equality.

As we have seen throughout this text, women do not agree among themselves on the meaning of equality, or even the desirability of equality, as defined by these two paths. Sex alone does not create a binding political identity among women, nor does it foster a group consciousness that mobilizes women around the issues of gender equality. Feminism, one manifestation of women's political consciousness, has not always provided an effective political mobilizing ideology because it too encompasses the paradox of gender equality. Feminism encourages unity among women even while recognizing and celebrating women's diversity. The same sorts of socioeconomic, demographic, and political cleavages that divide men from one another also divide women and have proven difficult to overcome in adopting a single approach to resolving the gender paradox.

Yet all women share one condition purely on the basis of their sex—a subordinate position within the gender hierarchy of patriarchy. Patriarchy privileges men over women, regardless of class, race or ethnicity, sexuality, or political ideology. The pernicious influence of the separate spheres ideology has combined with patriarchy's male privilege to render women's pursuit of equality an enduring political challenge. Private patriarchy (families) combined with public patriarchy (economy, politics, and public policy) creates a system that has historically submerged women in the private sphere, rendering them nearly invisible in the public sphere until the mid-1800s. The quest for women's rights can thus be characterized as a movement to gain women's autonomy and full citizenship in the public sphere. Full equality in the public sphere requires a substantial reordering of the private sphere. Although the legal equality approach has been effective in opening doors and dismantling barriers to women's full participation in the public sphere, the private sphere is far more impervious to legal mandates for change. Within the private sphere, the fairness doctrine may be a more appropriate approach, but because the notion of external forces infringing on the sanctity of family continues to meet fierce opposition, the private sphere remains virtually unreformed.

This book has traced women's historical progress in their fight for autonomy and equality. Early women activists had obvious hurdles to overcome, starting with the debilitating fact that women were not permitted to speak aloud in a public forum. Without a public voice, women could neither articulate their own interests nor expect their interests to be represented in politics or policy. The first manifesto of women's rights, the Declaration of Sentiments and Resolutions, adopted in 1848 at the Seneca Falls Convention, included the demand for women's voices to be heard within their marriages, their families, their communities, and the larger political system. Today it provides a good framework for evaluating women's progress toward equality. Exactly how far have women come in the pursuit of equality? Participants at the Seneca Falls meeting thought their demand for the vote was the most radical of the eleven resolutions that participants adopted. It was, as you recall from Chapter 2, the only resolution that was not adopted unanimously. In retrospect, the third resolution called for an even more fundamental transformation. It read, "Resolved, That woman is man's equal—was intended to be so by the Creator, and the highest good of the race demands that she should be recognized as such."

It took suffragists seventy-two years to win the elective franchise, but a clear declaration of equality between men and women—missing from the nation's founding documents—has yet to be embraced as fundamental US law. The Equal Rights Amendment, although first proposed in 1923 and considered by the states between 1972 and 1982, was never ratified as an amendment to the Constitution. Moreover, its international equivalent, the Convention on the Elimination of All Forms of Discrimination Against Women (CEDAW), has yet to be ratified by the US Senate since its adoption by the United Nations in 1979. Perhaps this does not matter if women have achieved equality by other means. Throughout the book we have examined a number of critical legal protections—the equal protection clause of the US Constitution, Title VII, Title IX, the Equal Pay Act, the Pregnancy Discrimination Act, the Violence Against Women Act, and various US Supreme Court interpretations of law as it applies to women's equality. Yet without that simple declaration of equality first proposed in the Declaration of Sentiments and Resolutions, the basis for women's equality remains nebulous and its very definition subject to variable interpretation, state and federal regulation, and intermittent enforcement depending on the character of the political climate.

This final chapter examines three areas in which women have demanded an expansion of rights, beginning with resolutions adopted at the Seneca Falls meeting. Each of the following sections briefly summarizes women's advances and identifies areas in which women are still struggling to define and achieve equality. In setting a future agenda for women's equality, we will evaluate the challenges that lie ahead in resolving the paradox of gender equality and identify ways for you to take action in the pursuit of gender equality.

ELECTIVE FRANCHISE AND POLITICAL REPRESENTATION

Although all women were enfranchised in 1920 with the ratification of the Nineteenth Amendment, it took more than seventy years and countless campaigns led by three generations of suffragists to win the vote. Having the vote is not synonymous with using the vote to promote women candidates or a women's political agenda. Women's votes have been highly sought after by both political parties, even though, as we have noted repeatedly, women rarely act as one homogeneous bloc. For example, unique efforts were made in 2008 to mobilize single women voters who did not participate in 2004, particularly women of color and young women. Although men and women voted differently in the 2008 and 2012 presidential contests, we cannot say that women voters alone determined the outcome in these elections.

In 2017, 83 women serve in the House of Representatives and 21 women serve in the US Senate—104 women out of 535 members, only 19.4 percent of the body overall and exactly the same number of women as in the previous congress. The rate of progress in increasing women's representation has been incremental and

Box 9.1

Seneca Falls Women's Rights Convention Resolutions

On the morning of July 19, 1848, the Declaration of Sentiments (see Chapter 2) was read, discussed, and approved by the convention. That afternoon, the following resolutions were then read and adopted:[1]

Whereas, the great precept of nature is conceded to be, "that man shall pursue his own true and substantial happiness," Blackstone, in his Commentaries, remarks, that this law of Nature being coeval with mankind, and dictated by God himself, is of course superior in obligation to any other. It is binding over all the globe, in all countries, and at all times; no human laws are of any validity if contrary to this, and such of them as are valid, derive all their force, and all their validity, and all their authority, mediately and immediately, from this original; Therefore,

Resolved, That such laws as conflict, in any way, with the true and substantial happiness of woman, are contrary to the great precept of nature, and of no validity; for this is "superior in obligation to any other."

Resolved, That all laws which prevent woman from occupying such a station in society as her conscience shall dictate, or which place her in a position inferior to that of man, are contrary to the great precept of nature, and therefore of no force or authority.

Resolved, That woman is man's equal—was intended to be so by the Creator, and the highest good of the race demands that she should be recognized as such.

Resolved, That the women of this country ought to be enlightened in regard to the laws under which they live, that they may no longer publish their degradation, by declaring themselves satisfied with their present position, nor their ignorance, by asserting that they have all the rights they want.

Resolved, That inasmuch as man, while claiming for himself intellectual superiority, does accord to woman moral superiority, it is pre-eminently his duty

slow. At the current rate, it will be 2121 before gender parity is reached in Congress. Whether "women's interests" will be effectively advanced as a result of these modest gains remains to be seen. By numbers alone, women have better descriptive representation in the 115th Congress than ever before based on numbers and diversity of members. Role models are essential to attracting women candidates and convincing young women that participating in politics is key to charting their own to encourage her to speak, and teach, as she has an opportunity, in all religious assemblies.

Resolved, That the same amount of virtue, delicacy, and refinement of behavior, that is required of woman in the social state, should also be required of man, and the same transgressions should be visited with equal severity on both man and woman.

Resolved, That the objection of indelicacy and impropriety, which is so often brought against woman when she addresses a public audience, comes with a very ill grace from those who encourage, by their attendance, her appearance on the stage, in the concert, or in the feats of the circus.

Resolved, That woman has too long rested satisfied in the circumscribed limits which corrupt customs and a perverted application of the Scriptures have marked out for her, and that it is time she should move in the enlarged sphere which her great Creator has assigned her.

Resolved, That it is the duty of the women of this country to secure to themselves their sacred right to the elective franchise.

Resolved, That the equality of human rights results necessarily from the fact of the identity of the race in capabilities and responsibilities.

Resolved, therefore, That, being invested by the Creator with the same capabilities, and the same consciousness of responsibility for their exercise, it is demonstrably the right and duty of woman, equally with man, to promote every righteous cause, by every righteous means; and especially in regard to the great subjects of morals and religion, it is self-evidently her right to participate with her brother in teaching them, both in private and in public, by writing and by speaking, by any instrumentalities proper to be used, and in any assemblies proper to be held; and this being a self-evident truth, growing out of the divinely implanted principles of human nature, any custom or authority adverse to it, whether modern or wearing the hoary sanction of antiquity, is to be regarded as self-evident falsehood, and at war with the interests of mankind.

futures. However, unless women in office also provide substantive representation by *acting* for women's interests, the status of women overall is unlikely to change. Since women's interests are not monolithic, substantive representation will require more Republican women candidates and officeholders. In addition, women must occupy several of the available leadership positions within the institution to be better able to shape the overall agenda to include women's issues. Representative

Nancy Pelosi (D.-Calif.) served as Speaker of the House of Representatives from 2007 to 2011—the first and only woman to achieve that position. Upon accepting the Speaker's gavel she remarked:

> It's an historic moment for the Congress. It's an historic moment for the women of America. It is a moment for which we have waited over 200 years. Never losing faith, we waited through the many years of struggle to achieve our rights. But women weren't just waiting; women were working. Never losing faith, we worked to redeem the promise of America, that all men and women are created equal. For our daughters and our granddaughters, today we have broken the marble ceiling. For our daughters and granddaughters now, the sky is the limit. Anything is possible for them.[1]

However, the optimism over what she could accomplish for women didn't last long. The protracted 2009 debate over health care reform made it clear that having a woman in the highest leadership position is not a guarantee that she will be able to act for women. Speaker Pelosi, who is prochoice, was heavily criticized by members of her own political party as well as feminist organizations for allowing new restrictions on abortion rights to be added to the House version of the health care reform bill. With the Democrats in the minority since 2011, Pelosi remains the Minority Leader.

Hillary Clinton's race for the Democratic nomination for president in 2008 and her achievement of that nomination in 2016 represent another significant advance for women in politics. Clinton won twenty-two states during the 2008 primary, attracting nearly 18 million voters (47.8 percent of the total votes cast) and 1,896 delegates to the Democratic National Convention. Barack Obama clinched the nomination by earning 2,229 delegates (2,118 required) with a margin of roughly 152,000 votes in a contest in which more than 35 million people participated.[2] Although there are countless examples of the ways gender played a role in the 2008 campaign, there is no way to know to what degree gender trumped race as a stereotypical obstacle for voters to overcome in making their decision, nor can we truly parse out the ways in which Clinton's strategic campaign decisions were influenced by gender stereotypes in politics, only to run up against an entirely new political landscape than the one she anticipated (see Chapter 4). Nonetheless, her strong candidacy opened doors for the next wave of female candidates and won her a place in the new administration as secretary of state. There are many who believe Clinton's run at the nomination also led to Sarah Palin's selection as the Republican vice presidential candidate—another first. In the 2016 Democratic primary Clinton won thirty-four contests and earned 2,220 delegates to Bernie Sanders' 1,831. Clinton sealed the nomination with a big lead among

IMAGE 9.1: *Former Speaker of the House Nancy Peloci (D-CA) takes the Speaker's gavel from Former House Minority Leader Rep. John Boehner (R-OH) after being elected as the first woman Speaker at a swearing in ceremony for the 110th Congress in the House Chamber of the US Capitol in Washington, D.C. on January 4, 2004.* Source: Chip Somodevilla/Getty Images.

party superdelegates (591 pledged to Clinton, 48 pledged to Sanders). Women's national visibility in both political parties in the 2008 and 2016 presidential contests is unprecedented. What impact will this have on women's willingness to wage a national campaign in the future? Hillary Clinton's loss to Donald Trump following a bitter campaign was a disappointment to many who felt that a woman was finally poised to become president. For the fifth time in American history, the winner of the presidency did not win the popular vote. Hillary Clinton achieved a 2.5-million-vote margin over Trump in the popular vote total indicating that a substantial majority of Americans is ready and willing to elect a woman to the highest office. In the five days following the general election more than 1,500 women joined the She Should Run Incubator, an online resource to promote women's public leadership and women candidates.[3] Perhaps the next woman candidate for president will emerge from among these highly motivated women.

Future gender equality activists have three primary tasks: recruit a greater number of gender-conscious women to run for office, elect them to positions in which they can have an effect on policy, and reelect female incumbents so that they will gain seniority and be eligible to assume positions of leadership. Given the recent research on the porous nature of the pipeline and women's inability to objectively assess their own qualifications for office, recruiting women candidates will require sustained attention and intervention. Parity will require women to seek elected office as a matter of course and to run in large numbers in every election and at every level of office. However, there is evidence that numbers of candidates have not increased significantly with each election. In 2008 four women sought governorships (all Democrats, and all faced male Republican opponents); two won and two lost. In 2014, nine women ran for governor (six Democrats and three Republicans), and five women were elected or reelected. In this group of five was Republican Nikki Haley, the first woman governor in South Carolina (first elected in 2010), and Republican Susana Martinez of New Mexico. Both are women of color and the first women of color elected governor of their respective states. Four women served as governor in 2017 (Nikki Haley was nominated US Ambassador to the United Nations by Donald Trump). The 2016 elections resulted in almost no growth for women in state legislatures or statewide office.[4] Since about 70 percent of women in Congress have served in lower elected positions first, more women must declare as candidates and seek elected positions at all levels of government. As we've noted repeatedly and as empirical evidence confirms, when women run they have a better than even chance of winning—but first they have to be candidates.

Taking Action: What Can You Do?

- *Test the waters and gain some experience.* If you are female, run for a position in your campus student government or for an office in a club or organization you are involved with, to gain experience. Help women see themselves as candidates for available positions on your campus and recruit them to run. Likewise, talk with your female friends about running for future political office in your local community and in your state. The more women envision themselves selves as qualified candidates, the more likely they are to actually become a candidate. The American Association of University Women (AAUW) sponsors a training program called "Elect Her" for young women who want to run for student government or student body president.
- *Get some leadership training.* Many colleges and universities have leadership centers or programs to identify and train young leaders. Some have leadership academic certificate programs or major programs of study that link course work with experiential internships, mentorships, or service learning opportunities. See what is available on your own campus and get involved. Whether your issue is immigration, women's health, or environmental sustainability, there are community organizations that also need your talents and time. Once you get some training, put yourself to work!
- *Get some political leadership training.* Chapter 4 includes a list of national political leadership and candidate training schools. Programs such as Running

Start are designed for college-age women and open to women of all political ideologies and parties. There are other programs open to men and women. You might not be ready to run for political office today, but the more training you get now and the wider your network of contacts, the more you will be prepared to run when you are ready. Look into local and state offices without age restrictions. Since most national officeholders gained experience in their local communities first, it is never too early to get started! Young women and men who believe in the value of gender equality are needed in public service—look for your opportunities to be allies for one another's political careers.

- ***Invite a woman to run and support women candidates.*** The most effective way to recruit women as candidates for public office is to ask them to run. Look around you and identify women you respect and whose work in the community you value, and ask them to run for political office. Register to vote! Give candidates (male and female) who support gender equality your vote as well as your time and talents in their campaigns. All campaigns need good volunteers to spread the message and get voters out to the polls. While you are working for a candidate, you are also gaining experience and building a network of contacts for your own political future.

MARRIAGE AND FAMILY RIGHTS

The Declaration of Sentiments and Resolutions was primarily concerned with changing the common-law practices associated with coverture that denied women the ability to exercise independent control over anything in their lives, including property, wages, household goods, and their children. Marriage reforms consistent with the legal equality doctrine now view men and women as equal partners in a marriage, and the Supreme Court's ruling in *Obergefell v. Hodges* in 2015 extended legal marriage equality to same-sex couples.

Resolving the division of family and workforce labor will be a primary issue facing men and women in the future. Policies consistent with the legal equality doctrine are more problematic in this area than in any other because of the weight that biological differences have when assigning reproductive responsibilities. Beyond the physical implications of pregnancy, attitudes about women's sociological responsibilities for children and the home also complicate developing gender-neutral family policies. Gender-specific policies consistent with the fairness doctrine carry the danger of reinforcing attitudes about women's natural fit in the private sphere at the risk of further exclusion from the public sphere. The "mommy track," a career path that makes a trade-off between fewer opportunities for job advancement and more-flexible work arrangements, was widely derided for downsizing women's ambitions, though it was actually first proposed as a way to make the workplace accommodate women's caretaking responsibilities at home. All

Burkinis and Bikinis:
Who Decides How Women Must Dress?

As the weather in France warmed and people flocked to the beaches, mayors of five seaside towns adopted bans on burkinis—a modest swim garment designed to cover a woman's legs, arms, torso, and head—worn by Muslim women. Supporters of the ban, including Prime Minister Manuel Valls, said the swimsuit "reflects a worldview based on the enslavement of women."[1] The minister of women's affairs, Laurence Rossignol, said "The burkini is . . . a particular vision of the place of the woman. It cannot be considered only as a question of fashion or individual liberty." Others argued that the message inherent in the burkini is inconsistent with a country that embraces *égalité* and *liberté*. France's highest administrative court suspended the ban in late August, but not before images of armed police requiring a woman to remove a portion of her clothing went viral on the Internet.

Writer Khadija Algaedi challenges the notion that equality requires that a woman forgo modesty in favor of nakedness: "We have forgotten that the expression of freedom lies in the choice, not the clothing of choice. It is not the burkini or the burka that is archaic but the definition that limits a woman's value and expression of freedom to her clothing or lack thereof. It is the thought process that allows a singular standard of dress for a woman to be considered acceptable."[2]

women experience some level of maternal discrimination whether or not they currently have or even plan to have children, since they all have the potential to become mothers. Employers continue to recruit and place employees based on gendered expectations that men will prioritize work over family responsibilities and women will place family and children first.

Aware of these forces, women cope rather than confront. Felice Schwartz offers a poignant example.[5] A group of female Wharton MBA students told her that it was common practice for married women in the MBA program to remove their wedding bands before going to job interviews, saying that "recruiters will not offer plum jobs to those women they believe will have commitments to their families." These students were not angry or outraged, but believed they were acting expediently and pragmatically to improve their job prospects. Thus women are significantly disadvantaged in the workforce because of the expectation that they continue to maintain primary responsibility for the children and home. A substan-

The 2016 Rio Olympics offered another juxtaposition of women's attire when the Brazilian women's beach volleyball team faced the team from Egypt. The Brazilian team's uniform is a sport bikini, while the Egyptian women are covered. Egypt's Doaa Elghobashy, age nineteen and participating in her first Olympic Games, said, "I wear a hijab because I am a Muslim but it doesn't stop me feeling a part of this game." Her partner, Nada Meawad, also wore long sleeves and long pants but did not cover her head.[3]

Source: REUTERS/Lucy Nicholson.

What do you think?

Why does women's dress attract the attention of so many? Why do governments feel that they can prescribe women's dress in modern times? Are there ways that men experience social judgment because of dress? Do you agree with Khadija Algaedi that "the expression of freedom lies in the choice, not the clothing of choice"? How is your response related to your understanding of gender equality?

tial portion of the pay gap is attributed to differences in men's and women's length of employment experience. The presence of children is associated with lower wages for women, but higher wages for men.[6]

It may be that many of these issues cannot be resolved by public policy. The political culture in the United States has not supported government's intervention into the private domain of family and children until relatively recently. Even now, government's participation is limited to protecting the health and safety of individuals within families and does not include providing financial and programmatic aid to families struggling to balance work and family responsibilities. The Family and Medical Leave Act of 1993 pales in comparison to family support programs provided in many other nations (see Chapters 7 and 8). Efforts to strengthen the legislation to provide paid leave funded by state unemployment insurance funds have been met with opposition, primarily from the business community. California became the first state to provide up to six weeks of paid family leave (up to

55 percent of a worker's wage) in 2014, financing it through the state's disability insurance fund. New Jersey and Rhode Island also provide paid family leave financed by a payroll deduction. San Francisco became the first US city to require employers of more than twenty people to cover the 45 percent of a worker's wage that the state of California does not. In April 2016, New York passed a paid family leave bill that will provide up to twelve weeks of paid leave when fully implemented. There is little evidence that a national child care policy tops any political agenda, even though both 2016 presidential candidates, Donald Trump and Hillary Clinton, presented policy proposals on this issue.

Until women and men reach the point where both are faced with the same challenges, it seems unlikely that a government policy will be the mechanism that produces real change. Policies that are designed to promote role equity (equality defined as fairness) have been more successful than policies designed to promote role change (equality defined as sameness). Balancing family with other public responsibilities presents a complicated case for this framework. Because men and women continue to hold traditional attitudes about the gendered division of labor within the family and private household (see Chapter 7), even women see their additional family responsibilities as "fair" up to a point. Until these attitudes change, it is unlikely that the public will pressure policy makers to produce solutions. Women must adopt change-oriented strategies of political participation rather than continue to cope privately as individuals.

The disadvantages women suffer as a result of children are made clear throughout this book. Women with children have fewer job prospects, they are likely to be paid less than men and women without children, they are less likely to be promoted to jobs with more responsibilities and greater pay, and they are less likely to have private pensions to support them in retirement. As a result, the best predictor of women's poverty is the presence of children. What does that say about gender, the prospects for gender equality, and for our culture in the United States?

Taking Action: What Can You Do?

- ***Think honestly about your own expectations of marriage and family.*** Think now about what you expect from yourself and your partner when and if you create a family. Because you likely do not face the immediate pressures of a decision, this is a good time to write down what you expect and what you want your future life to be like. If you are not already in the practice of writing a journal or blog, start one now to capture your expectations over time. Be sure that your expectations are grounded in empirical reality. Talk to your peers—both male and female—about their expectations. Armed with facts, confront myths and stereotypes about equality in the private sphere. Although people can argue over the source and the size of the wage gap, the difference in pay between men and women remains no matter who does the analysis or the number of control variables introduced. Women with children spend more hours per workday on child care and household chores than they did thirty years ago, and the United States is still among only four nations worldwide that do not guarantee paid family leave (the others are Liberia, Papua New Guinea, and Swaziland).

- *Lobby your state legislature and the Congress to adopt policies that support families and promote gender equality.* The Family and Medical Leave Act (see Chapter 8) is very limited in who is covered and in the unpaid benefits it provides. By comparison to other nations, the United States does not have a support system for working families. Do the research to identify promising approaches to supporting families and then lobby your state legislature and the Congress to pass appropriate policies. Our federal system of government allows the states to be policy laboratories and many of the most innovative approaches to assisting individuals in combining work and family can be found in the states or in the policies of private-sector employers. At the same time, states and companies differ, and so before you decide where you will live and work, do the research. Organizations such as the Institute for Women's Policy Research produce annual state-by-state report cards on gender equity.

- *Investigate the new activism around motherhood, fatherhood, and parenting.* Organizations such as MomsRising and Mothers and More have been founded to promote the interests of mothers in the workplace. As we've noted repeatedly, parenthood has historically been located in the private sphere in the United States, and too often parenthood has meant only motherhood. A new fathers' movement has emerged to support men in making demands on the public sphere for more time with their families. If men and women worked together to put pressure on the public sphere, perhaps more generous family policy would result. There is a long history of politicized mothers' movements in other nations (e.g., MADRE), and there are signs that similar political action in this country might elevate private sphere issues to public policy attention.

- *Investigate the policies of companies before you go to work.* Not all companies have family-friendly policies in place. Each year, *Working Mother* magazine publishes the "Top 100 Best Companies for Working Mothers." *Fortune* and *Black Enterprise* publish similar lists. The Sloan Work and Family Research Network at Boston College is another good source of information on workplace policies. Even if you do not plan to seek employment with one of these companies, research the policies that earned them a spot among the Top 100 Best so that you know what to look for when you pursue employment elsewhere and so that you know what to ask for when negotiating employment.

- ***Work to end unintended pregnancies.*** Attempting to control fertility—whether through pronatalist policies or population control efforts—is an ancient and enduring political interest. Nothing affects a woman's autonomy more than her ability to decide if and when she will bear children, how many she will produce, and how they will be spaced. Contraception enables women to avoid pregnancy, and yet nearly half of all pregnancies in the United States today are unintended. Educate yourself about reproduction and fertility, protect yourself from sexually transmitted diseases and unintended pregnancies, and inform yourself about reproductive choices available in your community. While abortion remains legal in the United States, it is increasingly difficult to access for most women, particularly for poor women and minorities. Promote education and fair access to health care for all women.

EDUCATION, EMPLOYMENT, AND ECONOMIC OPPORTUNITIES

Because women were legally excluded from all colleges and universities, as well as from most occupations, the Declaration of Sentiments and Resolutions demanded that women have access to education and employment opportunities. Today, Title IX (see Chapter 6) and Title VII (see Chapter 7) guarantee that access to educational institutions and most occupations cannot be denied on the basis of sex. These two pieces of legislation have been powerful tools for women in developing the human capital necessary to broaden economic opportunities. Human capital, which includes education and experience in the labor market, is often viewed as the most important determinant of wages. Wages, of course, are an important determinant of security, health, and quality of life. As we have seen in Chapters 6 through 8, gender-neutral access to education and employment does not necessarily ensure that the experience itself is comparable for men and women. Unless gender equity remains a priority in the changes that are being made to the way children are educated, gains in this area for women will be vulnerable.

The poverty rates for women in the United States, particularly among mothers and the elderly, remain startlingly high. Even as the nation has prospered, the proportion of women living below the poverty line has increased. There are a number of explanations for women's overrepresentation among the poor (see Chapter 7). The 1996 changes to the nation's welfare policy likely impacted women's poverty rate. There is ample evidence that families relying on minimum-wage or low-wage jobs, even with two workers employed full-time, cannot attain self-sufficiency. The Great Recession of 2008 affected both women and men, although differently. Men were more likely to lose their job and to lose better-paying jobs, leaving many women as the new primary wage earner in their family. Because women are concentrated in low-wage occupations and because of the wage gap, they earn less than men, and so the recession's impact on women and their families has been severe.

Although some communities have adopted living wage policies, they apply to very few workers and there is not currently a national debate on adopting a national living wage standard. At $7.25, the current minimum wage makes it likely that a family of three would be 18 percent below the poverty line, even with both parents working full-time and year round.[7] Addressing women's poverty will require attention to the impact of sex segregation in the workforce; disparate classroom experiences and counseling in grade and high schools; the limits imposed by the maternal wall, the glass ceiling, and the sticky floor; and, particularly, the pay gap.

The pay gap, although a strikingly consistent 20–25 percent across hourly and salaried occupations, remains the subject of debate. Some attribute the pay differential between men and women to "choices" each makes regarding employment, education, and family. The portion of the pay gap that remains unexplained by differences in education, occupation, union membership, and labor market experience, however, is estimated at roughly 12 percent.[8] This portion is attributed to sex discrimination, precisely the type of discrimination the Equal Pay Act of 1963 was designed to eliminate. But when "sex" is really "gender"—with all of the traditional gender stereotypes and societal norms—can a legal equality approach embodied in the Equal Pay Act ever be effective in closing the pay gap? Recall the research on starting salary differences between men and women. Individual experiences are most similar upon application for their first job, and yet a salary gap is already evident between male and female new college graduates. Part of that gap has been attributed to men's willingness to ask for more salary and women's tendency to accept what is first offered (see Chapter 7).

More than fifty years after equal pay policy was enacted, women still earn less than men even when performing the same job in the same sector of the economy. The pay gap has indeed declined over the past three decades, but it has not disappeared. Women with college degrees will still earn less on average than men with college degrees. Average annual earnings one year after graduation for men ($42,918) exceed those of women ($35,296).[9] The wage gap persists across all occupational fields. Over a forty-seven year work life, a woman with a college degree will lose more than $723,000. Women who don't finish high school can expect to lose nearly $300,000 because of the wage gap.[10] Like the wage gap itself, the amount of pay a woman can expect to lose over her working lifetime varies by state. The gap exceeds $300,000 in fifteen states, $400,000 in twenty-two states, and $500,000 in eleven states. The career wage gap also varies by occupation, with greater gaps found in occupations requiring more education and training. Women in the legal profession, for example, can expect to lose $1.5 million in lifetime earnings compared to male colleagues. Across all occupations, the widest gaps are found in finance and management, while the smallest gaps are found in construction and maintenance.[11]

A cosponsor of the Lilly Ledbetter Fair Pay Act as a senator, Barack Obama made it the first bill he signed into law as president. However, that law merely

Box 9.3 – Point of Comparison

The Best and Worst States for Gender Equality in the United States

Previous Point of Comparison boxes have featured data comparing several countries on a metric or central issue of gender equality. However, the vast majority of you will remain in the United States following graduation, and you might have the opportunity to decide where to live. Will a state's commitment to gender equality be a factor in that choice?

WalletHub, an online personal finance portal, has a variety of best/worst city and state rankings based on a robust methodology.[1] The presentation of the main findings is followed by a set of questions posed to a panel of nationally recognized experts and their responses interpreting the data. WalletHub investigated gender equality on measures roughly consistent with the World Economic Forum's 2015 Global Gender Gap report on which the United States ranked in twenty-eighth place: workplace environment, education, and political empowerment. Each area combines data on four to six measures to create an index. States are ranked from 1 to 50 based on each index.

For Critical Analysis

In what ways does it matter if there are small or large disparities in workplace environment, education, and political empowerment? How do you imagine that will shape the community you join? How might it shape opportunities for you to advance in your career, seek additional education or training, and get involved in politics? With a college education, your opportunities for geographic mobility increase. How will you make your decision about where to live? How important will gender equality be to that decision?

Workplace Environment

SMALLEST PAY DISPARITY	LARGEST PAY DISPARITY	SMALLEST WORK HOURS DISPARITY	LARGEST WORK HOURS DISPARITY
1: Hawaii	46: Kentucky	1: Nevada	46: Idaho
2: Tennessee	47: Alabama	2: Florida	47: Alaska
3: California	48: Montana	3: Delaware	48: Utah
4: Vermont	49: Utah	4: Maryland	49: Wyoming
5: Delaware	50: Wyoming	5: Hawaii	50: North Dakota

Education

SMALLEST EDUCATIONAL ATTAINMENT DISPARITY (BACHELOR'S DEGREE)	LARGEST EDUCATIONAL ATTAINMENT DISPARITY (BACHELOR'S DEGREE)
1 (tie): Alaska	46: South Carolina
1 (tie): Arkansas	47: Connecticut
1 (tie): California	48: New York
1 (tie): Colorado	49: Arizona
1 (tie): Delaware	50: Rhode Island
1 (tie): Hawaii	

Political Empowerment

SMALLEST POLITICAL REPRESENTATION DISPARITY	LARGEST POLITICAL REPRESENTATION DISPARITY
1: Hawaii	46: Oklahoma
2: Maine	47: Arkansas
3: New Hampshire	48: Mississippi
4: California	49: Georgia
5: Alaska	50: Louisiana

Overall Ranking

BEST	WORST
1: Hawaii	46: Louisiana
2: Alaska	47: Pennsylvania
3: Maine	48: New Jersey
4: California	49: Georgia
5: Vermont	50: Utah

restores the pre–*Ledbetter v. Goodyear* conditions under which an individual can file a claim for pay discrimination. It does not enhance the equal pay guarantees of the Equal Pay Act the way the Paycheck Fairness Act would, nor does it move toward a pay equity model, often referred to as "equal pay for comparable work" in recognition of persistent occupational gender segregation. Class action pay discrimination suits are difficult to mount. A more vigorous defense of equal pay standards by the EEOC would include more class action suits filed on behalf of women in occupational sectors other than retail.

Taking Action: What Can You Do?

- ***Make choices now that will improve your salary prospects later.*** In Chapter 6 we reviewed the statistics on women in STEM disciplines as undergraduates and later as graduate students and researchers in science, engineering, and technology fields. Think carefully about your choice of major and why you have selected it. Does it accurately reflect your interests and will it allow you to move into a career that pays wages sufficient to support you and your family? Could your choice of major have been conditioned by stereotypes and gendered expectations at any point in your life? Not everyone has an interest in science or the technology fields, but everyone can improve their math and technology skills now in a way that will expand their choices of occupations later. If you are majoring in a field in the humanities, social sciences, arts, or education, explore cognate majors or minors that will improve your earning power even as you explore your true interests. If you find that your major does not reflect your genuine interests but instead represents a gender-default choice, make an informed decision to change it.

- ***Research the wage gap and identify resources that will allow you to fight for wage equity.*** The information on the wage gap can seem overwhelming. Look for research and information sources from non-ideological sources and recognize the perspective of the authors of research you consume. The Institute for Women's Policy Research issues regular reports on the wage gap and makes research on its sources available on its Web site. The AAUW (American Association of University Women) published "Behind the Gap" in 2007 and "Graduating to a Pay Gap" in 2012, and both reports are available in full online. The WAGE (Women Are Getting Even) Project and AAUW have a collaborative project called Start Smart that sponsors workshops to teach junior and senior college women basic salary negotiation skills and how to benchmark the salary of the job they want when they graduate. The sponsors' goal is to conduct workshops on more than 500 college campuses in the next three years. Bring a Start Smart workshop to your campus.

- ***Protect Title IX.*** Stay informed about the status of Title IX, the legislation that opened doors for women in education as well as sports and ended discriminatory quotas in professions such as law, engineering, and medicine. The AAUW, founded in 1881 to advance equity for girls and women in education, is an advocacy and research organization with information on a wide range of Title IX issues. Likewise, the National Women's Law Center tracks legislative issues and court challenges related to Title IX. Male or female, if you play sports, volunteer to coach a girls' sports team for children in your community. Although the law now provides the opportunity for girls to play sports, only supportive adults can translate opportunities into reality. This is particularly important if you live in an urban area.

- *Advocate for gender equity in tax and pension reform and plan for retirement.* The National Council for Research on Women (NCRW) provides information, research, and publications on the impact of the tax code on women and tracks the implications of tax law changes for women. The National Women's Law Center and the AAUW (as well as others) provide information and sound research on Social Security, private pensions, and women in retirement. Educate yourself and start planning for your retirement now. Although it seems a bit absurd, now is the time to start investing for retirement even though you may not yet have secured your first "real" job! Financial security across the life span is a gender-equality imperative.

WHERE DO WE GO FROM HERE?

As we reach the end of this volume and our analysis of the gender paradox, where do men and women stand after nearly 170 years of effort toward a resolution of the paradox? We must conclude that men and women are more equal today than at any other time in US history, but the paradox has not been entirely resolved. In a variety of contexts, men and women lead very different lives, and in some cases women are decidedly disadvantaged because of their gender in addition to their sex. Public attitudes about gender roles in society have changed to support women as participants in the public sphere, although, as we've seen, there are limits to the autonomy women are extended. Feminism remains the most significant ideological challenge to the gender hierarchy that limits women's full participation and autonomy, but feminism faces a direct challenge to its own legitimacy as an organizing philosophy for women. There is a self-identified "third wave" of feminism under way. Notable for its decentralization and concern for a wide range of social justice interests, including many with a global scope, this branch of feminism is less focused on an advocacy consistent with the legal equality doctrine and more interested in humanist approaches that are consistent with, but not identical to, the fairness doctrine.

Today young women find themselves heirs to their mothers' and grandmothers' unfinished equality agenda.[12] That agenda is likely to include many of the same issues addressed by women at the Seneca Falls Convention in 1848—equality in work and wages; an effective public voice; political parity; accessible, quality child care; reproductive freedom; and educational equity. What is old is also new. Today's feminist agenda must be reshaped by the experiences of contemporary women of all races, ethnicities, sexualities, and ideologies, building on past successes and overcoming the remaining barriers to full participation in public life. Young women will need to craft their action strategies, find allies in men who value gender equality, choose their political leaders, and gain even greater entrée into the places where decisions are made. The opportunities are boundless, but not without challenges. As Lady Astor, the first woman to be elected to the British parliament, said, "When I came in, I left the door wide open!" The challenge of gender equality is now in your hands—and the door is wide open.

NOTES

Boxed feature notes appear at the end of the Notes section.

1 "Rep. Nancy Pelosi's Remarks upon Becoming Speaker of the House," *Washington Post*, January 4, 2007.
2 Real Clear Politics, "Election 2008," http://www.realclearpolitics.com/epolls/2008/president /democratic_delegate_count.html.
3 www.sheshouldrun.org/incubator. Accessed November 14, 2016.
4 Center for American Women and Politics, "For Women in State Legislatures and Statewide Offices, Not much Change," November 21, 2016. www.cawp.rutgers.edu/sites/default/files/resources /press-release-post-election-stateleg-2016.pdf.
5 Felice Schwartz, *Breaking with Tradition: Women and Work, the New Facts of Life* (New York: Warner Books, 1992).
6 Council of Economic Advisors, "Explaining the Trends in the Gender Wage Gap," 1998, www .whitehouse.gov/WH/EOP/CEA/html/gendergap.html.
7 Liana Fox, "Minimum Wage Increasingly Lags Poverty Line," Economic Policy Institute, January 31, 2007.
8 Ruth Leger Sivard, *Women: A World Survey* (Washington, DC: World Priorities, 1995), 9.
9 AAUW, "Graduating to a Pay Gap: The Earnings of Women and Men One Year After College Graduation," 2013.
10 Sarah Jane Glynn and Audrey Powers, "The Top 10 Facts About the Wage Gap: Women Are Still Earning Less than Men Across the Board," Center for American Progress, April 16, 2012.
11 Jessica Arons, "Lifetime Losses: The Career Wage Gap," Center for American Progress Action Fund, December 2008.
12 Cynthia B. Costello, Vanessa R. Wight, and Anne J. Stone, eds., *The American Woman 2003–2004: Daughters of a Revolution—Young Women Today* (New York: Palgrave Macmillan, 2003), 179.

Box 9.1: Seneca Falls Women's Rights Convention Resolutions
1 Elizabeth Cady Stanton, Susan B. Anthony, and Matilda Joslyn Gage, eds., *History of Women's Suffrage* (Rochester, NY: Charles Mann, 1881), 1:67–74.

Box 9.2: Burkinis and Bikinis: Who Decides How Women Must Dress?
1 Angela Charlton, "Are Burkini Bans Sexist, or Liberating?" Associated Press, August 18, 2016.
2 Khadija Algaedi, "The French Burkini Ban Is a Regression in Women's Rights," *Huffington Post*, August 24, 2016.
3 "Beach Volleyball: Egypt's Player in Hijab Gets Brazilian Support," Reuters, August 9, 2016.

Box 9.3: The Best and Worst States for Gender Equality in the United States
1 Richie Bernardo, "2016's Best and Worst States for Women's Equality," WalletHub, August 23, 2016, https://wallethub.com/edu/best-and-worst-states-for-women-equality/5835/#methodology.

Glossary

Aid to Families with Dependent Children (AFDC): A federal assistance program in effect from 1935 to 1996 (and known as AFDC since 1962) that provided financial assistance to children whose families had low or no income.

American Association of University Women (AAUW): Founded in 1881, a nonprofit organization that advances equity and education for women and girls through advocacy, education, philanthropy, and research.

American Equal Rights Association (AERA): Formed in 1866 to advance the cause of universal suffrage, including both African Americans and women. The organization dissolved when male suffrage took priority over woman suffrage in the Fifteenth Amendment.

American Woman Suffrage Association (AWSA): Suffrage organization led by Lucy Stone and Henry Ward Beecher that continued to fight for universal suffrage and supported the Fifteenth Amendment restricted to male suffrage; rival organization to National Woman Suffrage Association.

Androcentrism: The practice of overvaluing the male experience and undervaluing the female experience, whereby the male experience is understood to be the norm or universal standard by which all experiences are judged.

Black feminism: An expression of feminism that incorporates the dual oppressions of race and gender; themes include the legacy of struggle and the interdependence of thought and action.

Black women's club movement: Literary and social organizations formed to create solidarity among women of color and to promote activism around local issues facing Black women.

Bona fide occupational qualification (BFOQ): Under Title VII of the 1964 Civil Rights Act, jobs can be restricted to one sex (or gender) only if an attribute or characteristic of that sex/gender is determined to be essential to the performance of the job.

Campus SaVE Act (2013): An update to the Clery Act (1990) and complement to Title IX, this law requires that incidents of domestic violence, dating violence, sexual assault, and stalking be disclosed in annual campus crime statistic reports

417

and requires prevention education for all incoming students and new employees of universities.

Chilly climate: A male-dominated work or education environment where overt and subtle forms of discrimination may lead to women being treated differently, discouraged from pursuing particular careers or advanced degrees, or forced out of the classroom or workplace.

Clery Act: A 1990 law that requires all colleges and universities that participate in federal financial aid programs to keep and disclose information about crime on and near their respective campuses. Institutions are also required to give timely warnings of crimes that represent a threat to the safety of students or employees.

Combat exclusion: The Women's Armed Services Integration Act of 1948 excluded women from combat positions. The Combat Exclusion Policy was lifted as of January 24, 2013, following a unanimous recommendation by the Joint Chiefs of Staff. The deadline for each service branch to complete plans for full integration was January 2016.

Comparable worth: The idea that women and men should receive equal pay when their work requires comparable skills and training or when the tasks performed are of comparable worth to the employer. Occupational segregation leads to calls for equal pay for comparable work.

Comstock laws: The Comstock Act of 1873 likened contraception to obscenity and thus prohibited the distribution of any information on contraception or contraceptive devices. Supporters of the law believed that contraception violated nature in that it allowed women to engage in sexual intercourse for purposes other than procreation.

Concerned Women for America: A conservative Christian women's organization founded in 1979 by Beverly LaHaye in opposition to the National Organization for Women. An antifeminist organization that promotes the application of biblical principles to public policy.

Concrete ceiling: In contrast to the glass ceiling, where women can see but not reach the highest positions of leadership, women of color encounter a concrete ceiling that is more difficult to penetrate and obscures even the sight of the corner office.

Coverture: A legal doctrine whereby, upon marriage, a woman's legal rights and obligations were subsumed by those of her husband, in accordance with the wife's legal status of *feme covert*.

Critical mass: A theory of influence within organizations and institutions that argues a minority group can impact outcomes only when its numbers reach a critical mass. In gender politics, the concept is contested. Some scholars identify 15 or 30 percent as the point at which women exert influence over legislative outcomes, while other scholars find no empirical evidence in support of critical mass theory.

Cult of domesticity: An idea prevalent in the nineteenth century that encouraged middle- and upper-class women to dedicate themselves to homemaking as their proper social role consistent with separate spheres ideology.

Declaration of Sentiments and Resolutions: A statement of principles and claims to equality produced at Women's Rights Convention held in Seneca Falls, New York, in 1848. The resolutions adopted by those assembled call for women's suffrage, property rights, divorce, and employment.

Descriptive representation: A theory of representation in which descriptive characteristics of constituents are shared by the elected representative. Congruence of interests is assumed. When women are represented by other women in government, they are said to be descriptively represented.

Discrimination: The act of singling out a person for special treatment, not on the basis of individual merit but on the basis of prejudices about the group to which the person belongs. Laws designed to end sex discrimination in education and employment require that men and women be treated equally, without regard to sex.

Disparate impact: Practices in employment that adversely affect women or others protected by nondiscrimination policy even though the rules in question are formally neutral.

Disparate treatment: A form of employment discrimination when the actions of an employer deliberately favor or disadvantage one group compared to another. Women are subject to disparate treatment when they are denied access to certain high-paying positions due to fertility risks, for example.

Double shift: A term that recognizes the workload women have over and above what men have because their day's labor includes paid employment and the largest share of unpaid household labor. The term originates from sociologist Arlie Hochschild's book *The Second Shift*.

Eagle Forum: An antifeminist, anti–Equal Rights Amendment organization founded by Phyllis Schlafly in 1972.

EMILY's List (Early Money Is Like Yeast): A political action committee and organization dedicated to recruiting, screening, and funding Democratic, pro-choice women candidates for public office.

Equal Credit Opportunity Act (1974): A federal law that makes it illegal to deny credit to an individual on the basis of sex, age, race, color, religion, national origin, or marital status as long as they are otherwise creditworthy. This law allowed married women to apply for and receive credit in their own name rather than as a dependent of their husband.

Equal Employment Opportunity Commission (EEOC): The federal agency responsible for enforcing federal laws that make it illegal to discriminate against a job applicant or an employee because of race, color, religion, sex (including pregnancy, gender identity, and sexual orientation), national origin, age, disability, or genetic information.

Equal Pay Act: A 1963 law prohibiting sex-based wage discrimination between men and women in the same establishment who perform jobs that require substantially equal skill, effort, and responsibility under similar working conditions ("equal pay for equal work").

Equal Pay Day: The date each year symbolizing how far into the following year women must work to earn what men earned in the previous year. The date varies relative to the size of the wage gap between men and women.

Equal Rights Amendment (ERA): First proposed in 1923 as an amendment to the US Constitution prohibiting the denial of rights on account of sex, the ERA has never been ratified. It passed both houses of Congress and was submitted to the states in 1972, but fell three states short of the required three-fourths (thirty-eight) when time expired in 1982.

Equity in Athletics Disclosure Act (EADA): An enforcement tool for Title IX's guarantee of gender equity. Passed in 2008, the law requires colleges and universities that accept federal student financial aid and have an intercollegiate athletic program to prepare an annual report on athletic participation, staffing, and revenues and expenses, by men's and women's teams.

Fairness doctrine: The belief that treating men and women the same when they are in fact different is unfair. The fairness doctrine requires that law and policy account for the consequences of biological difference by treating men and women differently but fairly.

Family and Medical Leave Act (FMLA): A federal law adopted in 1993 that provides certain employees with up to twelve weeks of unpaid, job-protected leave per year and requires group health benefits to be maintained during the leave as if employees continued to work instead of taking leave. The United States remains one of four countries without paid family leave (the others are Liberia, Papua New Guinea, and Swaziland).

Feminism: There is no single definition of feminism. In general, feminism is a belief in social, economic, and political equality.

Formal representation: Mechanisms in a political system that ensure representation and allow constituents to hold representatives accountable for their actions.

Gender: Gender refers to the socially constructed characteristics of women and men—such as norms, roles, and relationships of and between groups of women and men. Although gender has in the past been understood as binary (man or woman), today gender is recognized as a more fluid identity.

Gender feminism: Gender feminists believe that the traits culture associates with women and femininity are superior in many respects to masculine traits. Because gender feminists argue that men and women are developmentally different, they are sometimes also known as difference feminists.

Gender gap: The gender gap in voting refers to the difference in the percentage of women and the percentage of men voting for a given candidate. A gender gap in voting for presidential candidates has been apparent in every election since 1980.

Gender harassment: An attempt to enforce gender or sex stereotypes. Victims of gender harassment are targeted for failing to follow norms that are typical for their sex or gender or for openly expressing a non-heteronormative sexual orientation.

Gender socialization: The process of learning the social expectations, role norms, and attitudes associated with one's gender.

Glass ceiling: A term that describes women's exclusion from the highest positions of leadership; women can see but not reach the top.

Glass cliff: A term that describes the phenomenon whereby women are most likely to achieve leadership roles during periods of crisis, when the chance of failure is highest.

Global feminism: The ways in which various forms of oppression interconnect and affect women has been the focus of many global feminists. They argue that economic and political forms of oppression are every bit as severe as sexual oppression.

Goldberg paradigm: A reference to bias in perceptions of men's and women's behavior relative to stereotypical expectations. When women occupy a male-dominated role (e.g., in politics) and behave "like men" in that domain, they are rated lower than their male counterparts. For example, a woman running for president must emphasize strength, experience, and mastery of policy details, but she runs the risk of being "unlikable."

Intersectionality: A term coined by Kimberlé Williams Crenshaw to describe the study of overlapping or intersecting social identities and related systems of oppression, domination, or discrimination.

Interspousal immunity: A common-law doctrine that prevents one spouse from suing another for personal injury. Although now abolished in most states, the doctrine is a legacy of coverture.

Legal equality doctrine: The belief that women and men must be treated the same in order to achieve equality. Therefore, differences must be erased by laws and public policies before equality can be achieved.

Liberal feminism: Contemporary liberal feminists believe that by reforming the legal and political system to allow women equal access to opportunities and resources, men and women can achieve a state of equality. Liberal feminists target laws that distinguish between men and women based on sex.

Marxist-socialist feminism: Marxist-socialists believe that capitalism, more than sexism, is at the root of women's oppression, and they advocate for public policy that aims to redistribute wealth and opportunity.

Maternalism: A subset of gender feminism, maternalism celebrates the power of women's reproductive capacity and assigns mothers unique social and political status.

Motherhood penalty: A term coined by sociologists who argue that in the workplace, working mothers encounter systematic disadvantages in pay, perceived competence, and benefits relative to childless women.

National American Woman's Suffrage Association (NAWSA): Women's suffrage organization founded as a result of the 1890 merger between the National Woman Suffrage Association (led by Elizabeth Cady Stanton and Susan B. Anthony) and the American Woman Suffrage Association. NAWSA and the National Women's Party orchestrated the last three decades of the campaign for suffrage.

National Organization for Women (NOW): Feminist organization founded in 1966 by people attending the Third National Conference of the Commission on the Status of Women. Betty Friedan served as the first president. Today the organization includes 550 chapters in all fifty US states and the District of Columbia.

National Woman Suffrage Association (NWSA): Suffrage organization founded when the AERA dissolved in controversy over the Fifteenth Amendment's inclusion of males only. NWSA was led by Elizabeth Cady Stanton and Susan B. Anthony, who urged supporters to make women's suffrage their highest priority.

National Woman's Party (NWP): Founded by Alice Paul in 1917 as an outgrowth of the Congressional Union to allow women to diversify their tactics in demanding suffrage and focus exclusively on women's suffrage. Members of the NWP led White House pickets demanding that President Wilson support the Anthony Amendment granting women the vote. By proclamation, President Obama established the NWP headquarters as the Belmont-Paul Women's Equality National Monument in 2016.

National Women's Political Caucus (NWPC): An organization founded in 1971 in order to increase women's representation in all aspects of political life. Today the NWPC recruits, trains, and supports women who seek elected and appointed office in the United States.

Oppression: A systematic mistreatment or exploitation of a group of people by a more powerful group of people or system of beliefs. Women's oppression refers to patriarchy's grip on all women regardless of race, class, or sexual orientation.

Patriarchy: Literally meaning "rule of" (*arch*) "fathers" (*patri*), patriarchy characterizes the pervasive control men exercise over social, economic, and political power and resources.

Patronymics: The practice of deriving names or parts of names from male lineage in a family.

Pay equity: Another term for "pay fairness," pay equity refers to a strategy for reducing the wage gap between men and women by assigning wages based on the content of jobs rather than the sex of the worker or gender stereotypes associated with the sex of the worker.

Paycheck Fairness Act: A legislative proposal to update the Equal Pay Act of 1963 by strengthening enforcement tools, encouraging transparency in salary and wage data, and requiring employers to prove that wage differentials between men and women are based on something other than sex.

Pink ghettos: A term used to refer to jobs dominated by women that describes the limits women face in furthering their careers, since the sex-segregated jobs held by women are often dead-end, stressful, and underpaid.

Postfeminism: The perspective that feminism has outlived its usefulness as an organizing ideology for women's advancement toward equality.

Pregnancy Discrimination Act (PDA): An amendment to Title VII of the Civil Rights Act of 1964 defining that discrimination on the basis of pregnancy, childbirth, or related medical conditions constitutes unlawful sex discrimination under Title VII.

Private sphere: Separate spheres ideology promotes the belief that because of women's role in reproduction, they are best suited to occupy the private sphere of home and family and restricted from economic or political activity found in the public sphere.

Public sphere: Separate spheres ideology assigns men to the public sphere of paid labor and political and social activity. Women's claims to equality over time have challenged their exclusion from the public sphere and advocated for equal social, economic, and political rights.

Radical feminism: A strand of feminism that believes it is the sex-gender system itself that is the source of women's oppression, and advocates women's liberation by a total revolution.

Second-generation discrimination: Subtle, perhaps even unconscious bias against women in the workplace; small incidents that viewed individually may seem trivial, but when viewed cumulatively point to a practice of insensitivity and devaluation that can get in the way of work performance.

Separate spheres ideology: The separate spheres ideology promotes the belief that because of women's role in reproduction, they are best suited to occupy the private sphere of home and family, whereas men are designed to occupy the public sphere of work and politics.

Sex: Sex refers to biological differences between male and female: chromosomes, hormonal profiles, internal and external sex organs.

Sexism: A form of prejudice, stereotyping, or discrimination against women on the basis of sex.

Sexual contract: Political theorist Carole Pateman argues that a sexual contract predated the social contract central to liberal political theory. The sexual contract required women to transfer their natural rights to men in exchange for protection, thereby leaving women without any independent rights to exchange with others in forming a social contract.

Sexual harassment: Unwelcome sexual advances, requests for sexual favors, and other verbal or physical conduct of a sexual nature constitute sexual harassment when this conduct explicitly or implicitly affects an individual's employment, unreasonably interferes with an individual's work performance, or creates an intimidating, hostile, or offensive work environment. A form of sex discrimination that violates Title VII's employment protections.

Stop-ERA: Phyllis Schlafly's organization founded in 1972 to campaign against ratification of the Equal Rights Amendment.

Substantive representation: Substantive representation occurs when women act for other women by pursuing distinctive interests and policy preferences unique to women.

Suffrage: The right to vote in political elections.

Surrogate representation: A representational relationship that exists outside the boundaries of an electoral district. Women members of Congress act as surrogate representatives for women outside the geographic boundaries of their districts by bringing something distinctive to their roles as representatives that most men do not provide.

Symbolic representation: Women's numeric representation in Congress, state legislatures, or other halls of power is important for symbolic reasons in the sense that women stand for other women. Symbolic representation adds an affective or emotional component to representation and offers women an opportunity to invest in the political system when they see other women in office.

Temporary Assistance to Needy Families (TANF): A federal program designed to provide temporary financial assistance for pregnant women and families with one or more dependent children. TANF provides financial assistance to help pay for food, shelter, utilities, and expenses other than medical. TANF replaced AFDC and represents an end to welfare as an entitlement program.

Third wave feminism: Third wave feminism developed in the early 1990s among young feminists interested in reclaiming the power of feminism and extending its reach and deepening its impact for women. Includes a broad focus and integrates women's concerns with larger issues related to justice, including racism, poverty, and environmental issues.

Title VII, Civil Rights Act of 1964: A federal law that prohibits employers from discriminating against employees on the basis of sex, race, color, national origin, and religion. Title VII makes it illegal to restrict jobs to one sex or the other based purely on sex or stereotypical assumptions about gender-linked abilities.

Title IX: Also known as the Educational Amendments of 1972, Title IX banned sex discrimination in education at all levels of formal education. Individuals may not be excluded from participation in or be denied the benefits of education on the basis of sex. The law ended quotas on women admitted to professional degree programs and opened competitive athletics to woman. Today Title IX is applicable to campus rape and sexual assault.

Title IX coordinator: All institutions must employ a Title IX coordinator whose responsibility it is to help a school ensure that every person affected by its operations is aware of his or her legal rights under Title IX, and that the school and all of its employees, through its policies, procedures, and practices, complies with its legal obligations under Title IX.

Trolling: Trolling is a form of baiting online that involves sending abusive and hurtful comments across all social media platforms. Women active on social media are far more likely than men to be targets of highly sexualized and violent trolling.

Violence Against Women Act (VAWA): A 1994 federal law that provides resources toward investigation and prosecution of violent crimes against women, imposes mandatory restitution on those convicted, and allows victims to access civil penalties if prosecutors decide not to bring criminal charges.

Womanist: A term intended to convey the shortcomings of feminism in capturing the full range of experiences of women of color. Alice Walker wrote, "Womanist is to feminist as purple is to lavender."

Women's Christian Temperance Union (WCTU): Founded in 1874 as an organization dedicated to social reform through temperance (abstinence from alcohol). Drunken husbands were a source of misery for women who could not earn wages through employment or seek a divorce.

Index

427

CPSIA information can be obtained
at www.ICGtesting.com
Printed in the USA
BVOW08s0237091017
497044BV00003B/4/P